Political Trials in Theory and History

From the trial of Socrates to the post-9/11 military commissions, trials have always been useful instruments of politics. Yet there is still much that we do not understand about them. Why do governments use trials to pursue political objectives, and when? What differentiates political trials from ordinary ones? Contrary to conventional wisdom, not all political trials are show trials or contrive to set up scapegoats. This volume offers a novel account of political trials that is empirically rigorous and theoretically sophisticated, linking state-of-the-art research on telling cases to a broad argument about political trials as a socio-legal phenomenon.

All the contributors analyze the logic of the political in the courtroom. From archival research to participant observation, and from linguistic anthropology to game theory, the volume offers a genuinely interdisciplinary set of approaches that substantially advance existing knowledge about what political trials are, how they work, and why they matter.

JENS MEIERHENRICH is Associate Professor of International Relations at the London School of Economics and Political Science. His books include *The Legacies of Law: Long-Run Consequences of Legal Development in South Africa, 1652–2000* (Cambridge University Press, 2008), which won the American Political Science Association's 2009 Woodrow Wilson Foundation Award for the best book on politics, government, or international affairs; *Lawfare: A Genealogy* (Cambridge University Press, 2017); and, as co-editor, *The Oxford Handbook of Carl Schmitt* (2016).

DEVIN O. PENDAS is Associate Professor of History at Boston College. He is the author of *The Frankfurt Auschwitz Trial, 1963–1965: History, Genocide, and the Limits of the Law* (Cambridge University Press, 2006) and the co-editor of *Beyond the Racial State: New Perspectives on the Third Reich* (Cambridge University Press, 2017).

Political Trials in Theory and History

Edited by
JENS MEIERHENRICH
London School of Economics and Political Science
DEVIN O. PENDAS
Boston College

CAMBRIDGE
UNIVERSITY PRESS

CAMBRIDGE
UNIVERSITY PRESS

University Printing House, Cambridge CB2 8BS, United Kingdom

Cambridge University Press is part of the University of Cambridge.

It furthers the University's mission by disseminating knowledge in the pursuit of education, learning and research at the highest international levels of excellence.

www.cambridge.org
Information on this title: www.cambridge.org/9781107079465

First published 2016

Printed in the United Kingdom by Clays, St Ives plc.

A catalogue record for this publication is available from the British Library

ISBN 978-1-107-07946-5 Hardback

Contents

Figures

Contributors

Catherine M. Cole is Professor and Chair of the Department of Theater, Dance, and Performance Studies at the University of California, Berkeley

Alexander C. Cook is Assistant Professor of History at the University of California, Berkeley

Lawrence Douglas is James J. Grosfeld Professor of Law, Jurisprudence, and Social Thought at Amherst College

Thomas A. Fudge is Professor of History at the University of New England, Australia

Ron E. Hassner is Associate Professor of Political Science at the University of California, Berkeley

Francine Hirsch is Professor of History at the University of Wisconsin, Madison

Marco Jacquemet is Professor of Communication Studies at the University of San Francisco

John E. Lopatka is A. Robert Noll Distinguished Professor of Law at Pennsylvania State University School of Law

Jens Meierhenrich is Associate Professor of International Relations at the London School of Economics and Political Science

Josiah Ober is Constantine Mitsotakis Professor in the School of Humanities and Sciences as well as Professor of Political Science and Professor of Classics at Stanford University

William H. Page is Marshall M. Criser Eminent Scholar and Professor of Law at the University of Florida College of Law

Devin O. Pendas is Associate Professor of History at Boston College

Richard Sakwa is Professor of Russian and European Politics at the University of Kent

Kenneth Sexauer received a BA in political science and history from the University of California, Berkeley

Mark V. Tushnet is William Nelson Cromwell Professor of Law at Harvard Law School

Christiane Wilke is Associate Professor of Law and Legal Studies at Carleton University

Laurence H. Winnie is Senior Lecturer in History and Director of Undergraduate Studies at Dedman College

1

"The Justice of My Cause Is Clear, but There's Politics to Fear": Political Trials in Theory and History

Jens Meierhenrich and Devin O. Pendas

PHILINTE: Then who will plead your case before the court?
ALCESTE: Reason and right and justice will plead for me.
PHILINTE: Oh, Lord. What judges do you plan to see?
ALCESTE: Why, none. The justice of my cause is clear.
PHILINTE: Of course, man; but there's politics to fear.

Molière, *The Misanthrope*, Act 1, Scene 1

Reflecting, three years before her untimely death, on the gestation of her 1964 book *Legalism*, Judith Shklar recalled thinking "that it might be interesting to take a good look at political trials generally."[1] In the five decades since that remarkable book's first publication, especially in the quarter century since Shklar's remark in 1989, a plethora of political trials have been staged. Especially in the context of transitions from authoritarian rule, this peculiar institution has been ascendant. Yet even in advanced industrialized democracies, political trials are a recurring feature of contention. In recent years, a host of actors – NGOs, governments, international organizations – have embraced trials ever more readily as useful instruments of politics.

The range of political trials is enormous, spanning the globe and much of human history. In addition to the cases analyzed in the individual chapters of the present volume, one might also think of trials as disparate as those of O. J. Simpson in Los Angeles, Saddam Hussein in Baghdad, or John Demjanjuk in Munich.[2] Nor are such political trials a particularly "Western" phenomenon,

[1] Judith N. Shklar, "A Life of Learning," Charles Homer Haskins Lecture for 1989, American Council of Learned Societies, ACLS Occasional Paper No. 9, p. 14.

[2] See, for example, Janet Cotterill, *Language and Power in Court: A Linguistic Analysis of the O. J. Simpson Trial* (London: Palgrave, 2003); Michael A. Newton and Michael P. Scharf, *Enemy of the State: The Trial and Execution of Saddam Hussein* (New York: St. Martin's Press, 2008); and Heinrich Wefing, *Der Fall Demjanjuk: Der letzte große NS-Prozess* (Munich: C. H. Beck, 2011).

as evinced by the Special Tribunal for Lebanon, established by the UN to investigate the assassination of Rafiq Hariri and others in Lebanon in 2005; the trial of Zulfikar Ali Bhutto in Pakistan in 1978; the proceedings before the Extraordinary Chambers in the Courts of Cambodia; or the Women's International War Crimes Tribunal held in Tokyo. Nor are political trials restricted to tribunals for murder and mass atrocities. For instance, various kinds of "free speech" trials would obviously fall into this category, whether for obscenity or libel.[3] Political trials can involve a range of economic cases as well, for instance, the various U.S. Supreme Court cases dispossessing Native Americans of their land.[4] If we believe the literary theorist Shoshana Felman, "the promised exercise of *legal* justice – of justice by trial and by law – has become civilization's most appropriate and most essential, most ultimately meaningful response to the violence that wounds it."[5] Against the background of these developments, it is time to take *another* good look at political trials generally, thereby critically revisiting what Shklar taught us about them almost five decades ago.

In the wake of *Legalism*, the social theorist Jürgen Habermas famously claimed that modern societies are marked by ever-increasing levels of juridification.[6] In his fairly abstract treatment, juridification means simply "the tendency toward an increase in formal (or positive, written) law," which manifests as both an "*expansion* of law" into new domains of social life and an "*increasing density* of law" in areas of traditional concern.[7] Habermas has little to say, however, about the venues in which law is performed. This is unfortunate because, as the political scientist John Ferejohn reminds us,

> Since World War II, there has been a profound shift in power away from legislatures and toward courts and other legal institutions around the world. This shift, which has been called "judicialization," has become more or less global in its reach, as evidenced by the fact that it is as marked in Europe, and especially recently in Eastern Europe, as it is in the United States.[8]

[3] See, e.g., Chris Hilliard, "'Is It a Book That You Would Even Wish Your Wife or Your Servants to Read?': Obscenity Law and the Politics of Reading in Modern England," *American Historical Review*, Vol. 118 (2013), pp. 653–678; or Richard J. Evans, *Lying about Hitler: History, Holocaust, and the David Irving Trial* (New York: Basic Books, 2001).

[4] *Worcester* v. *Georgia*, 31 U.S. (6 Pet.) 515 (1832); *U.S.* v. *Kagama*, 118 U.S. 375 (1886); or *Lone Wolf* v. *Hitchcock*, 187 U.S. 553 (1903).

[5] Shoshana Felman, *The Juridical Unconscious: Trials and Traumas in the Twentieth Century* (Cambridge: Harvard University Press, 2002), p. 3.

[6] Jürgen Habermas, *The Theory of Communicative Action*, vol. 2: *Lifeworld and System: A Critique of Functionalist Reason*, translated by Thomas McCarthy (Boston: Beacon Press, 1987), pp. 356–373.

[7] Habermas, *The Theory of Communicative Action*, vol. 2, p. 357.

[8] John Ferejohn, "Judicializing Politics, Politicizing Law," *Law and Contemporary Problems*, Vol. 65 (2002), p. 41. For an overview of the debate, see Ran Hirschl, "The Judicialization of Politics,"

Judicialization is a specific aspect of juridification, one that not only expands and deepens law but also increases the relative power of courts and trial attorneys at the expense of legislators and state regulators.

We believe that it is impossible to fully understand the diffusion of law in modern life unless one also understands how law operates at its key point of application: in the courtroom. Our concern here is with *judicialization* (as understood by Ferejohn) as a manifestation of a more general trend toward *juridification* (as theorized by Habermas). By examining a range of political trials, including several that might not at first glance seem to fit the paradigm as it is conventionally understood, we hope to illuminate select aspects of judicialization – the way it has operated on the ground and in lived experience, in both domestic and international trials.[9]

What Are Political Trials?

Although much has been written in the last decade on what Otto Kirchheimer long ago dubbed "political justice," a deeper comprehension of political trials as one institution capable of delivering political justice remains elusive.[10] We do not yet fully understand under what conditions trials become political, the social mechanisms by which this occurs, or with what effects. Much of the existing literature assumes "that we can recognize political trials when we see them."[11] Scholars more inclined to conceptual reasoning have interpreted the term in many different ways, sometimes haphazardly. Ronald Christenson, in an important article published more than three decades ago, put his finger on the crux of the conceptual matter: "Are political trials better classified as law or politics? If they are totally political, why have a trial? Since the courts are part of the 'system,' are all trials, therefore political?"[12] In answer, we propose that

in Gregory A. Caldeira, R. Daniel Kelemen, and Keith E. Whittington, eds., *The Oxford Handbook of Law and Politics* (Oxford: Oxford University Press, 2009), pp. 119–141.

9 For a review of scholarship addressing the determinants of judicialization, see Ran Hirschl, "The Judicialization of Mega-Politics and the Rise of Political Courts," *Annual Review of Political Science*, Vol. 11 (2008), pp. 93–118.

10 Otto Kirchheimer, *Political Justice: The Use of Legal Procedure for Political Ends* (Princeton: Princeton University Press, 1962).

11 The phrase is from Ronald Christenson, "A Political Theory of Political Trials," *Journal of Criminal Law and Criminology*, Vol. 74 (1983), p. 548. Examples of empirically rich but conceptually underdeveloped scholarship include Fowler Harper and David Haber, "Lawyer Troubles in Political Trials," *Yale Law Journal*, Vol. 60 (1951), pp. 1–56; Kermit L. Hall, "Political Power and Constitutional Legitimacy: The South Carolina Ku Klux Klan Trials, 1871–1872," *Emory Law Journal*, Vol. 33 (1984), pp. 921–951; Anthony W. Pereira, "'Persecution and Farce': The Origins and Transformation of Brazil's Political Trials, 1964–1979," *Latin American Research Review*, Vol. 33 (1998), pp. 43–66; and Adele Lindenmeyr, "The First Soviet Political Trial: Countess Sofia Panina before the Petrograd Revolutionary Tribunal," *Russian Review*, Vol. 60 (2001), pp. 505–525.

12 Christenson, "A Political Theory of Political Trials," pp. 547–548.

political trials are best thought of, first and foremost, as peculiar *legal institutions* that embody *political dynamics*. Before we further develop our own conceptualization of the term, it is worth pointing out what political trials are *not*. Here are a number of contending definitions, all of which we find wanting.

The most recent contribution to the study of political trials comes from Eric Posner. Posner, a prominent legal scholar who writes on both domestic and international law, defines a political trial as one

> whose disposition – that is, usually, a finding of guilt or innocence, followed by punishment or acquittal, of an individual – depends on an evaluation of the defendant's political attitudes and activities. In the typical political trial, a person is tried for engaging in political opposition or violating a law against political dissent, or for violating a broad and generally applicable law that is not usually enforced, enforced strictly, or enforced with a strict punishment, except against political opponents of the state or the government.[13]

The purpose of political trials in liberal democracies, according to Posner, is "to eliminate enemies of a system devoted to political tolerance. In a political trial, the normal constraints of liberal legalism yield, with judicial and public acquiescence, to the political imperative of self-preservation ..."[14] Although Posner captures a number of important attributes that we, too, consider important to a certain extent (e.g., the focus on enmity, which we develop below), his emphasis on criminal proceedings, on the one hand, and his preoccupation with the prosecution of political opponents, on the other, result in a conception of political trials that is too narrow to be useful for comparative historical analysis.

Posner's definition problematically excludes varieties of trials that are political in less confrontational a fashion. By effectively equating *all* political trials with partisan trials, Posner leaves little room for adopting a broader understanding of the concept of the political in the empirical study of political trials. The bluntness of his conceptual approach is exemplified by Posner's insistence that legal proceedings in the context of large-scale social change (what he calls "transitional trials") are inherently political. That is a reasonable argument, but not a very helpful one because it begs the question of *how* exactly these trials are political, *when* they tend to become so, and with *what* consequences. The point is to account for variation, not sameness. Posner remains stuck in the conventional, reductionist mold of thinking about political trials.[15]

[13] Eric A. Posner, "Political Trials in Domestic and International Law," *Duke Law Journal*, Vol. 55 (2005), p. 76.

[14] Posner, "Political Trials in Domestic and International Law," p. 150.

[15] Exemplary of this conventional mold is also Nathan Hakman, "Political Trials in the Legal Order: A Political Scientist's Perspective," *Journal of Public Law*, Vol. 2 (1972), pp. 73–126. Hakman, for one, uses the terms "ideological trials" and "political trials" synonymously.

For the last twenty years or so, Ronald Christenson has attempted to break this mold. Unlike Posner, he concedes that "[n]ot all political trials contrive to set up scapegoats."[16] Rather, says Christenson, "certain political trials are creative, placing before society basic dilemmas which are clarified through the trial. These trials become crystals for society."[17] This more inclusive conception of political trials, as we shall show in more detail below, is useful for refining Posner's rudimentary account. Most important, Christenson counterbalances the extreme instrumentalism inherent in Posner's conception of what political trials are. Among others things, he alerts us to the role of contingency in their creation and institutional development. By so doing, he opens the door for a consideration of the non-rationalist aspects of such trials, notably their performative dimensions. For, as he notes, "trials are not chess games which proceed according to exact rules, rigorous though the rules of evidence may be. Trials are, first and foremost, stories."[18] Or, as Felix Frankfurter, the former justice of the U.S. Supreme Court once put it, "We live by symbols."[19] It is for this reason that the humanities – in addition to law and the social sciences – also are essential for coming to grips with the multifaceted nature of political trials. That said, Christenson's definition is incomplete as well. Christenson does not offer a usable concept that could form the basis for comparative historical work because, while he is quite right that political trials "are not incompatible with the rule of law," he provides no analytical purchase for understanding the similarities *and* differences between political trials "within the rule of law" and those outside of it.[20]

Definitional problems are not the only challenge for the study of political trials. Our lack of systematic knowledge about the phenomenon stems from the fact that the vast majority of accounts of political trials are *rhetorical* rather than empirical or *descriptive* rather than analytical. By this we mean that the bulk of the existing literature fails, first, to look past the derogatory connotation of the notion of the political trial. It is regularly deployed pejoratively to pour scorn on a given legal proceeding rather than being used to elucidate the interaction of law and politics in the courtroom. A case in point is Danilo Zolo's recent treatise *Victors' Justice*, in which the author proffers an unconvincing critique of international legal order that lumps together a whole series of political trials without regard for theoretical subtlety, empirical specificity, or historical context.[21]

Second, we fault the existing literature for mostly lacking in theoretical ambition.[22] There exists little scholarship, for example, that inquires

[16] Ron Christenson, "What Is a Political Trial?," *Society*, Vol. 23 (1986), p. 26.

[17] Christenson, "What Is a Political Trial?," p. 26.

[18] Christenson, "What Is a Political Trial?," p. 26.

[19] *Minersville School Dist.* v. *Gobitis*, 310 U.S. 586, 596 (1940).

[20] Christenson, "A Political Theory of Political Trials," p. 554.

[21] Danilo Zolo, *Victors' Justice: From Nuremberg to Baghdad* (London: Verso, 2009).

[22] Exceptions are two important, yet dated, studies, namely Hakman, "Political Trials in the Legal Order," pp. 73–126; and Christenson, "A Political Theory of Political Trials," pp. 547–577.

rigorously – and comparatively – into questions of, say, institutional choice and design, the economic determinants of trial justice, or the relevance of communicative action for making sense of political trials. The handful of studies that single out political trials for closer inspection tend to forego the kinds of deep interpretative readings that are analytically ambitious *as well as* empirically grounded. Exemplary of this failing is Sadakat Kadri, whose popular history *The Trial* is rich in detail but of limited value for understanding trials, political and otherwise.[23] Of similar quality is Christenson's snapshot collection of political trials from antiquity to the late twentieth century.[24] Keeping these hurried studies company on the book shelf are popular treatments like Geoffrey Robertson's *The Tyrannicide Brief*, a historical yet ultimately slight tale of the trial of Charles I in England.[25] Similarly, David P. Jordan's standard history *The King's Trial*, about the trial of Louis XVI, explicitly rejects attempts to link it to broader phenomena of political justice, insisting that it was both sui generis and unrelated to the Terror in France.[26] Such treatments make for fascinating reading and contribute substantially to our understanding of the specific trials in question. However, they do not provide much help in constructing a more general account of how political trials operate or how they vary across time and space.[27] They offer anecdotes aplenty, but contribute little to the theory and history of political trials.

Studies that transcend the prism of a single perspective, that reveal both the social and doctrinal complexity of courtroom drama, and that seek to integrate theoretical sophistication and historical analysis are far and few in between. Three notable exceptions are Leora Bilsky's *Transformative Justice*, a close reading of four prominent Israeli trials that cut to the heart of the country's project of state-making; Lawrence Douglas's *The Memory of Judgment*, a sophisticated reading of select Nazi trials; and Richard Ashby Wilson's *Writing History in International Criminal Tribunals*, an anthropological inquiry into the didactic function of international proceedings at the International Criminal Tribunals for the former Yugoslavia (ICTY) and Rwanda (ICTR).[28] What all three studies have in common is

[23] Sadakat Kadri, *The Trial: A History from Socrates to O. J. Simpson* (London: Harper Perennial, 2006).

[24] Ron Christenson, ed., *Political Trials in History: From Antiquity to the Present* (New Brunswick: Transaction Publishers, 1991).

[25] Geoffrey Robertson, *The Tyrannicide Brief: The Story of the Man Who Sent Charles I to the Scaffold* (London: Vintage, 2006).

[26] David P. Jordan, *The King's Trial: Louis XVI vs. The French Revolution*, New edition (Berkeley: University of California Press, 2004), p. xix.

[27] Another recent example is John Laughland, *A History of Political Trials: From Charles I to Saddam Hussein* (New York: Peter Lang, 2008).

[28] Leora Bilsky, *Transformative Justice: Israeli Identity on Trial* (Ann Arbor: University of Michigan Press, 2004); Lawrence Douglas, *The Memory of Judgment: Making Law and History in the Trials of the Holocaust* (New Haven: Yale University Press, 2005); and Richard

a multidisciplinary sensibility and a healthy skepticism for conventional wisdom.

These contributions notwithstanding, much remains to be done when it comes to the study of political trials. This volume seeks to advance the agenda. It showcases exciting, deeply interpretive scholarship that has been informed by a new framework for analysis. To help deepen explanation and understanding of the ever more salient phenomenon of political trials, our volume is located at the intersection of law and related disciplines. Together with our contributors, we strike up intellectual conversations based on a foundation of insights from a variety of fields. Only on such a basis will we be able to come to terms with the logic of political trials, then and now. The past in our collection is represented by political trials ranging from those of Socrates to the French revolutionary trials. The present is under investigation in chapters on the Camorra trials in Italy, the Microsoft antitrust case in the United States, and the Khodorkovsky trials in Russia. Wedged in between these studies of the distant past and the recent present, readers will find innovative renderings of such diverse legal events as the Eichmann trial in Jerusalem, the Rivonia trial in South Africa, and the Gang of Four trial in China, to name but a few. By juxtaposing conventional and unconventional empirical cases from familiar and unfamiliar cultures, we hope to diversify and complicate the study of political trials. For not only do we believe that the politicization of trials is increasingly insidious, we also maintain that the meaning of the political in the courtroom is culturally specific.

The remainder of this introduction is organized into two parts. The first part explores theoretical foundations. It breaks the phenomenon of political trials into its two constituent parts: the concept of the political and the concept of the trial. Before we reassemble these moving parts, we critically reflect on a host of literatures that shed light, in whole or in part, on the two constituent phenomena. As far as the concept of the political is concerned, several questions are addressed: What is the essence of politics in the courtroom? What are the means of politics there? What are its ends? How do we know a phenomenon is political in the context of adjudication? Who is involved in law's politics? When we turn to the concept of the trial, other questions are raised: What are the defining characteristics of trials? What distinguishes trials from other institutions for the resolution (or pursuit) of political conflict? What social significance do trials enjoy? On the basis of these theoretical foundations, the second part builds a framework for the analysis of political trials. In addition to formulating a systematized concept, we introduce a typology of political trials. We contend that this framework offers a foundation for the study of political trials that allows them to be approached comparatively and historically.

Ashby Wilson, *Writing History in International Criminal Trials* (Cambridge: Cambridge University Press, 2011).

THEORETICAL FOUNDATIONS

The chapters collected in this volume "relate the political content to the juridical form," as Otto Kirchheimer once put it.[29] And yet we are not content to merely rehearse Kirchheimer's perspective on political justice. In fact, ours is a deliberate attempt to overcome a series of considerable shortcomings that we have detected in his magnum opus. Such corrections are important seeing that conventional analyses of political trials owe, unwittingly or otherwise, a tremendous debt to the exiled German jurist.

The Concept of the Political

We begin our attempt at reframing the field of study by charting – and contrasting – three different legal studies movements that have contributed meaningfully, albeit in different ways and to different degrees, to illuminating the politics of adjudication since the mid-twentieth century. These loose movements are Historical Legal Studies (HLS), Critical Legal Studies (CLS), and Empirical Legal Studies (ELS). These schools of thought are of direct relevance for this volume's subject matter despite the fact that their intellectual ambits all reach considerably beyond the phenomenon of political trials. By situating our project at the intersection of these important movements in legal studies, and by locating it in direct response to some of the perspectives that have emanated from them, we seek to reinvigorate the study of political trials for the twenty-first century.[30]

Historical Legal Studies in the 1950s and 1960s

A series of lawyers and social scientists, most of them émigré scholars based in the United States, turned to the subject of political trials in the 1950s and 1960s. This analytical turn, which was part of a wider intellectual current that we refer to as Historical Legal Studies (HLS), was far from surprising. Some of them had closely studied the political trials of Weimar Germany and the early years of the Nazi dictatorship, as well as the various postwar attempts to bring to justice major and minor "war criminals" (as the defendants were invariably, if often inaccurately, called). This prior interest helped generate a stream of publications on political justice in all its forms. It is worth taking a closer look at how two of these historically minded scholars – Kirchheimer and Judith Shklar – dealt with the concept of the political when writing about the role of law in modern society.

[29] Kirchheimer, *Political Justice*, p. vii.

[30] For a more general discussion of the concept of the political in the twentieth century than can be provided here, see, most recently, Samuel Moyn, "Concepts of the Political in Twentieth-Century European Thought," in Jens Meierhenrich and Oliver Simons, eds., *The Oxford Handbook of Carl Schmitt* (Oxford: Oxford University Press, 2016), pp. 291–311.

Kirchheimer, who after fleeing Nazi Germany revived his teaching career at Columbia University, related the essence of the political in the courtroom to the distribution of power in a given polity:

> Court action is called upon to exert influence on the distribution of political power ... [E]fforts to maintain the *status quo* may be essentially symbolic, or they may specifically hit at potential or full-grown existing adversaries. Sometimes it may be doubtful whether such court action really does consolidate the established structure; it may even weaken it. Yet that it is in both cases aimed at affecting power relations in one way or another denotes the essence of a political trial.[31]

In his early work, written in the Weimar Republic, Kirchheimer largely understood political justice in terms of class justice, and the power relations affected in the courtroom were invariably those between social classes. In his later work, Kirchheimer moved away from this earlier, relatively orthodox Marxist interpretation.[32]

Kirchheimer had been a doctoral student of Carl Schmitt, the infamous constitutional scholar and law professor whose body of thought had a more than random structuring effect on the law of Weimar Germany as well as the Third Reich. It should come as no surprise, therefore, that for Kirchheimer "the function of courts in political life ... in the simplest and crudest terms [was to] eliminate a political foe of the regime according to some prearranged rules."[33] This of course draws on Schmitt's famous assertion that the essence of politics is to distinguish friend from enemy. But for Kirchheimer, the more interesting question was why a regime would use the courts for such a process of elimination. After all, he recognized that "judicial inquest obtains neither the quickest nor by any means the most certain results."[34] Both formal political processes (such as elections) and collective violence could achieve the same results more directly and easily. The value of judicial proceedings in eliminating political foes lay, according to Kirchheimer, not in their efficiency but in their legitimacy. They "authenticated" political actions. In so doing, they helped contain the potentially boundless number of enemies a regime might generate. "By agreeing to a yardstick, however nebulous or refined, to cut down the number of occasions for the elimination of actual or potential foes, those in power stand to gain as much as their subjects."[35] Judicialized politics make the removal of political foes more acceptable to the polity at large, whether domestic or international.

Unlike authors of less sophisticated accounts, Kirchheimer is quite clear that political trials can be, and indeed are, characteristic of democratic polities as well as authoritarian ones. "Political trials," he says, "are inescapable."[36]

[31] Kirchheimer, *Political Justice*, p. 49.

[32] William E. Scheuerman, *Between the Norm and the Exception: The Frankfurt School and the Rule of Law* (Cambridge: MIT Press, 1997).

[33] Kirchheimer, *Political Justice*, p. 6.

[34] Kirchheimer, *Political Justice*, p. 6.

[35] Kirchheimer, *Political Justice*, p. 6.

[36] Kirchheimer, *Political Justice*, p. 47.

However, Kirchheimer is equally clear that not all trials are political (as they were thought to be by many representatives of the Critical Legal Studies movement, of which more in a moment). There are important differences between political trials and ordinary criminal trials. Critiquing those who would deny the possibility of political justice under the rule of law, who maintain that the proper application of due process depoliticizes the proceedings, Kirchheimer argues that it is more the *objective* than the method of trials that makes them political. True, all trials deploy forensic procedures for determining the truth of a given event (or, perhaps, *a* truth) and conclude with sanctions or vindication for the defendant(s). Ordinary criminal trials can be quite interesting in their own right, can even "disclose or expose hidden aspects and dimensions of contemporary civilization," but they are "cases rather than causes" and do not have the same kind of import as political trials. In a political proceeding, "the judicial machinery and its trial mechanics are set into motion to attain political objectives which transcend both the bystanders' curiosity and the governmental custodian's satisfaction in the vindication of the political order. Court action is called upon to exert influence on the distribution of political power."[37]

All trials, in other words, may be political in the generic sense that they uphold the state's right to adjudicate and resolve social conflicts. But political trials are political in a further and much more precise sense, in that they affect the distribution of power specifically within its political framework. Kirchheimer acknowledges this to be a narrow reading of power, recognizing that civil trials between major corporations or many kinds of ordinary criminal trials can have "decidedly political effects."[38] Yet this does not, according to Kirchheimer, make them political trials in the proper sense of the term, which deal only in the "direct involvement in the struggle for political power."[39] Socioeconomic conflict or the maintenance of ordinary order does not, on Kirchheimer's reading, directly implicate the distribution of power and trials concerned with such matters are therefore not to be considered political trials.

This implies a distinction between political and ordinary justice. While Kirchheimer is explicit that political trials need not entail any violations of due process nor devolve into show trials with foreordained outcomes, they are nonetheless clearly distinct from the ordinary workings of the courts. "The aim of political justice is to enlarge the area of political action by enlisting the services of courts in behalf of political goals. It is characterized by the submission to court scrutiny of group and individual action. Those instrumental in such submission seek to strengthen their own position and weaken that of their political foes."[40]

We certainly agree that trials of the sort described by Kirchheimer constitute political trials. We are less persuaded, however, by his exclusion of trials not

[37] Kirchheimer, *Political Justice*, p. 49.
[38] Kirchheimer, *Political Justice*, p. 50.
[39] Kirchheimer, *Political Justice*, p. 50.
[40] Kirchheimer, *Political Justice*, p. 419.

directly concerned with the distribution of (overtly political) power, ones with merely "political implications," which does not do full justice to the phenomenon of political trials. To begin with, the distinction between conflicts over political power and other conflicts with only indirect implications for the power constellation of a society or regime is not always easy to draw. The Microsoft antitrust suit analyzed in this volume, for instance, focused primarily on the distribution of *economic* rather than *political* power. Yet one need hardly be a Marxist to recognize the fungibility of economic capital in the political arena in contemporary democracies, the United States in particular. Money may not literally buy votes, but it comes close.[41] Similarly, "ordinary" criminal trials may not merely reveal something fascinating about the underbelly of civilization; they can change the way politics functions. Think, for instance, about the change in policing in Los Angeles in the wake of the back-to-back scandals of the Rodney King and O. J. Simpson trials. So, while Kirchheimer is quite right that there is a difference between trials with a directly political aim and ones with political effects, it seems overly narrow and rigid to deny that the latter can be viewed as political trials in a meaningful sense.

Then there is Shklar. Her *Legalism* was first published in 1964 and is deeply rooted in the scholarly tradition of the 1950s and 1960s.[42] The similarities can partly be accounted for by the biographical commonalities between her and Kirchheimer as well as other representatives of what we have called, for lack of a better term, HLS. Also relevant was the public law tradition in political science, the professional standing of which was considerable in the postwar decades but has been subject to steady decline ever since. In this sense, Shklar harked back to a different, European-inspired way of studying the relationship between politics and law, one embodied in the German tradition of *allgemeine Staatslehre* (the general theory of the state). Given these connections, Shklar's oeuvre, with its penchant for the Western canon of political thought, was already beginning to fall out of step with the times when *Legalism* was reissued in 1986. As we shall see, despite its forceful intervention, it was a movement of one. As a legal studies movement, History and Law, with its greater emphasis on empirical accuracy and careful archival research, had supplanted the more free-ranging – some might say cavalier – use of historical evidence that was germane to the relatively short-lived HLS.[43]

The limitations of Shklar's account of political trials become apparent very quickly. Her powerful chapter on the International Military Tribunal at Nuremberg (IMT) and the International Military Tribunal for the Far East

41 Thomas Ferguson, *Golden Rule: The Investment Theory of Party Competition and the Logic of Money-Driven Political Systems* (Chicago: University of Chicago Press, 1995).

42 Judith N. Shklar, *Legalism: Law, Morals, and Political Trials* (Cambridge: Harvard University Press, 1986).

43 For an overview of the vast field of legal history, see, for example, Andrew Lewis and Michael Lobban, eds., *Law and History: Current Legal Issues* (Oxford: Oxford University Press, 2004).

(IMTFE) is the scholarly analogue to Hannah Arendt's *Eichmann in Jerusalem*. It is perceptive and pathbreaking but ultimately underdeveloped in both theoretical and empirical terms. Theoretically speaking, it seems at times as if Shklar was more interested in indicting than in explaining or understanding international justice. Although she does recognize institutional differences within and between the IMT and IMTFE, it appears that her strong normative convictions prevented her from inquiring more deeply into the mechanisms of "victor's justice."

Shklar was clear that in her view, the international prosecutions after World War II were "political trials," which she considered broadly to be a bad thing, certainly a form of justice incompatible with the rule of law. Generally, she understood political trials to be those aimed at the "elimination of a specific sort of political enemy."[44] "What the principle of legality demands," she wrote, "is a law and also an act made criminal by law. In political cases either one or the other or both may be lacking."[45] Political trials, on her view, operated mostly in violation of the principle of legality by lacking either a prior law or a clearly illegal act (though she did acknowledge there might be some political cases, such as espionage trials, that did not). Even political trials that closely resembled ordinary proceedings were, in Shklar's opinion, different in that they could not be integrated into a "continuous process by which one case can be more or less assimilated into a pattern of similar cases."[46] So political trials generally and by their nature tend to be sui generis and hence in violation of the universality and generalizability characteristic of law properly understood. For Shklar, this meant that political trials always have the appearance of injustice – at least to some segments of a political community – even when they do not actually violate the principle of legality, e.g., by way of ex post facto prosecutions.

Under rare circumstances, however, it might be the case that trials in violation of the principle of legality – political trials in other words – are warranted. Such circumstances have occurred when there was no positive law prohibition on certain actions but "people have committed acts so profoundly shocking that something must be done about them."[47] The paradigm instance of such an occurrence was, of course, Nazi atrocities during World War II. It was (contra the American prosecution team) not the war but the specific, unprecedented character of Nazi mass atrocities that warranted prosecution. The war in the Pacific was different in this respect from the European war. For this reason, Shklar approved of the IMT but not the IMTFE. Nazi "crimes against humanity" may not have been, strictly speaking, illegal in accordance with the principle of legality, but they were of such a heinous nature that their political prosecution (and the elimination of the Nazi enemy thereby) was acceptable. "If the Nuremberg Trial can be justified as an act of legalistic

[44] Shklar, *Legalism*, p. 153. [45] Shklar, *Legalism*, p. 152. [46] Shklar, *Legalism*, p. 153.
[47] Shklar, *Legalism*, p. 153.

statesmanship and on the basis of its immediate effects on German politics, it is due to the revelations about crimes against humanity which it produced."[48]

In other words, for Shklar, the IMT was justified, not as a matter of law, but as a matter of politics, because it was in fact necessary to eliminate the Nazi enemy and because doing so in the legalistic (though barely legal) idiom of the tribunal served a valuable and necessary educative function for the Germans. Such conditions justifying political trials are rare on Shklar's reading. They are more likely to occur in international than in domestic settings, though as the unfortunate example of the IMTFE shows, even in the international arena, not all political trials are justified. The crimes of the Japanese were not so unprecedented as those of the Germans, thus making their ex post facto prosecution more dubious. More fundamentally, because the " 'situation ethics' of the Japanese are inherently unlegalistic," the trial could not hope to teach them any useful political lessons.[49] According to Shklar, the instrumental political benefit of a political trial justified the IMT, but not the IMTFE.

Shklar sets out a subtle and differentiated account of political trials. She is deeply skeptical of their value, but recognizes that they may at times be warranted. From our vantage point, she makes the same mistake as Kirchheimer. Both reduce politics to its Schmittian core – the opposition between friend and enemy – and see in political trials only "eliminative" proceedings. While these undoubtedly form a major category of such cases, political trials range more broadly and *can* serve functions above and beyond the mere elimination of political opponents. Recognizing this practical possibility opens up an analytical space for acknowledging the prevalence of political trials in liberal democracies and the diverse roles they play.

While Shklar recognized that there were degrees of legalism, she felt that political trials almost invariably violated the principle of legality. This generalization strikes us as overly simplistic. Clearly, not all political trials exhibit technical violations of the principles of legality. And if one recognizes that the politics served by political trials can be larger in scope than the straightforward elimination of enemies, then it is possible to restore to (some) political trials a "universal" character. After all, the practice of staging political trials without violating the principles of legality formed the focal point of Ernst Fraenkel's analysis of Nazi Germany's dual state.

What Fraenkel called a predictable "normative state" (which exhibited fidelity to law) coexisted with an unpredictable "prerogative state" (which generated wanton violence) in a hybrid regime that he famously dubbed "the dual state."[50] Curiously, most of the scholars who had been socialized during

[48] Shklar, *Legalism*, p. 170. [49] Shklar, *Legalism*, p. 180.

[50] Ernst Fraenkel, *The Dual State: A Contribution to the Theory of Dictatorship*, translated by E. A. Shils with an Introduction by Jens Meierhenrich (Oxford: Oxford University Press, [1941] 2017). For a contemporary engagement with Fraenkel, and an extension of his theoretical contribution to a broader range of cases, see Jens Meierhenrich, *The Legacies of Law: Long-*

Nazi dictatorship chose to disregard Fraenkel's ethnographic account initially written (unlike Franz Neumann's more famous *Behemoth*) inside of Germany.[51] This, in turn, draws attention to Shklar's selective engagement with legal theory. A more convincing (and usable) account of political trials might have been forthcoming if she had entertained in more depth the idea, courtesy of legal positivism, that the value of law is what actors make of it: "Although it is not a particularly inspiring or romantic description, the law is, in the end, an instrument. And like all instruments, it can be used for good or bad purposes."[52] We believe the same holds true for political trials, which is why we wish to complicate the categorically negative view popularized by Shklar – and recently revived by Eric Posner.

From the vantage point of legal history, it is worth pointing out that all kinds of odious regimes – apartheid South Africa and authoritarian Chile among them – have shown a considerable amount of respect for a legal way of doing things, even while they were using trials for the purpose of domination (and destruction). Empirically speaking, Shklar, like Kirchheimer, generalized on the basis of a selective evidence pool, gleaned in her case from the immediate post–World War II context. The thinness of Shklar's conceptualization is worth noting because her influence on the study of political trials is, for better or worse, still considerable. Most recently, Kathryn Sikkink, to whose work we will return below, invoked Shklar to dismiss the staged military trial (and immediate execution) on December 25, 1989, of Nicolae Ceausescu, the former president of communist Romania, and his wife as a "political trial." According to Sikkink, the case was "not a human rights prosecution but a political trial of the kind that has long been common during and after violent regime changes."[53] The Romanian proceeding most certainly was a political trial, conventionally understood. (It qualifies as an example of a particular subtype of political trial – the *destructive trial* – that we introduce below.) And yet, the pejorative use of the term that is so explicit in both Shklar and Sikkink is analytically problematic because it glosses over *both* the manifold ways in which supposedly ordinary trials, too, can be political *and* the ways in which perfectly adequate due process protections are compatible with highly politicized trials. Bilsky has shown as much in her study of the Kastner, Eichmann, Kufr Qassem, and Yigal Amir trials in Israel.[54] Christenson elaborated the same point three decades ago when he distinguished

Run Consequences of Legal Development in South Africa, 1652–2000 (Cambridge: Cambridge University Press, 2008).

[51] For a comprehensive account of the gestation and continued significance of Fraenkel's classic, see Jens Meierhenrich, "An Ethnography of Nazi Law: The Intellectual Foundations of Ernst Fraenkel's Theory of Dictatorship," in Fraenkel, *The Dual State*.

[52] Scott J. Shapiro, *Legality* (Cambridge: Belknap Press of Harvard University Press, 2011), p. 399.

[53] Kathryn Sikkink, *The Justice Cascade: How Human Rights Prosecutions Are Changing World Politics* (New York: Norton, 2011), p. 13.

[54] Bilsky, *Transformative Justice*.

conceptually, as noted above, between political trials "within the rule of law," as he put it, and those outside of it.[55] He called the latter "partisan trials," a helpful term that captures the negative bias associated with this particular subtype of political trial.

Yet trials need not be partisan to deserve the adjective political. Trials can be political without being partisan. Related to the prominence of the trope of partisanship in the existing literature on political trials is the trope of publicity. There appears to be a widely held but mistaken assumption that, in addition to a high degree of partisanship, a political trial will necessarily have a high profile. We do not think this to be a necessary attribute. Even ordinary trials can be extraordinarily political. Political trials are political *not* because they are unfair and not because they do nothing other than eliminate political foes, nor are they political mainly because they attract widespread publicity (although they may very well attract such attention). Rather, they are political because they involve political disputes of some social significance and are both reflective and constitutive of power relations in a given polity. Paul Schervish has put it well: "A political trial is an explicit occasion in which adversarial parties contend over the normative legitimacy of the legal order as a whole rather than just over the distribution of outcomes within the existing legal dispensation."[56] By adopting more value-neutral terms than some of our predecessors in the study of political trials, we are in a position to zoom in with more precision on the particular – and frequently changing – nature of the contentious politics of trials in a given setting. If we are truly serious about better comprehending the role of politics in the courtroom, we would be well advised to jettison outmoded notions of the concept of the political trial and embrace the complexity of the political. The CLS movement of the 1970s and 1980s set out to do just that.

Critical Legal Studies in the 1970s and 1980s

The CLS movement came to represent one of the most sophisticated – and controversial – intellectual efforts at excavating the meaning of the political in the law. It put new questions on the intellectual agenda, notably: Where exactly does power in law come from, who wields it, and how does it manifest itself in legal outcomes? In answer, CLS advocates called into question in more radical a fashion than HLS scholars ever felt necessary the ostensibly uncritical faith in law that pervaded the legal establishment in advanced industrial democracies. CLS, like many academic trends, was less a movement than a collection of loosely associated thinkers and ideas. Briefly prominent in the legal academy in the 1970s and 1980s, CLS represented one of the afterlives of the New Left. And like many such subsequent critical trends, it largely faded during the

[55] Christenson, "A Political Theory of Political Trials."

[56] Paul G. Schervish, "Political Trials and the Social Construction of Deviance," *Qualitative Sociology*, Vol. 7 (1984), p. 195.

conservative reaction in the decades since. At the same time, in light of recent discussions of the need for greater regulation of financial markets, and indeed, broader calls for reformist legislation more generally, it is worth asking whether CLS might not still have something useful to say about the law and its relationship to politics – critical and otherwise, especially when it comes to the study of political trials. After all, with Martti Koskenniemi, it was a leading CLS advocate who made one of the most enduring contributions to the theory of political trials in recent memory.[57]

In its most immediate – and critical, if not polemical – self-understanding, CLS saw its task as unmasking law as an inherently repressive mode of social organization, and trials as the most manifest expression of that repression. "Legal reasoning is an inherently repressive form of interpretive thought which limits our comprehension of the social world and its possibilities. This interpretive thought emerges within consciousness at moments of uncertainty about the legitimacy of the concrete world within which we find ourselves, and its function is to institutionalize ... the boundaries of a legitimate rationality."[58] This was a more radical critique than simply the orthodox Marxist assertion that law served class interests. More fundamentally, social actors gave themselves over to the limited rationality of law as they sought to legitimize and quite literally authorize their social experience. Peter Gabel compares this operation to "resistance" in the psychoanalytic sense. "Legal thought originates, of course, within the consciousness of the dominant class because it is in this class's interest to bring it into being, but it is accepted and interiorized by everyone because of the traumatic absence of connectedness that would otherwise erupt into awareness."[59] In this respect, law quite literally functions as a social "ego" censoring an illicit wish for social connectedness.

This quasi-psychoanalytic interpretation of legal repression created a certain interpretive dilemma for CLS, however. Insofar as Marx is right that the point of critique is to lead to action and transformation, casting law in the role of social ego obviates any such move. One approach – more or less explicitly psychoanalytic in nature – is to call actively for a return of the repressed, a polymorphously perverse release of legal desire. "The solution to this dilemma is to be found in the ontological meaning of each person of *experiencing* the intersubjective movement of socio-economic relations as a political communion of normative subjects."[60] This legal wish-fulfillment operates as individuals "imagine that we are actually disalienated in an harmonious socio-political connection that is also 'the law.' "[61] Such utopian

[57] Martti Koskenniemi, "Between Impunity and Show Trials," *Max Planck Yearbook of United Nations Law*, Vol. 6 (2002), pp. 1–35.

[58] Peter Gabel, "Reification in Legal Reasoning," *Research in Law and Sociology*, Vol. 3 (1980), p. 25.

[59] Gabel, "Reification in Legal Reasoning," p. 26.

[60] Gabel, "Reification in Legal Reasoning," p. 44.

[61] Gabel, "Reification in Legal Reasoning," p. 44.

fantasies seem sorely lacking as a program for social action. After all, Freud, though often ambivalent about repression, was clear that the ego was a structurally necessary and often beneficial component of human psyche. In this same way, law, as a necessary form of social mediation, one which represses the unfulfillable desire for direct, harmonious, and unmediated social interaction, seems difficult to simply wish out of existence.

A more plausible response to the repressive function of law arises from what is perhaps the best-known concept to emerge from the CLS movement: the notion of "legal indeterminacy." At its most basic, the idea of legal indeterminacy holds that legal rules, such as statutes, do not adequately predict legal outcomes.[62] The most obvious examples of this are when courts of first and second instance reach diametrically opposed rulings when examining the exact same case. In this broad sense, legal indeterminacy was not a new idea generated by CLS. A generation earlier, the so-called legal realists had first developed the concept.[63] The legal realists, however, had used this indeterminacy to buttress their calls for incorporating extra-legal considerations of policy into legal reasoning. Since the law could not in and of itself determine legal outcomes, they argued, something else had to do that work and that might as well be the policy preferences of judges. As Oliver Wendell Holmes put it: "You can give any conclusion a logical form. You always can imply a condition in a contract. But why do you imply it? ... [Because of] a concealed, half-conscious battle on the background question of legislative policy."[64] In this sense, the concept of legal indeterminacy – realist or critical – implies that all legal interpretations, all legal encounters, are irreducibly political.

The legal realist position is at least implicitly instrumentalist. The question was less what law is, than what law is for. (In this respect, the true heirs of legal realism are not so much CLS scholars but rather members of the so-called Law and Economics movement – like the aforementioned Eric Posner – who view economic efficiency as the most appropriate exogenous guide for legal reasoning.) This, in turn, implies that extra-legal policy concerns can be taken as both truly exogenous – independent of the law which they guide – and as coherent and knowable. So for legal realists, the politics of trials are indistinguishable from *policy*; the purposive quality of politics transfers directly to the courtroom. CLS scholars have rejected both of these claims – that policy is exogenous and that it is truly knowable.

Critical scholars don't see legal language as indeterminate *relative* to the social context to which it refers. Rather, they see legal language as indeterminate *because of* the

[62] Duncan Kennedy, "A Semiotics of Legal Argument," *Syracuse Law Review*, Vol. 42 (1991), p. 75.

[63] W. W. Fisher et al., eds., *American Legal Realism* (Oxford: Oxford University Press, 1993).

[64] Oliver Wendell Holmes, Jr., "The Path of the Law," *Harvard Law Review*, Vol. 10 (1897), pp. 457–478.

indeterminacy of the social context to which it refers. The indeterminacy of the social world frustrates instrumentalist efforts to explain or prescribe legal rules on the basis of their service to certain interests.[65]

According to CLS scholars, social reality is indeterminate in two senses. First, the application of policy is no more predictable or consistent than is the application of general rules. "If the application of formal legal criteria to particular cases requires the intercession of policy judgments, as the realists contended, so does the application of a general policy to a particular case. There is an infinite regress implicit in the need for a second policy with which to identify and apply a given policy."[66] Policy cannot serve as a *deus ex machina* to salvage legal reasoning from indeterminacy, since policy – and the interests which supposedly guide it – is no more determinate than law. So all law is politics, on this reading, yet all politics is indeterminate.

Yet the problem goes beyond this. As Duncan Kennedy observed, "the judge cannot claim that legislative acquiescence legitimizes his action because he himself creates, through his decisions of particular cases, the situation from which will emerge an as yet indeterminate constellation of legislative power."[67] In other words, law helps constitute, in unpredictable, indeterminate ways the very social context which could determine extra-legal criteria for legal reasoning. Law and politics are mutually constitutive, yet in ways that are unpredictable and inconsistent. (This is consistent with CLS's broader rejection of the orthodox Marxist reduction of law to class interests, which would constitute a highly *determinant* relation of law and politics.)

To put this in somewhat different terms, if rules do not determine legal outcomes, but policy preferences do, then the question arises as to what criteria could be applied to adjudge different policy options. One – descriptive – claim would be simply to say it is the personal policy preferences of the individual judge trying any given case, what Judge Joseph Hutcheson called a judicial "hunch."[68] This view has proven rather unsatisfactory to most legal academics (if not necessarily to judges) because its embrace of indeterminacy is perhaps a bit too blatant. The more typical approach, especially among the so-called post-realists, who dominate the contemporary American legal academy, has been to argue for some variation of a "balance" theory. This view asserts that the goal of legal decisions ought to be to balance an aggregate of competing interest positions, to be political, as it were, but pluralist. This has been framed as an explicitly "democratic" way of adjudicating legal conflicts. "The proper function of our law schools is, in short,

65 Guyora Binder, "Critical Legal Studies," in Dennis Patterson, ed., *A Companion to Philosophy of Law and Legal Theory* (London: Blackwell, 1996), p. 281.

66 Gary Peller, "The Metaphysics of American Law," *California Law Review*, Vol. 73 (1985), pp. 1152–1153.

67 Duncan Kennedy, "Legal Formality," *Journal of Legal Studies*, Vol. 2 (1973), p. 385.

68 Joseph Hutchenson, Jr., *Law and the Modern Mind* (New York: Brentano, 1930), p. 104.

to contribute to the training of policy-makers for the ever more complete achievement of the democratic values that constitute the professed ends of American polity."[69] This would be to acknowledge the irreducibly political nature of adjudication, without reducing politics to dominant power relations.

While by no means hostile to democracy, critical legal scholars reject the notion that policy can balance competing interests to achieve fair and democratic outcomes, because they view such interests as themselves partially the product of the legal process itself. They are not pre-given. The legal system only recognizes some interests as legitimate, while others are excluded. Lawyers will thus frame their clients' interests in ways the legal system will recognize, whether or not this is how the clients themselves would understand them. These legally recognizable interests then become "real." They may even become internalized by lay actors after their encounter with the legal system. Even if not, extra-legal interests that are not recognized by law cannot be balanced by juridified policy making; they simply do not exist, as far as the law is concerned.

> The ritual incarnation of social values is accomplished by the lawyers and the judge without any help from the litigants. It is the lawyers who perform the ceremony. It is they who assert rights and see their assertions recognized by the judge . . . Out of this interplay of performances, a sense of resolution or wholeness may emerge and be crystallized and confirmed by the judge. To be sure, he gives judgment only to one side, but he expresses his conclusion in terms established by both.[70]

Moreover, the "litigant, if he is well advised, will sit mutely and foolishly" throughout the proceedings. And if not, the judge will advise him or her to speak only through his/her attorney and, in extreme cases, may even hold the litigant in contempt for seeking to represent her own "interests" directly, without professional mediation.

Thus, the law cannot actually adjudicate and balance competing social interests, but only those which law itself constitutes. This is part of what systems theorists, like Gunther Teubner or Niklas Luhmann, mean when they refer to law as "autopoietic" or purely self-referential.[71] Consequently, for critical legal studies scholars projects for reform that operate within law – Peller's advocacy lawyering – are doomed to failure. Like Kafka's parable of the law, critical legal scholars see law as effectively inaccessible. For them, the key is to in effect reverse the process of autopoietic translation, to transform legal conflicts into social ones, to not stand before the gates of the law, waiting in vain for them to open, but find a side-door onto a different kind of terrain altogether. As with the post-legal realists, the goal for critical legal scholars is ultimately

[69] H. D. Lassell and Myres S. McDougal, "Legal Education and Public Policy: Professional Training in the Public Interest," *Yale Law Journal*, Vol. 52 (1943), pp. 203–295.

[70] William H. Simon, "The Ideology of Advocacy: Procedural Justice and Professional Ethics," *Wisconsin Law Review*, Vol. 29 (1978), pp. 97–98.

[71] Gunther Teubner, *Law as an Autopoietic System* (Oxford: Blackwell, 1993); and Niklas Luhmann, *Social Systems* (Stanford: Stanford University Press, 1995).

"democracy," which in their minds is more participatory than procedural, and as the utopian language of alternate imaginaries indicates, it is one which would ultimately transform law into something unrecognizable, because it is grounded in a profoundly different, albeit largely unspecified, social order.[72]

What does CLS offer by way of insight into the workings of political trials? The first and most obvious contribution is to break down the distinction between law and politics. While Kirchheimer and Shklar both acknowledged that law and politics were not always antagonistic, they nonetheless viewed them as distinct forms of social action, with divergent internal logics. The imbrication of one in the other meant, at a minimum, a distortion of its "true" nature, and at worst, a deep perversion. CLS, on the other hand, maintains, rightly in our view, that law and politics are mutually constitutive ways of organizing social power relations. As one scholar sympathetic to this intellectual stance writes, "it is readily apparent that political trials are not isolated collisions between courts and activists. These cases arise from fundamental, unresolved contradictions of capitalism, between movements for equality and the state's commitment to the unequal order, between the state's need both to repress dissent and maintain its legitimacy."[73] Politics, on this view, does not so much "use" law for extra-legal ends, as law internalizes political purposes and formulates them in proper legal terms. This broader understanding of the mutual constitution of law and politics obviously broadens considerably the range of proceedings that can be considered "political trials." CLS thus offers a way out of the overly reductive, Schmittian understanding of politics that shaped HLS.

If CLS is useful for broadening our understanding of the political in relation to law, it comes with two important limitations of its own. The first is that the CLS critique of law – notably the claim that law silences extra-legal actors by constituting their interests – is one-sided. The example of the ways in which litigants *can* be silenced by legal proceedings is a powerful one. Yet, as Elizabeth Mertz has shown, what she terms the linguistic ideology of law (its metapragmatics) is "double-edged."[74] For instance, the creation of a legal persona "is a double-edged process: the very same legal norms that may strip a story of arguably important social context may also require that we set aside biases against people based on background or past behavior that should not be part of the judgment in a particular instance."[75]

The abstract quality of legal personae, their status as mere tokens for argumentative positions stripped of their specific identities, also allows

[72] Binder, "Critical Legal Studies," p. 286.

[73] James P. Brady, "Fair and Impartial Railroad: The Jury, the Media, and Political Trials," *Journal of Criminal Justice*, Vol. 11 (1983), p. 246.

[74] Elizabeth Mertz, *The Language of Law School: Learning to "Think like a Lawyer"* (Oxford: Oxford University Press, 2007).

[75] Mertz, *The Language of Law School*, p. 101.

a degree of neutrality and egalitarianism to creep into legal reasoning that can, at times, be mobilized on behalf of the powerless.[76] At the same time, legal language, by abstracting social identities, obscures essential aspects of real-world context and variables that lay observers might find relevant for making moral judgments about "justice" in a given situation. As Mertz puts it, "linguistic filtering conceals the impact of social power, in the process contributing to the perpetuation of social inequalities through law ... At the same time, this metalinguistic level is not simply a reflex of power dynamics, transparently converting the interests of the powerful into legal results ... [Even] relatively powerless members of society have occasionally prevailed in legal settings."[77] So, while a critique of law's historical role is certainly warranted, we ought not to lose sight of the capacity of law – and the courtrooms associated with its practice – to enable progressive social change as well. The politics of political trials need not be repressive or "persecutory" in Shklar's phrase. They can be – and on occasion have been – progressive, even liberatory. In the present volume, Mark Tushnet's chapter on *Brown* v. *Board of Education* provides a powerful example of this historical fact.

Second, in arguing that law constitutes its own social context, CLS scholars have tended to be insufficiently dialectical. Duncan Kennedy's example of the way court verdicts shape the context for future legislation is correct, but he forgets to add that future legislation also shapes the context for future adjudication. In stressing the indeterminacy of law, CLS advocates have underestimated its capacity to set agendas, if not determine specific outcomes. In particular, CLS thinkers have tended, ironically, to focus on "law" in formal (and positivist) terms, as systems of rules, which cannot dictate specific outcomes. But law is more than just a set of rules. It is as much a place of procedures and a realm of rituals. And procedures and rituals are most certainly determinant, not in terms of outcomes, but in terms of enabling – or constraining – participation. The chapter on the Rivonia trial by Jens Meierhenrich and Catherine Cole, establishes this point very clearly.[78] The ritual dimension of law is about modes of participation and enactments of social dissensus and cohesion. Law, inside the courtroom or outside of it, has the capacity to stage social rupture and social order, and enables legal participants to (literally) reenact moments of discontinuity and reconstruction. In this respect, one is reminded of William Sewell's discussion of "events" as occurrences in which social structures, seemingly self-reproducing, generate the potential for their own transformation.[79] Law is, in a manner of speaking, both a structure *and* an event. Law indeed does generate its social context, and in so doing, reproduces

[76] Mertz, *The Language of Law School*, p. 213. [77] Mertz, *The Language of Law School*, p. 217.

[78] Jens Meierhenrich and Catherine M. Cole, "In the Theater of the Rule of Law: Performing the Rivonia Trial in South Africa, 1963–1964," in this volume.

[79] William Sewell, "Historical Events as Transformations of Structures: Inventing Revolution at the Bastille," *Theory and Society*, Vol. 25 (1996), pp. 841–881.

itself. But law also internalizes its social context in ways that it sometimes fails to digest. The law can fail to conquer social context. And when that happens, law can change, both itself and its social context. This is one major mechanism for social transformation. Because of its double-edged quality, and because of its capacity for failure, law offers a particularly potent resource for reconfiguring the distribution of social power within society, particularly in heavily juridified and judicialized modern polities.

Political trials are particularly likely to possess such transformative, "eventful" characteristics. The effect of political trials is less to "expand" the realm of the political, as Kirchheimer would have it, than it is to transform the terms of the political, by formulating power relations in legal terms and, in the process, altering them. The indeterminacy of legal outcomes, about which CLS scholars were quite right, means not only that politics operates *in* the courtroom but also that the politics *of* the courtroom can change the politics of the society in which it is embedded. But whether and how this will happen is complex. It depends not (certainly not exclusively) on the intentions of a trial's architects but on the constellation of forces in and around the trial, and the way these interact with the procedural and ritual aspects of the trial.

This brings us back to Koskenniemi, with whom we began our foray into CLS. As provocative as Koskenniemi's account of political trials is, it is unpersuasive in a number of respects. For one, Koskenniemi's dichotomous approach to the meaning of political trials significantly reduces the complexity of the role of the political. On his reading, political trials – a label that he reserves exclusively for high-profile prosecutions of individuals charged with international crimes in domestic or international jurisdictions – can only ever culminate in "show trials." The only alternative for coming to terms with the past, which seems to be the primary purpose of political trials on his account, is "impunity."

This portrayal does injustice to the rich and diverse universe of political trials, a significant number of which can be located on a continuum somewhere in between the two poles of impunity and show trials. To liken *a priori* all proceedings conducted at the ICTY to show trials "in the precise Stalinist sense of that expression" puts, methodologically speaking, the cart before the horse.[80] Just because the origins of the ICTY – and the invention of its jurisdiction – raise important questions about the legitimacy of international justice in the twenty-first century does not mean that all of the *ad hoc* tribunal's contributions to international law and politics have been a sham. It is high time that CLS scholars (as well as realist and neorealist scholars in both International

80 Koskenniemi, "Between Impunity and Show Trials," p. 18. Note that Koskenniemi has been influenced greatly by the controversial French-Vietnamese legal practitioner and theorist Jacques Vergès, notably his influential *De la stratégie judiciaire* (Paris: Éditions de Minuit, 1968).

Relations and International Law) open up the black box of international courts and tribunals.

Put differently, the meta-theoretical CLS critique of political trials would have considerably more purchase if it were underwritten by a comprehensive and systematic – rather than merely anecdotal – analysis of empirical evidence. It is certainly important to study, say, the event of "rupture" in the courtroom, as Emilios Christodoulidis wants us to do, or to examine how a political trial "establishes subject positions, delimits stakes and procedures and redeems these determinations by introducing a dimension of contestability to them according to the ideal of unconstrained discourse, as propounded by the Frankfurt School," but it is equally important to ask how these meta-theoretical conjectures relate to our expanding base of empirical knowledge about political trials.[81] If HLS ultimately failed to adequately recognize the mutually constitutive nature of law and politics, CLS responded to this problem by pitching its analysis at such a high level of abstraction that it can be difficult to see how it could possibly be relevant for understanding goings-on in courtrooms. Indeed, CLS as a whole has been conspicuously silent on empirical matters. A study in contrast is the "Empirical Legal Studies" movement that got underway in the 1990s.

Empirical Legal Studies in the 1990s and 2000s

Although ELS has not displayed any intrinsic interest in the study of political trials, its ontological and epistemological assumptions about how law works is of immediate relevance for the purpose of this study. As a research program, ELS emerged in the late 1990s. It developed rapidly and within a few years saw the creation of the *Journal of Empirical Legal Studies* at Cornell Law School in 2004. The hallmark of ELS (as opposed to empirical legal research more generally) is the use of quantitative methodology. Since its inception, ELS has established itself as a vibrant, if narrow, subfield under the broader umbrella of law and society scholarship.

Importantly, scholars steeped in ELS have no patience for CLS-style assumptions about the inherently political nature of law, and the indeterminacy of politics. Where CLS disputes the existence of knowable facts, ELS trades in them. Without a belief in an objectively verifiable world, the reliance on large-n data sets would be epistemologically unsustainable. The emphasis within ELS on the systematic nature of empirical research is shared by scholars who are more inclined to work qualitatively but who do take seriously the importance of methodological rigor. As Peter Cane and Herbert Kritzer recently put it,

[81] Emilios Christodoulidis, "Political Trials as Events," in Fleur Johns, Richard Joyce, and Sundhya Pahuja, eds., *Events: The Force of International Law* (London: Routledge, 2011), p. 131.

"empirical" research involves the systematic collection of information ("data") and its analysis according to some generally accepted method. Of central importance is the *systematic* nature of the process, both of collecting and analyzing the information. The information can come from a wide range of sources including surveys, documents, reporting systems, observation, interviews, experiments, decisions, and events ... The analysis can involve simple counting, sophisticated statistical manipulation, grouping into like sets, identification of sequences (in some circumstances called "process tracing"), matching of patterns, or simple labelling of themes. Ultimately, the analyst engages in a process of interpreting the results of the analysis in order to link those results to the question motivating the research.[82]

For the purpose this chapter, we follow Cane and Kritzer and conceive of ELS more broadly than is often the case. This notwithstanding, empirical legal research, as defined by its contemporary practitioners, excludes historical legal studies. As Cane and Kritzer put it, "Some empirical legal scholars use historical materials and may employ historiographical methods, but they tend not to label what they are doing as a 'legal history.' Typically such research begins with a hypothesis of the sort associated with social science and uses historical information as its data."[83] In the context of political trials, the writings of Eric Posner, whom we encountered at the outset of this chapter, are most pertinent as far as the promise and limits of ELS are concerned. The research program carried out over the last decade or so by Kathryn Sikkink on what she terms "the justice cascade" is illustrative of the hypothesis-driven ELS work of which Cane and Kritzer speak. Finally, Ron Hassner took the perhaps most historical of political trials – the trial of Jesus – and subjected it to an ELS-style analysis replete with a formal model. Let us briefly consider in turn the contributions of Posner, Sikkink, and Hassner to the study of political trials.

Posner's scholarship, heavily influenced as it is by the law and economics movement, has deep affinities with ELS. His recent treatise, coauthored with Alan Sykes, on the economic foundations of international law bespeaks an understanding of law that most ELS scholars, many of whom are economists, share:

Economists evaluate legal institutions by using two normative criteria. Under the Pareto criterion, a law is desirable if it makes at least one person better off without making anyone else worse off. Under the Kaldor-Hicks criterion, a law is desirable even though it produces losers as well as winners, as long as winners gain more than the losers lose.[84]

As we have seen, HLS and CLS use rather different criteria to evaluate legal institutions, notably political trials. But ELS brings something to the table that is

82 Peter Cane and Herbert M. Kritzer, "Introduction," in Peter Cane and Herbert M. Kritzer., eds., *The Oxford Handbook of Empirical Legal Research* (Oxford: Oxford University Press, 2010), p. 4.

83 Cane and Kritzer, "Introduction," pp. 4–5.

84 Eric A. Posner and Alan O. Sykes, *Economic Foundations of International Law* (Cambridge: Belknap Press of Harvard University Press, 2013), p. 13.

undeniably relevant when studying the politics of adjudication, namely a simplifying lens that allows one to abstract from the messiness of life, international and otherwise, that usually has an important structuring effect on political trials. As with most orthodox methodologies, any explanation developed purely on the basis of deductive reasoning will hardly be more than piecemeal. Having said that, the assumption that rational, self-interested agents use legal procedure in order to address domestic (or international) externalities and secure other benefits that might accrue on the basis of doing so is not altogether different from *some* of the assumptions that HLS and CLS scholars make about the function of law as a means to an end. The added value of being able to formalize or quantify (or both) the logic of politicization in the context of trials has the potential of advancing the study of political trials, notably by drawing our attention to previously unobserved connections or correlations, and by increasing the potential for generalization.

Posner is the most prominent ELS scholar to have addressed the topic of political trials. Based on a strong commitment to methodological individualism, Posner has advanced what he calls an instrumental theory of legalism. He regards the institution of the political trial through the lens of this theory. In a nutshell, Posner's instrumental theory of legalism, which he developed at greater length elsewhere, holds that a rational government in a democratic system with an interest in maximizing its political support will invariably pursue a strategy of "liberal legalism."[85] The theory is founded on the simplifying assumption that all actors in a given polity inherently are power-maximizers: "I assume that the government's main goal is to stay in power, and that a party's main goal is either to maintain power (if it has it) or obtain power (if it does not). All political actors know that they cannot maintain power unless they implement policies desired by the general public, including (but not exclusively) their political base."[86]

However, Posner's categorical assertion that "[p]olitical trials cannot occur in a regime of liberal legalism as long as legal institutions uphold this ideal" is unpersuasive.[87] It is sustainable only on the basis of an extremely reductionist understanding of what the concept of the political entails. Even if one understands political trials to comprise only destructive trials (in our sense) intended to eliminate political enemies, there is little reason to think that such cases are incompatible with the liberal rule of law. What, after all, were the Nuremberg trials but an attempt to destroy the Nazi enemy using the rule of law? And if one understands the political to encompass more than the elimination of enemies, as we do, then the claim that political trials are incompatible with liberal legalism makes even less sense.

[85] Posner, "Political Trials in Domestic and International Law," p. 98. For a more comprehensive statement, see Eric A. Posner, *The Perils of Global Legalism* (Chicago: University of Chicago Press, 2009).

[86] Posner, "Political Trials in Domestic and International Law," p. 99.

[87] Posner, "Political Trials in Domestic and International Law," p. 97.

This brings us to another scholar whose recent output brought her in the vicinity of ELS: Kathryn Sikkink. To be sure, Sikkink can only be subsumed under the movement if one applies an inclusive definition of what ELS entails, as we do, following Cane and Kritzer. Combining qualitative and quantitative methods, Sikkink and her coauthors have devoted a great deal of time to explaining the conditions affecting the creation and diffusion of human rights trials, with particular reference to the prosecution of human rights violations in countries that have undergone transitions from authoritarian rule. Interestingly, for our purpose, Sikkink categorically distinguishes "human rights trials" from "political trials," suggesting that the protection of the rights of the accused in the former is the key difference. Sikkink invokes Shklar in her defense, notably the latter's proclamation that "[p]olitical trials scorn the principle of legality."[88] We disagree with Sikkink, as her account is rather too truncated in historical terms to highlight the longer-term genealogy of "human rights prosecutions."

Sikkink argues that there has been a broad progression from what she terms an impunity model prior to 1945 to a state accountability model in the postwar period to an individual criminal accountability model beginning in the 1980s and 1990s. Obviously, these models are meant to be heuristic, yet her periodization is off in ways that make her "justice cascade" of the past twenty or thirty years seem more formidable and straightforward than it has been (or is likely to be going forward). The immunity model not only persists into the present (as Sikkink acknowledges) but was certainly challenged already in the early nineteenth century.[89] Indeed, the state accountability model – in which states, not individuals, were held accountable for atrocities – was enshrined in the so-called Hague Conventions. And far from characterizing the politics of the late 1940s, the UN explicitly considered and rejected a doctrine of state criminality in crafting instruments like the 1948 Genocide Convention. These oversimplifications of periodization make the tribunals of the 1980s look both more distinctive than they were and fail to account for earlier waves of international legalism that receded. Sikkink wants to tell a Whig story of the triumph of legalism and human rights prosecutions that is progressive and irreversible. A more nuanced history points to a much less teleological trajectory, with legalism alternating with realpolitik and often working side by side with it.[90]

By categorically declaring human rights trials (provided they adhere to the rule of law) as non-political, Sikkink skirts a most significant issue: the contentious politics that usually structure any domestic or international debate

88 Sikkink, *The Justice Cascade*, p. 13; Shklar, *Legalism*, p. 149.

89 See, e.g., the account of the pressure to try Napoleon I in Gary Jonathan Bass, *Stay the Hand of Vengeance: The Politics of War Crimes Tribunals* (Princeton: Princeton University Press, 2001).

90 See, e.g., Samuel Moyn, *The Last Utopia: Human Rights in History* (Cambridge: Belknap Press of Harvard University Press, 2010).

over the promise and limits of prosecutions for human rights violations. In fact, much of her own analysis of Latin American countries, especially Argentina, belies her claim that human rights proceedings are not political trials. They may not be show trials – although the performance of Luis Moreno Ocampo and colleagues in the 1985 "Trial of the Juntas" in Buenos Aires might persuade some to think otherwise – but it would be misleading to consider them anything other than political trials, for reasons to be explained in more conceptual detail below.

As a result of adopting a normative and pejorative conception of political trials, Sikkink is unable to appreciate the innumerable court proceedings in history during which the rule of law has been wielded as a weapon. Several of our chapters illustrate the danger of locating the phenomenon of political trials outside of the rule of law. They demonstrate that the principle of legality is often perfectly compatible with legal repression. Ernst Fraenkel was the first to make the point in his classic *The Dual State*. It has since been borne out repeatedly by scholarship on the politics of courts – and trials – in authoritarian regimes.[91]

Curiously, given their diametrically opposed epistemological and ontological positions, Posner and Sikkink on the one hand and Koskenniemi on the other misunderstand political trials for the very same reason: they work with a dogmatic concept of the political trial. On *both* types of accounts, political trials can only ever be partisan trials. By contrast, we believe that partisanship should be treated as a variable feature rather than a defining attribute of political trials. Political trials may exhibit high or low degrees of partisanship. We should not take partisanship as a given but try to figure out how it manifests itself inside the courtroom – and outside of it. By treating partisanship as a thing to be measured and explained rather than a thing to be assumed, we stand to gain more nuanced insights about the dynamics of legal contention because we automatically become more attuned to the social mechanisms and processes that are driving them. The work of ELS intersects with what Gregory Shaffer and Tom Ginzburg called "the empirical turn in international law scholarship." Shaffer and Ginzburg highlighted the difference between the empirical turn and the legacy of empiricism in the study of law. As they put it,

> The empirical turn is not atheoretical, but it generally is not aimed at building grand metatheory. Instead, it focuses on midrange theorizing concerning the conditions under which international law (IL) is formed and those under which it has effects in different contexts, aiming to explain variation ... By building theory from empirical study, it involves what one of us has called an "emergent analytics" – that is, analytics that oscillate between empirical findings, abstract theorizing, real-world testing, and back again. In this way, scholars help narrow the gap between abstract theory, empirical

[91] *Pars pro toto*, see Tom Ginsburg and Tamir Moustafa, eds., *Rule by Law: The Politics of Courts in Authoritarian Regimes* (Cambridge: Cambridge University Press, 2008).

research, and the world of practice. Theoretical engagement becomes part of a dynamic, recurrent, interactive process with empirical assessment of international law in action.[92]

This relatively new emphasis in the legal academy (at least outside of the law and economics subfield) on analytical rigor is of immediate relevance for the study of political trials. It points to a solution to the problem of pure description that we bemoaned earlier. For a not insignificant portion of the research output making up the empirical turn in international law has focused on the salience of political trials, notably in the province of international criminal law. This bodes well, in our estimation, for further deepening and broadening the study of political trials in the years to come. This requires, however, that the "mid-range theorizing" that emerges appreciates that law and politics are interrelated, not antithetical, structures. Empiricism, no matter how rigorous, is only valuable on a foundation of conceptual rigor and in the service of theoretical explication. Otherwise, it is simply a more quantitative form of description, less enjoyable to read but no more analytically productive.

Our interdisciplinary approach to the study of political trials owes a debt to *all* of the aforementioned legal studies movements, and it seeks to stimulate a vibrant interaction among them. Because the conventional wisdom on political trials is largely stuck in the 1950s and 1960s, it is incumbent for future scholars to engage with more recent perspectives on the role of law in modern society. It is also important to remember that what is at stake is not the entirety of the political or the legal worlds but a specific relationship between the two that is operating within the precisely circumscribed venue of the trial, itself only one of law's many operational sites. To properly understand the meaning of these sites in the larger context of the judicialization of politics, it is important to study them historically *and* critically *and* empirically. This does not mean taking on board uncritically any of the theoretical perspectives that we sketched in the preceding part, but it does require taking them seriously and placing them in dialogue with one another. For each offers a panoply of insights about the relationship between law and politics that are useful for studying political trials in theory and history.

The Concept of the Trial

While political trials certainly are a form of politics, they also remain trials. It is therefore imperative to come to terms with the nature and function of trials as legal institutions before we turn to their political dimensions. Given the significance of the trial as an institution of both civil and criminal justice – in domestic as well as international affairs – it is remarkable how little sustained theorizing exists regarding its substantive elements. This is far from a trivial matter, for as the legal historian Lawrence Friedman pointed out, "both critics

92 Gregory Shaffer and Tom Ginsburg, "The Empirical Turn in International Legal Scholarship," *American Journal of International Law*, Vol. 106 (2012), p. 1.

and friends of the modern trial operate from some notion of what the ideal trial is like."[93] Lindsay Farmer locates the reason for the marginalization of the trial as a conceptual variable in the development of law and society scholarship in recent decades. On the one hand, he notes that the sociology of law has turned its attention to various "means of diverting cases from the formal institutions of law [arguing] that in practice the trial is not central to the operation of law."[94] On the other hand, he argues that, while CLS rightly critiqued the formalism of much legal scholarship, its interest was "in the social and political forces that shape law making," and that it therefore accepted the formalist contention that trials are merely "a forum of rule application."[95] Both approaches neglect the trial itself.

Farmer might have added that ELS, too, has contributed to the neglect of trial-based scholarship, notably by popularizing, based on U.S. data, the idea of "the vanishing trial," i.e., the empirical finding that the absolute number of trials has been steadily declining in every case category, most dramatically since the 1980s.[96] If trials are less empirically salient, the impetus to take them seriously at the level of theory also declines.

Another reason why theorizing about the nature of trial is scant may have to do with the inherent complexity of doing so. Joseph Jaconelli cuts to the heart of the epistemological challenge: "To pose the question, 'What is a trial,' is to invite an answer which aims to transcend particular times, places and cultures. It is to suggest that, stripped of the rules that are peculiar to legal systems, those processes that are properly called 'trials' contain some inner essence."[97] This inner essence would thus transcend time and space, and trials from the ancient world to the modern would all share it.

Let us consider three widely used definitions of the trial. *Black's Law Dictionary* considers a trial to be a "formal judicial examination of evidence and determination of legal claims in an adversary proceeding." Similarly, the U.S. Supreme Court conceived of the institution of the trial, in the 1941 case of *Bridges* v. *California*, as follows:

[93] Lawrence M. Friedman, "The Day before Trials Vanished," *Journal of Empirical Legal Studies*, Vol. 1 (2004), p. 690. Institutional antecedents of the modern trial range from trial by ordeal to trial by battle. On the former, see, most famously, Robert Bartlett, *Trial by Fire and Water: The Medieval Judicial Order* (Oxford: Clarendon Press, 1986); on the latter, see, most recently, Peter T. Leeson, "Trial by Battle," *Journal of Legal Analysis*, Vol. 3 (2011), pp. 341–375.

[94] Lindsay Farmer, "Whose Trial? Comments on A Theory of the Trial," *Law and Social Inquiry*, Vol. 28 (2003), p. 547.

[95] Farmer, "Whose Trial?," p. 547.

[96] For an engagement with the topic in the U.S. context, see this contribution to a special journal issue on "the vanishing trial," Marc Galanter, "The Vanishing Trial: An Examination of Trials and Related Matters in Federal and State Courts," *Journal of Empirical Legal Studies*, Vol. 1 (2004), pp. 459–570.

[97] Joseph Jaconelli, "What Is a Trial?," in Maureen Mulholland and Brian Pullan, eds., *Judicial Tribunals in England and Europe, 1200–1700: The Trial in History*, vol. 1 (Manchester: Manchester University Press, 2003), p. 18.

The very word "trial" connotes decisions on the evidence and arguments properly advanced in open court. Legal trials are not like elections, to be won through the use of the meeting-hall, the radio, and the newspaper ... A trial is not a "free trade in ideas," nor is the best test of truth in a courtroom "the power of the thought to get itself accepted in the competition of the market" [as Justice Holmes had put it in *Abrams* v. *United States*, 250 U.S. 616, 630]. A court is a forum with strictly defined limits for discussion. It is circumscribed in the range of its inquiry and in its methods by the Constitution, by laws, and by age-old traditions.[98]

Finally, Lon Fuller, the influential legal philosopher, thought of trials as devices that afford disputants "an opportunity for the presentation of proofs and reasoned arguments" so as to give "formal and institutional expression to the influence of reasoned argument in human affairs."[99] As plausible as all of these definitions are, they obscure the fact that trials are "invested with a significance that goes beyond being an institution where wrongdoers are called to account or conflicts resolved."[100] Although trials are certainly not like elections, they are, *pace* the U.S. Supreme Court, sometimes won through the use of the meeting hall, the radio, and the newspaper. More serious defects of the above definitions are their treatment of rationality "as a given rather than a variable" in court proceedings, as well as their implicit assumption that trials are only neutral dispute settlement mechanisms, rather than viewing them also as institutions of legal contention beyond the courtroom, ones populated by actors with *agendas*, both legal and political. The latter insight is of fundamental importance for beginning to determine the various political dimensions of trials, as we are keen to do in this volume, since the politics of a trial take place as much outside as inside the courtroom. Given these shortcomings, we adopt as a working definition for our purposes Malcolm Feeley's definition of the trial as

a process by which proof is authoritatively established. Rationality can be but is not necessarily involved in the process, parties affected may or may not have an opportunity to offer proofs or to make reasoned arguments, and there may or may not be a "dispute."[101]

The advantage of Feeley's definition is twofold. First, his more general definition has jettisoned the normative perspective embedded in the instrumentalist definitions that we encountered above. Second, it "is useful in accounting for a greater variety of processes that are generally understood to be

98 314 U.S. 252, 271 (1941).

99 Lon L. Fuller, "The Forms and Limits of Adjudication," *Harvard Law Review*, Vol. 92 (1978), pp. 365, 366.

100 Lindsay Farmer, "Trials," in Austin Sarat, Matthew Anderson, and Catherine O. Frank, eds., *Law and the Humanities: An Introduction* (Cambridge: Cambridge University Press, 2010), p. 477.

101 Malcolm M. Feeley, "Trials: Cultural," in Neil J. Smelser and Paul B. Baltes, eds., *International Encyclopedia of the Social and Behavioral Sciences* (Amsterdam: Elsevier, 2011), p. 15897.

trials, although in widely different settings, including so-called simple or primitive societies, intensely religious societies, and modern Western societies. It also includes processes in which there are no 'disputes,' and where disputes are not 'resolved' so much as they are processed."[102]

In an effort to understand in more depth what trials are, what they do, and what they ought to be, Antony Duff, Lindsay Farmer, Sandra Marshall, and Victor Tadros recently embarked on a comprehensive analysis of the institution of the *criminal* trial.[103] Although civil trials are qualitatively different, and give rise to rather different trial dynamics, it is nevertheless helpful to start our exploration of the concept of the trial by focusing on the institution of the criminal trial. Seeing that a large proportion of political trials have revolved around the prosecution of municipal or international crimes – ranging from corruption to treason to war crimes – it is not entirely inappropriate to start out in this manner.

Theories of the Trial

According to Duff and his coauthors, the paucity of theorizing about the criminal trial is related to a widespread presupposition that the nature of the institution is too obvious to require intellectual elucidation. They critique what they call "the standard account" for the belief "that the aims and functions of the trial are already clear."[104] Quickly told, the standard account holds that criminal trials seek to establish "the truth" about a given transgression and "aim to establish whether defendants committed the offences with which they have been charged as defined by the criminal law, whether they are entitled to any defence, and to determine whether they can be punished."[105] Trials, on the standard account, are of purely instrumental value. Of course, anyone who has ever sat in a courtroom in the real world knows that the standard account captures the nature of the trial as a social institution only very superficially.

Duff and colleagues have rightly bemoaned the fact that on the standard account "[t]heorising about the trial ... quickly fragments into theorising about particular evidential and procedural questions, for instance about whether the contribution that a practice or rule makes to the probative values of the trial is outweighed either by its prejudicial potential or by particular rights of the defendant."[106] Another way of putting this is that a conception of trials as nothing more than technology favors doctrinal and jurisprudential engagement

102 Feeley, "Trials," p. 15897.

103 Antony Duff, Lindsay Farmer, Sandra Marshall, and Victor Tadros, eds., *The Trial on Trial*, vol. 1: *Truth and Due Process* (Oxford: Hart, 2004); Antony Duff, Lindsay Farmer, Sandra Marshall, and Victor Tadros, eds., *The Trial on Trial*, vol. 2: *Judgment and Calling to Account* (Oxford: Hart, 2006); and Antony Duff, Lindsay Farmer, Sandra Marshall, and Victor Tadros, eds., *The Trial on Trial*, vol. 3: *Towards a Normative Theory of the Criminal Trial* (Oxford: Hart, 2007).

104 Duff et al., *The Trial on Trial*, vol. 3, p. 4.

105 Duff et al., *The Trial on Trial*, vol. 3, pp. 4–5.

106 Duff et al., *The Trial on Trial*, vol. 3, p. 5.

over historical and empirical analysis; trials are treated as technologies, susceptible mainly to technical analysis to determine whether or not they function as intended. If the trial is conceived merely in terms of deploying means and delivering ends, much of the unpredictable everyday life of the courtroom will never register in their analyses. In order to highlight the centrality of these frequently non-legal dimensions for any conception of the criminal trial, Duff, Farmer, Marshall, and Tadros proposed to substitute a communicative account for the standard account, one that "calls the defendant to answer, and through which he can challenge the accusations of wrongdoing made against him, including the norms in light of which these accusations are made."[107] By conceiving the trial as a communicative forum, this conception draws our attention to relational dynamics inside the courtroom.

For the purposes of this volume, replacing the standard, instrumental account of trials with a communicative one offers several advantages. First and foremost, the communicative account of trials highlights their interactive character, and consequently drives home the point that any trial is embedded in a dense network of social practices – some legal, some not – that has a bearing on the origins and dynamics of trials. Changes in these networks invariably affect the social meaning(s) of trials. This relationship is exemplified by the fact that the twentieth-century criminal trial in the United States looks rather different from the nineteenth-century trial. "The modern trial is longer, more complex (as a result of the multiplication of procedural and evidential rules), and more legalistic than its predecessors, but it is also oriented toward the minute reconstruction of the pattern of events around the commission of a crime."[108] Even where nothing changes in the technical aspects of the proceedings, a shift in the constituent networks operating in trials can radically alter their dynamics, as is made apparent in Benjamin Hett's account of the impact of the development of professional autonomy among attorneys in private practice in nineteenth-century Germany.[109]

A communicative conception of the trial also forces us to ask what – aside from a given transgression – is being played out in the courtroom.[110] For criminal trials can be about many things alongside the alleged crimes of the accused, a fact of particular relevance to political trials. As Koskenniemi writes, "no matter how much judges may seek to proceed in good faith towards their judgements, the context of the trial cannot – unlike the history seminar – be presumed to manifest good faith on everybody's part. This is not a disinterested

[107] Duff et al., *The Trial on Trial*, vol. 3, p. 3. See also R. A. Duff, *Trials and Punishments*, New edition (Cambridge: Cambridge University Press, 2009), p. 143.

[108] Farmer, "Whose Trial?," pp. 549–550.

[109] Benjamin Carter Hett, *Death in the Tiergarten: Murder and Criminal Justice in the Kaiser's Berlin* (Cambridge: Harvard University Press, 2004).

[110] The account of Duff and colleagues has limitations as well, however. Most important, theirs is a normative account. Our objective, by contrast, is empirical. What is more, we are interested in exploring the relationship between politics and *all* trials, not just criminal trials.

enquiry by a group of external observers but part of the history it seeks to interpret."[111] But even in less overtly charged settings, the goings-on in courtrooms cannot be divorced from the societal dynamics – political, cultural, otherwise – surrounding them. By highlighting the communicative nature of trials, Duff and his coauthors bring the importance of contextual interpretation to the foreground. Their call for taking seriously norms and values – not just means and ends – when thinking about trials is well taken and undergirds our theoretical approach. It dovetails in a number of respects with the work of Robert Burns, the only scholar to date to have advanced a comprehensive theory of the trial. With particular reference to the American experience, Burns emphasized the importance of studying the everyday practices of trials, not just the rules that govern them. As he put it, "What lawyers *do* is important, ... and fundamental to an understanding of the nature of the contemporary trial. Trial law is a communal social practice."[112]

Burns has argued that the essence of the trial as an institution lies in its ability to place "different sorts of languages in the tautest tension with each other within sets of rules that guard specially against the traditional disease of sophism and against the yet more virulent and peculiarly modern diseases of ideologically driven amoral instrumentalism."[113] What he means is that the modern trial forces different realms of life to confront one another and thus serves an important non-legal function on top of the legal function of sorting out a given dispute:

> The modern trial respects the differences among these realms without sealing them off from one another; it acknowledges that most problematic situations have moral, legal, and political dimensions; and it creates a forum within which a judgment can be made about the relative importance of those dimensions to the concrete case that must be resolved; and, in particular, it provides a full range of normative resources for a practical reshaping of the basic structure in a careful case-by-case process.[114]

In this context, it is useful to think of trials as *translation procedures*, which enable communication across life-worlds (in Habermas's sense), while preserving at least the possibility of reference to norms at least potentially relevant across such boundaries. (Whether or not such norms are universal, or at least universalizable, is a different – and more purely philosophical – question.)

Needless to say, Burns, like Duff and his coauthors, dwells chiefly in the province of philosophy. He readily concedes that he, unlike this volume, does not deal in "messy specificity."[115] Any empirically minded scholar will

[111] Koskenniemi, "Between Impunity and Show Trials," p. 25.

[112] Robert P. Burns, *A Theory of the Trial* (Princeton: Princeton University Press, 1999), p. 35. Emphasis added.

[113] Burns, *A Theory of the Trial*, p. 242. [114] Burns, *A Theory of the Trial*, p. 244.

[115] Robert P. Burns, "A Response to Four Readings of A Theory of the Trial," *Law and Social Inquiry*, Vol. 28 (2003), p. 554.

therefore be well advised to think of non-instrumental theoretical perspectives as ideal types of the trial against which to compare court proceedings taking place in the real world. Such juxtaposition promises to sharpen our sensibilities for recognizing what is particular and what is generalizable about the trials we study. Although normative theories of the trial are usually colored by the legal norms and institutions most familiar to the authors who created them, they are nevertheless useful as heuristic devices. Although civil and criminal trials in the United States, for example, differ markedly from trials held in the context of most other legal traditions, Burns's account, for one, is relevant for our comparative historical undertaking because he homes in on "the concreteness of what the trial is," leaving largely to one side the very technical differences of, say, rules and procedures of evidence that separate jurisdictions. Although Burns's treatment is but an approximation of what makes for a trial, it is useful as a theoretical foundation in developing our framework for analysis. This being so, we have organized the remainder of this section around two broad dimensions of his analysis, namely what he calls the *linguistic practices* and the *constitutive rules* of trials. Although we borrowed the terms from Burns, we use them in a looser sense than he does so as to make them usable for comparative historical analysis.

Linguistic Practices

We have already seen that formal and informal practices account for much of what we consider trials. Many of these practices have a linguistic dimension because, as Burns insists, the trial as social institution is a "highly-structured language-centered event."[116] What could this possibly mean, and why should we care? Most simply put, it means that the logic of trials is heavily influenced by the relative weight accorded to the uses of language. Variations along the continuum from concreteness to abstraction matter as much as the performative space available for opening statements, closing arguments, and related lawyerly interventions. Furthermore, language matters at the level of narrative on all sides, most obviously in the decisions and judgments handed down by a given court at the conclusion of a trial, but also in the competing accounts offered by various trial participants – attorneys, witnesses, litigants, etc. There is a dramaturgy to all trials, and language is the most important linchpin. All trials follow a more or less regularized sequence of speech acts. As a consequence, as Burns puts it, "Generally, the trial works through the construction, then the deconstruction, then the attempted reconstruction of very different kinds of narrative."[117]

The participation of lay judges or juries may serve to heighten the drama in a trial. In the United States, for example,

[116] Burns, *A Theory of the Trial*, p. 35.

[117] Robert P. Burns, "What Will We Lose If the Trial Vanishes?," Northwestern University School of Law Public Law and Legal Theory Research Paper, No. 11–48, May 24, 2011, p. 7.

the battle for the jury's imagination that begins with [the] opening statement is not simply an argument about "what happened." It is a battle about the frameworks within which events should be understood – whether, for example, through the lens of traditional morality, on the one hand, or that of psychiatry, on the other. It is a battle about kind of "social ordering" the situation demands: legalistic, moral, bureaucratic, political. At another level, the opening invokes social and cultural values embedded in authoritative "scripts" and invites the jury to finish the story.[118]

But whatever the role of lay actors in a trial, this kind of extra-legal framing is a major component of trial lawyering, one heightened to be sure by adversarial procedures, but certainly not one alien to inquisitorial legal systems.[119]

Staying with the example of U.S. procedure, the opening statement is just one of several linguistic practices that are characteristic of trials there. Another practice is that of direct examination. Yet another is that of cross-examination. Finally, there is the closing argument as the routine culmination of the trial phase of any legal proceeding. All of these practices revolve heavily around language. Each practice is associated with a repertoire of linguistic devices that are available to bolster or undermine the credibility of competing stories. In this context, two related but different notions are important to introduce: truth and narrative.

Truth. Modern trials are, among other things, highly developed mechanisms for determining truth. Indeed, as Robert Summers contends, "[s]ome natural scientists, some social scientists, some philosophers, and many others regularly assumed that truth finding is the only important function of trial court procedures."[120] This is so because the forensic ability of trials to define, collect, collate, probe, evaluate, and, finally, classify evidence about the world we live in is unparalleled. No other institution of the modern state (or the international system in the case of international trials) enjoys the same reputation for separating "facts" from "fictions." In addition, the emphasis on truth in trials is central for creating and maintaining the legitimacy of law. "[W]ithout judicial findings of fact that generally accord with truth, citizens would, over time, lose confidence in adjudicative processes as fair and reliable tribunals of justice and as effective means of dispute resolution, both in civil and criminal cases."[121]

Trial lawyers often have a more cynical (some might say more pragmatic) understanding of the epistemological value of truth, sometimes expressed in the adage "Every fact has two faces."[122] Underlying this assessment is an

[118] Burns, *A Theory of the Trial*, p. 50.

[119] See, for instance, the entire career of the notorious French attorney Jacques Vergès, as chronicled in Bernard Violet, *Vergès: Maître de l'Ombre* (Paris: Seuil, 2000).

[120] Robert S. Summers, "Formal Legal Truth and Substantive Truth in Judicial Fact-Finding: Their Justified Divergence in Some Particular Cases," *Law and Philosophy*, Vol. 18 (1999), p. 497.

[121] Summers, "Formal Legal Truth and Substantive Truth in Judicial Fact-Finding," p. 498.

[122] As quoted in Robert P. Burns, "The Distinctiveness of Trial Narrative," in Duff et al., *The Trial on Trial*, vol. 1, p. 169.

instrumentalist conception of the trial. "On the simple instrumentalist view, the truth that trial seeks has no intrinsic significance: the only (or primary) reason for trying to establish it is that this will enable us to identify those who are to be punished."[123] Needless to say, many observers expect more from a trial, especially in instances where the underlying conduct is particularly egregious, or of national or international significance, or both. Perhaps unreasonably, many of us look to courts for guidance on substantive truth or at least historical truth.[124]

Yet the imperative of finality (i.e., the need for a conclusion to a trial) imposes considerable constraints on truth finding because it "puts pressure on the legal system to develop procedures and rules to justify the outcome reached."[125] The limited time and resources available for the conduct of a trial in most jurisdictions vitiates in principle against pursuing anything other than "formal legal truth," i.e., the information declared factual by the legal fact-finder (be it a judge, bench, jury, or any other alternative adjudicator), for the sole purpose of adjudicating the case before it. When it comes to the assessment of trials, it is therefore useful to explore the relationship between formal legal truth and substantive truth. Formal legal truth often coincides with substantive truth, but not necessarily so. Exploring the divergence (and the precise distance) between both kinds of truth can be truly illuminating. It forces us to engage with both the intervening effects of a trial's constitutive rules, as well as with the meaning of trials in a given polity. For the extent to which those within the reach of courts expect trials to enunciate, anything other than formal legal truth will vary across space and time. Without a doubt, a determining factor of such expectations is what exactly a given society deems legitimate types of authority, to invoke Max Weber.

Although trials are regularly faulted for their failure to supply substantive truth, the divergence between formal legal truth may not be as problematic as is sometimes thought. Various scholars have argued that legal truth and substantive truth may rationally diverge without our having to call into question the legitimacy of a given trial. John Jackson, a prominent scholar of the law of evidence, advances this argument: "[I]n the absence of a definitive manner of establishing the truth about a defendant's guilt, the strength of the

[123] Duff et al., *The Trial on Trial*, vol. 3, p. 78.

[124] On the question of historical truth in the context of domestic and international trials of Holocaust-related crimes, see, for example, Donald Bloxham, *Genocide on Trial: War Crimes Trials and the Formation of Holocaust History and Memory* (Oxford: Oxford University Press, 2001); Devin O. Pendas, *The Frankfurt Auschwitz Trial, 1963–1965: Genocide, History, and the Limits of the Law* (Cambridge: Cambridge University Press, 2005); and Devin O. Pendas, "Truth and its Consequences: Reflections on Political, Historical and Legal 'Truth' in West German Holocaust Trials," *Traverse*, Vol. 11 (2004), pp. 25–38.

[125] John D. Jackson, "Managing Uncertainty and Finality: The Function of the Criminal Trial in Legal Inquiry," in Duff et al., *The Trial on Trial*, vol. 1, p. 127.

trial has been that in the face of the uncertainty that attaches to making judgments about past events, it establishes a basis for resolving disputes about evidence and justifying the outcomes to the community."[126] Burns similarly believes that a "well-tried case can refine the community's common sense to the point where it can achieve a truth beyond story-telling."[127] More abstractly stated, although the production of formal legal truth may always exist in tension vis-à-vis substantive truth, its articulation in the course of a trial may nevertheless lead to a transcendental truth. Summers, finally, weighs in thus:

> It follows that the concept of "formal" legal truth, in those cases in which it diverges from substantive truth, is not necessarily something to be disparaged at all. If the system is well designed, and if, in a particular case of divergence, relevant rationales for such divergence are in play, the divergence is merely the price we pay for having a complex multi-purpose system in which actual truth, and what legally follows from it, comprise but one value among a variety of important values competing for legal realization.[128]

The upshot of our discussion is this. The *quest* for truth is linguistically routine in virtually all trials and intrinsically – not just instrumentally – important.[129] Yet whether or not a given trial can deliver anything other than formal legal truth is a question that can only be answered *ex post* and requires interpretive understanding. Carlo Ginzburg has argued that the quest for truth, for judges as for others concerned with questions of causation, such as historians and social scientists, hinges on questions of "proof."[130] The truth that trials seek is ultimately one of responsibility, which is to say, causes. Truth, on this account, is an account of causation derived from what Ginzburg elsewhere refers to as "clues."[131] One proves a given causal account with references to clues, traces left from the past, which serve to ground a given interpretation and disprove others. And yet, as he himself notes, such clues gain meaning only from the interpretive schema into which they are placed, what Ginsburg calls "working hypotheses."[132] Such interpretive schemata determine not only which clues will "count" in establishing chains of causation but also which *consequences* matter as well. Just as every complex event likely has multiple causes, so too does every cause have multiple consequences; chains of causation are therefore never innocent, never "simply there" to be discovered.

[126] Jackson, "Managing Uncertainty and Finality," p. 142.

[127] Burns, "The Distinctiveness of Trial Narrative," p. 177.

[128] Summers, "Formal Legal Truth and Substantive Truth in Judicial Fact-Finding," pp. 510–511.

[129] On this point, see also Duff et al. *The Trial on Trial*, vol. 3, pp. 78–87.

[130] Carlo Ginzburg, *The Judge and the Historian: Marginal Notes on a Late-Twentieth-Century Miscarriage of Justice*, translated by Antony Shugaar (London: Verso, 1999), pp. 17–18.

[131] Carlo Ginzburg, "Clues: Roots of an Evidentiary Paradigm," in Carlo Ginzburg ed., *Clues, Myths, and the Historical Method*, translated by John Tedeschi and Anne C. Tedeschi (Baltimore: Johns Hopkins University Press, 1989), pp. 158–209.

[132] Carlo Ginzburg, "Judge and Historia"; Duff et al. *The Trial on Trial*, vol. 3, pp. 35–36.

One could argue that the law itself is nothing but a particularly elaborate and sophisticated set of "working hypotheses" concerning relevant causation.[133]

All trials, thus, are linguistic interactions designed to elicit the "truth" of some action or event, which is to say its "cause," within a given set of working hypotheses. Many, but not all, of these working hypotheses or interpretive schemata will be legal in nature, such as notions of *mens rea*, but others will be extra-legal, political, or sociological in nature, as for instance when questions of racial profiling enter into a criminal case. Thus law, as a method for discerning or, perhaps more accurately, for generating truth, offers accounts of causes and effects that are always embedded in interpretive schemata. Many, though certainly not all of the conflicts in trials then manifest themselves as conflicts over the appropriate interpretive schema to be applied to an agreed upon set of "facts." Sometimes there may be a conflict between legal and extra-legal schemata – formal vs. substantive truth – but often enough the conflicting schemata will all be simultaneously legal and political in nature. The persuasiveness of a given position in a trial will tend to depend on its ability to mobilize clues to prove a specific causal account, or, to put it more succinctly, to turn clues into narrative.

Narrative. It has long been recognized that narrative – in the courtroom as well as in life – provides the "systematic means of storing, bringing up to date, rearranging, comparing, testing, and interpreting available information about social behavior."[134] Law is therefore fundamentally about telling stories, as Robert Cover taught us.[135] More specifically, trials are venues for telling competing and often contradictory stories and, in the end, adjudicating between them. Trials require a level of explicitness (due to an "austere epistemic demand on justification" associated with most legal proceedings) from all participants – witnesses, lawyers, judges – that we would not demand in most other social situations.[136]

Participants in trials tell purportedly true stories related to the issue under adjudication.[137] Many of these stories will be mutually contradictory, and thus not all of them can possibly be true in a substantive sense. (Indeed, none of them may be true, but that is not a possibility courts typically acknowledge.) It is the

[133] See, e.g., Herbert Lionel Adolphus Hart and Tony Honoré, *Causation in the Law*, Second edition (Oxford: Oxford University Press, 1985).

[134] W. Lance Bennett and Martha S. Feldman, *Reconstructing Reality in the Courtroom: Justice and Judgment in American Culture* (New Brunswick: Rutgers University Press, 1981), p. 5

[135] Robert Cover, "Nomos and the Word," in Martha Minow, Michael Ryan, and Austin Sarat, eds., *Narrative, Violence, and the Law: The Essays of Robert Cover* (Ann Arbor: University of Michigan Press, 1992), pp. 95–172.

[136] Duncan Pritchard, "Testimony," in Duff et al., *The Trial on Trial*, vol. 1, pp. 112, 113.

[137] For a valuable attempt to unpack the relation between performance and narration in trials, see Georg Wamhof, "Gerichtskultur und NS-Vergangenheit: Performativität-Narrativität-Medialität," in Georg Wamhof, ed., *Das Gericht als Tribunal, oder: Wie der NS-Vergangenheit der Prozess gemacht wurde* (Göttingen: Wallstein, 2009), pp. 9–40.

court's job to determine which of them is most relevant for a determination of formal legal truth, as defined above. Narratives are indispensable for making information appear true. "It is through narrative that we remember (re-member), and the internal characteristics of narrative, such as presence of extraneous details, can affect its plausibility even before any evidence is offered."[138] Burns therefore argues that "the existence, proper description, and meaning of even the most basic circumstantial evidence at trial is partly determined by its place in different levels of narrative."[139]

As Marco Jacquemet remarks about Italy's so-called Camorra trials in the 1980s, which involved some 800 defendants, "rational truth based on reason and methods proved not to be the main issue in the resolution of this legal process. The search for rational truth was in fact overshadowed by the synergy of locally dominant sociopolitical values with communicative performances based on dramatic affective displays."[140] Such performances often stand and fall with the persuasiveness of the stories told by way of narrative *both* in open court *and* in the documents filed as part of a trial proceeding and in the run-up to it. Burns demonstrates his faith in the power of narrative persuasion when he claims that "the acceptability of one narrative over the other ('the best story') can overwhelm the evidence in a particular case."[141] Oliver Wendell Holmes suspected as much, when, in 1907, he opined in *Chicago, B & Q Railway Co.* v. *Babcock* that "many honest and sensible judgments … express an intuition of experience which outruns analysis and sums up unnamed and tangled impressions – impressions which may be beneath consciousness without losing their worth."[142] Narratives are powerful devices for steering such impressions.

Here the issue of legal imagination, famously theorized by James Boyd White, comes into play. For in constructing what common lawyers call "a theory of the case," i.e., a preliminary, coherent, and reasonable narrative of how the law and the facts *might* relate in a given trial, they must rely as much on procedural rules as they must on argumentative rhetoric. This involves making choices about finding the right balance between legal reasoning and storytelling. But telling stories in a trial is about far more than simply straightforward legal tactics. Or rather, the tactical dimensions of narrative – its specific ability to frame and persuade, even beyond or against evidence – point to the ways courtroom stories extend to the outside world, and hence ineluctably connect to politics. There are two closely related dimensions to this: audience and normative experience.

White notes that "storytelling is both collective and individual," in that storytelling is a linguistic practice and "language itself is always social,"

[138] Burns, "The Distinctiveness of Trial Narrative," p. 170.

[139] Burns, "The Distinctiveness of Trial Narrative," p. 169.

[140] See Marco Jacquemet, "Anger, Honor, and Truth: The Political Prosecution of Neapolitan Organized Crime," in this volume, p. 298.

[141] Burns, "The Distinctiveness of Trial Narrative," p. 169. [142] 204 U.S. 585, 598 (1907).

dependent on communities of understanding (themselves constituted by language) to be meaningful. Consequently, "narrative, like rhetoric, is in this sense culture-specific."[143] Legal stories acquire meaning, and persuasive force, in the interaction between speakers and a properly acculturated audience, one capable of hearing the story in the "right" way. Where there is no audience, there can be no narrative. Before narrative can persuade it must be heard. Even where there is an audience, though, it is entirely possible for a story to be misheard or misunderstood. For a story to be heard, it must be told in an adequate language, one that renders the elements of the narrative (facts, characters, events, sequences, etc.) intelligible and persuasive to the audience. To a significant degree, this is true for all narratives (e.g., literature, sermons, anecdotes, etc.).

Legal narrative is distinctive, in that it is typically (though not always) openly competitive. There are multiple, incompatible stories being told, only one of which is supposed to be accepted by the audience. This highlights the element of choice involved in narrative. "[T]o tell a story is to choose a language in which it is to be told, and to choose a language is, at some level, to recognize that there are other possible languages, other possible meanings."[144] In a trial, there will almost always be different narrative languages in operation. Since distinct languages appeal to and help constitute distinct audiences, competing trial narratives can simultaneously succeed and fail, depending on the relevant audience. While the audience that matters most in the immediate term is typically the one that sits in judgment (judges or jurors or both), there may well be other audiences that matter as much or even more in the long term, audiences outside the courtroom. This is particularly true in political trials, where the fate of the defendant is often secondary to the "success" of an ideological message. It is entirely possible, in a political trial, to lose one's case and win the battle for public opinion; indeed, this is often precisely the point.[145] The persuasiveness of a trial narrative cannot be evaluated except in relation to its intended or actual audience.

Yet, since languages help constitute the communities that interpret them, the significance of narratives extends beyond mere persuasion, which implies an extrinsic, preexisting audience that "receives" a message. Rather, telling a story well can in effect create the proper audience to hear it. According to Cover, law both constitutes and is interpreted in relation to our *nomos*, the normative world we inhabit. This is comprised of interpretive commitments that "determine what law means and what law shall be."[146] Conversely, though,

[143] James Boyd White, *Heracles' Bow: Essays on the Rhetoric and Poetics of the Law* (Madison: University of Wisconsin Press, 1985), pp. 172–173.

[144] White, *Heracles' Bow*, pp. 172–173.

[145] For a powerful example, see Henning Grunwald, "From Courtroom to 'Revolutionary Stage': Performing Ideology in Weimar Political Trials," in Wamhof, *Das Gericht als Tribunal*, pp. 41–52.

[146] Cover, "Nomos and Narrative," in Minow, Ryan, and Sarat, *Narrative, Violence, and the Law*, p. 99.

"law is a resource in signification that enables us to submit, rejoice, struggle, pervert, mock, disgrace, humiliate or dignify."[147] So we both create law through our interpretations of it, and use law to respond to the moral claims of the world. This dual action, making and responding to law, constitutes a legal *nomos*. Such a *nomos*, "as a world of law" bridges, at least potentially, the is and the ought, fashions a moral world that is constituted simultaneously by our experience of its actuality and our intuition of its potential.[148] "The codes that relate our normative system to our social construction of reality and to our visions of what the world might be are narrative."[149]

Cover's account here is explicitly utopian. It is what law can be, not necessarily what it always is. "Not every divergent understanding of law is sufficient to withstand the coercive power of the state."[150] Indeed, in another essay, Cover goes further and argues that "neither legal interpretation nor the violence it occasions may be properly understood apart from one another." Legal interpretations – at least those of judges – are backed by the force of the state; they are *authoritative*, even when not *authoritarian*. Or, as Cover put it, "Interpretations in law also constitute justifications for violence which has already occurred or which is about to occur."[151]

When thinking about political trials, therefore, the role of narrative is particularly double-edged. On the one hand, legal stories authorize violence, typically, though not invariably, that of the state. This is most obvious in what we call *destructive trials*, where the state (prosecution and judges) tells a story of a threat averted to justify the violence exercised on a putative enemy. But even in *decisive* and *didactic* trials (see below), the *force* of law is operative, and there are consequences for a refusal to acknowledge law's power. (Not for nothing did the National Guard enforce the Supreme Court's ruling on *Brown* v. *Board of Education*.) On the other hand, legal stories can envision and attempt to enact a new normative reality. Since trial verdicts are typically performative in J. L. Austin's sense that they create the condition they enunciate, they are potentially well suited to this narrative act of normative transformation.[152] *Brown* v. *Board of Education* told a story of a more racially egalitarian society (equal, not separate) and sought to create the reality it described. This utopian moment in political trials, their *creative* capacity, is irreducibly normative because stories have morals.

This does not mean, obviously, that we (any given set of "we") necessarily have to approve of the moral of the story. Otherwise, there could be no dissenting from the judgment in political trials. One might think, just as

[147] Cover, "Nomos and Narrative," p. 100. [148] Cover, "Nomos and Narrative," p. 101.

[149] Cover, "Nomos and Narrative," p. 102. [150] Cover, "Nomos and Narrative," p. 152.

[151] Robert Cover, "Violence and the Word," in Minow, Ryan and Sarat, *Narrative, Violence, and the Law*, p. 203.

[152] John Langshaw Austin, *How to Do Things with Words* (Cambridge: Harvard University Press, 1962).

a counterexample to *Brown* v. *Board of Education*, of the enforcement of the anti-miscegenation provisions of the Nuremberg Race Laws by Nazi courts.[153] Indeed, because trials, political trials above all, encounter and constitute multiple, extra-legal audiences, the potential for dissent is innate. The specific characteristic of show trials, as a distinct sub-set of political trials, is that they seek – not always successfully – to stage manage the proceedings in such a way as to minimize this risk. They carefully frame the narrative in such a way as to constitute a highly determinant trial audience. Yet very often, political trials are characterized by multiple narratives appealing to and constituting distinct and divergent audiences, intentionally and otherwise. If political trials are political because they deal with the distribution of power, then this ability to shape, mobilize, and normatively convince distinct audiences gets to the heart of one dimension of their political character.

Constitutive Rules

As important as questions of truth and narrative are to understanding the nature of trials, it is equally critical not to lose sight of the fact that highly specific legal rules enable – and constrain – the construction of truth and narrative in most court settings. The manner in which this happens will differ dramatically from one context to another, which is why normative theories of the trial must be interrogated with the help of empirical studies of trials, and vice versa. We do not propose to rehearse similarities and differences in the constitutive rules of trials across legal traditions – the Western legal tradition, the East Asian legal tradition, the Islamic legal tradition, the sub-Saharan legal tradition, and so forth.[154] Rather, the purpose of this section is to draw attention to the fact that the procedural aspects, broadly defined, of trials matter. Two procedural aspects in particular – publicity and formality – are worth singling out. Both are recurring features of most trials, whether ancient, medieval, or modern.

Publicity. Generally speaking, trials are held in public.

What counts as being "in public" varies according to the media of communication available in the epoch in question. In its basic form, the rule allows for the admission to the trial of casual spectators who have no connection with the proceedings other than a wish to observe them. With the rise of the print medium, this was extended to the conferral of special facilities for the representatives of the press: both in seating specially set aside for them and in the legal privileges attaching to the publication of their

[153] Cornelia Essner, *Die "Nürnberger Gesetze," oder, Die Verwaltung des Rassenwahns, 1933–1945* (Paderborn: Schöningh, 2002).

[154] See, for example, H. Patrick Glenn, *Legal Traditions of the World: Sustainable Diversity in Law*, Fourth edition (Oxford: Oxford University Press, 2010), as well as the seven chapters in Part III of Mauro Bussani and Ugo Mattei, eds., *The Cambridge Companion to Comparative Law* (Cambridge: Cambridge University Press, 2012).

reports ... Finally, the growth of radio and television networks in the twentieth century has created the possibility of a global audience for the most prominent trials.[155]

The idea of publicity as a defining attribute of the concept of the trial reminds of Jeremy Bentham's hopeful observation from 1843: "By publicity, the temple of justice is converted into a school of the first order, where the most important branches of morality are enforced, by the most impressive means: into a theatre, where the sports of the imagination give place to the more interesting exhibitions of real life."[156]

Bentham, the legal philosopher and progressive reformer, was among those who provided moral underpinnings for publicity as a principle of adjudication. On his argument, allowing the public into the courtroom not only "keeps the judge himself, while trying, under trial" but also the witness in check: "Environed as he sees himself by a thousand eyes, contradiction, should he hazard a false tale, will seem ready to rise up in opposition to it from a thousand mouths."[157] Whether or not publicity always has the effects intended by Bentham is an open empirical question. For as Jaconelli notes, "trial proceedings may equally be perverted by being saturated in publicity, thereby gaining the stigma of a 'show trial.' "[158] On the other side of the equation, it is not uncommon for authoritarian regimes to use secret trials to prosecute, imprison, and even execute political opponents. But even granting this, publicity is germane to the concept of the trial as a social institution. Duff and his coauthors insist that "public justice must be seen as a core element of the process of calling to account."[159] One might invoke Bentham again: "Without publicity, all other checks are insufficient: in comparison with publicity, all other checks are of small account."[160] Indeed, in general terms, "[s]o close is the association between the idea of a trial and that of public access that the trial which takes places behind closed doors is regarded as fundamentally defective."[161] So too, one might add, are show trials in most instances. It is not necessary here to judge whether excessively public or needlessly secret trials

[155] Jaconelli, "What Is a Trial?," p. 27.

[156] Jeremy Bentham, "Bentham's Draught for the Organization of Judicial Establishments, Compared with that of the National Assembly, with a Commentary on the Same," in John Bowring, ed., *The Works of Jeremy Bentham*, vol. 4 (Edinburgh: Tait, 1843), p. 317.

[157] Jeremy Bentham, "Introductory View of the Rationale of Evidence; for the Use of Non-Lawyers as Well as Lawyers," in John Bowring, ed., *The Works of Jeremy Bentham*, vol. 6 (Edinburgh: Tait, 1843), p. 355; and Bentham, "Bentham's Draught for the Organization of Judicial Establishments, Compared with that of the National Assembly, with a Commentary on the Same," p. 317. Of course, various stages of trials (e.g., the deliberation of juries or judges; in camera witness testimony) are regularly being held under conditions of relative secrecy without necessarily violating the principle of publicity.

[158] Jaconelli, "What Is a Trial?," p. 28. [159] Duff et al., *The Trial on Trial*, Vol. 3, p. 261.

[160] Bentham, "Bentham's Draught for the Organization of Judicial Establishments, Compared with that of the National Assembly, with a Commentary on the Same," p. 317.

[161] Jaconelli, "What Is a Trial?," p. 28.

are "really" trials; we merely assert that most trials are public and that political trials in particular make frequent use of their very publicity as a core element of their politics.

Formality. Let us now turn to another constitutive rule of the trial as a legal institution: formality. For trials have specific rules and procedures governing who can speak and when, what kinds of speech are allowed, and how that speech is to be evaluated. Every trial to be worthy of the name is suspended in a tripartite tension occasioned by the institutionalized interactions of a *pursuer* (whether in the form of a prosecutor, a claimant, or a plaintiff), a *defender* (usually in the form of a defendant), and a *decider* (whether in the form of a judge, a bench, a jury, a hearing officer, or any authorized representative of a court or tribunal).[162] "There is, in the concept of 'trial,' a strong undercurrent of the idea of a contest. The trial is necessitated by the existence of a dispute – one that is resolved by the application of the law to the facts as authoritatively found and terminated by one side or the other securing the verdict of the court."[163] The rules of the game in a trial are formalized, sometimes by way of custom, often in a code of law. (We might think of the former as a form of "soft law," of the latter as an example of "hard law.")

Of course, legal formalism – the intellectual view that the application of legal norms to facts in a court of law is detached from normative or policy considerations – has been a long-standing, if controversial, current in the philosophy of law. "At the heart of the word 'formalism,' " Frederick Schauer reminds us, "lies the concept of decision making according to *rule*. Formalism is the way in which rules achieve their 'ruleness' precisely by doing what is supposed to be the failing for formalism: screening off from a decision maker factors that a sensitive decision maker would otherwise take into account."[164] The standard account of the trial is formalistic in this sense, which is why it is of very limited use for understanding the universe of political trials. This should not cause us to overlook, however, the explanatory significance of formality in the study of the trial.[165] As Feeley writes, "Differences in the structure of the trial process produce a number of important differences in effects."[166] Allow us to illustrate the importance of this explanatory factor with particular reference to a formal cleavage within the Western legal tradition, i.e., the differences in

[162] Inspired by the language of Scottish law, we have adopted the terms "pursuer" and "defender" as the most generic-sounding terms available.

[163] Jaconelli, "What Is a Trial?," p. 24.

[164] Frederick Schauer, "Formalism," *Yale Law Journal*, Vol. 97 (1988), p. 510.

[165] On formality more generally, see Arthur L. Stinchcombe, *When Formality Works: Authority and Abstraction in Law and Organizations* (Chicago: University of Chicago Press, 2001). See also Robert S. Summers, "The Formal Character of Law," *Cambridge Law Journal*, Vol. 51 (1992), pp. 242–262.

[166] Feeley, "Trials," p. 15899.

procedure concerning the allocation of responsibilities in the trial practices of the common law and the civil law.[167]

From a doctrinal perspective, Mirjan Damaska and John Langbein have perhaps done more than most to shed light on the nature and history of the institution of the trial – both civil and criminal – in these legal families.[168] In their long careers, both have been very much aware of the changing character of the trial across space and time. For a comparative historical endeavor such as ours, this insight cannot be overestimated because an important part of the analytical challenge that our contributors faced was to come to terms with the meaning of the trial in the empirical context of their case study. The kind of interpretive scholarship that we encouraged required careful contextual political analysis.[169] If scholars are steeped too deeply in a particular legal tradition, they can lose sight of the fact that the rules governing a courtroom are constitutive in the sense that they not only enshrine what is permissible but also shape the self-understandings of participants in the trial. As Judith Resnik explains, "rules of procedure embody, express, and help create values and attitudes about what constitutes fair decision making by, or through, the powers of the state. Procedure is laced with questions of legal policy and political philosophy."[170]

Simply put, procedure is concerned with the configuration of trials. Stewart Field, by focusing on the case of Europe, gives a good account of the manner in which procedural rules of the modern trial are simultaneously sticky *and* changing: "[O]ne can identify and specify certain central agreed ideas associated with the adversarial and the inquisitorial traditions. Most obviously there is the contrast between a vision of criminal process as something built around a contest between parties or around an active state investigation." There are also enduring differences in the preference for oral or written evidence, but beyond this, the distinction between common and civil law becomes more ambiguous. Field notes disagreement among scholars on the relative significance of lay jurors or negotiated settlements. In general, he concludes, "the richer and more complex the depiction of the institutional forms associated with the adversarial or the inquisitorial, the more scope appears to be left for disagreement as to whether particular features are

167 Traditionally, the topic of procedure was divided into civil, criminal, and administrative procedure.

168 See, most important, Mirjan Damaska, *The Faces of Justice and State Authority* (New Haven: Yale University Press, 1986); John H. Langbein, *The Origins of Adversary Criminal Trial* (Oxford: Oxford University Press, 2003).

169 Generally, see Robert E. Goodin and Charles Tilly, eds., *The Oxford Handbook of Contextual Political Analysis* (Oxford: Oxford University Press, 2006).

170 Judith Resnik, "Procedure: Legal Aspects," in Neil J. Smelser and Paul B. Baltes, eds., *International Encyclopedia of the Social and Behavioral Sciences* (Amsterdam: Elsevier, 2011), p. 12137.

intrinsically adversarial or inquisitorial."[171] What does seem incontrovertible is that there are different modes of formalism, different ways to formulate the procedural rules that govern a trial, but that virtually all trials have some kind of procedure.

If we believe Burns, the law of evidence as one particular set of formal rules (e.g., the so-called best evidence rule or the nonopinion rule in the legal procedure of the common law) is of utmost importance for grasping the concept of the trial. "The law of evidence provides the 'grammar' of the trial. Only those truths that can be said 'grammatically' can become part of the legal world."[172] Burns departs from the conventional account of the trial by insisting that the law of evidence does not only enable or constrain the interactions among pursuers, defenders, and deciders in the course of a legal proceeding but that it is also constitutive of their self-understandings and relations with one another. Consider the important role of judges.

Even in instances (of which there are many) in which it is law clerks (think the U.S. Supreme Court) or Associate Legal Officers (think the ICTY or ICC) who shoulder much of the burden of research and writing, or common law trials, where the verdicts are determined by jury, the legitimate (or illegitimate, depending on where you stand on a given trial) authority of judging rests with selected, elected, or anointed judges. Yet the institutional roles of judges differ across space and time. The rather divergent roles of judges in common law and civil trials illustrate the point. Generally speaking, the common law judge "will begin with the factual circumstances of the case and after examining, comparing and weighing the factual elements of the case, will attempt to find a rule that fits it. This [substantive] rule may be one of statutory law or derive from prior decisional law."[173] The procedural rules governing trials in the civil law tradition are usually very different:

> The civilian judge sees the case as a problem to be solved within the legal *structure* of the legal system. First, the problem at hand must be fitted into a legal category. Next, subcategories and sub-subcategories must be identified until "legal rule" or "concept" and the problem at hand match. Civilians proceeds by deductive reasoning, while the common law approach employs an inductive methodology.[174]

[171] Stewart Field, "Fair Trials and Procedural Tradition in Europe," *Oxford Journal of Legal Studies*, Vol. 29 (2009), pp. 368–369.

[172] Burns, *A Theory of the Trial*, p. 86.

[173] Peter Hay, "Civil Law," in Neil J. Smelser and Paul B. Baltes, eds., *International Encyclopedia of the Social and Behavioral Sciences* (Amsterdam: Elsevier, 2011), p. 1865. For a recent historical comparison of the role of judges in the common law and civil law traditions, see Paul Brand and Joshua Getzler, eds., *Judges and Judging in the History of the Common Law and Civil Law: From Antiquity to Modern Times* (Cambridge: Cambridge University Press, 2012).

[174] Hay, "Civil Law," p. 1865.

On the institution of the judge, Kirchheimer is also still relevant today, despite a certain lack of nuance. According to Kirchheimer, the judge "plays a dual role in the administration of political justice." He "presides over the trial as an arbiter of contending claims," on the one hand, and then, after the verdict, "engages in the business of sentencing," on the other hand. In other words, he serves first as an "umpire" and then as an "enforcement officer." Judges mostly find this shift straightforward because "the value structure embodied in the law enforced by the judge is not only his personal choice; what he expresses are the most cherished community values." This situation is imperiled if the political sovereign "manipulating law and administration alike, ceases to represent community values."[175]

Needless to say, the *specific* role of the judge in legal traditions other than the Anglo-American one often differs markedly from Kirchheimer's sketch – an empirical fact that continues to interfere not only with the making of, for example, an international criminal procedure but also with the more mundane matter of judicial cooperation among countries. Certainly, in inquisitorial courtrooms judges tend to replicate work more typically done by attorneys in the Anglo-American system. If anything, this heightens the significance (and the ease) of the transformation from umpire to enforcer, to which Kirchheimer points. At the same time, because the judge's inquisitorial role in continental law allows him or her to guide the proceedings more directly, it means that the identity between sovereignty and community values is both more important and more fragile than in common law, since the judge is a much more direct embodiment of the sovereign. It is in this sense that the legal rules governing trials are (or at least can be) socially (and sometimes politically) constitutive.

Other legal traditions have yet other understandings of the role of judges in trials. In earlier times and some contemporary settings, the function of judges is not formally prescribed but informally known by way of custom. But even in the Western legal tradition, a plethora of additional procedural rules come into play. Having said that, the *general* role of the judge (or a comparable decider) is an important explanatory factor that is essential to probe empirically on a case-by-case basis in the study of political trials. At present, the state of empirical scholarship is meager, to say the least. Many inferences are drawn exclusively on the basis of autobiographies. A more sophisticated approach is needed for coming to terms with the choices justices make while presiding over trials.[176]

[175] Otto Kirchheimer, "Politics and Justice," in Frederic S. Burin and Kurt L. Shell, eds., *Politics, Law, and Social Change: Selected Essays of Otto Kirchheimer* (New York: Columbia University Press, 1969), p. 424.

[176] For one comparative account, see David Robertson, *The Judge as Political Theorist: Contemporary Constitutional Review* (Princeton: Princeton University Press, 2010). Inspiration can also be gleaned from the reflections of U.S. practitioners. See, for example, David M. O'Brien, ed., *Judges on Judging: Views from the Bench* (Washington: CQ Press, 2004).

Our goal in this section was *not* to delineate conceptions of the trial in the inquisitorial and adversarial traditions but rather to drive home the point that the constitutive rules of trials everywhere – North, South, East, or West – are invented traditions. The point is neither to prioritize them nor to ignore them as explanatory factors but to inquire into their concrete significance for coming to terms with the goings-on in a given courtroom. In Weberian terms, we seek to understand trials characterized by different degrees of formality, with the formally rational trial of the modern democratic state representing but *one* ideal type of trial.[177] For as scores of legal anthropologists from Bronislaw Malinowski to Max Gluckman to Sally Engle Merry have shown through ethnographies of dispute settlement mechanisms in unfamiliar cultures, the inner logic of trials is culturally specific.[178] The constitutive rules of trials matter, but how they matter and why are questions for empirical inquiry.

A FRAMEWORK FOR THE ANALYSIS OF POLITICAL TRIALS

Having contemplated in some detail the two fundamental background concepts – the concept of the political and the concept of the trial – of the phenomenon with which this volume is concerned, we are now in a position to synthesize the insights gleaned for the construction of an integrated – and more nuanced – framework for the analysis of political trials than currently exists. We proceed in three steps. We first introduce our concept of political trials. We then elaborate a simple typology of political trials. In a final step, we lay out our analytical framework.

A Concept

Our understanding of political trials is simultaneously broader and more focused than Kirchheimer's classic definition of the political trial as "[c]ourt action ... called upon to exert influence on the distribution of political power."[179] In an effort to avoid conceptual stretching, we speak of a political trial only in instances in which at least one government is a claimant, an object of claims, or otherwise associated with the proceedings; the outcome of the

[177] *Black's Law Dictionary*, the U.S. Supreme Court, and Fuller, all are exclusively concerned with this ideal type. The three *other* conceivable ideal types are the formally irrational trial, the substantively rational trial, and the substantively irrational trial. On Weber's ideal types of law, see also Meierhenrich, *The Legacies of Law*, pp. 15–23.

[178] See, among other leading studies, Bronislaw Malinowski, *Crime and Custom in Savage Society* (New York: Harcourt Brace, 1926); Max Gluckman, *Politics, Law and Ritual in Tribal Society* (Chicago: Aldine, 1965); and Sally Engle Merry, *Colonizing Hawai'i: The Cultural Power of Law* (Princeton: Princeton University Press, 1999).

[179] Kirchheimer, *Political Justice*, p. 49.

proceedings crystallizes or communicates a political conflict, often but not necessarily, over the distribution of social resources of one sort or another; *or* courtroom proceedings are directed at the defeat of a political enemy, real or imagined. We are in agreement with Leon Friedman, who, in a little-known contribution more than forty years ago, argued that the concept of political trials encompassed three varieties of proceedings, namely "cases which are politically *motivated*, those that are politically *determined*, and those which in turn have substantial political *consequences*."[180]

The first variety is self-explanatory. A characteristic of the second variety is the manner in which political currents of the time influence the dynamics of an otherwise ordinary trial, elevating it, for example, from criminal justice to political justice. The infamous 1951 espionage trial of Ethel and Julius Rosenberg in the United States is a case in point. The third variety singled out by Friedman is related to the second in the sense that here, too, an ordinary trial takes on political significance. To the extent that one considers the legal proceedings of *Brown* v. *Board of Education* a trial, it certainly started out as a conventional trial but ended up altering the political fabric of the United States in a more fundamental manner than any other trial in the country's history ever before or since.[181] The *Brown* proceedings also drive home the conceptual point that trials can be political in more than one of Friedman's dimensions simultaneously. For his categories "are not mutually exclusive: a trial may be politically motivated, the result may be determined by the politics of the time, and it may in turn affect the distribution of political power. Law and politics may intermix at any one of these levels and not the others, but the trial is still political in the broadest sense."[182]

On this conceptual foundation, we disaggregate political trials along two major dimensions – what we call *purposes* and *practices*. To make sense of the category of purposes, we introduce a typology of political

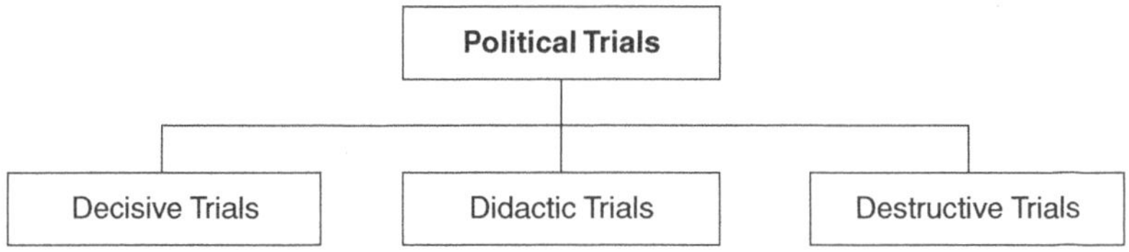

FIGURE 1.1 A Typology of Political Trials

[180] Leon Friedman, "Political Power and Legal Legitimacy: A Short History of Political Trials," *Antioch Review*, Vol. 30 (1970), p. 158.

[181] On the political consequences of *Brown* v. *Board of Education*, see, most recently, Martha Minow, *In Brown's Wake: Legacies of America's Educational Landmark* (Oxford: Oxford University Press, 2012); and Mark V. Tushnet, "*Brown* v. *Board of Education:* Private Civil Litigation as a Political Trial," in this volume.

[182] Friedman, "Political Power and Legal Legitimacy," p. 159.

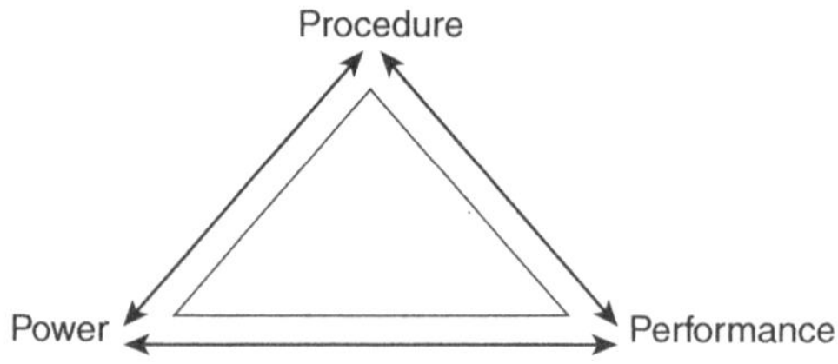

FIGURE 1.2 A Framework for the Analysis of Political Trials

trials, distinguishing among (1) *decisive trials*, (2) *didactic trials*, and (3) *destructive trials*, as already alluded to above (see Figure 1.1). This first conceptual differentiation allows us to hone in on variation in motivations. In terms of practices, our second dimension, we focus on the salience of three mutually constitutive explanatory factors that invariably shape, or so we claim, the operation of political trials as social phenomena: (1) *power*, (2) *procedure*, and (3) *performance* (see Figure 1.2). This second conceptual differentiation is directed at accounting for variation in outcomes.

Regardless of whether political trials are decisive, didactic, or destructive in nature, the peculiar dynamics of their contentious politics will be governed by the unique interplay among power, procedure, and performance. Needless to say, our dynamic framework for analysis demands a consideration of pre-trial, in-trial, and post-trial developments. It necessitates a contextual analysis that is more methodologically savvy than most scholarship on political trials that has come out of HLS, more empirically mindful of branching points and critical junctures than most contributions made by CLS, and more critically attuned to hegemonic discourses and related structural inequities than what passes for conventional wisdom in ELS.

Our conceptual refinement of the concept of the political trial was prompted by the increasingly undifferentiated use of the term in both popular and scholarly writings. What most of the ad hoc (and invariably post hoc) classifications of courtroom proceedings (domestic as well as international) lack is an explanation of how (and why and when) precisely politics enters the courtroom, or how (and why and when) the courtroom enters politics, in a given situation. Put differently, in short supply are subtle inquiries into the dynamics – the mechanisms and processes – of *both* the politicization of the judiciary *and* the judicialization of politics when it comes to adjudication of wrongdoing, civil or criminal, before municipal as well as international courts and tribunals. With this in mind, let us take a closer look at our typology and framework for the analysis of political trials.

A Typology

In order to capture the diverse universe of political trials, we distinguish among three subtypes of political trials: (1) *decisive trials;* (2) *didactic trials*; and (3) *destructive trials* (see Figure 1.1). All of these trials are political, but they are political *in different ways*. It is important to appreciate these differences – and the multiple meanings of the concept of the political – in order to be able to make analytical headway in the study of political trials. Among other things, we are keen to dispel the myth that political trials are incompatible with the rule of law or the related idea of the *Rechtsstaat*. We hasten to add that the three categories of political trials distinguished here are ideal types. They are standards against which to measure empirical reality. Consequently, we do not expect that historical and contemporary examples of political trials will embody any one type in full. With this caveat in mind, let us turn to our typological innovation.

Decisive Trials

Decisive trials are political because they seek, first and foremost, to settle a contentious legal question of political significance. Their *raison d'être* is political regulation. At the least contentious end of the spectrum are trials that require an independent court to settle a dispute, which cannot be – or has not been – resolved through other political mechanisms such as legislation or elections. Such failures to resolve can be structural (the dispute lies outside the proper realm of legislative authority, for instance) or more overtly political (the dispute is between relatively evenly balanced political factions, such that neither can generate the power necessary to impose a resolution). Perhaps the most famous of political trials in this rubric is *Oliver Brown et al.* v. *Board of Education of Topeka, Shawnee County, Kansas*, or *Brown* v. *Board of Education*, as it is commonly known.

In this proceeding, the court was seized by the simple yet politically explosive question of whether eight-year-old Linda Brown, born to African-American parents, and twenty other so-called Negro children in Topeka were entitled to receive their education in white schools. At the time, mixed schooling was prohibited under a Kansas law from 1879 which allowed cities to run separate school facilities for children of different races. A 1951 district court ruling found against the plaintiff, who was represented by the National Association for the Advancement of Colored Peoples (NAACP). It reached the U.S. Supreme Court on direct appeal shortly thereafter. Arguments were heard during three days in December 1952. On May 17, 1954, Chief Justice Earl Warren, after five months of deliberations among the nine judges, delivered the unanimous, eleven-page judgment: Separate educational facilities were inherently unequal and constituted a violation of the U.S. Constitution's Fourteenth Amendment.

It is undeniable that *Brown* v. *Board of Education* was a political trial, even though the famous legal proceeding was not a trial in the conventional sense but rather a suit for injunctive relief by thirteen plaintiffs against the Board of Education of the city of Topeka, Kansas, over that school district's policy of racial segregation in education. Yet we believe that *Brown* v. *Board of Education* (and legal proceedings like it) ought to be brought into the discussion about political trials, notably because the courtroom served as the principal site of contention. In terms of objectives and outcomes, the proceedings were highly political indeed.

At the same time, it would be misleading to lump the trial together with partisan trials or so-called show trials, which constitute only a small subset of political trials, properly understood. The nature of the political in *Brown* v. *Board of Education* was of a qualitatively different nature. The trial was political *not* because it was a charade but because it was *not*. Nor was the case about defining enemies, but rather about the distribution of resources, in this instance, access to education. Scores of legal scholars have since debated what *Brown* v. *Board of Education* should have said. The fact remains that the Warren Court intervened in U.S. state and federal politics in a decisive manner, yet hardly in a revolutionary one. As Allan Hutchinson has argued, "Thurgood Marshall [the NAACP's lead counsel at the time] predicted that school segregation would be completely abolished within five years. However, as important as the *Brown* decision was, it took much longer; a breakthrough in civil rights only occurred after much further time and struggle."[183]

Another political trial that owes its distinction primarily to the decisive quality of adjudication in the context of contentious politics is the International Court of Justice's (ICJ) 2007 judgment in the *Case* concerning Application of the Convention on the Prevention and Punishment of the Crime of Genocide (*Bosnia and Herzegovina* v. *Serbia and Montenegro*), or *Bosnia* v. *Serbia*, for short. In this landmark, albeit controversial, decision, the ICJ settled a long-standing disagreement between the two states over the application of the 1948 Genocide Convention to atrocities committed in the region in the early 1990s. The fifteen judges concluded (1) that the evidence before them did not show that the Serbian state had committed crimes of genocide in Bosnia (other than in Srebrenica), but (2) that the Serbian state had failed to comply with its obligations, pursuant to Article I of the Genocide Convention, to prevent and punish genocide.

Despite vocal protestations from Bosnian political and civil society organizations, the ICJ's decisive declaration about the empirical boundaries of state responsibility settled – though only legally – a political conflict that had pitted Bosnia and Serbia against one another ever since 1993, when the Republic of Bosnia and Herzegovina first brought suit against what was then

183 Allan C. Hutchinson, *Is Eating People Wrong? Great Legal Cases and How They Shaped the World* (Cambridge: Cambridge University Press, 2011), p. 102.

the Federal Republic of Yugoslavia. Although the ICJ found that the Serbian *state* was not guilty of genocide outside of Srebrenica, it did *not* simultaneously declare that other agents had not perpetrated genocidal acts outside of Srebrenica. The judges merely held that if and where such genocidal acts were committed, they had, based on the available evidence, not been carried out at the behest of the Serbian state. The case is of interest for the purposes of this volume because it represents, in our estimation, an international trial that was highly political in more senses than one, and yet it was neither destructive nor particularly didactic. By Friedman's yardstick, the case initiated by Bosnia in 1993 was politically motivated, and it was obvious to everyone involved that it would have substantial political consequences. It would therefore be disingenuous to pretend that politics played no part in the adjudication of state responsibility for genocide in The Hague. But because the case was legally determined, not politically, it would be equally misleading to lump this major ICJ case – and other domestic and international trials like it – together with political trials, pejoratively understood. Consequently, we believe that the category of the decisive trial does justice to the nature of *Bosnia and Herzegovina* v. *Serbia and Montenegro*.

A final example is the Microsoft case analyzed in some detail below by two of our contributors. Although few observers would rush to characterize the proceedings in Washington, D.C., a political trial, conventionally understood, the monopolization case against the software giant deserves closer scrutiny. And as William Page and John Lopatka demonstrate very clearly in their contribution to this volume, the trial was far from an ordinary proceeding in federal court. It was saturated with politics. Aside from having been called upon to decide a thorny question of antitrust law, the U.S. judges involved were faced with contending campaigns aimed at a politicization of the judiciary: "Political lobbying prodded the government to bring the case and shaped the litigation. But the purpose of the case was not simply to bring about an outcome favored by powerful economic interests. The more fundamental purpose, revealed only after trial and appellate procedures and even then only after extensive mediation and negotiation, was to ratify the essential claims of a powerful narrative with important political consequences. The outcome is political because it represents a victory for the intentional vision, which claims intervention in markets is necessary, even in the 'new economy,' to restore competition and ensure markets serve the public interest."[184] In that sense, aspects of *Microsoft* – as well as of *Brown* v. *Board of Education* and *Bosnia* v. *Serbia* for that matter – also exhibited traits of the didactic trial, to which we now turn.

Didactic Trials

Didactic trials are political because they seek, first and foremost, to spread a political message. Their *raison d'être* is political communication. It was once again Kirchheimer who first pointed to what he called the "didactic fictions" of

[184] William H. Page and John E. Lopatka, "The Microsoft Case as a Political Trial," in this volume, p. 368.

political trials.[185] The person who has done most for elaborating the concept of the didactic trial, however, is Lawrence Douglas. His sole focus, unlike that of this volume, has been the "perpetrator trial," which he described as a "specialized, unique breed of criminal trial."[186] According to Douglas, such perpetrator trials have "all aimed to do something more than render legal justice. They all explicitly embraced a didactic purpose." Their threefold pedagogical purpose is to "provide detailed and accurate representations of the larger sweep of historical forces that issues in acts of mass atrocity," to "locate in the historical record clear morals that could serve to shape the terms of collective memory," and, finally, to "honor the memory of victims and survivors" by providing a space for testimony.[187] Put more abstractly, for Douglas, the essence of the didactic trial is the goal "of actively re-imposing norms into spaces in which rule-based legality has been either radically evacuated or perverted."[188]

Unfortunately, this liberal conception of the didactic trial leaves out a large swath of illiberal history. Indeed, didacticism is at the heart of show trials in the pejorative sense of that term. What are we to make of the 1894 Dreyfus treason trial in France? What of the 1980 "Gang of Four" trial in China that took place before thirty-five judges and 880 "representatives of the masses," and which is analyzed in this volume?[189] What are the Moscow "show trials" of the 1930s if not prime examples of didactic trials? The substance of Stalin's communicated message we can certainly question normatively, but the method of the message was undoubtedly a didactic trial. Consequently, we modify Douglas's otherwise profound conception of the didactic trial with a friendly amendment: we conceive of didactic trials as legal proceedings with *no* inherent value commitment. As legal institutions of rule, they are value neutral until imbued with political meaning from the outside. Douglas's conclusion fits all kinds of didactic trials – those with liberal *or* illiberal agendas "[R]egardless of the processes by which the didactic trial shapes history and memory in the courtroom, the trial is unable to control the way in which it will become a cultural artifact and will pass into collective memory."[190]

[185] Kirchheimer, *Political Justice*.

[186] Lawrence Douglas, "The Didactic Trial: Filtering History and Memory in the Courtroom," *European Review*, Vol. 14 (2006), p. 514. For a slightly different version of this article, see Lawrence Douglas, "Perpetrator Proceedings and Didactic Trials," in Duff et al., *The Trial on Trial*, vol. 2, pp. 191–205.

[187] Douglas, "The Didactic Trial," pp. 513–514.

[188] Douglas, "The Didactic Trial," p. 514. Mark Osiel embraced the didactic trial for similar reasons. In his *Mass Atrocity, Collective Memory, and the Law*, he advanced a strong normative justification: "The orchestration of criminal trials for pedagogical purposes … is not inherently misguided or morally indefensible. The defensibility of the practice depends on the defensibility of the lessons being taught." See Mark Osiel, *Mass Atrocity, Collective Memory, and the Law* (New Brunswick: Transaction Publishers, 1997), p. 65.

[189] The figures were reported in Richard Bernstein, "The Gang of Four on Trial," *Time*, December 1, 1980.

[190] Douglas, "The Didactic Trial," p. 521. It is important to note in this context that normative arguments in favor of didactic trials – such as Osiel's endorsement of the use of trials as

Elaborating on Douglas's argumentation, we propose that didactic trials can be pursued from below as well as from above. Whereas both Kirchheimer and Douglas have given a great deal of thought to the latter, we feel that the former has been given short shrift in discussions of political trials. Yet one need only think of the phenomenon of cause lawyering to appreciate the fact that didactic trials can work in favor of *either* state or society. The didactic potential of political trials (whether educationally or ideologically motivated) is related to the idea of publicity as a defining attribute of the concept of the trial. It is reminiscent of Jeremy Bentham's hopeful observation that "By publicity, the temple of justice is converted into a school of the first order, where the most important branches of morality are enforced, by the most impressive means: into a theatre, where the sports of the imagination give place to the more interesting exhibitions of real life."[191]

One of the paramount examples of a didactic trial "from below" would be the so-called Scopes Monkey trial. The trial was instigated by the American Civil Liberties Union (ACLU, founded in 1920) in response to Tennessee's 1925 law making it unlawful to teach the theory of human evolution. In the wake of the legislation, the ACLU issued a press release, offering to challenge the Tennessee law, if it could find a client willing to serve as defendant in a test case. As Edward Larson has shown in his definitive account of the trial, the ACLU's goal was to find a case they could take to the Supreme Court in order to secure an expansion of the principle of academic freedom from higher to secondary education.[192] They had no direct interest in the subject of evolution one way or the other, though their more narrow agenda was not without its own political implications, given the tradition of local control over school curricula in the United States.

The case only took off, however, when civic leaders in the town of Dayton, TN, decided that bringing such a case locally, with all its anticipated publicity, would help revive the town's struggling economy. Local leaders on both sides of the case persuaded John Scopes, the local high school science teacher, to serve as defendant and contacted the ACLU to arrange the whole thing. Publicity and civic boosterism – not evolution, much less Scopes' alleged crime in teaching it – was the point of the case. The district judge in the case even moved up the grand jury session to preempt similar cases looming in other Tennessee jurisdictions. As Larsen has remarked, "everything about this case appeared upside-down,

"monumental spectacles" on behalf of a post-authoritarian agenda – have met with resistance. The gist of the critique is that didactic trials are inherently illiberal *regardless* of the worthiness of their cause or the "defensibility of the lessons" being taught. The phrase "monumental spectacles" appears in Osiel, *Mass Atrocity, Collective Memory, and the Law*, p. 3.

191 Bentham, "Bentham's Draught for the Organization of Judicial Establishments, Compared with that of the National Assembly, with a Commentary on the Same," p. 317.

192 Edward J. Larsen, *Summer for the Gods: The Scopes Trial and America's Continuing Debate over Science and Religion* (New York: Basic Books, 1997), p. 80. The following account of the trial is based on Larsen's magisterial work.

and no one seemed to care about upholding the law."[193] What they cared about was publicity.

In order to secure as much attention as possible, civic leaders sought to attract celebrity involvement from the start, inviting H. G. Wells, then engaged in a polemic with anti-evolutionists, to assist the defense, an offer he declined. One of Wells' intellectual sparing partners, William Jennings Bryan, however, offered his services to the prosecution in defense of the Tennessee law. Clarence Darrow, another nemesis of Bryan's and no stranger to publicity seeking himself, promptly offered his services to the defense, an offer they accepted despite the ACLU's own objections. "To me," Darrow subsequently remarked, "it was perfectly clear that the proceedings bore little semblance to a court case, but I realized that there was no limit to the mischief that might be accomplished unless the country was aroused the evil at hand."[194] The ACLU had lost control of its own case, which expanded from a narrow test of the legality of academic freedom into a full-fledged public debate over the scientific, moral, religious, and, above all, political validity of evolutionary theory and democratic education. It became a trial driven by civil society actors (Bryan and Darrow above all) who sought a forum to stage a polemical debate between revealed religion and scientific knowledge, one in which the merits of the case or even substantive legal principles such as academic freedom faded into insignificance. In the Scopes trial, the message became the medium.

While not all didactic trials, whether from above or below, are as extreme in their trivialization of the actual legal dispute at hand as the Scopes case, they do all tend to embed juridical disputation in a broad context of highly public discourse. In such cases, journalists are as important as lawyers, politicians can become star witnesses, and moviemakers can have the final verdict.[195]

Destructive Trials

Destructive trials are political because they seek, first and foremost, to eliminate a real or imagined political enemy. Their *raison d'être* is political destruction. The nature of destruction can be symbolic or physical or both. Perhaps the most notorious trials aimed at the physical destruction of presumed enemies – and which also served an important didactic function – were those conducted under the auspices of Roland Freisler at the *Volksgerichtshof*, the People's Court. The court meted out more than 5,000 death sentences in the course of its reign between 1934 and 1945. It targeted a whole host of enemies of the state, from

193 Larsen, *Summer for the Gods*, p. 92.

194 As quoted in Larsen, *Summer for the Gods*, p. 101.

195 Lawrence M. Bernabo and Celeste Michelle Condit, "Two Stories of the Scopes Trial: Legal and Journalistic Articulations of the Legitimacy of Science and Religion," in Robert Heriman, ed., *Popular Trials: Rhetoric, Mass Media, and the Law* (Tuscaloosa: University of Alabama Press, 1993), pp. 55–85.

members of the resistance in the occupied territories to domestic dissidents to suspected spies. It arguably represents the most destructive court in history.[196]

Although the term may be jarring, we developed the subtype of the destructive trial inspired by Shklar for whom *all* political trials were destructive in nature. As she put it in *Legalism*, "What, after all, is a political trial? It is a trial in which the prosecuting party, usually the regime in power aided by a cooperative judiciary, tries to eliminate its political enemies. It pursues a very specific policy – the destruction, or at least the disgrace and disrepute, of a political opponent."[197] The quintessential feature of destructive trials, we suggest, is their decidedly confrontational stance vis-à-vis their target. They are intended as weapons, no more and no less. Their deployment can be *ad hoc* or systematic.

We therefore continue with the assumption that a possible defining feature of a political trial is the use of legal procedure for the purpose of defeating a real or imagined enemy. This assumption retains Kirchheimer's emphasis on power relations but focuses on a sub-set of cases. This brings us back to Carl Schmitt's definition of the political as an existential conflict between friends and enemies. Schmitt, Kirchheimer's contemporary and one-time teacher, infamously put it thus:

> The political enemy need not be morally evil or aesthetically ugly; he need not appear as an economic competitor, and it may even be advantageous to engage with him in business transaction. *But he is, nevertheless, the other, the stranger*; and it is sufficient for his nature that he is, in a specially intense way, *existentially something different and alien*, so that in the extreme case conflicts with him are always possible.[198]

Even a cursory glance at the historical record would suggest that Schmitt, while not perhaps exhausting the meaning of the political, certainly hit on a recognizable element of political life. The same holds for political trials. As Kirchheimer put it, "[e]very political regime has its foes or in due time creates them."[199] One need only recall Robert Jackson's opening address as the U.S. Chief Prosecutor at the International Military Tribunal at Nuremberg, in which he emphasized the "otherness" of those in the dock: "What makes this inquest significant is that these prisoners represent sinister influences that will lurk in the world long after their bodies have returned to dust . . . Civilization can afford no compromise with the social forces which would gain renewed strength if we deal ambiguously or indecisively with the men in whom those forces now

[196] The most comprehensive analysis is Werner Wagner's 1000-page tome, *Der Volksgerichtshof im nationalsozialistischen Staat: Mit einem Forschungsbericht für die Jahre 1974 bis 2010* (Oldenbourg: De Gruyter, 2011).

[197] Shklar, *Legalism*, p. 149.

[198] Carl Schmitt, *The Concept of the Political*, translated by George Schwab (Chicago: University of Chicago Press, 1996), p. 27.

[199] Kirchheimer, *Political Justice*, p. 3.

precariously survive."[200] Jackson's oratory is founded on a concept of the political that is reminiscent of Schmitt's. Admittedly, the IMT proceedings are an extreme case. Convened in the immediate aftermath of World War II, with the allies "flushed with victory and stung with injury," it is not entirely surprising that Schmitt's concept of the political should have been invoked in a Nuremberg courtroom.[201] Granted, of course, this invocation was tacit and almost certainly unintentional, given that Schmitt was being interrogated by the allies as a potential defendant at the time. Of course, it would be misleading to claim that *every* political trial is political by virtue of the fact that two adversaries are waging an existential conflict in the courtroom. And yet we contend that instantiations of the friend/enemy distinction are germane to many political trials deserving of the name.

It is entirely conceivable, for example, to stage a political trial as part of a larger political campaign aimed at the destruction of a political enemy *tout court*, but this need not be the case. Examples of the surgical deployment of political trials for the purpose of destroying *individual enemies* are the legal proceedings against Henriette Caillaux in Paris, Herschel Grynszpan (or Grünspan) in Berlin, Alger Hiss in Washington, Adolf Eichmann in Jerusalem, and, in the context of our volume, the trials of China's Gang of Four in Beijing as well as of Mikhail Borisovich Khodorkovsky, the Russian oligarch and businessman, in Moscow.[202] The Rivonia trial in Johannesburg, examined in great detail by Meierhenrich and Broun below, also illustrates the general point. As one of us put it elsewhere,

> In May 1964, judgment was passed in the Rivonia Trial on six Africans, one Indian, and one white, among them Nelson Mandela. Fifteen months after his acquittal in the Treason Trial, Mandela was back in the dock, this time before the Supreme Court. He and ten others were held under the new ninety-day detention law, enacted in 1963. The charges were sabotage and conspiracy. Throughout the proceedings, at least seven nations were reported to have urged the apartheid government to exercise clemency. The trial is illustrative of the limits of the normative state. Nelson Mandela, Walter Sisulu and six other leaders of *Umkhonto we Sizwe* ("the spear of the Nation") – the recently established, armed wing of the ANC – were sentenced to

[200] International Military Tribunal, *Trial of the Major War Criminals before the International Military Tribunal, Nuremberg, 14 November–1 October 1946*, vol. 2 (Nuremberg: IMT, 1947), p. 99.

[201] The quote is Jackson's. See International Military Tribunal, *Trial of the Major War Criminals before the International Military Tribunal, Nuremberg, 14 November–1 October 1946*, vol. 2 (Nuremberg: IMT, 1947), p. 99.

[202] For relevant literature on the aforementioned political trials, see, for example, Edward Berenson, *The Trial of Madame Caillaux* (Berkeley: University of California Press, 1993); Helmut Heiber, "Der Fall Grünspan," *Vierteljahrshefte für Zeitgeschichte*, Vol. 5 (1957), pp. 134–172; Allen Weinstein, *Perjury: The Hiss Chambers Case*, Second edition (New York: Random House, 1997); and Hanna Yablonka, *The State of Israel vs. Adolf Eichmann* (New York: Schocken, 2004).

life imprisonment. The Treason trial defended the rule of law; the Rivonia trial marked its limits.[203]

Examples of political trials with the objective of destroying *collective enemies* also are plentiful in history. Most prominent among them, aside from the Salem Witch trials, perhaps are the various domestic and international proceedings against suspected Nazi war criminals, whether held at Nuremberg, in Germany, or in other European countries.[204] Stalin's show trials of the 1930s are of comparable interest to scholars of destructive trials.[205] A major difference lies in the procedural history of destructive adjudication in each of these examples. That "fair" trials, as much as procedurally dubious ones, may be used to destroy collective enemies is an often overlooked facet in the history of political trials. Of more recent pedigree are some of the U.S. attempts at coming to terms by way of trials with the threat of terrorism, including the infamous U.S. military commissions, as well as Rwanda's *gacaca* jurisdictions, which were created to come to terms with all but the most serious crimes perpetrated in the course of the 1994 genocide. Similarly, it is important to note that the enemies destroyed in such trials can be either quite real or purely imaginary. The "witches" of Salem and the Nazi elite in Nuremberg were both conceived by their judges as enemies, even if the threat posed by the former was entirely spurious, while that of the latter had been demonstrated all too dramatically.

Notwithstanding the popularity of destructive trials in history, Kirchheimer cautioned against their use because, as he put it, the "medium" of the trial was an "unpredictable" weapon. He pointed to the unreliable nature of witnesses and the possibility that cunning defense lawyers could persuade juries or judges of the innocence of defendants singled out for political destruction.[206] Indeed, given that, as we have insisted, political trials can operate under the most stringent due process protections, as well, obviously, as their most egregious violations, one question for scholars of political trials is the variable degree of risk they entail.

It is helpful to think in terms of these categories when evaluating the goals, procedures, and outcomes as well as the short-run and long-run consequences of political trials. Empirically speaking, political trials may exhibit traits of more than one of the aforementioned subtypes on any of these dimensions. (The exigencies of their operation may also cause them to evolve from one subtype into another.) For example, a political trial may be directed chiefly at

[203] Meierhenrich, *The Legacies of Law*, p. 138.

[204] Peter Charles Hoffer, *The Salem Witchcraft Trials: A Legal History* (Lawrence: University Press of Kansas, 1997); Devin O. Pendas, "Seeking Justice, Finding Law: Nazi Trials in Postwar Europe," *Journal of Modern History*, Vol. 81 (2009), pp. 347–368.

[205] See, e.g., Nathan Leites and Elsa Bernaut, *Ritual of Liquidation: The Case of the Moscow Trials* (Glencoe: Free Press, 1954).

[206] Otto Kirchheimer, *Politische Justiz: Verwendung juristischer Verfahrensmöglichkeiten zu politischen Zwecken* (Berlin: Luchterhand, 1965), pp. 183–185.

settling a contentious legal contest (exemplifying the decisive trial) but end up serving a communicative function as well (exemplifying the didactic trial). A case in point is the Microsoft trial in the United States. Alternatively, a political trial may well be designed to bring about the defeat of a real or imagined enemy (exemplifying the destructive trial) but simultaneously serve, for better or for worse, a public relations function (exemplifying the didactic trial). The trials of Adolf Eichmann in Israel and of members of the Red Army Faction, or RAF, in postwar Germany come to mind. Another, more recent example is the trial of Saddam Hussein in the immediate aftermath of the war in Iraq.

A Framework

The universe of political trials, as conceptualized herein, is wide and varied. In order to make sense of this institutional variety, we have assembled an accomplished roster of contributors, some of whom we already mentioned. We commissioned thick descriptions of trial proceedings that are theoretically aware whether or not they make direct use of the theoretical framework sketched here. With Burns we believe that "[t]his descriptive task is an important counterweight to some forms of social scientific investigation of the trial because the latter," as Ludwig Wittgenstein put it,

> naturally "see the method of science before their eyes, and are irresistibly tempted to ask and answer questions in the way science does." Excessive confidence in causal explanation under general laws or model building can stem from a "craving for generality" that is unhelpful in attempts to understand forms of human language, of which the trial is a particularly complex example.[207]

This is not to say that explanation is not important, as Burns concedes, but the institution of the political trial is so poorly understood – both theoretically and empirically – that a turn toward interpretative understanding is imperative. This task, in the words of the late Clifford Geertz, involves "a continuous dialectical tacking between the most local of local detail and the most global of global structures in such a way as to bring both into view simultaneously."[208] That is precisely our goal with this volume: to create a dialogue between theory and history about the study of political trials.

Such an interpretive understanding requires that political trials be analyzed along three interrelated dimensions: (1) *power*, (2) *procedure*, and (3) *performance*. By power, we mean the ability of compelling an adversary to go to court and to abide by the court's decision. By procedure, we mean the legal rules involved in reaching (or not) a verdict in the case at hand. By performance, we mean the various practices involved in staging and, where applicable,

[207] As quoted in Burns, *A Theory of the Trial*, p. 125.

[208] Clifford Geertz, " 'From the Native's Point of View': On the Nature of Anthropological Understanding," *Bulletin of the American Academy of Arts and Sciences*, Vol. 28 (1974), p. 43.

marketing the proceeding. We contend that only an integrative analysis of this kind will allow us to reveal, in all of their local and global senses, the meaning(s) of political trials in theory and history (see Figure 1.2).

These three dimensions are general, in that they provide an interpretive framework for political trials across time and space, but this does not mean that we conceive of such trials as a trans-historical or geographically restricted (e.g., "Western") phenomenon. Rather, the specific interplay of power, procedure, and performance themselves varies from one context to the next. Political trials are a general (though probably not universal) human phenomenon that change in character according to their specific context. In this regard, they might be thought of as similar to war, another human "universal" that nevertheless varies enormously across time and space. All wars share certain characteristics – collective violence, organized opponents, a broadly "political" purpose – without thereby ceasing to be distinctive. There are deep differences among World War II, the Taiping Rebellion, and the battles between Utes, Paiutes, and Navajos in the 1830s. Likewise, there are significant differences among the various trials analyzed in the present volume, yet they nevertheless all remain *political trials*.

Power

In recent decades, older definitions of politics that viewed it as essentially having to do with the exercise of state power have been in many ways superseded. The cultural turn in the social sciences and humanities and the rise of first structuralism and then post-structuralism have led to an emphasis beyond, below, and around the more manifest power of the sovereign. Michel Foucault, for instance, famously argued that to focus on the politics of the state, and with it, on questions of sovereignty, was to misapprehend power as being essentially negative and politics as being primarily about putting brakes on it. By contrast, he wanted to diagnose power as productive and networked. It is not something anyone *has*, not even (or perhaps especially not) a sovereign, but something which *flows* through and around human subjects.[209] This seems correct, but for political trials, misleading.

When dealing with political trials, it seems imperative to bring the state back in. While by no means all of the politics operating in political trials are state oriented, all trials – certainly all modern trials – operate as institutions of the state or of an international organization founded by states. None of the political trials featured in this volume, for example, despite the significant procedural and substantive differences among them, could do without the state. Even if the state has no specific stake in a given political trial, it has a general interest in seeing trials operate smoothly, effectively, and in a manner that legitimates the

[209] Michel Foucault, "Two Lectures," in Colin Gordon ed., *Power/Knowledge: Selected Interviews and Other Writings, 1972-1977* (New York: Pantheon Books, 1980), pp. 78–108.

state's authority to stage trials. Trials are often (though by no means always) among the best mechanisms at a state's disposal. For as Martin Shapiro has shown, trials and the courts that stage them have always also functioned as agents of social control.[210]

Procedure

Political trials are ritual venues for adjudicating contending truth claims. Like all rituals, they are governed by constitutive rules, as we have seen. First, there are the rules and procedures that structure legal action in any trial. This is the most obvious level of analysis. Unfortunately, it is not uncommon for scholars and other observers of political trials to have an inadequate comprehension of both the substantive criminal law and criminal procedure underlying the proceedings with which they are concerned. This is unfortunate because the rules of the game (from jurisdictional rules to rules of evidence) invariably affect the dynamics of any courtroom.

To start with the most obvious, it is important, for example, to consider the effects of common law versus civil law traditions of adjudication.[211] This must certainly be taken into account when contemplating the nature of the political, for institutional rules structure human behavior. It is worth considering, for example, whether adversarial systems of criminal procedure facilitate friend–foe conceptions of politics.[212] Next, in procedural terms, criminal trials play out very differently than civil trials. Also of note here are rules about time. For as Robert Burns notes,

> The American trial, especially the jury trial, occurs over a relatively compressed period of time. This is in stark contrast to the Continental model, where the trial evolves over a much longer period of time and ends only when the judge has determined that further investigation is not warranted. The Anglo-American compression has a number of effects. It elevates the opportunity for and necessity of thematic unities, the theory and theme of the case.[213]

Seeing what central role a thematic presentation often plays in political trials (consider, for example, the Salem Witch trials), it is essential that scholars of political trials interrogate the real-world effects of the rules governing trials. They are of immediate significance for coming to terms with the multifaceted nature of most political trials.

Performance

Political trials performatively enact an efficacious legal outcome with political import in Austin's sense. Yet mastery of the doctrinal and jurisprudential

[210] Martin Shapiro, *Courts: A Comparative and Political Analysis* (Chicago: University of Chicago Press, 1981).

[211] Glenn, *Legal Traditions of the World*. Obviously, one ought not to hypostatize these "traditions." There are shades and variations within and between each.

[212] See generally, Langbein, *The Origins of Adversary Criminal Trial*.

[213] Burns, *A Theory of the Trial*, p. 130.

challenges involved in political trials often comes at the expense of grasping the *social lives* of courts and tribunals, the ways in which they are performances as well as performatives (in the technical sense). For aside from the obvious procedural dimensions of adjudication, criminal or otherwise, there are, among many other things, the spatial and performative dimensions of courtroom behavior. These are of particular significance whenever the political is on trial. John Borneman observed quite rightly in the post-authoritarian context that sometimes trials "perform ... a successful 'final judgement' in the religious sense, a performance that would ultimately enable the state itself to function as a moral agent."[214] This dimension of analysis, in other words, speaks to the ritual nature and function of political trials.

Simply put, a ritual is a regularized social act that follows a prescribed, more or less precise pattern. Y always follows X. They assign roles. The priest (and only the priest) can consecrate the host. And they lay claim to effects that derive from their regularity. As rituals, trials are performative and this in a dual sense. In the first instance, as Victor Turner and other anthropologists have noted, there are strong similarities between rituals and theater. Not only do both have regularized sequences and assigned roles, but, equally important, both rituals and theater require an audience. The audience can be general or specific, narrow or broad, open or closed, as the case may be, but in order to "work," both need to be seen. Indeed, much of the efficacy and legitimacy of trials depends on their performative quality. To work, they must be seen to work, and to be seen to work, their regularity, forensic procedures, and role-playing must be performed properly before the relevant audience. (If the relevant audience rejects the performance, then the trial "fails socially" in White's sense, regardless of the truth content of the judicial outcome.) But trials are also performative in a second, more specific sense.

As previously noted, trials are also performative utterances in J. L. Austin's sense.[215] A performative utterance is, according to Austin, one that does not describe (or "constate") something, but one which enacts that which it states. Austin's classic example of a performative utterance is: "I christen this ship the 'Queen Mary'." The statement does what it says. At least in their adjudicative dimensions, trials (or more specifically, their verdicts) are performative in this sense. When a court declares a defendant guilty, he is, in the only relevant sense (legally), in fact guilty. This is quite independent of the "actual" extra-legal reality of his actions, which are no longer of legal relevance. Performatives, according to Austin, have no truth content, since they do not describe an external state of affairs that could be used to judge them. A performative can be "unhappy" or infelicitous, but not wrong or false. If I say "I promise to do

[214] John Borneman, *Settling Accounts: Violence, Justice, and Accountability in Postsocialist Europe* (Princeton: Princeton University Press, 1997), p. 23.

[215] Austin, *How to do Things with Words.*

X in future" and subsequently fail to do so (or never intended to do so in the first place), this does not make my promise untrue, since it was nonetheless enacted by my statement, merely unhappy. All three types of political trials seek, in this performative sense, to constitute a new reality, whether by resolving a contentious dispute, teaching a lesson, or destroying an enemy. Legally, this reality is performed by the trial. Whether that performance is taken up inside the courtroom or outside of it has to be determined on a case-by-case basis.

CONCLUSION

The three dimensions of political trials just outlined – power, procedure, performance – are mutually constitutive. Our empirical chapters make abundantly clear, however, that the interaction effect among the three dimensions is highly varied and frequently a structurally contingent outcome. The chapters to come either tackle little known but important political trials (e.g., the French revolutionary trials; Argentina's *ESMA* trials) or re-evaluate better known cases in a new and innovative way (e.g., the trial of the Major War Criminals at Nuremberg; the Rivonia trial; the Microsoft trial). We have organized the volume as a series of individual case studies that, when taken together, combine to a rich, comparative historical analysis of what exactly it means when politics enters the courtroom, and what happens when it does.

In keeping with the framework for analysis introduced above, our contributors illuminate the empirical diversity of political trials. By highlighting institutional variation in terms of the purposes and practices of political trials, they explode many of the persistent pejorative clichés that exist about the phenomenon. They highlight, *inter alia*, the variation in forms, functions, and effects of well-known and lesser known political trials. Yet, for all that the empirical chapters demonstrate the wide variation among political trials, they also show that all of these various trials remain deeply political. Political trials are more common than is often recognized, and that is what provides the common ground within the broad diversity identified by our contributors.

Because political trials are various, without ceasing to be political, it is imperative to approach them from a wide range of disciplinary perspectives and to engage in interdisciplinary dialogue concerning their form and content. Legal scholars, political scientists, historians, and linguistic anthropologists all have insights to contribute to the study of political trials. By bringing them together, we hope to initiate and deepen conversations across borders, disciplinary and otherwise.

2

The Trial of Socrates as a Political Trial

Explaining 399 BCE

Josiah Ober

In 399 BCE, Socrates, son of Sophroniscus of the Athenian township Alopece, was tried in Athens by a criminal court on the charge of impiety. He was found guilty by a slim majority (some 280 of 501) of the empaneled judges and executed in the public prison a few days later. The trial and execution constitute a defining moment in the relationship between law and politics, and between philosophy and democracy. Ever since, philosophers and historians have asked how a democratic community, committed to the value of free speech and public debate, could have come to convict and execute its most famous philosopher-citizen.[1]

Whether or not the trial was political in the *partisan* sense, there can be no doubt that, in the definition adopted in this volume, this was a political trial in the sense of being a formal legal procedure involving political disputes of social significance and reflecting and constituting power relations in the Athenian polity.[2] I will argue that, although the prosecutor may have intended it as a *destructive* trial, and the defendant, Socrates, may have intended it as a *didactic* trial, it actually performed the social function of a *decisive* political trial: The trial decided whether the definition of what is dangerous public speech was in the control of the speaker, the immediate audience, or the community as a whole. Given the importance of public speech in Athens, the trial of Socrates was decisive in setting the boundary between the democratic citizen's right to free expression and his duty to take responsibility for the results of that expression.[3]

[1] This chapter is adapted from Josiah Ober, "Socrates in Democratic Athens," in Donald R. Morrison, ed., *The Cambridge Companion to Socrates* (Cambridge: Cambridge University Press, 2010), pp. 136–175.

[2] Jens Meierhenrich and Devin O. Pendas, "'The Justice of My Cause Is Clear, But There's Politics to Fear': Political Trials in Theory and History," in this volume.

[3] Book-length treatments by classical philosophers, centered on Plato's account of the trial, include C. D. C. Reeve, *Socrates in the Apology: An Essay on Plato's Apology of Socrates* (Indianapolis: Hackett, 1989); Thomas C. Brickhouse and Nicholas D. Smith, *Socrates on Trial* (Princeton: Princeton University Press, 1989). Malcolm Schofield, "Socrates on Trial in the USA," in T. P. Wiseman, ed., *Classics in Progress* (Oxford: Oxford University Press, 2002), pp. 263–283,

The trial of Socrates was a notable and memorable event for the Athenians. It was a definitive moment for the Socratic tradition of philosophy and for writers who responded to that tradition. It quickly generated a substantial literature. The trial took place in a well-documented period of Athenian political and legal history. We know a lot about the historical context of the trial, and about the literary context of the Socratic tradition in which our accounts of the trial were written. We must, however, keep in mind that the "Socrates" who takes part in the story of the trial is, like a character in a historical novel, a conglomerate: in some part modeled on the real Socrates, in some part a fictional person invented by the authors of the tradition. There is no way to quantify how much of Plato's or Xenophon's Socrates is real, how much invented; respectable scholarly opinion on this subject covers a broad spectrum. My approach here is to place the events as portrayed in the tradition in their Athenian legal and historical context. I hope to show that the Socratic tradition engaged creatively with the Athenian context, and that "Socrates on trial" was a plausible Athenian character, deeply concerned with the moral values and political practices of the democratic city.

LEGAL PROCEDURE AND HISTORICAL CONTEXT

The chain of events that began with legal charges being lodged against Socrates and culminated in Socrates' execution unrolled according to the established judicial procedures of the democratic state. Meletus, a private citizen serving as voluntary prosecutor (*ho boulomenos*: "he who chooses to act"), brought charges against Socrates before the Basileus, a state official responsible for preliminary investigation of, among other matters, religious crimes. Meletus' brief was as follows: "Socrates does criminal wrong (*adikei*) by not recognizing (*ou nomizon*) the gods that the state recognizes (*nomizei*), and furthermore by introducing new divinities (*daimonia*); and he also does criminal wrong by corrupting (*diaphthairon*) the youth (*neous*)." The Basileus, employing his power as magistrate, summoned Socrates to his office in the Athenian *agora* (public square) for a preliminary hearing. Having interrogated Meletus and Socrates, the Basileus remanded the matter to an Athenian "people's court" (*dikasterion*). The case was tried over the course of a day by a panel of judges who had been selected randomly from a pool of Athenian citizens over age thirty.[4]

Athenian criminal law was decidedly adversarial, pitting the prosecutor against the defendant, with 501 voting judges standing in the place of the entire citizenry deciding the outcome. The Athenians who heard the case were

reviews the debate over Socrates' attitude toward democracy and his "quietism." The primary sources are assembled in Thomas C. Brickhouse and Nicholas D. Smith, *The Trial and Execution of Socrates: Sources and Controversies* (New York: Oxford University Press, 2002). Where not otherwise noted, I follow Plato's account of the proceedings.

[4] The version of the indictment cited by Diogenes Laertius (*Lives of the Philosophers* 1.5.40) is consistent with the main ancient accounts (Xenophon, *Memorabilia* 1.1.1; Xenophon, *Apology* 11–12, 19; Plato, *Apology* 24b, *Euthyphro* 2c–3b).

judges (rather than merely jurors) because they made substantive decisions about the meaning and applicability of the law itself, rather than merely determining matters of fact. Athenian written law, while very specific about procedural rules meant to ensure fairness (e.g., equal time for speeches by prosecutor and defendant), tended not to include definitions of the abstractions upon which the law's application hinged. It was, therefore, up to the judges to decide on their own, without expert assistance, the meaning of relevant terms as well as their applicability to particular cases. The best-documented example of this is the Athenian law on outrage (*hubris*): The law carefully specified the categories of persons against whom outrage may not be committed, the procedure to be followed in the case of trial, and the range of penalties that might be inflicted upon a guilty individual. Yet the law did not define *hubris* – it did not specify what behaviors or actions were outrageous. This meant that it was open to prosecutor and defendant to debate both facts (what the defendant purportedly did) and their legal meaning (whether what he did constituted a breach of the law). Precedent offered no firm guidance: Athenian judicial bodies were not bound by earlier decisions, although litigants often cited past judgments.[5]

The Athenian law on impiety appears to have been similar in form: detailing the legal procedure to be followed, but silent on the range of beliefs or acts constituting impiety. There was a strong consensus among Athenians that certain actions were impious and therefore merited prosecution: performing mock religious rites, defacing sacred objects, stealing goods stored in a temple, placing an olive branch upon an altar at an improper time, or removing the stump of a sacred olive tree from private land. Yet Socrates was accused of nothing of the kind. Meletus' charges of Socrates failing properly to recognize state gods, improperly introducing new gods, and corrupting the youth were quite vague, and we lack detailed evidence for Athenian impiety prosecutions on similar grounds. In light of the close vote, there is no reason to suppose that a strong normative consensus pertained to what constituted proper "recognition" of state gods, or what sort of actions would constitute improperly "introducing" new gods, or what counted as an "impious" sort of corruption.[6]

[5] On the law against *hubris*, see Nick R. E. Fisher, *Hybris: A Study in the Values of Honour and Shame in Ancient Greece* (Warminster: Aris and Phillips, 1992); on the procedural focus of Athenian law, see Stephen C. Todd, *The Shape of Athenian Law* (Oxford: Clarendon, 1993); and on precedents, see Adriaan M. Lanni, "Arguing from 'Precedent': Modern Perspectives on Athenian Practice," in Edward M. Harris and L. Rubinstein, eds., *The Law and the Courts in Ancient Greece* (London: Duckworth, 2004), pp. 159–172.

[6] On impiety law, see Douglas M. MacDowell, *The Law in Classical Athens* (Ithaca: Cornell University Press, 1978), pp. 197–202; Robert Parker, *Athenian Religion: A History* (Oxford: Clarendon Press, 1996), chapter 10. Ancient stories regarding other Athenian trials for "thought crimes" are probably spurious: Robert W. Wallace, "Private Lives and Public Enemies: Freedom of Thought in Classical Athens," in Alan L. Boegehold and Adele C. Scafuro, eds., *Athenian Identity and Civic Ideology* (Baltimore: Johns Hopkins University Press, 1994), pp. 127–155.

The judges listened to a carefully timed speech of accusation by Meletus, who, following ordinary Athenian prosecutorial practice, yielded part of his allotted speaking time to two associates. Next, Socrates, as defendant, was allowed an identical period of time in which to speak in his own defense. He used part of his time in a rare but legally unremarkable cross-examination of Meletus.[7]

Following Socrates' speech, the judges immediately voted on the verdict, by secret ballot. Because the majority of the judges voted for conviction, Meletus and Socrates each gave another timed speech, offering alternative penalties. Lacking discretionary sentencing authority, the judges were legally required to choose between these alternatives. Meletus proposed death. Socrates proposed a bizarre conglomerate "penalty": a substantial fine (30 minas: roughly ten years' wages for a craftsman) paid by his wealthy friends conjoined with the extraordinary honor of taking meals in the public dining hall for the rest of his life. A majority of the judges voted for death and Socrates was incarcerated in the public prison. A delay of several days ensued, due to a religious prohibition having nothing to do with the trial. In this interval Socrates' friends sought to have Socrates smuggled out of prison (Xenophon, *Apology* 23). Plato's *Crito* tells the story of Socrates' refusal, on ethical grounds, to cooperate with the escape plan. Socrates received visitors in his prison cell, some of whom stayed with him until the end (see Plato's *Phaedo*). The death sentence was carried out, via hemlock poisoning, as soon as the religious prohibition was lifted.[8]

The trial and its outcome were long remembered, both by sympathetic philosophers and by subsequent prosecutors in Athenian criminal trials who referred to the verdict as exemplary in one way or another. In order to grasp the kind of political trial this was, and the role of power, procedure, and performance in making it a socially significant event with long-term effects on the structure of Athenian power relations, we need briefly to consider the relevant historical background: The trial of Socrates was held in the aftermath of Athens' defeat in an external war and a brutal civil war.

In 404 BCE, four years before the trial of Socrates, Athens had surrendered to Sparta, ending the twenty-seven-year Peloponnesian War. Socrates' associates, Critias and Charmides, along with twenty-eight other antidemocratic Athenians, were soon installed as Athens' new governors by the victorious Spartans. The reign of "the Thirty" was short and brutal, featuring arbitrary arrests, judicial murder, property confiscation, and large-scale exile. Some

[7] For accounts of Athenian legal procedure, see MacDowell, *Law*; Adriaan M. Lanni, *Law and Justice in the Courts of Classical Athens* (Cambridge: Cambridge University Press, 2006). On Athenian law courts, see Alan L. Boegehold, *The Lawcourts at Athens: Sites, Buildings, Equipment, Procedure, and Testimonia* (Princeton: American School of Classical Studies at Athens, 1995).

[8] Stephen C. Todd, "How to Execute People in Fourth-Century Athens," in Virginia Hunter and Jonathan Edmondson, eds., *Law and Social Status in Classical Athens* (Oxford: Oxford University Press, 2000), pp. 31–51, reviews methods of capital punishment at Athens.

Athenians abandoned the city to join a pro-democratic army, based first at the Athenian border-village of Phyle and then in the port town of Piraeus. In 403 BCE, the government of the Thirty was overthrown by the democratic insurgency: Critias was killed in battle and others fled. The Spartan-brokered peace that followed allowed the reestablishment of a democratic government. The democrats proclaimed an Amnesty, protecting all but the Thirty and a few of their closest associates from legal prosecution aimed at their activities during the civil war.[9]

According to Socratic tradition (especially Plato, *Seventh Letter*, and the two *Apologies* of Plato and Xenophon), Socrates himself paid scant notice to this dramatic sequence of events. He remained in the city after the takeover of the Thirty, apparently continuing his ordinary round of philosophical engagements. Yet the Thirty were not content to leave him uninvolved: Along with four other Athenians, Socrates was ordered to arrest a certain Leon and to bring him to Athens for execution. Plato's *Apology* (32c-d) states that the other four obeyed the magistrate's order, but Socrates himself simply returned home, refusing to be frightened by the Thirty into doing something unjust. Socrates' principled refusal to cooperate did not save Leon, or other victims of the Thirty. In Socrates' ethics, actively aiding an unjust act was impermissible, but heroic action aimed at saving other men from injustice was not required.[10] Since Socrates acknowledged the legitimate power of valid laws to constrain his actions (see below), Socrates' decision to go home rather than to obey the order to arrest Leon suggests that he did not believe that the order was valid. Presumably, he considered the Thirty as lawless rulers, and regarded the Athenian law code under which he had grown up to be still valid (although not being enforced by the lawless rulers). If Socrates regarded the magistrate's order to be invalid under Athenian law, then his refusal to arrest Leon is consistent with a stance of obedience to legal authority.[11]

With the democratic restoration, Athens was freed from the Thirty, but remained in dire straits: Perhaps half the citizen population of Athens had been killed in the later years of the war and the civil war; the economy was a shambles; the fleet and walls that had protected the city were destroyed. Surviving Athenians had lost much: In many cases their ancestral property

[9] On this difficult period in Athenian history, see Peter Krentz, *The Thirty at Athens* (Ithaca: Cornell University Press, 1982); Andrew Wolpert, *Remembering Defeat: Civil War and Civic Memory in Ancient Athens* (Baltimore: Johns Hopkins University Press, 2002); Edwin Carawan, *The Athenian Amnesty and Reconstructing the Law* (Oxford: Oxford University Press, 2013).

[10] Socrates' passive response to the Leon affair is regarded by Isidor Feinstein Stone, *The Trial of Socrates* (Boston: Little, Brown, 1988) as proof of his fundamentally antidemocratic disposition.

[11] Xenophon, *Memorabilia* 1.2.34, humorously presents Socrates in a dialogue with Critias and Charicles over their new law forbidding him to discourse with the youth, and as open to the argument that he should obey. But Xenophon's Socrates is being ironic; the reader is not led to suppose that Socrates is given reason to obey.

was lost forever. Once-wealthy families struggled to make ends meet.[12] The Athenians held civic festivals stressing national unity. They honored the heroes who had begun the democratic resistance to the Thirty. And they completed the arduous task of re-codifying the laws. But these measures were carried out in an uneasy political environment. In the legislative citizen Assembly, proposals were advanced, and ultimately defeated, that would have radically altered the composition of the citizen body: disenfranchising the poorest Athenians, or enfranchising all non-Athenians who had participated in the anti-tyrannical resistance. Meanwhile, the Amnesty meant that the people's anger and pain at the losses suffered during the reign of the Thirty could not be satisfied by seeking justice through the legal system. It was an agonizing era; everyone's life was in disarray.

Everyone, it seemed, but Socrates. His response to the order to arrest Leon of Salamis, as reported in Plato's *Apology*, "going away from there [the magistrate's office], I went on home," might be taken as summing up his lack of concern with the chaos around him: That day was not, as it turned out, a good one for philosophical conversation in the *agora*; but there would be other days and other conversations. The Socratic tradition emphasizes Socrates' bravery in ignoring the arrest order: In Plato's *Apology*, Socrates claims that he himself might have been executed had the regime of the Thirty not fallen soon afterward. But to Athenians who had risked their lives to bring about the fall of the lawless rulers, Socrates' easy willingness to stay in the city during the worst of the excesses and his close relationship with some of the leaders were of greater moment than his principled refusal to collaborate in an arrest. Yet then again, many other Athenians had connections with members of the Thirty and many had stayed in the city during their reign. The Amnesty was intended to avoid implicating the legal institutions of the restored democracy in acts of private revenge upon those Athenians whose collaboration with the Thirty had been essentially passive – or even upon most of those who had actively collaborated. Although, as Critias' putative teacher, Socrates was no doubt a target of anger, that anger was blocked by the Amnesty from employing the law as its legitimate instrument.

SOCRATES' TRIAL: DESTRUCTIVE OR DIDACTIC?

I have suggested that Meletus launched what he intended as a destructive prosecution: That is, Meletus saw Socrates as an enemy of the Athenian state and intended to eliminate him as such. But Meletus was constrained by both the legal conditions of the Amnesty and by the legal risk to which he was subject as prosecutor. The Amnesty meant that Meletus could not openly prosecute

[12] Xenophon's *Memorabilia* sets Socrates in this milieu and, in its latter books, makes him a source of practical financial and military advice.

Socrates on the charge of being an oligarch's teacher and collaborator: One Athenian had already been put to death for violating the rule against seeking to prosecute in defiance of the Amnesty. Meanwhile, Athenian law mandated severe penalties for Athenian prosecutors who failed to secure one-fifth of the jury's votes.[13] There was no reason for Meletus to suppose that Socrates would be an easy target. Aristophanes' comedy *Clouds* shows that Socrates was renowned for his verbal cleverness. Meletus had to confront the possibility that Socrates would mount a rhetorically sophisticated and convincing defense.

Meletus' choice of the legal grounds of "impiety" ensured that he would not run afoul of the Amnesty. And impiety might, on the face of it, seem a safe charge for a prosecutor. Whether or not the late fifth and early fourth century was an era of "religious crisis" at Athens, as it is sometimes portrayed, there were a number of successful postwar prosecutions on the legal grounds of impiety. In some cases, these trials may be understood as political.[14] Yet the other well-known impiety trials concerned behavior that most Athenians would recognize as unambiguously impious. In Socrates' case there was no smoking gun of sacred mystery-mocking, sacred herm-smashing, sacred olive-tree-uprooting, or the like. If he were to convince a jury of Socrates' guilt, Meletus would need to expand the legal horizon of impiety. Since impiety was probably not defined in the written law, Meletus was free to seek to define impiety as failing to recognize the gods recognized by the state and introducing new gods. But this would be unfamiliar legal ground for the judges; there are no securely attested prior prosecutions under the impiety law employing Meletus' definition. Meletus must have counted upon political factors to tilt the decision in his favor.

The political factors most commonly adduced by the Socratic tradition, and especially by Xenophon, are the charges that Socrates was the teacher of Alcibiades and Critias, and that he was personally antidemocratic. Xenophon was eager to dispute both charges, and there has been much scholarly discussion about their actual weight in the trial and about their legitimacy.[15] While it seems indisputable that some Athenian judges would indeed have been prejudiced against Socrates on the basis of his earlier associations, it is also the case that others would be alive to the spirit of the Amnesty and respectful of their oath to judge according to the written law and according to justice when the law was silent.[16] Athenian dissatisfaction with Socrates stemmed, at least in part, from the fact that Socrates seemed unaffected, in his attitudes and in his public

[13] Execution for violation of the Amnesty: [Aristotle] *Athenaion Politeia* 40.2. Penalties for exceptionally weak prosecutions: MacDowell, *Law*, p. 64.

[14] On the "religious crisis," see W. Robert Connor, "The Other 399: Religion and the Trial of Socrates," in *Georgica: Greek Studies in Honor of George Cawkwell*, Bulletin Supplement (London: Institute of Classical Studies, 1991), pp. 49–56; Parker, *Athenian Religion*, chapter 10.

[15] See Schofield, "Socrates on Trial." [16] Athenian jurors' oath: MacDowell, *Law*, p. 44.

behavior, by the momentous events of the late fifth century. Yet I will argue that the vote to convict arose less from the "low politics" of resentment and revenge than from the "high politics" of normative conceptions of public duty and accountability. The jury's decision was not, in the first instance at least, either partisan or aimed at the destruction of an enemy, but rather it aimed to decide an essential question about the rights and duties of citizens in respect to potentially dangerous public speech.

The two extant *Apologies* give us strong reason to suppose that following the fall of the Thirty, Socrates went about his ordinary philosophical round: earnestly seeking conversation-partners in the public space of the *agora* as well as in private and elite gatherings, humiliating those who failed to avoid self-contradiction, and in the process gathering about himself a group of young men eager to be known as his students. In the years preceding the political crisis of the late fifth century, these young men had included Alcibiades, Critias, and other well-known enemies of democracy. Plato's Socrates emphasizes that his conversations were aimed at benefit, of himself and his interlocutors, and that he had no intention of corrupting anyone. Given that he was doing good and not harm, Socrates saw no reason not to pursue exactly the sort of life after the fall of the Thirty that he had pursued during and before their reign. But many Athenians had come to see things rather differently.

By 399 BCE, the immediate political crisis had passed, but so had public euphoria at surviving the war, at dodging the bullet of endless civil war, and reuniting the state under a reestablished code of law. The realization sunk in that reunification was only the beginning of a costly and uncertain rebuilding period, and that Athens remained fragile and vulnerable to its enemies. The Athenian willingness to tolerate potentially dangerous behavior and apparently irresponsible public attitudes reached a low point. And so, for Meletus the time was ripe: He could prosecute Socrates for impiety on relatively novel grounds with little concern of incurring the penalty for failing to gain a fifth of the votes.

Given the closeness of the vote, it appears likely that it was, however, only Socrates' idiosyncratic defense that enabled Meletus to gain a guilty verdict. The Socratic tradition holds that Socrates could not have given any other sort of defense while remaining true to his own convictions. But the question remains: Why did Socrates choose to defend himself in the first place? That is, why did he not only obey the procedural formalities but also willingly participate in the performative practices of the Athenian criminal trial?

The Socratic tradition was bothered by that question: In Plato's *Gorgias* (521c–22c), Callicles predicts that Socrates will be legally prosecuted by some evil man and that, lacking training in rhetoric, he will fail to defend himself and so will be killed. Socrates of the *Gorgias* concurs with this prediction. In his metaphor of a doctor being tried by a pastry-cook before a jury of children, he seemingly predicts that the inherent irrationality of the legal situation would leave him with nothing to say in his own defense. Maximus of Tyre's claim that Socrates stood silent at the trial translates this prediction into a spurious fact.[17]

Yet the historical Socrates certainly *did* address the Athenian judges. Perhaps he did so because he believed that even if the chances of acquittal were slight, he owed it to the continuation of his philosophical project to make the effort. But surely there was another reason, just as compelling: Socrates saw the trial as didactic. He believed that it was his civic duty to seek to educate (by stinging awake) his fellows – and especially his fellow Athenian citizens. Although the conditions of the trial, speaking at length before a mass audience and with time constraints, were far from optimal, the self-described gadfly owed it to his fellow citizens to offer them this last, best sting. When Socrates claimed that he could have presented no other defense, he must have meant (inter alia) that he was duty bound to present a speech that was more lesson than defense.

PERFORMING THE LAW IN ATHENS AND IN GREEK LITERATURE

Meletus' rhetorical strategy and substantive arguments can be hypothetically reconstructed by attending to the commonplaces used by other Athenian prosecutors and to the Socratic tradition regarding the trial. That tradition consists of two quite different *Apologies of Socrates* written some time after the trial by Socrates' followers, Xenophon and Plato; various remarks about the trial in the extensive body of "Socratic conversations" written by those two authors; and a miscellany of off-hand, fragmentary, and much later testimonies. Plato's *Apology* is the most important single item in the tradition. It takes the form of three sequential speeches: Socrates' defense proper (for which we have many near-contemporary comparanda in the corpus of Athenian legal orations), a speech at the sentencing phase of the trial, and a final address to the jurors who had voted to acquit. The main defense speech resembles real Athenian defense speeches; the two others are *sui generis*. Xenophon's *Apology of Socrates* is not modeled on actual Athenian defense speeches; it takes the form of a secondhand report of the trial and its aftermath. Xenophon's *Memorabilia* was written in response to a literary version of a prosecutor's indictment of Socrates.[18]

As prosecutor, Meletus and his two associates opened the proceedings of the trial with a series of speeches in which they laid out their case against Socrates. There were no strict rules of relevance in Athenian trials, but the prosecutors

[17] Maximus of Tyre, *Oration* 3.7 and passim.

[18] Literary version: below n. 21. Two references to the charges by the Athenian orators Aeschines and Hypereides are considered below. See Josiah Ober, *Mass and Elite in Democratic Athens: Rhetoric, Ideology, and the Power of the People* (Princeton: Princeton University Press, 1989) for an analysis of Athenian courtroom rhetoric. Mogens Herman Hansen, *The Trial of Sokrates – From the Athenian Point of View* (Copenhagen: Munksgaard, 1995) is historically well informed.

could expect vocal reprimands from the jurors – in the form of "uproar" (*thorubos*) if they were thought to be straying from the point. Attacks on the defendant's character, habits, and associates were common, but the case must be made that a law was broken – it was not enough to establish that Socrates was a social misfit. If Meletus were to succeed in his goal of destroying Socrates as an enemy of the state, using his expansive interpretation of the law on impiety as his tool, he had to demonstrate to the judges that the things he accused Socrates of doing or failing to do were *normatively* impious, as well showing *factually* that Socrates had done or not done them.

Meletus' legal burden bears directly on the question of Socrates' legal innocence or guilt. Given the apparent lack of a definition in the Athenian law on impiety, and in the absence of evidence for an Athenian consensus about what constituted improper recognition, introduction, and corruption, it is not possible to answer the question "was Socrates objectively guilty or innocent, according to Athenian law?" in any straightforward way – other than to assert, tautologically, that after the verdict he was certainly guilty, because the court's judgment, as a felicitously performed speech act, legally constituted him a guilty man. If there was no Athenian normative consensus on what constituted impious nonrecognition, introduction, and corruption, then the central question in much scholarship on the trial – "was Socrates (whether it is Plato's Socrates or the historical Socrates) *actually guilty*?" – is unanswerable.[19] I address instead a question that is more interesting from the perspective of looking at the trial of Socrates as a political trial: How and why did Meletus seek to prove to the judges that Socrates was guilty, and how and why did the early Socratic tradition seek to prove to posterity that Socrates was innocent – innocent, that is, in respect to justice and in the eyes of a reasonable Athenian judge?

Meletus' rhetorical strategy is largely lost to us – but it can be partly reconstructed by looking at how the Socratic tradition sought to exculpate Socrates. Plato's *Apology* and Xenophon's *Apology* and *Memorabilia* approach the task differently: Both acknowledge, either implicitly (Plato) or explicitly (Xenophon), that Socrates' speech of defense appeared extraordinarily boastful and unconvincing to the judges. Xenophon explains this by the assumption that, although innocent of impious behavior and of corrupting anyone, Socrates intentionally infuriated the jurors with a boastful speech because he planned to use the trial in order to commit judicial suicide.

Plato's Socrates, by contrast, presents a speech of outstanding rhetorical sophistication and filled with dazzling logical gambits. But Plato's Socrates is

[19] Guilty of impiety (qua harming the state by undermining traditional religion): Myles F. Burnyeat, "The Impiety of Socrates," *Ancient Philosophy*, Vol. 17 (1997), pp. 1–129; guilty of harming the democracy: Stone, *Trial*. Innocent of impiety: Reeve, *Socrates*; innocent of any antidemocratic tendencies: Gregory Vlastos, "The Historical Socrates and Athenian Democracy," in *Socratic Studies* (Cambridge: Cambridge University Press, 1994), pp. 87–108.

not just showing off: He is using the occasion of the trial for a specific didactic purpose. Socrates repeatedly lulls the judge/reader into thinking that the defense is developing according to the standard protocols of Athenian forensic rhetoric and then suddenly inverts those protocols in ways that are clearly intended to be shocking – thereby stinging the listener/reader into moral wakefulness. His sarcastic cross-examination of Meletus seeks to show that Meletus' views on politics and education are incoherent – and typical of those of most Athenians.

Plato's Socrates uses his defense speech to offer a critical assessment of the underlying assumptions of the democratic culture of Athens: He seeks to show the ordinary citizens of the jury that they were, as citizens, incapable of making important decisions and that the public institutions of the state were inadequate to train the youth in good civic values. Plato's Socrates claims to seek acquittal, but is pessimistic about the likelihood of this, and for good reason: He reveals his own commitments to truth-telling and moral value to be fundamentally at odds with the attitudes of most Athenians – and his life's work to be the painful process of bringing his fellows to acknowledge their individual and collective failings. And yet for all that, Plato urges his reader to suppose that a thoughtful and fair-minded judge *should* have voted to acquit: on the substance of the case, in his own genuine interest, and for the good of his city.[20]

In setting out to show that Socrates had violated a reasonable Athenian's conception of pious behavior, Meletus may well have accused Socrates of outright atheism, as Plato asserts (*Apology* 26e). He probably claimed that Socrates failed to participate in the ordinary round of state-sponsored religious practices (sacrifice, procession, cult ritual) – an argument that Xenophon sought to refute in his *Memorabilia*. Meletus almost surely accused Socrates of improper attention to a deity unrecognized by the state (Socrates' famous *daimonion*). If Meletus charged Socrates with corrupting specific Athenians (by name or implication), these likely included Alcibiades (an Athenian leader during the Peloponnesian War, whose treason contributed to Athens' loss in the war) and Critias (Plato's uncle and leader of the Thirty). Meletus may have implied that Socrates corrupted young men by teaching them to behave as he did, thereby making it more likely that they would willingly harm their fellow citizens (as Critias and Alcibiades had).[21] In developing his

[20] For a more detailed analysis of the rhetoric of Plato's *Apology*, see Josiah Ober, *Political Dissent in Democratic Athens: Intellectual Critics of Popular Rule* (Princeton: Princeton University Press, 1998), pp. 166–179.

[21] Non-participation in cult: Mark K. McPherran, "Does Piety Pay? Socrates and Plato on Prayer and Sacrifice," in Nicholas D. Smith and Paul Woodruff, eds., *Reason and Religion in Socratic Philosophy* (Oxford: Oxford University Press, 2000), pp. 89–114. The Athenian state allowed the introduction of new gods only by a legislative procedure: Robert Garland, *Introducing New Gods: The Politics of Athenian Religion* (London: Duckworth, 1992); Parker, *Athenian Religion*, chapter 9. The charge of "educating in badness" is a key part of the hostile portrait of Socrates in Aristophanes' *Clouds*. A half-century after the trial the orator Aeschines (1.173) reminded jurors that "you" convicted Socrates for having educated Critias, and Xenophon,

impiety case, Meletus was likely to have hinted at sundry other crimes and misdeeds, including a generalized hostility to the democracy itself. The judges were probably told that Socrates was arrogant (Xenophon, *Apology* 32), a diabolically clever speaker (Plato, *Apology* 17a–b), and an unpatriotic scofflaw with an inherently vicious character (Xenophon, *Memorabilia* 1.2.9). Meletus may have claimed that he was prosecuting only reluctantly, as a patriot performing a public service, and that a failure to convict would put the city at grave risk. To prove his case he may have cited the sworn testimony of witnesses (Xenophon, *Apology* 24), but he could also have called upon the judges themselves as informal witnesses, claiming that it was common knowledge that Socrates acted impiously.

Following the speeches of Meletus and his associates, Socrates delivered his speech of defense. In Plato's account of the trial, Socrates' defense hinged on two substantive claims intended to show that Meletus had utterly failed to build a case for impiety, and thus that Socrates could not reasonably be convicted. First, negatively, Meletus was incapable of recognizing impiety because he had no understanding of piety. Nor did he understand how the youth were either corrupted or benefited. His ignorance was demonstrated by his incapacity to avoid self-contradiction on these subjects under Socrates' cross-examination. Since Meletus could not explain what piety or education was without contradicting himself, he could not make a coherent case that Socrates had behaved impiously or had miseducated anyone. Second, positively, in accord with the beliefs of other Athenians, Socrates regarded piety as a virtue. Socrates' ideas about piety were, Plato argues, both internally consistent and fell within the range of reasonable Athenian opinion on the subject.

The tradition's argument for innocence is grounded in several claims: First, Socrates conducted his life in accordance with his moral commitments. Because he regarded piety as a virtue and his conception of piety conformed to reasonable Athenian opinion, Socrates would not, and did not, engage in actions that a reasonable Athenian would regard as impious. Next, Socrates had no motive to corrupt others, since by so doing he would have harmed himself. Finally, there was no evidence for corruption of the youth, since neither Athenian youths nor their parents testified that Socrates had corrupted them.

These arguments for Socrates' innocence might have convinced some of the judges but they did not directly answer the prosecutor's charges. A reasonable judge, listening to the speech of Plato's *Apology*, could hardly be blamed for concluding that the logic lesson given to Meletus was a cover-up and that Socrates actually disbelieved in state-approved gods and for that reason avoided participation in state religious rituals; that he promoted a personal deity unrecognized by the state; and that he corrupted entire families so thoroughly that they failed to recognize the harm they suffered and did. That

Memorabilia 1.2.12, claims that Socrates' association with Critias and Alcibiades was brought up by the prosecutors.

judge might well accept Meletus' argument that Socrates' behavior was impious. Plato sets Socrates' logical refutation of Meletus' conceptions of piety and education within a speech that challenged Athenian assumptions about what constituted a proper legal defense. And so the sympathetic reader is given to understand that Socrates truly *was* innocent, that the judges *should* have acquitted him accordingly, but also that many of the Athenian judges *would* have had reason to vote for conviction. A sympathetic reader of Xenophon's *Apology* was likely to reach a similar conclusion.

Plato's Socrates, like many actual Athenian litigants, spent a relatively small part of his allotted time answering the prosecution's charges; like other Athenian defendants, the bulk of his defense speech was devoted to a discussion of the conduct of his life and an assessment of his behavior and attitudes in respect to the democratic culture of the state. The choice to use much of the water in the clock on self-presentation was not inherently peculiar. Yet Plato presents Socrates as diverging radically from the standard practice of Athenian litigants in the *substance* of his self-presentation. Ordinary defendants sought to present their lives and attitudes as conforming closely to democratic norms. By contrast, Socrates presented himself as a long-standing and open critic of Athenian mores and as decidedly critical of certain core principles and practices of democratic politics. Socrates' goal in self-presentation was *not* that of the ordinary Athenian defendant: that is, persuading the judges to vote for acquittal on the grounds of his sound character and democratic way of life, whether or not they believed a law had been broken. Socrates' ultimate rhetorical goal was a matter of debate in antiquity: As we have seen, Xenophon suggests that he sought to assure his own conviction. In the philosophically and rhetorically richer account given by Plato, Socrates' goal in presenting himself as a social and political critic was the education (in its distinctively Socratic sense of "stinging into moral wakefulness") of the judges: Whether or not the historical Socrates treated the trial as a didactic occasion, there is no doubt that this is what it becomes in Plato's *Apology*.

The story of the trial is set in a compressed and dramatic narrative frame that would have been very familiar to Plato's and Xenophon's original Athenian readers. Socrates is the protagonist of this story, but the antagonist is not just Meletus but the state of Athens: its citizens (qua judges), its established laws, and its democratic political culture. From this perspective, we can see that, in the literature it spawned, the trial was a political trial in the fullest sense of the term. The stark confrontation between the moral philosopher and the democratic city in the dramatically satisfying narrative of the legal trial became a foundation story for Western civilization – and especially for moral philosophy. It is difficult to overestimate its impact. According to the *Seventh Letter* (325a–26a, a product of the early Academy if not by Plato), the trial and execution of Socrates was the decisive event that turned young Plato away from an engagement with democratic politics, and toward the philosophical project that resulted in the composition and circulation of Socratic dialogues and the foundation of the Academy. The events of 399 cast a long shadow across Plato's oeuvre; the trial theme notably recurs in the *Gorgias*, where Socrates' interlocutor, the aspiring Athenian politician Callias, predicts that Socrates will be unable to defend himself in court when unjustly charged with a crime.

The trial of Socrates spawned a new kind of Athenian literature: speeches of defense (*Apologiai*) and of accusation (*Kategoriai*) written for and against Socrates – the former by Socrates' followers and the latter by their intellectual opponents.[22] The trial was sufficiently notorious a half-century later to be cited in an Athenian courtroom by the politician and prosecutor Aeschines (1.173), who argued that the conviction of Socrates would be rendered unfair in retrospect if the judges were to allow the defendant's supporter, Demosthenes, to use the trial as a sophistical showcase. About a decade earlier (in ca. 352 BCE), the Athenian rhetorician Isocrates, whose school rivaled Plato's Academy, wrote an immense and fanciful super-*Apology*. In that speech (*Antidosis*) Isocrates cast himself in the role of an intellectual, falsely charged with "corrupting the youth," who faced capital charges if his defense failed to convince the judges: Isocrates' reader was obviously meant to recognize Plato's *Apology of Socrates* as the literary model that Isocrates sought to surpass in his lengthy and ornate legal fiction.[23] And a decade before that (361 BCE) the forensic orator Hypereides (fragment 44) reminded a jury that "your fathers" had punished Socrates "for his speeches" (*epi logois*).

Notably, in the trial scene in Plato's *Gorgias*, as in both Aeschines' and Isocrates' citations, the themes of the dissident intellectual confronting democratic political culture and the corruption of youth are prominent, but impiety as such has dropped from the picture. The specifically *religious* aspect of the trial proved to be its least enduring feature, at least for the classical tradition. This is perhaps because Athens had no independent religious establishment. The aspect of religion relevant to the trial was a facet of civic life, and so the trial of Socrates is relevant to the question of the compatibility of philosophical dissidence with democratic civic norms. The story of Socrates and Athens remains salient in modernity – in an era in which "democracy conjoined with law," as originally defined by the ancient Athenians, and "critical ethical inquiry," as originally defined by Socrates, are both regarded by many people as primary goods and basic to human flourishing. Although no retelling can ever hope to be definitive, by taking into account the relevant contexts – cultural, social, intellectual and philosophical, as well as political, and legal – we can hope to make sense of the story of the confrontation between philosophical Socrates and democratic Athens.

[22] The most famous *kategoria* was by the fourth-century BC sophist Polycrates, who is apparently the butt of Xenophon, *Memorabilia* Book 1, and Isocrates, *Busiris* 4. See further, Brickhouse and Smith, *Trial and Execution*, pp. 5–8.

[23] Isocrates and Socrates: Andrea Wilson Nightingale, *Genres in Dialogue: Plato and the Construct of Philosophy* (Cambridge: Cambridge University Press, 1995); Ober, *Political Dissent*, chapter 5.

SOCRATES' CIVIC DUTIES

The ways in which the trial was construed as political by later Greek tradition is elucidated by considering its aftermath: Socrates' behavior while in prison, awaiting execution. According to Plato's *Crito* – a dialogue which, like the *Apologies of Socrates*, puts Socrates into an active conversation with democratic norms and practices – Socrates refused to go along with an escape plan hatched by his friends because escaping from prison meant breaking the law. Escaping from prison would violate a legal order issued by competent public authorities. Moreover, escape, as Plato's Crito admits, would constitute a substantive harm to the edifice of Athenian law.[24]

Socrates of the *Crito* considers the harm consideration decisive. He brushes aside counterarguments regarding the bad effects of Socrates' death upon his friends and sons, and on the reputations of those who might have saved him but failed to do so. This carelessness about morally irrelevant conditions of life is typical of Socrates as portrayed in the tradition. More surprisingly, however, Socrates also refuses to take into consideration the substantive fairness of the judgment against himself. Both Crito and Socrates (and presumably Plato's intended reader) accept that the Athenian judges erred in convicting Socrates of impiety. As we have seen, in Plato's *Apology* Socrates had attacked the coherence of Meletus' conception of piety and sought to establish his own commitment to piety as a virtue. The philosophically inclined reader assumed by Plato's texts was likely to conclude that Socrates had been wrongly convicted in respect to justice. Yet Socrates had been rightfully convicted in respect to Athenian law. That is to say, the Athenian jury had made no procedural error in coming to its legal judgment. The power of the state had been used legitimately, and Socrates had acknowledged that legitimacy by his obedience to the lawful magistrate's lawful summons – just as he had refused to acknowledge the legitimacy of the authority of the Thirty when he disobeyed the unlawful order to arrest Leon. He further acknowledged the legitimacy of the proceedings by his performative participation in the trial – even while employing his performance for subversively didactic purposes.

Because the trial was procedurally correct, the decision of the court had legal authority for Socrates. Socrates believed that the verdict was based on the judges' acceptance of a logically flawed definition of piety. That meant that the verdict was substantively unjust, but the jurors' choice in accepting a faulty definition was strictly irrelevant in terms of the law and Socrates' obedience to it. In Athenian legal process there was no presiding magistrate who might declare a mistrial, no provision for legal appeal to a higher court, and

[24] For thoughtful book-length discussions of the *Crito*'s philosophical arguments, see Richard Kraut, *Socrates and the State* (Princeton: Princeton University Press, 1984) and Roslyn Weiss, *Socrates Dissatisfied: An Analysis of Plato's Crito* (New York: Oxford University Press, 1998).

certainly no provision for appeal to the authority of "absolute justice." The escape proposed by Crito was an extra-legal measure, to which Socrates' friends resorted in the absence of any obvious options for legal redress.[25]

Having discounted Crito's concerns about the negative effect of Socrates' death on individuals and reputations (harms without moral relevance), Socrates weighs the assumed *injustice of the conviction* against the potential *harm to the state's laws* and comes to an unambiguous conclusion: The consideration that escape would entail (morally relevant) harm to the laws decided the matter and so he refused to cooperate in the escape plan. But in Plato's dialogue Socrates comes to this conclusion in two stages: Harming the laws is initially rejected as an ethically acceptable course of action on the grounds that doing morally relevant harm is impermissible.[26] Socrates reminds Crito that they had previously agreed (in a conversation unavailable to Plato's readers) on the impermissibility of doing harm. If doing morally relevant harm is impermissible, and harming the law is morally relevant, then harming the laws is impermissible. So the discussion about what Socrates should do seems, philosophically, to be decided quickly and decisively. Yet the dialogue continues, taking the form of an imagined conversation between the "laws (*nomoi*) of Athens" and a Socrates who is (counterfactually) seriously contemplating breaking the law by escaping from prison. This "dialogue within a dialogue" continues the conversation between Socrates and the jury in Plato's *Apology*. The difference is that now Socrates' interlocutor is the law of Athens as he himself has come to understand it, rather than fallible and possibly educable Athenian citizens.

The imagined laws of Athens make what Socrates takes to be a powerful case regarding Socrates' duty of obedience in respect to themselves: Obedience to Athenian law is demanded on the grounds that, as a citizen, Socrates, like his forefathers, is the "son and slave" of the laws (50e). This argument, with its unexpected introduction of fundamentally unequal social positions (a father or master may do things to a son or slave that the son or slave may not do to the father or master), is concerned with harms (to the laws) and with what actions are permissible. It does not, however, hinge on the general impermissibility of doing morally relevant harms. It rests instead on the value of reciprocity within a political context: Were Socrates, a citizen of Athens, to harm the laws of his state, he would be returning evils for the goods he had previously received from the laws. Doing so would be analogous to the behavior of a son who struck his father (a common trope in Athenian literature) despite the goods he had received in the past from his parent. The strengthening of the paternal trope

[25] On Athenian "legal positivism," see Josiah Ober, "Law and Political Theory," in Michael Gagarin and David Cohen, eds., *The Cambridge Companion to Ancient Greek Law* (Cambridge: Cambridge University Press, 2005), pp. 394–411.

[26] It is important to distinguish between harm simpliciter and morally relevant harm. Socrates must have willingly accepted the possibility that he might inflict physical damage upon his opponents when he fought in Athenian wars.

implied by the reference to Socrates as son *and slave* of the laws rests on the claim that Socrates, qua citizen, had received from the laws of Athens benefits that exceeded even the benefits a son received from a parent. To wit, Socrates had received from the laws his birth (*genesis*), his upbringing (*trophe*), and his education (*paideia*).[27]

The relatively large amount of time that Socrates of the *Crito* spends in laying out the contractual relationship between citizen and laws suggests that the implied contract is a key to understanding the relationship between Socrates and Athenian democracy. It is important because Plato suggests that there was a general *agreement* between Socrates and the democratic political culture of Athens that the citizen had a substantial duty to his state, and an agreement on what that duty entailed in practice: It entailed obedience to the laws, customs, and magistrates of the state; public participation in support of the institutions of governance; and voluntary contributions on the basis of whatever special excellence he might possess. These duties were justly demanded by the state on the basis of a conception of reciprocal exchange that could be analogized as a just (although unequal) contract: The citizen's duties were an (inadequate) repayment for fundamental goods received by each citizen from the state and its laws.

Assuming that the real Socrates actually had such a conception helps to explain the ethical basis for a few seldom-disputed facts: Socrates' record of military and civic service, his habit of engaging in philosophical conversations with ordinary people in public (rather than limiting himself to private conversations with the educated elite), his willingness to answer the Basileus' legal summons and then to report to the people's court as ordered (rather than just going home), his willingness to make a speech of defense at the trial (rather than remaining mute), his choice to drink the hemlock (rather than escape from prison), and his decision, throughout his life, to continue living in Athens, rather than moving to somewhere with "better laws."

POLITICIZING CITIZENSHIP

The concern of the Socratic tradition with Socrates as a dutiful citizen brings us back to the fundamental question of why Socrates was convicted. If he had no fundamental quarrel with the laws of Athens, if he consistently did his duty as a citizen, how did "good citizen Socrates" come to be tried and executed by his fellow citizens? Scholarly answers can be roughly grouped into the partisan (an ambitious prosecutor mobilized popular anger at Socrates' antidemocratic behavior and/or that of his students) and cultural (postwar Athenian

[27] Parent-striking as an Athenian trope with special salience in the era of Socrates: Barry S. Strauss, *Fathers and Sons in Athens: Ideology and Society in the Era of the Peloponnesian War* (Princeton: Princeton University Press, 1993).

tolerance for intellectual nonconformism hardened and concern with piety grew).[28] Both partisan and cultural factors certainly played a part, but these should be set alongside the larger political context of civic obligation: The conviction was triggered by Socrates' idiosyncratic interpretation of, and persistent fulfillment (through his critical public speech) of, the citizen's duty to contribute to the state through whatever personal excellence he might possess. Socrates was convicted, I argue, because his refusal to take personal responsibility for the results of his speech (its effect on others) led the judges, in their role as representatives of the citizenry, to feel the need to clarify the community's authority to hold individuals accountable for effects of their speech.

The confrontation between Socrates and the community was set up by Socrates' distinctive understanding of the substance of his duty to serve the community. Rather than using his unique capacities to benefit the state in obvious and conventionally acceptable ways (e.g., through material contributions or good advice on state policy), Socrates consistently sought to benefit his fellow Athenians educationally by publicly criticizing democratic culture and its associated habits of thought, speech, and action.[29] The Athenians were quite used to political criticism; indeed they recognized criticism as essential to democratic flourishing. Socrates managed to be critical in ethical terms that were new, powerful, and ultimately profoundly disquieting to his fellow citizens. His stings were genuinely painful and sometimes untimely. Yet only in the special political and cultural circumstances of the era after the end of the civil war did the Athenians decide that it was necessary to slap their troublesome gadfly – not to destroy him, but to define the appropriate scope of public authority and individual responsibility.

By the 420s, a generation before the trial, Socrates was already well enough known as a "public intellectual" to stand in for the standard "mad scientist/conniving sophist," in the comedies of Aristophanes and other comic poets. But Socrates diverged from his contemporary Greek intellectuals in that he saw his relationship to himself, to others, and to his community in explicitly ethical terms and in that he initiated critical conversations with ordinary people in public places – thereby making the ethical inherently political. Because Socrates, unlike other Athenian intellectuals, carried on much of his critical work openly in public, Socrates was known to the Athenian public at large – and was thus

[28] Political explanations: Stone, *Trial*; Ellen Meiksins Wood and Neal Wood, *Class Ideology and Ancient Political Theory: Socrates, Plato, and Aristotle in Social Context* (New York: Oxford University Press, 1978). Cultural explanations: Connor, "Other 399"; Parker, *Athenian Religion*, chapter 10.

[29] Much of the scholarship is polarized around whether Socrates was a friend (Vlastos, "Historical Socrates") or an enemy (Stone, *Trial*) of democracy; see further Schofield, "Socrates on Trial," pp. 271–277; I suggest that the question is misconstrued: that Socrates was a critic and that being an engaged critic need entail neither friendship nor enmity.

a convenient butt of comic poets used to mocking public figures.[30] Socrates was also remarkable for conjoining his critical enterprise with his duties as a participatory citizen. As a councilor in charge of an Assembly meeting at which several generals were accused en masse of malfeasance in 406 BCE, Socrates refused – over the vocal objections of the assembled citizenry – to put the procedurally irregular matter to a vote. There can be little doubt that Socrates' reputation as an outspoken critic of the status quo was securely established well before 399 BCE.

Socrates was renowned in elite circles as well. Plato and Xenophon each wrote a *Symposium*, suggesting that Socrates was in great demand at exclusive gatherings of Athenian intellectuals. Socially, this was a heterogeneous society, composed of aristocratic citizens, wealthy resident foreigners, and distinguished foreign visitors. Some of these people came to regard themselves as Socrates' "students" – but that certainly does not mean that they took on board all of Socrates' attitudes and behaviors. Whereas certain of Socrates' elite friends and interlocutors were loyal supporters of the democratic regime, others (notably Alcibiades and Critias) came to despise the democracy and worked to overthrow it. The latter group clearly did not buy into the conception of the citizen's "debt to the laws of the state" that Socrates of the *Crito* subscribes to. Revolutionary antidemocrats eventually overthrew (with Spartan help) the democratic regime and its laws in favor of the regime of the Thirty.

Socrates denied that he had students on the grounds that he took no money for teaching. Nor did he accept that anyone could have been corrupted by his public or private conversations. But Athenian antidemocrats evidently focused on his critical view of democratic governance. Socrates' argument that ordinary persons, as opposed to experts in moral education, were incapable of improving others was grist for the mill of antidemocratic revolutionaries. That argument is compatible with the assumption that Socrates himself remained an obedient and participatory citizen of the democratic state: Socrates may have believed that no moral education experts existed, or that their authority could not be established without doing ethically impermissible harm to the laws. There was no *necessary* contradiction between being a critic of democratic ideology and a good citizen of the democratic community. After all, Athenian politicians, for their own part, were often sharply critical of Athenian political habits.[31] But that does not obviate the possibility that critical arguments, made in public, had pernicious effects when they were taken up by those already alienated from the democratic regime.

Like a democratic Athenian politician, although for somewhat different reasons, Socrates came to live in two worlds – in the open world of the public square, where his intellectual acumen and critical attitudes were on public view,

[30] Socrates in public: Xenophon, *Memorabilia* 1.1.10: Plato, *Apology* 17c, 19d, 33a-b; Maximus of Tyre 3.7.

[31] Ober, *Mass and Elite*, pp. 318–324.

and in the private world of exclusive elite gatherings. Yet, again like an Athenian politician, Socrates insisted that he always remained authentically himself – that he was the same over time and that there was no distinction between his "public self" and his "private self."[32] In Socrates' case, there is no reason to doubt that this claim to be always the same was sincere. Moreover, Socrates' contentions that he was a good citizen and "consistently at one with himself" in public and private were evidently accepted by most Athenians, through most of his life.

Despite his association with Alcibiades, and despite Alcibiades' (and others' of Socrates' acquaintance) entanglement in the notorious "Affairs of the Mysteries and Herms" in 415 BCE, there is no evidence that Socrates was accused – as they were – of impiously mocking the sacred Eleusinian mysteries in a private house or of defacing the sacred statues of the god Hermes erected in private and public spaces around the city.[33] By contrast, the Athenian politician Andocides, who was also prosecuted in 399 BCE on a charge of impiety, spent much of his defense speech (*On the Mysteries*) addressing the question of why he could not legitimately be prosecuted for his part in the events of 415. Socrates was evidently not regarded, in 415 or in the years thereafter, as the sort of politically discontented malefactor likely to be associated with antidemocratic activity. In sum, although he was very well known, and although any number of Athenians, as victims of his public interrogations, may have had reason to dislike him, and although he hung around with some dubious characters, there is no evidence that most Athenians regarded Socrates as a dangerous malefactor in the decades before 403.

Socrates of Athens – famous as a sophist, scientist, public philosopher, and all-round contrarian; friendly with the notorious, and conversation-partner with the ordinary man on the street; an obedient dissident; a critic of democratic culture who takes up public office and is a stickler for the legal rules – may appear to modern readers to be a mass of contradictions. But Athenian democratic ideology and discourse thrived on such apparent contradictions: Political leaders were expected to present themselves as at once extraordinary and ordinary, as at once the spokesmen for what "everybody knows" and as the fonts of highly original policy advice. Famously wealthy litigants could offer themselves in court as incapable of dowering their daughters. Athenians delighted in individual freedom of speech and thought, yet they also honored consensus as public ideal. So, if Socrates is paradoxical, he nonetheless fit within an Athenian political culture based on a capacity among the citizenry to embrace contradictions.[34] So why, in the end, was he convicted in a political trial

[32] Pericles as "always himself": Thucydides 2.61.

[33] Socrates' associates and the Affair of the Mysteries: Martin Ostwald, *From Popular Sovereignty to the Sovereignty of Law: Law, Society, and Politics in Fifth-Century Athens* (Berkeley: University of California Press, 1986), pp. 537–550.

[34] On these contradictions, see Ober, *Mass and Elite*, chapter 7.

in 399? The answer is that, although Meletus saw the trial as destructive, and Socrates saw it as didactic, the people of Athens, represented by the 501 men on the jury, came to see it as decisive: as deciding a key question about the rights and duties of citizens.

Socrates was famous for carrying out remarkable conversations about justice and responsibility (inter alia) in public places and before admiring audiences. The Athenians, for their part, were deeply disposed by their political culture to associate speech with action.[35] They believed that citizens should accept responsibility and pay for the consequences of their speech, even if those consequences were not intended or predictable. The Athenians accepted *parrhesia*, frank speech, and *isonomia*, the equal right to public speech, as cornerstones of their democracy. Yet free speech did not, for them, mean freedom from the consequences attendant upon speech: Citizens could say pretty much whatever they wished, but by the same token they were held responsible for the public consequences of their speech.[36]

That conviction ordinarily concerned speech in the context of legislative institutions. For example, he who employed his powers of frank and equal speech by successfully passing a decree in the Athenian citizen Assembly or a law before a panel of lawmakers was held personally responsible for his legislative act. The individual sponsor of a statute that turned out badly could be held legally liable on the grounds that he had proposed something illegal (*paranomon*) or inexpedient (*epitedeion*).[37] The key decision made by the judges in the political trial of Socrates was to treat Socrates' public speeches, the arguments he made when conversing with others in the *agora*, as analogous to the speeches made by a politician before a legislative body. This is, I think, why Hypereides (above) claimed that Socrates had been punished "because of his speeches."

By 399 BCE, it was well known that some of the young men who hung around Socrates during the war years subsequently went on to commit crimes against other citizens, and against the public order itself. Whereas Socrates renounced the idea that he was a teacher or intended to harm others, there was prima facie reason to relate the criminal actions of Socrates' followers to things that Socrates said in public and, by implication, in private. Although after the Amnesty Socrates could not be prosecuted as a proxy for the crimes committed by those who listened to him, his unwillingness to accept that he was in any sense liable for the effects of his speech on others was deeply

[35] Thucydides 2.40.2–3 with Ober, *Political Dissent*, chapter 2.

[36] Elizabeth Markovits, *The Politics of Sincerity: Plato, Frank Speech, and Democratic Judgment* (University Park: Pennsylvania State University Press, 2008), chapter 2, surveys Athenian conceptions of accountability, with special reference to *parrhesia* in both public and private contexts.

[37] Athenian laws governing proceedings against those who had sponsored illegal decrees and inexpedient laws: MacDowell, *Law*, pp. 50–52.

troubling to Athenian sensibilities – indeed it appeared indicative of a lack of concern with justice and evidence for personal irresponsibility. In brief, Socrates, the man who always remained true to himself, had come to look like a dangerous sort of hypocrite.

Many Athenians, convinced by the necessity for the Amnesty, were probably willing to give Socrates what was, in effect, a pass for what they regarded (rightly or wrongly) as the negative effects of his prior speech: that is, for his role in the formation of Alcibiades, Critias, and other enemies of democracy who had been suppressed by 403. But then, after the restoration of the democracy, Socrates blithely returned to his familiar practices. He acted as if nothing had happened in the meantime, carrying on exactly the same sorts of conversations in the same public spaces as he always had. He brushed aside criticism, asserting that his speech simply could not have had negative consequences. And he thereby made himself vulnerable to the charge that he was perversely and dangerously unwilling to accept responsibility for either the past or (potential) future effects of his own behavior. In such circumstances, his claim to be a public benefactor was likely to be taken by many judges as evidence of bad faith.

CONCLUSION

Socrates' behavioral constancy, the fact that he was indeed "always the same" in circumstances that had become very different, made him vulnerable to Meletus' prosecution. Socrates believed that he was ethically required to put his unique personal excellence to the service of his state in the form of beneficial "stinging"; nothing in the new external circumstances of the city changed that. And so it was that his unswerving and peculiar interpretation of his own public duty ultimately brought him into a fatal conflict with Athenian law. Although Socrates' philosophical convictions and the underlying values of Athenian democracy remained compatible, the political circumstances of the postwar years tipped the balance against him.

In 399, Socrates' reputation as an obedient and participatory citizen was no longer sufficient to convince enough of his fellow citizens that his distinctive public behavior fell within the expansive parameters established by Athenian democratic culture: Because he would not accept any connection between his speech and others' actions, Socrates, who had devoted his life to acting justly, seemed unwilling to accept his own responsibilities in respect to justice. Socrates had proved, by obedience to the procedural rules, that he accepted the legitimacy of the state's power to call him to trial and also to constitute him, through the jury's verdict, a legally guilty man, liable to punishment. His performance at the trial, however, made it clear that he would indeed remain himself and that he would not change his view on his responsibility for the effects of his publicly expressed speech.

By the end of the day, the majority of the Athenian judges came to recognize the need for a decisive judgment on the essential question of whether freedom and equality of speech meant that an individual citizen could decide on his own authority what counted as accepting responsibility for public speech. Their answer was "no": The state, through the judgments given in its law courts, must retain the authority to define that boundary, to determine when the exercise of free and equal speech *was* political – and thereby incurred the cost to the speaker of accepting responsibility for its public consequences. And so in the end, with whatever mix of emotions, the majority of Socrates' judges voted to convict and then to choose Meletus' death sentence over Socrates' hybrid alternative.

Because Socrates was in fact true to his convictions, and because he was true to his didactic mission, Meletus achieved his political purposes in employing the trial to destroy a man he saw as an enemy of the state. But Socrates also achieved his didactic purposes in the trial and in the long literary tradition that followed. And finally, the citizens of Athens achieved their decisive purposes by defining an essential boundary between civic rights and citizens' responsibilities.

Ironically, when we view this most notorious of ancient Greek trials as a political trial – employing the expansive sense of "political" proposed in the framework chapter of this collection – the trial of Socrates proves to be a win-win-win event. It obviously could not be regarded as such from the perspective of a contemporary *liberal* democracy, dedicated to the protection of rights as inherent attributes of persons. Approaching the trial of Socrates as a political trial helps to distinguish between a polity that is robustly democratic and a polity that is robustly *liberal and democratic*. Contrary to what is often claimed, the Athenian court's decision in 399 BCE, while certainly incompatible with liberal values, was not a betrayal of democratic values. The decision of the court shows us why it is, analytically, a mistake to conflate democracy simpliciter with liberal democracy. Moreover, it clarifies, as it was meant to, a political conception of civic responsibility that is lost with that conflation.

3

The Trial and Crucifixion of Jesus

A Formal Model

Ron E. Hassner and Kenneth Sexauer

The events surrounding the trial and crucifixion of Christ are the very foundation stone of the Christian faith. Following his rise to prominence in the Galilee, Jesus and his apostles journey to Jerusalem during the holy week of Passover. His arrival causes a stir among the Jewish authorities in the city. Judas Iscariot, one of his twelve disciples, offers to deliver Jesus to the chief priests in exchange for thirty pieces of silver. After Jesus predicts this betrayal at the Last Supper, he and his disciples travel to a garden to pray. Judas identifies Jesus with a kiss and a group of soldiers, retained by the high priests, arrest him. Jesus is brought before the Sanhedrin, or high Jewish court, and is questioned. The members of the court interrogate him, asking him if he is indeed the Christ and Son of God, to which he responds only cryptically and indirectly. The court then condemns Jesus and, claiming that it has no right to execute, delivers him to the Romans under Pontius Pilate for a new trial. Judas, witnessing this, is overcome with remorse and commits suicide. According to one account, Pilate first relinquishes Jesus to stand trial before King Herod, who finds no cause for execution and returns him to Roman control. Pilate then questions Jesus in person. Again Jesus fails to offer any direct answers to the charges against him.

This chapter is an expanded and updated version of Ron E. Hassner, "The Trial and Crucifixion of Jesus: A Modest Proposal," *Theory and Decision*, Vol. 54 (2003), pp. 1–32. Hassner wrote the original article as a protest and parody of game theory. In its pretense to normative neutrality, game theory has never sought to delimit its own boundaries or take responsibility for the wide-ranging normative implications of its findings. The humorous and critical nature of the original article was lost on its publishers and readers. Despite this covert motivation, the chapter is based on careful research and the arguments that follow are, on the whole, reasonable even if they are completely beyond the scope of game theory to substantiate. In the version prepared for this volume, we have replaced many of the game theoretic terms with more accessible language. For example, we use "optimal" instead of "Pareto optimal" and "rational outcome" instead of "Nash equilibrium." Sadly, this sacrifices much of the humor of the original, which rested in large part on the pseudo-scientific jargon espoused by game theorists. We thank *Theory and Decision* for their permission to draw on the original article.

Despite finding no fault in Jesus' actions or testimony, Pilate reluctantly puts the decision before the public, who calls for Jesus to be crucified.

In the introduction, the editors of this volume raise some difficult questions regarding the way legal institutions come to embody political dynamics through the process of judicialization.[1] What exactly does it mean for a trial to be political? What motivates the politicization of the judicial process? How do legal-political actors navigate these trials? How do political trials shape the movement of history? In this chapter, we hope to address these questions by providing a concrete, well-known example of a political trial and introducing a novel, rigorous, widely applicable analytic framework for understanding it. By applying game theory analysis to the trial and crucifixion of Jesus, we will demonstrate the centrality of strategic rationality to the judicialization of political conflict between competing religious and political institutions.

The trial and crucifixion of Jesus have undergone repeated reinterpretation since the composition of the four Gospels in the first century AD. Nevertheless, gaps within the narratives as well as discrepancies among the four versions, or between the Gospels and other available sources, have left large questions unanswered: Why does Judas betray Jesus and why, once successful, does he then commit suicide? Why are the priests, Pilate, and Herod all reluctant to try Jesus? Why does a crucifixion take place even though Pilate, and at times even Jesus, seems eager to avoid it?

Because most interpretations of this account focus on the motivations of individuals rather than on institutional decision-making, they have accepted irrational motivations and stereotypical characterizations of the participants. Instead, the games used in this chapter present the events as the outcome of rational decisions by institutions. The actions of Judas Iscariot specifically, which receive little explanation in the Gospel texts, are elucidated as attempts by a radical opposition movement, the Zealots, to drive a potential Messiah toward political and military action against a foreign regime.

These events have not been modeled previously. Brams (2003) has modeled a variety of biblical scenarios but has restricted himself to the Hebrew Bible.[2] In the introduction to his analysis of strategic interactions in the Bible, Brams explains the utility of game theory for penetrating complex decision-making situations:

[1] Jens Meierhenrich and Devin O. Pendas, "'The Justice of My Cause Is Clear, But There's Politics to Fear': Political Trials in Theory and History," in this volume.

[2] Steven J. Brams, *Biblical Games: A Strategic Analysis of Stories in the Old Testament* (Cambridge: MIT Press, 2003). A listing of game theoretic analyses of literary texts can be found in Barry O'Neill, "The Strategy of Challenges: Two Beheading Games in Medieval Literature," in Reinhard Selten, ed., *Game Equilibrium Models IV* (Berlin: Springer, 1991), pp. 124–149. See also Barry O'Neill, "Deception and Trickery in the Book of Genesis" (Talk for the Jerusalem Conference on Biblical Economics, 2000); S. Todd Lowry and Barry Gordon, *Ancient and Medieval Economic Ideas and Concepts of Social Justice* (Leiden: Brill, 1998); Barry O'Neill, "A Problem of Rights Arbitration from the Talmud," *Mathematical Social Sciences*, Vol. 2 (1982), pp. 345–371; and Steven J. Brams, "Game Theory and Literature," *Games and Economic Behavior*, Vol. 6 (1994), pp. 32–54.

Because its application requires the careful unraveling of a tangle of character motivations and their effects, [game theory] imposes a discipline on the study of these situations that is usually lacking in more traditional literary-historical-theological analyses of the Bible. These analyses often suffer, in my opinion, from their unrestrained arbitrariness in finding linkages, seeing parallels, and generally trying to tie things together – somehow – with valiant leaps of the imagination. An assemblage of random insights, unconnected by any structured view of the world that might be called a framework or theory, does not provide a parsimonious or compelling intellectual organization of the Bible. Understanding requires organization, and organization is given by a theory.[3]

Brams (1991) and O'Neill (1991) have argued that game theory can provide a parsimonious framework for analyzing literature and stories, just as familiar texts can be useful in highlighting game theoretic issues. Game theory can explain the rationality of characters' choices by enhancing the links between motives and action that make up the plot, even if the characters are fictional and their actions extraordinary. The resulting analysis can offer a coherent strategic interpretation of the work examined or compare the relative plausibility of existing interpretations. No less significantly, by revealing what information was available to participants and how they chose to use it game theory can bring to light the profound tragedy underlying an interaction.

Several students of the trial and crucifixion have focused on rational decision-making in their analyses. Prominent thinkers from Goethe through Kautsky have conceived of Jesus in political terms.[4] Haley (1971) offers an analysis of the "power tactics" of Jesus Christ at key junctions in his career, whereas Schonfield (1967) casts Jesus as a goal-driven calculator who aims at the fulfillment of Messianic prophecies and engineers events to suit his purposes.[5] "When we have grasped what considerations governed the activities of Jesus and compelled him to scheme to bring about a particular sequence of events," writes Schonfield, "it becomes easier to assess the relative worth of traditions. Of set purpose he embarked on a program calculated to fulfil what he believed the prophecies demanded of the Messiah. He was obsessed with this necessity. Its requirements shaped his every move and engaged his constant vigilance."[6] We depart from this individualist viewpoint by focusing not on the personal interests of Jesus but rather on the interests of the emerging Christian movement. In this respect, my approach is in agreement with Paul Winter's analysis of the trial of Jesus: "It is not individual enmities which come to light here, but antagonism of group against group."[7]

[3] Brams, *Biblical Games*, p. 7.

[4] Raymond E. Brown, *The Death of the Messiah: From Gethsemane to the Grave*, 2 vols. (New York: Doubleday, 1994), p. 679.

[5] Jay Haley, *The Power Tactics of Jesus Christ, and Other Essays* (New York: Avon, 1971); Hugh J. Schonfield, The Passover Plot: New Light on the History of Jesus (New York: Random House, 1965).

[6] Schonfield, *The Passover Plot*, p. 131; along similar lines, see Alan Watson, *The Trial of Jesus* (Athens: University of Georgia Press, 1995), p. 159.

[7] Paul Winter, *On the Trial of Jesus* (Berlin: De Gruyter, 1961), p. 113.

An institutional analysis is a promising approach for shedding light on the last days of Jesus Christ, for both empirical and normative reasons. First, as we show below, attempts to explain disparities in the Gospel account from an individualist perspective have generated inconsistencies and left gaps. Second, the available sources strongly indicate that Jesus, the High Priest, and Pilate were representatives and leaders of larger groups and that these groups shared certain common goals and preferences. Below we diverge from the strict text of the Gospels and, relying on historical evidence, depict Judas too as representing the interests of a group, namely the Zealot movement. Third, an analysis of these four individuals as representatives or leaders of groups can go beyond the psychological and personal motivations stated explicitly in the text and bring to light broader motivations. These hidden motivations could clarify ambiguities in the Gospel text as well as shed light on the political reality of a historical era. Generalizable motivations can be applied in a broad range of comparable situations, a clear advantage over reductivist analyses.

Conclusions from this study can be applied to an array of situations in which radical parties are trying to disrupt an understanding between a ruling government and a moderate opposition group, especially if party preferences resemble the structure of a "stag hunt." In a situation of this sort, each of the two players prefers mutual cooperation to mutual confrontation, but each also prefers such confrontation to acting cooperatively while the other player is confrontational. If the two players, the ruling government and the moderate opposition group, start the game at the optimal situation of mutual cooperation, then no party has an incentive to launch a confrontation on its own.[8]

A shift to the alternative outcome, the undesirable outcome of mutual aggression, can occur only if both actors confront simultaneously. Inducing this simultaneous move is the goal of radical elements within the government and radical elements within the opposition. These two players resent the status quo but must rely on each other to induce change, even though they do not have full information about one another's preferences. The game below shows that in order to succeed, these radical elements must overcome strong incentives for defection from their pact. They do so by sending encouraging signals about their identities and preferences, and thus their intentions, to one another. If each believes in its ability to subsume the other under its leadership once the ruling regime has been overthrown, then they will succeed in cooperating and demolishing the modus vivendi. It follows that governments can fortify a concord with the opposition by making public the degree to which the goals of various radical movements are incommensurable.

This chapter proceeds as follows: We begin with a background to the trial and crucifixion and highlight the puzzles that readers have faced so far.

[8] We use the term "optimal" as a shorthand for "Pareto optimal," a situation in which resources are distributed so that the benefit to one party could not be improved without decreasing the benefit to the other party.

We proceed to discuss the available sources and how the preferences of the four groups can be inferred from these sources. We then set up a game in four stages, based on the preferences and moves available to the four groups, and comment on the complexities of these games. Finally, we offer answers to several of the puzzles we face when reading the accounts of the Gospels, as well as some general implications regarding regime stability in the face of radical opposition.

THE TRIAL AND CRUCIFIXION OF CHRIST: UNANSWERED QUESTIONS

Christian theologians have argued that Judas Iscariot is the only sinner languishing in hell without any hope of redemption at the time of the Second Coming.[9] He is damned for all eternity for having betrayed the Son of Man, Jesus Christ, to his executors. God may forgive any man of his sins, except for Judas. In Dante's Inferno he languishes in the lowest circle of hell, trapped in the mouth of Satan – fitting company to this arch-traitor. His role in the death of Christ on the cross, as retold in Christian tradition throughout the ages, has had an immeasurable impact on the image of Jews in European communities throughout the Middle Ages. His evident hatred of Jesus, his greed for money, his betrayal and consequent suicide brand him as the ultimate figure of evil in the New Testament. No one, aside from the Apostle Peter and Jesus himself, has as much space dedicated to him in the Gospels. Yet we know little about his motivations and have difficulty explaining the sequence of events as they took place after the Last Supper and leading up to the crucifixion.

The motivations of other actors – Pharisees, Pilate, even Jesus himself – remain veiled in the Gospel sections treating the betrayal and trial of Jesus.[10] Gaps within the narratives as well as discrepancies among the four versions of the story, or between the Gospels and other available sources, leave the following questions unanswered:

1. Why did Judas betray Jesus? The Gospels offer two unsatisfactory explanations: The first, that "the devil entered into him," is at best descriptive and at worst tautological. The second motive, greed, is equally unsatisfactory since the sum is merely symbolic. Thirty pieces of silver fulfills a prophetic requirement but does not amount to a considerable sum of money. The sum involved would have sufficed for ransoming a slave, by one account, or constituted one-tenth of the value of a jar of ointment, by another account. In either case this amounts to a modest sum.[11]

[9] One notable exception is the fourteenth-century Dominican preacher Vinzenz Ferrer. See William Klassen, *Judas: Betrayer or Friend of Jesus?* (Minneapolis: Fortress Press, 1996), pp. 4–8.

[10] The relevant sections are Mark 14–15; Matthew 26–27; Luke 22–23; John 13:2; John 18; Acts 1. All biblical citations from *The Holy Bible*, King James Version.

[11] The prophecy in Zechariah 11:12 is puzzling and probably taken out of context by the Gospel authors. See Brown, *The Death of the Messiah*, pp. 1401–1404.

2. Judas and the religious establishment make for a most unlikely team. Why did the priests need Judas' help? The Gospels offer two explanations: Jesus was difficult to locate and had to be arrested in secret, so as not to arouse a public reaction. Both explanations are contradicted later in the text: Jesus expresses surprise at his clandestine arrest in light of the familiarity of his whereabouts.[12] The crowds, in turn, seem supportive of the arrest and execution of Jesus.
3. Why does money change hands between the priests and Judas? Why is a public burial ground bought with this sum (in one version by Judas himself) after Judas tries to return it to the priests?
4. If Judas betrays Jesus out of greed or pure evil, why does he commit suicide? If he committed suicide out of remorse, why does he do so just when the priests pass Jesus to the Romans, and not earlier or after the crucifixion?
5. What is the reasoning behind the strange dialogue between Jesus and the priests? Why does Jesus refuse to assert his Messianic authority by means of a miracle?
6. Why do the priests declare him a blasphemer, in spite of their failure to bring false evidence to bear against him, yet never condemn him?
7. Why do the priests hand Jesus over to the Romans? The Gospel's suggestion that the priests had no right to execute the death sentence contradicts other passages in the Gospels, as well as ample historical evidence.[13] In fact, the Jewish courts had the authority to execute criminals in four different ways: stoning, burning, slaying (stabbing), and strangling.[14]
8. What is the reasoning behind the strange dialogue between Jesus and Pilate? Why is Jesus reluctant to announce his mission? Why is Pilate in great pains to avoid executing Jesus?
9. Most importantly, why is crucifixion the outcome of this interaction? It seems that Pilate, and even Jesus at times, wishes to avoid this outcome. Judas commits suicide, apparently in remorse. How is it that only the priests accomplish their goal?

The game below offers a possible answer to these questions.

INFERRING PREFERENCES

Mentions of Jesus and his trial in first-century texts are extremely rare. Aside from the Gospels and the Acts of the Apostles, we have a single sentence in

[12] Matthew 26:55; Mark 14:48; Luke 22:52.

[13] Günther Bornkamm, *Jesus of Nazareth* (New York: Harper and Row, 1960), pp. 163–164; Winter, *On the Trial of Jesus*, p. 10; Tom A. Burkill, The Competence of the Sanhedrin, *Vigilae Christianae*, Vol. 10 (1956), pp. 80–96; Tom A. Burkill, "The Trial of Jesus," *Vigilae Christianae*, Vol. 12 (1958), pp. 1–18; Brown, *The Death of the Messiah*, pp. 368–371.

[14] Winter, *On the Trial of Jesus*, p. 70, pp. 100–112; with reference to Mishnah, Sanhedrin vii:1.

Tacitus' "Annals of Imperial Rome"; two minor references to Jesus in "Antiquities of the Jews" by the Jewish-Roman historian Josephus Flavius; and a mention of Pilate in the "Legatio ad Gaium" by the Jewish-Egyptian philosopher and historian Philo of Alexandria.[15] Additional background information can be found in Josephus' "The Jewish War," whereas the Mishnah supplies information on the Sanhedrin, the court of seventy-one that tried Jesus.

The Gospels are subjective versions of the events and are therefore problematic as factual resources. They were probably written within fifty years of the crucifixion, most likely in the order Mark (AD 65–70), Matthew (AD 70–80), Luke (AD 75–85), and John (AD 100). They display significant discrepancies on the very issues pertinent to this chapter: Judas' motivation for the betrayal, Jesus' response to the arrest and interrogations, the position of the priesthood and Pilate toward Jesus, and Judas' response to the events following the betrayal. Overall, the information at hand makes it difficult to draw hard conclusions as to the preferences, motives, and available moves of the parties involved in the trial and crucifixion. The Gospels do not offer precise historical detail, but a religious message.[16] Michael Grant advises:

> The extraction from the Gospels of evidence about the life and career of Jesus is a singularly difficult, delicate process. Students of the New Testament, it has been suggested, would be well advised to study other, pagan fields of ancient history first – because they are easier.[17]

In order to minimize circular reasoning and counteract the inherent bias of the texts, we infer preferences from a variety of sources, rather than accepting the motivations and goals as stated explicitly in accounts of the trial and crucifixion. The Gospels portray the events as driven by four individuals: Jesus, Pilate, Judas, and the High Priest. Instead, adopting an organizational approach, we model the events as an interaction between four interest groups or institutions: the young Christian movement led by Jesus (J), the Roman government in Judea (R), the radical Jewish political movement, also known as Zealots (Z), and the religious establishment represented by the priests (P). Given the institutional motivations of these groups and their previous interactions, we can infer preferences and interests.

[15] Tacitus, *Annals of Imperial Rome*, Book XIV; Josephus, *Antiquities of the Jews*, Book XVII, Chapter III, Sc 3 and Book XX, Chapter IX, Sc 1; Philo of Alexandria, *Embassy to Gaius*, segments 212, 301, and 307. Suetonius, Pliny the Younger, and Lucian mention Christ, but all wrote 50–100 years after the events and contribute no additional knowledge about his life or deeds. (Elmer. W. K. Mould, *Essentials of Bible History* (New York: Ronald Press Company, 1951), p. 486; James McLaren, *Power and Politics in Palestine* (Worcester: Sheffield Academic Press, 1991), pp. 34–38, 41, 45.)

[16] Winter, *On the Trial of Jesus*, p. 2. McLaren, *Power and Politics in Palestine*, pp. 90, 97.

[17] Michael Grant, *Jesus: An Historian's View of the Gospels* (New York: Charles Scribner's Sons, 1977), p. 197.

The Young Christian Movement: J

We must assume that the growing religious movement surrounding Jesus desired, as does any ideological organization, to prosper in size and authority.[18] Given the success and reputation of Jesus and his miracles, the movement seemed on a safe path to success. There was no need to fear a Roman response as long as it manifested no political goals – the Romans were as respectful of this religious movement as they were of its many competitors. In a period of foreign occupations, prophets and miracle workers such as Jesus were common. They were confronted by the authorities only if they caused civil unrest. Any attempt by Jesus to launch a political campaign to overthrow the Roman government would have been dealt with summarily.[19] Given the choice between confronting the Romans and maintaining the status quo, the movement would clearly opt for the latter. The ideal of coexistence between the two institutions is most prominently suggested in Jesus' demand to "render therefore unto Caesar the things that are Caesar's; and unto God the things that are God's"[20] and in the doctrine of the two swords.

If, however, Rome should attempt to eradicate the movement, Jesus and his followers would prefer to fight for the cause rather than allow the organization to be stamped out. This is implied in "Think not that I am come to send peace on earth; I came not to send peace, but a sword,"[21] as well as those segments suggesting the eventual victory of the kingdom of God over the kingdom of man. At times, the texts suggest that the leader of this movement, Jesus himself, wishes to avoid the painful implications of succumbing to Rome. Crucifixion was the slowest and most painful death available in the Roman legal code. In the minutes before his betrayal, his "complete humanity" comes to the fore as he pleads to "remove this cup" from him.[22] His pain and bewilderment during the crucifixion are expressed in his final words in the original Hebrew: "Eli, Eli, lama sabachtani." (My God, why hast thou forsaken me?)[23] In sum, the Christian movement prefers peaceful coexistence with Rome to mutual confrontation, but would struggle to survive rather than succumb, should Rome opt for conflict.

The Roman Government: R

The administration of Judea was in the hands of a procurator. He was chiefly a fiscal agent of Rome, as his title suggests, and his main goal was increased revenue.[24] In its rule over Judea, Rome exhibited extraordinary tolerance. Roman rulers respected and even protected the rights of Jews to practice their

[18] For a list of texts discussing the revolutionary politics of Jesus and his disciples, see Brown, *The Death of the Messiah*, pp. 679–693.

[19] Winter, *On the Trial of Jesus*, p. 140. [20] Matt 22:21; Mark 12:17. [21] Matt 10:34.

[22] Matt 26:39; Mark 14:36; Luke 22:42. See description in Bornkamm, *Jesus of Nazareth*, p. 162.

[23] Matt 27:46; Mark 15:34. [24] Mould, *Essentials of Bible History*, p. 466.

religion, as well as their rights to legislate, try, and enforce all religious and most civil matters. Roman procurators had supreme military and judicial authority within their provinces, but this was exercised in Judea only in extraordinary cases.[25]

The procurator, Pontius Pilate, had learned from his own experience to respect the religious rights of the Jews in Judea. An attempted transgression of the status quo by Pilate, so we are told by Philo, had led to a confrontation with the Jewish masses and an eventual withdrawal of the offending order.[26] Yet Pilate was also known to act ruthlessly against potential revolutionary leaders.[27] Given the nature of Christ's activities, he had as little reason to fear the Christian movement as he had any other of the many splinter groups that were appearing throughout Judea in these troubled times. This stance would have to be reversed if political claims or violent activities could be attributed to Jesus and his followers.

To summarize, the preferences of the Roman government of Judea are reminiscent of the preferences of the Christian movement. Player R prefers mutual cooperation with player J over all other outcomes, but should player J initiate conflict, player R will be forced to respond in kind.

The Religious Establishment: P

The Pharisees and Sadducees, which held the priestly positions, strictly observed the Jewish legal code. They opposed those religious movements that embraced Hellenism or Roman paganism, but they were equally opposed to any spirit of religious enthusiasm. Their highest priority was to maintain their position on the basis of a strict reading of Mosaic law.[28] Before the Roman occupation, they often clashed with reigning Jewish monarchs over interference in matters related to the Temple and the sacrifice. When these monarchs usurped the title of High Priest, direct clashes ensued – the Pharisees insisted on a stark separation of religion and state. They were strongly opposed to the Jewish nationalist movement, which sought to reunite these two realms under the leadership of a Messiah.

They did not, on the other hand, oppose Roman rule, since the Romans were respectful of Temple rites and deferred judgment in most civil and religious matters to the religious courts. By virtue of Roman support, they received and were able to maintain both wealth and civil authority.[29] The Sanhedrin, the Jewish legislature and judiciary, was granted legislative and executive rights

[25] Emil Schuerer, *A History of the Jewish People in the Time of Jesus* (New York: Schocken, 1961), p. 186.

[26] Schuerer, *A History of the Jewish People in the Time of Jesus*, p. 198–199.

[27] Louis Feldman and Gohei Hata, eds., *Josephus, Judaism and Christianity* (Detroit: Wayne State University Press, 1987), p. 48.

[28] Schuerer, *A History of the Jewish People in the Time of Jesus*, p. 75.

[29] Mould, *Essentials of Bible History*, p. 471.

beyond those common in most nonautonomous communities of the Roman Empire. It could pass and execute laws even over Roman citizens within its jurisdiction. Only death sentences for civil crimes required confirmation by the Roman procurator. The Romans went beyond tolerating Jewish worship: They protected the Temple and imposed the death sentence on those who entered its hallowed grounds, even when they were Roman citizens. No worship of the emperor was demanded of the priests who, in return, willingly sacrificed in his honor twice a day. Distinguished Romans were permitted to offer gifts to the Temple and even sacrifice there.[30]

The accelerating success of Jesus and his following challenged the authority of this group. The religious establishment was similarly threatened by the radical Jewish movements. These were continuously searching for a military and political Messiah to topple the foreign Roman rule and the corrupt priestly rule.[31] Yet given the limitations on the executive powers of the religious establishment and the modest political claims of Jesus and his followers, any attempt by the religious establishment to end the young Christian movement by itself entailed risks: A religious trial might establish the true Messianic identity of Jesus and lead to the downfall of the priesthood. The religious authorities could not, on the other hand, accept the status quo, given the charismatic power exhibited by Jesus, at first in the Galilee and now on their very doorstep, in Jerusalem. Jesus' entry into the city and his exclamations on the manner in which the Temple was run signaled that the priests needed to act decisively.[32] In order to avoid a religious trial, the priests had to find a way to bring Jesus before Pilate as a political criminal. The challenge facing the Sanhedrin was to find a way to arrest Jesus as a political activist contemplating an armed uprising, rather than accuse him of blasphemy and have to try him themselves.[33] Seen in this light, the *manner* of arrest, involving some form of armed confrontation, was more important than the circumstances of arrest. Judas was needed to initiate the proceedings against Jesus by orchestrating an armed confrontation against Jesus and the disciples.

In summary, the religious establishment wanted to eliminate the Christian movement by trying its leader in their courts and executing him for blasphemy. Yet they feared the possibility of Jesus revealing a true Messianic identity, since this would mean the end of traditional priesthood, their worst possible outcome. The higher the priests' confidence in Christ's Messianic identity, the more likely they were to forgo their first preference of trying him themselves and opt instead for a trial by the Roman authorities. This was less preferable than trying Jesus themselves, since they could not be certain of success, but still preferable to the prevailing status quo.

[30] Schuerer, *A History of the Jewish People in the Time of Jesus*, pp. 193–195.

[31] Bornkamm, *Jesus of Nazareth*, p. 159. [32] McLaren, *Power and Politics in Palestine*, p. 98.

[33] Schonfield, *The Passover Plot*, p. 122.

The Radical Jewish Political Movement: Z

The identity and motivations of Judas have intrigued researchers, starting with the early Church Fathers. Judas' surname, "Iscariot," and his introduction as "son of Simon" (possible Simon the Zealot, another disciple) have led to several curious theories about his background and the incentives for his actions.[34] Given the scarcity of information in the Gospels, the most convincing among these theories places Judas among the Sicarii, a violent faction within the radical Jewish political movement, the Zealots, who specialized in political assassination by means of short daggers (*sicae*).[35] Some evidence suggests that the Sicarii adopted a completely different interpretation of Judaism and became a "deviant sect," clashing with the religious establishment on both religious and political matters.[36] Several members of the emerging Christian movement may well have been Zealots: We learn in the scene of Jesus' arrest that some of the disciples were armed and were wont to use their weapons whereas one disciple, Simon Zelotes, is explicitly identified as a Zealot.[37]

Josephus describes this movement in detail as a group that showed unwillingness to await Messianic redemption but preferred to hasten its realization by means of conflict with the enemy. They resented Roman taxation and their resentment increased with the efficiency of Roman rule.[38] Their secondary opponents were the priests who collaborated with the Roman governor and assisted in the collection of taxes. The Zealots pinned their hopes on a Messiah who would play a political, even military, role leading to independence.[39] Jewish texts consistently demand that the Messiah be not merely a miracle worker but a political and military leader. The prevalent view of a Messiah at the time was a figure who would lead a political movement for independence.[40] The Slavonic version of Josephus describes the following reaction of the Jews to Jesus' miracle working:

> When they saw his ability to do whatever he wished by a word, they told him that they wanted him to enter the City, destroy the Roman troops, and make himself king; but he took no notice.[41]

Throughout Roman rule over Judea, such leaders gathered a following and arose in rebellion against Rome, most prominently Judas of Galilee, Eleasar Ben

[34] The most comprehensive sources on the identity and motivation of Judas are Klassen, *Judas*, and Appendix V in Brown, *The Death of the Messiah*. The latter includes an extensive bibliography on the subject.

[35] Schuerer, *A History of the Jewish People in the Time of Jesus*, pp. 229–230; Klassen, *Judas*, p. 32.

[36] Feldman and Hata, *Josephus, Judaism and Christianity*, p. 28.

[37] Matthew 10:4; Mark 3:18; Luke 6:15; Acts 1:13.

[38] Mould, *Essentials of Bible History*, p. 471. [39] Mould, *Essentials of Bible History*, p. 48.

[40] Feldman and Hata, *Josephus, Judaism and Christianity*, p. 48; Watson, *The Trial of Jesus*, p. 35.

[41] These passages in the Slavonic text of Josephus are absent from the Greek originals. Watson, *The Trial of Jesus*, p. 129, quoting from Josephus, *The Jewish War*, translated by Geoffrey A. Williamson (Oxford: Harmondsworth, 1959), p. 404.

Yair (of Masada fame), and Bar Kokhba. In Jesus' stead the crowds demanded that Pilate release Barabbas, described as one of "them who had made insurrection ... who had committed murder in the insurrection."[42] Barabbas may have been a rebel leader who had proved more successful than Jesus in physically confronting the Romans.

The notion of a Christian Messiah, one whose kingdom is "not of this earth," who refuses to engage in physical violence and willingly submits to torture and crucifixion, was alien to Jesus' Jewish followers. The medieval scholar Maimonides, the greatest Jewish authority on Messianism, stated the Jewish position on the role of the Messiah:

> The sole difference between the present and the Messianic days is the delivery from servitude to foreign powers ... If there arise a king from the House of David who ... prevails upon Israel to walk in the way of the Torah and to repair its breaches, and fights the battles of the Lord, it may be assumed that he is the Messiah ... But if he does not meet with full success, or is slain, it is obvious the he is not the Messiah promised in the Torah.[43]

If Judas was in fact a member of the Zealot movement, as his surname and lineage might suggest, his act of leading Jesus to the religious establishment may not have been a betrayal or an act of collaboration with the priests but a political move designed to bring the priests under the authority of Jesus. A closer analysis of the terminology used in the Greek version of the text, specifically the Greek verb *paradidomei*, suggests that Judas did not "betray" Jesus but merely "handed him over" for a trial, a trial designed to test and establish his Messianic identity.[44]

If Judas believed in the divine mission of Christ, as he must have after observing his acts for so many years, he also believed that this leadership would manifest itself not by means of a death on the cross but by means of a military uprising.[45] However, if Jesus could prove his divine mission to the high priest, all of Israel would unite behind him against the foreign conqueror. Judas was thus acting in response to Jesus' reluctance to assume a political role. To lead such an uprising Jesus would have to convince the religious establishment of his calling without falling into Roman hands. This demanded a deal between Judas and the priests – an agreement to conduct a religious trial and avoid a political trial. As we will show, given the incentives of the parties involved and the sequential nature of this game, this agreement was broken by the priests.

In sum, the Zealots wished to confront Rome under the leadership of a true Messiah. Confronting Rome under a false Messiah would be a disaster and would mean the end of the Zealot movement. A religious trial could determine whether Jesus possessed charismatic powers or was a mere impostor, a false Messiah and blasphemer. Depending on the ruling of the religious authorities,

[42] Mark 15:6; Luke 23:19.

[43] Moses Maimonides, *Mishneh Torah*, Book 14, uncensored version of Chapter 11. A direct reference to the false Messianism of Jesus and Muhammad follows.

[44] Klassen, *Judas*, throughout and Brown, *The Death of the Messiah*, pp. 211–213; 1399–1404.

[45] Grant, *Jesus*, p. 156; Watson, *The Trial of Jesus*, p. 14.

the Zealots would then follow Jesus into battle or seek a new leader, both outcomes preferable to the status quo.

THE GAME

Stage 1: Jesus versus Pilate

Given these preferences, we can model the events described in the scriptures as a game with four stages. The first stage is a coordination game between the Roman government (R) and the emerging Christian movement (J). It is a stag hunt, a game with two pure strategy equilibria of which one is Pareto optimal and the other Pareto suboptimal. The players move simultaneously, with each player choosing either to cooperate or to defect. Each party stands to gain from cooperating, but the costs of cooperating alone while the other defects are significant. As a result, players prefer to defect from cooperation if they believe that their opponents are likely to do the same.

In the case of this Roman–Christian relationship, this game structure entails the following logic: Although peaceful coexistence is the most desirable outcome for both Romans and Christians, each party stands to lose from pursuing a peaceful path while the other chooses conflict. Given the uncertainties and mistrust between the two movements, they might both choose conflict, even though mutual conflict is the less desirable equilibrium.

In this first stage both players make a simultaneous move: each chooses one of two moves. The Christian movement (player J) chooses between loyalty and revolt. The Roman government (player R) chooses between toleration and suppression (Figure 3.1). Payoffs are ranked $0<a<b<1$. The game has four

$0<a<b<1$

		R: C	R: D
J	C	(1,1)	(0,b)
	D	(b,0)	(a,a)

(The first payoff in each pair is Jesus'; the second is Rome's)

FIGURE 3.1 Jesus versus Pilate

possible outcomes with the following payoffs for the players (the first reward in each set represents the Roman reward; the second is the reward for the Christian movement):

CC: Mutual cooperation. This is the optimal outcome in this interaction with rewards (1, 1). The Christian movement could continue to gather a loyal following and gain acceptance within the Jewish community.
DC: A successful Christian revolt against Rome, matched by Roman passivity, with rewards (b, 0). This would be the worst possible outcome from a Roman point of view.
CD: A successful unilateral Roman move to eradicate the Christian movement, matched by Christian passivity, with rewards (0, b). This would be the worst possible outcome for the young Christian movement.
DD: Mutual confrontation – the Christian movement forcibly resists a Roman attempt at eradication, with rewards (a, a). While this scenario would be preferable to voluntary submission by R or J, it would most likely end in the death of the Christian leader. This is an undesirable outcome for all players. In the language of game theory, Crucifixion is a Pareto suboptimal outcome.

Both players clearly prefer the status quo (CC) over one-sided confrontation (CD or DC). Both also prefer mutual confrontation (DD) to one-sided submission (DC or CD). The rational outcomes of this interaction are either the status quo or mutual confrontation (i.e., crucifixion).[46] It is only in the interest of one party to change its behavior if it does so simultaneously with the other party.

This is precisely what the Zealots (Z) and the religious establishment (P) will attempt to achieve. Player P cannot move R to DD without Z moving J to DD at the same time. However, should Jesus and Pilate find themselves facing each other in a public trial, the modus vivendi between them will fall apart.

Stage 2: The Arrest

The second stage details the attempts by the extreme organizations within R and J to replace the status quo between R and J by mutual confrontation. The radical Jewish movement seeks to do so in order to overthrow the Roman regime; the religious establishment wishes to do so in order to eradicate the Christian movement. Key in this game is Judas' desire to confront Jesus with the religious establishment yet the priests' desire to avoid confronting a true Messiah in a religious trial. The resulting game is a signaling game of incomplete information, meaning that the beliefs and goals of one player are

[46] "Rational outcome" is my shorthand for "Nash equilibrium," meaning a solution to a game in which neither player would benefit from changing their strategy unilaterally, given what they know about the other player's strategy.

not known to the other player. The first player makes a move and the second player makes deductions about the first player's preferences (and consequently his identity) based on that move.

In this game, the priests (P) seek to determine the identity of Judas (Z) based on the manner of Judas' betrayal. The priests wish to learn about the identity and preferences of Judas in order to answer the question that troubles them most: Is Jesus the true Messiah? The priests would try Jesus only if they believed that he is not the Messiah, since a true Messiah might reveal his identity indisputably in court (by means of a miracle, for example) and thus signal an end to the religious authority of the priesthood. Thus, the priests pay attention to the manner of Judas' betrayal because they want to avoid trying a true Messiah. They interpret Judas' actions as follows: If Judas betrays Jesus for money, then Judas must be acting out of greed and is therefore a disloyal disciple to a false Messiah; if, however, Judas betrays Jesus without demanding money, then Judas is out to test his master, a true Messiah. Thus, Judas "signals" his own knowledge and goals by choosing between three courses of action: remaining loyal to Jesus, betraying him for money, or betraying him for no money (Figure 3.2).

Nature determines whether Jesus is the Messiah (M) or not (–M). That is to say, the players cannot know for certain what Jesus' true identity is at the outset of the interaction. Before Z makes the first move, P suspects that Jesus might be the Messiah (with some probability, p) or not (with probability, 1 – p).

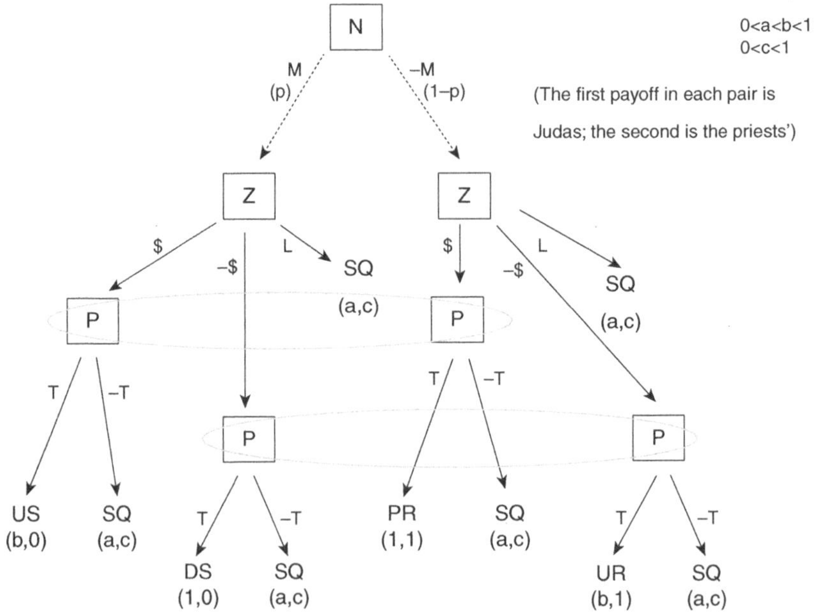

FIGURE 3.2 The Arrest

Judas (Z) makes one of three moves, based on his belief in the identity of Jesus and thus his motivation for loyalty or betrayal.

L: Z remains loyal to Jesus, does nothing, and the status quo (SQ) prevails.
–$: Z hands Jesus over to the priests but does not accept or demand money.
$: Z betrays Jesus for a symbolic sum of money.

If Z has chosen to act, P observes this move and responds in one of two ways:

–T: P chooses not to try Jesus, with outcome SQ.
T: P does try Jesus. This will lead to four possible outcomes (US, DS, PR, UR) depending on whether Judas accepted money and on whether or not Jesus is the Messiah.

The payoffs are ranked $0 < a < b < 1$ for player Z and $0 < c < d < 1$ for player P. The outcomes have the following payoffs (the first payoff in each set is the payoff for Z; the second payoff is the payoff for P):

SQ (a,c) – the Christian movement continues to prosper and no confrontation with Rome ensues, to the disappointment of both Z and P.
US: Undignified success for the Zealot movement (b,0) – Jesus is betrayed, tried, and, since he is the Messiah, officially recognized. This would mean an end to the current priesthood but success as far as the Zealots are concerned.
DS: Dignified success for the Zealot movement (1,0) – similar to undignified success but without Judas being tainted as traitor since no money has changed hands.
PR: Profitable Zealot reorientation (1,1) – Jesus is betrayed, tried, and, since he is not the Messiah, executed for blasphemy. The Zealots must search for a new leader but have avoided the danger of being led into battle by a non-Messiah.
UR: Unprofitable Zealot reorientation (b,1) – similar to profitable reorientation but Judas does not gain thirty pieces of silver.

There are several equilibria in the game. In other words, there are several rational combinations of strategies that the players could pursue, irrespective of the information they uncover during the game. The most robust of these equilibria is also the equilibrium which corresponds best with our evidence about players' beliefs and motives. It results from the following strategy combination: Judas demands money for handing over Jesus, no matter what he knows about his identity, and the priests respond with a trial if money was demanded and status quo if no money was demanded. Judas' move blurs the difference between a greedy and a loyal disciple by making it impossible to infer whether he is one or the other. A greedy disciple would demand money out of greed, whereas a loyal disciple would demand money to avoid sending a clear signal. This is known as a pooling equilibrium, because Judas' true knowledge is not revealed by his move. The thirty pieces of silver thus fulfill a double role:

They reduce the priestly belief in the Messianic identity of Jesus sufficiently to initiate a trial and they are tantamount to a pact between the two movements, the Zealots and the priests, to test the leadership potential of Jesus. This stage of the game ends with a trial, to the apparent satisfaction of Judas and to the potential consternation of the priests, who are about to discover the true identity of Jesus.

Our analysis diverges from the prevalent interpretation of the Gospel story on three points. First, we reject the notion of the priesthood as inherently corrupt.[47] The priesthood would not, and – as is evident from the pedantic proceedings of the subsequent trial – could not, execute Jesus if he proved his Messianic mission, just as they would not recognize him as the Messiah if he failed to do so. Trying Jesus thus entails some risk for the priests. The higher their initial beliefs in Jesus' Messianic identity, i.e. the higher p, the more likely they are to opt for the status quo.

Second, we do not assume that Judas is inherently evil or greedy. Instead, we posit two possibilities, as determined by "nature" at the outset of the game. We assume that Judas knows whether Jesus is or is not the Messiah, having followed him in recent years as a disciple and observed his activities, and values loyalty accordingly. A conscious follower of the true Messiah would be foolish to betray him for a small sum of money. A greedy follower of a false Messiah would be foolish to forgo payment for betrayal. By demanding money for initiating the game, Judas can signal or blur his own goals and the identity of Jesus. As opposed to a voluntary handing over of Jesus for a trial that would determine his Messianic qualification, the demand for money labels the act a betrayal, the perpetrator a traitor, and Jesus, evidently, a false Messiah.

Most importantly, as stated in the introduction to this chapter, we diverge from a literal reading of the Gospel text by conceiving of Judas as acting out of institutional interests, beyond immediate personal interests. Greed and loyalty aside, the main purpose of his actions was to assure the Zealots of a strong leader in their impending confrontation with the Romans. Judas' reward thus reflects indifference as to the outcome of the trial, be it a validation of Jesus' Messianic identity which establishes his leadership of the Zealots or refutation of his identity which would lead the Zealots to seek a new leader. Personal issues, such as profit or stigma attached to betrayal, merely skew these preferences one way or another.

Stage 3: The Trial

This interaction, between Jesus and the priests, hinges on the theological disagreement between Jesus on the one hand and Judas and the priests on the other hand as to the characteristics of Messianic leadership (Figure 3.3). As we saw

[47] See discussion in Brown, *The Death of the Messiah*, pp. 391–397. Winter, *On the Trial of Jesus*, p. 146, agrees and notes the Sanhedrin's responsibility for maintaining the public peace.

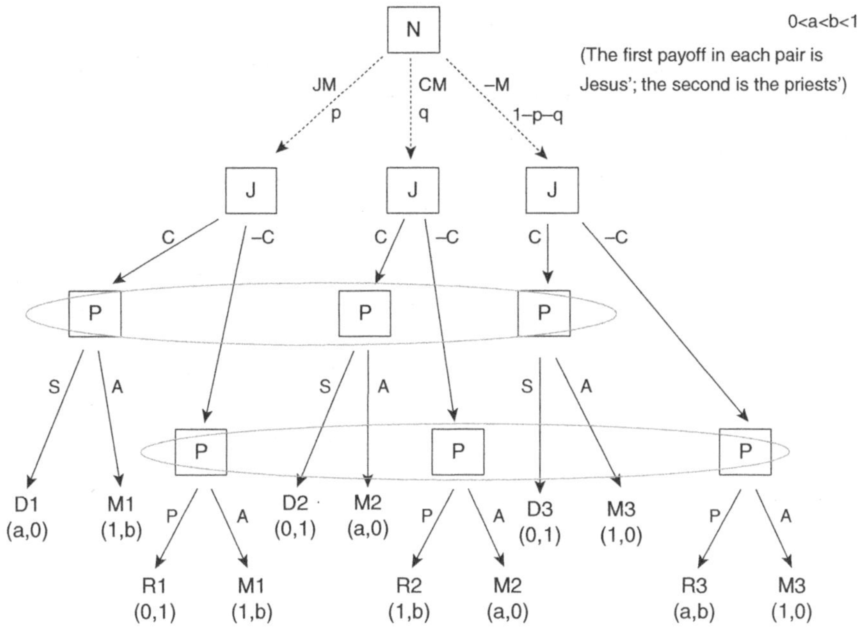

FIGURE 3.3 The Trial – Full Version

in the Gospels, Josephus, and Maimonides, above, traditional Jewish interpretation of the Messiah figure as held by the priests and the Zealots differed from the Christian interpretation by assigning a politically active, even martial, role to the Messiah. Contrary to this view of the Messiah as revolutionary leader, the young Christian movement stressed nonviolence and submission to existing authority, while emphasizing the otherworldly nature of their strivings.

As the game begins, the priests do not know the true nature of Jesus' Messianic identity. In the language of game theory, they do not know his "type." They suspect that he might be a Jewish Messiah (JM) with probability p, a Christian Messiah (CM) with probability q, or no Messiah at all (–M) with probability 1–p–q.

Jesus takes one of two courses of action:

C: He confronts the priests with evidence of his mission and demands to be recognized as the Messiah.
–C: He is nonconfrontational in order to avoid a verdict altogether.

The priests observe this move and respond:
If he is confrontational, they either

S: Stone him for blasphemy and he dies (D), or
A: Accept his leadership, recognizing that he is the true Messiah (M).

If he is nonconfrontational, they either

P: Pass responsibility for his fate on to the Roman authorities (R), or
A: Accept his leadership, recognizing that he is the true Messiah (M).

Note that the priests can only stone Jesus if he makes claims to being the Messiah (i.e., if he is confrontational) and they can only pass him on to the Roman authorities if he does not. Because each of three Jesus "types" (identities) chooses one of two moves, and the priests respond with one of two moves, there are twelve possible outcomes for this game. However, irrespective of whether Jesus was confrontational or not, payoffs for outcome M are the same (for each Jesus type but not across Jesus types). Therefore, there are only nine distinct payoff pairs for this game. Preferences are ranked $0<a<1$ for player J and $0<b<1$ for player P (the first payoff in each pair is the payoff for J; the second payoff is the payoff for P):

D1. The priests execute the Jewish Messiah (a,0)
D2. The priests execute a Christian Messiah (0,1)
D3. The priests execute a non-Messiah (0,1)
M1. The priests correctly recognize Jesus as a Jewish Messiah (1,b)
M2. The priests recognize a Christian Messiah as a Jewish Messiah (a,0)
M3. The priests recognize a non-Messiah as the Jewish Messiah (1,0)
R1. The priests have no evidence to recognize or execute the Jewish Messiah. They exploit this opportunity to lead him into a confrontation with the Roman authorities (0,1)
R2. The priests hand a Christian Messiah to the Roman authorities (1,b)
R3. The priests hand a non-Messiah to the Roman authorities (a,b)

In assigning preferences over the outcomes of this game, we made several simplifying assumptions: that the trial reveals the true identity of Jesus; that Jesus' beliefs about his own identity are correct; and that the middle values for payoffs (a and b) are the same for all identity types, e.g. the value of stoning (a) for a Jewish Messiah (JM) equals the value of being declared a Messiah for a Christian Messiah (CM) equals the value of being handed over to the Romans for a false Messiah (–M). Similarly, the value of (b) is constant across all Jesus types. These simplifying assumptions allow for comparisons between the three states and permit conclusions about equilibria outcomes.

The principal difference between the three types of Messiah lies in their preference regarding the three possible outcomes of the game. A Jewish Messiah wishes to confront the priests, even at the risk of a martyr's death by stoning. A Christian Messiah wishes to be nonconfrontational, avoids being declared a Messiah (a move tantamount to confronting Rome in the first game), and tries to work things out with Pilate. A false Messiah would like to be recognized as Messiah but prefers the uncertainty of being handed to the Romans over death by stoning.

Jesus' most reasonable strategy in this interaction is to signal his identity clearly.[48] Unlike Judas' strategy of blurring his identity ("pooling") in the previous game, the three Jesus types are easy to tell apart in this strategy because each type chooses a different move ("separating"): type JM is confrontational, CM is nonconfrontational, and –M is confrontational. Priests respond with P for confrontation and A for nonconfrontation. This outcome conforms to the observed outcome as related in the Gospels. Whereas a confrontational claimant to Messiahship would have been recognized as Messiah by the priests, Jesus' nonconfrontational stance leads the priests to conclude that he is not a (Jewish) Messiah. Since he has not committed blasphemy, they hand him over to the Romans.

Why does Jesus not confront the priests with overwhelming evidence of his Messianic identity? One answer, given directly by the Gospel according to John, confirms the preferences that we have assigned to the participants in this third game: Jesus preferred being handed over to the Romans because this would fulfill his earlier predictions of being delivered to the Gentiles and being "lifted up" – i.e., crucified.[49] This explanation, although rational from the point of view of an actor who can foretell the future and realizes that he cannot escape his own destiny, begs the question, to some extent. A more rationalist answer lies in the contrast between Jewish and Christian views of Messianism. Jesus exemplifies a new kind of spiritual leadership, unknown to his Jewish audience.

From the Zealot point of view, this interaction begins with a Jesus who is either a Messiah or not. By the end of this game, however, it is not at all clear whether the game determined Jesus' identity as a Jewish or Christian Messiah. As far as the priests are concerned, Jesus' nonconfrontational stance is evidence against his being a Messiah. From a Zealot point of view, the behavior of Jesus before, during, and after the trial also indicates that he is not the Messiah, or more precisely that he is not a Messiah by Jewish definitions prevalent in the first century. Our *ex post facto* understanding of his doctrine, however, sheds no such light on his identity. From a Christian point of view, Jesus' behavior becomes the very type of Messianic behavior in the face of adversity. From a game theoretical point of view, the two outcomes are identical.

[48] By "most reasonable strategy" we mean the subgame perfect, robust (with respect to p), trembling-hand equilibrium of the game. Trembling-hand equilibria in a game are those Nash equilibria that are not weakly dominated. See, for example, Eric van Damme, *Stability and Perfection of Nash Equilibria* (Berlin: Springer, 1991). In this game there is only one such equilibrium. It is robust for $p+q>2/3$, that is, for low likelihood of a false Messiah who could use this strategy to mask his identity. In a less robust equilibrium, JM, CM, and –M pool at confrontation. Priests respond with M for confrontation and –M for non-confrontation. This second equilibrium holds for $p>2/3$.

[49] Compare John 18:32 with the predictions in John 12:32–33 and Mark 10:33.

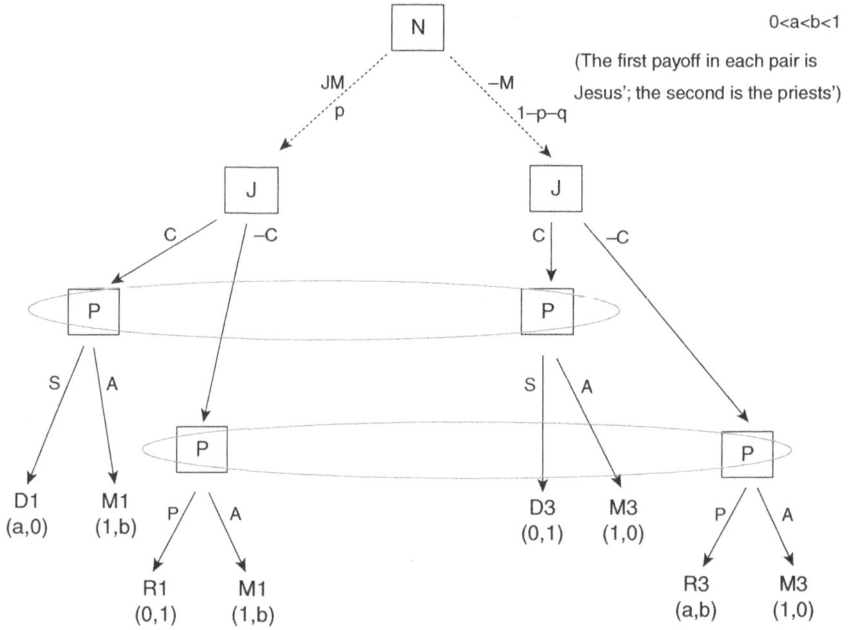

FIGURE 3.4 The Trial – Judas' Version

Judas may or may not have been present at the trial. If he does observe the outcome of the trial, it should be entirely unexpected given his previous beliefs.[50] Judas is familiar with Jewish expectations regarding the Messiah. But he is unfamiliar with the Christian-Messiah type and expects a particular version of this third game in which there is no Christian Messiah (q is set to zero) (Figure 3.4). In both outcomes of this version of the third game, Jesus confronts the priests, regardless of his identity ("pooling"), and the priests respond by declaring Jesus to be the true Messiah.[51] Given Judas' strong belief in the Messianic identity of Jesus, Judas would expect Jesus to emerge from this game as an acknowledged Messiah. There are only two possible outcomes in this game, as Judas sees it: death by stoning for a false Messiah or vindication for a true Messiah. Given Judas' point of view, the handing over of Jesus to the Romans is not a possible outcome. Since Jesus was neither declared Messiah nor executed for failing to assert his Messianic identity, something must have gone horribly wrong. Realizing that the priests reneged on their agreement to test

[50] Brown, *The Death of the Messiah*, pp. 638–640.

[51] In one equilibrium priests respond with M irrespective of J's previous move. In the second equilibrium the priests respond with M to a confrontational move and with R to a nonconfrontational move. Either way, the outcome is M and not R. These equilibria hold for $p>2/3$, which adequately describes Judas' beliefs in Jesus' Messianic identity.

Jesus themselves, Judas attempts to withdraw, unsuccessfully, from the deal struck earlier.[52]

Jesus is being handed over to a foreign authority. This means that Judas is no longer merely a disloyal disciple. He is something far worse – a *moser*, a halakhic category designating one who turns over another Jew to Gentile authorities. The penalty for this form of treason is death by hanging, a sentence that Judas proceeds to execute upon himself.[53]

Stage 4: Return to the First Game – Jesus and Pilate

The Zealots and the priests have succeeded, through uneasy collaboration, in bringing the young Christian movement and the Roman government into confrontation. The Gospel passages describe the trial of Jesus before Pilate in a manner that conforms to two actors attempting to withdraw simultaneously from an undesirable outcome. Jesus is presented to Pilate as an insurgent who, by claiming to be King of the Jews, has launched an attack against Rome's authority. As we argued above, Pilate's only rational move to this perceived provocation is to respond in kind. J and R find themselves at mutual confrontation (DD). This is a Pareto suboptimal outcome, yet the presence of the priests urging Pilate on and the cries of the crowd outside the palace prevent J and R from moving simultaneously toward the Pareto optimal outcome of mutual cooperation.

Both actors attempt in vain to rectify this situation. Jesus attempts to do so by refusing time and again to answer provocative questions that might brand him a political dissident; Pilate attempts to do so by refusing to try Jesus, by attempting to return him to the priests for trial, by passing him onto Herod for trial, and by offering the crowd a chance to ransom Jesus. All attempts having failed, Pilate consents to crucifixion, the standard death penalty for sedition. It is clear from the text that Jesus does not hold Rome responsible for this verdict. It is equally clear that Rome has no direct accusation against the Christian movement. Pilate can even be described as sympathetic to the Christian leader, refusing to bear the responsibility for the trial or its outcome by washing his hands in innocence.

CONCLUSION

The game presented above fills gaps in the Gospel accounts of the trial of Jesus and offers answers to questions raised in section 2 of this chapter. We have argued that Judas betrays Jesus not out of individualist interests but as

[52] Watson, *The Trial of Jesus*, throughout and pp. 38–40, hints that there may indeed have been foul play involved in the priests' refusal to try Jesus, their attempt to use false evidence against him, and the unexplained tearing of garments. He concludes that an early condemnation of Jesus was reversed the following day by dissenting members of the Sanhedrin.

[53] Brown, *The Death of the Messiah*, p. 1400.

a representative of a radical movement, the Sicarii, which adopted Jesus as their Messiah. This movement expected, as did parallel movements in this period, that Jesus would lead his followers to political and military victory over the foreign rulers of Judea. Judas' decision to deliver Jesus into the hands of the religious courts stemmed from his desire to accelerate the pace of events given Jesus' reluctance to forcefully claim his rightful position.

As far as Judas is concerned, the game is lost as soon as Jesus is handed over to the Romans. The models above indicate that Judas would not have initiated the game had he grasped Jesus' interpretation of Messianism. Had Judas known in stage 2 that a nonconfrontational Jesus was at all compatible with a Messianic Jesus, he would clearly have opted for the status quo rather than betray his master. Judas could not have understood Jesus' posture, given his own religious bias, just as he could not have predicted that his self-imposed execution by hanging would prove unnecessary three days later. His master's death was temporary – the betrayal, trial, and crucifixion a means toward the salvation of man.

Why does Jesus not assert his Messianic identity in his questioning before the priests? Doing so would have amounted to an unprovoked attack on Rome's political authority in Judea. His interests at this stage of the game are to be passed into Roman hands as quickly as possible, rather than score victory over the priests. Given the choice among succumbing to the priests, overwhelming them by means of a miracle or assuming an ambiguous stance, he chooses the latter. The priests, in turn, prefer a trial by Rome over a conclusive religious judgment. Although the Sanhedrin have the right to execute for blasphemy and may well have been absolutely sure of his guilt, they do not have the evidence necessary for executing Jesus. Jesus refuses to commit blasphemy in their presence by asserting his Messianic authority and the court fails to produce two independent witnesses who will testify that Jesus has committed blasphemy in the past, as required by Jewish law for the purposes of a death sentence. His behavior forces the priests to choose between an unwarranted declaration of Jesus as Messiah and an equally unwarranted execution by stoning. Instead, they choose to hand the accused over to another court on a different charge.[54]

The timbre of the dialogue with Pilate is remarkable. Here both sides show extreme and remarkable hesitation. Pilate repeats his questions over and over in order to give Jesus an opportunity to withdraw. Michael Grant describes his conduct as "an undignified feebleness and vacillation which one would not expect of a man who had already held down one of the worst trouble-spots in the empire for a number of years, and was destined to keep the post for a further considerable period."[55] Pilate refuses to condemn Jesus several times and,

[54] Watson, *The Trial of Jesus*, pp. 170–171, compares this move with the trial of Al Capone: "If you can't get him for murder, try tax evasion."

[55] Grant, *Jesus*, pp. 162–163.

according to one version, even passes him to Herod, who promptly returns Jesus to Pilate. This is their mutual attempt to reverse the game and return, simultaneously, to mutual cooperation. Their preference structure, past moves, and the presence of the priests as provoking agents make such a move impossible. Jesus is led off to crucifixion and Pilate washes his hands in innocence. It is indeed neither Pilate's nor Jesus' direct responsibility that a mutually undesirable outcome has been reached. Although they are the most powerful players, their preference structure offered opportunities for collaboration between mutual opponents. A combination of interactive preferences and partially veiled beliefs led to an outcome that none but the priests are content with.

The interactions between the four institutions examined here also entail broad lessons about the behavior of radical factions and opposition movements. A ruling government and a moderate opposition group can reach accord if neither side benefits from unilaterally challenging the status quo, irrespective of the other player's move. When the relationship between the ruling government and the opposition assumes the shape of a stag hunt, parties prefer mutual cooperation to mutual confrontation, but they also prefer mutual confrontation to unilateral cooperation. In such a case, neither party has an incentive to defect if the status quo prevails at the outset of the game.

In such a situation, discontent elements within the establishment and radical elements within the opposition have an incentive to cooperate in order to topple the status quo. Only by propelling their respective partners into a confrontation at the same time can they hope to induce change. However, since they have different capabilities and preferences, this cooperation takes the form of a sequential game, creating an opportunity for shirking.

As stages 2 and 3 of the game demonstrate, when the opportunity to shirk arises, the player who plays the final move has an incentive to defect and the player who plays the first move therefore has an incentive not to play. Because both parties are subversive, they cannot officially contract or use third-party enforcement to oversee their agreement. Both parties may share the goal of toppling the status quo but their long-term political interests could not be more different. Cooperation will only take place if either player believes that, once the status quo has been overturned, power will remain in his hands. In other words, each player must have strong beliefs in his own ability to subsume the other under its leadership after the revolution.

A word needs to be said about the aftermath of the events examined above. It is important to note that, while the outcome is suboptimal for all but one of the players involved, the events that followed the crucifixion of Christ and his death on the cross, according to Christian beliefs, achieve not only a mutual return to cooperation in the interaction between the Christian movement and the Roman government, and a renewed opportunity for the Zealot movement, but also an undesirable outcome for the priesthood. The resurrection completely reverses the outcome of the three games. Christ returns to lead his movement and his resurrection is harnessed as a key event in the theology of the group. This peaceful victory allows for a continued harmony between Christians and Rome for some time. Christians participated in none of the Jewish wars against the Romans. Only when the movement begins to openly challenge Roman authority does Rome respond with force.[56]

The Zealots are given new opportunities to lead insurrections. The resurrection confirmed the leadership of Christ to some Zealots within the Christian movement and allowed others to choose alternative Messiahs for purposes of an armed revolt. It is through such revolts that the Jewish wars against the Romans were instigated, as detailed in the works of Josephus: "What, more than all else incited them to the war was an ambiguous oracle, likewise found in the sacred scriptures to the effect that at the time one from their country would become ruler of the world."[57] Under the Messianic leadership of Judah of Galilee in 66 AD, and under the Messianic leadership of Bar-Kokhva in 115 and 132 AD, the Zealots and Sicarii faced Rome and even scored several decisive victories. The overall outcome, however, just as Jesus had prophesied it, was the destruction of Jerusalem and the Holy Temple in it, within a hundred years of the crucifixion. Thus, the priests are the long-term losers of a series of interactions in which, it seemed initially, they were the only beneficiaries. In this sense, crucifixion was a favorable outcome that permitted both Jewish and Christian believers to choose between following Jesus as the true Messiah and expecting the arrival of a different Messiah. It is difficult, however, to generalize from this final conclusion since it suggests that payoffs can be shaped after the fact by actors capable of resurrection.

[56] Feldman and Hata, *Josephus, Judaism and Christianity*, p. 54.

[57] Josephus, *The Jewish War*, VI, V, 4.

4

Jan Hus in the Medieval Ecclesiastical Courts

Thomas A. Fudge

> When the church perceives a threat, the principles of morality are suspended. With unity as the goal, everything to that end becomes sanctified: simony, duplicity, betrayal, imprisonment and death. Since order serves the community the individual must be sacrificed for the common good.[1]

The trial of Jan Hus was political. The trial of Hus was neither unfair nor illegal. In the early fifteenth century, the medieval church perceived a threat posed by Jan Hus, a priest in Prague. It has also been suggested that what followed was a teleological suspension of the ethical and moral principles, which were jettisoned in the effort to eliminate the perceived threat. We can find in the Hus case evidence of duplicity, betrayal, imprisonment, and death. Men intimately involved in the Hus case were convinced that the individual had to be sacrificed for the common good of the Christian community. The question remains: what was legal and what was political in the medieval ecclesiastical courts of Prague, Bologna, Rome, and Constance in the matter of Jan Hus? The distinction is crucial.

The trial of Jan Hus was a typical heresy trial in the sense that it followed established rules and legal procedure. At the same time, the process was a result of a highly specific political situation. Was there such a thing as political trials in the European Middle Ages? An examination of the legal histories in the later medieval period provides a welter of material that should not be set aside lightly. *Cui bono*? Who benefits from the trial of those considered dissenters, heretics, dangerous, and threats to the institutional security of the church? Serious inconsistencies in the evidence marshaled against such individuals advanced by the prosecutors and ratified by the courts to sustain accusations and formal charges are very much part of the fabric of these proceedings. Fraud

[1] This sentiment has been attributed to Dietrich Niem and his 1411 treatise *De scismate*. This is uncertain but the idea is also reflected by the canon lawyer Hostiensis.

and its cousins were sometimes regarded as salutary in the Middle Ages, and indeed one can locate falsehood based upon commendable motives. False charters and papal decrees were manufactured in order to settle questions of dispute concerning property or jurisdictional claims. Forgeries supported monks against episcopal interference or provided defense for popes enmeshed in struggles with secular rulers. It is possible to conclude that on account of so many forgeries and cases of fraud public morality was not offended by such tactics and the practice was not only condoned but expected.[2] We find evidence of the manufacture or manipulation of evidence in medieval courts. The procedures against the Knights Templar bear all the hallmarks. The papal bull *Faciens misericordiam* of August 12, 1308, issued by Pope Clement V, turned rumors about Templar misconduct into formal accusations.[3] Without warning, at dawn on a Friday morning, October 13, 1307, a coordinated raid across the kingdom of France resulted in the massive arrests of many of the estimated 2,000 members of the Temple. By the time it was over, the Templars had been exterminated.[4] Joan of Arc went to the pyre at Rouen under curious circumstances. Famously defended by Christine de Pisan and Jean Gerson, with the latter convinced she was of God and her accomplishments the work of God, it remains puzzling that her condemnation technically was based neither on military nor political charges but on heresy. This demonstrates the political uses of dissent.[5] Within a decade of her demise, one of her more significant colleagues was brought up on charges of sexual perversion and mass murder.[6] The evidence advanced in these legal procedures might not bear the weight of legal inquiry but it was sufficient to sustain the force of a politically inspired urge to purge. All of these cases ended in capital punishment, but when Bernard Délicieux came to trial in 1319, he was denied the opportunity for martyrdom because the authorities determined that rather than a salutary effect, that outcome was thought to be rather unhealthy.[7] Here we see the political dimensions of punishment. In the Hus case, there were men who believed

[2] Marc Bloch, *The Historian's Craft*, translated by Peter Putnam (Manchester: Manchester University Press, 1954), pp. 90–137.

[3] Oxford, Bodleian Library MS Bodley 454, fols. 1r–7r, now in a critical edition. Helen J. Nicholson, ed., *The Proceedings against the Templars in the British Isles*, vol. 2 (Aldershot: Ashgate, 2011) pp. 7–11.

[4] See the *Arrest Order* of 1307, in Georges Lizerand, ed. and translated by, *Le Dossier de l'Affaire des Templiers* (Paris: H. Champion, 1923), pp. 16–25, and Malcolm Barber, *The Trial of the Templars*, Second edition (Cambridge: Cambridge University Press, 2006).

[5] Jules Quicherat, ed., *Procès de condamnation et de réhabilitation de Jeanne d'Arc dite la Pucelle*, 5 vols. (Paris: Société de l'histoire de France, 1841–1849) and Daniel Hobbins, *The Trial of Joan of Arc* (Cambridge: Harvard University Press, 2005).

[6] Georges Bataille, *Le procès de Gilles de Rais* (Paris: Société nouvelle des editions Pauvert, 1997) and more recently Thomas A. Fudge, *Medieval Religion and its Anxieties: History and Mystery in the Other Middle Ages* (New York: Palgrave Macmillan, 2016), pp. 51–87.

[7] Alan Friedlander, *The Hammer of the Inquisitors: Brother Bernard Délicieux and the Struggle against the Inquisition in Fourteenth-Century France* (Leiden: Brill, 2000), p. 290.

steadfastly that if Hus had been permitted legal representation he would surely not have been burned.[8] That there were medieval political trials should not be doubted.

HERETICS AND POLITICS

The matter of Jan Hus has been explored in some detail.[9] The Hus process was a heresy trial. The definition of heresy was broadened by the court hearing the Hus case, especially during its final phases at the Council of Constance, to include simple disobedience.[10] This development appears to be a true and accurate reflection of trends in the later Middle Ages with respect to heresy. Heresy became an effectual tool of control for the later medieval church to enforce conformity, achieve its objectives, and get rid of dissenters. In that sense, heresy was political, and this is further demonstrated by the evolution of medieval heresy into witch-hunting. Before the Middle Ages came to an end that connection was unmistakable. The greatest *ketzerei* (heresy) was *hexerei* (witchcraft). When the *Malleus Maleficarum* was first published in 1486 it carried a bold statement on its title page: "to not believe in witchcraft is the greatest heresy."[11] Hunting and repressing heretics was, in the later Middle Ages, a judicial process wherein suspects were remanded to formal trial, and legal procedure and sentencing guidelines were established. *Pertinacia* and *contumacia* in the conciliar context are concepts closely related (indeed equivalent) to that of heresy. Jan Hus was charged with *heretica pravitas* (heretical sin, wickedness, depravity), which in the later Middle Ages had evolved into a complex matter. Doctrinally, Hus was deviant on a single point, that being ecclesiology. Efforts to establish dogmatic error in the Hus case generally become exercises in theological interpretation. Establishing theological error was not the basis for the Hus process. The Hus trial was a show trial to the extent that it came to its culmination before the greatest convocation known in medieval Christendom. It was a show trial because it aimed to use the Hus case to demonstrate to western Christendom that it was serious about reining heresy in, that the church was determined to overcome the liabilities created by the papal schism, and also that it could not be regarded as

8 Heinrich Finke, ed., *Acta concilii Constanciensis*, vol. 4 (Münster: Druck und Verlag der Regensbergschen Buchhandlung, 1896–1928), p. 352.

9 I have recently delineated his life and thought in three volumes: Thomas A. Fudge, *The Trial of Jan Hus: Medieval Heresy and Criminal Procedure* (New York: Oxford University Press, 2013); Thomas A. Fudge, *The Memory and Motivation of Jan Hus, Medieval Priest and Martyr* (Turnhout: Brepols, 2013); and Thomas A. Fudge, *Jan Hus: Religious Reform and Social Revolution in Bohemia* (London: I.B. Tauris, 2010).

10 Walter Brandmüller, "Hus vor dem Konzil," in Ferdinand Seibt, ed., *Jan Hus: Zwischen Zeiten, Völkern, Konfessionen* (Munich: Oldenboug, 1997), p. 237.

11 There is a modern critical edition. Christopher S. Mackay, ed. and translated by, *Malleus Maleficarum*, 2 vols. (Cambridge: Cambridge University Press, 2006).

soft on crime. The culmination of the trial was intended as a deterrent. The defendant was publicly condemned, defrocked in an elaborate ceremony, forced to walk in procession from the cathedral to the pyre, made to wear an opprobrious miter, and in the midst of considerable theater set ablaze before a multitude of onlookers.[12] Eyewitnesses recorded minute details.

What was the nature of politics in the five-year-long Hus trial? An examination of the existing dossier suggests didactic and destructive elements. In the case of the former, both sides in the struggle sought to convey important principles and thereby instruct those who saw, heard, or otherwise knew about the medieval church versus Jan Hus. The institution strove to use the Hus trial as a forum to teach the faithful that disobedience could not be tolerated, that heresy was a serious matter that infected the gospel with poison, and that it was divine will for all people to conform to the rules, laws, beliefs, and customs of the church. Jan Hus also regarded his trial, especially in its later stages, as an opportunity to provide an example of faithfulness to God, and commitment to truth, to all those who were involved in the court proceedings. Hus clearly stated that his intention was motivated by the opportunity to lead souls to salvation. Contemporary witnesses sympathetic to Hus testified that in his trials he demonstrated the work of love, witness to truth, and a godly example. Both didactic approaches stressed truth and obedience but diverged in lesson objective. The trial that culminated at Constance was also destructive in that Hus was burned alive and physically destroyed. The medieval church extended its teaching lesson by demonstrating that fidelity to God included a duty to cut out of the healthy body of faith whatever disease threatened the integrity of the whole. The destructive nature of the Hus trial included the elimination of danger, the curtailing of a threat, and the control of a subversive influence. The nature of the politics in the Hus case demanded the destruction of the defendant. Hus consented to this, enduring the process of defrocking, public humiliation, and death in order that through his own demise he might destroy falsehood and error.

In many respects, the trial of Jan Hus amounted to a power struggle that pitted reform against tradition. The culmination of the trial of Hus was a demonstration of ecclesiastical power and authority. Heresy investigations into the activities of Jan Hus reveal the relation of power and authority. Complicating the latter stages of the trial was the coming of age of an applied conciliar theory. Conciliarists, those who favored the authority of a general council over that of a pope, were no less concerned about heresy than papalists. The two parties collided at Constance and there the trial of Hus was conducted within a particular context. At Constance, this was determined by the understanding and definition of the conciliar claim to

[12] Petr Mladoňovice, "Relatio de Mag. Joannis Hus causa," in Václav Novotný, ed., *Fontes rerum bohemicarum*, vol. 8 (Prague: Nákladem nadání Františka Palackého, 1873–1932), pp. 112–120.

authority (*plenitudo potestatis*). What are the implications? It must not be forgotten that the trial of Hus at Constance was a continuation of the Curial process begun in 1410. The dramatic announcement of the decree *Haec sancta* in 1415, which declared that the Council possessed divine authority, did not alter the process against Hus significantly. The clandestine nocturnal flight of Pope John XXIII and the commensurate absence of a clearly defined presiding pontifical authority cannot be taken to suggest that established legal procedures were therefore jettisoned or underwent significant alteration. There is simply no evidence that legal procedures already in place did not continue to be scrupulously observed. Extant records reveal that the papal auditor John de Thomariis of Bologna took no note of John's departure or his ensuing deposition and continued to work on legal cases at Constance without any deviation from established law and legal procedure.[13] Assigning too much significance to *Haec sancta* in terms of the legal process of the Hus trial and its eventual outcome is a result of failing to take into account what had already occurred in the Hus case between 1410 and 1415. Since heresy was exceptional crime, the Council, on the strength of *Haec sancta*, claimed *plenitudo potestatis* and therefore matters concerning the faith were dealt with under the auspices of *Haec sancta*. But it is easy to make too much out of this. There can be little doubt that a papal court presided over by a duly elected and recognized pope would have yielded a different result.

Pursuant to *sede vacante* (when the papacy is vacant), jurisdiction is delegated to the power of the chapter, and the church through its bishops retains authority to judge people in matters of heresy.[14] There is no indication that the court at Constance did anything but recognize and thereby confirm the previous indictments, convictions, and judicial decisions handed down against Hus by the Curial court. From a legal point of view, the fact that Hus was in Constance still under penalty of excommunication and interdict posed a dilemma. Pope John XXIII did lift the sentences from Hus, but this was done only for the purposes of political expediency so that divine services would not have to be suspended in Constance during Hus' stay as ordinarily required by the canons.[15] Previous medieval heresy trials did not require the direct authority of papal approval in order to secure a verdict in a legal process. The Council also deployed the accusation of heresy to remove John XXIII from the papacy. There is no reason not to argue that this same motive and initiation was applied in the Hus case.

[13] Christopher M. D. Crowder, "Four English Cases Determined in the Roman Curia during the Council of Constance, 1414–1418," *Annuarium historiae conciliorum*, Vol. 12 (1980), pp. 366–367.

[14] X 3.9.1–3 *Ne sede vacante*, in Emil Friedberg, ed., *Corpus iuris canonici*, vol. 2 (Leipzig: Tauchnitz, 1879–1881), cols. 500–501.

[15] Mladoňovice, *Relatio*, pp. 34–35.

The politics surrounding the deposition of John XXIII might also qualify his abbreviated legal ordeal as a political trial. John was tried *in absentia* on an expansive dossier of charges and subsequently deposed from the papacy.[16] Unless it could be shown popes had acted against the faith, they could not be tried in a court of law.[17] Apart from heresy, medieval popes enjoyed immunity from human judgment.[18] Medieval canon law declared that popes possessed universal power, and this was generally not contested.[19] Dietrich Niem appears to have had his own agenda in spearheading the case against John and it was he who agitated the Council into taking action.[20] John's legal trial and deposition was brief because he chose not to contest the proceedings. That many of the allegations comprising the indictment against him amounted to boilerplate charges helps to situate the judicial procedure in the realm of a political trial. John was charged with perjury, simony, sexual misconduct, and murder. He did not fight the indictment and offered no resistance and did not attempt any semblance of defense. He was convicted of the charges and summarily sentenced to life imprisonment. Heresy plays a key role in the case against John, but the charge seemed so extravagant and specious that at least one cardinal and canon lawyer objected to the proceedings on the grounds that there was insufficient proof to sustain the case.[21] The deposition of John was regarded as an essential step in solving the papal schism. There is no indication that John XXIII would have acted differently than the Council toward Hus had he remained as pope. The Hus case had been declared a judicial matter long before the case against Pope John XXIII came to prominence. Therefore, it seems impossible to follow lines of argument which assert that there was a moment wherein procedural strategy for the defense of Hus collapsed.[22] Such hypothetical strategy was doomed from the beginning for it failed to take into account the legal process enacted at the Curia, the resulting decisions, and the failure of Hus and his attorneys to fulfill legal requirements by contesting the procedural irregularities in a timely fashion.

Doctrine, theological interpretation, and the relationship to recognized authority are important factors in situating heresy trials in the Middle Ages. According to canon law glosses, heretics include those men and women who

[16] Hermann von der Hardt, ed., *Magnum oecumenicum constantiense conciliorum*, vol. 4 (Frankfurt: Gensch, 1699–1742), pp. 237–248.

[17] D.40 c.6 *Si papa*, in Friedberg, *Corpus iuris canonici*, vol. 2, col. 146.

[18] C.9 q.3 c.13 *Nemo iudicabit*, C.9 q.3 c.14 *Aliorum hominum causas*, C.9 q.3 c.15 *Facta subditorum* and C.9 q.3 c.17 *Cuncta per mundum*, in Friedberg, *Corpus iuris canonici*, vol. 1, cols. 610–611.

[19] D.99 c.3 *Primae sedis* and D.99 c.5 *Ecce in prefatione*, in Friedberg, *Corpus iuris canonici*, vol. 1, cols. 350–351.

[20] Finke, *Acta concilii Constanciensis*, vol. 3, pp. 128–129.

[21] Heinrich Finke, *Forschungen und Quellen zur Geschichte des Konstanzer Konzils* (Paderborn: Ferdinand Schöningh, 1889), p. 177.

[22] Sebastián Provvidente, "Inquisitorial Process and plenitudo potestatis at the Council of Constance (1414–1418)," *Bohemian Reformation and Religious Practice*, Vol. 8 (2011), p. 110.

pervert the sacraments and offenders such as simoniacs (those who buy spiritual power). Heretics are also those who separate from the church. Heretics are those who have been excommunicated or expelled from the fellowship of the faithful. Heretics are those who commit error while interpreting scripture. Heretics encompass those who invent new sects or who align themselves with breakaway factions. Heretics are also individuals whose thinking departs from that endorsed by the Roman Church in matters concerning the articles of faith.[23] Other canonical glosses reflect similar convictions, but here we find additional items that add further nuance. A heretic is anyone who maintains persistent doubt about the faith. Heresy is the impulse to reduce the privileges of the Roman Church, while a heretic is anyone who violates a rule of the Roman Church.[24] The second gloss goes on to distinguish a broad and a strict sense of the term: "Sometimes a heretic is said generally to be anyone who does not hold the articles of faith, and in this sense Jews and Gentiles are heretics ... In the strict sense a heretic is anyone who has been removed from the church because that person errs in faith." The other types of heretics mentioned in these glosses are deviant in specific beliefs. All of this can be subsumed under one core concept. The common denominator present in each of these definitions of medieval heresy is a form of separation from the church based upon an identifiable error of faith and persistence therein.[25] While this is true for many canon lawyers dealing with the idea of heresy in the twelfth and thirteenth centuries, it would be folly to conclude that heresy was universally regarded by medieval theologians, canon lawyers, and ecclesiastics as simple doctrinal errors. Altogether, the Hus trial features in the crosshairs of canonical opinion on heresy. And the law is always political.

Medieval judicial practices generated a particular notion of truth and this is clearly evident in the Hus case. It is one thing to determine if the *ordo iudiciarius* (standard procedure) in the context of medieval canon law was followed. I have previously argued to the conclusion that both the *ordo* specifically and canon law generally were respected and generally adhered to. Therefore, Hus was rightly convicted of heresy. But within that legal process, can we find evidence that the trial might be evaluated from another perspective? Inquisitorial procedure in the Romano-canonical-based courts of later medieval Europe required as the law of proofs either confession, which was conceived as the *regina probationum* (the queen of proofs), by the accused, or the testimony of two witnesses. The latter was often problematic in cases involving heresy. Men such as Michael de Causis were sworn enemies of Hus and motivated at least in

[23] Relevant here is the gloss to X 5.7.3, s.v. *hereticum in* Friedberg, *Canon iuris canonici*, vol. 2, col. 778.

[24] C.24 q.3 p.c. 25, s.v. *heresim*.

[25] Othmar Hageneder, "Der Haeresiebegriff bei den Juristen des 12. und 13. Jahrhunderts," in W. Lourdaux and D. Verhelst, eds., *The Concept of Heresy in the Middle Ages* (Leuven: Leuven University Press, 1976), pp. 42–103.

part by malice. They were not above fraud, perjury, the subornation of witnesses, or procedural violations. Hus declined to confess to heresy in any sense believing that to do so was both unethical and perjurious.[26] These factors suggest the limitations of the law of proofs in matters of criminality such as heresy.

Positing the Hus case as a political trial in the context of repressing heresy helps to answer one important question. Why were the canonical admonitions for mercy generally ignored in the trial of Jan Hus?[27] Judges in medieval ecclesiastical courts were encouraged to follow the more humane path.[28] There were a range of options offered or allowed in heresy cases within the *ordo* and there was a measure of latitude within canon law. "There are many to be corrected, like Peter; many to be tolerated, like Judas; and many who are unknown, until the Lord comes, who will bring to light the hidden things of the darkness."[29] Why was Jan Hus adjudicated unworthy of the categories of Peter, or the unknowns, or even of Judas? He was neither to be corrected only nor tolerated, and at the culmination of a protracted judicial ordeal was judged unworthy of anything other than death. In this sense, the Hus process was destructive. There were definite implications of law and politics in the Hus trial.[30]

It is clear that the ecclesiastical courts had the option of dismissing the Hus case or of applying a lesser sentence. By the time the Hus trial reached the legal consideration of the Council of Constance, the judicial elements of the case were too far advanced to permit a decision allowing Hus to remain free, to return to Prague, to await the resolution of the papal schism. In effect, the judges were unwilling to put the matter off until 1418. The problem of the ghost of the English theologian John Wyclif (†1384) lingered over the trial of Hus, and this was a political shadow insofar as Wyclif was considered a heresiarch who had died unrepentant and whose malevolent influence had infected Bohemia and motivated Jan Hus to commit heresy. Wyclif had challenged the core of medieval religious practice, attacked church hierarchy, and advanced claims that gave the state precedence over the church. The salient question revolves around the query of why Jan Hus was considered such a threat to the Latin

[26] Thomas A. Fudge, "The One-Eyed Heretic? An Introduction to the Ethics of Jan Hus," in Zdeněk V. David and Karel Raska, Jr., eds., *Contributions of Czechs and Slovaks to Science and Technology in the Twenty-first Century* (New York: Publishing House of the Czech and Slovak Society of Arts and Sciences, 2011), pp. 56–70.

[27] C.23 q.4 cc.18–19 *Quidam vero*, in Friedberg, *Corpus iuris canonici*, vol. 1, cols. 781–782.

[28] *Glos. ord.* to C.23 q.4 and X 1.36.11 *Ex parte tua*, in Friedberg, *Corpus iuris canonici*, vol. 2, cols. 204–205.

[29] C.2 q.1 c.18 *Multi corriguntur*, in Friedberg, *Corpus iuris canonici*, vol. 1, col. 382.

[30] For the theory, see especially Jacques Chiffoleau, "Le crime de majesté, la politique et l'extraordinaire: Note sur les collections érudites de procès de lèse majesté du XVIIe siècle et leurs exemples médiévaux," in Yves-Marie Bercé, ed., *Les procès politiques (XIVe–XVIIe siècles)* (Rome: Collection de l'Ecole française de Rome, 2007), pp. 577–662.

Church. Heresy was a grave concern at the end of the Middle Ages, and there is little doubt that the Council, though willing to undertake more than the simple entertaining of a revolutionary idea, was prepared neither to harbor nor ignore heretics. Heretofore, I have imagined that Hus' sermon *De pace*, which he prepared for his court appearances, and his *quaestio* revealed his mistaken idea that the Council offered an opportunity for debate. This may not have been the case after all, but instead may have been part of a deliberate strategy to determine the nature of the hearings. However, I am not persuaded that the Council's determination to proceed judicially against Hus had anything to do with asserting its own authority thereby requiring submission to its power. This conviction depends to a great extent upon the nature of the process *before* the affair of John XXIII. I believe that a careful study of the Curial process in the Hus case does not support the idea. The political element in the Hus trial only deepened as it wound its way from Prague to the Curia and finally to the special commissions of the Council of Constance.

Was the fate of Hus at Constance substantially different from the fate of other accused heretics in the later Middle Ages? The profile of a heretic in the later Middle Ages was remarkably consistent. The suspect was an individual considered intellectually deviant, a failed reformer, an incorrigible contumax, a danger to institutional security, unbalanced, infected with contagious disease, a degenerate, and controlled by malevolent forces.[31] Evaluated against these eight characteristics, the legal records reveal that Hus was a typical medieval heretic. Faced with a demand to recant or die, Hus resolutely refused the opportunity to live citing the force of three arguments. First, he feared offending God. Second, he had no wish to commit perjury, and finally he was reluctant to act against conscience.[32] The final stages of the Hus trial coincided with an initiative to solve the protracted papal schism. The legal proceeding therefore was decisive. Hus was regarded as a political liability that could neither be ignored nor dismissed. He had to recant or die.

THEOLOGY AND ITS IMPLICATIONS

What are the political stakes of theological dispute in the later Middle Ages? Theologians and churchmen believed they dealt with ultimate truth. What makes the case of Jan Hus a political trial is the fact that the social and religious implications of his teachings challenged the foundations of medieval theology and clashed with prevailing political circumstances. The reaction to his book on the church was shrill and alarmed. Some argued it was more adverse to the Christian faith than the Islamic Qur'an.[33] Jean Gerson declared that only

[31] Fudge, *The Trial of Jan Hus*, pp. 44–72.

[32] Novotný, *Fontes rerum bohemicarum*, vol. 8, p. 13.

[33] Dietrich Niem, "De necessitate reformacionis ecclesiae," in Hardt, *Magnum oecumenicum constantiense conciliorum*, vol. 1, cols. 306–307.

judicial condemnation was appropriate. The book contained "notorious and obstinate heresy" amounting to "manifest mischief" and "open crime."[34] This is the language of medieval heresy trials. According to Hus, membership in the church was neither a legal right nor a matter of choice but a result of divine election. His judges regarded the church as a legal corporation, represented by the pope and council. Medieval theology considered the Roman Church ordained of Christ with the pope as head and the body made of the cardinals. As such, the church remained immune to all error concerning the faith. Everything taught by the pope was true. The papacy retained "the sacrament of anointing or unction." This implied an enormous claim to authority. This gift was not invalidated on account of sin and could not be forfeited due to wickedness. This anointing enabled the pope to function infallibly and guaranteed that supreme authority resided in the papal office and which extended into the social and political realm.

Hus refused this definition of ecclesiastical authority. His stubborn adherence to alternative ideas was judged subversive and injurious to the medieval church for the simple reason that it opposed the authority claimed by the church. The implications of Hus' theology applied broadly threatened the church as a legal entity along with its universal coercive powers. Medieval theology regarded prelates as possessing absolute jurisdictional power over the world with authority to pass judgment as a legal entity on all causes relating to the faith. Hus' ideas challenged the core identity of the church and its authority. The primacy of the Roman Church covered all ecclesiastical cases and many civil cases as well. It possessed authorization to judge, but it could neither be judged by its members nor by a lower court or authority.

Summarized in this fashion, Hus could not agree. Canon law defended and protected the authority and jurisdictional prerogatives of the institutional church. If the Latin Church followed Hus, this would have resulted in a shift of ecclesiastical essence away from its hierarchy and politico-legal jurisdiction. The implications were even more striking and immediate in the sense that popes, prelates, and priests might not even be members of the true church and in consequence might possess no spiritual power and therefore could be irrelevant. The possibility of such conclusion meant the institutional and legal church entity had neither meaning nor merit. The practical implications were unthinkable. Hus had to be stopped. The court at Constance became convinced that Hus' doctrine of the church nullified the medieval institution as most Christians knew it. Not even the conciliarists were prepared to pursue that model or run the risk of a Hussite ecclesiastical matrix challenging the *Romana ecclesia*. Hus advanced the law of God and scripture as the ultimate court of appeal. His detractors demanded unqualified submission to church authority. The perennial conflict over

[34] František Palacký, ed., *Documenta Mag. Joannis Hus* (Prague: Tempsky, 1869), pp. 187–188.

issues of authority intrudes. Medieval theologians struggled to find the balance between a fossilized scriptural emphasis that ignored tradition and arbitrary beliefs resulting from traditional practices that had little or no anchor in scripture.[35] The implications the court perceived in Hus' doctrine of the church were sufficient to warrant condemning his ideas. This was the basis for the politicizing of the Hus case. The political stakes in this theological dispute were beyond human calibration.

Hus' concept departed from the traditional late medieval doctrine of the church, especially as understood in the Bohemian province. By the time his trial shifted to the Council of Constance, the ecclesiology of many conciliar thinkers suggested another doctrine that is important in evaluating the unyielding resistance to Hus' *De ecclesia*, which led to his conviction as a capital offender and eventual designation as a felon. Conciliar theology is important for assessing the validity of the second categorical criminal charge lodged against Hus throughout his legal ordeal culminating at the ecclesiastical court in Constance. The Council argued that it had the authority to adjudicate all matters of faith and morals. It had the duty to judge cases within its purview even if it lacked a specific biblical mandate.[36] The men of the Council considered the synod representative of the Church as *congregatio fidelium* (or the community of baptized Christians). Conciliarists opposed Hus because they regarded the church as a legal entity under the jurisdiction of the papacy and a general council. Hus considered the church should impose limitations on ecclesiastical power codified in canon law. Unresolvable controversy over acceptable definitions of the church and the nature of spiritual authority between Hus and representatives of the Latin Church remained acute. The legal process concluded Hus' perspective was insubordinate and subversive. The finding was guilty as charged. Theories of power and authority separated them on crucial points and this, coupled with Hus' refusal to cease and desist, resulted in a political heresy trial. When diplomacy and reason failed to resolve the conflict, the next step involved legal proceedings.

PREVAILING LEGAL NORMS

The structural relationship between law and politics in the Middle Ages is not affected by modern assumptions about the desacralization of ideas. Fundamentally, during the time of Hus, both law and politics were infused with assumptions about the sacred. Law was an extension of the divine and politics were part of a divinely ordained social order. To understand the Hus process, it is necessary to outline the ideological foundations of the Hus case and

[35] Articulated succinctly in Paul de Vooght, *Les sources de la doctrine chrétienne d'après les théologiens di XIVe siècle et du début du XVe* (Bruges: Desclée de Brouwer, 1954), p. 262.

[36] *Tractatus de potestate ecclesiastica* in Louis Ellies Du Pin, ed., *Joannes Gersonii Opera Omnia*, vol. 2 (Antwerp: Sumptibus Societatis, 1706), cols. 225–256, especially cols. 247 and 249.

the meaning of legal norms within which the court procedures operated while keeping in mind the sacred component. The trial of Jan Hus was an inquisitorial process operating under the established rules of canon law and the *ordo iudiciarius*. That said, medieval trials were not all alike and it might be argued that each was unique depending upon political circumstances. Heresy trials are not homogeneous. Procedural law, described in the canons *Licet Heli* and *Qualiter et quando*, the process by which the church dealt with heretics, outlined in *Vergentis in senium*, and the relaxing of criminally convicted priests to secular authorities, articulated in *Novimus*, constitutes the basic legal doctrine in heresy cases.[37] *Vergentis in senium*, which considered heresy both criminal and treasonous, was the guiding legal principle for court cases at the time of the Hus trial.[38] The standard procedure, known as the *ordo iudiciarius*, included several phases within the inquisitorial process, ranging from oaths, witness testimony, the determination of a crime, the status of the accused, *indicia* (indications of criminal offense), *facti evidentia* (factual evidence), and so on.[39] A formal petition commenced the legal process before a canonical judge. This was a writ or valid formal accusation (*libellus*) that outlined relevant facts alerting the judiciary to the basis for the case and a reference point for the eventual verdict. This could include details such as the time, place, description of the circumstances, and other relevant factors in the alleged crime. Omissions were potentially prejudicial and might result in the case being dismissed.

Once a legal process began, a proper summons was issued by a judge. The defendant had the right to know the details of the charges. Names and testimonies of witnesses were included and opportunity for objections by the deponent was allowed.[40] The court summons (*citatio*) was delivered in the presence of two witnesses. Once the citation was issued, failure to appear resulted in provisional excommunication. The modern equivalent of an arrest warrant might be issued. If nonappearance persisted longer than one year, the censure became a definitive excommunication.

Presumption of innocence prevailed. This concept was well-known and established legal doctrine.[41] Following a formal citation, the defendant was

[37] X 5.3.31 *Licet Heli*, X 5.1.17, *Qualiter et quando*, and X 5.40.27 *Novimus expedire*, in Friedberg, *Corpus iuris canonici*, vol. 2, cols. 760–761, 738–739, 745–747, 924.

[38] Kenneth Pennington, "Pro Peccatis Patrum Puniri: A Moral and Legal Problem of the Inquisition," *Church History*, Vol. 47 (1978), p. 137.

[39] A review of procedural rules regulating the medieval *ordo iudiciarius* between the eleventh century and 1234 can be found in Wiesław Litewski, *Der römisch-kanonische Zivilprozeß nach den älteren ordines iudiciarii*, 2 vols. (Kraków: Jagiełłion University Press, 1999).

[40] X 5.1.24 *Qualiter et quando*, in Friedberg, *Corpus iuris canonici*, vol. 2, cols. 745–747.

[41] Based on Innocent III, X 2.23.16 *Dudum*, in Friedberg, *Corpus iuris canonici*, vol. 2, cols. 358–359. The commentary by Johannes Monachus on *Extrav. comm.* 2.3.1 (*Rem non novam*) exists in London, British Library MS Royal 10. E. I, fol. 214r and London, Lambeth Palace MS 13, fols. 363v–364r. I follow Kenneth Pennington, "Innocent until Proven Guilty: The Origins of a Legal Maxim," *The Jurist*, Vol. 63 (2003), pp. 104–124.

required to take an oath. This corresponds to entering a plea during arraignment. Refusal to take an oath constituted presumption of guilt. Generally, oaths were taken and the defendant either confessed to the charges or denied the charges. In the event of denial, the judge attempted to prove the charges by means of documentary evidence or on the basis of witness testimony. If insufficient evidence to sustain actual guilt on the charges was apparent, but witness testimony was deemed sufficient to establish *fama publica* (rumor), then purgation might be ordered. A finding of *fama publica* required the testimony of two reputable witnesses who affirmed that the defendant was guilty. Judges were required to establish *fama publica*. This was a preliminary inquest (*inquisitio generalis*) into the reputation of the suspect and was normally undertaken before a trial or hearing (*inquisitio specialis*) by an independent body. At the subsequent trial or hearing those findings could be taken under advisement.[42] While the defendant had to respond to the charges, they were not obliged to swear to anything further. The defendant had the right to silence and was under no obligation to respond to questions prior to formal arraignment. Moreover, the defendant had no obligation to plead if public infamy had not been established. Interrogations were recorded by notaries but details of depositions were not necessarily verbatim and amounted to a sum and substance of testimony.

Defendants were permitted to specify witnesses. A defendant could not be judged according to conscience but only on what was proven. Ecclesiastical courts cannot judge a matter apart from public accusations.[43] As noted, the accused submitted to formal interrogatory examination before duly appointed notaries and witnesses. The court hoped to establish guilt either by confession or evidence.[44] The presiding judge had considerable discretion in terms of deciding if witnesses were valid. Publicity was essential. In concert with that principle, the defendant had to be present when the inquisition began unless they were deliberately absent on account of contumacy. This was a critical factor in the Hus trial despite the fact his attorney tried to persuade the court that Hus' presence was not necessary and should be excused. The matter of contumacy is a central consideration in the judicial procedures in heresy cases. Contumacy carried the weight of conviction inasmuch as medieval lawyers and criminal courts considered contumacy and confession of equal weight. Defense lawyers were excluded. This is a striking difference from modern western

[42] Massimo Vallerani, *Medieval Public Justice*, translated by Sarah Ruben Blanshei (Washington: Catholic University of America Press, 2012), pp. 106, 113, and the recent study by Julien Théry, "*Fama:* l'opinion publique comme preuve judiciaire. Aperçu sur la révolution médiévale de l'inquisitoire (XIIe–XIVe siècle)," in Bruno Lemesle, ed., *La preuve en justice de l'Antique à nos jours* (Rennes: Presses universitaires de Rennes, 2003), pp. 119–147.

[43] Innocent III, decretal X 5.1.21 *Inquisitionis negotium*, in Friedberg, *Corpus iuris canonici*, vol. 2, cols. 741–742.

[44] Bernard Gui, *Practica inquisitionis heretice pravitatis*, ed., Célestin Douais (Paris: Picard, 1886), pp. 189–191, 214–215.

criminal proceedings. Witnesses might be anonymous and the depositions of unidentified testimonies were not necessarily revealed to the defendant. This also represents departure from modern court proceedings. The court did preclude known enemies of the suspect from giving testimony.[45] The judgment of the court (*sententia*) could only be passed in light of confession or if charges were sustained through due process. At this stage, the individual was considered *infamis* (infamous). Once a guilty verdict was returned, sentencing followed by means of a publicly delivered general sermon (*sermo generalis*).[46] The penalty incurred by impenitent heretics was capital punishment.[47] Bernard Gui tells us recalcitrant heretics were handed over to secular authorities for execution of sentence, which normally implied burning at the stake.[48]

The medieval appeal process and ecclesiastical court system consisted of four levels. In terms of an appellate process, one of two procedures might follow. The appellant could appeal to the next superior court or authority until reaching the Holy See, or the appeal might go directly to the pope at any time in the legal process. The right of appeal from the court to the pope was permitted if the defendant believed their rights were being violated. "Frivolous" appeals were prohibited.[49] It is not clear how or by what process an appeal might be dismissed as "frivolous." One cannot exclude subjective assessments. The Curia in the Middle Ages possessed the power of discretionary review (like modern supreme courts), meaning it could decide whether or not to hear the appeal. It is important to recognize that defendants in medieval courts had the right of appeal.

CURIAL COURT POLITICS

The Hus trial was structured around the political nature of the medieval church. The process involving Hus was political and the trial was conducted in a transnational setting (Bohemia, Italy, Germany) by a quasi-state entity. Certainly, the papacy was a state in the lands under its immediate jurisdiction, but outside the Papal States the political authority of the popes was not identical to the local state. The interplay of political and religious power, coupled with legal authority, is illuminated by the complexity of a multi-state conglomeration that emerges during the Hus trial. In application, the prevailing legal norms at the time Jan Hus appeared before the ecclesiastical courts can be better illuminated by reference to the Curial court politics in which the Hus case was heard. There are several factors including but not limited to disputes over papal

[45] Gui, *Practica*, pp. 214–215. [46] For a description of the sermon, see Gui, *Practica*, pp. 82–86.

[47] Gregory IX, X 5.7.13 *Excommunicamus*, in Friedberg, *Corpus iuris canonici*, vol. 2, cols. 787–789, and 4 Lat c.8 *De inquisitionibus*, in Norman Tanner, ed., *Decrees of the Ecumenical Councils*, vol. 1 (London: Sneed and Ward, 1990), p. 238.

[48] Gui, *Practica*, pp. 218–219.

[49] Innocent III, decretal X 2.28.53 *Pastoralis*, in Friedberg, *Corpus iuris canonici*, vol. 2, col. 432.

authority, suspicions of bribery, questionable legal *ex parte* practices, procedural irregularities, the political uses of the accusation of heresy, and systemic theological controversy, especially concerning indulgences and associated practices. Political fallout from the papal schism affected the Hus trial as three popes competed. Another issue involved Archbishop Zbyněk of Prague. In 1409, when the archbishop attempted to restrict access to the writings of John Wyclif, Hus opposed his ordinary and a protest was lodged at the Curia. Zbyněk was cited to respond to the complaint.[50] The plot thickened on Christmas Day when Pope Alexander appointed Zbyněk as his representative to deal with Wyclifite heresy via ecclesiastical censures.[51] From a legal perspective, this is problematic since the original protest citing Zbyněk to the Curia was a pending legal appeal, meaning the appellate process was now effectively subverted by papal action. An appeal was supposed to suspend lower court proceedings so that no sentence could be executed until the appellate court either dismissed the appeal or overruled the lower court. The papal bull appointed Zbyněk to oversee a situation in which he was a named defendant. Hus suspected bribery. Shortly thereafter, the attorney in charge of litigating the complaint against the archbishop was forced to admit defeat.

Empowered by the Curia, Archbishop Zbyněk excommunicated Hus. Full excommunication was lawful only after three warnings.[52] Had there been three admonitions? Records are inconclusive. Meanwhile, Zbyněk lobbied for increased Curial intervention in the Hus case. Bribery may again be suspected.[53] Since Pope Alexander had died, his successor John XXIII gave verbal instructions for the Hus matter to be handled with *auxilium brachii secularis* ("the aid of secular authority") if needed. Appeals were prohibited. Energized by these favorable developments, Zbyněk employed Curial mandates and applied the more serious censure of aggravated excommunication to Hus.[54] In the autumn of 1410, Cardinal Colonna summoned the already twice-censured Hus to the papal Curia in Bologna by means of a formal *citatio*.[55] Medieval law insisted a summons and citation of the defendant was so essential not even a pope could ignore them. If a defendant had not been properly cited, technically witnesses could not submit testimony.[56] The legal citation was

[50] Leipzig Chronicle, in Konstantin von Höfler, ed., *Geschichtschreiber der Husitischen Bewegung in Böhemen*, vol. 1 (Vienna: Hof-und Staatsdruckerei, 1856–1866), p. 11.

[51] Chronicle of the University of Prague, in *Fontes reum bohemicarum*, vol. 5, p. 570.

[52] C.17 q.4 c.21 *Quisquis inventus*, in Friedberg, *Corpus iuris canonici*, vol. 1, col. 820.

[53] Chronicle of Prague University, in *Fontes rerum bohemicarum*, vol. 5, p. 571 and Hus, *Knížky proti knězi kuchmistrovi*, in Amedeo Molnár, ed., *Magistri Iohannis Hus Opera omnia*, vol. 4 (Prague: Academia; Turnhout: Brepols, 1959), p. 321.

[54] Palacký, *Documenta*, p. 202.

[55] The Leipzig Chronicle, in Höfler, *Geschichtschreiber*, vol. 1, p. 12, and Palacký, *Documenta*, p. 734 make it October 1.

[56] X 4.17.13 *Per venerabilem*, in Friedberg, *Corpus iuris canonici*, vol. 2, cols. 714–716.

exactingly precise upon danger of the case being dismissed. Colonna's summons is problematic. In 1203, Innocent III said an excommunicate could not be a plaintiff in a church court. The question, then, has to do with the appeal against the excommunication. Such appeal could be filed on the grounds of unfairness or invalidity.[57] If the appeal was lodged on the former, the validity remained and the appellate required absolution before proceeding. If the appeal was on the basis of invalidity (because sentence was passed *after* appeal, or there were errors), this raised legal questions. It was incumbent upon the pope to absolve the appellant before hearing the case. Precedent mandated that absolution might be denied only if the judge showed the excommunication was for cause or if the excommunication came *after* an appeal had been filed. Other grounds for appeals against a writ of excommunication could arise if the authority behind the excommunication lacked proper jurisdiction for such action.[58] Absolution on these grounds was routinely granted.[59] None of this mattered because Hus refused to attend hearings at the Curia, citing personal danger. He later provided explanation for his refusal to comply.[60] Since Hus' grievance was directed at the ecclesiastical hierarchy it made no sense for those same people to preside over the appellate process. Hus expected the judges to recuse themselves from the case citing conflict of interest. Hus believed that going to Rome would invite summary execution.

Hus had legal grounds for refusing to appear at the papal court. Canon law allowed for appeal if the subject could not safely travel to the court.[61] Hus made this point fearing for his safety should he agree to travel to the papal court either at Bologna or Rome. That said, those who refused to appear could be charged with contumacy and disobedience, both serious matters in heresy cases.[62] Heresy suspects could be sentenced *in absentia*.[63] No one excommunicated for contumacy could appeal after the sentence had been issued and appeals were forbidden to heretics.[64] By the time of Hus, contumacy meant

[57] X 5.39.40 *Per tuas*, in Friedberg, *Corpus iuris canonici*, vol. 2, cols. 906–907.

[58] Raymond of Peñafort, *Summa sancti Raymundi de Peniafort* (Rome: Sumptibus Ioannis Tallini, 1603), 3.33.33, p. 413.

[59] Eugène Vernay, *Le "Liber de Excommunicatione" du Cardinal Bérenger-Frédol précédé d'une introduction historique sur l'excommunicatione et l'interdict en droit canonique, de Gratien à la fin du XIIIe siècle* (Paris: Rousseau, 1912), pp. 4–7.

[60] Initially in the *Ordo procedendi* in Václav Novotný, ed., *M. Jana Husi Korespondence a dokumenty* (Prague: Nákladem komise pro vydávání pramenů náboženského hnutí českého, 1920), pp. 228–231, and then in the 1413 Postil, in Molnár, *Magistri Iohannis Hus Opera omnia*, vol. 2, pp. 164–166.

[61] X 2.28.47 *Ex parte tua*, X 2.6.4 *Accedens* and Clem. 2.11.2 *Pastoralis*, in Friedberg, *Corpus iuris canonici*, vol. 2, cols. 428, 262, and 1152–1153.

[62] C.24 q.3 c.6 para.1 *De illicita*, in Friedberg, *Corpus iuris canonici*, vol. 1, cols. 990–991.

[63] Sext. 5.2.7 *Quum contumacia*, in Friedberg, *Corpus iuris canonici*, vol. 2, col. 1071.

[64] C.2 q.6 c.41 *Si quis appellat* para.11, and Sext. 5.2.18 *Ut inquisitionis*, in Friedberg, *Corpus iuris canonici*, vol. 1, col. 482, and vol. 2, col. 1077.

disobedience.[65] Those judged contumacious were subject to the full legal force of the medieval church. Hus sent three legal representatives to the Curia to argue to the court why he could not appear and simultaneously filed an appeal against the summons.[66] Lawyers, however, can only ask for exemption from appearance by the client; they cannot answer charges on behalf of the defendant. In criminal matters (i.e., heresy), representation was disallowed, and the law required the accused to appear in person.[67] Procedurally, defendants in criminal cases were required to attend the preliminary hearing and subsequent trial.[68]

Hus' legal team submitted a second appeal to the examining magistrate of the court questioning the partiality of the judge and framing a motion asking for *iudicis recusatio* – the magistrate to be recused from the case.[69] A partial judge should not legally preside over a case.[70] The appeal was lodged with John XXIII on the grounds of irregular proceedings.[71] The Curia did not respond, and by February 1411, Cardinal Colonna found Hus in contempt of court and excommunicated him for contumacy and for failure to appear.[72] Hus claimed the excommunication was secured through the malicious *ex parte* efforts of Michael de Causis.[73] Canon law considered the action by Colonna as malfeasance and illegal, as the second appeal should have been heard before further action on the initial summons took place. Papal rulings forbade the condemnation of anyone who had appealed to the pope.[74] A legal rebuttal arguing Colonna's action was valid might be advanced on the grounds that Hus' appeal had no judicial basis for effecting a legal suspension in the application of a sentence because the appeal was rooted in a response to a previous writ of excommunication. Medieval canon law recognizes that excommunication creates an exception-to-the-rule clause.[75] However, there is no record of the obligatory *canonica monitione* preceding the verdict which calls into question its validity.[76] Colonna's action was both controversial and problematic. The procedure can be criticized in three ways. First, Colonna made

[65] Pierre Torquebiau, "Contumacia, Contumax," in Raoul Naz, ed., *Dictionnaire de droit canonique*, vol. 4 (Paris: Librairie Letouzey et Ané, 1935–1965), cols. 507–525.

[66] *Ordo procedendi*, p. 228.

[67] X 5.1.15 *Veniens*, C.2 q.6 c.39 para.1 *Si autem* and C.2 q.6 c.40 *Si quando*, in Friedberg, *Corpus iuris canonici*, vol. 2, col. 737, and vol. 1, cols. 480–481.

[68] 4 Lat c.8 *De inquisitionibus*, in Tanner, *Decrees*, vol. 1, p. 238 and X 5.7.13 *Excommunicamus*, in Friedberg, *Corpus iuris canonici*, vol. 2, cols. 787–789.

[69] *Ordo procedendi*, p. 228.

[70] C.3 q.5 c.15 *Quia suspecti*, in Friedberg, *Corpus iuris canonici*, vol. 1, cols. 518–519.

[71] Novotný, *M. Jana Husi Korespondence*, pp. 88–89.

[72] Palacký, *Documenta*, p. 202.

[73] S. Harrison Thomson, ed., *Tractatus de ecclesia* (Boulder: University of Colorado Press, 1956), p. 231.

[74] Pope Gregory VII, "Dictatus papae," in Erich Caspar, ed., *Das Register des Gregors VII* (Berlin: Wiedmann, 1920), pp. 201–208.

[75] X 2.28.53 *Pastoralis*, in Friedberg, *Corpus iuris canonici*, vol. 2, col. 432.

[76] X 2.28.26 *Reprehensibilis*, in Friedberg, *Corpus iuris canonici*, vol. 2, col. 418.

no ruling on the reasons invoked by Hus for failing to appear. Second, the sentence was ratified by a judge who was himself the subject of an appeal. Third, allegations of corruption, based on judicial bias and suspicion of bribery, remained at issue.[77] Since no explanation was given for rejecting Hus' petition to avoid appearing, an appeal might well have been lodged suspending legal proceedings, resulting in the matter being referred to an appellate court based on the medieval equivalent of a writ of mandamus.[78] At the same time, Hus' enemies successfully had Hus' attorney disqualified by filing a motion amounting to a complaint of heresy against the lawyer.

Early in 1412, Cardinal Zabarella reviewed the case and wrote a dissenting opinion on the procedures, making an interlocutory judgment which substantially agrees with Hus' appeal. He admitted previously excluded evidence, set a new deadline for submission of evidence, and, perhaps shockingly for the prosecution, concluded that Colonna's decision not to allow a hearing of Hus' attorneys was inappropriate. Therefore, the excommunicating of Hus was unjustified because there was an appeal pending. These findings rested on solid legal precedent. Canon law permitted admission of all relevant evidence and specified that essential defenses could not be excluded.[79] Politics intruded when Pope John ordered the findings of the Hus inquiry be submitted to another cardinal, thereby removing it from Zabarella.[80] The possibility of lobbying by Hus' enemies cannot be excluded. Shortly thereafter, an *ex parte* petition reached the pope asking that the papal auditor assigned to the Hus case be replaced. That motion was also granted.

During these legal maneuverings, Pope John XXIII announced the sale of indulgences in Prague.[81] The chief motivation for the fund-raiser was to finance a crusade against one of the pope's political opponents. Hus objected, attacking the idea that money could produce "complete acquittal from the guilt and penalty" of sin.[82] Hus demanded to know how the pope presumed to usurp the place of God and grant plenary pardons. Priests and bishops had no business taking up physical weapons. The weapons of the spirit were preferred.[83] The two swords should not be confused. Now that John XXIII had acted improperly, Hus submitted he should not be obeyed. Arguing against the right and power of the pope to act in such manner,

[77] Jiří Kejř, *Husitský pravník: M. Jan z Jesenice* (Prague: ČSAV, 1965), pp. 48–49.

[78] X 1.29.27 para.5 *Super quaestionum articulis*, in Friedberg, *Corpus iuris canonici*, vol. 2, col. 172.

[79] Clem. 2.1.2 *Dispendiosam prorogationem*, in Friedberg, *Corpus iuris canonici*, vol. 2, col. 1143 and Clem. 5.11.2 *Saepe contingit*, in Friedberg, *Corpus iuris canonici*, vol. 2, col. 1200.

[80] *Ordo procedendi*, p. 229.

[81] Anon., *Historia et monumenta Ioannis Hus atque Hieronymi Pragensis*, vol. 1 (Nürnberg: Montanus and Neuberus, 1558, 1715), pp. 213–215.

[82] Anon., *Historia et monumenta*, vol. 1, pp. 216, 217, 223, 224, 225, 226, 228, 229, 234.

[83] Anon., *Historia et monumenta*, vol. 1, p. 218.

Hus declared it was "not only false but blasphemous." Therefore, it was incumbent to withstand the pope, to disobey and remain faithful to God.[84] The papal crusade bull was contrary to the law of God and contravened canon law. The indulgences controversy cannot be separated from the legal affairs of Jan Hus. His position deprived him of the king's support and raised the personal ire of John XXIII.

In the summer of 1412, Cardinal Peter degli Stephaneschi took charge of the Hus case. Handing down a decisive judgment, he affirmed Colonna's anathema against Hus.[85] He ignored the legally defensible findings of Zabarella. Once more, suspicion was voiced that the action of Stephaneschi may have been motivated by bribery.[86] Stephaneschi then issued a writ of major excommunication against Hus, meaning the full implementation of the legal and ecclesiastical sanction – the *aggravatio* – was now in place. This was the fourth excommunication issued against Hus. This constituted the *sententia*, or the formal court judgment. Rebutting the sentence, Hus' former lawyer argued that the sentence was invalid, suggesting the anathema was contrary to canon law. This assertion was based on the premise that without a specific admonition (*monitio canonica*) to the person in question, before witnesses, the anathema had no legal standing.[87] The anathema mentioned *monitio canonica* but there is no record of it having been issued separately in advance of the anathema itself.[88] Specific agendas in the Curial court system occasionally produced procedural irregularities and this brief summary draws attention to the structural relationship between law and politics which affected the Hus case. By the time the case reached Constance, didactic and destructive motives prevailed.

CONCLUSION

The language and dramaturgy of the court proceedings indicate how heresy trials may have unfolded. Loud voices shout in courtrooms patrolled by armed men. Officials engage in the painstaking examination of witnesses. Accusers hurl charges against the defendant despite orders for silence to be kept. There are threats about burning the defendant. Uproar and disorder convulse the process and exasperated judges call for order. The defendant appears in chains to face charges and counter-charges. Laughter, mockery, and references to law predominate. During one poignant moment, we read of the humane gesture of a brave man shaking the hand of the defendant and consoling

[84] Anon., *Historia et monumenta*, vol. 1, pp. 222, 223, 224, 232, 234.

[85] Palacký, *Documenta*, pp. 461–464.

[86] Jan Jesenice, "Repetitio," in Anon., *Historia et monumenta*, vol. 1, p. 418.

[87] Jesenice, *Repetitio*, in Anon., *Historia et monumenta*, vol. 1, pp. 408–419. Sext. 5.11.9 *Constitutionem felicis*, in Friedberg, *Corpus iuris canonici*, vol. 2, cols. 1101–1102. See also X 5.39.48 *Sacro approbante*, and X 2.28.26 *Reprehensibilis*, in Friedberg, *Corpus iuris canonici*, vol. 2, cols. 909–910 and 418–419.

[88] Palacký, *Documenta*, p. 407.

him as the latter is led from the court chambers. Bombastic speeches punctuate the trial and there is overt pressure to conclude the hearings, return a verdict of guilt, and be done with the troublesome priest. With no advocate, there was little chance Hus could persuade the judges of his innocence. Bishops thunder against the prisoner before an elaborate ceremony of defrocking with its ritual stripping and shaming. The convict is chained to the stake with wood piled to his chin, wearing a paper miter depicting demons. Then the fire, and the heretic dies to the sound of a song.[89]

The final court proceedings, especially those convened at Constance, were a means of publicly legitimizing the church's condemnation of Jan Hus. The court convened with the intention of destroying Hus whose sinister ideas were judged worthy of extermination. The procedures of the court authenticated the accusation of heresy. This is what Michael de Causis ardently longed for. The five-year legal ordeal for Hus was a political show trial. In medieval law, heresy was considered a *crimen mere ecclesiasticum*, which meant it was an offense reserved for judgment by the Church.[90] The right of the church to judge heresy could not be intruded upon even if secular legislation ruled otherwise.[91] Heresy trials by definition are examples of law in the service of an idea. The political uses are legion. Heresy trials intentionally sought to eliminate a particular type of enemy, and that enemy was described as those who threatened the identity and stability of the medieval church. The application of power and persuasion enter the scene and Hus' appearances in court amount to a trial of didactic and destructive agendas wherein issues of truth are at stake. The nature of the inquisitorial *ordo* shaped the perception of truth; its presentation and effect by the rules which enabled certain truths to advance and constrained other truths. In general, the Hus trial was not transacted at Constance outside of the rule of law even though it was convulsed by the political considerations noted above. What politicizes the Hus trial is the use of heresy, which must be understood in relation to the prevailing configuration of ecclesiastical power. The importance of the Hus

[89] Three main narrative sources written by men reliably placed at Constance during the Hus trial include Mladoňovice, *Relatio* in *Fontes rerum bohemicarum*, vol. 8, pp. 72–120, Thomas Martin Buck, ed., *Chronik des Konstanzer Konzils 1414–1418 von Ulrich Richental* (Ostfildern: Jan Thorbecke, 2010), pp. 60–66, and the *Passio etc secundum Iohannem Barbatum, rusticum quadratum*, in *Fontes rerum bohemicarum*, vol. 8, pp. 14–24. There is a translation of this last source with commentary. Thomas A. Fudge, "Jan Hus at Calvary: The Text of an Early Fifteenth-Century *Passio*," *Journal of Moravian History*, Vol. 11 (2011), pp. 45–81. There are two other sources, namely a Czech translation of the *Relatio* which adds to the original in places and there are additional useful remarks in this so-called *Passio* in *Fontes rerum bohemicarum*, vol. 8, pp. 121–149 and a Czech *Acta* in the Freiburg Codex, in *Fontes rerum bohemicarum*, vol. 8, pp. 247–318. The observations rely on all five sources. On the wider context of the handshake see Thomas A. Fudge, *Jan Hus Between Time and Eternity: Reconsidering a Medieval Heretic* (Lanham: Lexington Books, 2016), pp. 117–140.

[90] Sext. 5.2.18 *Ut inquisitionis*, in Friedberg, *Corpus iuris canonici*, vol. 2, col. 1077.

[91] *Glos. ord.* to Sext. 5.2.18.

trial was not just the verdict against the defendant but the broad social and ecclesiastical consequences which took its foundation from the court proceedings, that is, a complete condemnation of all things Wyclifite and Hussite and in this sense served as a policy-making principle which was then properly authenticated.

The Hus trial has continued to be politicized in the last few decades in the service of political correctness, ecumenical hopes, and in a tendency to control history rather than participate in it.[92] Allegations of judicial murder, betrayal, and procedural ineptitude are political reactions based more on modern commitments than conclusions drawn from medieval legal history and procedural law. Destructive and didactic political trials, like Hus', revolve around considerations of power, authority, and truth claims. In all of it, Jan Hus was not a passive victim. He was rather an active and willing participant in the lessons being taught by the legal proceedings. The church had to destroy Hus, because he was a political enemy who was a direct political subject of the medieval church. Hus agreed to be destroyed because he believed that his allegiance was not to the church in the first instance but rather to God. There was nothing passive about Hus' destruction. He rushed to the stake without complaint as though going to a feast.[93] Some who witnessed the culmination of the court case wrote that Hus had taught the faithful how to live and how to die.[94] As a destructive trial, the shaping of collective memory occurred in ways the court did not anticipate and which it could not control. As a didactic trial, perhaps the lessons of the defendant ultimately prevailed.

[92] I have elaborated some of this in two closely related essays. Thomas A. Fudge, "Whose Hus? Confronting the Challenges of Interpreting Jan Hus after 600 Years," in Jakoub Smrčka and Zdeněk Vybíral, eds., Jan Hus 1415 a 600 let poté, [Husitský tabor, supplementum 4] (Tábor: Husitské Museum v Táboře, 2015), pp. 265–290 and Fudge, Jan Hus Between Time and Eternity, pp. 225–47.

[93] Aeneas Sylvius, "Historia Bohemica," in Dana Martínková, ed., *Eneae Silvii, Historia Bohemica* (Prague: Koniasch Latin Press, 1998), chapter 35, p. 100.

[94] Fudge, "Jan Hus at Calvary," p. 72.

5

The French Revolutionary Trials

Laurence H. Winnie

Political trials have long been associated with the French Revolution. The French Revolution has often been thought of as the originator of many features of the modern political trial – especially revolutionary purge trials and broadly applied "revolutionary justice." In histories of the French Revolution, scholars emphasizing the French Revolution as the beginning, or at least the harbinger, of modernity, have often overplayed its claims as the exemplar, or incubator, of the contemporary. But in the matter of political trials and revolutionary justice, the abundance of characteristics is there. The theme of this chapter is that the French Revolution remains rich in examples of political trials; that they each show different emphases on the three dimensions of power, performance, and procedure; that these trials had powerful effects in France at the time, and on French history; and that, subsequently, whether famous or infamous, political trials were assumed to be inseparable from the modern revolutionary state. This has been an identification set in the public imagination, with a strong historical foundation (this latter is subject to debate, of course). And thus the political trials of the French Revolution have affected all of us who live in modern polities. In this way, as in many others, the French Revolution remains alive and vital.

Indeed, it should be said that political trials are, historically, sometimes hard to separate from the Revolution itself. The two have naturally been blended together for us in the historical imagination, as they often are in historical narratives. This is not hard to explain. In historical accounts, political trials occurred around important turning points of the Revolution; in the public imagination and in historical narratives, political trials brought together so much. They linked abstract political theory and the hard finality of the guillotine; the eternal ideals of the Revolution and the sudden break with life; the ideals of the Revolution for the Rights of Man and violence against those who were declared enemies of mankind. Placing political trials and punishment at the center of their thinking about the French Revolution was a strategy that unites two such unlike characters as the novelist Charles Dickens and the Robespierrist historian Albert Mathiez.[1] Condemnation of the Revolution was often undertaken using the trials as one of the central arguments to show how the Revolution went terribly wrong. Political trials are a prime piece of evidence for critics of the Revolution. For François Furet, the harsh justice of the Revolution was inherent in its beginnings and a template for justice in all revolutions.[2] Thus, it prefigured the justice in twentieth-century communist countries where, additionally, revolutionary justice was explicitly shaped by admiration for the French Revolution. The defense of political trials during the Revolution – almost always excused as a regrettable necessity – was equally important to supporters of the Revolution. For Mathiez, there were almost no examples of countries facing foreign war and civil war that did not have recourse to "summary and expedited justice" to deal with these sorts of threats.[3] In particular, repression of the countryside was for him a direct (and seemingly natural) response to the dangers of revolt.[4] For Albert Soboul, the trial and execution of the king "pointed the way to a new political order."[5] Wherever the historian looks, political trials are at the center of the discussion about the Revolution, for or against, in the past or in the present day. No one could escape commenting on them.

The effect and the importance of political trials in the French Revolution as it actually took place are more interesting and more fundamental. We may think of trials in the Schmittian sense that they reveal who is on which side, and show who is with the state and who is against it. This was an immensely important role for political trials to play. Occurring at critical moments during the French Revolution, political trials helped determine its direction. Trials meant decisions about guilt and innocence. They decided who would be future political actors and who would not. They decided who would survive and who would not. And most important, they established which political group would succeed and which would fail. This creation of political winners and losers had its most prominent role to play when trials decided definitive end of regimes or shaped the terms of their legitimacy. Trials were used as a wedge and a weapon – as a wedge by identifying those who were accused of sedition, of disloyalty to the Revolution, and who were forced, almost always as a group, on

[1] Charles Dickens, *A Tale of Two Cities* (Oxford: Oxford University Press, 1988). Originally published 1859, relying heavily on Thomas Carlyle, *The French Revolution: A History* (London: J. Fraser, 1837); Paul Schlicke, ed., *The Oxford Reader's Companion to Dickens* (Oxford: Oxford University Press, 1999), pp. 67, 549; Albert Mathiez, *La Révolution française*, 3 vols. (Paris: Librairie Armand Colin, 1978). Originally published 1922–1927.

[2] François Furet, *La Révolution de Turgot à Jules Ferry 1770–1880* (Paris: Hachette, 1988), p. 147.

[3] Mathiez, *La Révolution française*, vol. 2, p. 229.

[4] Mathiez, *La Révolution française*, vol. 2, p. 237.

[5] Albert Soboul, *A Short History of the French Revolution, 1789–1799*, translated by Geoffrey Symcox (Berkeley: University of California Press, 1977), p. 89. Originally published as *La Révolution française* (Paris: Presses Universitaires de France, 1965).

the defensive; and as a weapon where the penalty was death. The day after punishment was meted out the political landscape was changed. In general, then, political trials were both a shaper and a product of the Revolution, and the kinds of trials tell us a great deal about the nature of the French Revolution. This is because the nature of law, procedure, and trials were vitally affected by it.

THE NATURE OF TRIALS AND OF LAW

Revolutions are by definition periods in which the nature of legitimacy – what it is, who has it, and what kind of regime a state will have – is in flux. There are arguably no other moments of political uncertainty quite like it. The French Revolution, in its earliest years, changed the legal jurisdictions of the courts, abolished earlier courts of the Old Regime (thirteen *parlements* and four *conseils souverains* and the *seigneurial*, urban, and ecclesiastical courts under them), and rested the new, more uniform code of law on a new, enlightened basis, quite distinct from what was understood and practiced by the older courts for many centuries.[6] Under revolutions, then – that is, under this particular stress – legal institutions and the law are, for at least some time, at sea in social and political uncertainty. Revolution introduced novelty into the institutional roots of law, as well as into the procedures, practices, and assumptions needed to fill out these institutions. In the French Revolution the abolished forms of law were replaced via a series of fundamental changes. For example, in October 1792, the law was promulgated that Frenchmen were to choose their judges from among their fellow citizens. The professional judiciary was pushed aside. The new initiates would hardly have brought knowledge of formal and informal procedures into the courtroom. Here was a fertile field in which political trials might, and did, flourish. Then, in March 1793, the *tribunal criminel extraordinaire*, known as the *tribunal révolutionnaire*, was created to convict enemies of the Revolution not by ten votes of twelve jury members but by a simple majority of its handpicked, activist membership.[7]

[6] In the case of the French Revolution, this took place beginning with the law reorganizing judicial jurisdictions, August 16, 1790. Courts of appeal were defined by the law of November 27, 1790. The final parts of the new penal code and criminal code were voted September 26, 1791, and the first (jury) courts opened in Paris in February 1792. Edmond Seligman, *La Justice en France pendant la Révolution,* vol. 1: *1789–1792* (Paris: Plon-Nourrit, 1901), pp. 303, 450–451. January 24, 1791, was the last day of justice under the Old Regime in Paris (Seligman, *La Justice en France pendant la Révolution*, vol. 1, p. 351). Most of the elected new judges were chosen between fall 1790 and early 1791. The October 1792 law represented the drift away from the first wave of judicial reforms of 1791 under the Legislative Assembly. See Edmond Seligman, *La Justice en France pendant la Révolution,* vol. 2: *1792–1793* (Paris: Plon-Nourrit, 1913), pp. 352–362.

[7] Seligman, *La Justice en France pendant la Révolution*, vol. 2, pp. 360–361; 518–519.

Further, as the state was altered after some period of uncertainty, into first a constitutional monarchy (the Constitution of 1791) and then a republic (1792), which was in turn suspended in favor of an emergency government under a committee system of the Constitutional Convention, the central power (first of the monarch, then a monarch with a legislative assembly, then the Convention) was rethought and reshaped. As under the monarchies beginning with Louis XIV, the central power could overrule regional judicial bodies, so the refashioning of the state and its replacement of the old system of justice – one of the central goals of enlightened revolution – was not experienced as a smooth transition. This was true from the earliest moment of the Revolution. And the refashioning was significant: as the conservative historian Augustin Cochin once put it, once the forms of the Old Regime were no longer followed, the Revolution had begun – for the forms *were* the Old Regime.[8] The new regime took more than a decade, to 1804, with Napoleon's Code Civil and Code Criminel, to signal long-term legal and judicial stability.

Throughout, with adjustments, civil and criminal trials continued. They remained a part of public experience during the Revolution, just as they had before it – a source of gossip, entertainment, outrage, and prurient gratification. The well-documented explosion of newspapers during the Revolution went hand in hand with publishing trial accounts.[9] This amplified the didactic power of political trials. The issues and personalities seemed to reassure – or dismay – by showing how much human nature remained the same. This familiarity and reassurance arising from trials had terrible consequences in political trials. Under the stresses of internal opposition to the Revolution and invasion or the threat of war, political trials, no matter how unjust, could provide reassurance that there was respect for rules of evidence, procedure, examination of witnesses, and the proper application of law and just verdicts, against those who were enemies of the Revolution – when in fact these trials might be hollow. An execution with a trial and a guilty verdict was preferred by public power to one without them. Moreover, the execution of a political opponent could be broadcast via the publicity of a trial. It was an implicit threat to all allied with or sympathetic to the guilty party. In the desperate times of revolution, trials could be used to cast disagreement as disloyalty, opposition as sedition.

Once launched, the French Revolution, then, showed a double effect on political trials as it struggled to survive. The first concerned the nature of the state. The kind of state and the nature of its sovereignty were shifting at the same time there was an upsurge of new tribunals, committees, and agents to carry out

[8] Augustin Cochin, *Les sociétés de pensée et la Révolution en Bretagne (1788–1789)*, vol. 1: *Histoire analytique* (Paris: Plon, 1925), pp. 111–112.

[9] Carla Hesse, *Publishing and Cultural Politics in Revolutionary Paris, 1789–1810* (Berkeley: University of California Press, 1991), p. 176; Claude Bellanger et al., eds., *Histoire générale de la presse française*, vol. 1: *Des origins à 1814* (Paris: Presses Universitaires de France, 1969).

its policies. The instability of constitutional forms, the radicalization of its political discourse as groups contended for power within its legislative center, the fear of disunity, and the loss of control of the government over parts of the country made political trials more likely. Second, external threats to the government's continued existence made the resort to emergency powers or procedures even more tempting. Sometimes the latter were called for by popular pressure. This is how the Revolution deserved the reputation for occasionally capitulating to the justice of the crowd or the demands aired in political clubs of different kinds. These outside actors could be implicitly or even explicitly appealed to during political trials. Sometimes they demanded trials of whomever they conceived to be enemies of the body politic. Thus, as one can see, there were few anchors to avoid drifting into political trials.

FROM THRONE TO TRIAL

On December 11, 1792, Louis XVI appeared at the Convention in the first of only two personal appearances for his trial. He stood at the Convention bar, at the Manège, in Paris, the remodeled royal riding school, and responded to questions put to him by Bertrand Barère. Charles Valazé, as he read the charges, refused even to look at the accused. Louis looked well and calm despite several months in prison. His transportation from the Temple Prison to the Manège was carefully choreographed to ensure security in a hostile and volatile Paris. The charges were a long list, but amounted to treason against the French state. He had no lawyer present and his request for one at the end of the session was ignored.

Louis and the Throne had arrived at this moment through an immensely tangled route. Born in 1754, succeeded to the throne in 1774, he had convoked the Estates General by decree on August 8, 1788, to meet at Versailles. Representatives from the three Estates, the Clergy, the Nobility, and the Third Estate, were to establish reforms to set the powerful Bourbon throne back on the road to fiscal solvency. Suggestions via the *cahiers de doléances* for reform from all over the French kingdom would establish a basis, at least, for changes in taxation and the tax exemptions, which were part of the Old Regime social fabric. The course of events quickly veered out of his and his ministers' control, where it was supposed to remain. On June 17, 1789, the Third Estate declared itself to be the National Assembly and implored representatives to the other two estates to join them. They agreed not to disband, despite Louis's direct order to do so. In the end Louis relented and the restructuring of the French state, under the National Assembly, had begun.

From the beginning almost all of Louis's court was opposed to these changes. Many left the country. The National Assembly fundamentally reshaped the French state, abolishing the privileges of the nobility (and eventually nobility altogether), establishing law according to the principles of the Rights of Man, and legal equality. Beginning with the Civil

Constitution of the Clergy in July 1790, the Catholic Church in France was reformed (Church property had been nationalized in November 1789). These transformative measures alienated many of the clergy and nobility and they voted with their feet, either to exile abroad or to retirement back on their estates. The religious issue especially provoked deep splits in French society and laid the groundwork for violent opposition to the Revolution. Louis would watch and participate in these changes. But he was less in command of them than he was an unhappy hostage and then a prisoner of them. By and large Louis was kept under the suspicious eye of the French people, its new national governments, the Municipality of Paris, and the city's revolutionary sections and political clubs.

The Constituent Assembly finished work on the new Constitution of 1791 in August and September, and on September 14, 1791, Louis swore the oath to the Constitution as a constitutional monarch. But the experiment to hold onto the reformist gains of the early years of the Revolution and to incorporate the still-esteemed monarchy into a new parliamentary government did not last long. Among the many factors that played in this failure was, significantly, Louis's unwillingness to walk down this path in good faith. Surrounded by a rump of the court, the prisoner Louis was clearly under the influence of a wife and an entourage who would never accept this new type of monarchy, or government, nor the kind of society it implied or promised. Louis in fact played a double game, maintaining secret correspondence with friends and family (his two brothers, the Comte de Provence and the Comte d'Artois, had emigrated), who were working to overthrow the despised Revolution and bring about a return of the Old Regime. In June, 1791, Louis and his family tried to escape France and cross the border to join with family, friends, and supporters. They were stopped at Varennes. Caught and returned, he always denied that it was anything more than a trip. From that moment on, even those who had great stakes in maintaining the Constitution could never trust him, and they, at best, pretended that his flight was not serious. The truth was that Louis would have to be watched as a prisoner, one who, whatever he professed, meant to get away. The outlook for this marriage of the past and the present was bleak even before it began. Louis functioned as constitutional king for several months. The push to break with the Constitution of 1791 and to call a constitutional convention came from political action of the street.

By August, the Prussians had joined the Austrians against the French, and the Legislative Assembly had declared "the Nation in danger." The Brunswick Manifesto from the allies threatening destruction if harm came to the king was known in Paris by early August. Fear and anxiety and a heavy influx of patriots from other regions (*fédérés*) helped form an armed march on the Tuileries on August 10, 1792, the second one that summer. A bloody battle between the insurrectionaries and the Swiss guards (despite Louis's orders to surrender) ended with the king and his family escaping to the Manège and the protection of the Legislative Assembly. Surrounded by the angry attackers, the Assembly then declared The King of the French (according to the Constitution) deposed, and sent the royal family to be imprisoned in the tower of the Temple prison. The Parisian *journée* of August 10 had shown the power of the street and the sections; popular violence had re-entered the Revolution.

On August 10, with the end of the monarchy, the Legislative Assembly was forced to call for elections to a constitutional convention. The writing of the Constitution became only one of its tasks. Soon after its convocation on September 20, 1792, the Convention, as it came to be known, was faced with impending foreign invasions and the destruction of the Revolution. The leadership of the Convention was contested between two groups, the Girondins and the Mountain. The division was not between Left and Right (immortal political terms born during the National Assembly phase of the Revolution) but between two revolutionary constellations of delegates with differing views of how the revolutionary future should look. Historians' attempts to show the Montagnard and Girondin division as socially, financially, or class related have not held up. Pure political opinion, and tactics, distinguished them. The Girondins were in favor of finding a stopping point for the Revolution by the spring of 1793. For the Girondins, the revolutionary future should follow their more restrained view of the power of popular societies, the street, and restrictions on trade; for the Mountain, the Revolution must sever its ties with its enemies of the past and live up to what they developed as its ideals. But the distinctions between the two were as much oppositional as ideational. The two groups clashed for leadership. The majority of delegates, seated not on the benches above, but on the floor, was known as the Plain. The Girondins and the Mountain strove to win over this large, less mobilized, Plain. The ongoing struggle for power and control of the Convention, and consequently for the future of the Revolution, was a dominant factor in the trial of the now-deposed king of the French.

THE TRIAL OF THE KING

One of the greatest debates, important in its own right, was the most decisive overt issue about the trial: whether or not the king could be tried, what that meant for the future of the Revolution, and what penalty the king might have to pay.

Power

Except for Mountain and Girondin leadership, there was great hesitation among the majority of delegates about a trial of the king. Yet the fate of the king was an essential part of moving forward with the Revolution. Would France have a king or not? Could it be truly said that it had a Revolution and still had a king? Would the evidence show (and the majority were fearful that it clearly would show) that the king betrayed the Revolution, violated his oath as the executive power under the

Constitution of 1791? The Constitution of 1791 was explicit about his inviolability for his acts as king of the French. And there had been no explicit constitution before this, though there were agreements with the king. Nowhere were there provisions for the king being deposed, nor any for his being tried. Who had the power to try him? What should his punishment be? Should he suffer the penalty of death? For radicals, the killing of a king would show the true meaning of Revolution, serve as a symbol and a warning to the foreign invaders and the still-hopeful opponents of the Revolution that the Revolution had now truly been undertaken. These were the greater issues present as this political trial opened. The behavior of most deputies shows that they remained deeply ambivalent and reluctant to go on record in favor of trying and executing the king. It was the moment many members of the Convention had hoped for but more had dreaded.

Evidence there was in abundance against the king. A strongbox had been found in the walls of the Tuileries Palace on November 20, 1792. Its contents ended all doubts about Louis's duplicity concerning the Revolution and his constitutional oath. Louis maintained a secret correspondence with his family and the court across the border. He clearly referred to the dreaded Revolution and hoped for its termination – and his rescue. His embarrassed return to the capital after the flight to Varennes had not taught him to remain careful in hiding his views. He was, after all, the king under the Constitution. He was most upset over the Civil Constitution of the Clergy, the reorganization of the Catholic Church in France, which had been subsequently condemned by the Pope. He kept an illegal, nonjuring priest as his confessor, reason enough to mistrust him, for here, in a crucially important part of his life, he truly felt the Revolution and its lawfully established Church were wholly wrong. The documents showed that Louis, at heart a believer in the tradition of the absolute monarch, and raised in that belief, would never be content as a constitutionally established one.

Procedure

Still, the Convention agonized over whether Louis could be tried at all.

The constitutional safeguards had to be put aside in order to try Louis. A way was found. The Convention proceeded because, after a Girondin-dominated committee produced an ineffective report, it accepted, by vote, deputy Jean-Baptiste Mailhe's committee report. This recommended that Louis's constitutional immunity could be removed from him in trying him for his acts as king because immunity was originally a gift of the people and could be revoked by their representatives; and that the representative body of the people should decide by vote his guilt or innocence after a trial in the Convention; and, as the people's representatives, the Convention could determine his punishment and see it was carried out.[10] Mailhe's report

[10] David P. Jordan, *The King's Trial: Louis XVI vs. the French Revolution*, New edition (Berkeley: University of California Press, 2004), pp. 64–65, 101–102.

concluded that legal precedent need not be followed. Only the will of the nation limited the Convention in this matter. With the majority of members trained in the law, this was not accepted with wholehearted approval, but rather with a general reluctant assent.

Performance

Louis was brought to the Convention on December 11, 1792, to be formally charged. As the primary historian of the trial has noted, Louis shrewdly denied recognizing the pieces of evidence presented to him, including his own signature. This should have forced the prosecution to prove the provenance of each piece of evidence, according to the Criminal Code of 1791. In the end the tactic was futile, as the trial simply ignored this requirement of the law. In fact, as the historian David P. Jordan noted:

> Louis had not seen the accusation prior to his appearance in the Convention, he had no lawyer to advise him, and many of the charges were so complex that they defied a simple "yes" or "no" response. Louis accepted the offer of a legal dual and fought to save his life. He insisted that he could not be held responsible for any actions prior to his acceptance of the constitution, for, he maintained, he was not answerable to the nation before he became its constitutional monarch. Even as constitutional monarch, Louis said, he could not be prosecuted for vetoing decrees. The constitution gave him the veto . . . When he refused to recognize his signature or documents in his own hand, which infuriated the deputies, he was adhering to the legal guarantees of due process set out in the Criminal Code of 1791. His papers had been illegally seized and it was up to his accusers to prove that they were the king's papers, written in the king's hand . . . Louis was doing no more than honoring their commitment to a trial and protecting himself by insisting on a strict reading of the Criminal Code.[11]

The Municipality of Paris, a product of the radical sections, was the custodian of the prisoner, and the Jacobin leadership had, since the beginning of October, called for justice against the tyrant in the form of death. The Convention's trial took place in a Paris in the hands of those in search of revenge for the evils of the Old Regime, and also, finally, tired of the king and his opposition in a time of political and military crisis. The vast majority of the Convention felt Louis was guilty and must answer for his guilt. But the Girondins, especially, were reluctant to push for his execution. They understood that the trial energized the more radical forces outside the Convention, and they resisted, again and again, the Convention responding to these demands. The Mountain, on the other hand, saw this as their way to power and their responsiveness to these demands as the heart and meaning of the Revolution.

After Louis departed, the Convention returned to its deliberations. Marat, from the Mountain, declared that there was no need to adhere to the chicaneries of the Criminal Code. Pétion, of the Girondins, proposed Louis be given legal

[11] Jordan, *The King's Trial*, pp. 112–113.

counsel. The Mountain wanted Louis declared guilty and executed without a long, tedious trial; the Girondins resisted and demanded a proper trial for the king whose Old Regime judiciary was seen as arbitrary. The Convention agreed to allow Louis counsel and François-Denis Tronchet, Raymond DeSèze, and Guillaume-Chrétien Lamoignon de Malesherbes agreed to defend Louis. The defense was scheduled for December 26. The day-long hearing changed no minds. Louis and his lawyers would not have sufficient time for his defense – only two weeks. They were given no alternative.

DeSèze read Louis's *plaidoyer* for two hours on the morning of December 26. The claim was made that he had done no wrong, by any acts, either in the early stages of the Revolution or as constitutional king. The legal defense was solid, Louis's presence and his own few words were impressive, and yet this changed few minds. The arguments raged within the Convention on how to proceed. The Girondins endorsed the suggestion, first made in August, that the fate of the king be the subject of a referendum of all the people. They thought this would lead to clemency, and perhaps to peace with the allies (who, in actuality, were at best indifferent to Louis's fate). The Girondins wanted to lift so momentous a decision from the Convention. But further they wanted support from the moderate countryside, to help them remove the Jacobins or at least weaken the power they enjoyed in radical Paris. The Mountain countered that a referendum meant delay and opened the possibility that the king might not be punished with the only appropriate penalty and one they had urged from the beginning: death. As Robespierre had famously put it, if the king were ultimately found not guilty of betraying the Revolution, and not guilty of responsibility for shedding blood on August 10, then the Revolution must be guilty; and what then? The Mountain fought furiously for this either/or outcome.

Beginning January 14, 1793, the next procedural steps were debated. The Convention would vote, as a roll-call, the questions in the following order: (1) Is Louis guilty? (yes or no); (2) Whatever your decision, shall it be submitted to the ratification of the people? (yes or no); (3) What punishment shall Louis suffer? To the first, 745 deputies produced 693 yes votes and various other responses, but no negative votes were registered. The 717 present on January 15 for the second question voted 424 against and 283 for an appeal to the people. (Interestingly, in light of subsequent events, deputies from regions that would join in revolt against the revolutionary government voted 42 to 5 against appeal.) The Mountain had triumphed, and Louis was certainly doomed. The vote for death took an agonizing two days, from January 16 to 17. The deputies knew they would be forced to vote, by name, for the penalty; two amendments were proposed: one by Mailhe, suggesting postponement of any punishment; the other of the Girondin Jean-Denis Lanjuinais requested a 2/3 vote on so important a matter (a break with all precedents). Neither garnered many votes, and both amendments were from deputies convinced of Louis's guilt, but who wanted to avoid taking the last step. Of 721 deputies, 361 voted for death without conditions, while others voted with reservations or conditions of various kinds. At the end of a thirty-six-hour session, Louis Capet was sentenced by the Convention. His lawyers, present throughout the proceeding, then read a letter from Louis requesting an appeal to the people, but here was part of the Mountain's argument only too clearly confirmed: everything concerning the king had to be considered again and again, with no end in sight. Paris and the Convention, in a crisis of fear and dread, were in no mood to consider this.

> What mattered most was that the Convention had been through its greatest crisis and was still intact. The Jacobins were, it is true, now the dominant faction, but their ascension was incomplete in January ... And their victory in the king's trial was not the triumph of truth over falsehood, or rather political consistency over political flabbiness. The Jacobins triumphed, and Louis died, because they were able to articulate what the majority of the deputies felt yet could not express, and because their opponents, the Girondins, had bungled the trial. The struggle of the factions is inseparable from the king's trial and it is probably the most significant place to study the fight for supremacy in the Convention.[12]

Louis was notified by his lawyers and not given the extended time requested for him to prepare. Under heavy military guard, the execution was carried out in the Place de la Revolution at 10:22 on a cold morning of January 21, 1793. No part of France rose up at the news, nor did it seem to have much effect on foreign capitals, as many had feared or predicted.

THE PURGE OF THE GIRONDINS

The king had died, yet the struggle between the Girondins and the Montagnards, which had preceded, and propelled, the political trial of the king, continued. The struggle was for control of the Convention, and for direction of the Revolution in France. The articulation by the Mountain of the kind of revolution it was to be, and of the kind of governance that this meant, gave them a great advantage over the Girondins. The Girondins had been loosely defined as deputies from the provinces, especially in the west and south, who believed in a moderate revolution, and they represented the concerns, and even the fears, of the countryside that the Revolution would grow more and more radical in the control of urban activists and radical politicians. Robespierre and Marat had been vigorously attacked by the Girondin leadership in the debates of September and October 1792. At base the differences settled into clashing definitions of "The People," for whom, rhetorically, revolution had been made, and in whose name it continued to be carried out, as well as different notions of the nature of the rule of law.[13] These

[12] Jordan, *The King's Trial*, p. 204.

[13] Michael J. Sydenham, *The Girondins* (London: The University of London, 1961), pp. 209–211.

differences were present much earlier, in the Constituent Assembly, between Jacques Pierre Brissot de Warville of the Girondins and Robespierre of the Mountain; they would continue with lethal result.

Power

In the early months of 1793, after the execution of the king, the Girondins were tense and then fearful, first for their political future and then their safety. With the Allies pressing at the borders, the April treason of General Dumouriez (a former Girondin minister) at the northern frontier, the outbreak of rebellion in the west and central west against conscription, and the murder of local officials of the republic, the Revolution was under attack. As early as March 19, the Convention decreed that captured rebels should be killed.[14] By April, charges were more and more easily thrown about by the Montagnards impugning the Girondins' loyalty to the Revolution and to France. On April 1, a decree ended parliamentary immunity for any deputies suspected of being enemies of liberty, equality, and republican government.[15]

The sources of these beliefs, fears, and accusations were not only in the Convention itself. The Parisian sections were active centers of radical revolutionary politics, anxious that the Revolution not be sold out to monarchists or hindered by moderates. The Parisian sections and the municipal government were important extrajudicial actors, who so often play a role in political trials. Their well-timed interventions appear in retrospect to have been essential to moving events, as when the Convention's zeal for arrests and trials seemed lagging. Engaging a small proportion of citizens – males over twenty-one (each of the forty-eight sections of Paris had about 3,000 voters, but those engaged in these assemblies of direct democracy were few in number; for example, fewer than one in five voted for mayor) – the sections were the lifeblood of Parisians who could devote most of their day to political meetings. They were vitally concerned with provisioning (starvation and hoarding, or rumors of them, were rife, for they were thought to be the means of destroying the Revolution by literally starving "The People"). The Parisian sections and the National Guard played a role in the August 10, 1792, attack on the Tuileries that effectively ended monarchy and the Constitution of 1791. Their intervention had effectively created the Convention. The September massacres in the Parisian prisons, officially blamed on no one at all, were without a doubt known to the sections and the city government. The sections backed the Mountain, and they had on these two previous occasions flooded the floor of the Convention, mixing with deputies,

[14] David Andress, *The Terror: Civil War in the French Revolution* (London: Little, Brown, 2005), p. 162.

[15] Sydenham, *The Girondins*, p. 20.

fraternizing or threatening them. The threat of intervention or violence grew as the news from abroad worsened. Numerous circulars drawn up by sections of Paris named Girondin deputies as counterrevolutionaries. By the end of May the Revolutionary Committee of the sections decided to act, frustrated at the course of events.

Procedure

This began an unusual and extended form of political trial, with great consequences. On June 2, 1793, National Guard troops sent by the Central Revolutionary Committee of Paris (representing the sections in charge of the municipal government they had taken over on May 31) ringed the Convention – by then meeting in the Tuileries – with armed National Guardsmen and demanded the arrest of twenty-four deputies named the previous evening (earlier some had volunteered to step down). Bertrand Barère of the Committee of Public Safety asked that they resign voluntarily and suggested the Convention march outside to deliberate among the people. Amid protests from deputies, they marched out with the president of the Convention, Marie-Jean Hérault de Séchelles. They processed out to an almost silent corps of troops. General Hanriot, upon being refused his request to hand over the deputies, signaled his artillery to prepare to fire and his soldiers drew their muskets and swords. The Convention marched back into the hall (with a crowd of Parisians) and a majority voted the arrest of twenty-nine of its own deputies requested by the committee (the record of the vote is unclear). Some Girondins had already escaped; most were kept under lax arrest and some then fled to the provinces. The conspiracies of which they were charged expanded with time and debate. In June and July, the Convention finally charged them with creating divisions within the republic, and plots, both federalist and monarchist, as far back as July, 1791. A second list of twenty-nine more Girondin deputies for arrest was drawn up on July 28.

Performance

The formal *acte d'accusation* was not approved by the Convention until October 3, 1793. (There was then discussion of adding seventy-five more Girondins to the list, but this was dropped.) The twenty-one Girondins who had been rounded up and imprisoned then faced their trial on October 24. The Committee of General Security reported to the jurors that they were guilty of many crimes, but generally were counterrevolutionaries and agents of foreign powers. The accused were allowed to speak, and their eloquent and effective defense required an abrupt change:

> Alarmed at the inroads the defendants were making into the paper-thin case against them, the Committee of Public Safety (on Robespierre's proposal) obtained a change in the rules of the Revolutionary Tribunal from the Convention on October 29. Prosecutor

Fouquier-Tinville was now empowered to end a trial after three days by securing the jury's agreement that their "consciences had been sufficiently enlightened" as to the facts.[16]

They were guillotined together on October 31.

The escaped Girondins, now fugitives from a death sentence, fled to the west but found little of the support and refuge that they sought in the provinces. They tried to rally opinion for their view of the Revolution, but this generally met with little response because, as one observer put it, the Girondins preaching about the importance of the rule of law and rule by the capable competed, with little success, against the more potent political arguments from the Jacobins that the Revolution was centered on popular sovereignty. Though Lyons and Caens were in revolt against the Convention, most of France was indifferent or hostile to the Girondins' views and their fate.[17]

They moved from place to place, hunted by the authorities. Only Jean-Baptiste Louvet de Couvrai, who had escaped to Switzerland, survived. Alone, or several together, they were captured and guillotined. Some preferred suicide, the last of which were in June, 1794, by François Buzot and Jérôme Pétion, near Bordeaux. The Girondin fugitives left letters and *mémoires* (later published) decrying the turn of the Revolution that had produced this tyrannical Montagnard republic and detailed their suffering in flight, usually far from family and friends. Their view of the Revolution and their attempt to rally support to it, and their attempt to maintain control of the Convention and to destroy the Mountain, had collapsed. The Girondins left behind a trail of ink and blood.

A TALE OF TWO TRIALS

There were many political trials in the French Revolution, but this is an extraordinary example of arrests and eventual imprisonments and trials (and finally executions) as a purge of a representative body. Political purges of parliamentary bodies had of course occurred before, most notably in the English Revolution. Yet the trial of the Girondins has several poignant differences. First, Parisians had used the threat of violence to force an elected national body to purge itself. The sections and the Revolutionary Tribunal of the City, a de facto government of the radical sections, had called in the citizen's National Guard to enforce its political demands on the Convention. The Convention had feared some such action for some time. The direct democracy practiced in the sections meant that Paris sections, in a city swollen with immigrants, produced some of the most

[16] Andress, *The Terror*, p. 229; quoting David P. Jordan, "The Robespierre Problem," in Colin Haydon and William Doyle, eds., *Robespierre* (Cambridge: Cambridge University Press, 1999), pp. 25–26.

[17] Bette W. Oliver, *Orphans on the Earth: Girondin Fugitives from the Terror, 1793–1794* (Lanham: Lexington Books, 2009), p. 108.

radical politics, and a politics that demanded to be heard. Even the Mountain was pushed to act by the sections, not always willingly, for here was a force that was not always under control and could not always be directed to the political benefit of the Montagnards. Yet it must be assuaged where it could not be fulfilled, and Robespierre was one of the most skilled suitors in this delicate courtship. It should also be mentioned that the extra-parliamentary political clubs also produced resolutions and printed circulars and had an important role to play. On June 2, armed urban radical politics determined that there was to be a trial, not even the Convention's debate. The Convention itself bent to this force and voted the arrest of its own members, to be handed over to the city government, as they had agreed to hand over the king after August 10, 1792, for trial by the Convention. The king had been a prisoner of the city. Now, so too was the Convention itself. Every member had to be on guard after what happened.

What did it mean? The direct, declamatory democracy of the sections of Paris had broken the representativeness of the Convention. It gave up its central claim to legitimacy: once any member was removed for his opinions, his actions, or his affiliations, the Convention no longer represented the nation. Here was a crucial watershed. Protests from many cities and clubs at this change came too late. A precedent had been set. Once purged, the Convention was both more powerful and weaker. This acquiescence to a political trial was fatal to the Girondins but also fatal to the Convention's power. It was seen as a rump parliamentary body, ruling with, and never free from, the politics of the sections, the clubs, the press, and the street.[18] It had to contend with arguments from outside its walls. Its politics, however, were more aligned. The trial made the Convention more powerful, in that now after the trial of the Girondins, there were fewer barriers to the state fighting its enemies, internal and external. This is what the sections wanted. The trial was in one sense a development of the state in this direction of more absolute power. The trial and the pursuit of the Girondins heightened the sense of danger and the need for unity, as the Girondins had been found to be, by legal procedure, guilty as enemies within even the Convention itself. There were probably more. The state must look for enemies everywhere.

But where was, or who represented, the state? This could not be so easily answered after the trial of the Girondins as before. The capitulation of the Convention to the demand for the Girondins' arrest and trial meant further weakening of the rule of law. The content of the Revolution was thus redefined for all to see who did not see it on August 10. Law no longer defined or embodied the Revolution. The Revolution existed beyond law and procedure. Nor was the Revolution wholly within a representative body reflecting the will of the nation. After the purge of the Girondins the Convention was forced to compete for power with a Revolution not so clearly defined as before. It was now competing with a vision.

[18] Furet, *La Révolution de Turgot à Jules Ferry*, p. 135.

THE TERROR: JUSTICE FOR ENEMIES

The arrest and trial of the king in late 1792 and early 1793 and the arrest and trial of the Girondins in the second half of 1793 took place at the same time that the foundation was being laid for what became known as the Terror. Of all the uses of political trials, the Terror stands as the most vividly horrifying, and for some the most characteristic form of political trials during the French Revolution. Not a trial of a former sovereign monarch, nor a political purge of the legislative representatives of the people, the Terror was a long-lasting, numberless, group of modified trials and executions of those opposed to the Revolution, and those thought to be opposed to the Revolution, taking place, theoretically, everywhere in the country, but centered in Paris. The Terror included spectacular large-scale killings, such as the *noyades* (mass drownings) in Nantes, and the endless train of tumbrels to the guillotine lasting until the fall of Robespierre in July 1794 – its last victims its perpetrators.

Power

The power and finality of the republic's justice were there to see, by her enemies and anyone contemplating noncooperation (or nonobedience to Paris). The state would decide who were its enemies, bring them to light, and show them the terrible consequences for their guilt – guilt to be found in even kinds of people and in presumed opinions, as we have seen.

The trial records have been examined since Thermidor. About 17,000 persons were condemned to death, with a few escaping. This is not a large number, if one considers a single Napoleonic battle equaling or surpassing this.[19] Death at the guillotine was the death of the king and the queen and of almost all of the political opponents of the Mountain, and finally of Robespierre and Saint-Just of the Committee of Public Safety itself; the guillotine has become the symbol of the cruelties and divisiveness of the French Revolution. But however spectacular these deaths have remained in truth and in the imagination, they constituted only a tiny part of revolutionary justice. Capital verdicts were declared for only three and a half percent of all political prisoners. Here the extent of arrests and imprisonments, and, in smaller numbers, trials, becomes apparent. Most arrested under the Terror languished in makeshift prisons, holding a total of likely 500,000 prisoners in the period of the Terror.[20] Some awaited execution, of course. Many more simply waited. Detention served the state, and

[19] Donald Greer, *The Incidence of the Terror during the French Revolution: A Statistical Interpretation* (Gloucester: Peter Smith, 1966), pp. 25–29. The Law of Suspects of September 17, 1793, allowed the incarceration of "those suspected" of a variety of illegal or disloyal activities – a sweeping power given to the state.

[20] Colin Lucas, *The Structure of the Terror: The Example of Javogues and the Loire* (Oxford: Oxford University Press, 1973), pp. 26–31.

subsequent penalties might be fines, banishment, deportation, the galleys, or the pillory. Ironically, this justice system savored more of the Old Regime than the Enlightenment.

Nor were the patterns of this justice uniform over the country, or over time. Five departments (of eighty-seven total) accounted for 70 percent of all death sentences, and the next eight departments brought this proportion up to 89 percent. Death sentences were increasing over time in Paris because the Convention demanded, in the Terror's later months, to have more trials in the capital, and in the areas in revolt against the government (the Vendée, Loire-Inférieure, Maine-et-Loire, and the Rhône).[21] Six departments had no reported death sentences at all, and thirty-one more had from one to ten. Local habits and sympathetic officials and juries no doubt played a role in these statistics. But clearly many parts of France were quiescent or cooperative in contrast to those in open rebellion. Trials that led to imprisonment and executions occurred where there was resistance. The effect of these trials was complex. Where there was little resistance, there seemed no contagion of anger against the revolutionary government and its actions. Fear and a willingness to believe there were dangers to the republic must have played a part; so too, genuine belief in the Revolution and in the need for its defense. In the long term, on the other hand, the republic and republicanism were identified with the Terror and the guillotine, its most potent symbol. It would take the French republican movement almost a century to overcome this.

The Terror was not only unevenly spread throughout space in France; it also evolved through time. The historian Patrice Gueniffey has divided it into three phases. The first began on March 9, 1793, with the creation of the *Tribunal révolutionnaire* of Paris; the second with the law of September 17, 1793, the expanded Law of Suspects; and the third with the 22 Prairial II (June 10, 1794) law to the fall of Robespierre. During the first phase, there were about fifty convictions per month, 26 percent of which were capital; in the second, there were 300 convictions per month, 61 percent of which ended in a capital sentence; and in the third phase, there were over 700 per month, 80 percent of which were capital sentences.[22] This shows, in terms of trials, a great acceleration in convictions, a demand for justice swift and strong, exhibited by this vigorous rate of punishment for the guilty. Shortcuts were demanded and trials were sped up in the name of justice. Paris also demanded more trials be moved to the capital to ensure swift and severe justice; the provinces lacked sufficient vigor and conviction.

Yet the Terror went far beyond these patterns of legal retribution, justified, reassuringly, by the resort to and the use of juridical processes. For the Terror claimed more lives than the 17,000 capital cases, but likely consumed

[21] Lucas, *The Structure of the Terror*, pp. 145–147.

[22] Patrice Gueniffey, *La Politique de la Terreur: Essai sur la violence révolutionnaire, 1789–1794* (Paris: Fayard, 2000), p. 240.

200,000 to 300,000 lives in all (of a population of twenty-eight million). Since the Terror was used to subordinate the departments in revolt, and to maintain order in the other regions of France, inevitably the threat of imprisonment or violence affected a great many citizens. The Terror was also extrajudicial violence against the enemies of the regime, a kind of performance, a killing without trials, or via quasi-trials, a permitted killing based upon assumption or suspicion. The *colonnes infernales* of General Louis-Marie Turreau from the end of the summer of 1793 to the spring of 1794, when the Vendée was subject to scorched earth military destruction, was the period of the greatest killing, though not of the most trials.[23] Extrajudicial killing, the violence of the crowd, was as old as the Revolution. The first months of the Revolution included the taking of the Bastille in July 1789, and it sometimes relied on the street sense of justice against oppression at critical junctures, as we have seen, by action of the sections against the Girondins. The Revolution was never wholly separated from this justice of the crowd. But with the Terror this form of violence was channeled, or understood, for politically useful purposes by those who controlled the government. By declaring whole regions, or types of people (émigrés, nonjuring priests, nobles), guilty and worthy of imprisonment or destruction, the Convention passed judgment, as it were, on its enemies. And it welcomed and expected cooperation from all its loyal citizens.

Procedure

Very early in the Revolution laws were passed that defined the criminality in ways that became characteristic of the Terror. Almost all of them were definitions of who was to be considered an enemy of the state, and, eventually, of the Revolution, or those who were proved to be, or thought to be, associated with them. The law creating a Revolutionary Tribunal in Paris was passed by the Legislative Assembly on March 10, 1793. In the fall this was reorganized to speed up the arrest and trial of the accused, and modified on October 29, and then, finally the law of June 10, 1794, which "suppressed legal counsel for the accused and defense witnesses – phantoms, as Saint-Just remarked – ... made death the unique punishment for crimes within the Tribunal's competence and at the same time forbade the prosecutor to dismiss cases for lack of evidence."[24] Revolutionary tribunals were set up in other French cities on the Parisian model. But most of the victims of the political trials in the Terror were tried by civil or military commissions set up by the Convention in areas of war or resistance. The military commissions, from which there were no appeals, consisted of five judges, officers or soldiers, a clerk, and a prosecutor. The civil commissions operated on the same terms,

[23] Gueniffey, *La Politique de la Terreur*, pp. 240–241.

[24] Greer, *The Incidence of the Terror during the French Revolution*, p. 20.

with five civilian judges. These commissions tended to expand the types of infractions they considered, from armed action against the state to general counterrevolutionary activity. The criminal tribunals of the *départments* were also involved, but they were more scrupulous and were less trusted by Paris to act quickly against those accused of endangering the republic and the Revolution.[25] Extraordinary times called for special, extraordinary justice. Extraordinary justice called for special procedures for the judicial performances.

These commissions, or special tribunals, military and civilian, enforced the laws passed beginning in March, 1793, that defined further and without nuance the nature of criminal behavior. Most victims of trials in the Terror were convicted of sedition, always a capital crime. Sedition could be expressed as speech, cries in public, or writings. Anyone caught in a region of armed conflict against rebels who was captured with arms or monarchist insignia was to be executed within twenty-four hours. But the initial definition of what was criminal was expanded under the Legislative Assembly and then the Convention. The first laws were passed against refractory clergy, i.e., those who did not swear to uphold the Civil Constitution of the Clergy, passed in July, 1790. In the summer of 1792, nonjuring priests were banished; in the spring of 1793, any who returned or who remained and were caught were declared émigrés and liable to capital punishment. In April, 1794, merely concealing nonjuring clergy was made punishable by death. But there was more. The law of March 19, 1793, made death the mandatory penalty for sedition and was aimed especially against priests, former nobles, foreigners present in the country illegally, and their agents and servants, and called for the confiscation of all property of anyone found guilty under this law; hence trials under this law struck at categories of people, not acts; and it struck against entire families, not individuals. The law on émigrés was capacious and generally declared all those who had emigrated before July 1, 1789, and not returned before May 1792, as banished and their property was to be confiscated. Return meant death for them and their accomplices. Intentions, and even passivity, not acts, were all that was required for the justice of the Terror to work.[26] The Jacobin Louis-Antoine Saint-Just famously declared (and the Convention unanimously agreed) that counterrevolution in his time worked in secret, hid its true intentions, and took on the appearance of patriotism. Thus, in dealing with conspirators one must not judge by words or appearances. Instead one must judge these enemies of free government "by what honesty counsels [us] to do today" ("par ce que la probité conseille de faire aujourd'hui").[27] The Convention

[25] Greer, *The Incidence of the Terror during the French Revolution*, pp. 20–24.

[26] Gueniffey, *La Politique de la Terreur*, pp. 34–35.

[27] Marcel Reinhard, Georges Lefebvre, and Marc Bouloiseau, eds., *Archives Parlementaires, Premiere serie*, vol. 86 (Paris: Centre National de la Recherche Scientifique, 1965), pp. 434–442,

then passed the law of 23 Ventôse II (March 13, 1794), making traitors of anyone guilty of corrupting the spirit of the people, of the Revolution, all those who help them, and those who speak against the republican form of government. In sum, the Convention, via the Montagnards, had moved into broad ideas of criminality. This kind of law came to define these kinds of persons as not criminals in the normal sense, but declared them to be outside normal legal boundaries; they were, instead, *hors-la-loi* ("outside the law").[28] These "enemies of the human race" deserved not to live, and procedural justice for them was an act of civic generosity.

The most famous and important of the penalties was death on the guillotine. This was the usual punishment for sedition and for much of the Terror the penalty was in the ideal, and often in practice, to be carried out within twenty-four hours. There were supposed to be no appeals. This was an ideal repeated often in the revolutionary discourse, and one need only note that the special *représentants en mission* or *comissions*'s ideal was to utilize these swift (and often group) executions expressly to impress everyone with the firmness of revolutionary justice.

Performance

The didactic reach of these trials was very long. Terror included more than trials. The Terror was additionally a means of control over everyone, an expression of the Revolution not limited by the encumbrances of legality or legitimacy, and thus it was ideally a pure expression of sovereign power. It included the destruction of the Vendean revolt; from the summer of 1793 to the spring of 1794, large-scale murder, rape, and destruction of the land was inflicted on that unhappy region by the armies of the republic. These acts, as were the political trials, were known to everyone. And so thanks as well to the indifference or apathy of the populace of the French Republic, the Convention and its committees were able to use violence, and, just as effectively, the threat of violence, to maintain control of the nation and hence to have an effect on the direction and the nature of the Revolution. Exactly what the state was, what defined the content of the Revolution, and who were its enemies became a set of issues that grew more lethal as they became more vague. But no one could escape the threat.

The political trials that resulted from these principles of the revolutionary state and revolutionary justice can easily be imagined. But some mention should be made of the meaning and purpose of the Terror as a whole, of which these thousands of political trials (in short or elaborate form) are only a part.

and noted by Morris Slavin, *The Hébertistes to the Guillotine: Anatomy of a "Conspiracy" in Revolutionary France* (Baton Rouge: Louisiana State University Press, 1994), p. 129.

[28] Edelstein has linked this to the notion of natural right theories of justice. Dan Edelstein, *The Terror of Natural Right: Republicanism, the Cult of Nature and the French Revolution* (Chicago: University of Chicago Press, 2009).

The political trials were not all of the Terror. The Terror, rather, was a means of both fighting the enemies of the revolutionary government and instilling obedience and loyalty – and fear – in those who saw and knew about these measures for "public safety" and security in the midst of war and internal opposition. The Terror was a means of political decision-making and social control. Its trials were used to keep many others, not involved in the trial, obedient. The historian Colin Lucas noted in his study of a *commission* to the areas in need of enforcement that these were most successful when most "revolutionary": "For it was essential that revolutionary justice should be swift and implacable and, above all, that it should be seen to be so. This could not possibly be achieved by affixing verbose verdicts on a few isolated individuals to the Liberty Trees."[29]

Thus, the way the Terror was conducted reinforced the threat. The elemental fact was that, with law released from its anchor in orderly forms and procedures, trials could be used against anyone. They were used against both political opponents in the Convention (the Hébertistes and the Dantonists), but more especially against individuals and entire populations, men, women, and children, who were in cities (Lyon or Toulon) or whole regions (the Vendée) declared in revolt ("Federalism"). The Terror was the state in vengeance, openly crushing those who were its overt opponents, and pursuing its clandestine enemies, desperate to hide. This is the lesson these trials were meant to teach, again and again.

The idea of the Terror being an interval of time that contained these forms of official violence is a legacy of Thermidorians, anxious to distance themselves from recent events. But the Terror was never used as a term in this way during the event itself. As a recent work on the use of the term has indicated, "terror" was used in revolutionary discourse as a means to express both the state of mind produced in the hearts of loyal French citizens by the actions or words of their enemies and then, reflexively, as an ideal state to be produced in the enemies of the Revolution by the bold and violent acts of the government. "Terror" is what you want your enemies to feel, as you have felt terrified by them.[30] The performance, in trials especially, was essential for this result.

The pattern of the intensity of the Terror reveals the nature of its use and usefulness. Beginning with the exculpatory accounts of Jean-Baptiste Carrier or Bertrand Barère and many others, produced as soon as the fall of Robespierre, the Terror was claimed to be a response to the threats faced by the republic. It has been claimed that the greatest intensity of the Terror was due to its being a remedy undertaken only to save the Revolution and to save France in a time of crisis. However, the period of the *Grande Terreur*, from September 5, 1793, to 9 Thermidor II (July 27, 1794), when the laws and trials were at their most

[29] Lucas, *The Structure of the Terror*, pp. 254–255.

[30] Annie Jourdan, "Les discours de la terreur à l'époque révolutionnaire (1776–1798): Étude comparative sur une notion ambiguë," *French Historical Studies*, Vol. 36 (2013), pp. 51–81.

arbitrary and at the height of their production of capital convictions, came *after* the threats from allied armies or the revolt of the Vendée (which in the early part of this period was basically suppressed). The Terror used violence, and more importantly, the threat of violence, to warn and to control – for, as Gueniffey notes about the Terror: "s'il s'agit de punir pour réparer, il s'agit encore de punir pour prévenir."[31] This arbitrary universal "justice" had its purposes. Though clearly not a system of justice, as noted by its early opponents in the Legislative Assembly and then the Convention, the Terror never let go of its identification with notions of rightful punishments meted out to the deserving guilty. The Terror, as it became more centralized under the Committee of Public Safety in Paris, more and more bent the arc of justice until it could finally touch the other end. Here, procedure, the rigor of punishment, at the local level and carried out by the armies of the republic or by special *commissions* or *représentants en mission*, was key. For then the image of the state vigorously identifying and rooting out all of the guilty could appear to mean that all those who were punished were guilty. Note as well that each type of political trial described here was important to the other: the trial of the king; the arrest of the Girondins; and then the Terror. Yet none overtly referred to the others. Political trials here did not set clearly defined precedents. Political trials were like other important events of the Revolution: they served as portals through which one stepped into another political world, another part of the Revolution, where new things were possible – belying Georges Clemenceau's declaration near the end of the nineteenth century that the Revolution was all one thing ("un bloc").

CONCLUSION

The reality of political trials during the French Revolution was, as this chapter has noted, both more interesting and more fundamental than the ideological characterizations made of them. The French Revolution was not the creator of the high art of political trials. Nor did political trials "create" the Revolution. One indicator is that the three types of political trials described here have been described in very different ways. This is because they were, each kind, distinctively different. The trial of the king took place in the open, with great publicity, with members of the Convention obviously reluctant to misstep and even to face the choices that the trial would present them. The trial of the Girondins was undertaken under much different circumstances, initiated, again, by forces outside the Convention. And last, the Terror: while its trials maintained the care and detail of judicial forms, and though it became emblematic of the most absolute power of the revolutionary state, it actually began as a less centralized response to the failure rather than the success of the Revolution in restricted areas of the country. They were meant to coerce and

[31] Gueniffey, *La Politique de la Terreur*, p. 129.

frighten. These three political trials were decisive to the course of the Revolution in ways that are now obvious. They forced decisions at crucial moments, even as many actors may have recoiled from making a decision, and they gave the decision more or less a legal appearance. And the reader will note by now how each of these three examples from the French Revolution incorporate some of each of the three typologies of political trials identified in this volume.[32] The trial of the king, the trial of the Girondins, and the trials of the Terror were at once decisive, and predominantly destructive – and destructive with the higher purpose of building a better world. And in each case the revolutionary state wished to follow the principle of parsimony: that in all it did, it would not waste an opportunity to show its supporters and its enemies its actions; the didactic axis was also touched at almost every opportunity – for the Revolution had nothing to hide and much to live up to.

[32] See Jens Meierhenrich and Devin O. Pendas, "'The Justice of My Cause Is Clear, But There's Politics to Fear': Political Trials in Theory and History," in this volume.

6

The Soviet Union, the Nuremberg Trials, and the Politics of the Postwar Moment

Francine Hirsch

On its seventieth anniversary, the Nuremberg moment is being invoked to pursue a wide range of political ends throughout the world. In the West, the International Military Tribunal (IMT) of 1945–1946 continues to serve as a principal model for transitional justice – providing a precedent for international tribunals and for the International Criminal Court.[1] Politicians, journalists, and scholars refer to "the Nuremberg model" to describe how the courtroom can be used to foster peaceful political transitions and promote human rights. Meanwhile, in the Russia of Vladimir Putin, the Nuremberg trials – or at least invocations of the Nuremberg verdict – have played quite a different role, serving as a bastion of Russian patriotism. A 2009 Russian presidential commission, which declared it illegal to compare Stalinism with Nazism or to present an unfavorable interpretation of the Soviet Union's role in World War II, cited as its rationale "the findings of Nuremberg."[2] The Russian government withdrew the proposed

Support for this research was generously provided by the American Council of Learned Societies (ACLS), the International Research and Exchanges Board (IREX), and the Office for the Vice Chancellor for Research and Graduate Education at the University of Wisconsin-Madison.

[1] To be sure, in the West different governments have used the Nuremberg model to suit their own aims. The U.S. government continues to reject the International Criminal Court on the grounds that it may "engage in politically motivated prosecutions," but it had no problem invoking Nuremberg to argue for a special tribunal to try Saddam Hussein. See David Crossland, "International Criminal Court: Nuremberg Trials a Tough Act to Follow," *Der Spiegel*, November 23, 2005. On the "Nuremberg model," see Ruti G. Teitel, "Transitional Justice Genealogy," *Harvard Human Rights Journal*, Vol. 16 (2003), pp. 69–94.

[2] The Presidential Commission of the Russian Federation to Counter Attempts to Falsify History to the Detriment of Russia's Interests was set up by decree by former Russian president Dmitry Medvedev on May 15, 2009. Ukaz Prezidenta Rossiiskoi Federatsii ot May 15, 2009 N 549, "O Komissii pri Prezidente Rossiiskoi Federatsii po protivodeistviiu popytkam fal'sifikatsii istorii v ushcherb interesam Rossii." Also Proekt: Federal'nyi zakon "O protivodeistvii reabilitatsii v novykh nezavisimykh gosudarstvakh na territorii byvshego Soiuza SSR natsizma, natsistskikh prestupnikov i ikh posobnikov," available at http://regnum.ru/news/1153517.html. For an

law in 2012 and dissolved the presidential commission (at least partly in response to international pressure). But the law was soon revived. In April 2014, it went through, making it a punishable criminal offense "to deny facts which had been recognized by the International Military Tribunal" or to "approve of the crimes which this tribunal judged and to spread intentionally false information about the Soviet Union's activities during the Second World War."[3]

These current uses of "Nuremberg" are connected to present-day politics. Since 1991, the United States and Western Europe, no longer competing with the Soviet Union to define the form and scope of international legal institutions and legislation, have attempted to claim the language of human rights for themselves.[4] Meanwhile, as a number of post-Soviet successor states and their Eastern European neighbors turned westward and embraced European institutions (including NATO and the European Union), Russia bristled. Russia's assertions about the Nuremberg verdict mark an attempt to prevent reevaluations of the past at home or in the near abroad (i.e., Ukraine) that might further erode Russia's international position or prestige. At the same time, for Russian leaders to hearken back to the Nuremberg verdict is also to express nostalgia for an era when Russia was a great power, responsible for the defeat of the Nazis.[5] It holds up Russia's role as a "fighter of fascism" – rhetoric that Putin has skillfully manipulated in his current propaganda campaign against Ukraine.[6]

While the verdict, lessons, and model of Nuremberg have been called out to serve different ends, "Nuremberg" itself has remained more or less static: a set piece, utilized as needed in new narratives about the past. Meanwhile, the partial opening of the former Soviet archives and the release of documents about the role of the Soviets in the IMT have made it possible to reevaluate the on-the-ground and international politics of the IMT.[7] This chapter argues that bringing the Soviet Union – Soviet goals, motives, and perspectives – into

excellent analysis of the commission and its invocation of Nuremberg, see Nikolai Koposov, "Istoriia i pravosudie: Kak istoricheskaia politika pytaetsiia prikryt'siia Niurnbergom," Polit.ru, April 26, 2010, available at www.polit.ru/article/2010/04/26/koposov.

[3] Cited and analyzed in Peter Solomon, "Putin's Criminal Law: An Instrument of Authoritarian Rule," work-in-progress. The new law is Article 354-1 of the Russian Criminal Code. Also Ivan Kurilla, "The Implications of Russia's Law against the 'Rehabilitation of Nazism'," *Ponars Eurasia*, Policy Memo 331, August 2014, available at www.ponarseurasia.org/memo/201408_Kurilla.

[4] Thomas M. Franck, "Are Human Rights Universal?" *Foreign Affairs*, Vol. 80 (2001), pp. 191–204.

[5] See Irina B-Granik, "Rossii garantirovano proshloe: prezident sozdal komissiiu po bor'be s fal'sifikatsiei istorii," *Kommersant*, Vol. 88 (2009).

[6] Kurilla observes that "Russian state television has labeled the Ukrainian national movement as 'Nazis,' providing the pretext for seizing Crimea, supporting further interference in Ukraine, and justifying defense of the local population." Kurilla, "The Implications of Russia's Law against the 'Rehabilitation of Nazism'."

[7] Such a reexamination is first getting underway in Russia. See, for example, Natalia S. Lebedeva, ed., *SSSR i Niurnbergskii protsess. Neizvestnye i maloizvestnye stranitsy istorii: Sbornik dokumentov* (Moscow: Mezhdunarodnyi fond Demokratiia, 2012) and Natalia S. Lebedeva, Valeriy

our narrative of Nuremberg illuminates how the IMT was grounded in the politics of the postwar period and also helps provide a more comprehensive vision of the politics of the postwar development of the modern idea of human rights. It argues that Nuremberg was one of the first fronts of the Cold War, and that the Nuremberg model of transitional justice was, for better and for worse, a product of Cold War relations. The four victors that occupied Germany – the United States, the USSR, Britain, and France – were also the sole members of the prosecution of the IMT. The leaders of these countries saw the IMT as a forum not just to bring the Nazis to justice but also to transform the international order. And while all wanted to foster the transition from troubled past to hopeful future, the Western powers and the USSR (in particular) subscribed to different narratives of the past – and held different visions for the future.

Of course, the statement that Nuremberg was a "political trial" is a cliché. International law is in all cases political and war crimes tribunals are political events (which does not mean that such trials cannot also be legitimate and principled tools of international relations). This acknowledgment should not signal the end of the discussion, but can instead push us to make a thoughtful investigation of the politics that were at work. What did it mean, in practical terms, that the IMT was a political trial? What were the specific politics involved? And how did those politics influence the form, outcome, and ultimate impact of the trials? In the case of Nuremberg it is especially essential to look at the power dynamics among the multiple states making up the prosecution – and to examine how those power dynamics functioned not just in the courtroom (in the performative realm) but also behind the scenes.

Here in the West we are most familiar with American and British critiques of the IMT from the time of the trials. These critiques include the wholesale dismissal of the trials as victors' justice as well as the argument that the ex post facto creation of international law (which had precedent in the Soviet Union but not in the Western democracies) was an abomination.[8] These critiques also include the assertion that the IMT was corrupted from the start because the USSR, known for its kangaroo courts, was one of the countries of the prosecution.[9] Meanwhile, even as the Western powers fretted about the role that the Soviets would have in the trials, the Soviets had their own urgent concerns about the politics of the IMT. How would the Soviet Union, its leaders and its people, fare in the narratives about the past that were

I. Ishchenko, and I. Iu. Korshunov, eds., *Niurnbergskii protsess: Uroki istorii: Materialy mezhdunarodnoi nauchnoi konferentsii* (Moscow: Institut vseobshchei istorii RAN, 2007).

[8] The classic account of victors' justice is Montgomery Belgion, *Victors' Justice* (Hinsdale: Henry Regnery Company, 1949). For an indictment of political trials, see Judith N. Shklar, *Legalism: Law, Morals, and Political Trials* (Cambridge: Harvard University Press, 1986).

[9] In a number of recent accounts Soviet participation is held up as Nuremberg's main flaw. See, for example, Gary Jonathan Bass, *Stay the Hand of Vengeance: The Politics of War Crimes Tribunals* (Princeton: Princeton University Press, 2000) and Christopher J. Dodd, *Letters from Nuremberg: My Father's Narrative of a Quest for Justice* (New York: Three Rivers Press, 2007).

produced for, and in the course of, the trials? Would Soviet officials and experts be able to use the international forum of Nuremberg to the USSR's advantage? These particular issues became a major preoccupation, even an obsession, for Soviet leaders and for the members of the Soviet Union's secret Moscow-based Commission for Directing the Work of the Soviet Representatives in the International Tribunal (the Nuremberg Commission for short) – taking up thousands of pages of secret correspondence in the Soviet archives.[10]

What would it do to our understanding of Nuremberg if we gave serious consideration to Soviet concerns about the politics of the IMT? How might new materials from the former Soviet archives change our view of the trials and of the postwar moment in general? The rest of this chapter will attempt to answer these questions. The first part will look at the politics of history, focusing on the rival efforts of the USSR and the other countries of the prosecution to use the IMT to establish particular narratives about the causes and course of World War II. It will demonstrate how the Soviets attempted, with mixed results, to keep information that could hurt the USSR out of the courtroom and to bring in their own interpretation of events. The next part will consider the politics of the international stage, looking at the USSR's struggle to present itself as a major power in the courtroom, in the media, and on the ground in the American zone of occupation. It will show how Soviet political culture and practices handicapped the USSR in its dealings with the West. The concluding part will consider how a focus on the Soviet contribution to Nuremberg might change our understanding of the Nuremberg moment. It will also look at how the Soviets reacted to the Nuremberg verdict – and how Russia's current leadership has recast Nuremberg in an effort to pursue its own national and international agendas.

THE POLITICS OF THE HISTORICAL RECORD

All international tribunals engage in the work of putting together a record of the past. In the case of Nuremberg, all of the participants recognized that the IMT would do much more than establish the truth about Nazi atrocities and war crimes. All understood that the IMT would produce a broader historical record of the war and the international events that had preceded it: a record that would assess levels of blame and guilt, of suffering and damages, and of sacrifice and heroism – which would have real significance for the postwar political transitions that were already in the making. All four countries of the prosecution wanted to shape that record. The USSR's secret Nuremberg Commission worked hard to do so, making an exceptional effort to manage

[10] Materials relating to the formation of the commission, its membership, and its mission are stored primarily in the Archive of the Foreign Policy of the Russian Federation (AVPRF), the State Archive of the Russian Federation (GARF), and the Russian State Archive of Socio-Political History (RGASPI).

the Soviet delegation from afar and to influence the course of the trials. Joseph Stalin considered the work of this commission to be of immense importance, which is apparent from the high-level correspondence about its responsibilities and also from a list of its members, all distinguished Soviet officials. The commission included the Procurator-General of the USSR, the head of the Commissariat of Justice, and the head of the Counterespionage Division of the People's Commissariat of Defense (SMERSH), as well as major figures from the Commissariat of Internal Affairs (NKVD) and the Commissariat of Foreign Affairs.[11] It is telling that Stalin appointed as head of the commission none other than Andrei Vyshinsky, director of the USSR's Institute of State and Law and Deputy Commissar of Foreign Affairs, who had earned his political stripes as chief prosecutor in the three Moscow trials of 1936–1938.[12] The transcripts of these three show trials, excerpted in the Soviet press and then published in several volumes (in multiple languages), had successfully rewritten the historical record of the high politics of the 1920s and 1930s.[13]

What were the politics of the historical record at Nuremberg? And how did the Soviets shape – or fail to shape – the victors' larger narrative about World War II? Nuremberg was long ago described as "the greatest history seminar ever held in the history of the world," whose purpose was to provide an enduring record of Nazi atrocities.[14] In the decades since the IMT reached its verdict, Western scholars interested in questions of history and memory have looked at how Nuremberg facilitated the denazification of Germany and helped to

[11] It included the Procurator-General of the USSR Konstantin Gorshenin, Commissar of Justice Nikolai Rychkov, and President of the Supreme Soviet Ivan Goliakov. It also included head of SMERSH Viktor Abakumov and head of the People's Commissariat for State Security Vsevolod Merkulov, as well as NKVD officers Bogdan Kobulov and Sergei Kruglov. Other members were Ivan Lavrov from the People's Commissariat of Foreign Affairs and Pavel Bogoiavlensky from the Extraordinary State Commission for the Establishment and Investigation of the Crimes of the Fascist German Invaders and Their Accomplices. The Extraordinary State Commission compiled evidence about Nazi atrocities on Soviet soil. On the Nuremberg Commission and its members, see GARF f. 7445, op. 2, d. 391, ll. 49–56. On the Extraordinary State Commission, see Marina Sorokina, "People and Procedures: Toward a History of the Investigation of Nazi Crimes in the USSR," *Kritika. Explorations in Russian and Eurasian History*, Vol. 6 (2005), pp. 797–831.

[12] On Vyshinsky's roles in Soviet law and foreign affairs, see Arkady Vaksberg, *Stalin's Prosecutor: The Life of Andrei Vyshinsky* (New York: Grove Press, 1990); Peter H. Solomon, Jr., *Soviet Criminal Justice under Stalin* (Cambridge: Cambridge University Press, 1996); and Oleg E. Kutafin, ed., *Inkvizitor: Stalinskii prokuror Vyshinskii* (Moscow: Respublika, 1992).

[13] People's Commissariat of Justice of the USSR, *Report of Court Proceedings in the Case of the Anti-Soviet Trotskyite Centre* (Moscow, 1937) and People's Commissariat of Justice of the USSR, *Report of Court Proceedings in the Case of the Anti-Soviet "Bloc of Rights and Trotskyites"* (Moscow, 1938).

[14] The quote is from Robert M. W. Kempner, a member of the American prosecution team. Quoted in Lawrence Douglas, *The Memory of Judgment: Making Law and History in the Trials of the Holocaust* (New Haven: Yale University Press, 2001), p. 2.

establish an account of the Holocaust.[15] While these and other scholars have looked in detail at the politics of history from the American, British, and German perspectives, they have given far less attention to the Soviet side.[16] Materials from the former Soviet archives, now available to researchers, illuminate the actual depth and breadth of Soviet concerns. These materials make clear, for example, that Soviet leaders had hoped to use Nuremberg to make a powerful case for reparations. The Soviets maintained that the IMT should focus first and foremost on the Nazi crime of "launching an aggressive war" and should also look into specific Nazi violations of "the laws and customs of war."[17]

Stalin, Soviet Foreign Minister Vyacheslav Molotov, and the members of the Nuremberg Commission aspired to use the IMT to present a narrative of the wartime USSR that captured the depths of Soviet valor and sacrifice and that depicted the war as a crucible proving the great and irreversible achievements of the Bolshevik Revolution. They understood that courtroom speeches and critical documents such as the Nuremberg Charter and the Indictment Act would all become part of the permanent record about the war – and attempted to ensure that these materials reflected, or at least integrated, Soviet concerns and perspectives. Vyshinsky received drafts of Soviet speeches and official documents from London, Berlin, and Nuremberg through back channels, via Soviet agents and informants abroad. He forwarded these materials to commission members and other Soviet leaders, who wrote up their own comments and criticisms. For example, after looking over a draft of Soviet chief prosecutor Roman Rudenko's opening speech, Georgy Aleksandrov (the head of the Central Committee's Department of Agitation and Propaganda) sent Vyshinsky a long memo calling out and criticizing the speech's "hackneyed phrases," "repetition," and numerous "factual errors." Worst of all, Aleksandrov noted, the speech did not put a strong enough emphasis on the Soviet contribution to the Nazi defeat. Arguing that the speech needed "serious work," he recommended that it be rewritten to highlight the decisive role of "Soviet forces" in putting down "the Hitlerite

[15] See, for example Donald Bloxham, *Genocide on Trial: War Crimes Trials and the Formation of Holocaust History and Memory* (Oxford: Oxford University Press, 2003).

[16] A number of the classic works about Nuremberg written by observers and by scholars include some discussion of the Soviet side, albeit relatively superficial. See, for example, Whitney R. Harris, *Tyranny on Trial: The Trial of the Major German War Criminals at the End of World War II at Nuremberg Germany, 1945–1946* (Dallas: Southern Methodist University Press, 1954); Ann Tusa and John Tusa, *The Nuremberg Trial* (London: Atheneum, 1983); Telford Taylor, *The Anatomy of the Nuremberg Trials* (New York: Knopf, 1992); and Joseph E. Persico, *Nuremberg: Infamy on Trial* (New York: Penguin, 1994).

[17] See Francine Hirsch, "The Soviets at Nuremberg: International Law, Propaganda, and the Making of the Postwar Order," *American Historical Review*, Vol. 113 (2008), pp. 701–730. Also see George Ginsburgs, *Moscow's Road to Nuremberg: The Soviet Background to the Trial* (The Hague: Martinus Nijhoff, 1996) and Natalia S. Lebedeva, *Podgotovka Niurnbergskogo protsessa* (Moscow: Nauka, 1975).

armies" and "liberating the peoples of Europe."[18] After much discussion (and a round-robin of memoranda), the secret commission sent the Soviet delegation in Nuremberg a long list of line edits and directions for revision.[19] All in all, the existence of a Soviet secret commission whose express purpose was to supervise the Soviet delegation and meddle in the work of the IMT made for a complicated and awkward process: the Soviet legal team sometimes had to stall for additional time as it awaited word from Moscow, while representatives from the other countries of the prosecution faced no such constraints. Moreover, most of the documents for the court were joint-authored – and the French, American, and British prosecutors, who had the interests of their own countries to pursue, were not always receptive to the editorial requests of their Soviet colleagues.[20]

The Indictment Act, one of those joint-authored documents, prompted heated deliberation in Moscow and serious tension between the Soviet Union and the Western powers in September and October 1945, the two months before the start of the trials. Soviet leaders understood that the Indictment Act, which elaborated the four main counts against "the major war criminals" and established the basic framework for the IMT, was one of the most important documents for the case and for the historical record. Upon reviewing a draft of the act, key Soviet officials and the heads of the state security apparatus – members of a Moscow-based Indictment Commission that was also led by Vyshinsky – enumerated a long list of stylistic recommendations and "corrections in substance" and also expressed some serious misgivings.[21] Above all, they complained that the Indictment Act "belittled" the Soviet Union's critical role in the war and underestimated Soviet losses. "On the whole, the aggressive war against the USSR is shown palely in the Indictment Act and the USSR is given a significantly smaller place than the various small states," commission members complained. In the Soviet wartime narrative, the themes of valor and victimhood went hand in hand. Indeed, even as the Soviet regime worked to establish a heroic narrative about the resolve and strength of the Soviet people, it also endeavored to create a detailed record of the massive damage that the Nazis had inflicted on the lands, industries, institutions, infrastructure, and citizens of the Soviet Union at least in part in order to bolster Soviet reparations claims.[22] Soviet leaders had expected that the four chief prosecutors would make extensive use of the massive reports that Soviet experts and officials had compiled about Nazi crimes in Soviet territories – and that the Indictment Act itself would include

[18] AVPRF f. 07, op. 13, p. 41, d. 10, ll. 70–72.

[19] For example, AVPRF f. 082, op. 12, p. 178, d. 5, ll. 59–62. A similar process ensued back in Moscow to review and edit the speeches of the Soviet prosecution.

[20] For example, AVPRF f. 07, op. 13, p. 41, d. 3, ll. 121–123.

[21] GARF f. 8131, op. 38, d. 238, l. 71. This was the Commission for Preparing Indictment Materials for the Soviet Representatives in the International Military Tribunal.

[22] GARF f. 8131, op. 38, d. 238, ll. 87–90 and AVPRF f. 07, op. 13, p. 41, d. 10, ll. 63–64.

a comprehensive list of those places where the Nazis had committed war crimes and caused material damage in the USSR.[23] After learning that the Indictment Act would not comprise this level of detail, the Indictment Commission came down hard on Rudenko for allowing the Western powers to weaken the Soviet case – noting that as a consequence of "the shortening of the list of places where the German fascist aggressors committed evil deeds," the act "underestimates the damage" done to the USSR.[24]

In these deliberations, Soviet leaders expressed particular concern that the Indictment Act should provide extensive details about Nazi atrocities committed against Soviet civilians. In a secret October 1945 directive that saw the pens of Stalin and Molotov, Soviet leaders instructed Rudenko to insist that the document be revised to include summaries of Soviet data about the imprisonment, enslavement, and annihilation of the "peaceful population" of the Soviet Union.[25] Moreover, Soviet leaders wanted the document to make clear that the Nazis had targeted not just the Jews but also the Slavic peoples of the USSR with policies of annihilation and extermination. In a report to Vyshinsky, sent a few days earlier, Soviet Procurator-General (and Indictment Commission member) Konstantin Gorshenin had advised: "Regarding the enumeration of nationalities and racial groups against which the fascists on the whole conducted policies of mass extermination, it is necessary to also add the Russians (and not just Jews, Poles, and Gypsies)." When Vyshinsky read the report he crossed out "Russians" and replaced it with "Slavs."[26] It seems to have been Molotov who crafted the final Soviet wording for this revision, which he gave to Stalin for approval and which was ultimately forwarded to Rudenko in Nuremberg. It explained that the Nazis had carried out the "annihilation of adults, women, old people, and children, especially Russians, Belorussians, and Ukrainians, and the systematic extermination of Jews."[27] In the end, the published version of the Indictment Act did incorporate additional Soviet data about Nazi crimes in the USSR and called attention to the "annihilation" of Belorussians and Ukrainians in Nazi-occupied territories. It did not, however, include "the Russians" among the victimized nationalities. Nor did it list "the Slavs" (or the Russians, Belorussians, and Ukrainians) among the "nationalities and racial groups" that the Nazis had targeted for "deliberate and systematic genocide" or "extermination."[28]

[23] GARF f. 8131, op. 38, d. 238, l. 87. Soviet evidence about Nazi crimes was compiled by the Extraordinary State Commission.

[24] AVPRF f. 07, op. 13, p. 41, d. 10, ll. 40–43.

[25] AVPRF f. 07, op. 13, p. 41, d. 10, ll. 63–65.

[26] GARF f. 8131, op. 38, d. 238, l. 89.

[27] AVPRF f. 07, op. 13, p. 41, d. 10, l. 64. This report was labeled "Directives to Comrade Rudenko." It was sent from Molotov to Stalin for approval on October 16, 1945. AVPRF f. 07, op. 13, p. 41, d. 10, l. 54.

[28] Count Three of the Indictment accused the defendants of conducting "deliberate and systematic genocide, viz., the extermination of racial and national groups, against the civilian populations of certain occupied territories in order to destroy particular races and classes of people and

In their deliberations about critical documents for the IMT, Soviet leaders also focused on questions of historical interpretation related to international relations of the late 1930s and the origins of the war. Which events would be included, and which omitted, in a narrative of the war and its causes? What date would mark the "official" start of the war, and would the USSR's actions before 1941 (i.e., the invasion of Poland, Finland, and the Baltic states) factor into the record?[29] Here too the Indictment Act was of concern as it set out an authoritative narrative about the role of international organizations and treaties in failing to prevent, or even causing, the war. After reading a draft of the act, Vyshinsky and other members of the Indictment Commission voiced objections to its characterizations of the Munich Pact of 1938 and the Molotov–Ribbentrop Non-Aggression Pact of 1939. The latter elicited the most unease for Soviet leaders, who wanted to prevent the spread of information about the non-aggression pact's "secret protocols," in which the Nazis and the Soviets had together planned for and plotted out the conquest and division of much of Eastern Europe.

Complicating matters for the USSR was the fact that Soviet chief prosecutor Rudenko lacked basic information about the existence of these protocols (and their content), which the Nazi defendants of course did possess. A classified report from the Soviet consul in London Nikolai Ivanov, dated late September 1945, had impressed upon Vyshinsky the extent of the Soviet legal team's unpreparedness to navigate such politically sensitive issues. Ivanov, who had sat in on a session of the Committee of Chief Prosecutors that had been held in London a few weeks earlier, reported that Rudenko and his assistant lacked "sufficient knowledge about international relations" and also about "the internal affairs" of the German state. He advised that it was of particular importance to brief Rudenko about the diplomatic intrigues of the 1930s, to explain to him "the reasons for the war's origins," and to tell him "what position to take and how to respond to questions" relating to the non-aggression pact. Furthermore, Ivanov warned Soviet leaders that their failure to brief Rudenko and to provide him with competent advisors threatened the prestige of the USSR: that the Soviet prosecution would find itself "defenseless at the trial" if "the English or Americans or above all the defendants" attempted

national, racial, or religious groups, particularly Jews, Poles, and Gypsies and others." "Indictment: Count Three," *Nuremberg Trial Proceedings*, vol. 1, published online through the Avalon Project at Yale Law School, available at http://avalon.law.yale.edu/imt/count3.asp. Count One of the Indictment Act noted "the mass deportation of the Soviet citizens for slave labor to Germany, as well as the annihilation of adults, old people, women and children, especially Beilorussians [*sic*] and Ukrainians, and the extermination of Jews committed throughout the occupied territory of the Soviet Union." "Indictment: Count One," *Nuremberg Trial Proceedings*, vol. 1, available at http://avalon.law.yale.edu/imt/count1.asp. No explanation was given for these changes in the final version of the Indictment Act.

29 On Soviet policies in these regions, see Timothy Snyder, *Bloodlands: Europe Between Hitler and Stalin* (New York: Basic Books, 2010).

to forge or fake "one or another historical fact." In late October 1945, Soviet leaders heeded Ivanov's counsel to send "an experienced diplomatic worker" to Berlin to advise Rudenko on "political questions."[30] But this intervention seems to have been too little and come too late.

Indeed, well before Moscow's chosen diplomatic worker arrived in Berlin, Rudenko had begun to execute his orders to initiate discussions with the other chief prosecutors about points of dispute in the Indictment Act. He attempted, first and foremost, to insist on "concrete corrections" in the act's descriptions of the Munich Pact and the Molotov–Ribbentrop Pact and their relationship to the Nazi invasion of the countries of Eastern Europe and thus to the start of the war. Soviet leaders had complained that the act did not just "set forth facts" about these two treaties but also attempted to give "a certain" and "disputable" political interpretation of events – and that "political interpretations" in general did not have a place in such documents.[31] It is clear, however, that Soviet leaders in fact objected only to those political interpretations that were not in line with Soviet state interests. They took particular offense that the act did not treat the Molotov–Ribbentrop Pact and the Munich Pact in a parallel manner. While the draft suggested that the Molotov–Ribbentrop Pact had enabled, or was "the indirect reason" for, the Nazi "attack on Poland," it skirted the issue of French and British appeasement – and did not place similar blame on the Munich Pact for the Nazi invasion of Czechoslovakia.

Soviet leaders had given Rudenko firm orders to ensure that the act be revised so that the Molotov–Ribbentrop Pact "under no circumstances" could be interpreted as "the springboard for" Nazi actions. They had also directed Rudenko to insist that the act make clear that the "Hitlerite conspirators" had concluded this non-aggression pact with the Soviets in bad faith and had used it for cover while preparing an elaborate plan for "aggressive war against the USSR." At the same time, they had instructed Rudenko to argue for a more accurate account of the Nazi invasion of Czechoslovakia, noting that the document's description of events – that following "a dispute" between the German state and Czechoslovakia, the former had "intimidated the latter" into "handing its fate and the fate of its people" over to "the Fuehrer and the Reich Chancellor" – did not "correspond to the historical facts" and would insult "the Czechoslovak people."[32] Soviet leaders wanted the act to make clear that in the wake of the Munich Pact (i.e., once confident of French and British acquiescence), and without provocation from the Czechs, the Nazis had used massive violence to "seize Czechoslovakia" and thus commit a grave "crime against peace." It is obvious from secret correspondence that Stalin and Molotov cared most of all about the Molotov–Ribbentrop Pact. Indeed, the

[30] AVPRF f. 082, op. 27, p. 122, d. 23, ll. 16–18.
[31] AVPRF f. 07, op. 13, p. 41, d. 10, ll. 62–65.
[32] AVPRF f. 07, op. 13, p. 41, d. 10, ll. 40–43, 63–68.

Indictment Commission had ordered Rudenko to push hard for the revisions related to this non-aggression pact even if it meant conceding other points.[33]

The politics of the historical record remained a source of contention throughout the course of the trials. In the short term, Rudenko and the other chief prosecutors did reach a successful compromise about the Indictment Act's characterizations of the Munich Pact and the Molotov–Ribbentrop Pact. The final version of the act made a link between the conclusion of the Munich Pact and the Nazi seizure of Czechoslovakia. In deference to French and British concerns, it included a description of the "diplomatic crisis" that had compelled the Western powers to sign the pact and made clear that the Nazis had acted counter to "the provisions of" the pact itself.[34] The revised act also took into consideration some of the Soviet objections about the Molotov–Ribbentrop Pact. It omitted the line that had deemed this pact, and thus the Soviets, culpable for the Nazi invasion of Poland. It also characterized the Nazi invasion of the USSR in 1941 as a treacherous and premeditated "crime against peace," describing how the Nazis had broken their agreement with the Soviets and carried out acts of barbaric destruction in the Soviet Union in accordance with "detailed plans."[35] In the end, the Indictment Act trod with care around the issues of appeasement and collaboration and made clear that the Nazis alone, and none of the victors, would be tried in court. But as the IMT convened in November 1945, heated discussions continued about issues of historical interpretation, and these two pacts remained critical points of contention.

The Molotov–Ribbentrop Pact and its place in the historical record continued to rankle the Soviets. In subsequent weeks and months, both the Nazi defense team and the U.S. prosecution attempted to force a public discussion about the pact's secret protocols. In December 1945, the Soviets fought off a U.S. proposal for the IMT to examine the protocols in open court.[36] In April 1946, as the German defense team presented its case and brought witnesses before the court, the issue came up yet again – this time with less favorable results for the Soviets. Much to the consternation of Soviet leaders, the IMT permitted the defense to read out a statement from former German diplomatic adviser Friedrich Gaus about a secret agreement to divide Eastern Europe that German and Soviet leaders had concluded on the eve of the Nazi attack on Poland. To make matters worse, the IMT then allowed Joachim von

[33] AVPRF f. 07, op. 13, p. 41, d. 10, ll. 62–65 and AVPRF f. 06, op. 7, p. 20, d. 208, l. 22.

[34] "Indictment: Count One," *Nuremberg Trial Proceedings*, vol. 1, available at http://avalon.law.yale.edu/imt/count1.asp.

[35] "Indictment: Count One," *Nuremberg Trial Proceedings*, vol. 1, available at http://avalon.law.yale.edu/imt/count1.asp.

[36] AVPRF f. 07, op. 13, p. 41, d. 9, ll. 122–124. Also Grigorii P. Kynin and Ioahim Laufer, eds., *SSSR i germanskii vopros, 1941–1949: Dokumenty iz Arkhiva vneshnei politiki Rossiiskoi Federatsii*, vol. 2 (Moscow: Mezhdunarodnye otnosheniia, 2000), p. 84. Kynin and Laufer cite AVPRF f. 07, op. 13, p. 41, d. 8, ll. 58, 77, 79, 140.

Ribbentrop to corroborate Gaus's statement in open court and to attest that the USSR had been "prepared under certain circumstances to go to war" on the side of the Nazis. The Soviets were furious about the defense's "provocative attacks" on the USSR – and also about the fact that Gaus's statement had appeared in British and American newspapers even before the IMT had ruled on whether or not to allow it to be read in court.[37]

A "top secret" Soviet status report about the trials, sent from Nuremberg that April, described at length these and other difficulties that were bedeviling the Soviet prosecution at this "new stage" of the trials (i.e., "the presentation of the materials of the defense") and explained in detail how the German defense team had succeeded in "broadening the breach" between the Soviet Union and the other countries of the prosecution. "Dealing the final blow," the report noted, was the IMT's decision "to dismiss all materials related to [the] Munich [Pact]." The Soviets had thus lost important leverage, as the British and the French no longer had an incentive to compromise on matters relating to the Molotov–Ribbentrop Pact. This loss of leverage soon became apparent, the report continued, as the Soviet prosecution was no longer able "to establish the needed support from the other prosecutors" to keep "the events of 1939" out of the courtroom, even though "on these questions exists a prior mutual gentlemen's agreement."[38] Several weeks later the stakes were raised even further, as the German defense team gave the IMT an actual transcript of the secret protocols with a petition to introduce it as evidence. The Soviets made a successful bid on legal-technical grounds to keep this transcript out of the case, but not before the document had been circulated and reviewed in court.[39] The details of the Molotov–Ribbentrop Pact's secret protocols had thus become an open secret – and would remain so until Soviet leaders officially acknowledged their existence decades later.

All in all, the Soviets did have some success in using the IMT to shape the historical record about World War II and the course of international relations in the preceding decade – but not nearly as much as Soviet leaders had hoped for. Instead, it was the Western powers that managed to use the courtroom to shape and disseminate a historical narrative that isolated the USSR from the other victors and cast it as a co-conspirator of the criminal Nazi regime. The German defense team further undermined Soviet efforts, presenting damning evidence about Soviet policies and practices and thus taking advantage of and widening the rift between the USSR and its former wartime allies. Of course, all of these issues about historical interpretation, about the politics of the past (blame, guilt, suffering, damages, sacrifice, and heroism), were first and foremost about the future, linked to questions and claims about restitution, reparations, and the

[37] AVPRF f. 07, op. 13, p. 41, d. 9, ll. 113–114, 122.

[38] AVPRF f. 07, op. 13, p. 41, d. 9, ll. 112–116. This report was send by Mikhail Kharlamov, senior editor at the Soviet Information Bureau, diplomat, and informant.

[39] AVPRF f. 07, op. 13, p. 41, d. 9, l. 122.

shape of postwar Europe. What would become of Germany and its people? What would be the fate of Poland? And what roles would the Soviet Union and the United States play in the new European order? As the Western powers instituted new policies to rebuild Germany and proposed that the German people be spared major reparations, the Soviets saw the international situation shift unfavorably. Soviet leaders realized that the USSR likely would not receive the much-anticipated transfers of German cash, technologies, and labor as recompense for their wartime losses. Thus, as the Soviet delegation in Nuremberg lost control of the narrative about the war, the Soviet Union's postwar future loomed uncertain as well. Soviet informants in Nuremberg lambasted the Western powers for turning their backs on the USSR and abandoning it to the accusations of the defense. But these informants and the secret commission directed most of their criticism at the Soviet delegation and its lack of preparation for the pomp, circumstance, and politics of the international stage.

THE POLITICS OF THE INTERNATIONAL STAGE

Even before World War II had ended, Stalin and Molotov had come out in front of their wartime allies and argued for an international tribunal to bring the Nazis to justice. Soviet leaders believed in the educational and cathartic importance of such a tribunal for the Soviet population, and also hoped to use it to demonstrate Soviet power abroad and to shape the postwar order. The Soviets seemed to have imagined, at least at first, that the "scripting" and execution of an international tribunal would be more or less straightforward. All of the Allied powers had agreed that the Nazis alone would stand trial and that the public discussion and condemnation of Nazi crimes would have instructive or didactic value. It was not a coincidence that Soviet leaders had handpicked for their main delegation to the IMT individuals with notable "show trial" experience: men who were practiced in the staging of large-scale political trials within Soviet borders. The USSR's chief judge for the IMT, Iona Nikitchenko, had made his career as a judge in the infamous Moscow trials of 1936–1938. The USSR's chief prosecutor, Rudenko, had served as the prosecutor for show trials in Ukraine during the same era, and then more recently as chief prosecutor in a Soviet show trial of the sixteen leaders of the Polish Underground State.[40]

After the Nazi surrender, however, as preparations for an international tribunal began in earnest, Soviet leaders began to express apprehension about the political, practical, and logistical aspects of such an international venture. Where would the tribunal be held and who would preside? What rules would be

[40] The trial of the leaders of the Polish Underground State had been staged in Moscow over three days in June 1945. See Aleksandr Zviagintsev and Iurii Orlov, *Prokurory dvukh epokh: Andrei Vyshinskii i Roman Rudenko* (Moscow: OLMA-Press, 2001), pp. 212–213.

established for the introduction of evidence? Would the accused be permitted to call witnesses? What language or languages would be used in the courtroom and in related deliberations – and how would the court, not to mention the Soviet delegation, handle matters of translation and interpretation? What role would the media have in the trials? As the four countries of the prosecution attempted to work through their differences, and as the United States and Great Britain (and often France) stood united on critical issues, the Soviets were forced to compromise. Indeed, the decisions first to hold the tribunal in American-occupied Nuremberg as opposed to Soviet-occupied Berlin, and then to permit the Nazi defendants to take the stand as witnesses in their own defense, made clear to the Soviets the extent to which the IMT would be outside of their direct control.[41]

Moreover, as preparations for the IMT gained momentum, it became all too apparent that Soviet representatives overseas lacked critical experience and know-how. The Soviets saw their participation in the IMT as important international work of a new type.[42] But the Soviet delegation had received no special training in this work. In September and October 1945, when the chief prosecutors from all four countries of the prosecution met in London to prepare the Indictment Act, Soviet consul and informant Ivanov observed the Soviet delegation's shortcomings up close – and (as noted earlier) described them in his dispatches to Moscow. As Ivanov apprised Soviet leaders of the delegation's ignorance about Soviet–German relations and foreign affairs, he also reported that the Soviet representatives were at a marked disadvantage because of their "lack of experience" in the work of "international organizations." Ivanov noted that Rudenko and his assistants seemed uncertain about how to set meeting agendas, pose questions for discussion, and negotiate – all of which "impedes their work" at meetings of the Committee of Chief Prosecutors and in the subcommittees.[43]

To be sure, there were real reasons for the Soviet delegation's lack of know-how. Rudenko's ignorance about foreign affairs was in large part a consequence of Soviet policies and practices, which put a premium on controlling the flow of information into the Soviet Union – and which had attempted throughout the 1930s to keep even senior Soviet officials isolated from the rest of the world. Until 1934, the Soviet Union had defined itself outside of the existing international order, deriding international law and criticizing international organizations such as the League of Nations as "a disguise for

[41] On negotiations between the Soviet Union and the other countries of the prosecution about these and other questions, see AVPRF f. 07, op. 13, p. 41, d. 9, ll. 14–16 and AVPRF f. 07, op. 13, p. 41, d. 3, ll. 121–123. Also see Kynin and Laufer, *SSSR i germanskii vopros*, pp. 182–183. Kynin and Laufer cite AVPRF f. 07, op. 10, p. 8, d. 83, ll. 44–45.

[42] This idea is captured well in correspondence from Vishnevsky to Gorshenin, GARF f. 8131, op. 37, d. 2196, ll. 159–166.

[43] AVPRF f. 082, op. 27, p. 122, d. 23, ll. 17–18.

the imperialistic policies of certain great powers."[44] Even after the USSR formed alliances with the Western powers and chose to operate in the recognized realm of international relations (in large part in response to the Nazi threat), Stalin and his circle had remained suspicious of the West. Soviet officials with foreign-language expertise or experience abroad had come under attack in the Stalinist Terror of the late 1930s: large numbers of "international experts" (*mezhdunarodniki*) had been arrested or shot, and the USSR's Commissariat of Foreign Affairs had been decimated.[45] Indeed, most Soviet representatives to the IMT were part of a new and informal foreign relations apparatus: academics, officials, and cultural figures with little or no prior foreign relations experience.[46]

Moreover, it was not obvious to the Soviet team at Nuremberg how much initiative it should or even could take on the international stage. The Soviet regime's centralized command structure discouraged and prevented the true delegation of responsibilities. And Moscow's efforts to micromanage the Soviet delegation and the details of the Soviet case against the former Nazi leaders made matters even more awkward for Rudenko and his colleagues. The secret Nuremberg Commission sent the Soviet team a regular stream of detailed directives and instructions. One such communication reminded the team that "Soviet representatives" to the IMT were to make no "decisions on questions not envisioned in the present directives without the prior approval of the Soviet Government."[47] In order to seek and receive this official approval, the Soviet delegation had to smuggle extensive paperwork back to Moscow – with tight deadlines and through sometimes unreliable back channels. There were several instances, both before and during the trials, when critical materials (including a draft of the Indictment Act) were lost in transit.[48] There were also a couple of occasions when the Soviet prosecution did not receive directives from Moscow on time and was uncertain how to proceed. On one of these occasions, Rudenko even faked a case of malaria and absented himself from deliberations with the other prosecutors in an effort to hold up the proceedings.[49] Soviet leaders were

[44] Iu. V. Kliuchnikov and Andrei Sabanin, *Mezhdunarodnaia politika noveishogo vremeni v dogovorakh, notakh i deklaratziiakh*, Part 3, Issue 2 (Moscow: Litizdat NIKD, 1929), p. 238. Cited in Timothy A. Taracouzio, *The Soviet Union and International Law: A Study Based on the Legislation, Treaties and Foreign Relations of the Union of Socialist Soviet Republics* (New York: The Macmillan Company, 1935), p. 292. On early Soviet attitudes toward the League of Nations, see Aron N. Trainin, *Izbrannye proizvedeniia: Zashchita mira i ugolovnyi zakon* (Moscow: Nauka, 1969).

[45] On the Terror and the Commissariat of Foreign Affairs, see Teddy J. Uldricks, "The Impact of the Great Purges on the People's Commissariat of Foreign Affairs," *Slavic Review*, Vol. 36 (1977), 187–204. Also see Albert Resis, "The Fall of Litvinov: Harbinger of the German-Soviet Non-Aggression Pact," *Europe-Asia Studies*, Vol. 52 (2000), 33–56.

[46] I look in greater detail at this informal foreign relations apparatus in my book *Soviet Judgment at Nuremberg: A Cold War Story*, forthcoming with Oxford University Press.

[47] AVPRF f. 07, op. 13, p. 41, d. 3, l. 75. [48] AVPRF f. 06, op. 7, p. 20, d. 208, l. 21.

[49] AVPRF f. 07, op. 13, p. 41, d. 8, l. 62.

strict about the chain of command. In reaction to a couple of incidents on the eve of the trials, when Rudenko and Nikitchenko acted without official directives in hand, the two were called home to Moscow and reprimanded for "irresponsible actions." Back in Moscow, Soviet leaders criticized Nikitchenko for consenting to the American, British, and French recommendation that the British chief judge (Geoffrey Lawrence) serve as the chairman of the IMT: Vyshinsky noted with exasperation that "we did not give such directives!" He lambasted Rudenko for signing off on a draft of the "text of the Indictment Act in English, not knowing this language ... and not having corresponding instructions about it" from Moscow.[50]

The Soviet delegation's lack of experience and expertise also resulted in considerable problems with translation and interpretation. In his September 1945 memo to Soviet leaders, Ivanov lamented the lack of able Soviet interpreters and translators. He observed that the translator that Rudenko had "at his disposal" in London had poor English and German, and struggled to translate the evidence and other critical materials that the Committee of Chief Prosecutors was working with "to put together the Indictment Act." As a result, he warned, Rudenko was "unacquainted with an enormous amount of evidence that the Americans, French, and English have submitted for the prosecution." Ivanov added that Rudenko's translator was "even less" successful as an interpreter and often mistranslated his words. Ivanov expressed concern that unless the language problem was resolved, Rudenko would be "in a state of ignorance during the trials" – unprepared to object to the introduction of evidence that could send things "in an unfavorable direction" for the Soviet Union. In the same memo, Ivanov made a number of practical recommendations to improve the Soviet position – advising, for example, that Soviet leaders send skilled translators, interpreters, and other experts from Moscow to Berlin and Nuremberg to assist Rudenko and his colleagues.[51] Vyshinsky and Gorshenin did, in fact, attempt to follow through on some of Ivanov's suggestions. They took steps to select and screen Soviet translators and interpreters who knew English, German, and French; in December, four additional translators were sent to Nuremberg. But the number of able Soviet translators and interpreters assigned to the Soviet delegation still fell far short of what was needed (and of what had been requested), in all likelihood because the NKVD refused to clear most of the selected personnel for travel abroad.[52]

Ivanov's concerns about the delegation's lack of skilled translators and interpreters proved prescient. After the IMT convened in November 1945, Soviet informants reported that the Soviet interpreters, who now had the crucial job of providing the Soviet legal team with simultaneous interpretations of speeches and statements in the Hall of Justice, were making

[50] GARF f. 8131, op. 38, d. 238, ll. 17–21. [51] AVPRF f. 082, op. 27, p. 122, d. 23, ll. 16–18.
[52] AVPRF f. 07, op. 13, p. 41, d. 4, ll. 5–6; AVPRF f. 07, op. 13, p. 41, d. 8, ll. 88–89.

rudimentary mistakes all the time. This compromised the work of the entire Soviet delegation and was also a source of constant embarrassment. As one informant, a senior editor of the Soviet Information Bureau (Sovinformburo), Mikhail Dolgopolov, reported to Soviet leaders in late December 1945: "It must be said that the overwhelming majority of our translators do not provide a high quality of translation. Everyone is talking about this."[53] Another informant, the playwright and wartime correspondent Vsevolod Vishnevsky, writing to Nuremberg Commission member Gorshenin in late February 1946, lamented the low skill level of Soviet translators and interpreters – noting that most were uncertain and slow and that some made "the crudest mistakes."[54] Dolgopolov and Vishnevsky realized that these problems with interpreters and translators could have repercussions not just for the USSR's reputation but also for the success or failure of the Soviet case. And, indeed, when the defense took the stand in April 1946, it became all too apparent that Rudenko and his assistants were in fact unacquainted with a large amount of evidence that had been logged in not just for the prosecution but also for the defense. All of this created serious difficulties for the Soviets – especially when Ribbentrop, Hermann Goering, and other Nazi defendants took the stand. As correspondence between Nuremberg and Moscow made clear, the Soviet prosecutors' ignorance about critical documents made it exceedingly difficult for them to be proactive and to anticipate the legal arguments and maneuvers of the Nazi defense team.[55]

Soviet difficulties navigating the politics of the international stage extended to the press corps. The role of the press in covering, narrating, and publicizing the Nuremberg trials was an enduring concern of the secret Nuremberg Commission. Soviet leaders wanted to use the trials to disseminate the USSR's own narrative about the Great Patriotic War and "the crimes of the Hitlerites." Toward this end, the Soviets (like the other participants in the IMT) had assembled a team of talented journalists, writers, artists, cartoonists, photographers, and filmmakers for Nuremberg to bring the trials to the population back home as well as to an international audience. Their ranks included the writers Ilya Ehrenburg and Vishnevsky, the political cartoonist Boris Efimov, the photographer Evgeny Khaldei, the filmmaker Roman Karmen, and other major figures with reputations in the USSR and abroad.[56] At the same time, Soviet leaders were anxious about allowing such a cohort of Soviet journalists and cultural figures to spend months outside of

[53] GARF f. 7445, op. 2, d. 407, l. 2. [54] GARF f. 8131, op. 37, d. 2196, l. 165.

[55] AVPRF f. 07, op. 13, p. 41, d. 9, ll. 76–77, 112–116.

[56] On the Soviet correspondents at Nuremberg, see Boris Polevoi, *V kontse kontsov: Niurnbergskie dnevniki* (Moscow: Sovetskaiia Rossiia, 1969) and Arkadii. I. Poltorak, *Niurnbergskii epilog* (Moscow: Voennoe izdatel'stvo Ministerstva Oborony SSSR, 1965). Also see Leonid Trofimov, "Soviet Reporters at the Nuremberg Trial: Agendas, Attitudes, and Encounters, 1945–1946," *Cahiers d'Histoire*, Vol. 28 (2010), pp. 45–70.

Soviet borders and took measures to keep their numbers manageable, to monitor their operations, and to isolate them as much as possible from their American and European colleagues. Sovinformburo, the official Soviet press and propaganda administration that had been established in 1941 to cover the war, worked with the Nuremberg Commission to oversee the Soviet press corps in Nuremberg and also to ensure that Soviet press coverage of the trials remained on message.[57]

The Soviet press corps was supposed to bring news about the IMT not just to the Soviet population at home but also to audiences abroad. As such, it was in direct competition with the press corps from the other countries of the prosecution. Sovinformburo thus faced a formidable challenge. The NKVD sought to limit the size of the Soviet press corps abroad, while Sovinformburo worried that it would be outnumbered and thus at a disadvantage. It was with this concern in mind that the head of Sovinformburo, Solomon Lozovsky, wrote to Molotov in October 1945. Lozovsky reported that according to *World Press News*, the United States, Great Britain, and France had all been allotted far more spots for the press at the trials than had the USSR: the Americans would have about "100 places for journalists," the English would have 50, the French between 40 and 50, and the Russians between 25 and 30. He argued that "such a distribution of spots" was "unacceptable" since it indicated "the political belittling of the role and significance of the Soviet press" and would "give the advantage to the American, English, and French press in comparison with the Soviet press." Lozovsky further noted that almost all the Soviet journalists being sent to Nuremberg were from Russia. He suggested that "for political reasons" the Soviet Union should also send "journalists from the union republics that were victims in this war, such as: Ukraine, Belorussia, Moldavia, Lithuania, Latvia, Estonia, Karelia-Finland, and also from Leningrad." (Of course, the relationship between the three Baltic republics and the Soviet Union was an issue of contention at the time.) As Lozovsky himself realized, the Soviets had been allotted fewer spots for the press at least in part because Soviet leaders had planned to send fewer journalists than the other countries of the prosecution. By October 1945, Soviet leaders had approved just twenty-four journalists and writers for travel to the American zone. Lozovsky asked Molotov to speak with "the Americans and the English" about increasing the number of places for the Soviet press "to 50." Molotov ruled against this recommendation.[58] In the weeks that followed, however, Soviet leaders did concede the need to send more journalists, and the Central Committee ultimately approved a list of thirty-five writers and journalists and five cameramen for travel to Nuremberg.[59]

[57] In 1944, Sovinformburo was expanded to include a special bureau on propaganda for foreign countries.

[58] AVPRF f. 06, op. 7, p. 20, d. 208, ll. 34–35. [59] GARF f. 8131, op. 38, d. 238, l. 21.

Once in Nuremberg, the Soviet press corps did in fact find itself outnumbered. But this was perhaps the least of its problems. The Soviet Union had more than enough journalists on the ground to report on the course of the IMT. And once the IMT was in session, the Soviet newspapers *Pravda* and *Izvestiia* featured extensive news coverage and also printed partial transcripts of the trials.[60] But the Soviet press corps struggled to meet the demands of the secret Nuremberg Commission and found it difficult (and sometimes impossible) to communicate official Soviet narratives about the war, the trials, and postwar events to a broader international audience. Here too, the Soviets were not well equipped for the challenges they faced outside of their own borders. First of all, the same problems with interpreters and translators that hampered the work of the Soviet prosecution also beleaguered the Soviet press corps. Vishnevsky observed in his secret reports to Moscow that the shortage of qualified interpreters and translators was having a marked negative effect on the work of Soviet writers and journalists in Nuremberg. He also reminded Soviet leaders that the responsibilities of Soviet writers and journalists were not limited to writing "daily articles and essays" for newspapers but also included the fundamental work of producing a full written record of the trials themselves. "The leadership gave us directives about this," he noted. He warned that without "first-rate and swift translations" the Soviet press corps would not be able "to cope with" its crucial job of documenting the work of the IMT.[61]

The Soviet press corps in Nuremberg also faced significant difficulties on the propaganda and publicity front. Soviet journalists were supposed to communicate the official Soviet line about the course of the trials and about world events in their reportage and in their conversations with foreign correspondents. But the official line could, and often did, change, and the Soviet press corps found it difficult to keep up without a regular and reliable flow of information from Moscow. Sovinformburo editor Dolgopolov noted that the Soviet press corps did not receive Soviet newspapers for weeks at a time and did not even have a radio receiver. Meanwhile, "London, Parisian, and other newspapers, new magazines, and books" arrived at the press camp in the Faber Palace on a regular basis. As a result of all this, he observed, Soviet journalists found themselves "cut off altogether" from life back home, in a state of "disinformation," and unable "to answer the numerous questions of foreign correspondents" about "the appearance in their newspapers of one or another report about the Soviet Union."[62] Vishnevsky, in his memos to Soviet leaders, reported similar problems with the flow of newspapers, and information about life back

[60] Important articles from *Pravda, Izvestiia*, and other newspapers have been reprinted in Georgii N. Aleksandrov, Vladimir Velichko et al., eds., *Sud istorii: Reportazhi s Niurnbergskogo protsessa* (Moscow: Politizdat, 1966).

[61] GARF f. 8131, op. 37, d. 2196, l. 165. [62] GARF f. 7445, op. 2, d. 407, ll. 1–2.

home, from the Soviet Union to Nuremberg. He related how Soviet personnel were practically "hanging on the telephone wire to Moscow," attempting to establish a sense of connection to the homeland.[63]

Vishnevsky also complained about the Soviet legal team's inclination to hoard information and keep it from the Soviet correspondents. In a direct letter to Rudenko dated February 1946, just before the Soviet prosecution was about to take the stand, he complained (screaming in capital letters) that "FOR THE MOST PART, OUR LEGAL STAFF IN KEEPING WITH TRADITION HOLDS ALL THE MATERIAL IT HAS UNDER LOCK AND KEY." He recounted what had happened, for example, when he had asked the USSR's French translator to give him the texts of the testimonies of the witnesses Marie Valliant-Courturier and Hans Cappelen for publication in the Soviet journal *Znamia.* The translator "began the work with zeal," Vishnevsky explained, "but then his boss stopped him," forbidding him to share the materials. According to Vishnevsky, these were "staggering documents" that also "emphasized the courage and resolve of our Soviet people." As a result of the legal team's intransigence, "several hundred thousand Soviet readers" did not have the chance to read important materials "that would have underscored for them" the great esteem of "European soldiers" for "Russians and for the Soviet Union." Meanwhile, "foreign newspapers" have been printing "extraordinarily interesting documents that are damaging to Nazism and that help the Tribunal," he continued. He gave as examples a letter by the Nazi Air Force Colonel Bernd von Brauchitsch (about Nazi plans for Operation Barbarossa) as well as revelations about the details of the "1944 plot" to assassinate Hitler ("and about the fact that [Winston] Churchill, [Finnish President Gustav] Mannerheim ... and others participated" in it) – which both appeared in the Western press.[64]

According to Vishnevsky, the Soviet legal team's failure to share crucial information and materials with the press threatened the Soviet Union's international position. He suggested that at Nuremberg it was essential for the Soviets to depart from usual practices and provide as much material as possible "to the entire world press." Indeed, he went so far as to urge Soviet personnel to emulate "the Americans, English, and French" who "arrange meetings, press conferences, friendly conversations, dinners, and so on as necessary," in order to make sure that foreign correspondents "are continually in the know." He noted that the press bureaus of these countries also distributed summaries of essential speeches and other materials "to the world press and radio." "Even those documents that do not appear at the open meetings of the Tribunal are communicated" to the press, he added. Vishnevsky predicted that if current Soviet practices were to continue, "the entire corps of foreign correspondents will meet with difficulties" and "the speeches of the Soviet prosecution" will

[63] GARF f. 8131, op. 37, d. 2196, l. 166.
[64] Russian State Archive of Literature and Art (RGALI) f. 1038, op. 1, d. 2439, ll. 3–6.

likely be "spoiled" or "made a mess of" in the international press.[65] In the course of the trials the Soviet delegation in Nuremberg did begin to change some of its practices. The Soviet press corps did set up its own bureau in Nuremberg and began to prepare documents, photographs, summaries of major speeches, and other materials for foreign correspondents.[66] This attempt to emulate Western models had some success in the short term, but was later seen in Moscow as a political defeat.[67]

As the Soviet press corps attempted to negotiate the politics of the international stage, Soviet informants and other observers in Nuremberg also noted with distress that coverage of the IMT in the Western press was becoming more and more anti-Soviet as the trials unfolded. The Soviet appointee to the General Secretariat of the IMT, General Arkady Poltorak, later observed in his memoirs: "As the end of the war receded farther into the past, statements on the first signs of West-East tension began to appear in the Western, particularly the American, press." He recounted that the Nazi "defendants eagerly read the newspapers which they obtained from their defense counsels" and "kept an eye open for reports on divergences" between the Soviets and their former wartime allies. "Like hens dreaming of millet, Goering and Ribbentrop looked forward to reading about conflicts between the bourgeois West and the Soviet Union," he vividly noted.[68] Signs of tension between the Soviet Union and its former wartime allies were obvious even in general reporting about the trials in the Western press, Vishnevsky explained in his February memo to Gorshenin. In "political American magazines," such as *Time*, "information about the trials treats us unfavorably." The English and the French press also have an anti-Soviet "bias," and when reporting on the speeches of the Soviet prosecution omit "the most important political and statistical data" about Nazi crimes in the USSR, he observed. Most distressing of all for the Soviets was the fact that the Nazi defense was having far more success than the Soviet prosecution in bringing its message to the international press, through press conferences and other means. *The Associated Press* and other media outlets had published interviews with Nazi leaders who criticized the IMT as a one-sided "court of the victors," attempted to cast doubt on Soviet evidence, and brought up the issue of Soviet guilt.[69] In April 1946, the Nazi defense used the Western press to publicize information about the Molotov–Ribbentrop Pact (including Gaus's statement about the secret protocols) that the Soviets had been fighting to keep out of the courtroom.[70]

In addition to general problems with the mass media, the Soviet Union also faced a broader public relations dilemma at Nuremberg: Soviet informants reported that the USSR's representatives were making a poor impression on their foreign colleagues with their poor and tattered clothing and undignified

[65] RGALI f. 1038, op. 1, d. 2439, ll. 4–6. [66] GARF f. 8131, op. 37, d. 2196, ll. 159–160.
[67] RGASPI f. 17, op. 125, d. 386, ll. 30–34. [68] Poltorak, *Niurnbergskii epilog*, p. 89.
[69] GARF f. 8131, op. 37, d. 2196, ll. 160–162. [70] AVPRF f. 07, op. 13, p. 41, d. 9, ll. 113–114.

behavior.[71] Vishnevsky noted that some members of the delegation had not brought enough "clothes, undergarments, and so on" with them and were "turning to foreigners, to the black market" to attain necessary items. This "does not do," he added. According to Vishnevsky, the Soviet representatives were at loose ends in other respects as well. Reporting general "low morale" as well as drunkenness and brawling among members of the delegation, he noted that "the months out of contact with the homeland have affected our people." Vishnevsky observed that Soviet personnel were struggling without their accustomed "Soviet forms of relations." "Because of local conditions," Soviet representatives "do not have assemblies" or "local trade union committees" or "party committees" to meet and discuss current events. "We all get together infrequently and seldom talk with one another," he noted. "To me this is incomprehensible, even taking into account the special circumstances of the American zone." "We are a great country of victors," he reflected, and as such "we have a right" to bring "our customs with us" to the international stage.[72]

The Soviets went to Nuremberg to show the depths of Nazi guilt, to make a powerful case for reparations, and to celebrate their victory over fascism. Instead, the Soviets had a difficult time negotiating the politics of the international stage. The USSR was caught in a dilemma. The model of control that Soviet leaders saw as fundamental to the inner working of their state prevented the USSR from being an effective actor at Nuremberg. The classic techniques of the Soviet show trial could not be applied in this postwar venue. But of even greater significance, the Soviet Union's own logic of repression and control ended up undermining the Soviets abroad. The archival record gives a picture of the postwar USSR as a state whose legal personnel, journalists, translators, and other international experts lacked the essential skills, know-how, and polish to succeed in the work of international relations. It also shows how the basic elements of Soviet practices and political culture – a centralized command structure that discouraged initiative, a closed regime that put a premium on the strict control of information, a suspicion of Soviet citizens with foreign-language skills – handicapped the Soviets at Nuremberg and also in the more general Cold War competition that was unfolding between the USSR and the West. The IMT became a moment of taking stock for the Soviets. It showed the Soviet leadership what it needed to do to turn the USSR into a more agile international power. At the same time, though, it reconfirmed the Soviet leadership's distrust of international courts. In the postwar era, it would be this last lesson about the dangerous and unpredictable politics of the international stage that Stalin and other Soviet leaders would most take to heart.

[71] GARF f. 7445, op. 2, d. 407, l. 4. [72] GARF f. 8131, op. 37, d. 2196, ll. 165–166.

CONCLUSION

The Nuremberg trials have long been understood as a major political event and as a didactic trial writ large: intended to bring the major Nazi war criminals to justice, to reckon with the past, and to facilitate the transition to a new postwar order in Europe. But bringing in the Soviet perspective and Soviet materials about the trials makes clear the extent to which the USSR and its wartime allies came to the courtroom with different narratives about the causes of the war and with competing visions for the postwar order. When it came to thinking about the past, some of the most basic details about the war's origins proved to be matters of hot dispute. To what extent had the policies of the Soviet Union and the Western powers (as well as organizations such as the League of Nations) enabled the rise of Hitler and the march on Europe? Could the Munich Pact and the Molotov–Ribbentrop Pact be considered as possible indirect causes of the war? Of equal contention were questions about the war's heroes and victims. Which countries, and which peoples, would be remembered as the main victims of the Nazis? Which armies would be held up as the saviors of Europe?

It is not a surprise that these questions sparked passionate debate. Representatives to the IMT from the four countries of the prosecution, and also the Nazi defense, understood that how these questions were answered would be of critical importance not just for the historical record but also for the resolution of issues essential to the establishment of the postwar future. When the trials began, it was still uncertain how – or if – the politics of reparations and restitution would shape postwar Europe and postwar international relations. To be sure, the Soviet Union's role as one of the countries of the prosecution, as well as the decision to exclude the crimes of the victors from the purview of the IMT, influenced the narrative about the war that was related in the courtroom. In the end, however, the tensions between the Soviet Union and the Western powers, combined with Soviet inexperience and shortcomings on the international stage, turned out to be even more critical in shaping the wartime narrative and the course of the trials – and of even more enduring effect.

What might students of transitional justice learn from a nuanced account of the IMT as a forum of Cold War competition? Such a perspective reminds us that the broader international political context of a trial is often as important as the trial itself. It also makes clear that the behind-the-scenes politics of international tribunals are not background noise to the main event but are instead an integral part of it – and can shape outcomes. When analyzing the power dynamics of an international tribunal like Nuremberg, we would be remiss to focus primarily on the adversarial relationship between the defendants and the prosecution or to look solely at the courtroom proceedings. At Nuremberg, intense competition among the countries of the prosecution affected all aspects of the trials: the explication of the main charges in the Indictment Act, the atmosphere of the courtroom, the presentation of the case, the backroom meetings, the Western judges' decision to allow the Nazi defendants to introduce evidence that would embarrass the Soviets, the verdict, and more. Bringing in Soviet archival materials puts all of this into sharp relief and reminds us that even countries that are on the same side in a trial (in this instance, the prosecution) can use the courtroom to pursue separate or rival agendas, and that those agendas, whether open or unarticulated, can come to overshadow the actual case. Over the course of the trials, as four-power cooperation broke down, the German defense was able to exploit the rift between the Soviet Union and the Western powers to its own advantage and call world attention, in the courtroom as well as in the media, to Soviet crimes and breaches of international law.

An examination of the Soviets in Nuremberg and of the more general political framework of the IMT suggests additional lessons for students of transitional justice. New information about the Soviet Union's secret Nuremberg Commission, for example, reminds us to examine the internal politics of all of the countries involved in an international trial and to look, when possible, at back channels of information. After studying the Soviet archival record, it seems impossible to have a balanced view of what transpired at Nuremberg without an evaluation of this commission's hopes, fears, successes, and failures. A closer focus on the Soviet role also makes clear that practical decisions related to the organization of a trial are often also political decisions and can have a real impact on the outcome of a case – and on what the broader public learns about it. In the example of the IMT, the resolution of questions about the location of the tribunal, about the translation of evidence, about the role of journalists and cameramen in the courtroom, and so on turned out to be of critical importance. What's more, the fact that the Soviets found themselves at a disadvantage on the international stage vis-à-vis the Western powers, and the United States in particular, has had a lasting impact on how the Nuremberg trials are remembered. If Nuremberg helped bring about the modern human rights regime, it also produced the postwar politicization of human rights and human rights institutions.

Bringing Soviet materials and perspectives into our account of the Nuremberg trials lends important insights not just into the politics of international tribunals but also into the role of the law in shaping the political. The Soviets responded to the Nuremberg verdict with disappointment and disillusionment. The fact that the Western judges found several of the Nazi defendants to be not guilty of the formal charges on the grounds of "reasonable doubt" perplexed and angered Soviet leaders.[73] In the immediate wake of the trials, the Soviet regime criticized the verdict and

[73] The verdict was delivered in October 1946. Those deemed "not guilty" were Hans Fritzsche, Franz von Papen, and Hjalmar Schacht. All three were later tried and convicted by German courts. In addition, the court did not find the Reich Cabinet, the SA, or the General Staff and High Command to be criminal organizations. Soviet Judge Nikitchenko gave a dissenting

implemented secret plans to instigate a "massive campaign of protests against the freeing of the three criminals" in the Soviet zone of occupied Germany.[74] In the months that followed, Soviet leaders distanced the Soviet Union from Nuremberg and came to the (perhaps foregone) conclusion that future participation in international courts like the IMT would do the Soviet regime more harm than good. From late 1946 through much of the 1950s, Soviet leaders adopted a defensive position toward international law and a skeptical view of international institutions like the United Nations, even as the Soviet Union took its seat among the member countries.[75] Moreover, the same Soviet officials and experts who had advocated during the war for Soviet participation in an international tribunal to hear cases against the major Nazi leaders made a powerful case in this new context *against* proposals vetted in the United Nations to create a permanent International Criminal Court to hear cases about genocide.[76] In 1948, Soviet international law expert Professor Aron Trainin explained in a public lecture in Moscow that "the struggle against genocide as a crime directed toward the extermination of peoples and nations of course has the staunch support of the entire Soviet people." But "in current international conditions," he believed that an international tribunal would serve as a political weapon for the United States to use in its "slanderous campaign against the USSR."[77] Trainin himself had been a part of the Soviet team at Nuremberg, serving as an international law expert and advisor to the Soviet prosecution. He had also been one of the most eloquent and outspoken advocates of Soviet participation in the IMT and had authored the definition of "crimes against peace" that was used in the trials.[78] Trainin's critique of the proposed International Criminal Court was an unmistakable sign that the tide had turned. The postwar moment of four-power cooperation in the name of justice had turned out to be a chimera. Furthermore, the experience of Nuremberg had shown the Soviet Union, as well as the United States, that international courts could in fact be used for various political ends. In the wake of Nuremberg, both countries would try to steer clear of international conventions and institutions that challenged the principle of state sovereignty.

opinion in all of these cases. See "Judgment: Dissenting Opinion of I. T. Nikitchenko," *Nuremberg Trial Proceedings*, vol. 1, available at http://avalon.law.yale.edu/imt/juddiss.asp.

74 AVPRF f. 012, op. 7, p. 106, d. 178, l. 49, reprinted in Kynin and Laufer, *SSSR i germanskii vopros*, pp. 712–713. Also Hirsch, "The Soviets at Nuremberg."

75 See Alexander Dallin, *The Soviet Union at the United Nations: An Inquiry into Soviet Motives and Objectives* (New York: Praeger, 1962).

76 UN discussions invoked "the Nuremberg principles." See Benjamin N. Schiff, *Building the International Criminal Court* (Cambridge: Cambridge University Press, 2008), p. 27.

77 Aron N. Trainin, *Borba progressivnykh sil protiv unichtozheniia natsional'nykh grupp i ras (Konferentsiia v Niiu-Iorke po borbe s genotsidom), Stenogramma publichnoi lektsii prochitannoi v Tsentral'nom lektorii Obshchestva v Moskve* (Moscow: Vsesoiuznoe obshchestvo po rasprostraneniiu politicheskikh i nauchnykh znanii, 1948).

78 It was also Trainin who came up with the concept of "crimes against peace." See Hirsch, "The Soviets at Nuremberg."

So, how do we make sense of current Russian invocations of the Nuremberg verdict in light of the Soviet Union's efforts to distance itself from the IMT? How have Russia's current leaders attempted to recast the Nuremberg trials in an effort to pursue their domestic and international goals? Perhaps, Russia's attacks on "historical revisionism" and appeals to the "findings of Nuremberg" should be seen first and foremost as the latest rejoinder in the spirited dialogue among Russia, the former states of the socialist bloc, and the rest of Europe about the Soviet past. Indeed, with the end of the Cold War, Europe became Russia's main interlocutor on issues of historical interpretation, calling for a candid discussion of Soviet crimes and human rights violations. The European Union and the Council of Europe have compared Stalin with Hitler and have invoked the Nuremberg trials to call for the "international condemnation" of the "crimes of totalitarian regimes" and for a reassessment of the communist past. In 2006, the Council of Europe criticized the absence of an "international investigation" of the crimes of communism, noting that "the authors of these crimes," unlike the Nazis after World War II, have not faced an international tribunal.[79] In 2009, the European Union proclaimed August 23 to be "European Day of Remembrance for Victims of Stalinism and Nazism," noting that this date marked the signing of the Molotov–Ribbentrop Pact that "divided Europe into two spheres of interest by means of secret additional protocols." Here too, the European Parliament used the language of Nuremberg: It explained that "the mass deportations, murders and enslavements committed in the context of the acts of aggression by Stalinism and Nazism fall into the category of war crimes and crimes against humanity" and that "under international law, statutory limitations do not apply" to these types of crimes. It further maintained that such a day was necessary because "the influence and significance of the Soviet order and occupation on and for citizens of the post-Communist States are little known in Europe."[80] Eastern European leaders, in turn, have responded with enthusiasm to this call to expose the crimes of the Stalinist past – as doing so supports their own nation-building efforts.[81]

It is in this context and also in response to growing tensions with the United States that Russia's leaders have attempted to reclaim Nuremberg and the postwar moment as their own. Putin has argued that Russia is not responsible for the Soviet past, while other Russian leaders continue to praise Stalin as "an exceptional person" and to speak with pride about Soviet

[79] This was Council of Europe Resolution 1481. The Council of Europe's Parliamentary Assembly issued this resolution on January 25, 2006.

[80] "Declaration of the European Parliament on the proclamation of 23 August as European Day of Remembrance for Victims of Stalinism and Nazism," available at www.europarl.europa.eu/sides/getDoc.do?reference=P6_TA%282008%290439&language=EN.

[81] The Russian press has covered these developments. See, for example, Aleksei Fenenko, "Voennoe nasledstvo," *Nezavisimaia gazeta*, Vol. 210 (2009), p. 3.

accomplishments.[82] To be sure, the Russian government has released some critical documents about World War II that shed light on Stalinist transgressions. Most significantly, in a gesture of goodwill to Poland, Russia's leaders have posted on the Internet documents showing once and for all that the Soviets were responsible for the 1940 Katyn massacre of Polish officers; and the Russian State Duma has affirmed that the massacre "was committed on the direct orders of Stalin and other Soviet officials."[83] Russia's public revelations about Katyn, however, have been the exception to the rule. For the most part, Russia's leaders have eschewed openness in favor of avoidance, intimidation, and redirection. The new Russian law to combat "historical revisionism" has stipulated harsh penalties for scholars and writers who espouse historical interpretations that contradict the findings of the IMT on the grounds that doing so is akin to Holocaust denial. Russia's leaders, hiding behind the Nuremberg verdict, have embraced an approach to international relations that is oddly reminiscent of the Soviet approach at Nuremberg. Attempting to control the historical narrative about World War II and international relations more generally, Russia's leaders have opted for censorship and the suppression of information. Striving to master the shifting politics of the international stage, Russia's leaders have reverted to the political culture and practices of the closed state. Unwilling and perhaps unable to come to terms with the Soviet past, Russia faces the prospect of losing the propaganda struggle of Nuremberg all over again.

[82] The quote is from Russian politician and Speaker of the Russian Duma Boris Gryzlov. "Ot redaktsii: Vrozhdennye poroki," *Vedomosti*, Vol. 11 (2006).

[83] See www.rusarchives.ru/publication/katyn/spisok.shtml. The Russian government published these documents in April 2010 following the air crash that killed Polish President Lech Kaczynski. Kaczynski had been en route to a 70th anniversary commemoration of Katyn. Most of these documents were already available to researchers in Moscow. Many files on Katyn, however, still remain classified. The release of the documents came a few days after Putin gave a speech in which he seemed to justify the massacre. Simon Shuster, "Putin Says Stalin Massacred Poles Out of Revenge," *The Guardian*, April 7, 2010.

7

Brown v. *Board of Education*

Private Civil Litigation as a Political Trial

Mark V. Tushnet

Brown v. *Board of Education* ranks among the U.S. Supreme Court's most important decisions. The Supreme Court held unconstitutional the practice of segregating elementary and secondary school students by race, and opened the way for broader legal and political challenges to the Jim Crow (or apartheid) system in the American South. But Supreme Court decisions occur only because there have been hearings and trials in lower courts. *Brown* was the culmination of a sustained set of lower court cases seeking to undermine racial segregation, brought by the National Association for the Advancement of Colored People's Legal Defense Fund headed by Thurgood Marshall.[1] Each of those cases might be understood as a political trial, brought by private litigants seeking to disrupt the established racial order in the South. Yet, for reasons I discuss in the second section of this chapter, private civil litigation has some special characteristics that distinguish it from other incarnations of the political trial.[2]

Consider the trial – that is, the hearing held before a three-judge court – in *Briggs* v. *Elliott*. The Supreme Court decided five cases grouped under the heading *Brown* v. *Board of Education*, and *Briggs* v. *Elliott* was in many ways far more important than *Brown* itself, taking *Brown* to refer to the specific challenge to school segregation in Topeka, Kansas. Kansas was a border state in which racial segregation based on law was a relatively minor feature of the social order. *Briggs* v. *Elliott*, in contrast, challenged school segregation in Clarendon County, South Carolina, at the heart of the segregated Deep South.

[1] For a detailed discussion of the litigation preceding *Brown*, see Mark V. Tushnet, *The NAACP's Legal Strategy Against Segregated Education, 1925–1950* (Chapel Hill: University of North Carolina Press, 1987).

[2] Cf. Jens Meierhenrich and Devin O. Pendas, " 'The Justice of My Cause Is Clear, But There's Politics to Fear': Political Trials in Theory and History," in this volume.

By the time *Briggs* came to trial in 1950, the legal challenge to segregation had two components. First, the challenge accepted, provisionally, the stated law that segregation was constitutionally permissible if the facilities provided to whites and African Americans were substantially equal in quality.[3] The National Association for the Advancement of Colored People (NAACP) lawyers put on evidence demonstrating that, on virtually every measure of material quality – age, physical condition, availability of laboratories – the schools for African Americans were inferior to those for whites. Second, though, the lawyers challenged the premise that segregation, even in equal facilities, was constitutionally permissible. The first challenge required the presentation of evidence; the second was purely legal.

As in all civil litigation, the plaintiffs in *Briggs* v. *Elliott* put on their evidence first. The evidence came in through testimony by expert witnesses. And here one of the key features of *Brown* as a political trial emerged. On the first day of trial the NAACP's lawyers began by calling two whites to the stand – the county superintendent of education and the chair of the local school district. Their testimony provided only the broadest contours of the local school system's segregation policies and their effects. As Richard Kluger puts it in his account of the trial, one witness "was either genuinely ignorant about the details of his public responsibility or even more gifted than [the other] at dodging any question put to him."[4]

The real effect of their testimony was to set up that of the next group of witnesses. These were experts who testified in detail about the conditions of the schools in Clarendon County. And, what mattered for present purposes was not so much what they said but who they were. The first step in presenting an expert witness's testimony is to show that the witness actually qualifies as an expert. This involves laying out the expert's educational background and credentials and describing the scholarly work the expert has done. The NAACP's expert witnesses were highly credentialed: two taught at Howard University, one at Columbia University's education school. The contrast between their assured presentations and the stumbling by the white witnesses was stark. And, even more important, the witnesses from Howard were themselves African Americans. Just as the presence of African American *lawyers* in Southern courtrooms was a matter of political significance itself,[5] so was the presence of highly credentialed, self-assured African American witnesses. As expert witnesses they did not present evidence that was dramatic in itself, but their appearance alone – by which I refer in part to their physical appearance – contributed to the drama of the trial.

[3] The "separate but equal" rule derived from *Plessy* v. *Ferguson*, 163 U.S. 537 (1896).

[4] Richard Kluger, *Simple Justice* (New York: Vintage, 1977), p. 349.

[5] On the role of African American lawyers as representatives of their race, see Kenneth Mack, *Representing the Race: The Creation of the Civil Rights Lawyer* (Cambridge: Harvard University Press, 2012).

I will return to some of the dramaturgical aspects of the trial in *Briggs* v. *Elliott* below, but the foregoing may be enough to provide the basis for a more detailed inquiry into some of the analytic characteristics of private civil litigation as a political trial.

PRIVATE CIVIL LITIGATION AS LAWFARE: SOME PRELIMINARY DISTINCTIONS

Private civil litigation can be a form of what U.S. Air Force Colonel Charles Dunlap called "lawfare."[6] Government officials can call on the civil courts as well as the criminal ones to assist them in putting their political opponents at a disadvantage, and in the posture of defendants in civil cases, the opponents can put the cases to the same use that defendants in criminal cases do. Efforts by governments to prevent political parties from gaining access to the ballot or campaigning provide one example of this form of lawfare. So, for example, in the 1990s, the secular Turkish government responded to a challenge from an Islamist party by obtaining a judicial order finding the Islamist party's platform inconsistent with the Turkish Constitution. Similarly, in the 1950s, the Federal Constitutional Court in Germany held, in response to motions by the executive government, that the Communist Party and a neo-Nazi party were unconstitutional.[7] The widely noted use in Singapore of civil actions for libel (rather than criminal prosecutions for sedition) against opponents who criticize government policy is another example of civil litigation by government officials that functions as a means for imposing costs on political opponents.[8]

This lawfare occurs in the civil courts, but is otherwise not significantly different from the more usual examples of political trials in criminal cases, where officials of the governing regime seek to deprive their political opponents of their liberty. The sanctions imposed on the regime's opponents are monetary, not direct loss of liberty. But, the monetary sanctions can be severe. In Singapore, for example, damage awards escalate the higher up the plaintiff is in the government, on the theory that false imputations of a failure to

[6] The term came into widespread use after 2001, when Colonel Dunlap used it in a widely noticed essay, "Law and Military Interventions: Preserving Humanitarian Values in Twenty-first Century Conflicts," *Carr Center for Human Rights*, Kennedy School of Government, Harvard University, November 29, 2001, available at http://people.duke.edu/~pfeaver/dunlap.pdf.

[7] See, e.g., *Refah Partisi* v. *Turkey*, No. 41340/98, February 13, 2003, Eur Ct H R (Grand Chamber); KPD Case, BverfGE 5, 85 (Germany, Fed Const Ct. 1956). Note, though, that these cases tend to be brought by an organ of the government, sometimes an arm of the executive government and sometimes a body with some degree of independence from the executive government.

[8] See, e.g., *Lee Kuan Yew* v. *Jeyaretnam Joshua Benjamin* [1979–1980] S.L.L. (R.) 24. For a report on a subsequent, similar trial by an observer from Amnesty International (itself a signal that the civil trial had some characteristics of a political trial), see Judge Paul Bentley, "The Politics of Defamation in Singapore," available at www.singapore-window.org/80217can.htm.

serve the public damage the reputation of high officials more than they do that of lower-ranking officials. Regime opponents have been forced into bankruptcy, and one consequence of that is that until the debts are paid off the defendant is ineligible to serve in the parliament.[9] The structural similarities between criminal and civil forms of lawfare are suggested by the fact that the outcomes of libel cases in Singapore seem asymmetrical: Government officials win their cases claiming that opponents have libeled them, whereas the opponents lose the cases they bring claiming that government officials have libeled *them.*[10]

These political trials are private civil litigation in form. The plaintiffs seek two ends: exposure of their opponents' actions, and a legal judgment – didactic and destructive ends, respectively. In the libel cases, for example, the plaintiffs want to show that the defendants' statements (that they were corrupt, for example) are false, and they want to obtain a civil judgment against the defendants. And, as in political trials in criminal courts, the judges are aligned with the plaintiffs: They are judicial officials in the same regime in which the executive officials suing as plaintiffs serve.

In other configurations, the juxtaposition of private civil litigation and political trials presents two paradoxes. One is institutional. The plaintiffs seek the aid of one arm of a regime to disrupt the activities of another. The other is conceptual. The plaintiffs disrupt and destroy some practices within the legal system by legitimating other, deeper or more abstract, legal practices.

The institutional paradox is perhaps modest, but it arises because the alignment of the plaintiffs and the judges that we see in the Singaporean libel cases may not exist. The *Brown* litigants sought the same didactic and destructive goals of exposure and legal liability – exposure of the facts of inequality in the schools, and liability for maintaining segregated schools. But the litigation was an effort by a private party to deploy the power of one government institution, the courts, against another, the legislature or the executive. This is generally true of litigation of the sort typified by *Brown.* In that configuration an opponent of government policy challenges the policy in court on constitutional grounds. Yet, the idea of political trials centers around the thought that the state is reasonably unitary, in the sense that prosecutors – arms of the executive branch – seek to use the courts as weapons against the regime's political adversaries. In criminal lawfare, prosecutors see courts as their allies in that combat.

9 Const. Singapore, art. 45(1)(b).

10 See, e.g., *Workers Party* v. *Tay Boon Too and Another*, 1972–1974 *Singapore Law Reports* 621. In another case an opposition-filed libel case was withdrawn after the government officials whose statements were at issue apologized for them. See http://mothership.sg/2014/10/10-revelations-from-chiam-see-tongs-biography-that-will-interest-every-well-informed-sporean/, https://perma.cc/FH35-J2T4. There are few examples of opposition suits against government officials for libel, which may indicate the opposition's sense that chances for success are small.

How, then, could private litigants think that as plaintiffs they could enlist the courts on their side? They might draw some lessons from the more common form of political trial. First, sometimes criminal defendants in political trials successfully use the trial as the focus for political organizing outside the courts. The defendants' supporters can take to the streets, to editorial pages, and today to the social media to use the trial as an illustration of the reasons for overthrowing the regime. These trials are performances for audiences both inside the courts and outside them. Private civil litigation can have the same mobilizing effects, and notably the timing of such litigation is in the hands of the regime's opponents, not prosecutors. In addition, even in quite tightly controlled regimes there is sometimes some degree of independence in the courts. Defendants in criminal political trials sometimes are acquitted or have their convictions overturned by higher courts.[11] Private civil litigation can sometimes operate in the space within the courts not fully occupied by executive power.

The existence of that space suggests a broader point. Governments are complex institutions. Not only might "the center" – what I have been calling the regime – be unable to control every action down to the lowest level, but sometimes it might want to use one institution to develop information about how another institution is operating, communicate that information to the center, and discipline that institution. The regime might have the formal power to control all actions at the periphery, but it might find it helpful to use courts at the local level to discipline prosecutors at that level, rather than intervening directly against the local prosecutors. This sort of institutional complexity gives private civil litigants the opportunity to deploy the courts themselves, and sometimes to succeed in their litigation – when what they seek is consonant with the interests of the central government even though inconsistent with the wishes of government officials at the periphery, or when the central government fails to notice, perhaps only temporarily, what is happening in a nominally independent court in the periphery. In this aspect, the trial's audience consists of the institutions at the center.

The *Brown* litigation illustrates another form of that complexity. *Brown* and *Briggs* v. *Elliott* were challenges to *state* policies brought in the *national* courts (sometimes referred to as the federal courts). The form of federalism in the United States creates asymmetries. The central legislative and executive branches may be unable, mostly as a matter of constitutional law but with some practical features, to directly control the selection of local officials chosen by the subnational units, and as a result may find it difficult to control the

[11] As discussed below, in systems where criminal defendants receive trials by juries of lay persons, acquittals might result not from *judicial* independence but from the regime's inability to assert total control over the jurors. In such systems one might expect executive officials to attempt to transfer political trials from the ordinary criminal system to one where convictions can be obtained without lay participation.

substance of the policies those units pursue. Judges in the national courts, in contrast, are officials of the national regime. When the NAACP brought *Brown* and *Briggs* v. *Elliott* in the national court system, they were not – at least in form – asking the judicial officials of a unitary regime to act against other officials of the same regime.

The institutional paradox is not entirely dissolved by focusing on U.S. federalism. With specific reference to the *Brown* litigation, one of the cases the Supreme Court decided was initiated in the Delaware state courts – which held that state's segregation policy unconstitutional. Another was a challenge to segregation in the District of Columbia, where segregation was a policy adopted by agents of the national government which, as a matter of constitutional law, has the power "to exercise exclusive jurisdiction" in the District of Columbia.[12]

Before examining private civil litigation as a form in which political trials can occur, I raise some definitional questions by examining a classic political case in the United States – the Scottsboro case (or cases) – that fits awkwardly with some definitions of the category. The Scottsboro cases began with a series of three criminal trials in Alabama, conducted over a three-day period in April 1931.[13] The nine defendants, young African Americans who had been riding the rails as hoboes, were convicted of raping two white women on the train, and were sentenced to death. The substance of the crime was "ordinary," and the prosecution, of course with racial overtones, was a relatively ordinary form of exercising social control over African Americans in the apartheid South. The events of the trials themselves were routine and not "political" in the sense typically used when discussing political trials. On the days before and during the trials there were no large-scale mobilizations or indeed even much public attention beyond the trial venue. After the defendants were convicted, though, the cases came to the attention of the Communist Party, which decided to make the case a *cause célèbre*. The party organized mass demonstrations, speaking tours, and the like, all to the end of using the Scottsboro cases as a vehicle for an attack on the U.S. system of criminal justice. Eventually, the Supreme Court heard the Scottsboro appeals and found that the defendants' constitutional rights had been violated. The cases went back for retrial, and this time the trial events were widely publicized.[14]

Considered as political trials, as they should be, the Scottsboro cases show several features that can characterize political trials. First, the cases *became* political over an extended period. The events at the first trials were largely

[12] The Delaware case is *Gebhart* v. *Belton*, decided along with *Brown* v. *Board of Education*. The District of Columbia case is *Bolling* v. *Sharpe*, 347 U.S. 497 (1954).

[13] I rely in what follows on the account provided in Dan T. Carter, *Scottsboro: A Tragedy of the American South* (New York: Oxford University Press, 1969).

[14] The defendants were again convicted, the Supreme Court again vacated the convictions, and eventually most of the defendants were convicted and sentenced to prison terms of varying lengths.

unnoticed, and even the days of testimony at the second and third set of trials were a minor feature of the political dimension of the Scottsboro cases. Second, the cases became political not at the instance of the prosecution but because of the initiative taken by the defendants' supporters. The cases show the targets of ordinary trials can convert their trials into political ones. This is what those who use private civil litigation as a form of lawfare seek to do as well. And, finally, the Scottsboro cases show how what might seem at the moment an ordinary trial can be reconstructed in retrospect as a political trial. This constructed and retrospective view of political trials is important in understanding *Brown* v. *Board of Education* as a political trial.

THE BACKGROUND OF PRIVATE CIVIL LITIGATION AS A FORM OF POLITICAL TRIAL

Private civil litigation as a form of challenging the regime has a long history in Anglo-American systems. In 1762, annoyed at government criticism emanating from a newspaper called *The Monitor*, Lord Halifax, functioning roughly as an interior minister would today, directed his subordinates, led by Nathan Carrington, to search the home of John Entick, a writer for *The Monitor*. The search took four hours. Carrington and his assistants broke into locked drawers and cupboards, and took away a large number of books and pamphlets. A jury found that the search had caused forty shillings worth of damages to Entick's home and possessions, and that he had incurred £300 in costs associated with the litigation.[15] Entick sued Carrington for the civil tort of trespass, an unlawful breaking into his home. Finding that Carrington's actions were in fact not authorized by law, Lord Camden held in Entick's favor.[16]

Entick v. *Carrington* was widely known in the United States and Great Britain, and the form of action Entick used became the routine method by which plaintiffs challenged the legality and constitutionality of government action. The underlying theory in *Entick* was that such a severe intrusion on liberty could occur only if the statutory authorization for it were clear. The underlying theory in later cases was that the nation's people had not authorized government actions inconsistent with the U.S. Constitution. The form of this action was quite general: A search could be unconstitutional and the remedy was a civil action against the sheriff, a seizure of a ship could be illegal and the remedy was a civil action against the captain of the ship that captured the vessel, and – notably – an arrest could be illegal because the statute for whose violation the defendant was arrested was unconstitutional and the remedy was a civil action for false imprisonment.

[15] According to one calculation, forty shillings was the equivalent of something between £ 245 and £ 2,400 in 2011, and £ 300 the equivalent of somewhere between £ 36,000 and £ 489,000. For the calculation, see www.measuringworth.com/ukcompare/relativevalue.php.

[16] *Entick* v. *Carrington*, [1765] EWHC KB J98, 19 Howell's State Trials 1029 (1765).

The conceptual basis for these remedies was what today's public-choice theorists might describe as an agency problem. The U.S. Congress might have the power to direct captains to seize certain vessels, but it is in no position to supervise what they do while at sea. Some captains might go off on their own, seizing ships to see if they could get away with it. Civil litigation against ship captains is a mechanism that allows Congress to monitor the captains' behavior after the event (and to indemnify them for any damages awards they might face if Congress disagreed with the courts' evaluation of the legality of their conduct).[17] Translated to the level of actions claiming constitutional violations, the theory is that the nation's people had not authorized their agents – legislatures and executive officials – to act in ways inconsistent with the Constitution. The people create the power of constitutional review in the courts as a mechanism for supervising the actions of their agents in the other political branches.[18]

Now consider *Entick*. According to Lord Camden's holding, the King-in-Parliament could have authorized the search, but had not done so, either directly or by delegating the power to institute such searches to Lord Halifax. On the conceptual level there is the same agency problem: For all the King-in-Parliament "knew," Lord Halifax might have been pursuing Entick for purely personal reasons. Yet, of course, the conceptual structure did not map well on to the political reality. Nor would it in many cases with the same structure – a civil action by a private plaintiff claiming that a government official injured her by engaging in unauthorized action.

Two features of *Entick* v. *Carrington* deserve noting at this point. The first, perhaps obvious, is that the outcome depended on Lord Camden's willingness to say that Lord Halifax's action was unauthorized. That is, the outcome required that the judiciary possess some degree of independence from the executive government. The second is that the outcome also depended on the willingness of a jury to find the facts in Entick's favor.[19] Juries are drawn from the general public to serve, ordinarily, only once. So, though the political reality is that high public officials certainly did authorize and condone the search of Entick's home, those same officials lacked any real power to control what the one-shot jury would do. The independence of the jury was a hard-won gain in Anglo-American legal development,[20] but once it existed alongside some degree

[17] On indemnification, see James E. Pfander and Jonathan L. Hunt, "Public Wrongs and Private Bills: Indemnification and Government Accountability in the Early Republic," *New York University Law Review*, Vol. 85 (2010), pp. 1862–1939.

[18] Doing so creates its own agency problem, in that the people have few mechanisms they can use to ensure that the courts exercise the power of constitutional review in a manner consistent with the people's understanding (or, if you will, the correct understanding) of the constitution.

[19] In fact the jury in *Entick* v. *Carrington* returned a special verdict in which it laid out the facts as it found them to be, and left it to Lord Camden to determine whether, given those facts, Carrington was liable under the law.

[20] See Bushell's Case, [1670] 123 ER 1006, 6 Howell's State Trials 999.

of judicial independence of executive government, the structure was in place for civil plaintiffs to use civil litigation as a form of lawfare.[21]

SOME THEORIES OF PRIVATE CIVIL LITIGATION AS POLITICAL TRIALS

One theoretical basis for plaintiff-side lawfare was developed in the United States in conjunction with a strategy its proponents called "labor defense."[22] Labor defense was featured in the Scottsboro cases, where the Communist Party front organization that made them political trials was the International Labor Defense (ILD). As the term "defense" indicates, labor defense was a technique developed in connection with the defense in what its users described as criminal political trials, but the theory underlying labor defense could be extended to plaintiff-side lawfare. Labor defense responded to two dilemmas faced by political radicals of a Marxist bent. They were in an awkward position when they defended their actions by invoking their constitutional rights. Purporting to speak for "the masses," Marxist radicals faced the embarrassment of dealing with cases – often arising in the U.S. South – where the trials were a substitute for lynchings, which could be understood as a form of popular justice administered by the masses themselves. In the trials that took the place of lynchings, criminal defendants could hardly expect independent juries to find them not guilty (the jurors being drawn at random from the very population that would otherwise have lynched the defendants).[23]

Further, the radicals' theory of law and society implied that law, even constitutional law, was a reflection of basic power relations, a tool of the ruling class to suppress the working class. How could radicals expect judges, members of the ruling class elite, to interpret the law to immunize political radicals from persecution and prosecution? As *The New Republic* put it in commenting on a long sentence imposed by a Georgia court on a Communist organizer, "Even a paper as conservative as the New York Herald has protested

[21] Akhil Reed Amar gives the civil jury the central role in his account of remedies for constitutional violations, precisely on the ground that the civil jury was independent in the sense I have given. See Akhil Reed Amar, *The Bill of Rights* (New Haven: Yale University Press, 1998).

[22] For a discussion of labor defense, see Rebecca N. Hill, *Men, Mobs, and Law: Anti-Lynching and Labor Defense in U.S. Radical History* (Durham: Duke University Press, 2008). The following paragraphs are adapted from a work-in-progress on the Supreme Court from 1930 to 1941.

[23] The problems in cases where substantial segments of the public appeared to agree with the prosecution that the defendants were political radicals who deserved punishment might have been overcome by treating the juries as unrepresentative of "the masses." That resolution was available in part in the "legal lynching" cases, where the juries did not have any African Americans on them but would not fully address the problem in communities with white majorities (because, in such communities, whites would predominate even on demographically representative juries).

the outrageous injustice of this sentence, which goes far to prove what the Communists have long charged about capitalist-ruled courts, in the Deep South and elsewhere." Labor defense treated prosecutions as occasions for organizing support for radicals. Prosecutions demonstrated that capitalist "rule of law" was a sham, discarded as soon as the ruling class felt threatened by radical dissent. Labor defense exposed that sham through publicity and demonstrations.[24]

The best vehicles for labor defense were prosecutions that could be described as frame-ups of innocent defendants – at least, defendants who were innocent of the crimes with which they were charged. Campaigns against the continued imprisonment of Tom Mooney, convicted for setting a bomb that killed ten and injured forty at a "Preparedness Day" celebration in San Francisco in 1916, and of the execution of Joe Hill, for murdering a Salt Lake City butcher and his son in 1914, and of Nicola Sacco and Bartolomeo Vanzetti, convicted in 1921 of a robbery and murder in South Braintree, Massachusetts, foreshadowed the development of labor defense as a weapon for using prosecutions as an organizing device.[25]

The theory of labor defense worked best before a defendant was convicted, and in cases where its organizers could credibly claim that the victims were being framed, as they could in the cases prominent during the 1920s. Lawyers who accepted the theory could ask juries to acquit, even in the face of evidence, and thereby to demonstrate how working people could stand up to the ruling class. After conviction, the theory of labor defense had to confront the difficulty that the lawyers were attempting to persuade members of the ruling class to let political radicals go free in the face of a jury's decision that they had violated the law. This was even more awkward when the defendants were convicted of political offenses rather than ordinary crimes. Radicals were proud of their political positions, and were uncomfortable at best in claiming that they had not made the speeches or published the pamphlets that were at the basis of the charges against them. Mooney, Hill, and Sacco and Vanzetti might have been framed for murder, but political radicals were not being framed when they were charged with offenses that were defined by their radical views.

The advocates of labor defense never fully worked out how appeals to higher courts fit into radical political theory. Trumpeting one victory, Communist leader Earl Browder declared, "The higher court was forced by the pressure of aroused mass opinion and protest to set aside the verdict ..." Similarly, William Patterson, the leader of the ILD, asserted, "Not legal pressure alone, but

[24] "This Week," *The New Republic*, February 1, 1933, p. 309.

[25] Representative of a large literature are Richard H. Frost, *The Mooney Case* (Stanford: Stanford University Press, 1968); Gibbs M. Smith, *Joe Hill* (Salt Lake City: University of Utah Press, 1969); and Moshik Temkin, *The Sacco-Vanzetti Affair: America on Trial* (New Haven: Yale University Press, 2009).

mass pressure, into which the legal defense is merged, has forced the capitalist courts ... to grant a new trial."[26]

Yet, exactly how mass pressure could force capitalist courts to do anything was obscure. One promising path lay in describing political prosecutions as legal lynchings. Doing so allowed the lawyers to seek relief from one segment of the ruling class – the judges of the national courts, especially the Supreme Court – against decisions made by a more parochial segment of the ruling class, particularly judges in Southern courts. The idea was that sophisticated political elites would understand that legal lynchings undermined the credibility of the general claim that the capitalist rule of law was fundamentally fair, and generally involved defendants who posed no real threat to the capitalist economic, social, and political order. The contrast *The New Republic* drew between the conservative New York newspaper and the Georgia courts suggests this line of argument. Federalism and the hierarchical nature of a complex government provided the opportunity for higher courts to act independently of the wishes and interests of local ruling elites. Yet, even this approach was a bit schizophrenic. As historian Dan Carter put it in connection with the Scottsboro cases, advocates of labor defense "could not lose": "Had the Supreme Court affirmed the death sentences, [they] could have pointed to this as evidence that the courts were instruments of the ruling class. A reversal of the decision confirmed the correctness of the 'mass struggle' tactics."[27]

The NAACP developed a strategy with some resemblances to labor defense, at roughly the same time, and sometimes NAACP officials presented their strategy as "better" than labor defense because it was more consistent with American ideals. The strategy took the form of what was expected to be a sustained campaign against some manifestations of racial segregation in the U.S. South, with the ultimate goal of destroying the legal foundation for that system in the Supreme Court's decision upholding segregation as constitutionally permissible when separation was accomplished through the provision of "separate but equal" facilities for whites and African Americans.

That goal could be reached through two routes.[28] The first resembled the labor defense strategy. The NAACP hoped that its litigation could form the basis for organizational growth as African Americans came to see that the NAACP's actions were giving them material benefits. Those benefits would flow from success in litigation. The NAACP filed lawsuits on behalf of African American teachers in segregated schools, seeking to equalize their salaries with those of white teachers with equivalent credentials. It also pursued

[26] Quoted in Charles H. Martin, *The Angelo Herndon Case and Southern Justice* (Baton Rouge: Louisiana State University Press, 1976), p. 15.

[27] Carter, *Scottsboro*, p. 165.

[28] This following account of the NAACP strategy and its functions is based on Tushnet, *NAACP's Legal Strategy*.

litigation to obtain graduate and professional education for African Americans, in states where doing so would require either the creation of entire new programs such as law schools or the integration of existing institutions. Success in these cases would, the NAACP hoped, show its constituents – especially the teachers – the value of supporting the organization. In addition, the litigation had a modest amount of the kind of dramatic value that attached to political trials in criminal cases, because the mere appearance of African American attorneys in white-dominated courts demonstrated to the local African American community how racial equality could be acted out in public spaces.[29] The "mobilization" component of the NAACP's strategy required legal victories, because the material benefits would occur only if the lawsuits succeeded. Here the strategy was didactic in a specific way – not to inform the community about the practices being challenged, with which the audience was of course entirely familiar, but to inform it about the NAACP's value to the community.

As with labor defense, the NAACP's strategy was to use litigation for mobilization, but the mobilization was rather more limited – building organizational capacity rather than mobilization of the masses throughout the nation. The litigation had goals beyond mobilization, though. Successful litigation would increase the cost of segregation by obtaining court orders directing that the separate facilities for African Americans actually be equal and thereby make maintaining segregation too expensive. It was in this sense destructive. The success the NAACP sought was a single goal – destroying the legal basis for segregation – that could be reached via two paths. The first was increasing the cost of segregation. The second, always implicit in the equalization lawsuits but emerging as a distinct theme only in the 1940s, was a challenge to the "separate but equal" doctrine itself.

Both paths to ultimate victory required winning cases, and the theory behind them consisted mostly in simple faith in the fairness of the U.S. legal system. This was especially true of the salary equalization cases, which were "small" ones that the U.S. Supreme Court was unlikely to consider or use as a vehicle for a broad ruling about segregation's constitutional status. Yet, to some extent both paths were strengthened by the hierarchical structure of the U.S. courts and the theoretical possibility that the Supreme Court – a national court – might take a broader perspective than the courts in the Southern states. And, the possibility of review cast a shadow over the lower courts' actions. Again, the complexity of "the government" provided room for plaintiff-side lawfare.

The challenge to school segregation was simultaneously destructive and preservationist, presenting the conceptual paradox described briefly above. It was destructive, because legal successes would undermine the Southern

[29] For a discussion of the performative dimension of African American lawyers' work, see Mack, *Representing the Race*.

system of apartheid, but it was preservationist because the localized disruption would occur when, and because, national courts held that the existing Constitution itself condemned segregation. Considering only the goal of winning legal victories (and putting aside the goal of mobilization), plaintiff-side lawfare generally has this dual character: It seeks to destroy a discrete practice, though of course one that might be of large social significance, by invoking "the law" as it currently "is" to condemn the practice. Critical legal scholars pointed out that that invocation implicitly relied on the indeterminacy of the law, but also suggested that overall the preservationist effect of plaintiff-side lawfare might outweigh its disruptive effect.

BROWN V. BOARD OF EDUCATION AS A POLITICAL TRIAL

In the late 1940s, after winning a series of cases involving graduate and professional schools, and facing increasing pressure from NAACP members and other lawyers within the NAACP, Thurgood Marshall decided the time was right to pursue a "direct attack" on segregation – lawsuits challenging segregated education in elementary and secondary schools. Local activists, informed of the NAACP's interest in a direct attack, generated four cases; a fifth, in the District of Columbia, was generated by activists loosely associated with the NAACP but not formally part of the strategic decision-making. The goal was a Supreme Court decision holding segregation unconstitutional, but that goal could be reached only after trials in the five cases. And, those trials had some features that resembled aspects of classic political trials, especially the exposure of factual material casting segregation in a bad light.

Before returning to *Briggs* v. *Elliott*, to illustrate both the promise and the difficulties of using civil trials as political forums, I turn again to the Scottsboro cases to emphasize the dramaturgical coordination of trial evidence for purposes of political mobilization. As mentioned earlier, the cases attracted little attention until the defendants were convicted in a first round of trials. The Supreme Court vacated those convictions on the ground that the defendants had not been adequately represented by counsel. The original trials, then, were not "political trials" of the classic sort.

The retrials were different. The ILD procured the services of Samuel Liebowitz, a prominent criminal defense lawyer from New York. Liebowitz developed a strategy for pretrial motions and for the trials themselves. The immediate audience in the courtroom was entirely white, because the community's African Americans had been intimidated by the "lynch law" atmosphere associated with the cases. Liebowitz's trial strategy involved a relentless attack on the credibility of the woman who the defendants were said to have raped. Within the courtroom that attack was badly received by the audience. Notably, it was not straightforwardly disruptive of the Southern system either, except to the extent that it challenged an implicit and rarely acknowledged position among Southern whites that the word of a Southern white woman charging rape by African Americans had to be taken as true no matter what her character or inherent credibility was.

Liebowitz's pretrial strategy, in contrast, was fully destructive, consisting of a challenge to the composition of the grand jury that indicted the defendants and the jury rolls for their trials. The challenge was that African Americans had been deliberately excluded from the jury rolls. Liebowitz staged this challenge in two acts, which Marshall's use of expert witnesses in *Briggs* v. *Elliott* unconsciously echoed.

The first act – actually this occurred twice, because the defendants had been indicted in one county and were being tried in another – involved testimony from the counties' jury commissioners and associated officials, all of course white. Liebowitz asked them to describe the statutory requirements for jury qualification, then asked them whether there were African Americans in their communities who satisfied those requirements. The officials testified that there were none. They suggested that African Americans were uneducated; when Liebowitz pointed out that the jury rolls had illiterate whites on them, one witness responded that that might be so, but African Americans "will nearly all steal." After the official admitted that it was unlikely that an African American minister would steal, Liebowitz got him to acknowledge that he would keep even such a person off the jury rolls, "partly" because of race. Overall, Liebowitz was able to show that the white officials did not take seriously their constitutional duty to place all qualified citizens, of either race, on the jury rolls.

The second act consisted of testimony from African American residents, none of whom had ever served on a grand jury or a trial jury. These witnesses testified that they knew of African Americans who fit all the statutory requirements, and many themselves were clearly qualified to serve. One was a dentist with a degree from Howard University, another a physician who had graduated from the University of Illinois. *The Birmingham News* described these witnesses as "unusually intelligent in appearance" and, indicating something of white Southern views about African Americans, thought it worth noting that they "employed good English."[30]

Liebowitz's target was not the audience within the courtroom. Rather, one audience was the large number of people around the country who had become interested in the Scottsboro cases through the ILD's labor defense activities. The contrast between the white witnesses, who Liebowitz was able to present in self-discrediting ways, and the African American witnesses not only made the legal point that the jury commissioners had acted unconstitutionally but also showed the virtues of the Southern African American community. Another audience, of course, was the U.S. Supreme Court. When the cases returned there, Chief Justice Charles Evans Hughes's opinion explicitly referred to the

[30] The hearings, testimony, and comments are summarized in Carter, *Scottsboro*, pp. 194–201.

competing testimony from the white and African American witnesses. According to Hughes, Liebowitz had shown that no African Americans had served on juries for decades. "The case thus made was supplemented by direct testimony that specified negroes, thirty or more in number, were qualified for jury service. Among these were negroes who were members of school boards, or trustees, of colored schools, and property owners and householders." The jury commissioners' testimony that there were no African Americans in the counties qualified for jury service "cannot be divorced" from the "direct and specific" "testimony, not overborne or discredited, that there were, in fact, negroes in the county qualified for jury service."[31]

The courtroom performance in the Scottsboro retrials shows that the audiences for labor defense were outside the courtroom, but also that what happened within the courtroom was an essential predicate for some of labor defense's disruptive and organizational effects. The same can be said about the trial in *Briggs* v. *Elliott*, where Marshall was in charge.[32] As a good lawyer, Marshall knew that he had to prepare a case showing that the separate schools in Clarendon County, South Carolina, were unequal in material terms, because he could win his case by succeeding with the direct attack on segregation or by showing that the school district violated the "separate but equal" rule. He compiled a lot of evidence about inequality he hoped to introduce at the trial. In contrast to the courtroom in the Scottsboro cases, the one in *Briggs* was filled with African Americans, brought there by community organizations.

Marshall was prevented from introducing the most dramatic evidence of material inequality when the school board's lawyer conceded that the facilities were unequal. As we have seen, Marshall did put on several expert witnesses who described terrible facilities, with broken chairs, outdoor toilets, and no dining rooms or gymnasiums. There was, however, no jury. The NAACP sought an injunction directing the elimination of segregation, which meant that it had to persuade judges, and (in the courtroom) judges only, that its legal position was correct. Yet, in addition to the judges, there was an immediate audience for the trial evidence: A line of African Americans wound its way through the courthouse, each one waiting for a chance to enter the courtroom itself.[33]

After the NAACP lawyers put on their expert witnesses who detailed the physical conditions at the Clarendon County schools, they called Kenneth Clark to the stand to present what came to be seen as the most important evidence at the trial. Clark's testimony dealt with the psychological harms caused by

31 *Norris* v. *Alabama*, 294 U.S. 587, 592, 594 (1935).

32 For additional detail and references, see Mark V. Tushnet, *Making Civil Rights Law: Thurgood Marshall and the Supreme Court, 1936–1961* (New York: Oxford University Press, 1994), pp. 158–159.

33 Kluger, *Simple Justice*, pp. 346–347.

segregation. With help from his contacts at Columbia University, Robert Carter, Marshall's principal deputy, had located the work of social psychologist Clark and his wife Mamie. The Clarks conducted what came to be known as "doll tests." They presented African American children with a number of dolls with different skin tones, some "black" or "brown" and others "white," and asked which ones the children preferred and which were most like them. Typically, the African American child described the white dolls as "nicer" than the others, and the black dolls as more like themselves. The Clarks concluded that African American children had impaired self-images: In their own eyes they were not as "nice" as white children.

Eventually, the Supreme Court included a reference to the doll studies in a footnote in its unanimous opinion finding segregation unconstitutional.[34] The footnote was appended to the assertion that "modern authority" supported the statement made by one of the courts hearing the five cases that "Segregation of white and colored children in public schools has a detrimental effect upon the colored children ... for the policy of separating the races is usually interpreted as denoting the inferiority of the negro group." The reference to "modern authority" directs attention to yet another audience for the *Brown* trial: the community of generally liberal social scientists whose authority Clark and the Supreme Court invoked.

Critics of the decision seized upon the footnote to claim that it demonstrated that the Court's ruling rested on "sociology" rather than "law." Using the Clarks' evidence at trial had been controversial within the NAACP, with some lawyers, probably including Marshall, somewhat skeptical about using such "soft" evidence. The criticism eventually took a more academic form, with critics of the studies pointing out that they really were about African American self-images, not about the effects of segregation in the public schools, and that they did not meet the scientific standards that eventually came to be demanded by social psychologists.

The criticisms of the doll studies transformed the way in which *Brown* v. *Board of Education* was a political trial. The decision's supporters came to believe that the Clarks' conclusions were almost certainly correct, though perhaps not well-supported by their studies, but were also almost certainly unnecessary in a constitutionally well-founded decision finding segregation unconstitutional. The decision's critics believed, to the contrary, that the Court's references to "modern authority" impaired the constitutional legitimacy of its decision. This transformation shifted the political valence of the trial evidence: Introduced to show why segregation was unconstitutional, the evidence came to be taken as showing why the Court's way of addressing the constitutional question was mistaken. The trial evidence did not precisely backfire, because the NAACP won its cases, but in the decision's aftermath the doll studies came to work against rather than for the plaintiffs.

[34] *Brown* v. *Board of Education*, 347 U.S. 483, 494 n. 11 (1954).

SOME LIMITATIONS ON PRIVATE CIVIL LITIGATION AS POLITICAL TRIALS: BROWN'S AFTERMATH AND ITS INFLUENCE ON LITIGATION FORMS

After the Supreme Court held segregation in public education unconstitutional, the question remained, what to do about it? Concerned about the possibility of Southern resistance to immediate desegregation, the Court required only that Southern school boards proceeded toward desegregation "with all deliberate speed." A decade of experience showed that recalcitrant school boards were not proceeding toward desegregation at all. As a result, the Supreme Court encouraged lower courts to enter orders directing school boards to do something immediately. By the time this happened, latent ambiguities in the constitutional doctrine *Brown* articulated had come to the surface. The decision could have meant "only" that school boards could not use race as a basis for assigning children to schools – could not "segregate" the children. That would imply that school boards could develop pupil assignment systems using other bases for assignment such as neighborhood residence or parental choice even when doing so would produce schools that were racially identifiable. And, that is what many school boards did. The lower courts came to think that these were merely techniques to evade the Supreme Court's ruling, as they certainly were in many instances. The result was that an alternative reading of *Brown*, one that had existed from the day it was announced, became more attractive. The mandate, it came to be thought, required integration of the schools, the elimination of racially identifiable schools.

In 1968, the Supreme Court wrote that the Constitution required that schools be neither white nor African American but "just schools."[35] Lower courts understood this to mean that they had to enter orders that would have the effect of eliminating racially identifiable schools. In light of residential segregation and "white flight" from cities to suburbs that was no easy task. The lower courts entered comprehensive orders dealing with a wide range of school practices: student assignment plans, teacher assignments, school location, educational programming, and eventually transportation of students to schools that would as a result not be racially identifiable. Occasionally, the hearings leading up to these orders exposed to wider view practices that many ordinary people had not known were occurring, and so, again, served some of the functions of political trials. Most notably, perhaps, was the experience in Detroit, Michigan. The desegregation case there was assigned to a quite conservative judge, initially skeptical about claims that the city's authorities had deliberately made decisions to exacerbate the racial segregation that resulted from residential segregation. The judge found the record of deliberate acts to make school segregation worse so compelling that he entered an order essentially directing the consolidation of the city's schools

[35] *Green* v. *County School Board of New Kent County*, 391 U.S. 430 (1968).

with those in the suburbs, though the U.S. Supreme Court later reversed his decision.[36]

The experience with comprehensive remedies in school desegregation cases generated a new form of plaintiff-side civil litigation, given the name "public law litigation" by Harvard Law School's Abram Chayes.[37] Civil plaintiffs used the courts to obtain reforms in prisons and police departments, and again the trials in these cases sometimes fit the image of the classic political trial, useful for political mobilization and public education. A notable example came in a long-running case challenging overcrowding in California's prison system. When the case reached the Supreme Court, a sharply divided Court affirmed an order directing that the state implement a plan that included releases of prisoners before their terms had been completed. The opinion was routine in form, but Justice Anthony Kennedy's opinion for the majority included photographs dramatically illustrating the overcrowded conditions to which the courts were responding.[38] A New York federal judge held that the city's police department engaged in racial profiling when it selected people to stop and question on the streets. The facts developed at the hearings, along with some of the judge's preliminary rulings, induced some changes in public views about the city's "stop and frisk" practices. The judge ordered systemic changes in the department's practices and appointed an outside "monitor" to ensure compliance with the order. After a new mayor took office, the city dropped its opposition to the order.[39]

International human rights NGOs in the United States saw the opportunity for something akin to public law litigation in their field as well.[40] Here private civil litigation as a form of political trial occurs in litigation under the Alien Tort Act. Recent developments show how the two goals of plaintiff-side lawfare – mobilization and obtaining enforceable legal judgments – sometimes are separated. The statute, enacted in 1791, provides that U.S. courts can impose liability in the form of money damages on non-U.S. citizens, including corporations, for actions that take the form of torts – private civil wrongs – made unlawful by international law. The modern origin of Alien Tort Act litigation is *Filartiga* v. *Peña-Irala*, decided in 1980, in which a lower court allowed a tort claim against agents of the Paraguayan dictatorship for

36 *Milliken* v. *Bradley*, 418 U.S. 717 (1974).

37 Abram Chayes, "The Role of the Judge in Public Law Litigation," *Harvard Law Review*, Vol. 89 (1976), pp. 1281–1316. The term has spread internationally, with the Indian Supreme Court being especially involved in public law litigation.

38 *Brown* v. *Plata*, 563 U.S. 493 (2011).

39 Benjamin Weiser and Joseph Goldstein, "Mayor Says New York Will Settle Suit on Stop-and-Frisk Tactics," *New York Times*, January 30, 2014.

40 Harold Hongju Koh, "Transnational Legal Process," *Nebraska Law Review*, Vol. 75 (1996), pp.181–207, provides a useful short introduction to the theories underlying public law litigation in international human rights.

kidnapping, torturing, and murdering the son of a political dissident.[41] The U.S. Supreme Court has interpreted the Alien Tort Act quite narrowly. In *Sosa* v. *Alvarez-Machain*, the Court held in 2004 that the torts to which it referred were a quite limited list of universally condemned and specifically defined wrongs such as piracy and torture – and did not include the concededly unlawful kidnapping of a Mexican citizen by Mexican mercenaries cooperating with the U.S. Drug Enforcement Agency.[42] In 2013, the Court unanimously held that the courts could hear Alien Tort Act cases only "where the claims touch and concern the territory of the United States."[43] The justices disagreed about what it would take for a claim to do so, but apparently injuries to U.S. citizens or substantial corporate activities in the United States that had some connection to the wrongs committed elsewhere might qualify.

Alien Tort Act litigation is private civil litigation often conducted primarily for purposes of mobilization. As in *Filartiga*, the underlying wrongs are of course quite real, but the litigation's primary purpose may not be obtaining compensation for wrongs. The 2013 case, for example, involved a claim brought against Shell Oil for destroying the ecosystem and cultural heritage of the indigenous people of a region in Nigeria, not through its ordinary oil extraction processes, but rather through cooperation with the Nigerian military's allegedly brutal campaign to clear the area of indigenous opposition. The primary point of the litigation was to bring Shell's actions to the world's attention, in the hope not so much of actually winning the lawsuit but rather in the hope of generating public pressure on Shell and other oil companies to change their ecologically and culturally unfriendly policies.

Alien Tort Act litigation differs structurally from the private civil litigation discussed earlier in the chapter because it does not, in form, involve an attempt to use the regime's courts against another component of the regime: Structurally, the cases pit the United States against Paraguay or Nigeria. But, again, the complexity of government means that the formal description of the litigation structure fails to capture the political reality.

The U.S. executive branch became increasingly uncomfortable as the number of Alien Tort Act cases grew, even though the absolute number was always rather small. In part that resulted from decreasing sympathy with the international human rights system. *Filartiga* was decided in 1980, when official U.S. endorsement of that system was at its height. By 2004, when *Sosa* was decided, U.S. government enthusiasm for international human rights had diminished markedly, with Republican policy-makers particularly dismayed

41 630 F.2d 876 (2d Cir. 1980).

42 *Sosa* v. *Alvarez-Machain*, 542 U.S. 692 (2004). After being kidnapped, Alvarez-Machain was taken to the United States, where he was tried – and acquitted for lack of evidence – for his supposed participation in the killing of a DEA agent.

43 *Kiobel* v. *Royal Dutch Petroleum Co.*, 569 U.S. (2013).

over the scope of the claims made on behalf of international human rights. Transnational corporations were troubled by Alien Tort Act litigation, and they had the legal resources to develop well-presented legal arguments against expanding the scope of the Alien Tort Act. Finally, the U.S. State Department took the position that expansive Alien Tort Act jurisdiction complicated diplomatic relations with allies and adversaries. As to allies, Shell Oil is a Dutch company, and there are other examples of Alien Tort Act cases brought against transnational corporations chartered in allied nations. As to adversaries, the State Department complained that Alien Tort Act litigation, which they could not control, impeded its ability to work out systems of incentives and sanctions that, in its view, were more likely than the litigation to produce change in the adversaries' policies. With the introduction of the State Department into the picture, we can see how the formal structure of Alien Tort Act litigation conceals the reality that it too involves an attempt to use the courts as one branch of government against another.

Until recently, it could be said that Alien Tort Act litigation had been a reasonably successful element in a larger strategy of expanding public support for international human rights. News stories about the cases and demonstrations outside the courts when hearings occurred drew attention both to specific human rights violations and to the international human rights regime more generally. The Supreme Court's obvious hostility to an expansive Alien Tort Act will almost certainly limit the effectiveness of litigation. With the possibility of legal success remote, the cases will be dismissed at an early stage, making it extremely difficult to use the litigation for mobilization. That fact in turn suggests one of the limitations on private civil litigation as a form of political trial: Successes depend upon the willingness of the national government as a whole to make space – in this context, time – even for mobilization around such litigation.

CONCLUSION

Brown and the Alien Tort Act litigation, seen as political trials, clearly share some of the general characteristics of political trials. *Brown* was decisive in the sense used by Meierhenrich and Pendas. It brought into the judicial arena a question of public policy that was being controverted in multiple venues – and in doing so it transformed, at least within that arena, the policy question into a question of constitutional law and rights. Similarly, Alien Tort Act litigation seeks to obtain a judicial declaration that certain practices violate international human rights law. *Brown* and the Alien Tort Act lawsuits of course sought and seek actual remedies, but the history of implementation after *Brown* suggests real limitations on that possibility. So, in addition to judicial declarations, these lawsuits seek to educate the public about the practices they bring into court. Importantly, though, as the Scottsboro litigation shows, the education *accompanies* the trial but need not be part of it. That is, the facts as brought out within the courtroom play some role in the educational function of this litigation, but extra-curial mobilization extends farther than the facts inside the courtroom. Advocates will refer to material perhaps excluded from the judicial record for technical reasons, or material perhaps going well beyond the specifics of the case at hand to show why the case being litigated is typical or representative of some broader policy problem. And, of course, the goal of the litigation is the destruction, not so much of political enemies, but of policies the plaintiffs believe to be incompatible with human rights or the Constitution. But, as I have observed, reaching that goal has a preservationist or legitimating – non-destructive – effect.

8

The Eichmann Trial in Law and Memory

Devin O. Pendas

In the past few years, in connection with the fiftieth anniversary of the 1961 trial of Adolf Eichmann in Jerusalem, there has been a wave of interest in the trial, with commemorative academic conferences taking place from Melbourne to Toronto. Much the same thing took place ten years earlier with the fortieth anniversary.[1] Why this interest? Why have cosmopolitan intellectuals from throughout the world – Anglophone, German speaking, Hebrew speaking – been so interested in this particular trial? Why, fifty years after the legal proceedings and seventy years after the crimes adjudicated, does this trial continue to attract global attention? This is, after all, highly unusual. Few trials, even the most prominent, have that kind of cultural staying power. Most "trials of the century" are forgotten as soon as they are over.[2] Aside from the International Military Tribunal at Nuremberg (and for related reasons), there may be no better-known twentieth-century trial than Eichmann's.

WHY THE EICHMANN TRIAL?

So what is it about the trial of Adolf Eichmann that distinguishes it from other highly publicized, historically significant trials, most of which no one remembers? Another way of framing this question is to ask if the Eichmann trial was, in our terms, a didactic trial – and Lawrence Douglas is surely right that it was in many ways the paradigmatic didactic trial – then what is it about

[1] The conferences around the fortieth anniversary produced a number of important scholarly works focused mainly on Arendt's relation to the trial. See, e.g., Gary Smith, ed., *Hannah Arendt Revisited: "Eichmann in Jerusalem" und die Folgen* (Frankfurt: Suhrkamp, 2000) and Steven E. Aschheim, ed., *Arendt in Jerusalem* (Berkeley: University of California Press, 2001).

[2] For instance, one legal blog listing the top trials of the twentieth century includes a half-dozen trials of obscure celebrities or political figures unknown to any but the most well-informed experts. See: www.crschools.net/blog/20-trials-of-the-century.

its lessons that has proved to be so enduring?[3] As Douglas describes didactic trials, they seek first "to provide detailed and accurate representations of ... historical forces" and to "teach history lessons."[4] But of course didactic trials may also seek to teach other kinds of lessons at the intersection of law and politics. These might be the scientific lessons of the "Scopes Monkey trial" or the lessons in U.S. race relations at the heart of the O.J. Simpson trial. They might also, however, be legal lessons. We tend to forget that legal precedent is a kind of pedagogy, albeit of a particular sort. In articulating binding precedent, courts seek to "teach" subsequent tribunals the proper interpretation of some legal doctrine or statute. The power of that lesson depends, in part, on the power of the court issuing the ruling, but it also depends in part on the didactic persuasiveness of the legal lesson in later contexts. (One might think, here, of the *Dred Scott* case as an example of failed legal pedagogy.)

So to ask why the Eichmann trial has proved as enduring as it has is to ask about the specific admixture of law and politics in its pedagogy. Is it remembered because it articulated a particularly powerful interpretation of legal norms, or because of its "detailed and accurate depiction of historical forces?" I will suggest here that, although the Eichmann trial did to a limited extent break new legal ground in the interpretation of certain legal norms, it is not – unlike Nuremberg – recalled mainly for its legal pedagogy, but neither is it ultimately remembered for its historical lessons. While these were certainly detailed and reasonably accurate, their impact on the memory and historical understanding of the Holocaust was indirect, highly mediated, and ultimately created an ironic universalization of the highly specific genocide of European Jewry.

One possible explanation for the enduring interest in the Eichmann trial could be its role as a legal precedent in a direct sense. The trial is cited with some frequency by subsequent tribunals dealing with mass atrocities, and William Schabas has argued that the trial played a significant role in the development of international law.[5] Yet even if one agrees that the trial had a significant impact on international law – and there are reasons to be skeptical on this count – it seems unlikely that legal precedent explains much of the trials' continued fascination for a broad public.

Alternately, the Eichmann trial might serve not as a precedent but as a legal model for how to properly prosecute mass atrocities. Such an explanation would emphasize not so much the specific legal principles enumerated in Jerusalem or their applicability to subsequent prosecutions. Rather, one

[3] Lawrence Douglas, *The Memory of Judgment: Making Law and History in the Trials of the Holocaust* (New Haven: Yale University Press).

[4] Lawrence Douglas, "The Didactic Trial: Filtering History and Memory in the Courtroom," *European Review*, Vol. 14 (2006), pp. 513–514.

[5] William Schabas, "The Contribution of the Eichmann Trial to International Law," *Leiden Journal of International Law*, Vol. 26 (2013), pp. 667–699.

could argue that the *kind of trial* Eichmann had, a trial conducted in the national courts of the victim community, offered a powerful example of how to do justice for past atrocities. The contrast, obviously, would be with deracinated international trials held at some remove from the victim (and perpetrator) societies. This explanation is ultimately no more satisfying than the precedential interpretation, and for related reasons. Ultimately, the Eichmann trial was simply too *sui generis* as a legal event for it to have much relevance to subsequent legal actors, much less for the specifics of its juridical character to matter to global civil society. As Oliver Wendell Holmes once said, "great cases are called great not by reason of their real importance in shaping the law of the future, but because of some accident of immediate overwhelming interest which appeals to the feelings and distorts the judgment."[6]

This suggests that it is the politics of the Eichmann trial that matter more than the jurisprudence. At the most basic level, the trial clearly had a profound impact on Israeli identity.[7] Yet this alone hardly explains the level of international interest in the case – for it is hardly just Israelis (or diaspora Jews) who continue to find the Eichmann trial an object of fascination. Rather, something more must be going on. In particular, it is imperative to explain why the Eichmann trial has come to acquire a kind of "universal" significance that extends beyond the specific political context of Israel in the early 1960s. Clearly, this is related to the Eichmann trial's role as a didactic trial, but I would like to suggest that the results are rather more complicated than a straightforward reading of the didactic purposes of the trial would indicate. One of the ironies that frequently haunt didactic trials is that the intended students learn the wrong lessons or that the wrong students learn the intended lessons. In the Eichmann trial, a bit of both took place. In the Eichmann case, rather than Jews learning the lachrymose history of Jewish suffering and the attendant need for a nation-state, as the Israeli prosecution intended, it was mainly non-Jews in the West who learned to adopt a subject-position of universal victimhood. The lachrymose history of modernity might be said to have been the dominant lesson the world learned from Eichmann, which was, from the vantage of the prosecution at any rate, entirely the wrong lesson and, in many ways, the wrong audience.

POLITICS AND THE EICHMANN TRIAL

To say that politics matter more to the persistent relevance of the Eichmann trial than law is not, however, to draw an artificial or absolute distinction between politics and law. Such a distinction would obviously run counter to

[6] *Northern Securities Co.* v. *United States*, 193 U.S. 197 (1904), pp. 400–401.

[7] Tom Segev, *The Seventh Million: The Israelis and the Holocaust* (New York: Picador, 2000), p. 11.

the project of the current volume. Although she herself was perhaps not as punctilious in overcoming this distinction as one might like, Judith Shklar was quite right to observe that one of the unfortunate characteristics of legalism as an ideology was "the tendency to think of law as 'there' as a discrete entity, discernibly different from morals and politics ..."[8] Trials for past atrocity are always political in our sense of the term, either as didactic or as destructive trials (and often as both). Yet trials like Eichmann's embody a more specific kind of politics as well, what I have elsewhere referred to as a "juridical politics of the past."[9] This term is intended to highlight the way that criminal trials for past atrocities embed policies of lustration and reintegration (the destructive aspect) and normative-political pedagogy (the didactic dimension) in the performativity of trials. After the demise of an oppressive regime, it has become commonplace to turn to criminal trials to exclude past perpetrators and to teach moral lessons. This is the essence of what Kathryn Sikkink refers to as "the justice cascade," and why such trials are in fact preeminently political.[10]

In much of postwar Europe, trials for Nazi perpetrators and their collaborators served both destructive and didactic functions. Criminal trials were used either in conjunction with or as alternatives to administrative purges (e.g. Denazification) to remove potential enemies of the postwar order from positions of power. Importantly, this destructive function necessarily carried with it its antithesis. Procedures for exclusion are always also simultaneously mechanisms for inclusion. Increasingly, over the late 1940s and the early 1950s, it became clear to postwar societies that it would be neither practically feasible nor politically wise to exclude all former Nazis and collaborators. Criminal trials were particularly useful for identifying a (generally small) group of "intolerable" cases which facilitated the reintegration of the (much larger) group of "ordinary" followers who could be rehabilitated into the postwar order.[11] While many of the more minor trials, of which there were tens of thousands throughout Europe, can hardly be accorded a significant didactic function, since they were typically brief, fragmentary, and received little or no public scrutiny, these mundane Nazi trials were punctuated by periodic high-profile trials. Whether the Nuremberg trials or the Polish trial of Auschwitz commandant Rudolf Höss in the 1940s, the Ulm or Frankfurt trials of the 1950s and 1960s, or the

[8] Judith N. Shklar, *Legalism: Law, Morals, and Political Trials* (Cambridge: Harvard University Press, 1964), p. 9.

[9] Devin O. Pendas, "Seeking Justice, Finding Law: Nazi Trials in Postwar Europe," *The Journal of Modern History*, Vol. 81 (2009), p. 352.

[10] Kathryn Sikkink, *The Justice Cascade: How Human Rights Prosecutions Are Changing World Politics* (New York: Norton, 2011).

[11] This was particularly acute in the formerly occupied countries of Europe. See the essays in István Deák, Jan Tomasz Gross, and Tony Judt, eds., *The Politics of Retribution in Europe: World War II and Its Aftermath* (Princeton: Princeton University Press, 2000).

Barbie/Trouvier/Papon troika of trials in the 1980s and 1990s, there was a steady stream of heavily mediatized trials geared more or less deliberately toward public pedagogy.

What differentiates the Eichmann trial from this broader history of Nazi trials is that the destructive dimension is almost wholly absent. While clearly, Eichmann could reasonably be considered an enemy of the Jewish people, it seems exaggerated at best to say that the point of his trial was to define and eliminate an enemy of the people. Not only was Eichmann clearly no longer a credible threat, which after all is often true of enemies destroyed in political trials, but neither was the political force (Nazism) he represented. To be sure, part of the didactic purpose of the trial was to demonstrate the perennial threat of anti-Semitism by way of Eichmann's biography, but this merely reinforces the fact that the didactic clearly predominated over the destructive in this case. The setting of the Eichmann trial, in Israel rather than Europe, also differentiated it significantly from other prominent Nazi trials. It was the only perpetrator trial conducted by Jewish victims and, for reasons I outline below, this had a profound although somewhat surprising impact on the way the trial has been remembered subsequently.

In thinking about the politics of the Eichmann trial, it is crucial to think about them in temporal terms. The politics of the trial *at the time* both inform the politics of the trial's legacy and are rather distinct from the politics of the trial in its aftermath. The past informs the present but does not dictate it. In a legal context, this relationship is often summarized in terms of the concept of "precedent," in which past decisions shape future ones. The principle of *stare decisis* notwithstanding, even in the common law tradition, precedent hardly *determines* the present. It does, however, help explain the interest the present has in the past in a legal context. What a court inclines to do now will – at least nominally – be informed by what courts have done in the past, and part of the jurisprudential project is to determine which past court actions are relevant.

THE NAZI AND NAZI COLLABORATORS (PUNISHMENT) LAW

It is worth starting with a consideration of the ways in which the Eichmann trial has served, or more relevantly, mostly failed to serve, as a legal precedent. Certain trials, of little intrinsic interest in terms of subject matter, continue to have important consequences long after their end, simply because they establish important legal principles or enduring precedents. Precedent can in itself be political. The *Somerset* case ending slavery in England in 1772 or *Marbury* v. *Madison* which established the principle of judicial review under the U.S. Constitution in 1803 would be examples of this sort of trial, one that established legal precedents with decisive political implications. Whether we are talking about the doctrine of "free soil" or of judicial review, these were important legal principles that informed subsequent legal interpretations for many generations and in both cases had a profound effect on the distribution of political power.[12] The Eichmann trial was not a case of this sort. It broke no new jurisprudential ground and established no significant legal precedent.

To understand why, unlike the Nuremberg trials, the Eichmann trial has had only a very restricted usefulness as a legal precedent for subsequent prosecutions of mass atrocity at either the international or domestic level, it is worth considering the nature of the legislation under which Eichmann was prosecuted. After he was seized in Argentina in May 1960 and transported to Israel, Adolf Eichmann was indicted for his role in the so-called Final Solution to the Jewish Question under the Nazis and Nazi Collaborators (Punishment) Law. This was a somewhat odd law. Although unacknowledged, either in the Knesset debates or in Israeli trials, its earliest precursors lay in the unofficial trials conducted in the postwar Displaced Persons (DP) camps of Jewish collaborators (mainly Kapos) who had aided the Nazis.[13] In these early trials, Jewish survivors of the Holocaust sought to both come to terms with the fact of Jewish collaboration and to create a postwar Jewish community cleansed of the "traitors" who had not only been responsible for the deaths of their fellow Jews but who had broken the bonds of Jewish solidarity and shattered any possible sense of unified community. The "saving remnant" as the DPs themselves termed it had, in part, to save itself from the stain of Jewish collaboration.[14]

With the founding of Israel, this project – of reconstituting community by punishing those who had violated it from within – took on even larger significance because the goal of communal reconstitution was now linked to the process of state formation. Debate on the Nazi and Nazi Collaborators (Punishment) Law began in late 1949, and the government presented the bill to the Knesset in March 1950. The debate was stormy; the main issue was how "Jewish" the law should be. There were two dimensions to this. First, should the law deal only with Jewish collaborators? And second, should it punish only crimes against Jews? The initial government draft "made no specific mention of Jews."[15] Yet it was clear from the start that the real target of the law was not Nazis but Jewish collaborators. When Pinhas Rosen, the Israeli justice minister, introduced the bill to Knesset, he said:

> Finally, another word about the practical implications of the law ... The law applies also to those who carried out the orders of the Nazis, and we cannot, unfortunately, be sure

[12] On the *Somerset* case, see Steven M. Wise, *Though the Heavens May Fall: The Landmark Trial That Led to the End of Human Slavery* (Cambridge: De Capo Books, 2005). On *Marbury* v. *Madison*, see William E. Nelson, *Marbury* v. *Madison: The Origins and Legacy of Judicial Review* (Lawrence: University of Kansas Press, 2000).

[13] Rivka Brot, "Julius Siegel: A Kapo in Four (Judicial) Acts," *Dapim*, Vol. 25 (2011), p. 75.

[14] Atina Grossman, *Jews, Germans, and Allies: Close Encounters in Occupied Germany* (Princeton: Princeton University Press, 2009), p. 131. See also Zeev W. Mankowitz, *Life between Memory and Hope: The Survivors of the Holocaust in Occupied Germany* (Cambridge: Cambridge University Press, 2007).

[15] Hannah Yablonka, *The State of Israel* v. *Adolf Eichmann* (New York: Schocken, 2004), p. 8.

that such people are not among us, although they are certainly few in number ... The proposed law may furthermore contribute to clearing the air among the survivor remnant that has immigrated to Israel. Everyone who is familiar with its problems knows how painful is the issue of suspicions and mutual accusations that to this day hover over some of those liberated from the camps and ghettos who have immigrated to the country ... Let our camp be pure.[16]

This was a "practical implication" for two reasons. Firstly, the goal was to consolidate and unify Israelis, who could not afford to be internally divided by old rivalries and enmities in light of their hostile environs. It is important to recall that, as Hanna Yablonka has put it, "due largely to their demographic attributes, from the moment of their arrival in Israel the survivors were an exceptionally active and – more importantly – influential group of immigrants."[17] And this group was particularly adamant that Jewish collaborators be punished. To this end, some forty trials were held against Jewish collaborators in the period between 1950 and the start of the Eichmann trial a little more than ten years later.[18]

The emphasis on punishing Jewish collaborators was "practical" in another sense as well. In the first decades after the war, the Israeli government was making no systematic effort to locate German Holocaust perpetrators, whether Eichmann or anyone else. Indeed, it was a German, the Hessian Attorney General Fritz Bauer, who pushed the Israelis to begin to seriously pursue Eichmann.[19] It was Bauer who discovered Eichmann was in Argentina, who informed the Israelis of this fact, and who pressured them to act on that information.[20] Quite simply, it never occurred to Israeli officials in the first decades after the war that they might have the chance to prosecute a major Holocaust perpetrator.

The second issue was whether the law should focus on crimes against Jews. Israel had signed the United Nations Genocide Convention shortly after becoming a sovereign state and had incorporated that convention into Israeli law. Yet, as Orna Ben-Naftali and Yogev Tuval note, "it was nevertheless felt by Knesset members that something was amiss in the Genocide Law – it did not address the unique plight of the Jewish people, it did not single out the Holocaust for its unique horror and it did not enable Israel to bring the people responsible for the Holocaust to justice."[21] The Nazi and Nazi Collaborators (Punishment) Law offered a chance to redress this problem.

[16] Knesset Proceedings 4, p. 1148 (1950), as cited in Brot, "Julius Siegel," p. 12.

[17] Yablonka, *Israel* v. *Eichmann*, p. 6.

[18] Hanna Yablonka, "HaHoq le'Asiyat Din beNatzim uve'Ozreihem: Heibet Nosaf leShei'elat HaYisra'elim, HaNitzolim veHaSho'ah," *Qatedra*, Vol. 82 (1997), p. 135.

[19] Tom Segev, *Simon Wiesenthal: The Life and Legends* (London: Jonathan Cape, 2010), pp. 136–138.

[20] Irmtrud Wojak, *Fritz Bauer: Eine Biographie* (Munich: C.H. Beck, 2013), pp. 294–298.

[21] Orana Ben-Naftali and Yogev Tuval, "Punishing International Crimes Committed by the Persecuted: The *Kapo* Trials in Israel (1950s–1960s)," *Journal of International Criminal Justice*, Vol. 4 (2006), p. 134.

As a consequence of these factors, and after much debate in the Knesset, the final draft of the law punished not only war crimes and crimes against humanity, as envisioned in the initial government draft, but also "crimes against the Jewish people."[22] This category parallels the language of the genocide convention, except that instead of criminalizing acts against any ethnic, racial, or religious group, it singles out crimes against the Jewish people, and unlike the Genocide Convention, this crime was to apply retroactively.[23] This was a crucial addition that was to have profound implications for the Eichmann case. Given the prospective nature of the Genocide Convention and its incorporation into Israeli law, it would not be possible to prosecute Eichmann for this crime (genocide). He would have to be tried on the basis of the Nazi and Nazi Collaborators (Punishment) Law, including for "crimes against the Jewish people."

While both war crimes and crimes against humanity – the other two crimes punishable under the law – are defined in significant ways with respect to the status of the victims, they are obviously not framed with any specific victim group in mind. Rather, both cover crimes against noncombatants, war crimes against foreign nationals, and crimes against a state's own citizens or stateless persons (and eventually coming to include crimes committed outside the context of war). Crimes against the Jewish people encompasses a different logic altogether. Although it was presumed that the Jews victimized by the Nazis were noncombatants, it was their identity as Jews that was relevant in this context. While the goal of the Israeli government to inculcate Jewish solidarity is hardly irrelevant to this formulation, it is also worth noting that the logic of the law was to highlight that Jews were killed and otherwise persecuted by the Nazis *as Jews*, not as noncombatants. It was felt that failing to highlight this would be to obfuscate the reality of the Nazi genocide of the Jews. In other words, while the law undoubtedly (and intentionally) distinguished and specifically emphasized Jewish victimization, it did this in part because that was a central element of Nazi policy.

Eichmann was indicted on fifteen counts, four of them for crimes against the Jewish people, seven for crimes against humanity, one for war crimes, and three for membership in a hostile organization. In many instances, the exact same act was covered under different counts of the indictment. For instance, Count Five indicted Eichmann for Crimes against Humanity because,

> the Accused committed acts, during the period between 1939 and 1945, in Germany and the other countries of the Axis, in the occupied territories and also in the areas which were in practice subject to their authority, which are to be defined as crimes against

[22] Nazis and Nazi Collaborators Punishment Law, text available at www.mfa.gov.il/MFA/MFAArchive/1950_1959/Nazis+and+Nazi+Collaborators+-Punishment-+Law-+571.htm.

[23] Ben-Naftali and Tuval, "Punishing International Crimes Committed by the Persecuted," pp. 132–133.

humanity, when, together with others, he caused the murder, extermination, enslavement, starvation and expulsion of the Jewish civilian population in those countries and areas.[24]

The first four counts of the indictment, all "crimes against the Jewish people," likewise accused Eichmann of "caus[ing] the deaths of millions of Jews" (Count One), "subject[ing] many millions of Jews to living conditions which were likely to bring about their physical destruction" (Count Two), "caus[ing] grave harm to millions of Jews, physically and mentally" (Count Three), and "adopt[ing] measures calculated to prevent births amongst the Jews" (Count Four). Indeed, Counts Five through Eight merely characterized the crimes outlined in the first four counts as crimes against humanity, rather than crimes against the Jewish people. To be sure, Counts Nine through Twelve did indict Eichmann for crimes against non-Jews (Poles, Slovenes, Gypsies, and the Czech citizens of Lidice), while Counts Thirteen through Fifteen accused him of criminal membership in "hostile organizations." On the indictment's formulation, crimes against humanity were simply another way of describing crimes against the Jewish people. While there is nothing legally improper about this (European Jews most certainly were victims of crimes against humanity under the Nazis), the identification of the two categories would have major implications for the trial's relevance outside Israel. It also helps to explain the ways the trial has served – or more relevantly failed to serve – as a useful precedent under international law.

THE EICHMANN TRIAL AS PRECEDENT AND MODEL

The Eichmann case has been cited on a number of occasions by international criminal tribunals, but in many cases these pertain to ancillary procedural issues, rather than anything significantly affecting the substance of international criminal law. For instance, the International Criminal Tribunal for the Former Yugoslavia cited the Eichmann case in a ruling concerning the doctrine of *male captus, bene detentus*, or wrongly captured, properly detained. Citing the Eichmann case among many others, the tribunal rejected a motion to dismiss by Dragan Nicolic, who claimed to have been wrongly arrested.[25] Likewise, the appeals chamber in the case against Dusko Tadic cited the Eichmann case in rejecting the defendant's plea of sovereign immunity. The tribunal held: "The right to plead violation of the sovereignty of a State is the exclusive right of that State. Only a sovereign State may raise the plea or waive

[24] *Attorney Gen. of Israel* v. *Eichmann*, 36 I.L.R. 5, available at: www.vex.net/~nizkor/hweb/people/e/eichmann-adolf/transcripts/Sessions/Session-001-01.html.

[25] *Prosecutor* v. *Nikolic (Decision on Defense Motion Challenging the Exercise of Jurisdiction by the Tribunal)* IT-94-2 (October 9, 2002), available at www.icty.org/x/cases/dragan_nikolic/tdec/en/10131553.htm.

it, and the accused has no right to take over the rights of that State."[26] The appeals chamber rejected this part of the trial court's reasoning, but nonetheless upheld its rejection of Tadic's plea of sovereign immunity, in part by itself citing the Eichmann case, on the grounds that the primacy of international tribunals must be upheld in instances where the case "involve[s] the perpetration of an international crime which all the nations of the world are interested in preventing."[27]

More significant than these fairly minor jurisdictional and procedural matters is the question of whether the Eichmann trial had a significant impact on the substantive development of international law. Here there are two areas of interest: genocide and universal jurisdiction. William Schabas has argued that the Eichmann trial made important contributions to the jurisprudence of genocide. He notes that the wording of the Nazi and Nazi Collaborators (Punishment) Law "closely resembles" that of the United Nations Genocide Convention, except that it substitutes the term "Jewish people" for "national, ethnical, racial, or religious group" in its category of protected persons.[28] On his reading, this substitution did little to isolate the jurisprudence of the Eichmann case from the broader development of the international law of genocide, given the broader overlap in statutory wording. "The judges in *Eichmann* were," he contends, "the first to consider the definition of the crime of genocide, the appropriate jurisdiction for its prosecution, and related issues."[29]

There are two core problems with this argument. First, Schabas asserts that "*Eichmann* remained the only significant judicial application of the Genocide Convention until the late 1990s," with the creation of the International Criminal Tribunal for Yugoslavia (ICTY). Yet, as he himself acknowledges, the court in the Eichmann case was not, in fact, applying the Genocide Convention, which was incorporated into Israeli law only with *prospective* jurisdiction, and thus could not be (and was not) used in the Eichmann case, but rather the Nazis and Nazi Collaborators (Punishment) Law.[30]

More fundamental is the second issue. Schabas points out, rightly, that the Jerusalem court distinguished between acts of physical extermination, which it held to constitute "crimes against the Jewish people" (genocide), while crimes committed against Jews prior to the invasion of the Soviet Union in 1941 were

[26] *Prosecutor* v. *Tadic (Appeals Chamber Decision on the Defence Motion for Interlocutory Appeal on Jurisdiction)* IT-94-1 (October 2, 1995), available at www.icty.org/x/cases/tadic/acdec/en/51002.htm.

[27] *Prosecutor* v. *Tadic (Appeals Chamber Decision on the Defence Motion for Interlocutory Appeal on Jurisdiction)* IT-94-1 (October 2, 1995).

[28] Schabas, "The Contribution of the Eichmann Trial to International Law," p. 670.

[29] Schabas, "The Contribution of the Eichmann Trial to International Law," p. 671.

[30] Schabas, "The Contribution of the Eichmann Trial to International Law," p. 670, where Schabas notes the prospective restriction for the Israeli incorporation of the Genocide Convention.

held to constitute crimes against humanity, since they fell short of the intent to physically destroy the Jewish people. As Schabas points out, distinguishing crimes against humanity from genocide in this way, with the latter being restricted to instances where the intent was physical destruction, became the norm in the jurisprudence of the ICTY.[31] At the same time, however, this neglects the fact that Eichmann was not actually convicted of genocide. The Knesset decided, as we have seen, to distinguish crimes against the Jewish people from genocide, with only the former being subject to retroactive prosecution. The purpose here was explicitly to highlight the specificity, indeed in the minds of many in the Knesset, the uniqueness of the Final Solution. So using Eichmann's conviction as a precedent for the jurisprudence of genocide in effect thwarts the legislative intent of the Knesset. It might also be noted that it goes against the intentions of Raphael Lemkin, who wanted "genocide" to include any number of policies that stopped short of physical annihilation.[32] So while Schabas is correct that the Eichmann case has been cited in support of a narrow interpretation of genocide, this has been in some ways a misreading of both the Eichmann case and the origins of the idea of genocide.

Of perhaps more substantive impact has been the use of the Eichmann case as a precedent for universal jurisdiction.[33] Obviously, Israel did not exist at the time of the Holocaust. Therefore, it could not claim territorial jurisdiction over Eichmann. Because the Genocide Convention does not contain a proviso for universal jurisdiction, the Jerusalem court, in considering its own jurisdiction in the Eichmann case, creatively interpreted the Genocide Convention as mandating territorial jurisdiction, but allowing universal jurisdiction.[34] On one level, this did not matter, since Eichmann was not being prosecuted for genocide, but for "Crimes against the Jewish People" under Israeli law.

Yet, aware that the manner of Eichmann's capture in Argentina and the nature of the Nazi and Nazi Collaborators (Punishment) Law risked delegitimating the trial in the eyes of world opinion, the Jerusalem court was at pains to emphasize that its jurisdiction rested on multiple foundations.

[31] Ibid., pp. 674–676.

[32] John Cooper, *Raphael Lemkin and the Struggle for the Genocide Convention* (Houndmills: Palgrave Macmillan, 2008).

[33] This another central contention in Schabas, "The Contribution of the Eichmann Trial to International Law" but see also Gary J. Bass, "The Adolf Eichmann Case: Universal and National Jurisdiction," in Stephen Macedo, ed., *Universal Jurisdiction: National Courts and the Prosecution of Serious Crimes under International Law* (Philadelphia: University of Pennsylvania Press, 2006), pp. 77–90, and Kenneth Randall, "Universal Jurisdiction under International Law," *Texas Law Review*, Vol. 66 (1988), pp. 810–813.

[34] Schabas points out that this is a fairly clear misreading of the genocide convention. Schabas, "The Contribution of the Eichmann Trial to International Law," pp. 687–690.

We have said that the crimes dealt with in this case are not crimes under Israeli law alone, but are in essence offences against the law of nations. Indeed, the crimes in question are not a free creation of the legislator who enacted the law for the punishment of Nazis and Nazi collaborators, but have been stated and defined in that law according to a precise pattern of international laws and conventions which define crimes under the law of nations.[35]

Because Eichmann's crimes "offended the whole of mankind and shocked the conscience of nations," they constituted violations of international as well as Israeli law and, "in the absence of an International Court, the international law is in need of the judicial and legislative authorities of every country, to give effect to its penal injunctions and to bring criminals to trial. The jurisdiction to try crimes under international law is universal."[36]

This decision to buttress Israel's jurisdictional claim with appeals to universal jurisdiction has given the Eichmann trial some purchase in later cases under international law. For instance, the Eichmann case, specifically the Israeli Supreme Court's upholding of jurisdiction based on universal jurisdiction, was cited by the ICTY in its judgment in *Prosecutor* v. *Furundzija* in laying claim to jurisdiction over a case of torture, even though the tribunal's authorizing statute made no specific mention of that offense. Citing the Eichmann case, the tribunal held, "it has been held that international crimes being universally condemned wherever they occur, every State has the right to prosecute and punish the authors of such crimes."[37]

It is fair to say, then, that the Eichmann case has helped consolidate the legitimacy of universal jurisdiction for crimes under international law. This achievement is, however, relatively modest, in that there are many sources of universal jurisdiction, dating back to the law of piracy, and the Jerusalem precedent is merely one among many. To be sure, Schabas is correct to note that the trial helped expand the "narrow frame" of jurisdiction established by the UN genocide convention, though since Eichmann was not, in fact, indicted for genocide, there is an element of analogical reasoning involved in this application of the Eichmann judgment.

More fundamentally, though, it remains to be seen to what degree universal jurisdiction establishes itself as a common practice under international law. To begin with, as Leora Bilsky has pointed out, "without introducing some requirement of a link to a living community, the pure concept of universal jurisdiction introduces many dangers of politicization."[38] If prosecuting

[35] *Attorney Gen. of Israel* v. *Eichmann* 36 I.L.R. 1, available at www.nizkor.org/ftp.cgi/people/k/ftp.cgi?people/e/eichmann.adolf/transcripts/Judgment/Judgment-002.

[36] Ibid.

[37] ICTY, *Prosecutor* v. *Furundzija*, December 10, 1998, p. 60, available at www.icty.org/x/cases/furundzija/tjug/en/fur-tj981210e.pdf.

[38] Leora Bilsky, "The Eichmann Trial and the Legacy of Jurisdiction," in Seyla Benhabib, Roy Tsao, and Peter Verovsek eds., *Politics in Dark Times: Encounters with Hannah Arendt* (Cambridge: Cambridge University Press, 2010), p. 213.

nations are not required to establish some link to the crimes in question, the potential to prosecute foreign nationals for unrelated, political reasons is substantial. Bilsky argues, following Hannah Arendt, that by not highlighting its communal link to the victims of Nazi crimes in its claim of universal jurisdiction, the Jerusalem court set a rather poor precedent for subsequent courts.

In fact, the Eichmann trial was an exercise in universal jurisdiction only in a very narrow sense. The Jerusalem court laid claim to universal jurisdiction for political reasons, to buttress an otherwise potentially controversial prosecution. Since Israel had not existed at the time of the Final Solution, there was the risk that jurisdictions based on either the protective or the passive personality principles might be regarded as technically invalid – although the district court claimed all three. It was the appeals court that insisted on the centrality of universal jurisdiction, while also accepting the claim of protective jurisdiction. They did so because the court convicted Eichmann of crimes against non-Jews as well as Jews.[39]

Yet, it is obvious that Israel's interest in the Eichmann case rested primarily not on a sense of universal justice but on a sense of wrong done to a specific community, albeit one that did not at the time have sovereign national status. Could one really believe Israel would have kidnapped Eichmann and brought him to Jerusalem for trial had his crimes exclusively affected Sinti and Roma? The Appeals Court's insistence on universal jurisdiction seems intended to cover incidental, rather than essential, elements in the trial. In the end, Theodor Meron's contention to the contrary notwithstanding, it seems clear that what was fundamentally at stake in the Eichmann trial was, as Israeli law stated, crimes against the Jewish people, and therefore the core jurisdictional claim by the Jerusalem court rested on passive personality principles.[40]

Schabas is correct to note that the Eichmann appeals verdict has been influential in generating a broad consensus in international law that genocide is subject to universal jurisdiction, but he is also correct to note that universal jurisdiction has been "rarely exercised."[41] On the one hand, the creation of the permanent International Criminal Court with broad jurisdiction over mass atrocity crimes would seem to obviate much of the need for states to individually deploy universal jurisdiction. On the other hand, the actual experience of universal jurisdiction in the 1990s proved to be a rather unhappy one. Pinochet, famously, was arrested on the basis of universal jurisdiction while convalescing in England, but was never delivered to Spain

39 See Schabas, "The Contribution of the Eichmann Trial to International Law," pp. 691–692.

40 Theodore Meron, "Public International Law Problems of the Jurisdiction of the State of Israel," *Journal du droit international*, Vol. 88 (1961), p. 1058.

41 Schabas, "The Contribution of the Eichmann Trial to International Law," p. 693.

for trial. This was ostensibly because of his poor health, but it seems certain that politics played as big a role in the decision as medicine.[42] Similarly, after ten years, Belgium repealed its universal jurisdiction law in 2003.[43] This law, which had allowed victims to file complaints for human rights abuses in Belgian courts, had been a political headache for the Belgian government from the start, and while U.S. authorities put considerable pressure on Belgium to repeal the law in the context of the "war on terror," it seems likely the government was only too happy to have an excuse to step back from vigorous universal jurisdiction.[44] So while the Eichmann trial may have helped validate universal jurisdiction under international law, there is reason to doubt whether this is a precedent that will actually see much application in practice. Certainly, its use by the ICTY is a rather restricted example, given that tribunal's status as an *international* court authorized by the UN Security Council and in only modest need of universal jurisdiction to buttress its more ordinary claims of subject-matter jurisdiction under its authorizing mandate.

More broadly, although Eichmann was indicted for crimes against humanity as well as against the Jewish people, the trial has been rather difficult to mobilize for international legal purposes because of the specificity of the latter charge. The use of the Eichmann precedent mainly on procedural and jurisdictional grounds, rather than for interpretation of substantive international criminal law reflects this. The precedential significance of the Eichmann trial is, in the end, limited.

The other possible way that the Eichmann trial could be legally significant is not as a precedent in the strict sense but as a model. Lawrence Douglas, for instance, has recently argued *apropos* of the Eichmann trial that it might be an example of the value of domestic, as opposed to international, prosecutions for past atrocities. He notes that the principle of complementarity as applied by the International Criminal Court enshrines the preferability of domestic over international jurisdiction. He asks, rhetorically, "if justice can be impaired by insufficient distance, can it also be impaired by too much distance? Can a case be so far removed as to erode the efficacy, if not the possibility, of justice?"[45] Certainly, he is right that there is a risk that international trials, far removed in time and place from the crimes which they seek to judge, can fail to arouse any support or even recognition among the perpetrator or victim nations.

Yet the Eichmann trial shares very little with other domestic trials for past atrocities. The defining feature of domestic trials in transitional justice settings is

[42] Naomi Roht-Arriaza, *The Pinochet Effect: Transitional Justice in the Age of Human Rights* (Philadelphia: University of Pennsylvania Press, 2006).

[43] www.hrw.org/news/2003/08/01/belgium-universal-jurisdiction-law-repealed.

[44] Roozbeh B. Baker, "Universal Jurisdiction and the Case of Belgium: A Critical Assessment," *ILSA Journal of International and Comparative Law*, Vol. 16 (2009), pp. 141–167.

[45] Leora Bilsky, Donald Bloxham, Lawrence Douglas, Devin Pendas, and Annette Weinke, "Forum: The Eichmann Trial Fifty Years On," *German History*, Vol. 29 (2011), p. 281.

that the perpetrators and the victims continue to coexist in the same territory and generally within the same polity. The problems facing such tribunals are well known. There is, on the one hand, the risk that the perpetrator group, which is frequently the military, as in Argentina or Chile, could exercise violence or even stage a coup. On the other hand, there is the potential for victim groups to use trials for past atrocities to consolidate a new authoritarian regime, as was done within Eastern Europe after World War II and appears to be happening in contemporary Rwanda. None of this applies to the Eichmann trial. By trying Eichmann in a new country created by and for victims, but without any perpetrator presence, the proceedings could succeed in mobilizing public support without any of the emotional or political ambivalence that is so marked in other domestic tribunals. One need only think of the recent controversies surrounding the Mixed Tribunal for Cambodia, where first the presiding judge and then the chief prosecutor both resigned in protest over political interference, to see this.[46] For obvious reasons, Eichmann had no allies in Israel.

THE EICHMANN TRIAL AND THE POLITICS OF COSMOPOLITAN MEMORY

So if we are not interested in the Eichmann trial because of its significance for the development of international law or as a model for domestic jurisdiction, why are we interested in it? Here, it becomes necessary to think less about law directly and more about history. It is sometimes asserted that the Holocaust was "forgotten" or "neglected" in the immediate aftermath of World War II. This is overly simplistic. At Nuremberg, for instance, substantial evidence pertaining to the genocide of the Jews was presented, albeit in a framework that emphasized the primacy of the Nazi's waging of aggressive war.[47] And of course, among the Nuremberg successor trials, one, the so-called Einsatzgruppen trial, dealt almost exclusively with the Holocaust in the Soviet Union.[48] Historians – especially Jewish survivor historians – began writing the history of the Holocaust even before it was over.[49] As early as 1953, Gerald

[46] Seth Mydans, "Judge Quits Tribunal in Khmer Rouge Inquiry," *New York Times*, October 10, 2011, available at www.nytimes.com/2011/10/11/world/asia/judge-quits-cambodia-tribunal.html and Colin Meyn, "International Prosecutor Resigns from KR Tribunal," *The Cambodia Daily*, September 10, 2013, available at www.cambodiadaily.com/archives/international-prosecutor-resigns-from-kr-tribunal-41982/.

[47] Michael Marrus, "The Holocaust at Nuremberg," *Yad Vashem Studies*, Vol. 26 (1998), pp. 5–42.

[48] Hilary Earl, *The Nuremberg SS-Einsatzgruppen Trial, 1945–1958: Atrocity, Law, and History* (Cambridge: Cambridge University Press, 2009).

[49] Laura Jockusch, *Collect and Record! Jewish Holocaust Documentation in Early Postwar Europe* (New York: Oxford University Press, 2012).

Reitlinger wrote the first comprehensive history of the "Final Solution to the Jewish Question."[50]

Still, it would be fair to say that starting in the late 1940s, the Nazi genocide of the Jews was significantly blocked in global public opinion. The Germans obviously had a strong interest in suppressing any substantial engagement with that history.[51] The Soviets were, by the early 1950s, descending into a wave of anti-Semitic agitation and repression of their own and, besides, had never had any interest in highlighting Nazi racial crimes, since they saw fascism as an outgrowth of capitalism, not racism. And in the context of the burgeoning Cold War, the Americans were more interested in rehabilitating than in condemning Germans – as evinced by the "amnesty fever" (Robert Kempner) that freed virtually all Nazi perpetrators from allied prisons by the mid-1950s.

So by the time of the Eichmann trial in 1961, the Holocaust had been marginalized in the global discussion of World War II. This was the context in which the Eichmann trial took place, one in which the memory of the Nazi genocide of the Jews had become mainly a Jewish memory, and in which the memory of the war years subsumed the extermination of the Jews into a broader history of generalized suffering. In response, one of the explicit goals of the trial was to highlight and publicize the specificity of Jewish suffering at the hands of the Nazis. Indeed, in a way that even the Einsatzgruppen trial or the trial of Auschwitz Commandant Rudolf Höss in Poland had not been, the Eichmann trial was (and was intended to be) about the Jews – what the Nazis had done to them, how they had responded, and, by implication at least, what lessons ought to be drawn for the present from this. As Shklar put it in 1964, "the Eichmann case ... does not really create new problems for legal theory. Eichmann, alas, was always a Jewish problem. Once he landed in Jerusalem his trial became an issue of Jewish politics and interests, both in Israel and in other Jewish communities."[52]

Israeli attorney general, Gideon Hausner, serving as chief prosecutor in the Eichmann case, sought to stress the essential Jewishness of the Holocaust.[53] In his opening speech, he proclaimed: "When I stand before you here, Judges of Israel, to lead the Prosecution of Adolf Eichmann, I am not standing alone. With me are six million accusers ... I will be their spokesman and in their name I will unfold the awesome indictment."[54] Hausner, in other words, claimed not to be

[50] Gerald Reitlinger, *The Final Solution: The Attempt to Exterminate the Jews of Europe, 1939–1945* (New York: Beechhurst Press, 1953).

[51] Jeffrey Herf, *Divided Memory: The Nazi Past in the Two Germanys* (Cambridge: Harvard University Press, 1997) and Ulrich Brochhagen, *Nach Nüremberg: Vergangenheitsbewältigung und Westintegration in der Ära Adenaur* (Hamburg: Hambuger Edition, 1994).

[52] Shklar, *Legalism*, pp. 154–155.

[53] On Hausner's strategy, see Douglas, *The Memory of Judgment*, pp. 123–149.

[54] *Attorney Gen. of Israel* v. *Eichmann*, 36 I.L.R. 5, available at www.vex.net/~nizkor/hweb/people/e/eichmann-adolf/transcripts/Sessions/Session-006-007-008-01.html.

speaking for the state of Israel or even for justice, much less the law.[55] He claimed to be speaking for the Jews of the world, those who were murdered in the Holocaust, those still alive, and even those of the past, noting that "The history of the Jewish people is steeped in suffering and tears. 'In thy blood, live!' (Ezekiel 16:6) is the imperative that has confronted this nation ever since it made its first appearance on the stage of history."[56]

Thus, for Hausner, the Eichmann trial was at its core not just about the recollection of Jewish catastrophe but also the imperative of Jewish survival. This emerges quite clearly in the kinds of seemingly extraneous testimony that Hausner elicited; these were of little forensic value but of tremendous experiential interest. For instance, on May 3, 1961, Rahel Auerbach from Yad Vashem, herself a survivor of the Warsaw ghetto, testified about the Holocaust in Warsaw. At the start of her testimony, however, Hausner asked her for "a general description, and a very concise one, of Warsaw as it was, from the Jewish point of view, before the outbreak of the War?" To this Auerbach responded:

> I would want to speak mainly about Warsaw from the spiritual aspect, about the cultural world of Jewish Warsaw. When I came to Warsaw for the first time . . . I was astonished at the intensity of the Jewish life. It was especially the Orthodox Jews who made an impression on me . . . this Jewry, Orthodox Jewry, was the great reservoir of Jewish life. Jews from modern social strata, the intellectual elite, all the time were leaving Jewish life, but these Orthodox Jews remained and they continually produced new strata of cultural creation.
>
> There was a complete Jewish state there.[57]

Auerbach's description of Warsaw as a "complete Jewish state" was hardly coincidental. It highlighted the breadth of Jewish life before the war and the fact that the Nazis had murdered not just Jews, but Jewishness.

> It was known that the enemy wanted to destroy us also from the spiritual point of view; this was also a prelude to physical destruction, to humiliate us and to convince their own people and the world at large that this was a nation of parasites who were not fit to live in the world, that they were a kind of gypsies.[58]

She went on then to describe the incredible efforts made by Jews in the Warsaw ghetto to preserve their cultural and educational institutions in the face of German hostility and about various efforts at Jewish self-help in the ghetto. Aside from the unfortunate racism implicit in her reference to the gypsies, what is most telling about Auerbach's testimony is the way that hers is a testimony

[55] Yechiam Weitz, "In the Name of Six Million Accusers: Gideon Hausner as Attorney-General and His Place in the Eichmann Trial," *Israel Studies*, Vol. 14 (2009), pp. 26–49.

[56] Ibid.

[57] *Attorney Gen. of Israel* v. *Eichmann*, 36 I.L.R. 5, available at www.vex.net/~nizkor/hweb/people/e/eichmann-adolf/transcripts/Sessions/Session-026-01.html.

[58] Ibid.

not about personal trauma, not about self-knowledge, but about institutions, about the state-like character of Jewish life in Warsaw before and even during the Ghetto.

The Zionist implications of Auerbach's testimony could hardly be clearer. Her central political message – tacit but quite clear – was that the pseudo-state of pre-war Jewish Warsaw was utterly incapable of protecting Jews from the Nazis. Its state-like attributes were admirable, part of a fully flourishing Jewish life, but without the full powers of sovereignty, most obviously the capacity for armed self-defense, they were ultimately inadequate, an illusion. Only a "real" state could fulfill the promise of pre-war Warsaw.

Ironically, by putting Jewishness at the center of the story of Nazi atrocities and World War II, the Eichmann trial allowed for a universalization of the Holocaust without imbricating it in the logic of the Cold War. This is not to imply that the Middle East was not important to the Cold War. Obviously, in the wake of the Suez crisis, it was.[59] Although in this period of the run-up to the building of the Berlin Wall, Central Europe still loomed larger in the Super Power confrontation. The crucial point here, though, is that by re-narrating World War II in terms of the Holocaust, the Eichmann trial created a way of understanding Nazism that lowered the strategic stakes for both the Soviets and the Americans. At Nuremberg, especially in the International Military Tribunal, the core issue had been aggressive war. As Sidney Alderman, Robert H. Jackson's deputy prosecutor at the IMT, put it at the very start of the proceedings:

> After all, everything else in this case, however dramatic, however sordid, however shocking and revolting to the common instincts of civilized peoples, is incidental to, or subordinate to, the aggressive war aspects of the case. All the dramatic story of what went on in Germany in the early phases of the conspiracy – the ideologies used, the techniques of terror used, the suppression of human freedom employed in the seizure of power, and even the concentration camps and the Crimes against Humanity, the persecutions, torture, and murders committed – all these things would have little jurisdiction of international significance except for the fact that they were the preparation for the commission of aggressions against peaceful neighboring peoples.[60]

The British prosecutor Hartley Shawcross went further: "the place of war in international law had undergone a profound change [prior to World War II]. War was ceasing to be the unrestricted prerogative of sovereign states."[61]

[59] Odd Arne Westad, *The Global Cold War: Third World Interventions and the Making of Our Times*, New edition (Cambridge: Cambridge University Press, 2007), pp. 124–130.

[60] International Military Tribunal (The Blue Series), vol. 2,available at http://avalon.law.yale.edu/imt/11-23-45.asp.

[61] International Military Tribunal (The Blue Series), vol. 3, available at http://avalon.law.yale.edu/imt/12-04-45.asp.

This understanding of Nazi criminality as residing in essence in its aggression against its neighbors, and linking this to efforts to criminalize aggressive war, was the essence of the so-called Nuremberg paradigm.[62] This view of World War II was deeply implicated in the project to reforge international society after 1945, through various international projects, including the United Nations, the International Military Tribunal, efforts to set up a permanent International Criminal Court, and attempts to codify international criminal law, especially that against aggressive war.[63] For instance, in a draft report in April of 1950 on the Nuremberg Principles and the development of a draft code of international criminal law, the Greek rapporteur for the International Law Commission, Jean Spiropoulos, argued that any code of international criminal law ought to refer only to "political" crimes, not other kinds of international criminality. The code "is intended to refer to acts which, if committed or tolerated by a State, would constitute violations of international responsibility … These are offenses which, on account of their specific character, normally would affect international relations in a way dangerous for the *maintenance of peace*."[64] Of the nine offenses listed in Spiropoulos' draft code, the first four concerned various forms of aggressive action against other states, while only the last two (genocide and war crimes) concerned crimes against individuals. The remaining three articles (5–7) concerned the observance of international treaties. On this vision, war remained the supreme matter of concern for international law; atrocities were derivative.

Plans to develop international criminal law also considered the question of enforcement mechanisms, in ways that would presage the Jerusalem court's resolution of this issue. In Spiropoulos' report, he argued there were three options: ad hoc international tribunals, a permanent international court, or enforcement by domestic courts. The first would reduce international law to a list of offenses with no intrinsic means of enforcement. This was not ideal in his view, but preferable to nothing. It would be "unrealistic," he insisted, to reject an international law code simply because one with institutionalized enforcement mechanisms proved "unobtainable." Spiropoulos doubted that a permanent international criminal court could be created in the foreseeable future and thought it "very unrealistic" to imagine states would hand their citizens over to such a court for trial, should one be created.[65] Spiropoulos' preferred option was to have domestic courts, acting on the basis of domestic legislation incorporating the draft code of international offenses, enforce

[62] Donald Bloxham, *Genocide on Trial: War Crimes Trials and the Formation of Holocaust History and Memory* (Oxford: Oxford University Press, 2003).

[63] Devin O. Pendas, "Toward World Law? Human Rights and the Failure of the Legalist Paradigm of War," in Stefan-Ludwig Hoffmann, ed., *Human Rights in the Twentieth Century* (Cambridge: Cambridge University Press, 2011), pp. 215–236.

[64] UN Doc A/CN.4/25. "Report by J. Spiropoulos, Special Rapporteur," *Yearbook of the International Law Commission*, vol. 2 *1950* (New York: United Nations, 1957).

[65] UN Doc A/CN 4/25, "Report by J. Spiropoulos."

international law. In part, this was because he followed the genocide convention as "a *decisive* precedent," but also because he felt this was the most realistic option, given the current state of international affairs. Obviously, the Jerusalem court agreed with him in matters of jurisdiction, even if it did not apply international law.

Much of this project of regulating war through international law was deeply American, part of what Elizabeth Borgwardt has called "America's New Deal vision for the World."[66] It is worth adding that, alongside American idealism, there was no little British imperialism embedded in the new multilateral institutions, as the United Nations and its emerging "human rights" agenda were explicitly conceptualized by its influential architects, like Jan Smuts from South Africa, as a substitute for decolonization.[67]

Equally relevant in this context is the fact that this entire project was all but stillborn. The Soviets and their satellites would have none of this, since they perceived it, not wrongly, as part of an agenda to, at a minimum, constrain their freedom of action. The Soviets stymied any efforts to codify international criminal law or to create a permanent international criminal court. Efforts broke down in 1953, mainly over the issue of defining aggression, which was a highly contentious issue in the midst of the Korean War, with each side accusing the other of that offense. Thereafter, the development of international law came to a standstill. It was into this Cold War context that the Eichmann trial erupted, offering an alternative – not just jurisdictionally, in the form of domestic courts, but more fundamentally, in shifting the emphasis from war to atrocity.[68]

By reframing the issue of Nazi criminality not in terms of aggression or the maintenance of international peace and stability – issues that inevitably raised the question of whose peace and stability on whose behalf – the Eichmann case disconnected Nazi criminality from the issue of world order and even from the development of international criminal law, despite the fact that Eichmann was, among other things, charged with crimes against humanity. It is not that the trial forced a recognition of the specificity of Jewish suffering on the East Block, which remained wedded to its narrative of Fascism as the last gasp of capitalist imperialism down to 1989. Rather, what the highlighting of the Holocaust *strictus sensus* did was allow the West – the Germans and the Americans in particular – to reach a common, moralized narrative of World War II that marginalized the Soviets entirely. This new account was no longer about the

[66] Elisabeth Borgwardt, *A New Deal for the World: America's Vision for Human Rights* (Cambridge: Belknap Press of Harvard University Press, 2007).

[67] Mark Mazower, *No Enchanted Palace: The End of Empire and the Ideological Origins of the United Nations* (Princeton: Princeton University Press, 2009).

[68] Lawrence Douglas has called this the emergence of the "atrocity paradigm" of international law. Lawrence Douglas, "From IMT to NMT: The Emergence of a Jurisprudence of Atrocity," in Kim C. Priemel and Alexa Stiller, eds., *Reassessing the Nuremberg Military Tribunals* (New York: Berghahn, 2012), pp. 276–295.

war between nations, but about the "war against the Jews," as the historian Lucy Davodovich termed it.[69] In this analysis, Americans were rescuers and Nazis (but not Germans) were perpetrators.

Obviously, because the fate of the Jews in World War II was intimately connected with the founding of the state of Israel, which in turn was deeply tied to the recurring turmoil in the Middle East, it would be overly simplistic to say the Eichmann case had no implications for contemporary international politics. It may be, as Peter Novick has argued, that in the United States in particular, the Holocaust was used to mobilize political support for Israel.[70] I would suggest, however, that the Eichmann trial helped effect a larger shift, in which the Holocaust came to stand in for a pathological modernity, one that could be combatted by the normative order of law and American-style liberalism. The Holocaust was not so much *instrumentalized* as it was *universalized*. Here is where the trial's verdict becomes crucial.

Gideon Hausner sought to craft a profoundly Zionist narrative in the trial, one in which Jewish weakness and vulnerability in the European diaspora was used to justify the need for a Jewish state. This was a major subtext for the witness testimony.[71] As Hanna Yablonka puts it:

> The witnesses related, in agonizing detail, heartrending stories that revealed the helplessness of the European Jews, the betrayal of the nations, the heroism of the resistance fighters, the depth of the trauma, the cruelty of the Germans, and the pride of the Zionists. The overt message was the Jewish nation. The hidden message was the Jewish state.[72]

But this was not all there was to the Eichmann trial. This Zionist narrative clearly had its own political stakes, and had Hausner succeeded in getting the trial he wanted, the Eichmann trial would likely have been swept up in the passions of Middle East politics and Cold War maneuvers and we would have no more to say about it today than we do the Kastner trial, or the Höss trial, or countless others like them. The judges in the Eichmann case, German speaking and deeply imbued with a Central European sense of the rule of law, largely reinterpreted Hausner's agenda in a legalist idiom. They did so by disciplining witnesses, by limiting his digressions, by bringing the case time and again back to Eichmann and his deeds.[73]

[69] Lucy S. Dawidowicz, *The War against the Jews, 1933–1945* (New York: Free Press, 1975).

[70] Peter Novick, *The Holocaust in American Life* (New York: Mariner Books, 2000).

[71] Leora Bilsky has argued the trial marked a major step in the development of a jurisprudence of atrocity, in which the role of the witness changed, bringing the didactic and jurisprudential dimensions of the trial into closer dialogue and allowing a confrontation between victims and perpetrators. See Leora Bilsky, "The *Eichmann* Trial: Towards a Jurisprudence of Eyewitness Testimony of Atrocities," *Journal of International Criminal Justice*, Vol. 12 (2014), pp. 27–57. This is clearly correct, but it does not change the political subtext of the witness testimony.

[72] Yablonka, *Israel* v. *Eichmann*, p. 120.

[73] Douglas, *The Memory of Judgment*, pp. 123–150.

The judgment in this regard is a masterpiece of restrained and substantive jurisprudence. The court began by noting that the Holocaust had come up in earlier trials, "but this time it has occupied the central place in the court proceedings, and it is this fact which has distinguished this trial from those which preceded it."[74] The pressure to provide a detailed history of the Holocaust, and to answer pressing historical questions concerning the origins of the Holocaust, the activities of the Jewish diaspora, the history and psychology of anti-Semitism, and countless others, was, according to the judges, perfectly understandable. It was also profoundly misplaced.

In this maze of insistent questions, the path of the Court was and remains clear. It cannot allow itself to be enticed into provinces which are outside its sphere. The judicial process has ways of its own, laid down by law, and which do not change, whatever the subject of the trial may be. Otherwise, the processes of law and of court procedure are bound to be impaired, whereas they must be adhered to punctiliously, since they are in themselves of considerable social and educational significance, and the trial would otherwise resemble a rudderless ship tossed about by the waves.[75]

In adhering to their rigorous legalism, the judges created a narrative of the Holocaust that was less Zionist than it was universalist. As much as Hannah Arendt complained about the Eichmann trial, and the prosecution's failure to realize, as she put it, that Eichmann was guilty of "crimes against humanity perpetrated on the body of the Jews," this is precisely what the court articulated in its verdict.[76] As a result, the trial highlighted Jewish suffering in a universal idiom and made it accessible to non-Jews. The profound resonance of the trial globally – due in no small part, of course, to Arendt's own controversial but enormously popular account – was possible because the trial ended up prioritizing crimes against humanity in the form of crimes against the Jews.[77] As a result, the universalization of the Holocaust, its status as the metaphor for human evil, for political crime, and for genocide, dates from the Eichmann trial. The plasticity with which the Holocaust has been treated in the past fifty years, its cosmopolitan presence in all sorts of odd places – like the national mall in Washington DC with its Holocaust Museum, or in Australian courtrooms in the 1990s, or in Canadian Holocaust denial cases – originates in the Eichmann trial.

Indeed, it is worth emphasizing that while the witness-driven narrative may have dominated the initial press reports, especially in Israel itself, in the longer

[74] *Attorney Gen. of Israel* v. *Eichmann*, 36 I.L.R. 1, available at www.nizkor.org/ftp.cgi/people/e/eichmann.adolf/transcripts/ftp.py?people/e/eichmann.adolf/transcripts/Judgment/Judgment-001.

[75] Ibid. [76] Hannah Arendt, *Eichmann in Jerusalem* (New York: Viking, 1963).

[77] On the controversies surrounding *Eichmann in Jerusalem*, see Anson Rabinach, "Eichmann in New York: The New York Intellectuals and the Hannah Arendt Controversy," *October*, Vol. 108 (2004), pp. 97–111 and Michael Erza, "The Eichmann Polemics: Hannah Arendt and Her Critics," *Democratiya*, Vol. 9 (2007), pp. 141–165.

run, it was a combination of legal and historical analysis that gave the trial its enduring legacy. And here, I would argue, Arendt really does become crucial. The Eichmann trial was able to serve a very useful function in integrating Germany into the Western anti-communist alliance more fully and smoothly than before because it came to be viewed in a broadly Arendtian frame – as being about totalitarianism and pathological modernity, to which anti-communism and liberalism were the antidote. Arendt's profoundly influential book on the Eichmann trial, derived from her reportage for the *New Yorker*, was blessed by a title that encapsulated a whole set of ideas and resonated with the *Zeitgeist* as few concepts do. Arendt entitled her book *Eichmann in Jerusalem: A Report on the Banality of Evil.* Her core thesis was that Eichmann was not evil in a traditional sense, not a "villain" as Iago or Richard III had been. Rather, he was a dutiful, if unimaginative and morally obtuse, bureaucrat. His moral failing was literally "thoughtlessness."[78] In this respect, he was a typical product of impersonal, bureaucratized modernity. To the extent that this was true, the Holocaust was not primarily about *Germans* or about anti-Semitism but about the dynamics of modern violence, as embodied not only in the Third Reich but also in the USSR. Eichmann was the classic totalitarian subject. And although Arendt herself was not a classic "Cold Warrior," her image of Eichmann could easily be accommodated within the frame of Cold War liberalism. The implication, then, was that combatting Russians today had the same moral valence as combatting Nazis twenty years previously. The Holocaust, on Arendt's interpretation, could be mobilized as a justification for the Cold War. The popularity of Arendt's account, and its lasting intellectual influence, should not be underestimated.[79] This is one major reason why the Holocaust came in the course of the 1960s to serve as the metonym for political evil in the West.

In other words, to answer the initial question – why the continuing interest in the Eichmann trial? – I would argue that it exists because the Holocaust has come to be less about the specific history of the Nazi genocide of the Jews than it is about the human capacity for evil under dictatorship and the need to prevent genocide and other mass atrocities. The "jurisprudence of atrocity" that begins with the Eichmann trial paints a generic portrait of the politics of atrocity, in which one genocide is much the same as any other, and the motives of the perpetrators can be determined by social-psychological generalizations. In this sense, the Holocaust has become a cosmopolitan and, indeed, rather

[78] Devin O. Pendas, "*Eichmann in Jerusalem*, Arendt in Frankfurt: The Eichmann Trial, the Auschwitz Trial and the Banality of Justice," *New German Critique*, Vol. 34 (2007), pp. 77–109.

[79] Richard I. Cohen, "A Generation Responds to Eichmann in Jerusalem," in Aschheim, ed., *Hannah Arendt in Jerusalem*, pp. 253–280 and Daniel Maier-Katkin, "The Reception of Hannah Arendt's *Eichmann in Jerusalem* in the United States, 1963–2011," *HannahArendt. Net: Zeitschrift für politisches Denken*, Vol. 6 (2011), available at www.hannaharendt.net/index.php/han/article/view/64/84.

promiscuous symbol for any number of messages.[80] The reinterpretation of Hausner's Zionist narrative by the Eichmann trial judges helped make this possible. Law, in this sense, universalized what was initially a narrow political message and made it relevant – politically, morally, and perhaps even metaphysically – to the whole world, even as it rendered it legally marginal to the future development of international law.

[80] Natan Sznaider, *Jewish Memory and the Cosmopolitan Order: Hannah Arendt and the Jewish Condition* (Cambridge: Polity Press, 2011).

9

In the Theater of the Rule of Law

Performing the Rivonia Trial in South Africa, 1963–1964

Jens Meierhenrich and Catherine M. Cole

The social drama that became known as the Rivonia trial began on July 6, 1963, when seven men were arrested at Liliesleaf Farm in the Johannesburg suburb of Rivonia.[1] Six of those men and four others were eventually charged with various crimes against the Republic of South Africa, notably sabotage and conspiracy. *The State against Nelson Mandela and Nine Others* was one of the most iconic trials of the twentieth century, not least because convictions could have resulted in the defendants being hanged, a result widely expected in South Africa and the world at large when the momentous trial began. The Rivonia trial was intended to be both destructive and didactic, to use the analytical language of this volume.[2] By prosecuting some of the most influential leaders of the African National Congress (ANC) under the new Sabotage Act, the racial state sought to deal a decisive blow to the insurgent movement that was slowly gaining strength in the townships. In addition to removing an increasingly painful thorn from its side, the National Party-led government also endeavored to discredit anti-apartheid resistance in general and Nelson Mandela in particular in the court of world opinion. At the trial's conclusion, most of the defendants were found guilty, but none were executed. Not only did the apartheid government fail to destroy by way of law some of the most influential leaders of the ANC, it also inadvertently provided a stage for one of law's most capable orators. In the eyes of much of the world, Mandela's performance in the Rivonia trial memorably and lastingly *de*legitimated the project of apartheid and *re*legitimated the opposition movement despite the latter's embrace of the strategic use of violence.

1 The term "social drama" was first theorized in Victor Turner, *The Anthropology of Performance* (New York: PAJ Publications, 1988), p. 33.

2 Jens Meierhenrich and Devin O. Pendas, "'The Justice of My Cause Is Clear, But There's Politics to Fear': Political Trials in Theory and History," in this volume.

Why did the apartheid regime hesitate to put to death those it considered guilty of preparing the ground for "an armed invasion of, and violent revolution in" South Africa, those who aspired to bring "the present Government to its knees and thus violently overthrow it," as Percy Yutar, Transvaal's deputy attorney general, put it in his opening address for the prosecution? And what happened in this political trial that led to Nelson Mandela's star turn? In answer to these and related questions, this chapter develops an argument that revolves around what we call "the theater of the rule of law," by which we mean *the contending performances – legal and otherwise – of interacting adversaries that are staged in a courtroom on the procedural foundations of formally rational law*. We show that the Rivonia trial turned into a performative and theatrical struggle over ideas, not unlike the political trials of the Black Consciousness era in the 1970s, in which, to use Michael Lobban's apt formulation, "two cohesive but rival ideologies confronted each other."[3] Building on a legacy of South African political trials from the 1950s, the Rivonia trial was aimed at communicating larger – albeit deeply contested – truths about the nature of apartheid and resistance to it that went well beyond the facts of the case. Not surprisingly, the various histories and memories that adherents and opponents of apartheid filtered into the Pretoria courtroom over the course of nine months were deeply at odds with one another.

Although history is rich with performances of law, there has been "no sustained theoretical articulation of the nature of legal performance or the meaning of legal theatricality" in the existing literature.[4] Like Julie Stone Peters, we are in pursuit of "an alternative legal historiography, more narrative and descriptively 'thick' (in Clifford Geertz's famous formulation), more sensitive to law's paratexts, both complement and corrective to the doctrinal or institutional historiography of law."[5]

Drawing on court records – including recently recovered Dictabelt recordings of Mandela's famous statement from the dock – and interviews with key protagonists, we explain how legal adversaries in the Rivonia trial came implicitly and explicitly to orient themselves toward others "as if they were actors on a stage seeking identification with their experiences and understandings from their audiences," to use Jeffrey C. Alexander and Jason L. Mast's definition of symbolic action.[6] Taking place against a background of deepening political repression and resistance, the Rivonia trial was considerably

[3] Michael Lobban, *White Man's Justice: South African Political Trials in the Black Consciousness Era* (New York: Oxford University Press, 1996), p. 21.

[4] Julie Stone Peters, "Legal Performance Good and Bad," *Law, Culture and the Humanities*, Vol. 4 (2008), p. 181.

[5] Peters, "Legal Performance Good and Bad," pp. 181–182.

[6] Jeffrey C. Alexander and Jason L. Mast, "Introduction: Symbolic Action in Theory and Practice: The Cultural Pragmatics of Symbolic Action," in Jeffrey C. Alexander, Bernhard Giesen, and Jason L. Mast, eds., *Social Performance: Symbolic Action, Cultural Pragmatics, and Ritual* (Cambridge: Cambridge University Press, 2006), p. 2.

more performative and theatrical in nature than any of the politicized court proceedings of the previous decade and most that followed in its wake. We explain why this was so and propose that the expressive function of the trial accounts for much of what has been deemed political about *The State against Nelson Mandela and Nine Others*. In theoretical terms, we argue that the *performativity of law* can be revealed only by relating insights about the *textuality of law* to insights about the *theatricality of law*. In empirical terms, we maintain that a performative analysis of the Rivonia trial must take account of the peculiar structure of apartheid law at the time of the proceeding. Without a focus on the institutional determinants of legal performance, any analysis of the famous trial would fall short. A purely performative analysis would be as inadequate as a purely institutional analysis, which is why a collaboration that synthesizes insights from law, the social sciences, and the humanities seems so promising to us.

In the early 1960s, the apartheid state was in a period of transformation, both legally and politically, into an ever-more-authoritarian regime. At the same time, the fledgling anti-apartheid movement, particularly the ANC, was transitioning from a decades-long commitment to nonviolence to a new policy of selective violence, including sabotage. For each side, the Rivonia trial served as a platform on which to portray its respective views about the polity's future and strategies for attaining its vision. How the state and the resistance movement were characterized in the eyes of the nation and the world mattered a great deal symbolically to the future. Public legitimation of the use of violence was a didactic goal for both the prosecution and the defense, and each used the trial to communicate to external constituents. The apartheid government sought the re-equilibration of a racist dispensation in the wake of numerous challenges to its legitimacy. For its part, the clandestine anti-apartheid movement maintained its long-standing commitment to civil disobedience while at the same time it embraced the new tactic of using sabotage as a response to the state's ever-escalating recourse to violence.

However, internal divisions within both the state and the anti-apartheid movement complicated the pursuit of didactic aims. As Jens Meierhenrich has argued elsewhere, the country was governed by a dual state.[7] This dual apartheid state consisted of a normative and a prerogative state, in Ernst Fraenkel's sense of the terms, in which a rule-guided way of law coexisted with an institutional logic founded on violent arbitrariness. While by the

[7] For a theoretical and empirical treatment of the concept of the dual state, see Jens Meierhenrich, *The Legacies of Law: Long-Run Consequences of Legal Development in South Africa, 1652–2000* (Cambridge: Cambridge University Press, 2008). See also Jens Meierhenrich, "The Intellectual Foundations of Ernst Fraenkel's Theory of Dictatorship," in Ernst Fraenkel, ed., *The Dual State: A Contribution to the Theory of Dictatorship*, translated by Edward A. Shils with an Introduction by Jens Meierhenrich (Oxford: Oxford University Press, [1941] 2017).

1960s, the balance was shifting noticeably in favor of the prerogative state, the normative state nevertheless persisted, albeit in weakened form. Thus, the country was nonetheless still governed by both halves of the dual state.

Interestingly, it was not just the apartheid state that was governed by a dual logic. The apartheid resistance, too, was concurrently pursuing strategies of law and violence. The pursuit was not tactical, however. It was the product of internal ambivalence over the most appropriate form of resistance. We argue that what made the Rivonia trial so exceptional as a space of legal performance was the transitional character of both the apartheid government *and* the resistance movement in this period of South African history. Both organizations operated under the influence of contending normative and prerogative impulses. Both were struggling with institutional dissonance. Actors on both sides were torn between embracing law or violence as strategy of conflict. This ambivalence was a structural feature of incumbent and insurgent collective action alike.[8] As a consequence, the courtroom in the Rivonia trial became a space of *agon* not only between the prosecution and the defendants (and, by analogy, white and black South Africa) but also between the conflicting normative and prerogative logics inside both the government and the ANC. The proceedings thus came to reveal what is often concealed: how the law *produces* the subject before the law. Mandela, as a trained lawyer with considerable respect for his vocation, seized upon the institutional remnants of the normative state in South Africa. In the process of performing in the courtroom, he emerged as an icon.

In our analysis, we make explicit the social meanings and political effects of various performative repertoires, including spoken narratives, bodily enactments, spatial configurations, and other forms of dramatic representation that interacting adversaries brought to bear in their quests to outperform the other, both literally and figuratively. By tracing in some detail the legal performances of Nelson Mandela in particular and by hinting at counter-performances, we illuminate the role of symbolic action at a critical juncture in the making of apartheid. For Mandela and his co-accused, the act of performing the law was a continuation of the struggle by other means.[9] The empirical and rhetorical and the theatrical, affective, and embodied truths the defendants and their defense lawyers communicated in the courtroom provided agency to otherwise powerless individuals at a time in South African history when racial domination was reaching its zenith. At the same time, the apartheid state was attempting to manipulate the theater of the rule of law to conceal an expanding prerogative state, one

[8] On the latter, see Elisabeth Jean Wood, *Forging Democracy from below: Insurgent Transitions in South Africa and El Salvador* (Cambridge: Cambridge University Press, 2000).

[9] Nelson Mandela, *Long Walk to Freedom* (Boston: Little, Brown, 1994), p. 56.

that was increasingly authoritarian and used force excessively, detained people arbitrarily, and engaged in torture wantonly.[10]

Such were the "given circumstances" of the Rivonia trial, and they set the stage for it to become one of the most political, theatrical, and performative trials of the century, one as notable for certain acts of oratory as for its transformative impact on history.[11] Certain agents in the Rivonia trial did things – big things – with words. They also did things with their bodies and voices and with space and time. By analyzing the relationship between the effective and affective dimensions of the trial, between the performative and the theatrical, between textuality and orality, and between temporal and spatial dimensions, we present an argument aimed at furthering the often discussed but seldom deeply analyzed relationship between performance and the law. Even though the law's primary event, the trial, is frequently discussed in theatrical terms, the confluence of the law and performance generally – and during political trials specifically – deserves far deeper and more thorough investigation than we have seen to date.

THE LIMINAL TRIAL

The State against Nelson Mandela and Nine Others marked a liminal period that lay "betwixt and between" in the institutional development of both apartheid law and anti-apartheid resistance.[12] The trial was staged during the apartheid regime's transition to a more authoritarian rule of law. While political trials in the South Africa of the 1950s were generally restrained and conducted in the context of a criminal justice system whose liberal features were still notable, political trials in the 1960s were more overtly – and destructively – political, not least because of the political fallout from the 1960 Sharpeville massacre.[13] In the wake of the violence, *Umkhonto we Sizwe* ("Spear of the Nation"), the ANC's military unit, also known as MK, and *Poqo* ("Pure"), the armed wing of the PAC, and other insurgents carried out more than 200 bomb attacks on government buildings, transportation routes, and electrical installations.[14] Many of these acts of sabotage were part of the indictment

[10] Catherine M. Cole, "Justice in Transition: South Africa Political Trials, 1956–1964," in Awol Kassim Allo, ed., *The Courtroom as a Space of Resistance: Reflections on the Legacy of the Rivonia Trial* (Farnham: Ashgate, 2015), p. 102.

[11] On the term "given circumstances," see Konstantin Stanislavski, *An Actor's Work: A Student's Diary*, translated by Jean Benedetti (Abingdon: Routledge, 2008), pp. 52–53.

[12] On liminality, see Victor W. Turner, *The Ritual Process* (New York: Penguin, 1969).

[13] Most recently, see Tom Lodge, *Sharpeville: A Massacre and Its Consequences* (Oxford: Oxford University Press, 2011).

[14] The prosecution at the Rivonia trial depicted MK as the "military wing" of the ANC, and indeed, this is how it came to be generally characterized subsequently in South African history. However, the Rivonia defendants disputed this conflation of the ANC and MK, asserting that they were two separate organizations with different goals and strategies. The point is not trivial, for it relates to our argument about the dual nature of the ANC-led resistance.

against the accused in the Rivonia trial. Of particular significance was "Operation Mayibuye." Members of the high command of MK conceived this strategy for "protracted war" in early 1962. The Sharpeville massacre, in other words, marked a critical juncture, and the Rivonia trial, especially for the white regime, was essentially about the adjudication of this juncture. Virtually all of the legal performances that could be witnessed on the courtroom stage were about *the moral economy of law*. The re-balancing of the dual apartheid state – the restraining of its normative half, the toughening of its prerogative half – was an attempt by the architects of separate development to configure the rule of law as a weapon.[15] In the wake of the Rivonia trial, and because of it, the courtroom ceased to be the primary stage for enactment of power by the apartheid regime. "As the 1960s wore on," Catherine M. Cole has shown, "the state's methods became more clandestine, calculated to avoid the theatrical and highly public encounters staged by political trials."[16]

But the Rivonia trial was also liminal in another respect. It coincided with the ANC's strategic retreat from legalism and its embrace of armed struggle.[17] Although Mandela had previously believed in the possibility of fairness in apartheid courts, his rhetoric took on more revolutionary overtones in the 1960s. He put it thus during his 1962 Incitement trial: "In a political trial such as this one, which involves a clash of the aspirations of the African people and those of Whites, the country's courts as presently constituted, cannot be impartial and fair ... To have a White judicial officer presiding, ... however strong his sense of fairness and justice, is to make whites judges in their own case."[18] The combination of Mandela's gradually changing attitude toward the legitimacy of armed struggle and the far-reaching success of the apartheid state's judicial, legislative, and executive interventions to combat anti-apartheid protests in the 1960s inaugurated a relative decline in the salience of courts as strategic institutions in South Africa.

In the case of the Rivonia trial, the apartheid regime was intent on staging both a destructive trial and a didactic trial, as defined in this volume. The regime's apparent goals in bringing the men to trial were to further advance the destruction of the ANC's organizational foundations and to legitimate its own judicial and extrajudicial tactics by exposing the defendants' links to communism. The attorney general of Transvaal Province

[15] See also Catherine Hester Albertyn, "A Critical Analysis of Political Trials in South Africa 1948–1988," Ph.D. dissertation, University of Cambridge, 1991, pp. 176–177.

[16] Catherine M. Cole, *Performing South Africa's Truth Commission: Stages of Transition* (Bloomington: Indiana University Press, 2010), p. 62.

[17] The retreat was temporary because the ANC returned to legalism in the 1980s, as did other collective actors in the struggle against apartheid. For important empirical evidence of this development in the evolution of legal contention, see Richard L. Abel, ed., *Politics by Other Means: Law in the Struggle against Apartheid, 1980–1994* (London: Routledge, 1995).

[18] Nelson Mandela, *No Easy Walk to Freedom* (London: Heinemann, 1965), p. 126.

ultimately charged all the defendants with violating the newly enacted, so-called Sabotage Act and the Suppression of Communism Act.[19] Crucially, the testimony of a *single* witness was enough to prove violations of the Sabotage Act. In addition to lowering the burden of proof, the apartheid government also did away with the procedural requirement of a three-judge panel that still was the norm, for example, in treason cases. Consequently, only a single judge presided over the Rivonia trial, Quartus de Wet.[20]

Despite the removal of institutional constraints under the Sabotage Act, it is important to appreciate that the Rivonia trial was not a sham trial. While the trial was no model for procedural justice, it was not a kangaroo court either. The defense was permitted to make its arguments to the court and conduct effective cross-examination of the witnesses. Throughout the proceeding, the surviving remnants of the normative state enabled the defense and constrained the prosecution. It is for this reason, more than any other, that Mandela was able to deliver the most important legal performance of his life. Mandela and the banned ANC-led liberation movement were given what they had sought for many years but had been violently denied: visibility and voice. Mandela's textual and theatrical performances, in other words, were *structurally contingent*. The power of his legal performance did not derive solely from the performative genius of Mandela, as is commonly assumed: It was institutionally determined.

The complicated relationship between authoritarianism and the rule of law in South Africa matters because it is often overlooked and significantly complicates conventional wisdom about the nature of political trials more generally. The politicization of the courtroom in Pretoria (where the Rivonia trial was heard by the Transvaal Division of the Supreme Court of South Africa) inadvertently empowered the anti-apartheid movement. James Boyd White explains how the trial's legalism opened up a unique performance space for Mandela's statement from the dock:

> The condition of Mandela's speech is a public trial, presided over by a judge and attended by journalists. The government could simply have murdered him, or tried him in private, or turned the proceedings into a show trial. But they did not, and their decision had consequences against their immediate interest, for it enabled Mandela to speak and be heard. The trial created a moment of rhetorical equality between the state and the accused, and as such enacted a political value inconsistent with the regime of oppression of which it was a part.[21]

Without the institutional remnants of the normative state, the Rivonia trial would have turned into a one-sided show trial. Instead, the worldwide audience

[19] General Law Amendment Act of 1962; Suppression of Communism Act of 1950.

[20] Kenneth Broun, *Saving Nelson Mandela: The Rivonia Trial and the Fate of South Africa* (Oxford: Oxford University Press, 2012), pp. 30–31.

[21] James Boyd White, *Acts of Hope: Creating Authority in Literature, Law, and Politics* (Chicago: University of Chicago Press, 1994), pp. 293–294.

stepped into the theater of the rule of law. The fact that the rules of the game were unjust but not arbitrary accounts for the success of some of the insurgent legal performances Mandela and his colleagues offered up. The rules of the game were unjust because they were a reflection of racist mores. They were not arbitrary, however, because legality was, by and large, honored and the country's law of criminal procedure was adhered to during the proceeding. In 1963, the applicable law in the Rivonia trial, to use Max Weber's helpful terminology, was *substantively irrational* but *formally rational*. The conflicting imperatives of the prerogative and normative halves of the dual apartheid state existed in a rough equilibrium. This important institutional fact also explains why some of the prosecution's legal performances fell flat: The state's performers played roughshod with the legality of law so often that judge de Wet felt compelled to repeatedly – though not consistently – reprimand Percy Yutar, the legal representative of the regime that he himself was serving. With his inconsistent behavior from the bench, de Wet performed the institutional logic of the dual apartheid state: the conflicting imperatives of governing by rules and governing by rifles. De Wet's partial commitment to the rule of law and his occasional and unexpected insistence on the sanctity of the rules of procedure and evidence provided important legal space for the defense in general, and for Mandela in particular, thereby making possible the legal performance that made the Rivonia trial so memorable.

This performance, more than any other, established Mandela as a great orator. It contained some of the most famous words ever spoken in a courtroom, words that fortified resistance to white domination not just in South Africa but the world over. Our analysis subjects Mandela's remarkable speech to a close reading that is especially attuned to the interplay between theatricality and legality. Mandela's dual personality – which united his persona of the revolutionary with his persona of the lawyer – mirrored the dual nature of the apartheid state (and that of his own, dual-natured organization, the ANC). As Tom Lodge observed, "the structured world of courtroom procedure itself shaped Mandela's political practice, restraining it even in its most theatrically insurgent phases, and reinforcing his respect for institutions, traditions, and history."[22] This unique relationship between a black agent and a white structure, at a liminal moment in the history of apartheid, we argue, is crucial to understanding what the world came to witness on April 20, 1964.

IN THE THEATER OF THE RULE OF LAW

How did the Rivonia trial become both performative and theatrical inside and outside the courtroom, and to what effect? We address this question with the help of a number of vignettes, asking how the most important adversaries in the

[22] Tom Lodge, *Mandela: A Critical Life* (Oxford: Oxford University Press, 2006), p. viii.

legal proceeding transformed from litigants into performers, with particular reference to Nelson Mandela. In so doing, we fill an analytical gap, for as Elleke Boehmer observed, "Mandela's mastery of performance, though often taken as a given, is rarely ... analyzed in any depth."[23] This is especially true for his statement from the dock on April 20, 1964, which opened the defense case with a bang. As Joel Joffe, one of Mandela's attorneys, recalls, "Yutar was behaving as though he could not believe his ears. As Nelson rose slowly, adjusting the spectacles which he wore only for reading, Yutar jumped to his feet. His voice rose to that of a falsetto which we came to know as the crisis call of the prosecution."[24] Yutar was right to be concerned, because what transpired during the following three hours was by all accounts "the most dramatic moment in the trial – the moment that would come to symbolize South Africa's struggle against oppression in the eyes of the world for all time."[25] In addition to allowing for an analysis of the social mechanisms that drive textual performance and theatrical performance, and the contributions of each to law's performativity, Mandela's appearance in the dock serves as a useful case study with which to illuminate the relationship between instrumental and expressive functions of legal performance.

Textual Mechanisms

The textuality of Mandela's legal performance can be explored through his use of narrative and the distribution and salience of performatives relative to constatives in his speech. The former focus is undergirded by theoretical insights from historian Hayden White and sociologist Jeffrey Alexander, the latter by recourse to J. L. Austin and other linguistic philosophers. According to White, any narrative "entails ontological and epistemic choices with distinct ideological and even specifically political implications."[26] The conception and arrangement of Mandela's statement from the dock amounted to a special discursive form, one that reimagined in crucial ways the political order of things in South Africa. The construction of his narrative was critical to establishing the authenticity and legitimacy of this new way of seeing.

The transcribed text of Mandela's statement from the dock can be divided into seven distinct sections. The introductory section (pp. 4–7) provides a glimpse of the man – both the lawyer and the revolutionary – and previews in short, declarative sentences the nuanced argument to come. Mandela

[23] Elleke Boehmer, *Nelson Mandela: A Very Short Introduction* (Oxford: Oxford University Press, 2008), p. 125.

[24] Joel Joffe, *The State vs. Nelson Mandela: The Trial that Changed South Africa*, introduction by Nelson Mandela (Oxford: Oneworld, 2008), p. 157.

[25] Broun, *Saving Nelson Mandela*, p. 70.

[26] Hayden White, *The Content of the Form: Narrative Discourse and Historical Representation* (Baltimore: Johns Hopkins University Press, 1987), p. ix.

admitted that he had "planned sabotage." He provided reasons for his, as he claims, reluctant turn to limited violence but denies that either he personally or *Umkhonto we Sizwe* were responsible "for a number of acts which clearly fell outside the policy of the organization, but which have been charged in the indictment against us."[27] Mandela then embarked on a history of the ANC from its founding in 1912 until the organization "went underground" after the government banned anti-apartheid organizations (pp. 7–10).[28] In a third and closely related section, Mandela contrasted the ANC's previously absolute commitment to nonviolence with the gradual emergence of a violent discourse in the context of the formation of *Umkhonto we Sizwe* in November 1961 (pp. 10–24). It is here that Mandela sought to establish what he called "sabotage" as the least destructive of "four forms of violence" and as a response that was proportionate to the government's resort to violent repression. This is why it was adopted as *Umkhonto* policy, Mandela explained.

In a fourth section (pp. 24–33), Mandela continued the conceptual discussion by addressing "the question of g[ue]rilla warfare."[29] This section combines a brief travelogue with a detailed refutation of some of the evidence provided by the most important state witness, "Witness X." In it, Mandela projects a legal-rational authority, and his mechanical form of address gradually but steadily paves the way for the emotional crescendo on which the statement will end. The use of "telegraphic, empirical language" in this qualified justification of armed resistance drives home the rationality of the ANC strategy and the reasonableness of its objective.[30] The affect-less, lawyerly form of the narrative in this section only accentuated its subversive content. Boehmer explains the logic of this aspect of Mandela's performativity, "*See!* his court appearances announced, here is a black man outdoing the white at representing the very civilized values that he, the white man, would deny me. The impact was extremely subversive, precisely because in making his claims, Mandela was incarnating the principles of law and liberty that white authority attached exclusively to itself."[31] The fifth section (pp. 34–47) deals with several specific allegations in the indictment, most important the government's assertion that the aims of the ANC and the Communist Party were identical, which Mandela categorically denied. He also contrasted at length his own political values with those of his Communist comrades and professed admiration for "the parliamentary system of the west."[32] Having sought to

[27] Official Trial Transcript, April 20, 1964, Document A19, "Defence Opening Address and Nelson Mandela's Statement," Collection AD1844, State vs. Nelson Mandela and 9 Others (Rivonia Trial), Historical Papers, University of the Witwatersrand, pp. 5–6, available at www.historicalpapers.wits.ac.za/inventories/inv_pdft/AD1844/AD1844-A19-text.pdf.

[28] Official Trial Transcript, April 20, 1964, p. 10.

[29] Official Trial Transcript, April 20, 1964, p. 24.

[30] Boehmer, *Nelson Mandela*, p. 136.

[31] Boehmer, *Nelson Mandela*, p. 131.

[32] Official Trial Transcript, April 20, 1964, p. 44.

establish the moral imperative of resorting to limited violence in the preceding sections, he tempered this commitment with a mention of the importance of democratic institutions, especially legal institutions. This section gains its performative power from the authenticity of the claim that is advanced. Mandela was not enacting what he had rehearsed; he was embodying what he lived. Throughout his long life, Mandela admired the norms and institutions of law, which is why Jacques Derrida dubbed Mandela "a man of the law *by vocation*."[33] By laying claim to this vocation very concretely in his statement from the dock, Mandela convincingly positioned himself as a politically moderate member of the National Liberation Movement.

The sixth section (pp. 48–55) is an indictment of the apartheid regime. Here, Mandela turns from defendant to prosecutor, bringing charges for a finding of political and moral guilt. In support, he draws on a litany of examples of the state's structural violence. Despite its dramatizing function, the section is carefully reasoned. Its claims are not merely asserted but supported by socio-demographic data. The seventh and most frequently cited section (p. 55) consists of just one paragraph. It contains some of the most famous words ever spoken in a courtroom:

> During my lifetime I have dedicated my life to this struggle of the African people. I have fought against White domination, and I have fought against Black domination. I have cherished the ideal of a democratic and free society in which all persons live together in harmony and with equal opportunities. It is an ideal which I hope to live for, and to see realised. But my lord, if needs be, it is an ideal for which I am prepared to die.[34]

Mandela, when contemplating the possibility of a death sentence in the Rivonia trial, reportedly recalled the following lines from William Shakespeare's *Measure for Measure*:

> DUKE: Be absolute for death: either death or life
> Shall thereby be the sweeter.[35]

These words are said to have informed Mandela's composition of the final lines in his statement from the dock.[36] In fact, as Boehmer has shown, Claudio's words directed at Duke Vincentio in the passage directly preceding the command above not just informed but actually appeared, in slightly amended form, as Mandela's final words:

[33] Jacques Derrida, "The Laws of Reflection: Nelson Mandela, in Admiration," in Jacques Derrida and Mustapha Tlili, eds., *For Nelson Mandela* (New York: Seaver, 1987), p. 29.

[34] Official Trial Transcript, April 20, 1964, p. 55.

[35] William Shakespeare, *Measure for Measure*, edited by Brian Gibbons, Updated edition (Cambridge: Cambridge University Press, 2006), p. 137.

[36] Sampson, *Mandela*, p. 196.

CLAUDIO: The miserable have no other medicine
But only hope.
I've hope to live, and *am prepared to die.*[37]

Perhaps also on his mind was Shakespeare's *Julius Caesar*, whose protagonist invokes death as "a necessary end" that "[w]ill come when it will come," an invocation that Mandela would later describe as his favorite Shakespeare passage.[38] The salience of Shakespeare in Mandela's life is suggestive of his penchant for drama in more ways than one. And yet emotion was rarely more than an undercurrent in the text of his statement from the dock.

In the course of his narrative, Mandela repeatedly – and presumably deliberately – changed the style of narration. In certain parts, he narrated like a storyteller. In others, he reasoned like a lawyer. In yet others, he invoked the rhetorical style of the revolutionary. And elsewhere, he reasoned in a style akin to that of a dispassionate chronicler of events. What was the textual purpose – and communicative effect – of these stylistic choices? Importantly, the statement of the dock was not just a text. It also served as a "script" for Mandela's theatrical performance in the courtroom on April 20, 1964. The key challenge of a script centers on the imperative to plot a powerful representation of either facts or fiction that is capable of projecting cultural meanings and of doing so to emotional and moral effect. As Alexander reminds us, "If the scripted narrative is effective and if the performance of the plot is powerful, the audience experiences catharsis, which allows new moral judgments to form and new lines of social action to be undertaken in turn."[39] According to Alexander, an effective script "compress[es] the background meanings of culture by changing proportion and by increasing intensity."[40] In his theoretical model, four rhetorical techniques are associated with an effective script: cognitive simplification, time-space compression, moral agonism, and twisting and turning.[41] What follows is an illustration of some of these techniques in the context of Mandela's written statement from the dock.

There is ample evidence of cognitive simplification in the text, which can be achieved by condensing and repeating facts and assertions. One of the most striking aspects, as far as repetition is concerned, is the fact that Mandela uses

37 Shakespeare, *Measure for Measure*, p. 137. Emphasis added. See also Boehmer, *Nelson Mandela*, pp. 146–147.

38 William Shakespeare, *Julius Caesar*, edited by Marvin Spevack, Updated edition (Cambridge: Cambridge University Press, 2004), p. 112; Boehmer, *Nelson Mandela*, p. 146.

39 Jeffrey C. Alexander, "From the Depths of Despair: Performance, Counterperformance, and 'September 11,' " in Jeffrey C. Alexander, Bernhard Giesen, and Jason L. Mast, eds., *Social Performance: Symbolic Action, Cultural Pragmatics, and Ritual* (Cambridge: Cambridge University Press, 2006), p. 95.

40 Jeffrey C. Alexander, *Performance and Power* (Cambridge: Polity Press, 2011), p. 59.

41 Jeffrey C. Alexander, "Cultural Pragmatics: Social Performance between Ritual and Strategy," in Alexander, Giesen, and Mast, eds., *Social Performance*, pp. 59–63.

"African" as a keyword. It appears 139 times in the text, an indication that Mandela, by repetitively naming an oppressed collectivity, is seeking to imbue it with agency in a country where it has none.[42] By contrast, the words "white" and "government" appear forty-nine and forty-one times. And whereas Mandela describes black South Africans with a modicum of detail, the oppressive "other" is presented with less nuance. Perhaps, the most prominent metaphor in the statement from the dock is that of "struggle," aided by the term "fight," which occupies the same semantic field.

Mandela also introduces a number of starkly polarized binaries, another stylistic device for achieving cognitive simplification. He implicitly compares the authoritarian regime of apartheid with the democratic regimes in the United Kingdom and the United States. Mandela announces that he regards "the British Parliament as the most democratic institution in the world" and asserts that "the independence and impartiality of its judiciary never fail to arouse my admiration."[43] He named the "Magna Carta," the "Petition of Rights," and the "Bill of Rights," concluding by stating that the "doctrine of separation of powers, as well as the independence of its judiciary arouse in me similar sentiments."[44] Notwithstanding the fact many of his comrades at the time had far less positive things to say about the two capitalist democracies, Mandela glosses over this fact and introduces an assessment of democracy. The rhetorical effect is powerful: Few impartial spectators could doubt that the apartheid regime, whose atrocities Mandela has chronicled in his statement, fell short considerably in terms of the standards of civil and political rights of the advanced industrialized democracies like the United Kingdom and the United States.

Mandela introduces another binary when he contrasts the ANC's "policy of non-violence" with the "violence [that] had ... become a feature of the South African political scene."[45] Even though he admits to a reluctant turn within the organization to an embrace of "properly controlled sabotage," Mandela endeavors to minimize the potential for destruction of this strategy of conflict by creating a stark contrast between the ANC's "preparations" for "g[ue]rilla warfare" and the purported responsibility of "the Government" for "the blood of in[n]ocent Africans" with which, he claims, "the soil of South Africa" was

42 We are grateful to Cora Lacatus for her expert research assistance regarding word frequency and usage in Mandela's statement from the dock.

43 Official Trial Transcript, April 20, 1964, p. 44.

44 Official Trial Transcript, April 20, 1964, p. 44. Here is an overview of the incidence-related terms in the statement from the dock: "constitution" (three times), "law(s)" (fourteen times), "resolution" (four times), and "rights" (thirteen times). The semantic usage could be seen as evidence for a commitment to, or at least respect for, "a legal way of doing things." On this behavioral mode in the anti-apartheid movement, see Meierhenrich, *The Legacies of Law*, pp. 208–264, 279–281.

45 Official Trial Transcript, April 20, 1964, pp. 9, 14.

"already drenched."[46] Mandela delves even more deeply into the semantics of violence, when he constructs, for obvious reasons, a conceptual distinction between types of insurgent violence, notably between "revolution" and "sabotage," the former most certainly treasonous under apartheid law, the latter, with some luck, not.[47]

Here is another example of stylistic repetition: Mandela created considerable intensity by repeating the phrase "We want." He does so eleven times in quick succession. He repeats the declaration nine times verbatim, twice using the variation "Africans want," once the phrase "African men want," and once "[o]ur women want."[48] He adopts the same technique earlier in the text, when he interchanges the words "died" and "killed" five times in one and the same paragraph. Each usage is tied to a specific year, from 1920 to 1960, and serves to drill into the audience a memory of the death toll of apartheid.[49] The monotonous repetition of synonyms and syntax conveys stylistically the mounting of this toll. For the reader/observer, it amounts to a visceral experience. The statement in this section of the text is palpably angrier than in other sections, but the tone is nonetheless controlled. The simmering outrage is an attempt to affect the audience's psychological identification with the plight of the oppressed. Another rhetorical device for bringing about cognitive simplification is the compression of language. Speechwriters insist that sentences of successful scripts "must be short and sayable."[50] By virtue of education or instinct, Mandela was aware that brevity and simplicity are critical to ensuring comprehension, and he reduced the form of his narrative to essentials. It is dominated by declarative sentences; the number of sub-clauses is kept to a minimum. No clutter and very few extraneous words halted the enactment of his 1964 script. It was mechanical, but it was instantly comprehensible and often gripping, despite its length.

This brings us to the technique of moral agonism, the idea that the progression of a script must follow a dynamic movement that hinges, as Alexander argues, "on a conflict pitting good against evil, creating a wave-like dialectic that highlights the existential and metaphysical contrast between sacred and profane."[51] Mandela conjures the sacred by reference to the wars "fought by our ancestors in defence of the fatherland."[52] In contrast, he repeatedly associates the profane with the everyday violence of apartheid,

[46] Official Trial Transcript, April 20, 1964, pp. 16, 25.

[47] Official Trial Transcript, April 20, 1964, pp. 17–25. Not coincidentally, the term "sabotage" appears thirty-one times in the statement from the dock; the term "revolution" a mere seven times.

[48] Official Trial Transcript, April 20, 1964, p. 54.

[49] Official Trial Transcript, April 20, 1964, p. 24.

[50] Peggy Noonan, *On Speaking Well: How to Give a Speech with Style, Substance, and Clarity* (New York: Harper, 1998), p. 35

[51] Alexander, "Cultural Pragmatics," p. 61.

[52] Official Trial Transcript, April 20, 1964, p. 5.

from "poverty" to "malnutrition" to the miseducation and institutionalized "inferiority" of blacks.[53] He juxtaposes the "glory of the entire African nation" with "the many years of tyranny, exploitation and oppression of my people by the Whites."[54] Whereas the ANC "[f]or 37 years – that is until 1949 – ... adhered strictly to constitutional struggle," Mandela claims, a succession of white governments established conditions for black South Africans "similar to those of the serfs of the Middle Ages."[55] Reminding his audiences, at home and abroad, of the most violent repression of anti-apartheid resistance up until that point, Mandela asks rhetorically, "How many more Sharpevilles would there be in the history if our country? And how many more Sharpevilles could the country stand without violence and terror becoming the order of the day?"[56] To most impartial spectators in 1964, the answers would have been obvious. But Mandela made sure that his audiences could not only *hear* his argument from self-defense but also psychologically identify with it. To this end, he employed some of the most emotionally charged language in the entire text:

> Experience convinced us that rebellion would offer the Government limitless opportunity for the indiscriminate slaughter of our people. But it was precisely because the soil of South Africa is already drenched with the blood of in[n]ocent Africans that we felt it our duty to make preparations as a long-term undertaking, to use force in order to defend ourselves against force.[57]

Although the statement from the dock is replete with moral binaries of this kind, Mandela's textual genius lay in the fact that he never completely severed his ties to the profane world of apartheid, notably its law. In the opening section of his statement, for example, he delivers a striking act of antagonistic self-definition that *simultaneously* acknowledges an institution of the profane world that he resists. As James Boyd White has argued, "he is an African patriot engaged in a defensive war. Such are his commitments and his motives: but they are expressed in English, and in a manner and tone that enact a commitment to certain aspects of European culture as well."[58] Not condemning in its entirety the European culture from which apartheid sprang, Mandela introduces the persona of the *reasonable revolutionary*. An invented tradition, it served him well throughout his life. In the statement from the dock, it "runs through the speech as a whole, generating much of its energy."[59] By complicating his narrative of good and evil, Mandela achieves an authenticity that few revolutionaries before him or after managed to convey. "If the performance is energetically and skillfully

[53] Official Trial Transcript, April 20, 1964, pp. 48–54.
[54] Official Trial Transcript, April 20, 1964, pp. 5, 6.
[55] Official Trial Transcript, April 20, 1964, pp. 7, 48.
[56] Official Trial Transcript, April 20, 1964, p. 24.
[57] Official Trial Transcript, April 20, 1964, p. 25.
[58] White, *Acts of Hope*, pp. 280–281.
[59] White, *Acts of Hope*, p. 280.

implanted in moral binaries," Alexander writes, "psychological identification can be achieved and elements from the background culture can be extended dramatically."[60] The statement from the dock bears out this theoretical logic, but Mandela went one step *farther* on the road to authenticity by avoiding the histrionics of ordinary morality tales. This rhetorical self-restraint was one of the reasons why Yutar's portrayal of Mandela as a revolutionary firebrand appeared unconvincing to many audience members. International observers who came to support Mandela sometimes forgot that his personality was evenly split between the persona in the dock (Mandela the lawyer) and the persona in the indictment (Mandela the revolutionary). He was not quite as restrained as he sometimes portrayed himself for strategic advantage. And yet he shared with another revolutionary, Mahatma Gandhi, the ability to perform self-restraint, the "supremely Victorian quality of self-mastery and operation within the rule of law which they derived from the British colonial education they shared."[61]

In sum, the text of Mandela's statement from the dock is a perfect example of script-craft. The blueprint for his speech was highly effective because, as a script, it successfully "fused," as per Alexander's theoretical model, the text with background representations on the one hand and with the audience on the other. The former ensured cultural signification of, the latter the possibility of psychological identification with, the narrative content of the text of Mandela's speech.[62] These elements of the script were instantiated in the courtroom, which brings us to the *mise-en-scène* of Mandela's legal performance – the confrontation of text and theatricality.

Theatrical Mechanisms

Focusing solely on the textual aspects of Mandela's intervention overlooks the critical role of the body and voice, which were also performatives. Existing analyses of his statement from the dock are problematic because they provide incomplete accounts of what arguably constitutes the most important example of role-play in Mandela's long and distinguished life. Bringing the body and voice back into performative analysis and inserting it squarely into the study of the Rivonia trial reveal the theatricality of law as an indispensable feature of law's performativity.[63]

[60] Alexander, "Cultural Pragmatics," p. 61. [61] Boehmer, *Nelson Mandela*, p. 103.

[62] Generally, see also Alexander, "Cultural Pragmatics," p. 59.

[63] Jack Balkin and Sanford Levinson have gone as far as suggesting that law is about "the acting out of texts rather than the texts themselves." Jack M. Balkin and Sanford Levinson, "Interpreting Law and Music: Performance Notes on 'The Banjo Serenader' and 'The Lying Crowd of Jews,'" *Cardozo Law Review*, Vol. 20 (1999), p. 1518. This argument, however, overlooks the fact that words, even without oral delivery, matter in legal performance.

What can be said about Mandela's embodied enactment of the statement from the dock? And how does attention to a legal performance as an event, as a live form that is durational, ephemeral, embodied, oral, affectively expressive, and situated in space and time, help us understand the unique circumstances that made Rivonia one of the most political trials of the twentieth century? In answer, we have singled out four dimensions of theatricality: spatiality, physicality, temporality, and orality. We take *physicality* to refer both to the look of Mandela, from his clothing to his gestures, and to his comportment, from his posture to the aura he conjured. Our analysis of *temporality* explores the bodily exertion that was required for the delivery of a 176-minute monologue and the significance of this physical feat for the effects of legal performance. By *orality*, we mean the nature of his delivery from the dock, such as tone, rhythm, intonation, pacing, accent, volume, and modulation. We begin with *spatiality* because it is relevant to an understanding of the theatrical effects of physicality, temporality, orality, and of Mandela's role in constructing them.

Spatiality

The dimensions of the stage and its adornment are the physical parameters that delimit all physical activity in theatrical performance. In the case of legal performance, courtrooms often play a role that is functionally equivalent to that of the theatrical stage.[64] Whether the spatial dimensions of courtrooms are exploited quite so instrumentally or simply create meaningful separations and sightlines, they have a structuring effect on the theater of the rule of law. As Milner Ball points out, "The design and appointment of the courtroom, enhanced by costuming and ceremony, do create a dramatic aura which has even been described in hyperbolic religious terms. Theatrical effects are such dominant factors of a courtroom that their absence may raise doubts about whether a court which lacks a properly theatrical aspect is really a court at all."[65] Scholars in law and the social sciences have come to similar conclusions and emphasized the communicative function of both architecture and courtroom design.[66] In a word, a courtroom is, following Jeremy Bentham, a staging ground for "actors in the judicial drama," a principal site of "judicial theatre."[67]

[64] See, most recently, Henning Grunwald, *Courtroom to Revolutionary Stage: Performance and Ideology in Weimar Political Trials* (Oxford: Oxford University Press, 2012).

[65] Milner Ball, "The Play's the Thing: An Unscientific Reflection on Courts under the Rubric of Theater," *Stanford Law Review*, Vol. 28 (1975), p. 84. See also Katherine Fischer Taylor, *In the Theater of Criminal Justice: The Palais de Justice in Second Empire Paris* (Princeton: Princeton University Press, 1993).

[66] See also Linda Mulcahy, *Legal Architecture: Justice, Due Process and the Place of Law* (London: Routledge, 2010); Linda Mulcahy, "Architects of Justice: The Politics of Courtroom Design," *Social and Legal Studies*, Vol. 16 (2007), pp. 383–403; and Keith J. Bybee, "Judging in Place: Architecture, Design, and the Operation of Courts," *Law and Social Inquiry*, Vol. 37 (2012), pp. 1014–1028.

[67] Jeremy Bentham, *The Works of Jeremy Bentham*, vol. 7, edited by John Bowring (Edinburgh: William Tait, 1839), p. 23.

The fact that the Rivonia trial took place in the Palace of Justice in Pretoria is meaningful. The previous high-profile trials that were arranged to quell mounting resistance to apartheid were held in far less imposing settings, what one scholar described as "converted judicial outpost[s]."[68] The Treason trial, for example, was staged in two locations: a converted military hall in Johannesburg known as the Drill Hall and the Old Synagogue in Pretoria. Despite their poor acoustics and out-of-the way locations, both spaces turned into places of noisy and colorful resistance at least from the vantage point of black audiences living in Johannesburg's townships. Because the courtrooms were improvised sites, the repertoires of performance on display were considerably more varied than during the Rivonia trial. Architecture was one of the factors that shaped the nature of legal performances in these earlier trials.

The enormous building that is the Palace of Justice dates back to the late nineteenth century. Proceedings were first heard there in 1902. The imposing architecture was meant to symbolically establish the supremacy of law over frontier politics, as envisaged by John Kotzé, chief justice of the High Court of the Republic of Transvaal. Ultimately, Kotzé's architectural vision – not unlike his progressive legal vision, which called for the introduction of judicial review to South Africa – had powerful detractors and was largely defeated.[69] As a result, the architectural design of the Palace of Justice was altered to aggrandize it. First and foremost, the three-story building with its neoclassical façade became a paean to the power of Afrikanerdom. Replete with an imposing set of stairs and other vestiges of the classical world, the Palace of Justice has been described as "a magisterial landmark in the capital city."[70]

In 1963, the space of the Palace of Justice would have been imposing, even intimidating, to black audiences who wanted to support the accused in the Rivonia trial. The city of Pretoria at the time was racially cleansed, far from the mixed city that it has become since. Dennis Davis and Michelle le Roux remind us that in at the time of the legal proceeding,

> Pretoria was the white capital of the Afrikaner kingdom. Huge, white men, many with epaulettes weighed down with small crowns distributed by the police and army, strode the streets of the city. Pretoria was the centre of apartheid power; its white inhabitants were supremely confident of the future of their city.[71]

One white onlooker at the time, sympathetic to oppressed black South Africans, remembered the atmosphere vividly:

[68] Cole, *Performing South Africa's Truth Commission*, p. 53.

[69] Wessel le Roux, "Studying Legal History through Courtroom Architecture: Scattered Comments on the Palace of Justice, Church Square, Pretoria," *Codicillus*, Vol. 44 (2003), p. 62.

[70] Dennis Davis and Michelle le Roux, *Precedent and Possibility: The (Ab)use of Law in South Africa* (Cape Town: Double Storey Publishers, 2009), p. 40.

[71] Davis and Le Roux, *Precedent and Possibility*, p. 36.

The display of armed force is chilling beyond words. Uniformed and plain-clothes police mass around the Palace of Justice; leather-strapped khaki uniforms, service revolvers, grim, antagonistic faces, eyes noting every move of the spectators, watching who greets whom, heavy thick men pressed among us listening to each whispered word. A trial conducted in such an atmosphere can have only one outcome. These are the guardians not of peace and order, but of suppression and death.[72]

The state's attempt to control the atmosphere was a direct response to the public dimensions of the political trials that had preceded the Rivonia trial (the Defiance trial, the Treason trial, and the Incitement trial). In these earlier trials, as Cole has argued, "there was an acute sense of the audience outside the courtroom: in the Treason trial, it was the masses standing at the door of the Drill Hall; in the Incitement trial, it was the growing international attention the trial was garnering in the world at large. The Rivonia trial represented a progression as global spectatorship became even more intense and the range of performative repertoires available to both spectators and the accused narrowed significantly."[73] One manifestation of this narrowing was the apartheid government's tight control of spectator movement.

This exercise of control was visible inside the Palace of Justice. The apartheid government changed the physical layout of the courtroom, apparently in an attempt to interrupt direct sight lines between the accused and their supporters. As Cole describes, "A special dock was constructed to change the physical layout of the courtroom so that the accused had to sit with their backs to the audience. The dock had been made with sufficient room that each defendant could be guarded by two private warders."[74] Bruno Mtolo, a former *Umkhonto* operative who, under the pseudonym "Mr. X," was the prosecution's star witness during the Rivonia trial, recalled the spatial dimensions of the proceedings on the day he was called to give testimony against his former comrades:

The court was [as] big as a city hall. It was quite a distance to walk from the door to the witness box. When Captain Van Wyk pointed out the way and the box where I must go, I looked up and saw somebody sitting on a high seat wearing red robes like a Roman Catholic priest. When I looked at him he was also looking at me. He was terrifying ... I got into the box facing the accused, who were quite a distance away. In between us there was a table where the prosecuting council and the defence team were sitting. On my right, I would say five or six feet from the witness box, was the judge. I was shivering like a reed, and kept leaning against the box to stop shivering but it was useless.[75]

[72] Hilda Bernstein, *The World That Was Ours: The Story of the Rivonia Trial* (London: Heinemann, 1967), p. 115.

[73] Cole, *Performing South Africa's Truth Commission*, p. 53.

[74] Cole, *Performing South Africa's Truth Commission*, p. 53.

[75] Bruno Mtolo, *Umkonto we Sizwe: The Road to the Left* (Durban: Drakensberg Press, 1966), p. 147.

Hilda Bernstein, the wife of one of the defendants, described additional features of the courtroom in her 1967 memoir *The World that Was Ours*:

> The judge's bench is an elaborate pulpit of wood, carved and posted like an old-fashioned bed, at one end of the 60-foot court. He is enthroned there, dwarfed in his scarlet robes. On either side of this structure are beige curtains, draped and pleated from floor to ceiling, into which the voices of prosecutor, defending counsel and judge alike disappear and are lost.[76]

Such was the setting in which Mandela rose to speak on Monday, April 20, 1964. It represented an element of what Alexander refers to as the "means of symbolic production" in social performance.[77]

Physicality

While the courtroom setting provided a unique platform, Mandela's first theatrical intervention relied on a prop: his clothing. "He was in an elegant suit and tie and looked imposing and every bit the leader he was," recalls attorney Joel Joffe.[78] In legal performance, especially when undertaken in a formal setting, clothing can help dramatize utterances and other performative acts. As Boehmer has argued, "The predominant aspect of the many eye-catching performances that distinguish Mandela's career is the strong emphasis given to sartorial display: not only acting the part, but also donning the right costume."[79]

Mandela's choice of conventional attire for his statement from the dock contrasts markedly with his clothing style in the 1961 Incitement trial, when he stunned everyone in attendance by appearing, day in and day out, in traditional Thembu dress. But not just that, he chose the leopard skin traditionally reserved for royalty. Zolani Ngwane explains the valence of the imagery during the Incitement trial:

> The most important visual inscription of Mandela's body during the trial was his costume … In that costume Mandela not only reached back, but reached higher in stature than even his father, who was a headman, to the ruling princely line of the Thembu. No longer simply the counselor to kings that he was groomed to be as a young man, he was now, in that witness box, as if on his throne meting out justice on the system that put him on trial.[80]

It was a case of strategic aggrandizement. Something similar transpired in the Rivonia trial.

The fact that the style of Mandela's clothing in 1964 was inconspicuous is precisely what made it stand out. It is safe to assume that Mandela's choice of

[76] Bernstein, *The World That Was Ours*, pp. 125–126.

[77] Alexander, "Cultural Pragmatics," pp. 35, 65–69.

[78] Joel Joffe, personal correspondence with Jens Meierhenrich, August 21, 2014.

[79] Boehmer, *Nelson Mandela*, p. 128.

[80] Zolani Ngwane, "Mandela and Tradition," in Rita Barnard, ed., *The Cambridge Companion to Nelson Mandela* (Cambridge: Cambridge University Press, 2014), p. 128.

a conservative ensemble was deliberate because by the time the proceeding began, he had "developed a public image that centered on his body – a corporal icon with phantasmal amplifiers."[81] Mandela's choice of attire for the Rivonia trial was a theatrical gesture par excellence. It can be interpreted on multiple levels.

First, the selection of the suit can be seen as an assertion of dignity, a recovery of status after the humiliations that accompanied his imprisonment following the conviction in the Incitement trial. Denis Goldberg describes Mandela's first court appearance in the Rivonia trial: "He was in leg irons and handcuffs, wearing sandals, no socks, short trousers, a jacket that looked like a house boy's jacket. Now, you know, to put a man into the dock like that is to create an immediate prejudice."[82] By parading Mandela in shorts and sandals, the authorities diminished his status to that of an inferior being, to that of a boy, because grown men would not be caught wearing either in a professional setting. Mandela may have felt the humiliation even more strongly because in *Long Walk to Freedom*, he commented on the importance that he attached throughout his life to proper attire and especially to carefully maintained footwear, which for him was associated with professionalism and respect. After he was denied such respect during his first court appearance in the trial, Mandela's donning of a suit for his statement from the dock can be read as an iterative performative response.

Second, while Mandela's referencing of Thembu royal dress during the Incitement trial momentarily decentered "the conventions of South African courts of law with an affected ritual elaboration," this enactment also inadvertently reinforced the apartheid regime's racist portrayal of the country's African population as "other," as the ostensibly more "primitive" members of the land. Mandela's return to suit and tie for the purpose of delivering his statement from the dock can be read as an attempt to argue on an equal footing with those who accused him and his comrades of a conspiracy to overthrow the country. Clothing was an equalizer in this regard. By following the dress conventions of white society everywhere, which he personally deemed desirable as well, Mandela may have sought to diminish any perception of a difference between him and some of his audiences. On another level, the Western suit can also be read as a sign of respect for and affiliation with the institution of the rule of law. This goes hand in hand with James Boyd White's textual interpretation of the opening section of Mandela's statement from the dock:

> The opening is a striking act of self-definition. Mandela is a lawyer and speaks with the confidence of one. He belongs in court and knows that he is entitled to be heard. In his respectful and objective tone, muted in feeling and focused on the facts, he seems almost to be speaking about a client, not himself. His legal training and manner, like his earlier degree in arts, mark him as "one of us," as a member of the community

[81] Ngwane, "Mandela and Tradition," p. 127.

[82] Goldberg quoted in Cole, *Performing South Africa's Truth Commission*, p. 53.

defined by law – English law – and reason. This is not the voice of a hotheaded revolutionary or saboteur but of an educated lawyer.[83]

His presentation at the Rivonia trial was not that of a revolutionary either, in contrast to the choice he had made for his first television appearance in 1961, a dark zippered jacket, or the khakis he wore for a photograph with the Algerian Liberation Army in 1962.[84] We can interpret the suit as the costume most befitting the role Mandela sought to embody at this moment and in this particular legal context: that of the reasoning and reasonable man. It, too, made him "one of them," one of the white elite ruling the South African bar, partially reversing the otherness his previous trial performance had created. Boehmer comes to a similar conclusion, noting that Mandela translated "his respect for Westminster democracy and gentlemanly values … into a liking for the 'trappings of British style and manners.' "[85] The power of performativity in Mandela's statement from the dock partially derives from the contrast between form and content: his delivery of incendiary words in a gentlemanly manner while wearing inoffensive and even stylish garb.

The defense team's decision to have Mandela deliver a statement in open court instead of testifying and being subject to cross-examination heightened the theatrical effect of Mandela's formal regal look. This was both a legal and theatrical decision that created the most effective staging of the intersecting legal performances that would constitute the case for the defense. As Joffe wrote, his clients

had begun to realize that the case which they wished to put to the world – their side of the case – would not emerge forcibly through Mandela in the witness box. It would come out in a jumble of bits and pieces, led in the spasmodic fashion which question and answer necessarily provides. There would be no cohesive statement which they and their supporters in the country and abroad would be able to build upon or even to understand.[86]

The defendants were worried, in short, that they might not be able to connect with their intended audiences, to establish the kinds of affective ties that bind. Even though the Rivonia trial was a legal proceeding involving multiple defendants, Mandela's solo appearance before the beginning of the defense case proper further enhanced the aura of authority that he, as "Accused No. 1," already possessed, at home as well as abroad. It contributed immeasurably to the iconography of Mandela. As in the Incitement trial, Mandela's body was once again "the dominant icon" in a political trial, albeit

[83] White, *Acts of Hope*, p. 280.

[84] For Mandela's first TV interview, see the ITN Roving Report news program about apartheid, which aired on October 21, 1961: "First Nelson Mandela Interview," YouTube video, available at www.youtube.com/watch?v=fPofm50MHW8.

[85] Boehmer, *Nelson Mandela*, p. 126.

[86] Joffe, *The State vs. Nelson Mandela*, pp. 148–149.

in a very different way.[87] The man in the impeccably tailored suit, the man who spoke without hesitation for three hours straight, the man who maintained composure and focus was also the lawyer who presented his own case – one coherent, well-presented suit.

Temporality

Temporality is a crucial theatrical dimension of Mandela's statement from the dock. By speaking for 176 minutes, Mandela demonstrated staying power, both literally and figuratively. He stayed put, stretching time, inscribing resistance with his body into the trial transcript. The performative power of his text in the dock combined with the performative power of his body. In the 1960s, Mandela was in the best physical shape of his life, as numerous photographs from the era attest. His "charisma and the enigma were enhanced ... by his physical appearance, including his height, and the aesthetic dimensions of his bodily control, projection, and movement. That he was willing to maintain his body and enhance it through physical exercise and acutely nuanced sartorial practices only helped to accrue its powers."[88] Even though Mandela had lost a considerable amount of weight in prison following his incarceration after the Incitement trial, these powers were very much on display during the statement from the dock. The theatrical effect was considerable: At a time when the ANC was banned and reporting on its activities was prohibited by law, the insurgent organization's figurehead stood tall and strong and firm in the most important city that Afrikaners built and spoke at unprecedented length about the ills of their rule and the duty of black South Africans to resist white domination. For more than three hours, the captive of the apartheid state held the apartheid state captive.

Few, if any, defendants in the history of political trials have spoken truth to power for as long as Mandela did on April 20, 1964. The physicality of this performance was so impressive that until very recently trial participants and scholars unwittingly exaggerated the actual length of Mandela's appearance in court. Instead of the actual 176 minutes he spent delivering the statement from the dock, Martin Meredith writes that the delivery lasted "more than four hours," Tom Lodge has Mandela "speaking for four hours to complete the text he had prepared," and Joffe even for "five hours."[89] Mandela himself thought he "had read for over four hours."[90] The overall impression of listening to what we call Mandela's "filibuster for dignity" is like

[87] Ngwane, "Mandela and Tradition," p. 126.

[88] Sarah Nuttall and Achille Mbembe, "Mandela's Mortality," in Barnard, ed., *The Cambridge Companion to Nelson Mandela*, p. 275.

[89] Martin Meredith, *Mandela: A Biography* (London: Hamish Hamilton, 1997), p. 268; Lodge, *Mandela*, p. 112; Joffe, *The State vs. Nelson Mandela*, p. 160. The length of 176 minutes was reported by the Nelson Mandela Centre of Memory and was calculated on the basis of the digitized audio files created from the original Dictabelt recordings.

[90] Mandela, *Long Walk to Freedom*, p. 322.

witnessing a marathon. This is a man of purpose who has trained long and hard for this performance. He will not be interrupted. He will not be rushed. His speech claims his right to occupy the dock and to speak for whatever duration and at whatever pace he wishes. There is a consistency here with his comportment later while in jail. When Mandela was imprisoned on Robben Island, the jailers tried to rush Mandela and his cohorts as they processed each day to and from the worksite. An early test of will and status was how he and his comrades managed to set their own pace with their wardens. Mandela said later in an interview, "You must fight the battle for dignity on the very first day you go to jail."[91]

As with his walking pace on Robben Island, Mandela set his own pace with the Rivonia statement from the dock, and by any measure of theatrical time, this is a tour de force of endurance performance art, one that certainly demanded an extraordinary stamina from the speaker, yes, but also from his listeners who sat in a cavernous hall on wooden benches for a very long time. Mandela created a visceral experience of the passage of time. By stretching time, he may have wanted to remind the audience of the extraordinary endurance that was required of the oppressed peoples of South Africa to *physically* cope with the country's long history of racial domination.

Orality

In the many books and articles devoted to Mandela, little attention has been paid to his distinctive voice and his theatrical use of it. Once he had entered the dock, he "began very slowly, very quietly, reading the statement which he had prepared, in a flat even voice. At no stage did he raise his voice very much, or change from the slow, measured speech with which he had started. His voice carried clearly across the court. Gradually as he spoke the silence became more and more profound, till it seemed that no one in the court dared move or breathe."[92] Other supporters of the ANC were less impressed by Mandela's oral embodiment of a well-crafted text:

> The address, after going through many changes, returned (I thought) to the simple verity of the second version, and read much better than it was spoken: Mandela's delivery was very disappointing indeed, hesitant, parsonical (if there is such a word), boring.[93]

The source of this frank assessment, the late Nadine Gordimer, has a point. The Dictabelt recordings of his statement from the dock acquaint the listener with a slow, deliberate speaker who for much of the address proceeds in

[91] See Ted Koppel, "Nightline," *ABC News*, June 21, 1990, available at www.youtube.com/watch?v=W2BSGjg4bwU.

[92] Joffe, *The State vs. Nelson Mandela*, p. 157.

[93] Nadine Gordimer, as quoted in Ronald Suresh Roberts, *No Cold Kitchen: A Biography of Nadine Gordimer* (Johannesburg: STE Publishers, 2005), pp. 155–156.

a distinctive, predictable pace, phrasing a few words at a time with regular breaks and pauses, delivering sentences in a staccato, percussive manner. Mandela's timbre is also distinctive, as is his nasalization and the placement of sound within his mouth. He has a halting and yet deliberate delivery and a surprising placement of caesura. Mandela speaks as one accustomed to delivering speeches at political rallies with poor acoustics and without aid of amplification: he phrases a few words at a time, enunciates them clearly, and then pauses between segments to let his words fully carry across the room.[94] These speech patterns were consistent throughout his lifetime, equally evident in his scripted speeches as they were in his more improvisational encounters with television journalists, such as the time Mandela flummoxed U.S. anchorman Ted Koppel at a town hall in New York shortly after his release from prison.[95]

Some have called Mandela's vocal patterns "wooden," and indeed while listening to the entirety of this three-hour speech, one is struck by its lack of dramatic tonal modulation. Also notable are his emotional restraint and emphatic spoken rhythms. However, these details underestimate the theatrical impact of his speech in the larger context of the trial, especially in comparison to some of the other legal performers in the Rivonia trial. "Yutar is reported to have squeaked, whined, and crackled his way through the Rivonia Trial, often resorting to the falsetto registers," says Cole. "Mandela was, in contrast, calm, unwavering, and steady, the antithesis of a hot-headed radical revolutionary."[96]

Mandela performed as a man of purpose, conviction, stature, and endurance. Listening to this recording of Mandela, one experiences a "long walk" to the end of each of his sentences. As the speech goes on, he does modulate his vocal intensity and the percussiveness of his diction, especially at moments when the subject matter of his speech becomes more personal. In the courtroom, Mandela's precise vocal pattern demanded attentive listening and concentration from the audience. Perhaps the very feature of Mandela's delivery to which Gordimer objected may have been its most ingenious, whether by design or happenstance. Restraint in an actor is a well-known strategy for producing a dramatic affective response for the audience. What is more, it is not quite true that Mandela spoke evenly and steadily throughout. A closer listen to the Dictabelt recordings of his statement from the dock reveals considerable changes in the pace and tone and volume of his delivery and its emotional expressiveness.

[94] Mandela's voice is instantly recognizable on the recordings, although it requires concentration to listen for more than a few minutes at a time, which attorney Joel Joffee believes is more symptomatic of the quality of the recordings than of Mandela's projection in the Palace of Justice.

[95] Koppel, "Nightline." [96] Cole, *Performing South Africa's Truth Commission*, p. 54.

Take, for example, Mandela's discussion of what he calls "the question of guerilla warfare," upon which he embarks about halfway through his speech.[97] In it, he refers to the African lives lost in the Sharpeville massacre a few years earlier. Throughout this segment of 4:43 minutes, which is equivalent to just over one page of text in the official trial transcript of the statement from the dock, his delivery is anything but measured.[98] It is brimming with barely suppressed anger. Although he starts out softly and evenly, having just addressed de Wet formally and announced the topic of the next part of his speech, Mandela's delivery picks up in vigor and volume. In his enumeration of five massacres of Africans white authorities perpetrated in the period 1920–1960 in South Africa and South-West Africa, he put great emphasis on his pronunciation of the verbs "killed" (which he used three times) and "died" (which he used twice) to communicate his outrage. He then used the next section of rhetorical questions to extend the dramatic mood he had just created, before returning to a more analytical tone presumably designed to make the defendants' decision "to make preparations as a long-term undertaking, to use force in order to defend ourselves against force" appear rational and reasonable.[99] The audio segment is suggestive of Mandela's ability to modulate his voice for theatrical gain. The changes in inflection enhance the independent power of his textual performance.

One section where Mandela's affective volubility was vividly evident came when he refuted the prosecution's allegation that the "ANC and the Communist Party are one and the same." He begins this section by categorically stating that the accusation is false, which he does in a measured, matter-of-fact way. He follows this by pursuing several lines of refutation, each beginning in a soft, low tone and then building to a series of peaks, each more emotionally intense than the last. He speaks of the Freedom Charter and how it is far from a blueprint for a socialist state – it calls for redistribution, but not nationalization of land. He then frames the relationship of the ANC and the Communist Party as being similar to the cooperation of the United States, Great Britain, and the Soviet Union against Hitler. In a peak of irritation, Mandela declaims, "*Nobody* but Hitler would have *dared* to suggest that such co-operation turned Churchill or Roosevelt into communists or communists['] tools."[100] Each time Mandela reaches a crescendo it is higher than the last, and each time he follows this immediately by pulling back, returning again to a soft, low tone as he pursues the next sub-point. His command of spoken dynamism demonstrated emotional mastery.

97 Official Trial Transcript, p. 24.

98 Recording 1CDR0028062 BD2 NSA, Collection Rivonia Trial, South Africa, 1963–1964: Nelson Mandela Dictabelt Dubbings, British Library, available at http://britishlibrary.typepad.co.uk/sound-and-vision/2013/12/rescuing-the-rivonia-trial-recordings.html.

99 Official Trial Transcript, April 20, 1964, p. 25.

100 Official Trial Transcript, April 20, 1964, p. 25. Emphasis added.

The climax of the entire section was at the moment when the argument became most personal. Mandela speaks of friendship and his own banning. At this point, he asserts not just an alliance of political interests between Communists and African politicians but also a personal alliance of friendship based upon a recognition of common humanity. This is because "communists were the *only* group in South Africa who were prepared to treat Africans as *human beings* and as their equals; who were *prepared* to eat *with us*, live *with us*, and work *with us*. They were the *only* political group which was *prepared* to work with the Africans for the attainment of political rights and a stake in society." He repeats the words "with us" three times, matching this with basic human functions: eat, live, and work. The repetition of "prepared" also foreshadows the use of that word in his legendary final sentence of the speech ("prepared to die"). Mandela brings the entire section to a head by personalizing the argument further, speaking of his own story: "My lord, I am *not a communist* and *I have never been a member of the communist party*. I myself have been *banned*, have been named under that pernicious Act because of the role I played in the Defiance Campaign. I have also been banned and *convicted* under that Act." At the conclusion of this section, Mandela rapidly de-escalates and shifts to a new line of argument, one that commences with the deferential address "my Lord." Mandela's rapid modulation between different registers of intensity imbued quieter moments with an added drama, since one could see that his restraint came at a price. Likewise, intense emotional outbursts were imbued with a gravity because of Mandela's ability to rapidly de-escalate and shift gears. Righteous fury juxtaposed in such close proximity with rational legal argument demonstrated one thing utterly and completely: Mandela was fully in control.

This evidence underscores the importance of relating textuality to theatricality. It partially contradicts Joffe's and Gordimer's recollections of Mandela's delivery and presents a speaker whose oral repertoire was both more varied and less boring than these two trial observers thought. Perhaps, the best example is the final minutes of the statement from the dock, which concluded with the famous sentence "But my lord, if needs be, it is an ideal for which I am prepared to die."[101] As Gordimer recalls,

> Only at the end did the man come through; and when he had spoken that last sentence the strangest and most moving sound I have ever heard from human throats, came from the "black" side of the court audience. It was short, sharp and terrible; something between a sigh and a groan. Afterwards, silence.[102]

Gordimer thought Mandela properly embodied the powerful words she had helped him edit with their journalist friend Anthony Sampson. In theatrical terms, the long silence following Mandela's statement was as memorable (and

[101] Official Trial Transcript, April 20, 1964, p. 55.
[102] As quoted in Roberts, *No Cold Kitchen*, pp. 155–156.

as frequently remarked upon) as the words themselves. For silence, as Marianne Constable reminds us, "is not always an absence of voice."[103]

The power of textuality, on the one hand, and of theatricality, on the other, amplified one another. After speaking eloquently, deliberately, persuasively for three full hours and providing within this speech such a sophisticated analysis of history and the law, Mandela, through his measured and unwavering delivery, gave a very particular performative force to the phrase "I am prepared to die." A man of education, royalty, stature, endurance, and deliberateness had just delivered an extraordinary and unprecedented act of oratory that took a Herculean three hours to convey. The form of his delivery *showed* the audience that Mandela was a man who knew fully what it meant to "prepare." The speech itself performed the capacity of its speaker to prepare diligently, deliberately, and decisively for the unknown, speaking with calm equanimity even in the face of death.

Mandela could not know that the much-remarked-upon silence would come over the courtroom at the conclusion of his speech, but his performance was most certainly calculated to culminate in a dramatic finale. His description of these last two minutes of his courtroom appearance in *Long Walk to Freedom* provides important clues:

> I had been reading my speech, and at this point I placed my papers on the defense table, and turned to face the judge. The courtroom became extremely quiet. I did not take my eyes off Justice de Wet as I spoke from memory the final words. The silence in the courtroom was now complete. At the end of the address, I simply sat down. I did not turn and face the gallery, though I felt all their eyes on me. The silence seemed to stretch for many minutes. But in fact it lasted probably no more than thirty seconds, and then from the gallery I heard what sounded like a great sigh, a deep, collective "ummmm," followed by the cries of women.[104]

This description attests to Mandela's awareness of how deliberate bodily activity (putting papers on the table, turning to the bench, eyeing the judge, dropping the voice, sitting down) and the use of engineered silence could be used for extraordinary dramatic effect. Mandela's reliance on theatrical strategies, however, must not be misunderstood. Our suggestion that his statement from the dock amounts to a legal performance is not to suggest that it was "just" theater "or that the values or ideas informing" his text and delivery "were insincere or merely pretended."[105] As Henning Grunwald writes, "Performance in its substantive sense (i.e. apart from the 'all the world's a stage' generalities) has little to do with make-believe, and nothing at all with 'fakeness.' Authenticity *is* performance."[106] Mandela's appearance bears this out. His ability to convey

[103] Marianne Constable, *Just Silences: The Limits and Possibilities of Modern Law* (Princeton: Princeton University Press, 2005), p. 59.

[104] Mandela, *Long Walk to Freedom*, p. 322.

[105] Henning Grunwald, "Justice as 'Performance'? The Historiography of Legal Procedure and Political Criminal Justice in West Germany," *InterDisciplines*, Vol. 2 (2012), p. 72.

[106] Grunwald, "Justice as 'Performance'?" p. 74.

authenticity – by way of both text and theater – was at the heart of the power of his courtroom appearance. The statement from the dock would have been less powerful if it had not felt authentic. The fact that it did – and still does to those who hear the famous words spoken for the first time fifty years later – has to do with the carefully conceived textual performance that served as the script for the theatrical performance. These two halves *in conjunction* were responsible for the fact that Mandela's statement from the dock turned into the legal performance of a lifetime, if not a century.[107]

THE LEGACIES OF PERFORMANCE

If the trial did things – big things – with words, what were the long-term effects of Mandela's legal performance? The Rivonia trial was a threshold event: It redefined the rules of the political game in South Africa, but in largely unexpected ways. To begin with, the proceeding enacted (in all senses of the term) the anti-apartheid movement's detachment from its earlier, less confrontational self. As the dramatis personae in the Rivonia trial performed the law in the Palace of Justice, new repertoires of contention became thinkable.[108] Because the proceeding marked the *third* performative defeat for the apartheid regime in its courts of law within a few years, it, too, began to revise its strategy of conflict. At a fundamental level, it began to prioritize the prerogative state over the normative state in the administration of "separate development." As a direct consequence, the number of political trials substantially decreased, and those that were held operated according to a very different logic. In a comprehensive study of political trials in South Africa, Catherine Albertyn has shown that "the massive campaign of repression and trials in the early sixties constituted a major defeat for the extra-parliamentary movements. The consequent decline in political conflict coincided with a dramatic decrease in political trials between 1967 and 1976."[109] The nature of legal contention up until the Rivonia trial was "gentlemanly," according to the late Joe Slovo, a senior ANC member and longtime leader of the South African Communist Party. "There was still a rule of law. You had a fair trial in [the apartheid regime's] courts. Nobody could be kept in isolation. Up to 1963, I know of no incident of any political prisoner being tortured."[110] But the long-term consequences of the Rivonia trial were more varied than both Albertyn and Slovo allowed. We therefore must distinguish several different institutional effects over the long term.

107 For a sociological discussion of the role of "scripts" in social performance, see Alexander, "Cultural Pragmatics," pp. 33, 58–59.

108 See generally Anthony W. Marx, *Lessons of Struggle: South African Internal Opposition, 1960–1990* (New York: Oxford University Press, 1992).

109 Albertyn, "A Critical Analysis of Political Trials in South Africa 1948–1988," p. 277.

110 Joe Slovo, as quoted in Thomas G. Karis and Gail M. Gerhart, *From Protest to Challenge: A Documentary History of African Politics in South Africa, 1882–1990*, vol. 5: *Nadir and Resurgence, 1964–1979* (Stanford: Hoover Institution Press, 1997), p. 24.

Destructive trials, as defined in this volume, are political because they seek to defeat a real or imagined political enemy. As the editors put it, "They are intended as weapons, no more and no less."[111] On this score, the South African government could rightly proclaim that the Rivonia trial was a significant success for the regime. The heart of the leadership of the ANC, the Communist Party, and their joint enterprise, MK, ended up in prison, many for life. The Rivonia arrests, trial, and sentences, coupled with continued aggressive action by the police and draconian laws, broke the back of anti-apartheid resistance for nearly a generation. Some important second-line leaders were imprisoned in what came to be known as the "Little Rivonia trial" in 1964. Much of the rest of the leadership of the anti-apartheid movement fled the country to avoid prosecution or detention under the ninety-day detention law.[112] Resistance floundered for more than a decade after the trial until the emergence of new and youthful leaders in the mid-1970s, most notably Steve Biko and the Black Consciousness Movement and various young activists after the 1976 Soweto uprising.[113] Certainly in the short term, the Rivonia trial had one of the political effects its architects intended: It figuratively decapitated the leadership of the anti-apartheid movement. In this sense, the trial was utterly destructive.

At the same time, the anti-apartheid movement experienced victory in defeat. The Rivonia trial bears out Lawrence Douglas's observation that "regardless of the processes by which the didactic trial shapes history and memory in the courtroom, the trial is unable to control the way in which it will become a cultural artifact and will pass into collective memory."[114] This is precisely what transpired in Pretoria. The defense team's didactic maneuvering won out over the prosecution's attempt to control the message about the trial. Although the trial at least temporarily gave the South African government some breathing space from militant opposition, its international propaganda efforts were far less successful.

The trial was good publicity only to the extent that much of the Western media gave a grudging nod of respect to the independence of the South African judiciary. But most of the world sympathized with the defendants' motives and the oppression that spurred them to commit sabotage and plan for guerrilla warfare. Although Justice de Wet may have gotten kudos from the world press, the ruling powers in Pretoria continued to be castigated at every opportunity. The failure of the trial to generate support abroad for the South African government removed an incentive for similar trials in the future. There would

111 Meierhenrich and Pendas, "'The Justice of My Cause is Clear, But There's Politics to Fear,'" p. 57.

112 For a history of anti-apartheid resistance from abroad, see Stephen Ellis, *External Mission: The ANC in Exile, 1960–1990* (London: Hurst, 2012).

113 On the rise of Black Consciousness, see Gail M. Gerhart, *Black Power in South Africa: The Evolution of an Ideology* (Berkeley: University of California Press, 1978).

114 Lawrence Douglas, "The Didactic Trial: Filtering History and Memory in the Courtroom," *European Review*, Vol. 14 (2006), p. 521.

be very few public trials as long as the Nationalists continued to rule the country. Enemies of the regime were dealt with by long detentions without trial and – as in the case of Steve Biko – by murder. The publicity the Rivonia trial generated in the world press had an effect that was very different from what the regime intended. Instead of generating strong support for the government as a bulwark against dastardly communist plots, the already strong opposition to apartheid in the developing and communist world gathered momentum in the West.

Some of the tropes in international reporting contributed to the political legitimation of the convicted defendants in the wake of the Rivonia trial, as in this hyperbolic example from the *New York Times*: "As the debates and votes in the United Nations this past year have shown, most of the world regards the convicted men as heroes and freedom fighters. They are considered the George Washingtons and Benjamin Franklins of South Africa, not criminals deserving punishment."[115] The United States and the United Kingdom were not ready immediately to approve meaningful sanctions against South Africa, but pressure on both governments was building. The Rivonia trial had fully exposed apartheid for the repressive regime that it was. Anti-apartheid activists referred to that exposure over and over again in various international fora – most importantly at the United Nations.[116] On October 11, 1963, for example, in Resolution 1881, the UN General Assembly called upon the government of South Africa "to abandon the arbitrary trial now in progress and forthwith to grant unconditional release to all political prisoners and to all persons imprisoned, interned or subjected to other restrictions for having opposed apartheid."[117] Remarkably, 106 of the 107 states that deliberated over Resolution 1881 voted in favor; only South Africa voted against it. On June 9, 1964, two days before the announcement of the verdict in the Rivonia trial, the UN Security Council urged the apartheid regime "to end forthwith the trial in progress, instituted within the framework of the arbitrary law of apartheid."[118]

The convictions in the Rivonia trial strengthened resolve in the UN to move toward declaring apartheid a crime against humanity, which finally occurred in 1973. Perhaps the same pressure would have built had there been no trial and no statements from the leaders of the anti-apartheid movement at the Rivonia trial. But the articulation of the plight of the wretched of South Africa in the proceeding most certainly accelerated the delegitimation of white supremacy.

[115] "Verdict in South Africa," *New York Times*, June 14, 1964.

[116] See Audie Klotz, "Norms Reconstituting Interests: Global Racial Equality and U.S. Sanctions against South Africa," *International Organization*, Vol. 49 (1995), pp. 451–478; and Audie Klotz, *Norms in International Relations: The Struggle against Apartheid* (Ithaca: Cornell University Press, 1999).

[117] "The Policies of *Apartheid* of the Government of the Republic of South Africa," UN General Assembly Resolution 1881, October 11, 1963.

[118] UN Security Council Resolution 182 (1963), December 4, 1963.

CONCLUSION

In our analysis of the performative dimensions of Mandela's statement from the dock, we have focused on the roles of linguistic performatives, dramatic performances, and the legal constraints that are the "given circumstances" framing the mutually constitutive relationship that often exists between them. By so doing, we have related textuality to theatricality in a broader attempt to transcend the still-influential – yet in our view misguided – interpretation that posits the two concepts as oppositional terms.[119] This is a move toward an integrated understanding of performativity, one that is satisfactory to multiple users in diverse disciplines and fields of inquiry, especially in the province of law.

We argue that the performativity of law hinges on the kinds of things that actors do with words *and* bodies, legal procedure *and* expressive embodiment, physical presence *and* spatiality.[120] Focusing on one aspect of performativity at the expense of another risks misrepresenting the nature of legal performance. We hope that our analysis of the Rivonia trial has demonstrated empirically what David Apter has posited theoretically:

> It is performance that, when at its best, enables a politics as theatre to endow a particular space with a certain clarity, miniaturizing, focusing, concentrating and intensifying public attention, by magnifying a symbolic register. Political theatre then becomes a way of defining and communicating preferred and alternative political interpretations, a twofold process in which conventional knowledge may be emptied of content but ritually reinforced, and/or replaced by new referential and more gripping signs, symbols, and signals.[121]

With his statement from the dock, Mandela told a people's history of South Africa. Because this history lesson was immediately embraced as authentic by a sizable portion of the audience, the country's most important political trial ended up being, against all odds, didactically successful for the defendants. The Pretoria courtroom served as an important space of resistance.[122]

In the long run, the Rivonia trial proved more transgressive than the apartheid regime thought possible. By communicating transubstantiating and believable truths, it inverted the racial order of things, even though the political consequences of this inversion did not make themselves fully felt for several decades. Anthony Sampson writes that "Pretoria was confident that within a few years [Mandela] would be out of sight and out of mind, the ANC forgotten and abandoned."[123] This was not to be. Instead, the world became

[119] See Marvin Carlson, "The Resistance to Theatricality," *SubStance*, Vol. 31 (2002), pp. 239–240.

[120] Austin, *How To Do Things with Words*.

[121] David E. Apter, "Politics as Theatre: An Alternative View of the Rationalities of Power," in Alexander, Giesen, and Mast, eds., *Social Performance*, p. 227.

[122] See also the contributions to Allo, *The Courtroom as a Space of Resistance*.

[123] Sampson, *Mandela*, p. 199.

his stage. Not only his message, but Mandela himself became sign, symbol, and signal. His moral standing became deeply intertwined with his legal performance in the Rivonia trial, as Stephen Curkpatrick argues:

> Mandela is admired because he admires the law, reflects the law, reflects on the law, experiences the mirror reflections of the law as defendant and prosecutor, is an exemplary reflection of the law's necessary supplement in justice, and reflects the spectral nature of the law by prosecuting the law through the law. Mandela mirrors the law's need for supplementation, and makes visible the force of its violent foundations by contesting the law in his witness to the suffering of his people under apartheid.[124]

The achievement of his extraordinary court appearance was that he demonstrated "how an oppressive situation can be withstood through a process of strategically repeating and exceeding the oppressor's self-justifying discourses of rationality."[125]

In our argument, the power of Mandela's legal performance can be best understood by considering the structurally contingent interplay of three explanatory factors: *legality, textuality*, and *theatricality*. The first element set the stage, the second element provided the script, and the third element created the social drama that shook the world. When viewed from the vantage point of the twenty-first century, it is clear that the Rivonia trial undermined the state more than it reinforced it. By lending institutional visibility to the larger question of historic injustice in South Africa in the middle of the twentieth century, the Rivonia trial was "jurisprudentially dramatic," to borrow a phrase from Shoshona Felman.[126] The theater of the rule of law during the 1963–1964 period highlighted the complicated – and changing – relationship between the prerogative and normative halves of the apartheid state.

Despite the ritual of procedure, the institutional remnants of the normative state that served Mandela and nine others so well, the strength of the racial state loomed large in the Pretoria courtroom, and the apartheid regime deployed its infrastructural power with destructive force in the wake of the trial. Emblematic of this resurgence of the prerogative state was the adoption, in 1967, of the Terrorism Act, which bestowed far-reaching powers of warrantless detention and interrogation on the police, "thus effectively shutting down the courtroom as a primary stage for the state's enactment of power."[127] As Cole writes, "Thereafter, torture became the new staging ground for confrontation between the archive and the repertoire, between the document and the body. Unlike trials, these

124 Stephen Curkpatrick, "Mandela's 'Force of Law,' " *Sophia*, Vol. 41 (2002), pp. 69–70.

125 Boehmer, *Nelson Mandela*, p. 13.

126 Shoshona Felman, *The Juridical Unconscious: Trials and Trauma in the Twentieth Century* (Cambridge: Harvard University Press, 2002), p. 162.

127 Cole, *Performing South Africa's Truth Commission*, p. 60.

confrontations took place behind closed doors, with no rules and with virtually no witnesses beyond the police and prison warders and the victims themselves."[128] Anti-apartheid activists have therefore referred to the years before to the Rivonia trial as "the legal days."[129]

Following the trial, the apartheid regime ensured that these days were over. And in the short run they were. The long-run consequences of the trial, however, were different and unexpected. Mandela's legal performance, but also those of his lawyers and of some of his co-defendants, exemplified the continued power of the rule of law as a weapon in the struggle against apartheid. These performances, as Wessel le Roux has shown, "were inspirational to a younger generation of lawyers who joined in the work [of political resistance] ... Through their skill, these liberation lawyers managed to turn the already politicised courts into sites of resistance."[130] Recent findings suggest that the institutional effects of the Rivonia trial reached even farther into the future. We believe that the proceeding and the other political trials in the period 1956–1964 must be seen "as central to the performance genealogy" of the Truth and Reconciliation Commission of South Africa, which marked another liminal period in the country's history.[131]

When analyzed in performative terms, the Rivonia trial becomes much more than the trial that put Nelson Mandela in jail for life. It marked a critical juncture in the consolidation of apartheid, but it also, and more crucially, underlined the political power that can be generated in the theater of the rule of law. It is no hyperbole to suggest that Mandela's legal performance provided "a manifesto for anti-apartheid campaigners everywhere."[132] At least as significantly, Mandela's charismatic authority ensured that the ANC retained a commitment to legal contention, not just violent contention – an achievement that proved crucial in the resolution of apartheid's endgame.[133] Nelson Mandela legitimated the strategy of legal contention within the ANC by demonstrating in no uncertain terms the efficacy of the insurgent use of legal procedure for political ends.[134]

[128] Cole, *Performing South Africa's Truth Commission*, p. 60.

[129] Albie Sachs, "Foreword," in Ruth First, *117 Days* (New York: Monthly Review Press, 1989), p. 11.

[130] Wessel le Roux, "Conscience against the Law: Mahatma Gandhi, Nelson Mandela and Bram Fischer as Practising Lawyers during the Struggle," *Codicillus*, Vol. 42 (2001), pp. 34–35.

[131] Cole, *Performing South Africa's Truth Commission*, p. 30. For a foundational analysis, see Richard A. Wilson, *The Politics of Truth and Reconciliation in South Africa: Legitimating the Post-Apartheid State* (Cambridge: Cambridge University Press, 2001).

[132] Sampson, *Mandela*, p. 194.

[133] For this argument, see Meierhenrich, *The Legacies of Law*, esp. pp. 175–291.

[134] Ours is a tweak of the subtitle of a public law classic: Otto Kirchheimer, *Political Justice: The Use of Legal Procedure for Political Ends* (Princeton: Princeton University Press, 1961).

10

China's Gang of Four Trial

The Law v. *The Laws of History*

Alexander C. Cook

The most famous trial in Chinese history took place in Beijing in the winter of 1980–1981, four years after the death of Chairman Mao. Ten recently deposed leaders stood before a special tribunal, indicted on charges of orchestrating a counterrevolutionary conspiracy to seize control of the Chinese Communist Party (CCP); its state apparatus, the People's Republic of China (PRC); and its military force, the People's Liberation Army (PLA). The ten defendants had carried out the radical politics of Chairman Mao's Great Proletarian Cultural Revolution (CR) (1966–1976), and now stood accused of hijacking the movement as a vehicle to persecute rivals and usurp power.

Among the accused were five military officers implicated in an alleged coup d'état and assassination attempt against Chairman Mao in 1971. The leader of the plot was Lin Biao, then the supreme commander of China's military and Mao's designated successor. (Lin, along with his wife and grown son, died in a plane crash allegedly fleeing the country after the plot was hastily aborted.) Also on trial was Mao's former political secretary, Chen Boda, who had been purged in a leadership struggle between radical factions in 1970. Most notorious of all, however, was the "Gang of Four," a clique of radical cultural revolutionaries that fell from power shortly after Mao's death in 1976. It was this small but extraordinary clique – led by Mao's then wife (now widow) Jiang Qing – that gave the trial of the Lin Biao and Jiang Qing Counterrevolutionary Groups its colloquial misnomer: the Gang of Four trial. Absent from the dock of course was the late Chairman Mao himself, whose legacy soon would be dealt with in a separate but related CCP resolution on the history of the party.

The basic facts about the Gang of Four trial were well publicized in China at the time, and are available to Western readers in the Chinese-produced propaganda work *A Great Trial in Chinese History*.[1] The lengthy indictment,

[1] *A Great Trial in Chinese History* (Beijing: New World Press; distributed by New York: Pergamon Press, 1981); English reprint edition (Honolulu: University Press of the Pacific, 2003). Versions were also published in French, German, and Spanish.

prepared by a special prosecutor, listed forty-eight charges in four categories: (1) the systematic framing and purging of party, state, and military leaders up to the very highest levels; (2) the persecution of more than 700,000 lower-level party cadres and regular citizens, resulting in the unlawful death of nearly 35,000 people; (3) the unconsummated assassination and military coup (in which the Gang of Four proper was not involved); and (4) the Gang of Four's failed plan to stage an armed rebellion in Shanghai during the succession crisis that followed Mao's death. The case was tried by a special court, established under the auspices of the Supreme People's Court.

The court worked six days a week for six weeks, from late November to late December, examining the ten accused, hearing testimony from forty-nine witnesses, and weighing 651 items of evidence.[2] The defendants were generally compliant, with the notable exception of Mao's widow Jiang Qing, who defended herself vigorously. "To rebel is justified!" she announced in open court, arguing that her actions had taken place in a heroic revolutionary context beyond the reach of legal codes. She also provided the trial's most memorable moments, summoning the ghost of Mao in her defense: "I was Mao's dog. What he said to bite, I bit!" she proclaimed, and "To vilify me is to vilify Mao!" The verdict, issued in late January following four weeks of deliberations, found all ten defendants guilty. The court imposed sentences ranging from sixteen years' imprisonment to death, though the two death sentences (including one for Jiang Qing) were immediately suspended and later commuted to life imprisonment.

From beginning to end, daily broadcast and print coverage brought the legal drama to a mass audience, providing a curious Chinese public with the most detailed picture yet glimpsed of the destructive political intrigues of the Cultural Revolution.[3] Outside the courtroom, this spectacular legal event became the focal point for a larger cultural conversation about history, justice, and the fate of Chinese socialism.

The present chapter aims to analyze China's Gang of Four trial in light of some issues raised in the introduction to this volume.[4] The chapter will first

[2] "Zuigao renmin fayuan tebie fating guanyu shenpan Lin Biao, Jiang Qing fangeming jituan an zhufan de xiaojie" [Brief summary of the trial of the main culprits in the Lin Biao and Jiang Qing counterrevolutionary groups by the Special Court under the Supreme People's Court], February 9, 1981, in *Zhonghua renmin gongheguo zuigao renmin fayuan tebie fating shenpan Lin Biao, Jiang Qing fangeming jituan an zhufan jishi* [Records of the Special Court of the Supreme People's Court of the PRC trial of the main culprits in the Lin Biao and Jiang Qing counterrevolutionary groups] [henceforth abbreviated *TBFTJS*] (Beijing: Falü chubanshe, 1982), pp. 480–492.

[3] English translations of select Chinese media coverage can be found in the Foreign Broadcast Information Service (Daily Report) for China (FBIS-CHI).

[4] Jens Meierhenrich and Devin O. Pendas, " 'The Justice of My Cause Is Clear, But There's Politics to Fear': Political Trials in Theory and History," in this volume. For a broader discussion of this complicated event, of the official discourse that interpreted the trial to the public, and of alternate discourses of justice that emerged contemporaneously in the cultural realm, please see Alexander

introduce the historical background to China's Cultural Revolution and its aftermath. Knowledge of this background is essential to understanding the political significance of the Gang of Four trial. Following these preliminaries, the chapter will classify the Gang of Four trial within the proposed typology of didactic, destructive, and decisive political trials. The Gang of Four trial was primarily a didactic trial, and its main lesson was that the unaccountable political violence of the Cultural Revolution was to be replaced by socialist law and order. Although the Gang of Four trial has usually been dismissed as a political "show" trial, the content of its didactic show makes it more useful to think of the trial as an example of transitional justice in a uniquely Chinese and socialist context.

The chapter will then turn to the interrelation of power, procedure, and performance in the Gang of Four trial. The concept of socialist legality emerging in post-Mao China unabashedly presented legal procedure as an instrument of state power. Next we will introduce the element of performance, showing how the post-Mao political transition was staged and enacted (and mediated to the public) on the very first day of the trial. In the last part of this chapter we will examine the connection between the legal verdict and the historical resolution on Mao, and the resulting claim about the connection between the law and the so-called laws of history.

THE CULTURAL REVOLUTION: AN INTRODUCTION

In October 1949 the Chinese Communist Party (CCP) founded the People's Republic of China (PRC). The end of a long civil war marked the victorious conclusion of the socialist revolution as a political revolution. In other ways, it was only the beginning of the struggle. CCP Chairman Mao Zedong accepted Lenin's prediction that the socialist era, the era of transition to communism, would be "a period of unusually violent class struggles in their sharpest possible forms."[5] This meant that under socialism the revolutionary classes must exercise strict dictatorship over the enemies of the people. Thus, on the eve of founding the socialist state, Mao cautioned his comrades against complacency in victory:

> The imperialists and domestic reactionaries will certainly not take their defeat lying down and they will struggle to the last ditch. After there is peace and order throughout the country, they will still engage in sabotage and create disturbances in various ways

C. Cook, *The Cultural Revolution on Trial: Mao and the Gang of Four* (New York: Cambridge University Press, 2016).

[5] Vladimir Ilyich Lenin, "The State and Revolution," in Henry M. Christman, ed., *Essential Works of Lenin: "What Is to Be Done?" and Other Writings* (New York: Dover, 1987), p. 295.

and will try every day and every minute to stage a comeback. This is inevitable, beyond all doubt, and under no circumstances must we relax our vigilance.[6]

The revolution, if not secured, could be reversed. In the decades that followed, Mao took an increasingly pessimistic view of China's prospects for completing the revolution in his lifetime. Instead Mao came to view revolution as a continuous struggle to be fought again and again over a long period of time.[7]

In the years leading up to the Cultural Revolution, Mao perceived the specters of "revisionism" and "capitalist restoration" materializing within the socialist camp, both domestically and overseas. He pointed with alarm to de-Stalinization in the Soviet Union and the retrenchment of agricultural collectivization after the Great Leap Forward in China.[8] Mao suspected that the old guard of Chinese revolutionaries was degenerating into a new privileged class of bureaucrats, and he warned of this danger in a high-level party document issued in January 1965: "[A]fter the socialist transformation of ownership has been basically completed, the class enemies of socialism will use the means of 'peaceful evolution' to seek the restoration of capitalism. This sort of class struggle inevitably will be reflected in the Party."[9] The urgent task, he concluded, was to "grasp the struggle between the two roads of socialism and capitalism" and identify "those in positions of authority in the Party taking the capitalist road."[10] This task – the political and cultural struggle against the restoration of capitalism from within the communist party – was the basic program of the Cultural Revolution.

The Cultural Revolution spanned the decade from 1966 to 1976.[11] The first couple of years was the most active period, including phases of mass mobilization, the purge of existing leadership structures, the creation of new structures, armed factional clashes, and demobilization. This active period was followed by a new round of conflicts among the radicals over the spoils of victory. Through these struggles the Gang of Four precipitated the downfall of fellow Special Court defendants Chen Boda and the Lin Biao group, and

[6] Mao Zedong, "The Chinese People Have Stood Up!" (Opening address at the First Plenary Session of the Chinese People's Political Consultative Conference), September 21, 1949, available at www.marxists.org/reference/archive/mao/selected-works/volume-5/mswv5_01.htm.

[7] Nick Knight, *Rethinking Mao: Explorations in Mao Zedong's Thought* (New York: Lexington Books, 2007), pp. 249–269.

[8] Roderick MacFarquhar, *Origins of the Chinese Cultural Revolution*, 3 vols. (New York: Columbia University Press for the Royal Institute of International Affairs, the East Asian Institute of Columbia University, and the Research Institute on Communist Affairs of Columbia University, 1974–1983).

[9] CCP Central Committee, "Nongcun shehuizhuyi jiaoyu yundong zhong muqian de yixie wenti" [Some current problems in the rural socialist education movement], January 14, 1965, available at http://news.xinhuanet.com/ziliao/2005-02/02/content_2539348.htm.

[10] CCP Central Committee, "Nongcun shehuizhuyi jiaoyu yundong zhong muqian de yixie wenti."

[11] For a fuller history of the Cultural Revolution, see Roderick MacFarquhar and Michael Schoenhals, *Mao's Last Revolution* (Cambridge: Belknap Press of Harvard University Press, 2008).

themselves emerged as the standard bearers of the radical line in Chinese politics.

A party circular dated May 16, 1966 initiated the Cultural Revolution. The circular took aim at the Group of Five, an informal panel appointed by the Central Committee in 1964 to oversee the revolution in culture. The group of establishment politicians and intellectuals, headed by Beijing mayor Peng Zhen, was exposed an "anti-Party clique" and summarily dissolved. It was replaced by a more powerful and far more radical body, a Central Cultural Revolution Group (CCRG) to be convened by Premier Zhou Enlai and reporting directly to the Politburo's Standing Committee. Mao's former political secretary Chen Boda headed the new group, whose roster counted Mao's wife Jiang Qing, radical Shanghai politician Zhang Chunqiao, and chief of the national intelligence apparatus Kang Sheng, among others. A June 1 editorial in *People's Daily* called on the Chinese people to "sweep away all monsters."[12] From there, the situation escalated rapidly.

Though Mao had his critics among the top leadership, he enjoyed great prestige among the Chinese people, owing in part to a cult of personality fostered by PLA leader Lin Biao.[13] Thus Mao was able to rally a coalition of revolutionary forces from outside the party-state apparatus to assail the revolution's enemies, real or perceived. He hailed the younger generation as "revolutionary successors" and over the coming months throngs of students were encouraged to challenge authority at higher and higher levels. Numerous officials were dragged from their homes and paraded before jeering crowds. Eventually the two biggest "capitalist roaders" would be revealed as State Council President Liu Shaoqi and Party Vice-Chairman Deng Xiaoping. In January 1967, a clash between labor organizations brought down the Shanghai municipal government. Mao praised this "January Storm" as a seizure of power by the masses, and urged the military to support similar seizures of power elsewhere across the country.

Violent skirmishes became endemic, and it was not always clear to the military brass which among the many competing rebel groups deserved their backing. Local armed conflicts grew in intensity, sometimes even pitting military units against each other. By the summer of 1967, China teetered on the brink of civil war. It was time to consolidate gains, declare victory, and bring the active phase of the Cultural Revolution to a close. The consolidation would take another year and a half of struggle and bloodshed. Zhou initiated an open-ended campaign to root out troublemakers and "purify the class ranks." The campaign would drag on for years, implicating millions of people. By the end of the summer of 1968, the new Revolutionary Committees were in place in

[12] Chen Boda, "Hengsao yiqie niugui sheshen" [Sweep away all ox-ghosts and snake-spirits], *Renmin Ribao* [People's Daily] [hereafter abbreviated as *RMRB*], June 1, 1966.

[13] Daniel Leese, *Mao Cult: Rhetoric and Ritual in China's Cultural Revolution* (New York: Cambridge University Press, 2013).

every province of China, and normalcy had been restored under de facto martial law.[14] Millions of radical students and intellectuals were demobilized – exiled to the countryside, not knowing when they might return. The purge of party leadership was confirmed in October 1968, when a skeletal party plenum formally expelled Liu Shaoqi, dismissed Deng Xiaoping from office, and designated Lin Biao as Mao's future successor.

In his summary report at the opening of the Ninth Central Committee in April 1969, Lin Biao declared that although "a great victory has been won in the Great Proletarian Cultural Revolution," it was "too soon to speak of final victory." He urged that the study and dissemination of the basic lessons of the Great Proletarian Cultural Revolution, of the history of the struggle between two lines [capitalism and socialism], and of Chairman Mao's theory of continuing the revolution under the dictatorship of the proletariat were lessons that would have to be relearned and repeated "every year, every month, and every day."[15]

Almost as soon as victory had been claimed, the radical coalition began to turn against itself. Chen Boda, the head of the Central Cultural Revolution Group, was the first to fall. The presidency had remained vacant since the purge of Liu Shaoqi. Chen Boda and Lin Biao insisted that Mao should resume the office, which he had held before, while Mao proposed that the post be eliminated. In any case, Mao did not want the largely ceremonial role, which he considered tiresome. Mao resented the hectoring. Lin Biao also wanted to add to the party constitution a phrase from his Foreword to *Quotations from Chairman Mao*, in which he asserted that Mao had developed Marxism-Leninism "with genius, creatively, and comprehensively."[16] Mao countered that genius was a bourgeois concept, and Chen Boda was dismissed as a "phoney Marxist."[17]

It was Lin Biao who had put up Chen Boda to pester Mao, and now Mao grew distant from his erstwhile "closest comrade-in-arms." This was a fatal mistake for Lin, who had lost the Chairman's trust and confidence. The split between Lin Biao and Mao Zedong set in motion the mysterious events of September 1971, in which Lin died in a plane crash after discovery of an aborted assassination plot against Mao. After his death, Lin Biao was exposed as one half of the "Lin and Chen [Boda] Anti-Party Clique" and later became the central target of the Gang of Four's stultifying campaign to "Criticize Lin and Confucius."[18] In the final years of the Cultural Revolution, the Gang of Four – Jiang Qing, Zhang Chunqiao, Yao Wenyuan, and Wang Hongwen –

[14] MacFarquhar and Schoenhals, *Mao's Last Revolution*, pp. 245–246.

[15] Lin Biao, "Report to the Ninth National Congress of the Communist Party of China," April 1, 1969, available at www.marxists.org/reference/archive/lin-biao/1969/04/01.htm.

[16] Lin Biao, "Foreword to the Second Edition of Quotations of Chairman Mao Tse-tung," December 16, 1966, available at www.marxists.org/reference/archive/lin-biao/1966/12/16.htm.

[17] Quoted in MacFarquhar and Schoenhals, *Mao's Last Revolution*, p. 356.

[18] "Circular and Materials of the CCP CC on Organizing the Distribution and Discussion of *The Struggle to Smash the Lin-Chen Anti-Party Clique's Counterrevolutionary Coup* (Materials, Part 1)," December 11, 1971 [Zhongfa #77 (1971)]; Tien-wei Wu, *Lin Biao and*

held firm control of the radical wing of the party, and Wang Hongwen was put forward as a candidate to succeed Mao.

Though Mao became increasingly frail and isolated in his old age, he continued to maintain among the top leadership a delicate balance of power that he could tip to meet his purposes. Thus the Gang of Four was held in check by other factions: by other senior cadres who had benefited from the turnover in leadership in the late 1960s, by supporters of the elder statesman Zhou Enlai, by entrenched interests in strategic economic sectors like the petroleum industry, and even by periodically rehabilitated moderates such as Deng Xiaoping.

A few months before his death, a frail and ailing Chairman Mao reflected back on his life and counted two great accomplishments. His first great accomplishment, he said, had been to beat back the Japanese invaders and defeat Chiang Kai-shek's Nationalist regime in the subsequent civil war. The second great accomplishment had been to launch the Cultural Revolution. Mao had initiated this second (cultural) revolution in order to safeguard the first, but he had to concede that its greatness was not widely recognized: "Not many people support this thing, and more than a few oppose it. The matter is not yet resolved. It is a legacy to be handed down to the next generation – if not in peace, then in turmoil."[19] Thus Mao went to his deathbed fearing a "reversal of correct verdicts" and an end to continuous revolution. His fear proved prescient.

When Mao died, power initially passed to the capable but colorless Hua Guofeng, a doctrinaire Maoist who represented the senior beneficiaries of the Cultural Revolution. One of Hua's first actions, just weeks after Mao's death, was to "smash" the Gang of Four. The radicals were placed under house arrest and subjected to criticism in a series of political campaigns. Hua Guofeng did not criticize the Cultural Revolution, however. That would be left to the regime of Deng Xiaoping, who outmaneuvered Hua to take control of the party in late 1978. Deng Xiaoping had a reputation as a pragmatist, as well as the résumé of a Long March veteran, deep connections in the military, and the support of other senior leaders who had survived the purges of the past decade. Now the party declared the class struggle over and turned to the business of "socialist construction" – the development of productive forces and the social accumulation of material wealth.

Confronting the legacy of the Cultural Revolution, the new regime undertook a comprehensive "reversal of false, unjust, and incorrect verdicts." Whereas Mao had believed such a reversal would be a betrayal of the socialist

the Gang of Four: Contra-Confucianism in Historical and Intellectual Perspective (Carbondale: Southern Illinois University Press, 1983).

[19] This anecdote is oft repeated but not well documented. On attribution of this quote, see Jiang Yihua, "Perspective 1: On Mao Zedong," in Timothy Cheek, ed., *A Critical Introduction to Mao* (New York: Cambridge University Press, 2010), p. 342; and Frederick Teiwes and Warren Sun, *The End of the Maoist Era: Chinese Politics During the Twilight of the Cultural Revolution, 1972–1976* (London: Routledge, 2007), p. 595.

project, the post-Mao reformers claimed the reversal to be a redemption of it. At the center of the reversal of verdicts was the courtroom trial that brought a legal verdict against the most notorious leaders of the Cultural Revolution – and set the stage for a final, historical verdict on Mao.

The Special Court faced enormous challenges. The trial was expected to model a new political culture, to triage open wounds and mend a tattered social fabric, to assign meaning to dimly understood historical events, to determine personal liability for mass harm, and to usher in a new era of sober rationality. The political challenges alone were formidable. It was easy enough to shield Mao from a posthumous legal reckoning, since the late Chairman could not be called to testify in court about the events that he had set in motion. But it was impossible to separate the Cultural Revolution from Mao, or Mao from the larger history of Chinese socialism. (A subversive joke from the time of the trial referred to the Gang of Four with four fingers held up and a wiggling thumb outstretched.) The floodgates of violence had been opened in the name of "continuing the revolution" and the resulting ruin left the legitimacy of Chinese socialism badly damaged. It was imperative now for Chinese socialism to offer justice.

Inevitably, the trial that ensued was inadequate to meet all of these challenges. Nevertheless, the court's orderly legal proceedings posed a stark contrast to the rough, summary justice handed out by unruly mobs during the Cultural Revolution. As such, the trial announced a new political culture and a new way of dealing with the sharpest contradictions in society.

THE GANG OF FOUR TRIAL AS TRANSITIONAL JUSTICE

The Gang of Four trial was both the most important legal case and the most memorable cultural event of the post-Mao transition. Nevertheless, our view of the trial so far has been narrowly limited to the show trial interpretation. In China, politics made it all but impossible to express any view divergent from the official interpretation of the trial's meaning. More surprising perhaps is the scant attention paid to the trial in Western scholarship. Despite its symbolic significance for the fate of Chinese socialism, and for the actual lives of millions of Chinese, the Gang of Four trial has been mostly overlooked.[20] In the absence of scholarly work on the trial in both China and the West, the images crafted by popular media accounts have framed our perception of the

[20] The main scholarly works on the trial appeared shortly after the event. These include the essays in James C. Hsiung, ed., *Symposium: The Trial of the "Gang of Four" and its Implication in China*, Occasional Papers/Reprints Series in Contemporary Asian Studies 40 (Baltimore: University of Maryland, 1981); Ross Terrill, *Madame Mao: The White-Boned Demon*, Revised and expanded edition (Stanford: Stanford University Press, 1999), pp. 13–19, 374–394; David Bonavia, *Verdict in Peking: The Trial of the Gang of Four* (London: Burnett, 1984). More recently, several Chinese participants in the trial have published personal, retrospective accounts.

trial. Now, more than three decades later, it is time to re-examine our assumptions.

Western media coverage of the trial was generally good, both in quality and quantity, but the reports were also tinged with condescension. This postscript to the trial from the pages of *Newsweek* is typical:

> To no one's surprise Jiang Qing ... and the other three were convicted. After all, the Chinese are still running a dictatorship. But the trial was a signal that the legal system is important, a reminder that perhaps in China the law can evolve, guaranteeing a modicum of liberty for its citizens. It's not Jeffersonian democracy, but for the people who live there it's no small accomplishment.[21]

Seeing a socialist court press former socialist leaders on charges of counterrevolution recalled for many the notorious Moscow trials of the 1930s and other such kangaroo courts. Without a second thought, critics in the Western media wrote off the trial as a crude Stalinist farce adapted to the Chinese stage – a show trial. This interpretation was and is entirely reasonable. The Gang of Four trial was a purge of disgraced political leaders, a legal spectacle staged by an authoritarian state with a well-deserved reputation for grand political theater. The selective prosecution of politically palatable defendants, the retroactive application of laws, the numerous procedural irregularities, the widespread assumption of guilt, the limited opportunities for defense, the strongly pedagogical tone – all of these elements rightly contributed to the impression that the Gang of Four trial used the barest of legal trappings to conceal a raw demonstration of political power. Hindsight further confirms the suspicion of contemporary observers that the trial was far less important legally than it was politically. The trial failed to establish a robust and lasting precedent for socialist rule of law, as proponents claimed it would, and criminal prosecution continues to be used in the PRC today as an instrument to suppress political opposition.

Nevertheless, the standard interpretation of the Gang of Four trial as a show trial, correct as far as it goes, is also severely limited. The pejorative term "show trial" deems whatever the trial purported to show as unworthy of serious consideration. Calling the trial "just a show" implies that it was not a *real* historical event but merely a staged pseudo-event, a performance "staged or managed (or co-opted) by an existing configuration of power or authority, rather than spontaneously generating any new such configuration."[22] But the event was no less real for being staged. If we are to learn anything of historical value from a history of this trial, then we need to take the "show" seriously.[23]

[21] ARIC Press, "China Lays Down the Law," *Newsweek*, September 7, 1981, p. 47.

[22] Scott Newton, "Post-war to New World Order and Post-socialist Transition: 1989 as Pseudo-Event," in Fleur Johns, Richard Joyce, and Sundhya Pahuja, eds., *Events: The Force of International Law* (London: Routledge, 2011), pp. 106–107.

[23] This is also true of the original Soviet show trials. See Elizabeth A. Wood, *Performing Justice: Agitation Trials in Early Soviet Russia* (Ithaca: Cornell University Press, 2005), pp. 193–207.

Unlike the worst of the Soviet show trials, the Gang of Four trial was not "just a show" in the sense of a mere fiction spun by the state. Although the continued inaccessibility of archival sources prevents a full and independent assessment of the case, our knowledge so far confirms the initial impression of David Bonavia, a Western journalist who followed the proceedings closely: The trial was "[not] even remotely a fair one," he concedes, but still the show seemed to be "only to some extent stage-managed" and it was "rooted in fact, even if tendentiously presented."[24] The Gang of Four trial was a show trial to be sure, but we must take this fact as the impetus for further inquiry and not as the final judgment. To press forward, we need to find a more capacious interpretive framework – one that allows us to understand the greater significance of the event in its cultural and historical contexts. That framework is transitional justice.

Transitional justice "focuse[s] on how societies address legacies of past human rights abuses, mass atrocity, or other forms of severe social trauma, including genocide or civil war, in order to build a more democratic, just, or peaceful future."[25] It refers to both a field of activity – that is, to a range of political and cultural practices – and to a field of scholarly inquiry. As a field of scholarly inquiry, transitional justice is relatively new.[26] The term first gained currency in the early 1990s, as governments and scholars inquired into the process of de-communization in Eastern Europe, often in direct comparison with the collapse of authoritarian regimes in Latin America over the previous decade. It entered common usage in the 2000s in connection with the work of the South African Truth and Reconciliation Commission. Due to the political orientation of the transitions under way when the field took shape, early studies often embraced normative assumptions about liberal democracy, human rights, and the rule of law as the desirable outcomes of transition.[27]

As the field of transitional justice has developed, scholars have begun to resist this overly narrow approach.[28] More recent analytical works have used the conceptual framework of transitional justice to inquire retrospectively into a broader field of activity promoting post-conflict transitions in many times

[24] Bonavia, *Verdict in Peking*, p. 12.

[25] *The Encyclopedia of Genocide and Crimes against Humanity*, vol. 3 (New York: Macmillan Reference, 2004), p. 1045.

[26] The field of inquiry coalesced quickly. An important milestone was publication of Neil J. Kritz, ed., *Transitional Justice: How Emerging Democracies Reckon with Former Regimes*, 3 vols. (Washington: United States Institute of Peace Press, 1995).

[27] For a normative statement of this type, see Charles D. Smith, "Introduction," to Kritz, *Transitional Justice*, vol. 1, p. xv.

[28] David A. Crocker, "Reckoning with Past Wrongs: A Normative Framework," *Ethics & International Affairs*, Vol. 13 (1999), pp. 43–64. For more recent critical perspectives, see Phil Clark and Nicola Palmer, "Challenging Transitional Justice," in Nicola Palmer, Phil Clark, and Danielle Granville, eds., *Critical Perspectives on Transitional Justice* (Cambridge: Intersentia, 2012), pp. 5–8; Paige Arthur, "How 'Transitions' Reshaped Human Rights: A Conceptual History of Transitional Justice," *Human Rights Quarterly*, Vol. 31 (2009), pp. 321–367.

and places.[29] Jon Elster, a leading scholar in the field, has stated flatly that transitional justice "is *not* limited to modern regimes or to democratic regimes."[30] Expansion of this very recent field of inquiry into a much older and richer field of transitional justice activity has produced the crucial insight that "the particular histories, social norms and cultural practices of affected communities must shape how transitional justice is conceived and will inevitably determine its impact" in real circumstances in specific, diverse, and culturally contingent ways.[31]

The Gang of Four trial was presented, understood, and evaluated in China as transitional justice, even if commentators of the time did not use that precise term. Not only was the trial consistently depicted as a way to address the abuses of the violent past so as to build a more just and peaceful future, but also the trial was even claimed to inherit the legacy of the post–World War II war crimes tribunals at Nuremberg and Tokyo.[32] The language of transition filled the air, albeit inflected with the accents of Chinese socialism. In an editorial published in *People's Daily* just days after the verdict, a judge on the tribunal reflected on the spirit of the moment:

> From a historical perspective, this trial signals the ending of a truly unfortunate period in the history of socialist China. When the Gang of Four was smashed in October 1976, the decade of catastrophe ended, as well, but the trial and sentencing of the accused may be seen as the formal ending to that period. In its wake a new period has appeared, a period marked by stability and unity, by democracy and the rule of law, a period in which the nation works together heart and soul for the realization of socialist modernization. We explore and strive so that China's one billion people might build a better society.[33]

29 See Neil J. Kritz, ed., *Transitional Justice,* vol. 2: *Country Studies* (Washington: United States Institute of Peace Press, 1995). For examples in a broader temporal range, see Jon Elster, *Closing the Books: Transitional Justice in Historical Perspective* (Cambridge: Cambridge University Press, 2004); and Carla Hesse and Robert Post, eds., *Human Rights in Political Transitions: Gettysburg to Bosnia* (New York: Zone Books, 1999).

30 Elster, *Closing the Books*, p. 1, emphasis added.

31 Clark and Palmer, "Challenging Transitional Justice," p. 8.

32 The Republic of China (ROC) and PRC states both prosecuted cases against alleged Japanese war criminals in the decade following World War II. China's Nationalist ROC regime sent delegates to the International Military Tribunal of the Far East at Tokyo, then later conducted its own national trials under the auspices of the Far Eastern and Pacific Sub-Commission of the United Nations War Crimes Commission; see Chang Cai, *Trials of Sovereignty: Chinese Nationalist Trials of Japanese War Criminals, 1946–1949*, Undergraduate honors thesis, University of California, Berkeley, 2010. Likewise, the nascent PRC conducted numerous trials of Japanese war criminals in the 1950s; see Adam Cathcart and Patricia Nash, "War Criminals and the Road to Sino-Japanese Normalization: Zhou Enlai and the Shenyang Trials, 1954–1956," *Twentieth Century China*, Vol. 34 (2009), pp. 89–111. For two examples of explicit comparisons of the Gang of Four trial to the Nuremburg and Tokyo trials, see *Zhongguo qingnianbao*, November 11, 1980; and Fei Xiaotong, "Yi ge shenpanyuan de ganshou" [Impressions of a judge], *RMRB*, January 30, 1981.

33 Xiaotong, "Yi ge shenpanyuan de ganshou."

These sentiments very clearly express the core ideals of transitional justice: transition to a new era, punishment of wrongdoers, reconciliation and social stability, democracy and the rule of law, and hopes for creating the good society.

It must be emphasized that the transitional justice framework can accommodate and by no means excludes the show trial interpretation. Because transitional justice trials aim to make a strong social impact, they necessarily involve politically charged public performance. Therefore, we should avoid the pitfall of reserving transitional justice as a positively connoted label for show trials whose political ideologies we find palatable and whose legal outcomes we find agreeable.[34]

The Gang of Four trial was part of the Chinese party-state's larger efforts to confront the harmful legacies of the Cultural Revolution.[35] These efforts included a more comprehensive campaign to re-assert legal normalcy under a reformed legal system; criminal trials of scores of Gang of Four accomplices; and lustration, meaning the exclusion from office of political radicals from the government, the military, and the communist party. The official reassessment of the past entailed the review of nearly 3 million "false, incorrect, and unjust cases." This review resulted in the (sometimes posthumous) nullification of penalties handed down by the previous regime, as well as the provision of various kinds of reparations to exonerated victims and their families.[36] As for the assessment of perpetrators, Deng Xiaoping cautioned that the party should not get bogged down in retribution: "Our ideal is that every wrong should be righted, [. . . but] we cannot possibly achieve – and should not expect – a perfect settlement of every case. We should have the major aspect of each problem in mind and solve it in broad outline; to go into every detail is neither possible nor necessary."[37] The basic principles, he said, should be leniency for past mistakes

[34] On "trials by fiat of successor regimes" as a variety of political trial, see Otto Kirchheimer, *Political Justice: The Use of Legal Procedure for Political Ends* (Princeton: Princeton University Press, 1961), pp. 304–347. For a sympathetic but critical discussion of the liberal political ideology underpinning transitional justice, see Judith N. Shklar, *Legalism: Law, Morals, and Political Trials* (Cambridge: Harvard University Press, 1986).

[35] For previous scholarship on transitional justice after the Cultural Revolution, see Alexander Cook, "Settling Accounts: Law as History in the Trial of the Gang of Four," in Andrew Lewis and Michael Lobban, eds., *Law and History* (Oxford: Oxford University Press, 2003), pp. 413–432; Susanne Weigelin-Schweidrzik, "Coping with the Cultural Revolution: Competing Interpretations," in Agnes Schick-Chen and Astrid Lipinsky, eds., *Justice Restored?: Between Rehabilitation and Reconciliation in China and Taiwan* (Frankfurt: Peter Lang, 2012); Sue Trevaskes, "People's Justice and Injustice: Courts and The Redressing of Cultural Revolution Cases," *China Information*, Vol. 16 (2002), pp. 1–26. Amnesty International, *China's Ultra-Left on Trial: Unfair Legal Procedure and Political Imprisonment in the Anti-Gang of Four Purge, 1976–1987*, pp. 25–30 and Appendix 2, pp. 58–60.

[36] He Zai, ed., *Yuan jia cuo an shi zheyang pingfande* [This is how unjust, false, and wrong cases were reversed] (Beijing: Zhonggong zhongyang dangxiao chubanshe, 1999), p. 3.

[37] Deng Xiaoping, *Deng Xiaoping Wenxuan (1975–1982)* [Selected works of Deng Xiaoping], vol. 2 (Beijing: Renmin chubanshe, 1983), pp. 140–153.

and severity for recidivism, leniency toward the rank and file and severity toward the ringleaders. The Gang of Four trial was only the most visible aspect of transitional justice in post-Mao China. The Gang of Four trial was a discrete historical event that became the focal point on which the issues of transition were momentarily concentrated. However, the actual (as opposed to merely judicial) resolution of those issues was a complex and protracted process that played out across society over a long period of time.[38] A history of this kind could not be, and was not, confined to the courtroom.

As far as the regime was concerned, the most important contribution of the trial was the lessons it could convey to the public. According to the typology of didactic, destructive, and decisive political trials, the Gang of Four trial was primarily a didactic trial. The Gang of Four trial marked a change in the normative order, but not in the decisive sense of mediating between two possible competing visions. Rather, the trial was a demonstration and endorsement of a decision already taken: the Cultural Revolution was over and the transition to a new political order well under way. Likewise, the trial's purpose was not primarily destructive, since the defendants had already been destroyed politically. The Gang of Four had been removed from power four years prior, and during that interval they were subjected to indefinite incarceration, removal of official titles and party membership, systematic criticism, as well as vicious public calumny and private innuendo. Elimination of the Gang of Four from the political scene was now entirely redundant, and could have been demonstrated with more finality and less expense by simply killing them. This trial consolidated victory in a battle already won. Its significance lay in the public performance of state power and legal procedure.

POWER AND PROCEDURE

Marxist-Leninist regimes regard law as an instrument of state power. According to this view, law is the codification and institutionalization of the self-serving norms that the dominant class uses to justify its repression of the dominated class, and it must be used as such by the proletariat. Mao shared this view, unapologetically describing the law as a tool of the socialist dictatorship: "The state apparatus, including the army, the police, and the courts, is the instrument by which one class oppresses another. It is an instrument for the oppression of antagonistic classes. It is violence and not 'benevolence.' "[39]

[38] Daniel Leese of the Institute of Sinology at the University of Freiburg is presently conducting a major research project funded by the European Research Commission called "The Maoist Legacy: Party Dictatorship, Transitional Justice and the Politics of Truth, 1978–1987."

[39] Mao Zedong, "On the People's Democratic Dictatorship" (1949), available at www.marxists.org/reference/archive/mao/selected-works/volume-4/mswv4_65.htm.

Since laws existed as instruments for practical use, piecemeal codes and ad hoc institutions were made to order as needed – and just as quickly discarded. Moreover, the state did not exercise monopoly over the legitimate use of violence; the party, the military, and the masses all actively participated in the maintenance of social order following a bewildering and often inconsistent array of laws, codes, rules, regulations, directives, and customs. This meant that law was not the only means for justice. The regime also relied on social practices such as mediation, mutual surveillance, organizational discipline, struggle sessions, and reform through labor, as well as techniques for education, indoctrination, and persuasion. This informal, societal approach was especially useful for handling non-antagonistic contradictions among the people.[40]

As part of its post-Mao reassessment of the Cultural Revolution, the Deng Xiaoping regime looked to strengthen and rationalize formal legal institutions. An official party communiqué announced the regime's renewed commitment to socialist legality:

> In order to safeguard people's democracy, it is imperative that we strengthen the socialist legal system so that democracy is systematized and codified, and that these democratic institutions and laws possess stability, continuity, and great authority. We must have laws to follow; the laws that we have must be obeyed; enforcement of the laws must be strict; and violations of the law must be investigated. From now on, legislative work should be high on the agenda of the National People's Congress and its standing committees. Prosecutorial and judicial organs must maintain proper independence; they must be faithful to laws and institutions, to the interests of the people, and to the truth; and they must ensure that the people enjoy equality before their laws, and that no person enjoys special authority above the law.[41]

The agenda outlined here meets the essential criteria for what is sometimes called the "thin" definition of the rule of law: Law is systematized in codes and institutions, made transparent and accessible to the public, administered and adjudicated by trained professionals, and applied equally and universally to all citizens of the state.

China's post-Mao legal reform belonged to a larger process of bureaucratic rationalization. This meant the institution of a well-ordered hierarchy of offices, staffed by skilled technocrats capable of efficiently and impersonally executing specialized tasks. China's post-Mao reformers considered rationalization so important because it called for the replacement of arbitrary, charismatic authority with regular, rule-based authority. The Deng Xiaoping regime

[40] Mao Zedong, "On the Correct Handling of Contradictions among the People," February 27, 1957, available at www.marxists.org/reference/archive/mao/selected-works/volume-5/mswv5_58.htm.

[41] "Zhongguo gongchandang di shiyi jie zhongyang weiyuanhui di san ci quanti huiyi gongbao" [Communiqué of the Third Plenum of the Eleventh Central Committee of the Chinese Communist Party], December 22, 1978, available at http://cpc.people.com.cn/GB/64162/64168/64563/65371/4441902.html.

viewed a functional and efficient legal system as a cornerstone of a rational, prosperous, and modern society. Therefore, restoration of the formal legal system that had been criticized, neglected, and dismantled during the Cultural Revolution period was an integral part of the post-Mao agenda.

Responsibility for legal reform was placed in the hands of Peng Zhen, an early victim of the Cultural Revolution. Undertaken with breathtaking urgency and speed, legal reform provided the institutional and structural prerequisites for the Gang of Four trial. Thoroughgoing legal reform entailed revision of the state and party constitutions; the rebuilding of basic legal institutions such as courts; rehabilitation of dismissed legal personnel and training of new personnel, from lawyers and judges to police and prosecutors; as well as the drafting and promulgation of the first comprehensive criminal code and criminal procedure code in the history of the People's Republic. The new criminal code contained statutes specifically prohibiting crimes characteristic of the Cultural Revolution period, such as mob activity, incitement of violence, unlawful detention, torture, and frame-ups.[42] Likewise, the new criminal procedure code set limits on evidence collection, stressed the reliability of material evidence over personal accusations, and carefully qualified the use of confessions. Together, the new laws narrowed the scope of political activity that could be criminalized, and also rationalized the standards for establishing legal facts.

The criminal code set the normative standard of behavior against which the Gang of Four would be judged. Just as important, the criminal procedure code enabled the regular and systematic exercise of state power in its formulation of legal truth. Formal legal processes shape the ways that trials may interpret the past. As Christopher P. Gilkerson explains, legal codes and procedures tend to structure and determine acts of "legal storytelling": "[T]he law and its institutions establish form and substance requirements for stories that claim rights and express needs. Elements include a specified vocabulary for invoking claims, a paradigm of argumentation, formulae for proof, and narrative conventions for reconstructing individual and collective stories."[43] Moreover, legal truths enjoy an authoritative status that other stories do not; to reiterate: legal truths are built on the discovery and interpretation of facts whose ostensible facticity is backed by the power of the state.

The Deng Xiaoping regime took preparations for the trial very seriously. In March 1980, the Secretariat of the CCP formally recommended a closed trial with results to be publicized at its conclusion.[44] The case would be tried

[42] Harold M. Tanner, *Strike Hard! Anti-Crime Campaigns and Chinese Criminal Justice, 1979–1985* (Ithaca: Cornell University East Asia Program, 1999), pp. 14–19.

[43] Christopher P. Gilkerson, "Poverty Law Narratives: The Critical Practice and Theory of Receiving and Translating Stories," *Hastings Law Journal*, Vol. 43 (1992), pp. 861–945.

[44] Xiao Sike, *Chaoji shenpan: Tu Men jiangjun canyu shenli Lin Biao fangeming jituan qin liji* [Super trial: a personal account of the trial of the Lin Biao counter-revolutionary group], vol. 1, 2 vols. (Jinan: Jinan chubanshe, 1992), pp. 197–199; Tumen and Xiao Sike, *Tebie shenpan: Lin Biao, Jiang Qing fangeming jituan shoushen shilu* [Special trial: True account of the trial of the

according to the new legal codes.[45] The Secretariat's proposal emphasized that the trial must not be a Stalinist farce:

> The case – indictment and evidence and such – must be irrefutable and stand firmly on its own feet, so it can be passed on to posterity and never be toppled. If done in this way, the trial will have a positive effect on strengthening government unity and implementing the Four Modernizations with one heart and one mind. It will also have a good influence on our international standing.[46]

In April 1980, as a matter of procedural regularity, the case files were transferred from the party's Central Commission for Discipline Inspection to the state's Ministry of Public Security and the Supreme People's Procuratorate for pre-trial investigation.[47] Thus far, investigators had collected evidence from more than 1 million documents and 178,000 persons, and had whittled down a list of 500 suspects to just eleven names.[48] The Ministry of Public Security concluded its own investigation in September 1980 and formally recommended prosecution of the ten living main conspirators, including the Gang of Four.[49] On September 29, 1980, the National People's Congress established a Special Procuratorate to prosecute the case and a Special Court to try the defendants publicly.[50] Thus the trial would be staged for maximum didactic effect. We turn now to the stage and its performers.

THE PERFORMANCE OF LEGAL TRUTH

The Special Court was meant to be broadly representative of society so that the case could be judged symbolically by the whole of the people. As a result, the

Lin Biao and Jiang Qing counterrevolutionary groups] (Beijing: Zhongyang wenxian chubanshe, 2003), pp. 135–136.

45 Wu Jianfan and Ouyang Tao, "Lun shenpan Lin Biao, Jiang Qing fangeming jituan de jige falü wenti," [Discussion of a few legal questions in the trial of Lin Biao and Jiang Qing counter revolution groups], *Faxue yanjiu* [Research in jurisprudence] June 1980, pp. 4–5.

46 Quoted in Tumen and Sike, *Tebie shenpan*, p. 135.

47 Li Haiwen and Wang Yanling, eds., *Shiji duihua: yi Xin Zhongguo fazhi zunjiren Peng Zhen* [A century of conversations: remembering Peng Zhen, the key figure in New China's legal system] (Beijing: Qunzhong chubanshe, 2002), p. 90.

48 Wang Wenfeng, *Dou Mo: Mian dui mian shencha Jiang Qing fangeming jituan qin liji* [Battling demons: personal memoirs of investigating the Jiang Qing counter-revolutionary group face-to-face] (Beijing: Zhongguo shehui kexue chubanshe, 2000), pp. 96–97 and 88.

49 *Law Annual Report of China 1982/3* (Hong Kong: Kingsway International, 1982), p. 179; *TBFTJS*, p. 70.

50 "Di wu jie quanguo renmin daibiao hui changwu weiyuanhui guanyu chengli zuigao renmin jianchayuan tebie jianchating he zuigao renmin fayuan tebie fating jiancha, shenpan Lin Biao, Jiang Qing fangeming jituan an zhufan de jueding," September 29, 1980 [Resolution of the Standing Committee of the Fifth National People's Congress Regarding Establishment of the Special Procuratorate of the Supreme People's Procuratorate and the Special Court of the Supreme People's Court to Investigate and Try the Main Culprits of the Lin Biao and Jiang Qing Counterrevolutionary Groups] *TBFTJS*, p. 1.

Special Court's panel of judges was unusually large. Under the socialist legal system, a typical case would be tried by one to three judges and audited by two to four common people called assessors, but the Special Court had a president, three vice-presidents, and a blue-ribbon panel of thirty-one lay judges selected from diverse backgrounds.[51] The Special Court divided into two tribunals: the First Tribunal to try the five civilian defendants, and the Second Tribunal to try the five military defendants. Presiding over the full court was Jiang Hua, who was concurrently Chief Justice of the Supreme People's Court. He was assisted by three vice-presidents: Huang Yukun, concurrently Major General and Deputy Director of the Political Department of the PLA; Zeng Hanzhou, concurrently Associate Justice of the Supreme People's Court, who would serve as chief judge of the First Tribunal; and Wu Xiuquan, concurrently Deputy Chief of Staff of the PLA, who would serve as chief judge of the Second Tribunal. Two to five of the lay judges were assigned to focus on each defendant, with the two female judges among the five assigned to the only female defendant, Jiang Qing.[52] Unlike the assessors found in the regular people's courts, the lay judges of the Special Court could actively participate in and even lead court inquiry.[53]

The panel of judges included representatives from all eight minority political parties, as well as diplomats, jurists, and experts on party and military discipline. Scientists, industrialists, agriculture experts, and military personnel personified the regime's commitment to the Four Modernizations. Though it is obvious the panel was chosen to be representative, the NPC offered no explanation of how it selected the individual judges. Some of the judges were fairly prominent in their fields, and others seem to have been more or less common people. One of the more prominent judges, who emerged to become a sort of informal public spokesman for the court, was Fei Xiaotong, a leading sociologist and legal theorist. Like several other judges on the Special Court, he

[51] "Quanguo renda changweihui guanyu chengli tebie fating gei zuigao renmin fayuan de tong zhi" [Notification by the Standing Committee of the National People's Congress Given to the Supreme People's Court Regarding Establishment of the Special Court] [Standing Committee of the National People's Congress Document No. 27] September 29, 1980 *TBFTJS*, p. 433.

[52] "Zuigao renmin fayuan tebie fating guanyu shenpan renyuan fengong de yijian" [Suggestions of the Special Court of the Supreme People's Court Regarding Division of Work among Judges (Passed by the First Meeting of the Special Court of the Supreme People's Court, dated November 6, 1980)] *TBFTJS*, pp. 455–456. Gan Ying and Liu Liying were both members of the Central Commission for Discipline Inspection. Liu Liying went on to become a famous jurist. See Haiwen and Yanling, *Shiji duihua*, p. 94; Liu Guohang, "Yu Jiang Qing da san nian jiaodao 'nü baogong' Liu Liying chenzhuo yingdui feibang" [Three years of dealings with Jiang Qing, female "Judge Bao" Liu Liying handled slander with calm], December 11, 2002, available at http://news.tom.com/Archive/1002/2002/12/11-38889.html.

[53] The Special Court held its first organizational meeting on November 6, where it established the special rules and procedures by which the indictment would be examined and adjudicated. "Zhonghua renmin gongheguo zuigao renmin fayuan tebie fating shenpan Lin Biao, Jiang Qing fangeming jituan an zhufan jishi," pp. 70–73.

had been branded a "Rightist" in the late 1950s and then persecuted during the Cultural Revolution. Similarly, the president of the Special Court was a victim named in the indictment, and his wife had died from mistreatment at the hands of her political persecutors. One of the vice presidents of the court had spent seven years as a political prisoner. These judges were not recused, on the logic that nearly everyone had suffered during the Cultural Revolution; on the contrary, the inclusion of these judges seemed that much more just, since through them other victims could vicariously fulfill their desire to condemn their tormentors. This inclusiveness was important symbolically: the Special Court would be a court of the people.

Even the address of the Special Court was symbolic: No. 1 Justice Road. The building that housed the courtroom was actually the Ministry of Public Security's Ceremonial Hall, located on the grounds of the police headquarters in a restricted-access area just east of Tiananmen Square. This large hall had more suitable facilities than the nearby Supreme People's Court building; however, Peng Zhen was concerned that using a police building might compromise the appearance of judicial autonomy. He suggested therefore that the location simply be described as "Justice Road," since a service entrance to the building did in fact open onto that street. Ren Lingyun, Deputy Chief of the Ministry of Public Security, also a lay judge on the Special Court, erroneously reported the address to the media as No. 1 Justice Road (the service entrance was actually at No. 7).[54] Once reported, the name stuck in the public imagination: "What profound significance!" observed *People's Daily* reporter Hu Sisheng, "We have taken many twists and turns; now at last we walk the road of upholding justice!"[55]

The courtroom's interior was a symbolic space for China's transition to legal modernity. The courtroom was designed by special legal advisor to the court Qiu Shaoheng (Henry Chiu), who held degrees in both law and literature and served as a delegate to the Far Eastern War Crimes Tribunal in Tokyo in April 1946.[56] Reporter Wu Kailiu described the impressive effect of the room. He wrote,

> The first thing to catch your eye was, in the very center of the bar, a brightly colored national emblem hanging high upon the curtain. Below the national emblem was the bench, formed of a stepped platform arrayed with two sets of crimson upholstered seats ... Red carpeting adorned the aisles of the bench, and the entire bar looked particularly solemn and imposing in the brilliant lights.[57]

[54] Ren Lingyun as quoted in Haiwen and Yanling, "Shiji duihua," p. 94.

[55] Hu Sisheng, "Kaiting zhi ri" [Opening day of court], *RMRB*, November 21, 1980.

[56] Qiu Shaoheng was brought on as an advisor in mid-September 1980. See Ma Lingguo, "Tebie Fating de falü guwen Qiu Shaoheng" [Special Court legal consultant Henry Chiu], *Shiji* [Century] (September 1999), pp. 18–21.

[57] Wu Kailiu, "Renmin de shenpan, lishi de shenpan" [The people's trial, history's trial], *Guangming ribao* [Guangming Daily], November 21, 1980.

A deep red velvet curtain, interwoven with golden thread, set the backdrop to the bar.[58] This sea of red and velvet conveyed the majesty of the Special Court in the symbolic color of Communism. The national emblem heralded the power of the state.

Like the stylized performance of Chinese opera, each role on the stage had a conventional costume and place. Members of the Special Court and the Special Procuratorate addressed the audience and defendants from the authority of a raised dais. An aisle divided the platform, with Chief Justice Jiang Hua flanked by the three associate justices and Chief Procurator Huang Huoqing by his two deputy chiefs. The remaining judges and procurators were arrayed in rows behind them. A metal-railed dock for the defendants sat recessed in the orchestra pit, divided into ten stalls and furnished with wooden chairs and green carpeting. Thus defendants occupied the lowest position in the Special Court, with their backs turned to the people assembled in the gallery. Wooden placards with black lettering designated their seating areas within the courtroom. In this staging, the inclusion of the procurators on the platform with the judges signaled their close relationship as unified representatives of the people and the state. By contrast, locating the defense on a lower level and off to the side set them apart. The clothing worn by the court personnel and the accused established similar distinctions. The judges wore black uniforms, the clerks and procurators dark gray, and the defense light gray. The defendants wore clothes of their own choosing. In the weeks leading up to the trial, the Special Court had held several dress rehearsals, sometimes with mock defendants. Through these practice sessions, the judges learned to anticipate and handle many situations that might arise during this unprecedented trial.[59] Now the real trial was set to begin.

On November 20, 1980, the courtroom was ready to open with real defendants in the dock. In mid-afternoon, ticketed audience members and reporters filed into the courtroom gallery, which could accommodate more than 880 spectators at a sitting. The spectators were carefully selected and included representatives from every province, provincial-level municipality, autonomous region, political party, people's organization, CCP Central Committee organ, national-level state organ, and the People's Liberation

[58] Lingguo, "Tebie Fating de falü guwen Qiu Shaoheng," p. 19. The curtain is described as silver-gray in Sun Haogang and Qian Gang, "Kaiting di yi tian" [First day of trial], *Jiefang junbao* [Liberation Army News], November 21, 1980; perhaps this report is based on a black and white photograph? Most Chinese would have viewed the trial on black and white television sets and in black and white print news. However, the events were filmed and photographed in color, and print reports did take care to describe colors when significant. Seating layout based on photographs and video and descriptions in Sisheng, "Kaiting zhi ri"; and "Lishi de shenpan, renmin de shengli" [History's trial, the people's victory], *Beijing ribao* [Beijing Daily], November 21, 1980.

[59] Lu Hong, *Zhonggong zhengzhi wutai shang de "Fu Jiang": Wu Xiuquan chuanqi* ["Lucky General" on the government stage: the legend of Wu Xiuquan] (Beijing: Zhongguo qingnian chubanshe, 2000), pp. 215–216.

Army. Also present were the widows of prominent Cultural Revolution victims such as Premier Liu Shaoqi and Vice Premiers He Long and Luo Ruiqing.[60] Shortly before 3:00 p.m., a series of electronic bells toned, alerting the audience to take their seats in silence and signaling court personnel to take their positions. Court police in smart blue uniforms took their positions at either side of the dock. The clerks of the court entered, followed by the prosecution and the acting counsel for the defense. When all had been seated, Clerk Guo Zhiwen read aloud the regulations of the Special Court. Finally, the justices and judges were announced by name as they entered. The clerk notified the chief justice that the Special Procuratorate was on hand to initiate public prosecution against the ten defendants held in custody.[61] The trial was about to begin.

At 3:00 p.m. sharp the bell toned again and the room was flooded with lights. Reporters Sun Haogang and Qing Gang described the moment for readers of the *Liberation Army News* as if it were a theatrical production:

> Suddenly the mercury-vapor stage lamps were illuminated and the atmosphere turned solemn. The movie and television cameras hissed and hummed in unison. With this dazzling flash of light, the ten defendants of the Lin Biao and Jiang Qing counterrevolutionary groups were led in custody onto the scene of this historic trial, and one by one they came into focus.[62]

In the glow of the lights, Chief Justice Jiang Hua called the Special Court into session. The Chief Justice summoned defendant Wang Hongwen, handing a billet to the Clerk of Court. This was passed to an officer of the court police, who went to the holding room to fetch this disgraced former Vice Chairman of the CCP. At 3:03 p.m. the court police returned and led the first defendant down the middle aisle of the gallery. It had been more than four years since the Gang of Four had appeared in public, and even longer for Chen Boda and the Lin Biao group. Everyone was curious to see them. In a hush, the spectators craned to look.[63]

One at a time, ten former Party leaders and military officials were called by the Chief Justice and paraded into the courtroom in manacles. First Wang Hongwen and Yao Wenyuan were summoned, followed by each of the five Lin Biao defendants and Mao's personal secretary Chen Boda. Finally the Chief Justice called the two most important defendants, Zhang Chunqiao and Jiang Qing. One of the few ways the defendants had to present themselves was through their personal bearing and dress. However, the state had the advantage of interpreting the scene to the public. The official papers glommed

[60] Kailiu, "Renmin de shenpan, lishi de shenpan."

[61] "Zhonghua renmin gongheguo zuigao renmin fayuan tebie fating shenpan Lin Biao, Jiang Qing fangeming jituan an zhufan jishi," pp. 79–80.

[62] Haogang and Gang, "Kaiting di yi tian."

[63] Composite description based on reports from Sisheng, "Kaiting zhi ri"; Haogang and Gang, "Kaiting di yi tian"; and Kailiu, "Renmin de shenpan, lishi de shenpan."

onto every detail of each the defendant's appearance, never shying away from using figurative descriptions to editorialize on their characters.

The youngest defendant, Wang Hongwen, entered first. As a factory worker, Wang had led his peers to overthrow bureaucratic managers and eventually the whole Shanghai Party apparatus. He had come to represent the young upstart faction of the CCP. On this day he was visibly thinner, looking humbled and forlorn. The once energetic Wang sat motionless in his chair for the reading of the indictment.[64] Reporters Sun Haogang and Qing Gang captured the contrast between "Wang Hongwen, rebel" and "Wang Hongwen, defendant" in their description. They wrote, "Wang Hongwen wore a grey pantsuit with crew-cut hair and a jaundiced complexion, his two listless eyes blinking mechanically. The confident swagger of the Shanghai Bund's erstwhile 'Rebel Commander' had dissipated, leaving only the residue of his native mediocrity."[65] By exposing Wang Hongwen's illusory swagger, the description implied he was part of a dysfunctional political system that had failed to nurture real talent and instead promoted criminals.

Propagandist Yao Wenyuan entered next. Presentation did not work in his favor. If the vicissitudes of time revealed a telling change in Wang Hongwen's outward appearance, Yao looked much the same as always: toady and squat, with large watery eyes. The papers took pains to note that Yao had lived well off the fruits of his writings, which had caused suffering and starvation for so many others. Only since receiving the indictment had his hearty appetite for sleep and food finally waned.[66] Again, *Liberation Army News* provided a particularly colorful description, noting, "Yao Wenyuan was bald as ever, and fat made his fish-eyes seem to bulge out even more. He could be seen to put on a sanctimonious and dignified appearance, even remembering to clip a fountain pen into his shirt pocket when in court. But his eyes revealed trepidation and dejection."[67] Perhaps the pen was intended to remind us that whatever his crimes, the wordsmith had never wielded an actual sword. But the newspapers played up his haughty carriage, stout frame, and ridiculous visage.

The military defendants, all now elderly, wore close-cropped hair and one of them, Huang Yongsheng, wore a green military-style uniform stripped of insignia. Mao's former political secretary Chen Boda looked weak and ashen, needing assistance to walk to the dock. Grizzled old theoretician Zhang Chunqiao shuffled into the courtroom wearing a grimy shirt hanging loose at the collar. Throughout the session he sat silent and despondent, his unshaven jaw and sagging eyelids betraying impatience, boredom, or annoyance in turn. *People's Daily* described his bizarre behavior:

> Zhang Chunqiao, who plotted all sorts of tricks during the ten years of chaos, today continually bobbed his head about – if not to this side, then to that – never once keeping

[64] Sisheng, "Kaiting zhi ri." [65] Haogang and Gang, "Kaiting di yi tian."
[66] Sisheng, "Kaiting zhi ri." [67] Haogang and Gang, "Kaiting di yi tian."

still. His lips curled downward, eyes darting left and right, [he looked] the very image of the masses' epithet: "the traitorous official" ... Several times he supported his body with the back of the chair, dumbstruck as a wooden chicken, ... and though he wore only a thin Chinese-style placard shirt with the collar hanging open, sweat gathered continuously on his face.[68]

His attitude would be interpreted later as an act of defiance, but at this stage in the trial the media saw Zhang Chunqiao as defeated and disengaged.

Finally, at 3:15 p.m., the star of the show made her much anticipated entry. Chairman Mao's widow and alleged Gang of Four ringleader Jiang Qing wore a conservative, ankle-length, and long-sleeved dress, rather than her jaunty trademark cap and scarf. She declined to appear in the elaborate Tang Dynasty finery of the "female emperor" Empress Wu Zetian, whose style she was said to have admired, nor in her own special "Jiang Qing shirt," which she had supposedly commissioned in imitation of the Sun Yat-sen jacket or Mao suit.[69] Nevertheless, the newspapers persisted in describing her as a conniving female usurper, writing, "Two female court police brought into the courtroom the fanatic Jiang Qing, in her own mind a 'female emperor.' Today she wore a black outer-garment and black cotton-upper flats. Her hair as always was combed to glossy sheen, and on the bridge of her nose sat a colorful pair of wide-rimmed tortoise-shell glasses."[70] The *People's Daily* emphasized Jiang Qing's careful accoutrement, including expensive eyewear and carefully coifed hair. This description was typical in its insistent reminder that Jiang Qing was above all else an *actress* – spry and wily, and in her younger days even charming enough to beguile the Chairman. But today in court, her affected manner held no charms. The report continues, "With her every movement she maintained her customary arrogant posture. Still employing performance techniques from her time as a movie actress, she deliberately cocked her head and advanced with slow paces under everyone's eyes, in a manner that made you sick."[71] Reporter Shi Hongdao of the *Beijing Daily* echoed this crude reaction to Jiang Qing's insincerity, "Seeing her performance really made you want to vomit."[72]

By 3:17 p.m. all ten defendants were standing in the dock, separated from the gallery by a cordon of court police. Jiang Qing put in a hearing aid and listened intently. Chief Justice Jiang Hua, with his close attention to procedure, instructed the defendants to be seated and informed them that the trial would begin. After calling the roll of court personnel, the chief justice invited the chief

[68] Sisheng, "Kaiting zhi ri."

[69] Jiang Qing's sartorial tastes were much criticized in the years leading up to trial. Her alleged sketch of a model "Jiang Qing shirt" (in the spirit of Sun Yat-sen's Zhongshan jacket or its progeny, the Mao jacket) was seen as presumptuous in the extreme. Furthermore, her alleged adoration of capable Chinese empresses was taken to reveal her autocratic imperial ambitions. See *Liang Xiao zuizheng cailiao* [Material on the crimes of the Liang Xiao group] (Beijing: Liang Xiao Special Case Group, unpublished, 1978), pp. 116–118.

[70] Sisheng, "Kaiting zhi ri." [71] Sisheng, "Kaiting zhi ri."

[72] "Lishi de shenpan, renmin de shengli."

procurator to read the indictment aloud. It took three hours to read the document in its entirety, and at 5:20 p.m. court was adjourned. This public reading of the indictment added nothing from a textual standpoint, but the performance and especially the media coverage of it created an audience and a model response. The next morning's newspapers ran several reaction pieces featuring prominent victims' family members, including an interview with the widow of Marshal Peng Dehuai – the modern paragon of the virtuous official, who had earned Mao's wrath by speaking out against the Great Leap Forward, and who was the subject of the historical allegory that set off the Cultural Revolution. "This is a trial by the people, history's trial," reported Marshal Peng's widow, "I'm thrilled to see [the defendants] with my own eyes being led in shackles to the dock, and now I can console Old Peng's spirit in heaven."[73]

The performance also engaged the desire for justice of those assembled outside the courtroom, according to *People's Daily* reader Li Demin. He watched the opening session of the trial from the packed television lounge at his office and described the reactions of his fellow viewers in a "Daily Chat" column called "In Front of the Television Set, Viewing the People's Hearts." " 'See! The wicked Jiang Qing is a shameless actress.' 'Zhang Chunqiao looks like he's been exhumed from a tomb.' 'Look at that Wang Hongwen – where is the authoritative air of the Rebel Commander?' "[74] These published responses modeled judgments for other members. "In front of that glowing screen, we felt like we ourselves were sitting on the judges' bench."[75] As *Liberation Daily* reported, in that moment the people began to form their own verdict. "History has firmly nailed [the defendants] into the pillory; no matter how they dissemble and connive, they will never be set free."[76]

The reading of the indictment provided the script for the opening act of the dramatic trial. Media coverage of the indictment seems to have prejudged the case and short-circuited the ability of the public to give a fair hearing. It is also clear that even for the court, the guilt of the defendants was largely a foregone conclusion.

The state used mass media to project the symbolic courtroom drama to reach the largest possible audience, which extended far beyond the Special Court's gallery. Those who could not pack into the courtroom followed the trial through every form of mass media at the state's disposal, including posters, print, radio, and broadcast television. Among these forms, television deserves

73 "Lishi de shenpan, renmin de shengli."

74 "Dianshiji qian kan minxin" (In front of the television set, watching the people's heart), *RMRB*, November 23, 1980.

75 "Dianshiji qian kan minxin."

76 Haogang and Gang, "Kaiting di yi tian." Similar rhetoric is repeated in Social Commentary editorials for November 21, 1980, such as: "Renmin de shenpan, lishi de shenpan" [The people's trial, history's trial], *Gongmin ribao* [Workers' Daily]; "Zhengyi de shenpan, renmin de xinyuan" [Justice's trial, the people's aspiration], *Jiefang junbao* [Liberation Army News]; and "Jiuyi renmin de shenpan" [900,000 people's trial], *Renmin ribao* [People's Daily].

special attention. The Gang of Four trial, in addition to being an unprecedented legal event, was also a pioneering media event: coverage of the proceedings might rightly be considered the first Chinese-produced television serial.[77] Every night throughout the trial, Central China Television's (CCTV) *Network News* program featured six minutes of highlights from that day's testimony and an hour-long *Special Report* covering of the previous day's events.[78] The official Xinhua News Agency even arranged satellite television programming for foreigners and overseas Chinese. As a tool for propaganda (or for advertising), television is a major advance over print and sound media. Television provides unparalleled audiovisual verisimilitude: the combination of sound and image makes for a more vivid and immediate experience. The small screen's simulacrum of "real-life" social interactions is said to exert a strong normative influence on viewers. In this case, viewers received constant cues from the interactions of the judges, the prosecution, the defense, the live courtroom audience, and a chorus of news commentators. In China at the time, this normative influence would have been amplified by group viewing habits. Watching the trial unfold on television each night was an important social occasion. In 1980 the family television set remained a novelty outside the most prosperous urban areas; more often the members of a work unit would watch together on a common set.[79] Thus we have no figures to reliably gauge audience size over the course of the proceedings, but the anecdotal evidence is clear: ask any Chinese of age at the time and they are likely to remember viewing at least some portion of the trial.[80]

Though we have no space here to detail the long courtroom drama that unfolded, it is useful to consider the defendants' various strategies for defense. Only a few of the defendants availed their right to legal counsel, either because legal defense seemed pointless or in order to appear more compliant. (Chinese culture traditionally takes a dim view of lawyering.) Defense options were

[77] China's first domestically produced drama series, *Eighteen Years of Disguisement in the Enemy Camp*, debuted in May 1981, several months after the trial's conclusion. See also Mary Farquhar and Chris Berry, "Speaking Bitterness: History, Media, and Nation in Twentieth Century China," *Historiography East and West*, Vol. 2 (2004), pp. 116–143, 129.

[78] As announced in a Xinhua wire report, November 19, 1980.

[79] In 1981, 57 percent of urban households had television sets, compared to less than 1 percent in rural areas. CCTV estimated a total television audience of 210 million in 1980 and 270 million in 1981, up from just 18 million in 1975. Figures cited in Jingyu Lu, "The Structure and Function of Chinese Television, 1979–1989," in Chin-chuan Lee, ed., *Voices of China: The Interplay of Politics and Journalism* (New York: Guilford Press, 1990), pp. 73–74.

[80] Television coverage of the trial exemplified the careful and extensive application of a mass medium just reaching huge new audiences. The trial aired at a unique moment, in the midst of Chinese television's initial growth spurt but before the commercialization and decentralization that soon ended the national government's monopoly over programming. See Hong Junhao, *The Internationalization of Television in China: The Evolution of Ideology, Society, and Media since the Reform* (Westport: Praeger, 1998), pp. 145–147; and Zhao Bin, "Greater China," in Anthony Smith and Richard Paterson, eds., *Television: An International History*, Second edition (Oxford: Oxford University Press, 1998), pp. 247–248.

severely limited, as well: defendants first saw the indictment just weeks before trial, there was no period of discovery, most evidence was introduced in written depositions, and those witnesses who did appear in person could not be properly cross-examined. Defendants had to rely on their responses to court inquisition and their closing statements. Within this narrow range of options, the defendants took different approaches. Wang Hongwen and the five Lin Biao group defendants submitted completely to the normative order of the law, freely confessing to their crimes, implicating others, and begging for leniency. Yao Wenyuan and Chen Boda mounted arguments against specific charges, attempting to use the legal codes to mount a legitimate defense. Zhang Chunqiao remained silent throughout the entire trial, refusing to answer questions or make statements. This was a total negation of the legal order. Jiang Qing's performance was most dramatic, invoking the abandoned normative order of the Cultural Revolution. She accused the judges of complicity in past violence, berated witnesses as bourgeois reactionaries, and repeated radical slogans that denounced the legal order of the state: "To rebel is justified!"

MAO AND THE VERDICT OF HISTORY

In late June 1981, six months after the Special Court verdict, the Chinese Communist Party (CCP) released its much anticipated "Resolution on Certain Questions in the History of the Party since the Founding of the People's Republic of China." The state's legal verdict and the party's party resolution were devised together as complementary parts of a coherent interpretation of the past. The public trial of Cultural Revolution leaders would become a showcase for the new socialist legal system, enabling the state to deliver legal retribution, create closure, and establish a factual record of past crimes. Likewise, the official reevaluation of history would provide an opportunity for the party to acknowledge its mistakes, control damage to its reputation, and put forward a vision for moving forward. In the wake of mass violence over which they themselves had presided, the state and party crafted these two narratives to re-establish their legitimacy to govern.

These two official interpretations of the Cultural Revolution were separate but related attempt to settle accounts, in the sense of establishing a definitive account of the violent and contested past. The two official accounts were complementary, issuing a binding and authoritative interpretation of the past in separate but related registers: the law, and the laws of history. The verdict provides an account of the Cultural Revolution in terms of crimes at the level of law. Meanwhile, the resolution analyzes the Cultural Revolution at the level of objective historical laws as a series of "errors" in revolutionary thought and practice. Taken together, the verdict and the resolution attempted to characterize the Cultural Revolution in such a way as to demonstrate that Chinese socialist law and historiography are capable of interpreting and drawing lessons from the violent past and are just as worthy of leading the way to the future.

To succeed, the party's resolution on history would have to achieve a number of difficult goals. First, it would have to protect the historical legacy of the CCP without shirking responsibility for its failures. The good of the party's historical accomplishments would have to outweigh the bad of the "decade of disaster." Second, the party would have to analyze and explain the failures of the Cultural Revolution in socialist terms, in a theoretically coherent and defensible way. In other words, the interpretation would have to demonstrate that socialist ideology could provide solutions to its own problems. Third, the historical model would have to isolate and contain the failures of the Cultural Revolution era, putting brackets around the period as an aberration or rupture that has now ended. At the same time, it would have to provide continuity around that rupture, connecting the past glories of the CCP to the present. Finally, it would have to explain why Chinese socialism was the best option for moving forward into the future.

The basis for this double judgment was a distinction between crimes and errors. On December 22, 1980, as the Special Court concluded its inquiry in preparation for deliberations, the authoritative Special Commentator byline headed a major theoretical article in *People's Daily*, called "Milestone in Socialist Democracy and Legality."[81] The commentary reminded readers that the Special Court would only address the crimes of the Cultural Revolution and not non-criminal errors. The article explained that mistakes in revolutionary theory or strategy, even very grave errors with disastrous consequences, must be considered as fundamentally different in nature from crimes. In essence, a crime is "an action harmful to society that is subject to punishment under the law," while an error is "a discrepancy between the subjective and the objective, an action that does not conform to objective laws."[82] These parallel definitions refer to parallel normative standards: the statutory laws (*falü*) that govern a particular society, and the objective laws (*guilü*) that govern social and historical development in general.[83] Violations of the former are crimes, while violations of the latter are errors. The nature of this distinction would figure in several important projects: in the exculpation of Chairman Mao from legal responsibility, in the official condemnation of the Cultural Revolution as an erroneous disaster, and in the authorization of law as a valid tool for analysis under socialism.

[81] Special commentator, "Shehuizhuyi minzhu he fazhi de lichengpai: ping shenpan Lin Biao, Jiang Qing fangeming jituan" [Milestone in socialist democracy and legality: on the trial of the Lin Biao and Jiang Qing counterrevolutionary groups], *RMRB*, December 22, 1980.

[82] Special commentator, "Shehuizhuyi minzhu he fazhi."

[83] According to advisers to the Special Court Wu Jianfan and Ouyang Tao, errors are "mistakes in ideology"; see Jianfan and Tao, "Lun shenpan Lin Biao, Jiang Qing fangeming jituan de jige falü wenti," p. 2.

It is the system of Mao Zedong Thought that defines errors as violations of *guilü*, or the objective "laws of history." In reviving the Maoist maxim, "seek truth from facts" (*shishi qiushi*), the post-CR reformers reaffirmed Mao Zedong Thought as a correct and scientific system, to be distinguished from its flawed and all-too-human progenitor. Basically, "seek truth from facts" describes the inductive process of social science, by which one studies specific examples in order to divine general principles. In Mao's own explanation of "seek truth from facts," he defines truths as expressions of *guilü*: " 'truth' means the internal relations of objective things, namely their regularities (*guilüxing*) [i.e., their *guilü*-ness, or the extent to which their internal relations constitute *guilü*]."[84] By this definition, truths are those constant or regular principles ("laws") that govern how society works: in Marxism, the law of class struggle; in liberal economics, the law of supply and demand; in Maoism, the law of the unity of opposites; and so on. Maoism is concerned in particular with discovering certain kind of laws, namely, the laws of historical development. Mao's central project was the "Sinification of Marxism" – the application of abstract Marxist theories to concrete Chinese realities. Mao recognized that the complexity and contingency of history make it impossible to replicate and "mechanically apply" the laws induced from European history to other places and times.[85] Since the objective laws of history (*guilü*) are universal only to the degree that they are abstract and devoid of specific content, therefore the truth of abstract theories constantly must be tested in practical application. This is the meaning of the second important epistemological slogan of the post-Mao period: "practice is the sole criterion for testing truth." Because it relies on practice to test inductive reasoning, Mao Zedong Thought is neither predictive nor infallible. Inevitably, errors will arise from imperfect knowledge or the misapprehension of true facts and conditions, leading to the subjective misinterpretation of objective laws. If crime and punishment was the central concern of the verdict, the Maoist understanding of error assumed paramount importance for the drafters of the resolution.

The verdict and resolution sought to mark with perfect clarity the relationship and distinction between crimes (violations of statutory laws) and errors (violations of objective laws). The Chinese character *lü*, common to the terms "statutory laws" (*falü*) and "objective laws" (*guilü*), links the two concepts. At the most basic etymological level, *lü* denotes a restraint; in classical usage, *lü* refers to the formal codification of abstract normative principles: most commonly legal codes, but also codified systems of pitch and tone in music, and rules of tone and rhyme in regulated verse. Correlating statutory law with the objective laws of history implicitly places both within a broader spectrum of normative orders or restraints: the self-discipline or

[84] Quoted in and translated by Nick Knight, "The Form of Mao's 'Sinification of Marxism,'" *Australian Journal of Chinese Affairs*, Vol. 9 (1983), p. 19.

[85] Mao Zedong's phrase, quoted in Knight, "The Form of Mao's 'Sinification of Marxism,'" p. 20.

autonomy of the individual (*zilü*), the group discipline of the Party or other social unit (*jilü*), the legal discipline of society as a whole (*falü*), the objective laws of history (*guilü*), and finally the immutable laws of nature (*dinglü*). This correlative model, which has ample precedents in the long history of Chinese thought, lends socialist legal thought a moral authority similar to that of natural law.[86] Mao Zedong Thought provides that revelation of the higher order is accessible to human beings through practical experience and applied reason. The conceptual and etymological connection between law and restraint is not unique to the Chinese tradition. For example, St. Thomas Aquinas notes in the introduction to his "Treatise on Law" (1269–1270): "Law is a rule or measure for action by which one is led to action or restrained from acting. The word law (*lex*) is derived from *ligare*, to bind, because it binds one to act."[87] It is the binding necessity of law that is normative or repressive.

Just as the creation of a legal indictment against the Gang of Four elevated the violence of the CR from an issue of Party discipline (*jilü*) to a matter of law (*falü*), so too did the party's resolution elevate the discussion of transgressions yet another level, from law (*falü*) to the laws of history (*guilü*). The conflation of human laws and scientific laws is a powerful ideological concept, which Northrup Frye has rightly called "a violent and foolish pun."[88]

The Gang of Four trial and the historical resolution were planned simultaneously. Deng Xiaoping and his reformist protégé Hu Yaobang were put in charge of the project, while party veteran Hu Qiaomu and leading theoretician Deng Liqun were tasked with drafting the document. At the outset, Hu Qiaomu identified two major difficulties: on the one hand, to not only identify the errors of the Cultural Revolution but to explain why they occurred, and on the other hand, to define the [correct] essence of the party's guiding ideology and its relationship to Mao Zedong Thought. In March 1980, in the same meeting at which the Secretariat approved plans to conduct the Gang of Four trial, party leaders also discussed the resolution. Deng Xiaoping suggested to Hu Qiaomu three basic principles to uphold in drafting the document: First, the resolution must acknowledge the historical importance of Mao Zedong Thought and reaffirm its value as an ideology to be adhered to

86 According to Benjamin Schwartz, correlative cosmology was well established in Chinese thought by the third century BCE and reached its height in the Huang-Lao syncretism of the Han dynasty, "leaving its lasting mark on the entire subsequent development of the 'philosophy of nature' in China." Schwartz notes that while correlative thinking is "considered by some to be a primordial and quintessential expression of the Chinese mind," he agrees with A.C. Graham that correlative cosmology as an expression of general proto-scientific thinking along the lines of Levi-Strauss' primitive "science of the concrete." See Benjamin I. Schwartz, *The World of Thought in Ancient China* (Cambridge: Belknap Press of Harvard University Press, 1985), pp. 350–352.

87 Compare St. Thomas Aquinas, *Summa Theologica*, electronic edition (e-artnow, 2013), Vols. I-II, Qu. 90, 1, Qu. 91, 3 and Qu. 93, 3.

88 Northrop Frye, *Myth and Metaphor: Selected Essays, 1974–1988*, edited by Robert D. Denham (Charlottesville: University Press of Virginia, 1990), p. 265.

and developed. Second, the document must "seek truth from facts" to analyze the events of past thirty years, including a fair evaluation of correct and erroneous policies as well as the merits and demerits of responsible cadres. Third, the resolution must provide a basic but comprehensive summary of events, painted in broad strokes rather than close detail, in order to help people understand the past and "unite as one and look toward the future." Deng Xiaoping also noted that the party leadership must accept some measure of collective responsibility for past errors, which were certainly not all the errors of a single person.

The complete text was publicized on July 6, 1981.[89] The new resolution was consciously patterned after the earlier "Resolution on Certain Historical Questions" passed by the Seventh Plenum of the Sixth CCP Central Committee in April 1945.[90] This original 1945 resolution, also drafted by Hu Qiaomu, was the first document of institutionalized party history and solidified the new orthodoxy of Maoist historiography. The resolution "shows that the [Central Committee] still conceived of itself as being the only source of authoritative interpretations of Party history."[91] An important feature of party history or any kind of historical writing whatsoever is periodization. Periodization performs the basic narrative and interpretive function of setting beginnings, middles, and ends. In short, periodization marks ruptures and continuities. The periodization put forth in the resolution still dominates the study of party history today, both in China and the West, dividing the era of state socialism into smaller periods: "basic completion of the socialist transformation" (1949–1956), "beginning to build socialism in all spheres" (1956–1966), "the ten years of the 'Cultural Revolution' " (1966–1976), and the present "great turning point in history" (1976–1981).

The feature of interest to us here is the decade of the Cultural Revolution, formally dated from May 1966 to October 1976 (§19), for it is the integrated narrative of the verdict and the resolution that holds together the complex

89 The trial and the resolution were devised to be the final business of the Eleventh Central Committee. The first stable draft was dated November 22, 1980, coinciding precisely with the start of Gang of Four trial, with revisions to be postponed until conclusion of the trial. A revised draft was put before an enlarged session of the Politburo in late May 1980 and formally approved by the plenary session in late June of that year. For a recent account of the drafting process, see Huang Li, "Guanyu jianguo yilai dang de ruogan lishi wenti de jueyi" qicao taiqian muhou [Behind the scenes of the drafting of the "Resolution on Certain Questions in the History of Our Party since the Founding of the People's Republic of China"] from Zhongguo Gongchandang xinwen wang [CCP News Network] April 2, 2009, available at http://dangshi.people.com.cn/GB/85040/9070755.html.

90 See Tony Saich, "Writing or Rewriting History? The Construction of the Maoist Resolution on History," in Tony Saich and Hans van de Ven, eds., *New Perspectives on the Chinese Communist Revolution* (London: M.E. Sharpe, 1995), pp. 299–338.

91 Susanne Weigelin-Schwiedrzik, "Party Historiography," in Jonathan Unger, ed., *Using the Past to Serve the Present: Historiography and Politics in Contemporary China* (London: M.E. Sharpe, 1993), p. 171.

decade of the Cultural Revolution as a single, coherent period of rupture between the early years of the People's Republic and the historical present. Recall that the crimes listed in the indictment fall into three categories: persecution of Party and state leaders and incitement of mass violence by the Gang of Four in 1966–1969; the attempted coup d'état and assassination of Chairman Mao by the Lin Biao group in 1971; and various moves to consolidate political power by the Gang of Four in 1974–1976 (slandering political rivals to Mao, suppression of popular expressions of grief for the late Zhou Enlai, amassing a cache of weapons in Shanghai). There are two major problems here: first, the connection between Gang of Four and the Lin Biao group was tenuous; and second, even in this official account there is a five-year gap in the criminal activities of the Gang of Four. However, the court case (and eventually the verdict) bridged all of these events into a single counterrevolutionary conspiracy. The narrative force of the resolution is attested by the fact that soon after it was issued, in official discourse the term "decade of internal chaos" supplanted the term "decade of catastrophe."[92] The resolution completed the rhetorical work of positioning the chaotic Cultural Revolution as entirely erroneous in orientation. The resolution does not hold back in describing the magnitude of the disaster, calling the Cultural Revolution "a grave Left-deviation error comprehensive in nature and protracted in scope" (§ 22). Utterly unlike the truly progressive revolution of 1949, the Cultural Revolution was interpreted as a chaotic rupture in the history of socialism characterized by violations of both positive (statutory) and natural (objective) law. Such an abnormal and regressive "Left-deviation error" demanded explanation in terms of the socialist laws of history. Accordingly, the resolution's explanation of the Cultural Revolution rested on the concept of "error":

> Owing to our Party's meager experience in leading the cause of socialism and to subjectivist errors in the Party leadership's analysis of the situation and its understanding of Chinese conditions, prior to the Cultural Revolution there were mistakes of enlarging the scope of class struggle and of rash, premature development in economic construction. Afterwards, there occurred the comprehensive, protracted, and grave error of the Cultural Revolution. (§ 8)

[92] Based on frequency of usage in *RMRB*. The phrase *shinian haojie* (decade of catastrophe) first appeared June 8, 1979; usage peaked from July 1980 through June 1981 (more than twenty-five usages per month). However, the phrase *shinian neiluan* (decade of internal chaos) appeared with equal frequency in July 1981 and thereafter with much greater frequency. The phrase *shinian neiluan* (decade of internal chaos) became common only after mid-June 1981: there are only five examples prior to June 15, 1981, the earliest on October 28, 1980, compared to 137 examples from the latter half of 1981. "Decade of internal chaos" remained a common phrase throughout 1982–1983, before declining in 1984. Note that the term "catastrophe" (*haojie*) does not appear at all in the *Resolution* as adopted, while the term "internal chaos" (*neiluan*) does appear in the section on the CR period (see resolution, § 20).

The Party leadership's lack of practical experience, its limited knowledge of objective facts, and its mistaken analysis of the overall situation resulted in unintended violations of the objective laws governing historical development. Such violations could not but result in disaster. However, these errors were fundamentally different in nature from crimes, those violations of law described in the verdict.

The resolution characterized as the four erroneous theses that formed the general political theory of the CR. The four erroneous theses were: (1) The Cultural Revolution was a struggle against the revisionist line or the capitalist road. This had no grounding in fact, and many of the policies negated had been correct. (2) The confusion of right and wrong led to the confusion of friends and enemies. The facts show that many of the people attacked and persecuted had been wrongly labeled. (3) The Cultural Revolution was supposed to rely on the masses for support. In fact, the movement was divorced from Party organizations and the masses and even had been resisted or rejected by people at all levels. (4) The Cultural Revolution was said to be a revolution. Here the refutation is very strong: "Practice has shown that in fact the Cultural Revolution did not – and indeed *could not possibly have* – constituted a revolution or social progress *in any sense*" (§ 20). The errors made were contrary to fact, contrary to the objective laws of history, and contrary to the great tradition of Mao Zedong Thought.

Nor does the resolution stint in its criticism of Chairman Mao.[93] On the other hand, the resolution also stresses Mao's lasting and overwhelmingly positive contributions to the cause of Chinese socialism, even citing his good intentions in launching the Cultural Revolution. The resolution urged a balanced view of history, equally condemning those who supported or attacked Mao without qualification: "These two attitudes fail to draw a distinction between Mao Zedong Thought, a scientific theory formed and tested over a long period of time, and the errors made by Comrade Mao Zedong in his later years. Yet this distinction is absolutely necessary" (§ 31). This is to say that in evaluating history, the distinction must be drawn between the person and his thought, between the subjective and the objective; people's actions must be measured separately against the law and the objective laws of history.[94] The resolution affirms that the enduring historical philosophy of Mao Zedong Thought can and must be salvaged and applied to the challenges ahead: only through the guiding principles of Marxism-Leninism and Mao Zedong Thought – seeking truth

[93] Party leaders Ye Jianying, Deng Xiaoping, and Huang Kechang all provided critical evaluations of Mao Zedong that predated the Resolution; see Brantly Womack, "Where Mao Went Wrong: Epistemology and Ideology in Mao's Leftist Politics," *Australian Journal of Chinese Affairs*, Vol. 16 (1986), p. 25, n. 2.

[94] Haiyan Lee, "Mao's Two Bodies: On the Curious (Political) Art of Impersonating the Great Helmsman," Unpublished paper, applying the metaphor developed by Ernst Hartwig Kantorowicz, *The King's Two Bodies: A Study in Mediaeval Political Theology* (Princeton: Princeton University Press, 1957).

from facts, and testing it through revolutionary practice – can the nation achieve unity, stability, and modernization as it moves forward. In summary, even as the resolution sharply criticized the later content of Mao Zedong Thought, it reaffirmed the ostensibly scientific method of socialist governance according to the laws of history.

From the ambition of the party's historical resolution, and from its direct and complementary relationship to the earlier legal verdict, it is clear that the Gang of Four trial aimed to achieve much more than a public shaming of Cultural Revolution leaders. The trial attempted to define the scope and function of law in socialist society, to demonstrate its proper exercise by state power, and to render a judgment on the past rooted in the ostensibly law-like and scientific regularities of human history.

11

Anger, Honor, and Truth

The Political Prosecution of Neapolitan Organized Crime

Marco Jacquemet

From 1973 to 1982 criminal organizations in southern Italy controlled, according to the most prudent estimates, at least one-third of the economic activity in the region. In those years Naples witnessed the spectacular evolution of an internecine warfare between two cartels: the *Nuova Famiglia* (New Family, a corporation of all the main criminal families in Naples) and the *Nuova Camorra Organizzata* (or NCO, Newly Organized Camorra, a loose confederation of various gangs from the Neapolitan hinterland). By 1981 the NCO had become, according to Italy's Justice Department, one of the most powerful criminal organizations in the nation, providing a living for at least 200,000 people in the Neapolitan area alone. It also set itself up to muscle out the Nuova Famiglia from its traditional territory in downtown Naples. As a result, in the early 1980s the number of gang-related murders skyrocketed and the NCO seemed to be poised to wipe out the Nuova Famiglia altogether. Murders in Naples went from 85 in 1979 to 148 in 1980, to 235 in 1981, and peaked in 1982 at 265, an increase of 300 percent in four years.[1] This war was fought every day and on every corner, and nobody felt safe. A "state of emergency" was declared for the Neapolitan region and the Italian government passed a law allowing the Justice Department to prosecute people solely on the basis of "belong to a Mafia-like organization." Using this law, the Italian police increased its rate of arrests, and this led to a game-changer event: the desertion of some of NCO's key men who, once arrested, broke the code of silence (*omertà*), turned against their former associates, and collaborated with the Justice Department. These people came to be known as *pentiti* (lit. "repenters"). They were the first Italian equivalents of the American Mafia's government witnesses, a.k.a. turncoats or stoolies. Using the information provided by these pentiti, the Italian state finally decided to crack down hard on organized crime, striking at the core of the NCO structure. On June 17, 1983

[1] Osservatorio sulla Camorra, *1985 Year Report* (Naples: OSC, 1985).

(a day labeled by the Neapolitan press as "the Black Friday of the NCO"), the Neapolitan police arrested 856 people. Overall, more than 1,000 would later be indicted on the crime of association with a "Mafia-like organization called NCO." The Nuova Famiglia cartel, on the other hand, was left relatively untouched, allowing it to regain absolute control over all criminal activities in the area. Without a rival to fight, in 1984 the murder rate fell to pre-1980s levels (or just a little more than a hundred a year).

The mass trial (or *maxi-processo* as it was called) resulting from the blitz against the NCO lasted three years and required the participation of nine different judges and scores of legal clerks, attorneys, witnesses, and military policemen. The legal records – which included audiotapes of the entire proceedings – filled an entire room at Naples' Hall of Justice. Apart from the extraordinary number of people tried and the complexity of the proceedings, the trial derived its political significance from the pentiti's presence.

In this chapter I document the problematic, and inherently political, relationship between pentiti and the Justice Department – especially trial judges. The confessions the pentiti delivered to law-enforcement agents had to be reenacted in the courtroom in order to be accepted as judicial evidence. In the courtroom the pentiti had to produce a "true" discourse: that is, a discourse recognized as truthful by its recipients. However, in this quest for credibility, they drew on the communicative strategies available to them – those acquired over the years in everyday interactions within their local networks, which were mainly made up of people involved in "State-disapproved" activities.[2] In an unfamiliar role and under stress from close scrutiny, they based their performance on the witness stand upon locally recognized social values – above all, the code of honor. In this code, credibility is assigned on the basis of social reputation rather than referential accuracy. They therefore sought to establish their credibility with the Justice Department by presenting themselves as "men of honor," thus emphasizing their social reputation, rather than by producing factual and accurate testimony.

However, the combination of the pentiti's local street talk with interactional strategies dictated by the code of honor was ill-suited for the courtroom. They came to court with their own epistemological expectations of how to act and react, but these expectations often conflicted with the ones embodied by courtroom communication. As a result, they clashed with the courtroom environment: their presence in the courtroom broke the judicial routine, and everybody, especially the presiding judge, had to readjust and renegotiate his role.[3] A curious pas de deux developed between judge and pentito, in which the

[2] In keeping with Neapolitan understanding of local practices, I prefer to use this somewhat awkward label to more semantically precise but locally contested terms, such as "criminal" or "unlawful."

[3] Since all pentiti and all judges were male, throughout this chapter I will use the masculine form to refer to them.

latter's credibility came to depend on how a particular judge perceived him, on the pentito's ability to negotiate the judge's expectations of his performance, and on the degree of rapport between an individual judge and an individual pentito. These unique interactions between judge and pentito produced legal proceedings shaped by locally dominant sociocultural norms – most of the times at odd with national norms based on rationality and logic. In this context, the judge–pentito relationship became the determinant axis in the construction of judicial evidence and in the determination of the truth. Depending on the personalities of the participants and the sociopolitical factors underlying this relationship, their rapport was highly subjective and varied over time.

Drawing upon this Neapolitan case, I want to argue that this particular trial is relevant for understanding the broader phenomenon of political trials for four reasons: it prioritized local sociopolitical concerns (such as restoring honor) over more abstract values (such as truth); it was mainly concerned with finding a new balance of power between the state and various criminal groups through the selective prosecution of one organization (the NCO); it evaluated defendants' and witnesses' behavior based on their stance vis-à-vis locally constructed sociopolitical values (such as honor and credibility); and it attempted to legitimize the prosecution through a dramatization of the struggle against organized crime. In this chapter, I want to focus on the performative aspects of political trials by illustrating how in this particular criminal case the final judgment was constructed and regulated through the two imperatives any political trial faces when confronted with conflict: prioritizing the reestablishment of dominant social relationships ruptured by the conflict even at the expenses of material evidence (i.e., constructing a "sociological truth" rather than establishing "what truly happened"),[4] and securing control over the production and reproduction of social power through public performances.[5] As such, this trial points to a particular feature of all political trials: judicial procedures and political goals are ultimately decided by communicative performances able to impose themselves over competing claims through their appeal to restore the social order and uphold existing power relations.[6] In other words, control over these trials was achieved through communicative performances that defined the veridical status of

[4] Peter Just, "Let the Evidence Fit the Crime: Evidence, Law and 'Sociological Truth' among the Dou Douggo," *American Ethnologist*, Vol. 13 (1988), pp. 43–61.

[5] Marco Jacquemet, *Credibility in Court* (Cambridge: Cambridge University Press, 2009). See also Michel Foucault, *Discipline and Punish: The Birth of the Prison* (New York: Pantheon, 1977); John Comaroff and Simon Roberts, *Rules and Processes: The Cultural Logic of Dispute in an African Context* (Chicago: University of Chicago Press, 1981); and Richard Bauman and Charles Briggs, "Poetics and Performance as Critical Perspectives on Language and Social Life," *Annual Review of Anthropology*, Vol. 19 (1990), pp. 59–88.

[6] Cf. Jens Meierhenrich and Devin O. Pendas, "'The Justice of My Cause Is Clear, But There's Politics to Fear': Political Trials in Theory and History," in this volume.

conflicting and competing statements based not on rational reasoning but on concerns over maintaining (or regaining) the status quo.

In the remaining sections of this chapter I will look in detail at a particular courtroom performance to document how rational truth, based on reason and logical methods, proved not to be the main concern in the resolution of this legal process. The search for rational truth was in fact overshadowed by the synergy of locally dominant sociopolitical values with communicative performances based on dramatic affective displays.[7]

MEN OF ANGER, MEN OF HONOR, MEN OF TRUTH

Politically motivated trials feature emotional states contextually selected as most pertinent to the achievement of the dominant political agenda. This process of individuation, selection, and representation of emotional states leads to what I called "affective posturings."[8]

Affective posturings (i.e., the communicative displays of emotions) lie in the domain of effective communicative performance – as such they are one of the means through which dominant discourses find their legitimacy. This is the case for two reasons. First, affective posturings are evidence of interactional control – what is acceptable in the representation of what a body can do, how it can move, freeze, stare, tense or relax, is derived from the social environment a person is allowed, or is able to penetrate in his/her quest for legitimacy. When animated, people stand, their voices tense, their communicative behavior intensifies to show the embodied connection between emotions and language, between bodily functions and discourse strategies for dominance. Moreover, these emotional displays conjure to construct a social and ideological consciousness made up of sets of opposing moral values: good/bad, right/wrong, true/false. This moral yardstick is then applied to our understanding of other people's intentions. As a result of an occupation of the moral consciousness by these semi-symbolic systems, we inject into these categorizations of communicative behavior our ideological evaluation (determining for instance that one was "right" in being angry), thus providing a moral cover to social behavior.

Second, while emotions permit a representation of social action which account for our responses to them, let us not forget that truth is the pivoting

[7] This case has been selected following Llewellyn and Hoebel's dictum that situations in which a system breaks down often yield the richest information about the nature of the system, cf. *The Cheyenne Way: Conflict and Case Law in Primitive Jurisprudence* (Norman: University of Oklahoma Press, 1941). The extreme case discussed here provides the best available evidence to uncover some of the basic features of any political trial, otherwise obscured by taken-for-granted institutional routines.

[8] Jacquemet, *Credibility in Court*. See also Elinor Ochs, "Introduction to the Pragmatics of Affect," *Text*, Vol. 9 (1989), pp. 1–25.

narrative of courtroom communication. Affective posturings not only evolve around questions of truth, but are often assumed to be true, the "instinctual," supposedly unmonitored, motion of the body being recognized as the primary locus for authenticity.

Among the affective posturings usually associated in Western societies with authenticity and an undeniable "physical state," anger has always played a leading role. When angry, people posture themselves "as if" out of control, the body unrestrained, the voice out of range; in so doing they tap into the "natural," lived connection between intentionality and authenticity, between interactive strategies for dominance and bodily displays. Depending on the social environment and the cultural values of a society these affective posturings can be more or less accentuated and can be more or less invested with moral determinations (they range from the concealment of the Yamatos to the expressive neutrality of the Eskimos to the understatement of the Anglo-Saxons to the overstatement of southern Italians).[9]

Criminal networks in general stand out as privileged zones where representations of being unrestrained assume great moral qualities. In southern Italy in particular, resorting to "angry" posturing is not perceived as necessarily a character flaw but as a mark of the man of honor facing a challenge: "having a hot temper" signals the power of the individual, his threatening potential for destruction, the freedom afforded him in his ability to go beyond, to be out of control. In this sense, the representation of anger becomes another tool in the struggle for supremacy within a social hierarchy continuously testing the strengths and the weaknesses of its members. How often this anger is released depends on the social position of the individual (his need to assert, or reassert, a dominant role vis-à-vis challengers), on the environmental conditions in which this social hierarchy operates, and, most especially, on outside pressure.[10]

It should not come as a surprise that in court, the institutional zone par excellence for competition over representations, the pentiti asserted freely and frequently their violent and aggressive side. The simple fact of having "snitched," of having violated the code of honor (*omertà*), had stripped them of their social status, thus exposing their weakened self to the attacks of their opponents. When confronted by challengers (other pentiti, defendants, opposing counsels, judges) during courtroom interactions, they often resorted to angry posturings in an attempt to reclaim their honorable and superior position vis-à-vis the opponent. In their logic, they needed to have their anger recognized as legitimate behavior of a man of honor as the first step to be judged credible witnesses (i.e., "men of truth").

[9] See Catherine Lutz and Geoffrey White, "The Anthropology of Emotion," *Annual Review of Anthropology*, Vol. 15 (1986), pp. 405–436.

[10] See Diego Gambetta, *Codes of the Underworld: How Criminals Communicate* (Princeton: Princeton University Press, 2009).

The aggressive, and sometimes violent, clashes which erupted in the Neapolitan courtrooms were the result of pentiti's attempts to reopen a conflict over who could claim a superior position based on honor. Because of their communicative behavior, the courtroom environment came to be colonized by a local code of honor, morally and concretely constituted through pragmatic moves shared by all—judges, defendants, and witnesses.

ON BEAUTY, VIRGINITY, AND AGE

The case under consideration happened during the final days of the trial, when it became very clear that one of the biggest problems the prosecution faced was the overabundance of government witnesses called to testify. This overabundance had in fact created contradictory and at times contrasting testimonies. It was at this point that the court decided to identify the government witnesses who in their testimony had presented radically different versions of particular events and have them testify at the same time and face to face, setting up a direct confrontation between them. This confrontation turned out to be an additional strain on the pentiti's communicative performance, and led to an internecine struggle to have one's own reconstruction of events trump that of other government witnesses. Forced into an increasingly awkward position—testifying as government witnesses against other government witnesses in a court that seemed to distrust them—the pentiti became less and less capable of maintaining control, quickly reaching the point of communicative meltdown.

The confrontation between Gianni Melluso and Pasquale D'Amico, which took place on June 3, 1986, best exemplified this tension. Although both men were among the first group of pentiti to come forward in 1983, they played a significantly different role in the trials against the NCO. Gianni Melluso (a.k.a. *Il Bello*, the Beautiful) was neither a Neapolitan nor an active member of the NCO. Melluso, an active pimp and small drug dealer in Milan, worked under the command of Francis Turatello an affiliate of the Sicilian Mafia and was never directly involved in NCO business. He came to play a significant role once the investigation of the NCO began to explore NCO connections with organized crime in northern Italy. Defense attorneys, defendants, and other pentiti routinely attacked Melluso and tried to undermine his credibility. One of the most vocal of Melluso's opponents was Pasquale D'Amico (a.k.a. *O'Cartone*, the Cardboard). This underboss for the area of downtown Naples was one of the more prominent men of the NCO. In 1982 he had total control over all activities in his area. When he became a pentito, he provided sound evidence against his former employees (e.g., drug dealers, killers, numbers runners, smugglers, pimps). During his testimony, he also declared that Melluso, a Sicilian who had migrated to Milan as a teenager, could not have been in a position to know the business of the NCO, and he attacked him mercilessly.

In the exchange described in detail below, the two pentiti were put in direct confrontation to determine who was telling the truth. The stakes were particularly high for Melluso and this exchange constituted his chance to refute D'Amico's charges against him. Melluso's strategy, in order to account for the discrepancy in their testimony, was to convince the presiding judge that D'Amico was not interested in the truth, but was attacking Melluso simply on personal grounds. Melluso attempted to convince the presiding judge that this was strictly a case of personal enmity resulting from a breach of a fiduciary contract established between them. In order to prove this animosity, Melluso told the story of this accord and of the resulting breach of trust responsible for triggering D'Amico's hostility in the first place. Melluso's carefully constructed narrative was designed to allow the court to understand the implications behind D'Amico's relentless attack on Melluso's testimony.

Melluso's story revolved around the moral value of hospitality among men of honor – the notion of offended honor combined with the social context for the eruption of anger and the desire for revenge. Once upon a time (the time reference left vague in the tradition of good storytellers), Melluso had formed a protection pact with D'Amico, since they both knew that when an NCO member became a pentito his family would be in great danger of *vendetta trasversale*, a feud in which people belonging to the corporate group of a wronged person seek vengeance on any reachable members of the wrongdoer's family. Melluso had asked D'Amico, who was already a pentito, to provide a safe haven for Melluso's brother and brother-in-law. D'Amico agreed to hide the brother in the house of his lover, Patrizia Petrucciano. In this house, Melluso's "beautiful" brother met D'Amico's daughter and he deflowered her. According to Melluso, after this episode, the trust between Melluso and D'Amico was shattered forever and D'Amico's attacks on Melluso's credibility had to be understood in the light of this animosity.

Melluso's interactional goal was to goad D'Amico into expressing in court a personal grudge against him, in that way reproducing in front of the judges the alleged animosity. In order to do so, Melluso deliberately provoked D'Amico to try to make him loose his "cool," showing his anger toward Melluso. But to lead D'Amico into this emotional trap, he had to cautiously and gradually reveal the highly sensitive material in public, so that he would be allowed to reach the climax of the story – the deflowering charge – before triggering an adverse reaction from D'Amico or the presiding judge. He needed to let the court and the public grasp, little by little, the importance of his revelation. As we will see, his plan worked perfectly, but the aftermath of D'Amico's explosion would prove catastrophic for Melluso.

To fully appreciate the complex link between narrative performance and moral work, it will be necessary to go through an extended narrative analysis in stages. Since storytelling is achieved in a sequential fashion through the deployment of complex conversational strategies, the deployment of

Melluso's performance will be analyzed through the communicative tactics he activates in his narrative.

The following section will look in detail at some passages from the courtroom exchange. Participants in the exchange include the presiding judge (JP4), the associate judge (JP5), the prosecuting magistrate (PM4), the two pentiti (Mel and DA), and various lawyers (law).

COMMUNICATIVE TACTICS DURING CONFLICT TALK

While verbal opponents rely on discourse strategies for the overall plan of their dispute, various verbal tactics are deployed throughout the sparring of the battle. Among the many techno-political devices employed on this level, Melluso utilized particular speech moves able to elicit sympathetic responses from the judges and establish new conditions for the reception of his performance. Two such devices of primary importance in his performance were *contextualization tactics* and *story characters deployment*.

Contextualization Tactics

Contextualization tactics are communicative practices that both produce representations of the social world in accord with a given ideology and seek to persuade others to comply with these representations.[11] We can think of two forms of contextualization practice: context-evoking and context-producing.

Participants in a communicative event must be able to guide each other's interpretation of what is being said, evoking the cultural background and social expectations necessary to interpret speech. During storytelling, lexical expressions have the task of contextualizing the flow of narration and projecting a particular disposition on the listeners for what still has to come.[12]

At the start of his testimony, Melluso uses a contextualization tactic to forewarn the court of the problematic nature of his relationship with D'Amico: "unfortunately I have a beautiful brother":[13]

[11] Bauman and Briggs, "Poetics and Performance as Critical Perspectives on Language and Social Life," pp. 59–88. See also Marco Jacquemet, "Verbal Conflict," in Keith Brown, ed., *Encyclopedia of Language and Linguistics*, Second edition (London: Elsevier, 2005).

[12] John Gumperz, in *Discourse Strategies*, call this discourse feature a "contextualization cue" (Cambridge: Cambridge University Press, 1982).

[13] The three participants in this transcript are Melluso (Mel), D'Amico (DA), and the presiding judge (JP4). In the transcripts below I marked overlapping turns with dashes (-) at the beginning and end of the overlap on two successive lines; equal signs (=) are used at the end of one line and the beginning of the next to mark latching turns. Extra prominence (or loudness) is marked with CAPS. Unclear passages are marked as (xxx). Pauses and silences are marked with parenthesis and dots (...). Other transcription symbols include: ~ / ? and ∧ for pronunciation; [h] for laughter. For a detailed description of transcription conventions in Conversational Analysis, see Marjorie Goodwin, *He-said-she-said: Conversational Practices in Urban Black Children* (Bloomington: Indiana University Press, 1990).

01	Mel	= mio fratello ^vittorio	01	Mel	my brother Vittorio,
02		(. . .) io purtroppo presidente/	02		unfortunately Your Honor
03		C'ho dei fratelli,	03		I have some brothers,
04		dei bei ragazzi =	04		beautiful boys
05	JP4	= va-bbbè -	05	JP4	all right
06	Mel	-non ci nascondo la- le ^bugie =	06	Mel	I won't hide the- the lies from You.
07	DA	= e c'ERA LA MOGLIE/	07	DA	and once his wife
08		signor pre -siden-te,	08		Your Honor
09	JP4	- sshh-	09	JP4	shut up
10	DA	c'era la MOglie	10	DA	there was his wife
11		- (xxxx xxxx) -	11		(xxx xxx)
12	Mel	- e fammi parl-ARE	12	Me	and let me speak
13		e dico la verità/	13		and tell the truth
14		e non se ne parla più =	14		and that'll be the end of it
15	DA	= non metto la famiglia in mezz-	15	DA	I don't bring the family into it
16		(xxx -xxx xxxx xx)-	16		(xx xxx)
17	Mel	- STAI ZITTO-	17	Mel	SHUT UP
18		presidente/	18		Your Honor
19		(. . .) io ci ho dei ~fratelli	19		(. . .) I have some brothers
20		ci dico la verità	20		I tell You the truth
21		perchè questo signore ce l'ha con me,=	21		about why this man has a beef with me
22	DA	= non metter la famiglia in mezzo-	22	DA	don't bring the family into it
23	Mel	e mi ha coinvolto	23	Mel	and he turned
24		tutti gli ~altri ~pentiti =	24		all the other pentiti against me
25	JP4	= e diciamola questa ve- (rità) -	25	JP4	and let's say this truth
26	Mel	- ecco -	26	Mel	right,
27		diciamola e non se ne parla più.	27		let's say it and then we can drop it.
28	Mel	(. . .) io ci ho dei fratelli/	28		(. . .) I have some brothers
29		presidente dei belli-ssimi-	29		Your Honor, very beautiful
30	JP4	- sono-	30	JP4	they are
31		belli ragazzi,	31		beautiful boys
32		abbiamo -sentito-	32		we heard it
33	Mel	- belli - ragazzi,	33	Mel	beautiful boys
34		come me presidente,	34		just like me Your Honor
35		e gli stavo di[h]cen[hh]do [ride] =	35		and I was telling You [laughter]
36	JP4	= -vabbene -	36	JP4	okay
37		- [urla] -	37	def	[screams from the holding pens]

Here Melluso uses two contextualization cues: the first one – a lexical interjection (line 02 "unfortunately") – framing the second – a metaphorical cue of the beauty motif. Melluso uses the beauty theme as a powerful conversational tool to play with his opponent (and incidentally with the court) and to keep everybody hanging on his words. Throughout the text, the theme is invoked by Melluso with regard to his brother, and incidentally, to himself, to set up conversational suspense and raise the expectations of the recipients. It is introduced as a contrastive element to forecast trouble ahead, some ugliness to come: the "unfortunately I have some beautiful brothers" (lines 02–04) already warns of something bad to come – otherwise one could not understand the harm in having beautiful brothers.

In the other corner, D'Amico does not have a single clue as to where Melluso's contextualizing tactic is leading; he passively reacts to the latter's turns by trying to divert him from his story. However, Melluso is not distracted and returns to the main theme of his brothers' beauty, who have, by now, become "very beautiful" (lines 29–30).

Although the presiding judge objects to this repetition, Melluso, in his next turn, continues on this theme by equating their beauty with his own (line 34: "just like me"), delivered in a joking mode to which both the judge and the defendants in the cages respond, the latter with ridicule and sarcastic comments. Sensing the judge's impatience, Melluso then withdraws from this theme, reserving it for later use, and returns to the events being narrated. The narrative tension is nevertheless set up; something unfortunate is linked to this beauty, forewarning of a troubling context ahead.

The second contextualization tactic—found in most societies—usually consists of three parts: the decontextualization of an event from its occurrence in a particular space and time, its entextualization into a discourse with a more controllable set of truth-values, and the recontextualization of this discourse within a communicative frame set up to legitimize it.[14] For instance, the speaker may elect to embed an opponent's statement within her own speech while inverting its referential value or adding a negative comment through intonational coloring. Most instances of reported speech in argumentative situations conform to this tactic: the embedded segment, which usually takes the form of a short quotation from the opponent's previous talk, serves the speaker in the unflattering representation of the opponent, in its representation of the relationship between the two sparring partners, and through the cues it presents to the audience about how to read the conflict.

Through reported speech speakers not only animate the story, but give clear indications of their attitude toward the situation in which the story is

[14] Michael Silverstein and Greg Urban, eds., *Natural Histories of Discourse* (Chicago: University of Chicago Press, 1996).

performed. In particular ego's reported speech is used in reference to a third party called upon to provide either the speaker's truthfulness or moral rectitude. As such, reported speech functions as a mechanism to reinforce social values.

01	Mel	una volta/	01	Mel	one time
02		presidente mi riferisc-	02		Your honor I refer-
03		ci si- ci ho detto/	03		I- I said to him
04		al carcere di campobasso,	04		in the prison of Campobasso
05		d'amico.	05		"D'Amico,
06		mi dovresti fare una ~cortesia	06		you should do me a courtesy
07		mi ~minacciano la ~famiglia in ~sicilia	07		they are threatening my family in Sicily
08		ho bisogno che mio fratello/	08		I need for my brother
09		o qualche mio ^fratello	09		or some of my brothers
10		se ne va a na-poli-	10		to go to Naples"
11	DA	-vede-te qua	11	DA	let's see it
12		vedete se è vero. =	12		let's see if it's true
13	Mel	= vabbene un attimo. =	13	Mel	okay just a second
14	DA	= eh.	14	DA	right

Melluso is back to using the story format based on vague temporal references and a more structured spatial one. The two main characters, Melluso and D'Amico, are in the pentiti's prison of Campobasso, a town 200 miles from Naples. It was there that Melluso had to ask a *cortesia* (line 06: "courtesy") of D'Amico. Note that Melluso reports that he asked a simple cortesia, not a *favore*, favor. This lexical choice is crucial since, in this highly structured world of patrons and clients, the first term reflects a symmetrical relationship, while the latter presupposes an asymmetrical one between a pledger and a provider of services able to command respect and obedience through his position as power broker. Melluso needs a safe haven for his family and wants them to go to Naples.

Deploying Story Characters

The success of a story depends in large part on the ability of the storyteller to inhabit its world with characters. While telling a story, a speaker not only portrays events, but also animates characters able to produce talk of their own and provide indications on their own alignment toward the events being recounted.[15]

[15] Marjorie Goodwin in *He-said-she-said* refers to this phenomenon as "participation framework." See also Erwin Goffman, *Frame Analysis: An Essay on the Organization of Experience* (Cambridge: Harvard University Press, 1974).

In the middle of a multiparty communication, the introduction of characters constructs a narrative framework signaling that the dialogical exchange has been replaced by a story structure in which everybody but the narrator becomes a recipient. In a story involving conflictual issues, the storyteller's main task is to place the blame for the conflict on a third party – evoked as character. In the following segment, this is achieved by means of a shift from the I/you confrontation to a narrator/originator-of-the-story pair.

01	Mel	= no, è ^importante	01	Mel	No (. . .) it's important..
02		siccome/	02		since-
03		questo signore,	03		this man,
04		con questa faccia così grossa,=	04		with this big face
05	JP4	= ezzitto per continuare/	05	JP4	be quiet and from now on
06		non fare n'osservazione, =	06		don't make remarks
07	Mel	= eh/ ha detto,	07	Mel	eh.. he said,
08		che:: mio ~cognato mio ~fratello	08		that my brother-in-law, my brother
09		{[ff] eccetera eccetera}	09		etcetera etcetera
10		sono gente di napoli,	10		are people from Naples,
11		l'avete se-ntito-	11		You heard him
12	DA	- no::-	12	DA	noo
13	Mel	oppure gente dalla SICIlia/	13	Mel	or people from Sicily
14		che viene a napol[h]e, =	14		that come to Naples
15	DA	= bravo bravo.	15	DA	bravo bravo
16	Mel	voglio dirvi la verità,	16	Mel	I want to tell You the truth
17		perchè questo signore ce l'ha con me,	17		why this man has it in for me,
18		presidente,	18		Your Honor,
19		così/	19		so that
20		finalmente si chiarisce tutto =	20		everything is cleared up.
21	JP4	= [h]e,	21	JP4	well,
22		perchè ce l'ha con voi? =	22		why does he have it in for You?

In this segment, Melluso moves into the story mode by introducing a prototypical story starter (line 02: "since") and shifting to the third person in referring to D'Amico (line 03: "this man"). Through these devices Melluso signals that what he has to tell has officially started and will extend over several turns. Immediately thereafter, however, he elects to attack D'Amico on the subject of his "big face" (line 04). While this lexeme is ridden with multiple meanings – from commenting unflatteringly on appearance to linking it with the honor/reputation of the target, observation of subsequent talk clearly indicates that Melluso is after something more than looks (although to this pentito nicknamed "The Beautiful," this theme also provides an opportunity to counterpose his beauty to the appearance of his opponent). What is at stake here is D'Amico's honor. By acknowledging his rival's important reputation through the "big face," Melluso is hinting that his revelation has something to do with this reputation.

When the presiding judge interrupts him impatiently, Melluso goes back to the story format, introducing two new characters, one of whom will play the role of initiator of the story (the brother, line 08). These characters are introduced as pieces of D'Amico's previous testimony (line 07: "eh ... he said"), using again reported speech to establish a direct link between them and his opponent. Melluso relates that D'Amico claimed that they came from Naples, which prompted the latter to counter, directly addressing his knowledge of these men and denying this statement (line 12). When Melluso then rephrases it by acknowledging that they are Sicilian, he has successfully established that D'Amico had a more than superficial knowledge of these people.

Moreover, secondary characters are brought into a story to provide additional information about the main characters. Given the polemical format of any story, these minor characters find their niche in one of the two fields that polarize the narration (the hero's positive side versus the anti-hero's antagonistic, negative side). In so doing, they allow an interactional representation of the main characters. By providing a sense of the main characters' relationships with others, a narrator explores the moral attributes of these two fields, determining the listeners' alignments.

01	Mel	e allora che ^succede	01	Mel	and then what happens
02		LUI/	02		HE
03		(. . .) mi dice non ti ~preoccupare	03		(. . .) he tells me: "don't worry
04		fai salire a tuo ^cognato	04		bring up your brother-in-law
05		e a tuo fratello ^Vittorio	05		and your brother Vittorio
06		che li faccio ospitare di mia moglie.	06		I'll fix them up at my wife's place."
07		(. . .) sua moglie/	07		(. . .) his wife,
08		{[lo] poverina/}	08		poor thing
09		una brava donna perchè la conosco/	09		a good woman, I know her,
10		no- non ha ~potuto	10		she couldn't do it,
11		e e- lui me li ha fatti ~mandare	11		and, and he had me send them
12		della sua ~donna =	12		to his lover
13	DA	= euh/	13	DA	right!

(*continued*)

14	Mel	petrucciano patrizia/	14	Mel	Petrucciano Patrizia
15		la scriva, =	15		write it down
16	JP4	= si =	16	JP4	yes
17	Mel	= che fa/	17	Mel	she is
18	Mel	(. . .) la prostituta pro-	18		a prostitute just-
19		in coppa ai ^quartieri	19		on the top of the Spanish quarter
20		lo sanno tutti presidente/	20		everybody knows that Your Honor
21	JP4	Eh	21	JP4	all right,
22	Mel	lo sa anche la questura, =	22	Mel	even the police station knows it

Directly quoting D'Amico (lines 03–06), Melluso provides referentiality to the latter's reported speech by introducing a new character, D'Amico's wife, who should have provided a haven for Melluso's kin. In his process of story animation, Melluso keeps commenting on it, giving to his courtroom opponent the ungrammatical voice (line 04: *fai salire a tuo fratello* instead of grammatically correct *fai salire tuo fratello*; line 06: *ospitare di* instead of *ospitare da*) of an accomplice. Through this reported speech, Melluso wants to establish that the two men had entered into a fiduciary contract. By declaring that D'Amico has extended his hospitality to Melluso's relatives through a female kin, Melluso is tapping into the highly charged dimension of hospitality as prescriptive behavior. In essence, D'Amico's hospitality has engaged Melluso's relatives (and consequently Melluso) to fully comply with the rules that govern the presence of a non-kin male within his host's household, including the rule of female avoidance.

Furthermore, in the story D'Amico's situation is complicated by the fact that Melluso's brother could not be sent to his primary household (ruled by D'Amico's wife) but to a secondary one, built around the figure of a longtime lover (Patrizia Petrucciano), here stigmatized by Melluso as a prostitute in the downtown district of the Spanish Quarter.

Melluso's narrative about D'Amico's female kin provides a dynamic deployment based on an opposing pair: the good wife ("good" simply because Melluso "knows her," line 09) is in direct opposition to the lover, a necessarily bad person for stealing other women's men through her profession (lines 18–19). The already polarized universe of hero versus anti-hero is here enriched by this oppositional pair, the wife entering into the field of Melluso's allies, the lover into the dissolute world of D'Amico's vices. Notice how Melluso interrupts the story to make sure, by use of a directive, that the presiding judge has noted the lover's name, and when the latter complies, he switches to

Neapolitan dialect to characterize the profession of D'Amico's lover, whose behavior is public knowledge (line 20) and a source of such continuous gossip that "even" the police know it (the highly ironic line 22).

D'Amico's bigamy, combined with the profession of the lover, constitutes a departure from accepted cultural norms and signals slackness in his code of honorable behavior. This, in turn, forecasts a weakness in D'Amico's ability to protect his family in the event of an attack, which is exactly where Melluso is leading his captive audience.

Throughout the entire story, Melluso has invested the figure of problematic beauty with the task of keeping a leitmotif running, of contextualizing the narration, and of cueing its characters at the moment of their appearance. The effect is the production at the interactional level of a situation in which Melluso can toy with his opponent (and incidentally with the court) and keep everybody hanging on his words. All characters brought into the story have been qualified through this figure: the first time this is used to describe D'Amico negatively – as a man with an incredible "big face," which sets him on the opposite side from this handsome pentito, nicknamed, let us not forget, *Il Bello*. It is then invoked in regard to his brother, thus setting up conversational suspense and raising the expectations of the recipients. In that case, the figure of beauty is treated as a contrastive element to forecast trouble ahead, some ugliness to come – "unfortunately I have some beautiful brothers." It resurfaces as a way to regain the floor after D'Amico has launched a series of obscure allegations against Melluso's wife, when Melluso indulges in a brief switch of frame to remind everybody that his nickname is Il Bello and his brothers take after him. Then, after introducing D'Amico's wife as unattractive, he returns to this theme with a new reference to the handsome brother and finally to D'Amico's ugly lover. In her final appearance D'Amico's lover is additionally labeled as *cordiale*. This term – derived from the Latin *cor* [gen. *cordis*] heart, to mean both a warm and friendly person but also a sweet liquor given to visiting guests as a sign of hospitality – is strategically deployed by Melluso to lay over the beauty configuration a new semantic field constructed through two cultural values related to honor: hospitality and friendliness.

The scene has been telescoped down to a specific location (Petrucciano's apartment), the actors are almost all in place, and, still, most of the participants, especially D'Amico, do not have a clear clue as to the thrust of Melluso's story. While an exasperated D'Amico offers, out of the blue, that he did not kill the brother, the alerted judge is now suspicious that a crime of honor has occurred but his own imagination can only go as far as to propose a sexual assault scenario between Melluso's brother and D'Amico's lover. Through the combination of an underlying code of honor and hospitality, the mention of a loose environment and the unfortunate reality of having a beautiful brother, Melluso has prepared the stage for the final touch, the introduction of the proverbial sacrificial lamb, D'Amico's own "little daughter":

01	Mel	= siccome questa ragazza ~presidente	01	Mel	since this girl, Your Honor,
02		disgrazia vuole,	02		unfortunately
03	Mel	è una bruttissima ~ragazza =	03	Mel	she is an ugly girl
04	DA	= eh =	04	DA	right
05	JP4	= e vabbene =	05	JP4	okay
06	Mel	= però è una ragazza ^cordiale	06	Mel	but she is very friendly,
07		(. . .) mio fratello/	07		(. . .) my brother
08		ha conosciuto la ~figliolina/	08		met the little daughter
09		di Pasquale D'Amico,	09		of Pasquale D'Amico,
10		e l'ha sverginata.	10		and he deflowered her.
11	JP4	no no no	11	JP4	no no no

[D'Amico – shaking off a frozen look of disgust from his face – throws his microphone at Melluso and tries to jump him. The military police promptly intervene and restrain D'Amico to his chair. All the defendants are shouting from their holding pens. The presiding judge begins to shout. Equally shocked, the lawyers start to complain.]

12	Mel	[a DA] come la verità non la vuoi sapere?	12	Mel	[to DA] so you don't want to know the truth?
13	DA	(BASTARDO/	13	DA	BASTARD
14		MIA FIGLIA CI HA DODICI ANNI)	14		MY DAUGHTER IS TWELVE YEARS OLD
15	JP4	ci ha dodici anni,=	15	JP4	she is twelve years old
16	Mel	=NON E' VERO PRESIDENTE/	16	Mel	THAT'S NOT TRUE YOUR HONOR!
17		CE NE HA DICIOTTO=	17		SHE IS EIGHTEEN!
18	JP4	=però non dovete offendere.=	18	JP4	but You don't have to be offensive
19	Mel	=presidente/	19	Mel	Your Honor,
20		allora facciamo una cosa/	20		then let's do something,
21		presidente,=	21		Your Honor
22	JP4	=se tiene dodici anni/	22	JP4	if she is twelve
23		*nun seppò fà*=	23		that's not feasible
24	Mel	=presidente/	24	Mel	Your Honor,
25		ce ne ha DICIOTTO/	25		she is eighteen
26		porca miseria,	26		geez,
27		ma lei va appresso alle chiacchiere sue=	27		but You are swallowing his chatter.

The permissive, morally lax, and cordial lover has allowed the beautiful young brother to meet D'Amico's daughter. D'Amico could not stop the handsome spoiler of his daughter's virginity, could not perform his duty of guardian, being himself guarded by state-paid guardians. With no other male relatives around to protect the virgin and save D'Amico's honor, beauty, youth, and passion easily overcome any moral imperatives: she is deflowered (line 10). To this revelation, a stunned and frustrated D'Amico can only react by resorting to the ultimate weapon of the code of honor: anger and raw violence. He throws his microphone, hitting Melluso with his word, undoubtedly a word of honor, technologically entrapped in a microphone.

D'Amico's verbal reaction to Melluso's allegation consists of a direct insult to Melluso, followed by an angry disclaimer regarding his daughter's age: she is twelve years old (line 14). At this disclosure the presiding judge promptly relays this disturbing piece of information to Melluso (line 15) and then proceeds to declare the "unfeasibility" of the matter (line 23). In his next turn, Melluso is quick to counter, abandoning the story framework to claim that D'Amico's daughter is eighteen (16–17). The exchange has finally hit bottom. In the emotional environment created by Melluso's revelation, the pentiti have now produced two contrasting pieces of information about the age of D'Amico's daughter. This was finally an element that could be easily investigated, proving one of them correct. Unfortunately, life in the Neapolitan courtrooms would never be this simple.

THE POLITICAL POWER OF CULTURE

Most communicative tactics (such as contextualization or reported speech) are intentionally staged and performatively acted to acquire *interactional power*, i.e., the ability to shape the course of an interaction and lead people to follow such course even against their will. All speakers, including those in positions of dominance, need to perform their power, to stage the speech acts able to convey their will to power. In so doing, interactional power allows for a dynamic and flexible structure of power relations, where a skillful performer in a weaker structural position could still achieve his or her agenda. Thus the outcome of any attempt to gain control over communicative resources is never predetermined: power in interaction (especially during verbal conflict) must be claimed through the use of communicative resources – asymmetrically distributed but always negotiable in performances.

Most dominant classes can, however, count also on *authority*, as the institutionally invested capacity to carry out the dominant agenda. People in positions of power, such as judges, deploy strategies that endow them with better opportunities to talk, establish certain regions of knowledge as authentic and meaningful at the expenses of others (usually endorsed by their opponent), and link this authenticity to systems of power that can boost their claims to credibility. Moreover, they increase their credibility through their ability to evoke and use relevant domains of knowledge, and by clashing over the rules, conditions, and procedures that establish what is believed to be true and what is believed to be false.[16]

Melluso proved to be the superior performer through his dexterity in keeping the floor, his ability to prevent D'Amico's moves by withholding significant information until the last possible moment, and his competence in building the climax through tensive narrative devices. His plan to provoke D'Amico into losing his "cool" and becoming angry worked beautifully: D'Amico, indeed, appeared to have lost control, letting his anger pour forth freely and unrestricted. Melluso was clearly hoping that the judges would interpret this angry eruption in the courtroom as evidence of D'Amico's long-held animosity against him as a consequence of the deflowering. In addition, he was able to have D'Amico commit to an objective fact (the age of the daughter) that could be easily verified. Unfortunately for Melluso both of these scenarios never materialized.

From his position of authority, the presiding judge in fact reacted angrily, showing his displeasure with Melluso through his interpretation of the story and his siding with D'Amico. He immediately made his moral indignation known, based on the daughter's age ("if she's twelve / that's not feasible"). The judge's indignation was stylistically marked by constituting a moral community through code-switching: in his turn, the judge aligned himself with D'Amico, the Neapolitan pentito, by switching to Neapolitan dialect to address Melluso, the pentito from Sicily, to declare that the fact "was not possible/feasible." This established a confrontational "we" (Neapolitans) vs. "you" boundary. Melluso's revelation of seduction was clearly offensive, and Melluso was the main culprit for the chaos in the courtroom (this, while D'Amico was throwing microphones, banging his notebook on the table, threatening the military police, and shouting obscenities at Melluso). Moreover, later on he will refer to the sexual encounter as a "violent act," in a striking departure from Melluso's depiction of the intercourse between an unfortunately beautiful man and the innocent, love-stricken daughter.

This moral alignment with the offended father will become even more evident when the two witnesses next engage in a fight for the record. When Melluso asks the judge to have the daughter's age put on record (an element that could be easily verified later), D'Amico responded by asking the judge to put on record that Melluso is claiming that his daughter is no longer a virgin and to verify this claim. This was one of the more puzzling moments of the whole exchange: D'Amico demanded that the same allegation that just a couple of minutes before put him into a fit of rage because it was made in a public arena, should go onto the legal

[16] See Pierre Bourdieu, *Language and Symbolic Power* (Cambridge: Harvard University Press, 1991).

record, the most public and permanent of all official documents. The judge, however, quickly acknowledged D'Amico's request, pointing out that, in the case the virginity could be verified, he could look for satisfaction from Melluso's offense by filing a defamation suit. By reminding D'Amico of his constitutional rights, the judge is clearly signaling his support for the offended father. Moreover, by reminding the father of his legal prerogatives he is asking this powerful criminal to keep his response within the limits of normative courtroom procedure, instead of resorting to the traditional means of the "man of honor."

This tension between national rules and local norms was thus clearly revealed in court, leaving the presiding judge stranded by these two poles: a rational search of the daughter's age based on logic and birth certificates or seeking to determine through unorthodox but locally accepted methods her virginal status. Instead of opting for the relatively easy task to find out D'Amico's daughter's age, the judge sought as legal evidence a *certificato d'illibatezza*, a certificate of the virginal status of the girl (whose name and age remained indeterminate). This certificate, produced by D'Amico's family doctor and accepted as evidence by the court, "proved" Melluso a liar: D'Amico's daughter was declared a virgin (Tribunale di Napoli 1990, personal communication).

Local practices, based on the cultural value of honor, trumped national procedures, based on rational syllogisms and impartial decisions. D'Amico's honor had become the judge's honor and the honor of his courtroom. Melluso's story had caused a breakdown in local values, and the judge's priority was to fix this breakdown and heal the local community.

If one looks back at the exchange, it is clear that the presiding judge's shock justified D'Amico's ordeal, neutralizing Melluso's attempt to discredit him by proving he had a personal ax to grind. On purely narrative grounds, one can say that Melluso was successful in his performance: he had been able to tell the entire story with minimal interruption, to override the president's call for silence, and to force the latter to acknowledge a basic contradiction between the two "truths" about the age of the daughter. His conversational skills proved once again his talent as a verbal duelist, but unlike what happened earlier in the trial, here he did not have the court on his side. His rational account paled when compared with D'Amico's ordeal, and the judges clearly sided with the offended father.

Melluso's successful story was determined to be just that, a well-told story; not only did it not sway the judge's decision, but it backfired, causing a backlash against Melluso's violation of the local code of honor. As a result, Melluso was ignominiously stripped of his government witness status and thrown back into prison, to wait for D'Amico and others to take their revenge – perhaps through a libel suit, as suggested by the presiding judge, or more likely through practices customarily used to respond to an offense to one's honor, like a knife in the ribs.

CONCLUSION

In a series of lectures Foucault delivered in 1973 and 1974, subsequently incorporated into several of his texts, he distinguished two divergent approaches to "truth," one emphasizing a family of practices that he defined by their common use of *l'enquête*, the other emphasizing a group of esoteric rituals that he defined by their recourse to *l'épreuve*. Enquête can be rendered into English as "examination," or "inquiry"; épreuve can be translated as "ordeal," "test," or "trial." [17]

The idea of a truth that could be approached through an examination was distinctly modern, and one of the methodological foundations of modern science. In an examination, evidence is gathered on the assumption that truth is objective and can be confirmed by anyone with the appropriate training and type of knowledge (or discipline). Such a model of inquiry became central to the judicial process in the modern state, and also to scientific procedures for gathering information about the natural world (from physics to medicine).

But this scientific truth has always been flanked by another idea of truth "repugnant to both science and philosophy" which is the singular product of "propitious moments" and "privileged places" where a ritualized "ordeal" can unfold.[18] Delphi's oracle, the Christian desert hermitage, the medieval tournaments, or the art of torture belonged to this tradition of determining the "truth-by-trial:" "Suffering, confrontation, and truth" were linked, as he wrote in *Discipline and Punish*, in a kind of "battle" or "duel;" and it was only the "victory of one adversary over another that 'produced' truth according to the ritual" (1977: 38). While most of the time it was the will of the sovereign that emerged triumphant, if the suspect "held out," if the poison did not kill him or he did not drown, his innocence could then be assumed proven. The magistrate had to drop charges, the tortured man might win back his life. This truth, Foucault continued, "is not given by the mediation of instruments, it is rather produced directly, inscribed in the body and soul of a single person, it is attained through strategy, not method." Truth provoked by rituals creates a relationship between truth and the individual who lies in wait for it, and is struck by it: "this relationship is always ambiguous, reversible, bellicose in its mastery, its domination, its triumph – a relationship of power."[19]

Foucault's assumption that modern judicial discourse was based upon logic and concrete evidence proved in Naples to be highly problematic. In many instances during the so-called "maxi-trial against the NCO," it was the "ordeal" kind of truth that became the pivotal narrative of courtroom interactions. As other legal

[17] Michel Foucault, "La maison des fous," in Franco Basaglia and Franco Basaglia-Ongaro, eds., *Befriedungsverbrechen uber die Dienstbarkeit der Intellektuellen* (Frankfurt: Europäische Verlagsanstalt, 1980); see also the section on "The examination" in Part III of Foucault's *Discipline and Punish*.

[18] Foucault, *Discipline and Punish*, p. 197.

[19] Foucault, "La maison des fous," p. 146.

anthropology studies have pointed out, rational truth based on reason and method proved not to be the main issue in the resolution of this legal process; instead, the rational process was overshadowed by the body politics of affective posturings.

This focus on the ordeal highlights the inherently political character of the "maxi-trial." The prosecution of this criminal organization was in fact carried out because of strictly political concerns, above all the preoccupation with local sociopolitical values (such as honor) and with the political consequences of a new balance of power among criminal groups. The prioritizing of local values over national interests led to a phenomenon typical of political trials: the evaluation of defendants' and witnesses' behavior based on personality rather than evidence. In this case, defendants and witnesses were evaluated based on their reputation and honor. This approach produced a predetermined, almost liturgical, trial, scripted by judges who were more interested in validating the Ministry of Interior's repressive policies than in determining the factual validity of the pentiti's statements. The maxi-trial became, in Moore and Myerhoff's words, a "secular ritual" in which participants performed and dramatized social values (such as honor) which were both potent and uncertain.[20] This potency and uncertainty allowed for a conflict resolution carried out through communicative performance which, far from having any objective validity, reflected the goal of the state to reestablish political relationships and connections disrupted by the aggressive rise to power of the NCO.

A second step of its politicization was the Ministry of Justice's attempt to seek the political legitimization of the prosecution through a dramatization of the struggle against organized crime. The decision to place the pentiti center stage ensured a continuous string of spectacular courtroom confrontations. Italian media, both the public TV networks and local and independent radio stations, avidly covered the trial. The national news channels brought the theatrics of the trial into every Italian home by broadcasting excerpts of the trial (such as the conflict between Melluso and D'Amico) at dinnertime, and by producing multiple shows broadcast at all hours of the day. Some news radio networks broadcast the trial in its entirety (albeit in the middle of the night) and provided uninterrupted judicial commentary. [21]

The final feature this trial shared with trials considered strictly "political" concerned its management of public support through selective prosecutions. As I mentioned in the introduction, the Italian state intervened in the affairs of organized crime only during a particularly violent phase in the war between cartels. It did so, however, by being selective: no known member of the Nuova Famiglia was arrested at that time, so its business continued unperturbed. This

[20] Sally Falk Moore and Barbara Myerhoff, "Introduction: Forms and Meanings," in Sally Falk Moore and Barbara Myerhoff, eds., *Secular Ritual* (Assen: Van Gorcum, 1977).

[21] Because they were allowed to keep radio receivers in their cells, most inmates, including defendants in the case, were thus able to follow the trial, with potentially devastating consequences for the trail itself.

caused the murder rate to drop to pre-1980s levels (or just a little more than a hundred a year) but only because the state removed one of the two cartels from the territory. The Nuova Famiglia, and in particular the Casalesi clan, reasserted its control over the entire Neapolitan area, a domination that continues well into the new millennium.[22]

On September 16, 1986, more than three years after Black Friday, the First Court of Appeals in Naples acquitted 114 of the 187 defendants who had made it to the first of the three appeals of "maxi-trial" against the NCO. The not-guilty verdict included all those convicted in the first degree solely on the basis of the pentiti's testimony. At the reading of the sentence, the prosecuting magistrate shouted: "This is the victory of the camorra!" He was swiftly put on probation (*Il Mattino*, September 17, 1986).[23]

[22] Roberto Saviano, *Gomorrah* (London: Picator, 2008).

[23] Of the 1,013 people arrested in 1982, 301 were cleared during the *istruttoria*, the Italian discovery phase conducted in secret by the prosecuting magistrates (a procedure that lasted more than two years – during this time the defendants were imprisoned and their lawyers were prevented from seeing the accusatory evidence). In the first-degree trial, 83 people were cleared of all wrongdoings, 263 were found not guilty, and 66 were found guilty solely on the testimonies of the pentiti. Of the 349 people who appealed, 204 were found not guilty and only 145 (all well-known felons) were convicted. Overall, the initial 1,013 arrests produced a conviction rate of a mere 15.9 percent. See Bruno Rubino, *Tortora: I Mille Giorni* (Naples: Edizioni Dick Peerson, 1988).

12

"This Following Orders Thing Is Very Relative"

Ascriptions and Assumptions of Responsibility in the Causa ESMA, *1983–1987*

Christiane Wilke

What does it mean to be responsible, to be held responsible, or to claim responsibility? How are responsibility and irresponsibility ascribed in political and judicial decisions? This chapter examines contentions over responsibility for the enforced disappearances of thousands of people during the 1976–1983 dictatorship in Argentina with a focus on the relationship between one specific politicized case – *Causa ESMA* – and the national political debate and legislation. Argentina was one of the first countries to stage trials of former dictators and military officers, but the trials were followed by military unrest, legislation limiting criminal responsibility for violence committed under the dictatorship, and eventually pardons. The 1985 trial of the juntas – the highest military commanders who had governed the country – attracted enormous attention because it found most of the highest commanders guilty without absolving the subordinate officers from criminal responsibility. This first trial was followed by trials of officers who were responsible for specific detention centers or military zones, among them *Causa ESMA*. Congress responded to ensuing military unrest by passing a law stipulating that most officers had acted under duress when they participated in the atrocities.[1] While authors disagree whether the law was President Alfonsín's direct concession to the rebels, most accounts present the shift between different models of military responsibility from 1983 to 1987 as a struggle between different ideological and political positions.[2] I argue here that the trajectory of the trials can be better understood if we pay attention to the performative work that assumptions and ascriptions of responsibility themselves do. Responsibility norms shape the subjects that act on the politico-legal scene.

[1] See, for example, Carlos Santiago Nino, *Radical Evil on Trial* (New Haven: Yale University Press, 1996).

[2] Nino, *Radical Evil on Trial*; Mark Osiel, "Constructing Subversion in Argentina's Dirty War," *Representations*, Vol. 75 (2001), pp. 119–158.

The military crisis of April 1987 was widely viewed as a disturbing performance of disobedience and a rupture of military norms of hierarchy and order. In its aftermath, legal stipulations of "due obedience" as an excuse became more palatable as the political elites sought to subordinate the armed forces to civilian authority. Present obedience was sought by creating legal fictions that sanctified past obedience.

Causa ESMA is one of the largest and most complex trials for state violence in Argentina. The case file was opened in 1983, temporarily closed in 1989, and reopened in 2003. The case is currently in the trial stage.[3] From 1983 on, the fate of *Causa ESMA* hinged on the shifting ways in which national legislation and jurisprudence contemplated the responsibility of junior officers in response to changing political contexts. This chapter focuses on the 1983–1987 phase of *Causa ESMA*. It draws on publicly available judgments, legislation, and media coverage of *Causa ESMA* and the 1987 military crisis. In addition, I make use of notes and excerpts from the *Causa ESMA* case file that were made available to me by the staff of the *Centro de Estudios Legales y Sociales* (Center for Legal and Social Studies, CELS) in Buenos Aires.[4]

The chapter proceeds with a reconsideration of responsibility as a concept and practice in relationship to military organizations and periods of political change. I argue that especially in times of (attempted) political change, responsibility practices can become crucial tools for inculcating new political norms and subjectivities. The subsequent sections travel back and forth between tracing the national political and legal developments in the ascription of responsibility for dictatorship-era violence and analyzing the effects of these larger developments on specific proceedings in the *Causa ESMA*. The case was indelibly marked by the shifting political contexts. This is not to suggest illicit interference. Rather, the proceedings were shaped by concurrent legislation and political discourses that instituted, suggested, prohibited, or otherwise shaped the ascriptions of responsibility that the participants in the proceedings brought to bear on the case. The deep societal disagreements on the legitimacy of the dictatorship and its violence were not directly articulated. Instead, legal and political actors debated the ascriptions of legal responsibility for acts of violence whose existence and criminality itself was contested.

THE PLACE AND POLITICS OF RESPONSIBILITY

In *Causa ESMA*, ascriptions of responsibility worked in specific modes and context: the case deals with (1) criminal responsibility for (2) military violence

[3] See CELS, Weblog Juicios, available at www.cels.org.ar/wpblogs/ingles.

[4] CELS lawyers represent victims in *Causa ESMA* and took notes on the original case files for their work in the trial phase that started in 2003. In addition, they requested photocopies of parts of the files. The notes are complete, and the photocopies of motions and testimonies I consulted are selective but extensive. They include much of the testimony that military officers gave in the case.

in (3) times of (attempted) political transition. This section takes up these aspects in turn.

Responsibility and Criminal Law

Responsibility – as a concept, ascription, assumption, or practice – is not confined to criminal law. Yet the logic of criminal law easily becomes a model for responsibility practices in other spheres – political, moral, or metaphysical.[5] Western criminal law generally requires two elements in order to attribute a crime to a person: first, proof that the alleged acts occurred and were caused by the accused; and second, a mental element such as intention to kill. This second element ensures that persons are held liable only if they had the capacity and opportunity to act otherwise.[6] This concern resonates with liberal ideals of the self as an autonomous, rational agent that can be held responsible for voluntary actions. This liberal ideal of the "self-determining moral agent"[7] fails to capture crucial dimensions of selfhood, for example, vulnerability, dependency on others, or the constraints to action and imagination posed by hegemonic norms.[8] In addition, even societies with a strong liberal ethos carve out spaces in which the ideal of the autonomous reasoning subject is not meant to apply, for example, military institutions.

Ascriptions of responsibility are based on understandings about the kind of persons who can or cannot be responsible subjects. In accounts of violence, the narrative frequently culminates in a judgment about responsibility, in a condemnation, or in an explanation.[9] Since many concepts of responsibility presume a liberal autonomous subject as the only possible responsible agent, the search for responsibility is not the same as the search for causes: the conditions, norms, and forces that shape individual action are easily excluded from the picture if the goal is to find liberal legal responsibility. A search for responsibility that remains within the confines of this liberal framework needs to anchor the cause of an injury in a subject that is imagined as autonomous and "produced first and foremost as the accountable originator of an injurious deed."[10] The turn to criminal law and its discourses of responsibility implies the search for subjects that can be criminally responsible: individual human beings, not institutions,

5 For a division of guilt into four categories, see Karl Jaspers, *The Question of German Guilt*, translated by Ernst B. Ashton (New York: Capricorn, 1961 [1947]).

6 See Nicola Lacey, "In Search of the Responsible Subject: History, Philosophy and Social Sciences in Criminal Law Theory," *Modern Law Review*, Vol. 64 (2001), pp. 352–353.

7 Nicola Lacey, "Responsibility and Modernity in Criminal Law," *Journal of Political Philosophy*, Vol. 9 (2001), p. 251.

8 See Chad Lavin, *Politics of Responsibility* (Urbana: University of Illinois Press, 2008); Judith Butler, *Bodies That Matter: On the Discursive Limits of Sex* (London: Routledge, 1993); Judith Butler, *Giving an Account of Oneself* (New York: Fordham University Press, 2005).

9 See Butler, *Giving an Account of Oneself.*

10 Judith Butler, *Excitable Speech: A Politics of the Performative* (New York: Routledge, 1997), pp. 45–46.

not nations, and not "history that, by its very temporality, cannot be called to trial."[11] Thus, ascriptions of responsibility do not simply make a violent past manageable and prosecutable; they also produce subjects that can be responsible, irresponsible, or non-responsible. Assessments of responsibility interact with the people who have been stipulated to have been responsible or irresponsible: the ascriptions "have effects on the people classified," but "the classified people can take matters into their own hands" as well.[12] This is, I argue, what happened when Argentine junior officers who found themselves classified as responsible and therefore unable to invoke the due obedience excuse for past atrocities started to practice disobedience in the present.

Responsibility, Obedience, and Hierarchy: The Military

Military organizations pose distinct problems for ascriptions of responsibility. First, militaries are large organizations that rely on the cooperation of many persons to produce specific outcomes. Second, armed forces are hierarchical: their members interact with one another as superiors and subordinates, not as the equal and autonomous citizens that criminal law otherwise envisages. Obedience is central to the identity, cohesion, and ethos of a military as an institution. In the standard view, subordinates owe their superiors obedience, and superiors assume responsibility for the actions they ordered their subordinates to perform.[13] In this scheme, soldiers occupy a position parallel to the one that Roman law reserved for children and slaves: they are not responsible because they are not assumed to be the true authors of their actions; their actions are commanded by a will that is not their own.[14]

In the aftermath of the atrocities of World War II and the Holocaust, this distribution of responsibility within the military was increasingly questioned. In *U.S.* v. *Ohlendorf*, a U.S. Military Tribunal convicted commanders of German *Einsatzgruppen* who had jointly killed 1 million civilians in Eastern Europe. The court rejected the plea of superior orders: "The obedience of a soldier is not the obedience of an automaton. A soldier is a reasoning agent. He does not respond, and is not expected to respond, like a piece of machinery."[15] Only genuine coercion and duress can excuse participation in massacres, and "when the will of the doer merges with the will of the

[11] Butler, *Excitable Speech*, p. 50.

[12] Ian Hacking, *The Social Construction of What?* (Cambridge: Harvard University Press, 1999), pp. 58–59.

[13] Argentina, Code of Military Justice, Article 514. See Paula Speck, "The Trial of the Argentine Junta: Responsibilities and Realities," *University of Miami Inter-American Law Review*, Vol. 18 (1987), pp. 517–526.

[14] See Speck, "The Trial of the Argentine Junta," p. 521.

[15] *U.S. v. Otto Ohlendorf et al., Military Tribunal II. Trials of War Criminals before the Nuremberg Military Tribunals under Control Council Law* No. 10, Vol. 4. (Washington: U.S. Government Printing Office, 1951), p. 470.

superior in the execution of the illegal act, the doer may not plead duress under superior orders."[16] These rulings are often hailed as universal principles regarding military atrocities,[17] but they were based on specific understandings of the workings of the German military and the personalities of the defendants. The court observed:

> The defendants are not untutored aborigines incapable of appreciation of the finer values of life and living. Each man at the bar has had the benefits of considerable schooling. Eight are lawyers, one a university professor, another a dental physician, still another an expert on art. One, as an opera singer, gave concerts throughout Germany before he began his tour of Russia with the Einsatzkommandos. This group of educated and well-bred men does not even lack a former minister, self-unfrocked though he was.[18]

The juxtaposition of lawyers and opera singers with "untutored aborigines" demonstrates that the court's understanding of the soldiers' agency and reasoning was context-specific: the U.S. tribunal assumed that educated and well-bred Germans must have known that massacres of civilians were crimes, and established that these educated officers resembled liberal autonomous subjects rather than the cogs they pretended to have been.[19]

U.S. v. *Ohlendorf* was a key decision in the post-war adjudication of criminal responsibility for state atrocity. It did not, however, end the debate about what militaries are like. Michel Foucault's study on discipline generalized disciplinary institutions from a military in which the soldiers appear as "automata" that "were also political puppets, small-scale models of power,"[20] as "meticulously subordinated cogs of a machine."[21] Recent studies in military sociology suggest that many military organizations rely on small-group cohesion rather than hierarchical coercion or abstract patriotism.[22] Martha Minow, upon reviewing literature on military sociology and behavioral psychology, argues that given the hierarchical structure of militaries, the current training, and group pressure, soldiers can be expected to obey orders regardless of their legality.[23] She summarizes the dilemma: "telling soldiers that they face punishment unless they disobey illegal orders means telling them to think for themselves and question authority, yet directing them to do that risks

[16] *U.S.* v. *Ohlendorf*, p. 480.

[17] See Martha Minow, "Living Up to Rules: Holding Soldiers Responsible for Abusive Conduct and the Dilemma of the Superior Orders Defence," *McGill Law Journal*, Vol. 52 (2007), p. 17.

[18] *U.S.* v. *Ohlendorf*, p. 500.

[19] For an analysis of concepts of civilization in a parallel case, see Christiane Wilke, "Reconsecrating the Temple of Justice: Invocations of Civilization and Humanity in the Nuremberg Justice Case," *Canadian Journal of Law and Society*, Vol. 24 (2009), pp. 181–201.

[20] Michel Foucault, *Discipline and Punish: The Birth of the Prison* (New York: Vintage, 1995), p. 136.

[21] Foucault, *Discipline and Punish*, p. 169.

[22] Philip Smith, "Meaning and Military Power: Moving on from Foucault," *Journal of Power*, Vol. 1 (2008), pp. 275–293.

[23] Minow, "Living Up to Rules," p. 35.

undermining their training to follow orders, work as a cohesive whole, and subordinate their own desires and views to the collective enterprise."[24] Nonetheless, Minow insists that punishing soldiers for obeying and executing illegal orders "remains important for symbolic reasons"[25] such as making clear that such acts "are blatantly wrong."[26] Individual responsibility of subordinate officers would "express the symbolic importance of individual accountability central to democratic ideals."[27] In other words, Minow proposes an ascription of responsibility that does not start with reasoning liberal subjects but instead tries to produce them. Seen from this angle, trials that address the responsibility of soldiers for violence cannot help to be didactic: they "spread a political message" about responsibility in addition to settling legal questions of wider social and political importance.

Transitional Trials: Responsibilizing Future Citizens

Causa ESMA raised the question of individual responsibility for military violence in the context of a society in transition: away from authoritarianism and military dictatorship, toward democracy and the rule of law. *Causa ESMA* was adjudicated at a time of competing big political projects, a time of molding new subjectivities that could sustain democratic politics, a time in which the relationship between the military and civilians was negotiated through distributions of responsibility within the military. *Causa ESMA* was a *transitional political trial*: it negotiated responsibility for past atrocity, grappled with legal and political uncertainty in the present, and pointed to a future in which the "never again" promised by the Argentine Truth Commission Report would be fulfilled.[28] Transitional trials "have decidedly *not* been simple and unmediated reflections of moral sentiments already universally felt within society towards the accused."[29] Instead, these trials have been vehicles through which government and defendants, respectively, try to advance their narrative of the recent past, their assessments of the transitional present, and their normative visions for the future.

Ascriptions of responsibility in transitional contexts aim to bring about new relations and subjectivities. For example, in their responses to Nazi atrocities, Karl Jaspers and Hannah Arendt gestured toward responsibility and guilt as vehicles for changing self-knowledges. Hannah Arendt acknowledged that from a functional perspective, Nazi perpetrators appeared as cogs of a gigantic bureaucracy. Yet "if the defendant happens to be a functionary, he stands accused

[24] Minow, "Living Up to Rules," p. 5. [25] Minow, "Living Up to Rules," p. 7.
[26] Minow, "Living Up to Rules," p. 39. [27] Minow, "Living Up to Rules," p. 54.
[28] See CONADEP [Comisión Nacional sobre la Desaparición de Personas], *Nunca Más* (Buenos Aires: Eudeba, 1985).
[29] Mark Osiel, "Making Public Memory, Publicly," in Carla Hesse and Robert Post, eds., *Human Rights in Political Transitions: From Gettysburg to Bosnia* (New York: Zone Books, 1999), p. 218.

precisely because even a functionary is still a human being, and it is in this capacity that he stands trial."[30] The "transformation of a cog into a man" in the courtroom allows for questions of agency and constraints that might otherwise not arise.[31] Karl Jaspers, in turn, proposed to see the political liability of citizens as a beginning of a transformation. He suggested "[t]hat in fact all the people pay for all the acts of their government ... is a mere empirical fact; that they know themselves liable is the first indication of their dawning political liberty. It is to the extent of the existence and recognition of this knowledge that freedom is real."[32] The subject of "inner political unfreedom," he continued, "obeys on the one hand, and feels not guilty on the other."[33] For Jaspers, "[t]he feeling of guilt, which makes us accept liability, is the beginning of the inner upheaval which seeks to realize political liberty."[34] If citizens realized that they are collectively responsible for the deeds of the state, Jaspers hoped, they would start to act as if they were free, thus becoming able to be responsible and self-governing. Responsibility is productive and performative; assumed rather than given. To use a parallel to Butler's discussion of the "assumption of sex": to assume responsibility means to act within the constraints of dominant models of responsibility and agency, to refer to norms, and to possibly re-signify them.[35] Thus, assumptions of responsibility are not (necessarily) "performed in compliance with the law" but rather "mobilized by the law";[36] they have a creative relationship to the law. Taking of responsibility is performative in the sense that the speech act itself, if intelligible in relationship to existing norms, brings about what it names.[37] Yet the effects of performatives such as assumptions of responsibility are contingent and never predictable: on the one hand, the legal norms about responsibility can produce "a set of consequences that exceed and confound what appears to be the disciplining intention motivating the law."[38] On the other hand, the officers who *assume* responsibility (or irresponsibility), who thereby invoke military norms about agency and obedience that are not necessarily shared by their civilian interlocutors, do not know how their invocations of obedience and honor will be taken up. In Argentina, as the next section shows, legislative stipulations as well as individual pronouncements of responsibility were intended to be performative and to produce subjectivities appropriate for democracy, but they often ended up "signifying in excess of any intended effect."[39] The trials, intended

[30] Hannah Arendt, "Personal Responsibility under Dictatorship" [1964], in Hannah Arendt ed., *Responsibility and Judgment*, ed. Jerome Kohn (New York: Schocken, 2003), p. 30.

[31] Arendt, "Personal Responsibility under Dictatorship," p. 32.

[32] Jaspers, *The Question of German Guilt*, p. 77.

[33] Jaspers, *The Question of German Guilt*, p. 77.

[34] Jaspers, *The Question of German Guilt*, p. 77.

[35] Butler, *Bodies That Matter*, p. 12.

[36] Butler, *Bodies That Matter*, p. 12.

[37] See John L. Austin, *How to Do Things with Words* (Cambridge: Harvard University Press, 1962).

[38] Butler, *Bodies That Matter*, p. 122.

[39] Butler, *Bodies That Matter*, p. 122.

to settle some politically contentious legal issues, became more than just decisive trials: they were widely perceived to have didactic and destructive potential. In this context, questions of responsibility were not settled, but rather became unsettling and unsettled.

ASCRIBING RESPONSIBILITY IN ARGENTINA: 1983–1987

The 1976–1983 Argentine military dictatorship was preceded by political radicalization, social tensions, and calls for the military to restore order. On March 24, 1976, the armed forces forced the President into exile, took over government, and proclaimed their desire to restore the country to tranquility and honor. The so-called *Process of National Reorganization* outlawed any possibly dissident political and social activity. Many citizens initially welcomed the coup. Behind the facade of order and morality, the armed forces divided the country into military zones and subzones, established about 350 clandestine detention centers, abducted thousands of people, tortured and detained most of them, killed many of them, and categorically denied any knowledge of the whereabouts of any of them.[40] Human rights organizations now estimate that up to 13,000 people remain disappeared.[41] In response to the unsuccessful 1982 war against the United Kingdom over the Malvinas/Falkland Islands and escalating economic problems, the military negotiated its way out of power and made space for presidential elections in 1983.

As long as the armed forces controlled what counted as knowledge about the disappearances, their discourses on responsibility were not concerned with criminal responsibility, but with highlighting agency, honor, and dignity. This strand of responsibility discourse remains important throughout the 1980s. In April 1983, the military issued a "final document on the anti-subversive struggle" in which it denied the disappearances, affirmed a broad institutional responsibility, admitted that mistakes might have been made, but reserved judgment for God.[42] In September 1983, weeks before the scheduled election, the junta passed an amnesty law that covered the time between May 25, 1973, and the end of the Falklands War on June 17, 1982.[43]

Raul Alfonsín, the winner of the 1983 elections, challenged the amnesty law. In making the case that a self-amnesty law passed by a military government

[40] See EAAF, *2007 Annual Report*, pp. 14–15, available at http://eaaf.typepad.com/annual_report_2007/An07_Argentina-8.pdf.

[41] See EAAF, *2005 Annual Report*, p. 14, available at http://eaaf.typepad.com/ar_2005/4aArg-pt 1_p14-59_rev.pdf.

[42] Reprinted in Stella Maris Ageitos, *Historia de la Impunidad: De las actas de Videla a los indultos de Menem* (Buenos Aires: Adriana Hidalgo editora, 2002), pp. 96–114.

[43] Law of National Pacification, Law 22.924, September 22, 1983, available at www1.umn.edu /humanrts/research/argentina/ley22-924.html.

cannot claim validity, Alfonsín relied on arguments by his advisors, the legal philosophers Carlos Nino and Jaime Malamud Goti.[44] Instead, Alfonsín promised, there would be trials of those who had violated basic human rights. As Nino recounted, "Alfonsín wanted to try the commanders and high-ranking officers, although he was skeptical about trying too many lower-ranking officers, fearing a dangerous reaction among the armed forces."[45] Alfonsín planned to limit the number of trials by dividing the perpetrators into three groups with different degrees of responsibility. Only two of these three groups would be prosecuted. According to memoranda written by Alfonsín's advisors, the first group would consist of those who gave the orders. The second group was made up of those who "exceeded the orders they received, committed additional crimes, often motivated by cruelty, perversity, or gain," and the third group consisted of those who "had strictly complied with the orders they received, acting in a context of general mistakes and coercion that made them assume that their actions were legitimate and that they should obey the orders they received, knowing that disobedience might have grave consequences."[46] These three categories of actors with the respective ascriptions of responsibility were adopted by President Alfonsín and circulated throughout the period of the trials in the 1980s in legislation and public discourse.

By sorting the participants in the dirty war into three distinct groups, Nino and Malamud suggested two dividing lines: one line separated the military leadership from those who directly committed violence. The second line divided the lower-ranking officers: on the one hand, there are the paradigmatic "bad apples" who exceeded orders and who presumed to have been motivated by private motives such as "cruelty, perversity, or gain," not by institutional motives such as internalized anti-communism. These officers might be prosecuted, and they are simultaneously cast outside the military community because their excesses are private, not institutional. The majority of junior officers, on the other hand, are described as coerced and indoctrinated: their actions are presumed to have originated solely in the orders they received, not in any independent individual agency. This stipulated "due obedience" would not be punished, and individual responsibility for excessive violence would not implicate the military as an institution.

What were these categories meant to do? At the time that these categories were crafted, there was little empirical knowledge about the organization of the dictatorship's violence. Alfonsín's categories and ascriptions of responsibility did not translate established facts into judgments on responsibility. Instead, the categories of responsibility were, as Nino recounted, "a legal mechanism to

[44] Nino, *Radical Evil on Trial*, pp. 65–66. [45] Nino, *Radical Evil on Trial*, p. 63.

[46] Nino and Malamud memorandum, reprinted in Horacio Verbitsky, *Civiles y Militares: Memoria Secreta de la Transición* (Buenos Aires: Edición Sudamericana, 2003), p. 265; also see Nino, *Radical Evil on Trial*, p. 63.

facilitate Alfonsín's wishes" that not too many perpetrators would stand trial.[47] In their memorandum to Alfonsín, Nino and Malamud had pointed out that "reasons of political prudence suggest limiting the responsibility of the third category [of obedient junior officers] with the view to win these officers back for the democratic reconstruction of the country."[48] When President Alfonsín introduced the bill that resulted from these discussions in Congress, he emphasized: "it is … imperative to offer the opportunity of loyal service to the constitutional democracy to those members of the armed forces and security forces who have not acted on their own initiative in acts that violated human dignity."[49] Implicit in Alfonsín's reasoning is the assumption that trials would not only settle important legal questions of political relevance and establish a record of the violence, but that they would be understood by the military as "public degradation ceremonies" – even more so when military officers would have to answer to civilian judges.[50] Trials for the disappearances could not help but be divisive: not because the President intended them to be an exercise in identifying enemies, but because the military would not easily cede the right to question, judge, and convict its officers to civilian courts. Fine-tuning the definitions and ascriptions of responsibility was a way of calibrating how many perceived indignities the military would have to put up with.

Viewed from this angle, it is clear that President Alfonsín aimed to elicit the military's *loyalty in the present* by offering a *legal fiction of due obedience in the past*. This offer was challenged from different perspectives: First, junior officers, steeped in the military's ethos of pride, honor, and dignity, were notably reluctant to invoke the due obedience defense. They demanded a vindication of their actions, not a legal categorization of their deeds as irresponsible: they wanted justifications, not excuses.[51] Second, given that the President wanted to make the due obedience defense available for crimes such as torture and killings of prisoners, human rights groups and their allies in Congress demanded that "atrocious and aberrant acts" should never be covered by the due obedience defense. Congress decided that obedience couldn't be an excuse "when [the acts] consisted in the commission of atrocious or aberrant acts."[52] This amendment to the bill introduced by Alfonsín subverted the carefully crafted tripartite division that Nino and Malamud had envisioned in order to limit the number of trials. Many acts committed by the military could be considered

[47] Nino, *Radical Evil on Trial*, p. 63.

[48] Nino and Malamud Goti in Verbitsky, *Civiles y Militares*, p. 266.

[49] Quoted in Verbitsky, *Civiles y Militares*, p. 269.

[50] See James Cockayne, "Hybrids or Mongrels? Internationalized War Crimes Trials as Unsuccessful Degradation Ceremonies," *Journal of Human Rights*, Vol. 4 (2005), pp. 455–473.

[51] See John L. Austin, "A Plea for Excuses," *Proceedings of the Aristotelian Society*, New Series, Vol. 57 (1956–1957), pp. 1–30.

[52] Law 23.049, February 9, 1984, Art. 11, available at www1.umn.edu/humanrts/research/argentina/ley23-049.html.

atrocious or aberrant and therefore subject to prosecution. The law was passed on February 9, 1984.

Causa ESMA, 1983–1984: "Everyone Has a Conscience"

The case file of *Causa ESMA* starts rather inconspicuously, on August 23, 1983, with a grainy photocopy of testimony that retired police officer Rodolfo Peregrino Fernández gave at the Argentine Human Rights Commission. At that time, the military still governed the country. When the military's self-amnesty came into force in September 1983, the fate of the case seemed sealed.[53] The case received its next impulse not from the judiciary, but from a series of magazine interviews given by David Raúl Vilariño, who had served at the ESMA as an officer. A public prosecutor forwarded the interviews to the court.[54] The interviews are noteworthy not only because they became evidence in the case, but also because they offer a window into the responsibility discourses and practices of junior officers in the immediate post-dictatorship period.

Vilariño was frank about the violence employed by the Navy in the ESMA in general, but he shied away from naming specific incidents. His view of the ESMA was based on sharp distinctions: on the one hand, there were teams of good soldiers that abducted people, risked their lives, and "occasionally" killed victims in these clandestine "operations"; and on the other hand, there were officers who brutally and cowardly tortured the detainees. Vilariño disassociated himself from the immorality of torture while taking limited responsibility for the abductions themselves.[55]

When Vilariño was asked "who was responsible" for the atrocities at the ESMA, he named mid-ranking officers who served directly at the ESMA, and not the admirals in the Navy command that the President determined were the most responsible for the abuses.[56] According to Vilariño, ESMA director Rubén Chamorro "gave the orders."[57] In his account, Vilariño reflected on his responsibility for the disappearances through the lens of Alfonsín's three levels of responsibility, but he also cautioned that these categories did not match his experience of participating in violence. For example, the distinction between orders and excesses that was crucial for Alfonsín was not clear to Vilariño: "this following orders thing is very relative." In the beginning, the actions and membership in the squads were voluntary, but over time, the

53 Supreme Council of the Armed Forces, Resolution. November 24, 1983. *Causa 761/ESMA*, Vol. 1, p. 152.

54 Julia A Sanchis Ferrero, letter to Federal Appeals Chamber of Buenos Aires, January 10, 1984. *Causa 761/ESMA*, Vol. 1, p. 193.

55 Similar for Scilingo, see Horacio Verbitsky, *The Flight: Confessions of an Argentine Dirty Warrior* (New York: New Press, 1996).

56 Ricardo Ibarlucía, "La Confesión de un asesino," *La Semana*, January 5, 1984, p. 36.

57 Ibarlucía, "La Confesión de un asesino," p. 40.

fear of not returning alive elicited a kind of obedience that was no longer voluntary.[58]

While Vilariño stressed the institutional responsibility of the Navy, his relationship with the institution was strained: "of course," he said, he felt betrayed by his superiors whose orders he had followed and who now changed their language about the disappeared or remained silent altogether.[59] "I feel like I'm falling apart," he added, "and maybe I'm the only stupid one who will reveal his face and deal with the consequences, while the rest remains living in impunity."[60] Vilariño held his superiors to a standard of military honor, and observed their failures with a mix of shock and bemusement. They, who had "hidden behind their desks" during the fight against the subversion, were now the ones who were afraid to tell the truth about the disappearances. When asked about answering for his deeds in a court of law, Vilariño responded that he was ready to go: "If I have to pay for the crimes I committed, I have no problem. But I will not go alone: we will all go."[61]

For Vilariño, the interview became an arena for performing a new kind of subjectivity, agency, and willingness to assume responsibility. He played with the power of giving and withholding names and details about the disappearances: he gave some names of perpetrators, hesitated, then gave some more, and finally explained that he would never give the names of his close associates because "everyone has a conscience." Vilariño's interview performance was not concerned with minimizing his own criminal responsibility, but with enacting his interpretation of military values and engaging with ascriptions of responsibility that were circulating. His interviews suggest the pacts of obedience that had underwritten the actions of the junior officers during the dirty war were unraveling in a new social context.

In response to the nullification of the amnesty law and the revelations by Vilariño and others, the military court in charge of *Causa ESMA* initiated new investigations. Starting in February 1984, the court took testimony from a number of admirals who had served high in the chain of command.[62] Vilariño was the only junior officer who was asked to testify. However, the military court did not intend to use his testimony as evidence of the disappearances. Instead, it filed a criminal complaint against Vilariño for giving false testimony.[63] The military was still in a position to suppress dissident accounts of the events by legal means, but the contestation would soon shift from the facts of violence to the legal responsibility for them.

58 Ibarlucía, "La Confesión de un asesino," p. 42.
59 Ibarlucía, "La Confesión de un asesino," p. 43.
60 Ibarlucía, "La Confesión de un asesino," p. 46.
61 Ibarlucía, "La Confesión de un asesino," p. 42.
62 *Causa 761/ESMA*, Vol. 2, pp. 257–330.
63 Supreme Council of the Armed Forces, November 21, 1984. *Causa 761/ESMA*, Vol. 6, p. 1101.

The Trial of the Juntas, 1985: "I Feel Responsible But Not Guilty, Quite Simply Because I Am Not Guilty"

Causa ESMA was only one of the cases concerning disappearances that military courts dealt with. President Alfonsín had established the primary jurisdiction of military courts over the disappearance cases in order to give the military a chance to distance itself from the disappearances by casting out those responsible for the atrocities.[64] His intention was precisely not to make these trials into "destructive trials"[65] in which the civilian courtroom becomes the site in which the military is castigated, but to allow the military to perform rituals of transition and renewal by trying their own members. Yet in the event that military courts were not taking these tasks seriously, the civilian Federal Appeals Chamber of Buenos Aires would act in a supervisory capacity and could take over cases if they were handled improperly.[66] In the proceedings against the nine former highest commanders, the Supreme Council of the Armed Forces had exhausted all the deadlines and extensions given by the Appeals Chamber in August 1984. The Supreme Council reported: "As a result of the studies performed to date, the decrees, directives, and operational orders that mandated the military against subversion are, with regard to their content and form, unobjectionable."[67] In response, the Appeals Chamber took charge of the proceedings.

The 1985 trial of the nine members of the military juntas was the most anticipated and publicized trial for disappearances. In adjudicating the responsibility of the former highest commanders, the case would have ripple effects on cases such as the *Causa ESMA* in which the defendants could point to the orders of the highest commanders. The court convicted five of the nine accused. Sentences ranged between four and a half years and life in prison. Following the evidence and analysis of the prosecution, the court portrayed the military as a strictly hierarchical organization and the commanders as the sole sources of orders. What did these findings imply for the trials of lower-ranking officers such as *Causa ESMA*? Although the court recognized that "in order to establish the mode in which the accused participated in the crimes, it is not necessary to determine the possible responsibility of the executors" because "the accused always maintained control over them,"[68] it treated the due obedience problem with considerable detail. The account of the background conditions for the crimes showed considerable sympathy for the lower-level officers:

[64] See Nino, *Radical Evil on Trial*, p. 78.

[65] Jens Meierhenrich and Devin O. Pendas, "'The Justice of My Cause Is Clear, But There's Politics to Fear': Political Trials in Theory and History," in this volume.

[66] See Nino, *Radical Evil on Trial*, p. 75.

[67] As quoted in Nino, *Radical Evil on Trial*, pp. 77–78.

[68] Cámara Nacional de Apelaciones en lo Criminal y Correccional Federal de la Capital Federal, *La Sentencia en la Causa 13/84*, Vol. II (hereinafter "*La Sentencia*"), p. 802.

The illegal orders were intertwined with the legal structure of the antisubversive struggle and were accompanied by intense indoctrination to the effect that this was the only way of fighting the revolutionary criminality. Under these conditions, *it can be presumed that many subordinates can claim the excuses of due obedience or an inevitable mistake about the legitimacy of the orders that they received.* Still, there is no doubt that there were also *some* who, given their position in the chain of command, knew about the illegal character of the orders, and there were also some who committed atrocities.[69]

The judges recommended trying the higher-level officers who "knew about the illegal character of the orders due to their position in the chain of command" and those who committed "atrocities."[70] The court specifically ordered the prosecution of officers who had been in charge of military zones or subzones, as well as those officers who had exercised "operational responsibility" in the disappearances.[71] Thus, the case that found the highest commanders criminally responsible for the disappearances established a hierarchical image of the military. It mandated other courts to investigate officers who commanded military zones and sub-zones, as well as others who had operational responsibilities. At the same time, the court's decision gestured toward the availability of the due obedience defense for junior officers.

How did the junta members themselves articulate ideas about responsibility? Both Jorge Videla, de-facto President from the coup until 1981, and Eduardo Massera, commander in chief of the Navy 1976–1978, instructed their lawyers not to make any arguments that would shift responsibility from the commanders to subordinate members of the armed forces. For the highest commanders, responsibility was not merely a concept in criminal law, but part of the patriarchal military ethos and the distinguishing mark of the superior officer: "love of responsibility has to be among the qualities of the commander."[72] Former Navy commander Eduardo Massera explained in his final statement that he had not "come here to defend myself," but "to take the responsibility for all the actions that the men of the Navy undertook."[73] This honor of being responsible was not to be confused with an admission of criminal responsibility. Massera continued: "I feel responsible but not guilty, quite simply because I am not guilty."[74] If Massera was not guilty, however, no one was: he would absorb everyone else's criminal responsibility:

If this court, in order to relieve all my subordinates of all responsibility, I repeat, in order to relieve all my subordinates of all responsibility, needs that I would have to accept that all that occurred was based on precise and concrete orders that I have given personally . . ., I also accept that. *I – and only I – have the right to sit on the bench of the accused. Having others sit on this bench would be like placing Argentina on the bench of the accused.*[75]

[69] *La Sentencia*, p. 802. Emphases added. [70] *La Sentencia*, p. 802. [71] *La Sentencia*, p. 865.
[72] Army Manual, as quoted in *El Diario del Juicio*, Vol. 21 (October 15, 1985), p. 1.
[73] Eduardo Massera, *El Diario del Juicio*, Vol. 25 (November 12, 1985), p. 7.
[74] Massera, *El Diario del Juicio*, p. 7. [75] Massera, *El Diario del Juicio*, p. 7. Emphases added.

For Massera, responsibility is an honor and a privilege. It is predicated upon one's capacity of judgment and on one's authority to leave traces in the world for which one can be held responsible. At the same time Massera's offer of responsibility is a defense of a particular vision of military order that is underwritten by a patriarchal pact of hierarchy and obedience. This pact was undermined by trials of junior officers such as the *Causa ESMA* and more generally by the junior officers' widespread perception that they had been betrayed by their superiors.

Causa ESMA, 1985: "I Was a Repressor Because This Is What My Conscience and My Superiors Ordered Me to Do"

While public attention focused on the trial of the juntas, the military court in charge of *Causa ESMA* displayed only moderate activity. Prompted by the civilian judges who oversaw the proceedings, the court took declarations without oath from forty-two officers, starting with the high-ranking admirals, and slowly working its way down to the junior officers.[76] These testimonies reveal how officers of different ranks performed responsibility and agency in front of military judges who were perceived as relatively nonthreatening, as evidenced by the questions they asked and didn't ask.

All of the officers denied the disappearances, understood as abductions followed by illegal detention, torture, and withholding of information about the detention. Some admitted that there might have been some coercion employed to get "subversives" to give names of their comrades. The officers collectively drew a picture of the distribution of responsibility within the Navy that complicates and questions the hierarchical distributions of responsibility from the trial of the juntas: according to them, the Navy as a whole participated in the fight against subversion. "All the actions of the Navy before and during my command were absolutely organic and institutional and no one can say that they were removed from the phenomenon of subversion and the battle against it," as the Navy's former Commander of Operations Pedro Santamaría put it.[77] Given the nature of this unconventional war, stated Antonio Vañek, another former Navy Commander of Operations: "each commander of the task forces was assigned a wide and almost complete liberty of action for deciding which procedures correspond to which moment, because these procedures needed to be taken almost immediately, ... they could not be asking for orders."[78] Santamaría added, "I do not recall having reprimanded any subordinate commander, and if I don't recall this, it is because they did not commit errors that would have needed to be punished. And this is because the supervision of

[76] *Causa 761/ESMA*, March 15, 1985, Vol. 6, pp. 1125–1127, Vol. 7, p. 1579.

[77] Testimony Pedro Santamaría, March 20, 1986. *Causa 761/ESMA*, Vol. 8, p. 1607.

[78] Testimony Antonio Vañek, March 22, 1984. *Causa 761/ESMA*, Vol. 2, p. 321.

the actions that were undertaken would have made it impossible that anyone could have done something illegal without it being detected."[79]

Lower-ranking officers emphasized that their actions were authorized by orders, that they had wide latitude in their operations, and that they were never reprimanded by their superiors. Rubén Chamorro, the director of the ESMA from 1975 to 1979, stated that he had received orders to "annihilate the subversion." In the unconventional war that ensued, he was guided by written general orders, which were supplemented by special verbal orders.[80] These directives were the basis for his own responsible actions: "I gave my own directives that turned out to be almost completely in verbal form because of the changing and unforeseeable nature of the events."[81] The form of supervision was dictated by the circumstances, Chamorro explained:

> I exercised a constant supervision. Normally, I was present at all the planning meetings before the operations, as well as at the post-operation meetings upon return. I constantly received information about ongoing operations; often ... supervising their development through means of communications and in some special cases being present at the place of action. In this way, I could ensure the compliance with the given orders; and, as the commander, I could modify them if necessary. I could control the development of the action. I also supervised almost all of the interrogations and constantly visited the installations of the Task Unit 3.3.2.[82]

Chamorro took pride in his control over his troops much in the same way that Massera tied his own dignity and honor to his responsibility.[83] Yet in both cases, the assumed responsibility is not criminal responsibility: both denied any acts for which they could be held criminally responsible. There were no deaths in the ESMA, Chamorro maintained, and interrogations were never conducted with physical pressure.[84] Suspected "subversives" were brought to the ESMA and kept there for at most a few hours, he claimed. The suspects were interrogated and they made a "spontaneous confession," decided to collaborate with the Navy in the "fight against the subversives," or were handed over to the police.[85] Chamorro emphatically claimed a responsibility that resonated with his military ethos but made no reference to the acts that he was accused of. Instead, his assumption of responsibility in front of his former military colleagues was a vindication of his own agency and military honor.

79 Testimony Pedro Santamaría, March 20, 1986, p. 1611.

80 Testimony Rubén Chamorro, April 22, 1986. *Causa 761/ESMA*, Vol. 8, p. 1761.

81 Testimony Rubén Chamorro, April 22, 1986, p. 1761.

82 Testimony Rubén Chamorro, April 22, 1986, p. 1787. Chamorro died in June 1986, less than three months after making these statements. It is possible that it was apparent that he would not be able to stand trial.

83 Testimony Rubén Chamorro, April 22, 1986, p. 1775.

84 Testimony Rubén Chamorro, April 22, 1986, p. 1771; and Testimony Rubén Chamorro, February 29, 1984. *Causa 761/ESMA*, Vol. 2, p. 269.

85 Testimony Rubén Chamorro, April 22, 1986, pp. 1771, 1778.

The junior officers – many of them on active duty – were not only concerned with the reputation of the institution, but also with their own careers. They did not want to defend themselves by shifting the blame to their superiors. Juan Carlos Rolón declared: "I have participated in operations of war that were ordered by my superiors, and if I have committed any violation of the Military Code of Justice or any other norm, I was never told about it. This is why I don't understand why I am facing this court."[86] Jorge Acosta, who had been in charge of the interrogations and torture as ESMA chief of intelligence, also emphasized the institutional organization of the violence but insisted on not merely being an obedient cog: "I was a repressor because this is what my conscience and my superiors ordered me to do. No one can soil our good name and honor."[87] For Acosta, individual agency and institutional structures reinforce one another without adding up to criminal responsibility. Overall, the defendants' testimonies in the *Causa ESMA* reveal no shortage of claims to agency and responsibility: the officers speak of agency, pride, and control over their actions within a hierarchical institution and under close supervision, but they do not offer any acknowledgment of individual or institutional wrongdoing.

Causa ESMA, 1986–1987: After the Full Stop

In late 1986, the conflict between military and civilian judges in *Causa ESMA* escalated. In December, the Supreme Council of the Armed Forces cited 15 retired admirals to testify as potential defendants. The statements were short and terse, spanning only two to three pages per admiral.[88] On December 23, 1986, the day after the last of these declarations, the Supreme Council decided that there was not sufficient evidence that any of the accused gave, transmitted, or executed orders as had been described in the judgment against the juntas. Rather, the Supreme Council asserted, the accused had legal and legitimate authority for their actions and supervised their subordinates at all times to ensure that no excesses were committed.[89] In response, the Appeals Chamber prepared to take control of the case.

This transfer of jurisdiction from a military to a civilian court took place amid a rapidly changing political context. On December 2, 1986, the Federal Appeals Chamber that supervised *Causa ESMA* had convicted General Ramón Camps and four other military and police officers of participation in the disappearances.[90] On December 5, President Alfonsín sent a bill to Congress that was meant to limit the number and duration of the remaining trials.

86 Testimony Juan Carlos Rolón, January 12, 1987. *Causa 761/ESMA*, Vol. 12, p. 2686.
87 Testimony Jorge Eduardo Acosta, June 21, 1986. *Causa 761/ESMA*, Vol. 9, p. 1907.
88 See *Causa 761/ESMA*, Vol. 12, pp. 2461–2553.
89 Supreme Council of the Armed Forces, Resolution, December 23, 1986. *Causa 761/ESMA*, Vol. 12, pp. 2555–2558.
90 See Nino, *Radical Evil on Trial*, p. 93.

It established a sixty-day deadline for initiating criminal trials for the disappearances.[91] Past this deadline, only persons who had either been cited as accused or were fugitives from justice could still be subject to trial. The so-called *Full Stop Law* was passed on December 23, 1986. Instead of limiting trials, the law prompted a new frenzy of cases: civilian courts became much stricter in their supervision of the military courts and took over many cases. In January 1987, human rights organizations filed criminal complaints naming 650 persons "responsible for state terrorism."[92] Due to the *Full Stop Law*, *Causa ESMA* was no longer a standout case, but became part of an avalanche of cases that the legal system as well as the public were not prepared to handle.

On January 19, 1987, the Supreme Council of the Armed Forces issued its final report to the Federal Appeals Chamber in the *Causa ESMA*, refusing to prosecute anyone in the Navy for the disappearances at the ESMA.[93] On February 4, 1987, the Federal Appeals Chamber formally took control of the case, chided the Supreme Council for failing its duties, and suggested that the military court was at least guilty of negligence, if not obstruction of justice.[94] On February 20, a mere two weeks later, the assigned prosecutors Julio Strassera and Luis Moreno Ocampo, who had already prosecuted the juntas, filed the indictment. Relying on the decision in the *Camps* case, they emphasized that due obedience is only available to those officers who could not know that their actions contributed to the torture and disappearance of persons. Working under the time pressure imposed by the *Full Stop Law*, they matched the short profiles of 286 victims with equally formal accounts of the positions and duties of 34 officers who served at the ESMA or in positions of influencing events at the ESMA. The prosecutors attributed responsibility to higher-ranking officers by matching each case with the suspects who in were positions of authority over the site at which the violations occurred at the relevant time. The prosecutors relied on the officers' own emphatic assumptions of organized and hierarchical responsibility.

Upon receiving the indictment, the court immediately cited seventeen officers to testify as potential defendants. Due to the *Full Stop Law*, this was not the only case in which civilian courts suddenly cited military officers to testify. Instead of a slow trickle of citations and indictments, the military experienced a flood of demands from the judiciary. The civilian courts were anxious to assert their authority. When six retired admirals asked for a postponement of their court date in the *Causa ESMA*, the court did not hesitate to declare them "in

[91] Law 23.492, December 23, 1986, available at www1.umn.edu/humanrts/research/argentina/ley23-492.html.

[92] Request for the indictment of 650 persons responsible for state terrorism, January 1987. *Causa 761/ESMA*, Vol. 12, pp. 2619–2665.

[93] Supreme Council of the Armed Forces, Report. January 19, 1987. *Causa 761/ESMA*, Vol. 13, pp. 2735–2737.

[94] Federal Appeals Chamber of Buenos Aires, Resolution. February 4, 1987. *Causa 761/ESMA*, Vol. 13, pp. 2866–2867.

contempt" and ask the Federal Police for their capture.[95] The Court indicted 17 of the 34 officers named by the prosecution[96] and ordered pre-trial detention for 12 of them.[97] For the first time since the beginnings of the post-dictatorship trials, a civilian court detained active duty officers.[98] These developments, triggered as much by the deadlines of the *Full Stop Law* as by the intransigence of the military courts, were met with considerable anxiety.[99] While the defense lawyers suggested, via conservative newspapers, that the testimonies by ESMA survivors were unreliable and contradictory,[100] government officials and liberal journalists alike worried about possible confrontations triggered by active duty officers called to testify in civilian courts.[101] In *Causa ESMA*, the citations were met with limited confrontations and evasions: in addition to the six admirals who dragged their feet but hurried to the court when declared "in contempt," two junior officers refused to testify. Raúl Vildoza, a former ESMA associate director, and Pedro Horacio Estrada, a junior officer, were declared fugitives from justice on March 23, 1987.[102]

When civilian courts cited active duty junior officers, they breached two norms that the military insisted on: first, military officers were adamant that for military acts, only military judges could be the "natural judges" as guaranteed by Art. 18 of the Argentine Constitution.[103] Second, the military demanded that junior officers, and especially active duty junior officers, should be sheltered from individual accountability. Junior officers, in turn, feared for their careers. Since the law did not allow a due obedience defense for "atrocious and aberrant" acts, they could no longer expect that their superiors could absorb all responsibility. The commanders stressed that they supported all of the officers who would be indicted, but junior officers explicitly demanded *protection from* trials, not *help in* the trials.[104] The ire of the junior officers was not only directed against the courts, but also "against the

95 Federal Appeals Chamber of Buenos Aires, *Causa 761/ESMA*, Vol. 16, p. 3436.

96 List of Defendants, February 25, 1987. *Causa 761/ESMA*, Vol. 17, p. 3496.

97 See "Fundamento de las prisiones dictatdas en la *Causa ESMA*," *La Razón*, March 1, 1987.

98 See Bradley Graham, "Added Rights Cases Disturbing Argentine Military," *Washington Post*, March 2, 1987; "Fundamentos de las prisiones dictadas en la *Causa ESMA*," *La Razón*, March 1, 1987.

99 See Martín Granovsky, "Siete Días de politica," *La Razón*, March 1, 1987.

100 "Estimó Siro de Martini que los testimonios son contradictorios," *La Prensa*, March 2, 1987.

101 See, for example, Granovsky, "Siete Días de politica"; Graham, "Added Rights Cases Disturbing Argentine Military"; James Neilson, "La Hora de los Almirantes," *La Semana*, March 4, 1987.

102 "El próximo lunes concluirá las indagatorias de la *Causa ESMA*," *La Razón*, March 7, 1987; *Causa ESMA*, March 23, 1987. Vol. 19, p. 3958; "Podrían ser dados de baja dos marinos declarados 'en rebeldía,' " *La Razón*, April 1, 1987.

103 See, for example, Osiris G. Villegas, "Cuando los juzgadores no son los jueces naturales," *La Prensa*, March 17, 1987.

104 See "Finaliza hoy la ronda de citaciones por la Escuela de Mecánica de la Armada," *La Prensa*, March 11, 1987.

high ranks of the forces, who are accused of 'weakness' in facing the civilian government."[105]

Civilian courts became an arena in which conflicts within the military as well as between the armed forces and the government were played out. Ascriptions of responsibility occupied a central place in these contentions: The government's initial strategy for limiting trials had centered on limiting responsibility of junior officers for past violence. At the time of the trials, the government and the military commanders were also keenly interested in military obedience in the present. Junior officers who found that their obedience in the past was not honored became more inclined to disobey in the present. Beginning in mid-March 1987, there were "almost permanent assemblies"[106] and "meetings" in which officers "analyzed the situation."[107] As fault lines between the junior officers and their superiors deepened, observers feared that the "state of deliberation"[108] would turn into disobedience. A group of retired admirals shared their fear that trials of junior officers for past violence would incite disobedience in the present: Punishment for junior officers "who followed military orders in a context of war" would "gravely damage the principles of discipline and subordination" within the Navy.[109]

April 1987, Military Rebellion: "The Commanders and Officers of the Armed Forces Only Have One Obligation: To Obey the Orders of Their Superiors and of the Highest Commander"

On March 7, 1987, newspapers reported that 218 officers were cited to testify in civilian courts.[110] By March 15, 39 officers were in pre-trial detention, another 12 officers were convicted of crimes committed during the dictatorship, and nine were fugitives from justice.[111] By March 25, 400 officers were affected by the trials, a third of them on active duty.[112] By mid-April, newspaper reports relayed rumors about pardons and amnesty laws.[113] Ramón Camps, the former chief of the Buenos Aires Police who had just been sentenced to twenty-five years in prison, wrote an editorial in the conservative newspaper *La Prensa*, asking, ominously, "How much longer, Alfonsín, will you abuse our patience?"[114]

[105] "Finaliza hoy la ronda de citaciones por la Escuela de Mecánica de la Armada."

[106] Jesús Iglesias Rouco, "La hora de la verdad," *La Prensa*, March 17, 1987.

[107] "Finaliza hoy la ronda de citaciones por la Escuela de Mecánica de la Armada."

[108] See Daniel Lupa, "¿Juicio político a la Cámara Federal?" *La Prensa*, March 20, 1987; Jorge Raventos, "¿Qué pasa con los militares?" *La Semana*, March 25, 1987.

[109] "Consejo de Almirantes 1975–1981" [Advertisement], *La Prensa*, March 20, 1987.

[110] "Formuló nuevas citaciones la Cámara de La Plata," *Clarín*, March 7, 1987.

[111] "Situación de los detenidos, procesados y condenados, y solicitudes de extradición," *La Prensa*, March 15, 1987.

[112] Raventos, "¿Qué pasa con los militares?"

[113] See Claudia Acuña, "Vision military sobre los juicios," *La Razón*, April 16 1987.

[114] Ramón J. A. Camps, "Alfonsinaria," *La Prensa*, April 16, 1987.

Camps and his fellow generals did not trigger the rebellion that followed, nor were they able to control it. On April 15, 1987, Ernesto Guillermo Barreiro, a junior officer in the Army, refused to be flown to Córdoba to testify at a trial about the disappearances. He was immediately discharged from duty.[115] Although Barreiro was not the first officer who refused to testify, he was the first who made his refusal public and thereby forced his peers to choose between siding with him and obeying their superiors. Barreiro explained that he took the decision "personally, on the basis of my own convictions" and did not want to "change the constitutional order."[116] This was not a coup, but a rebellion against the superior officers' refusal or inability to protect him and others from the civilian courts. Barreiro's disobedience caught on: the officer whose task it was to take Barreiro to the court date declared that he was not in a position to force him.[117] What started as a "military insubordination" in Córdoba soon spread to other units.[118] Aldo Rico, a junior officer stationed in the interior of the country, convinced some of his troops to follow him to Buenos Aires and occupy the Army's Infantry School.[119] At a press conference, the rebellious officers declared "no one is in the position to put down [the rebellion] because no one is going to obey them" since "we believe that this is a just cause."[120] The commander of the Third Army Corps, it was reported, "found himself virtually deprived of his command since he ordered the detention of the ex-Major Barreiro."[121] The Third Army Corps had operated the clandestine detention center *La Perla* during the dirty war, and Barreiro had served as an intelligence officer and chief interrogator in torture sessions.[122]

The civilian courts' insistence that junior officers like Barreiro should be legally responsible for their violence during the dictatorship triggered a crisis in which junior officers acted on their own account in the post-dictatorship context, exercised disobedience, and defiantly assumed responsibility for their acts of rebellion. Junior officers like Barreiro reemployed different discourses of responsibility: they saw the pacts of obedience that tied them to their superiors unravel, and they responded with disobedience. They saw themselves interpellated by the law as responsible agents, and they responded with spectacular displays of agency, discourses of conscience, and proclamations of responsibility. In the 1987 rebellion, legal and military responsibility discourses were not only challenged but also cited, recycled, and mobilized for new purposes.

115 "Fue dado de baja un mayor que se rebeló ante un llamado judicial," *La Razón*, April 16, 1987.
116 "Fue dado de baja un mayor que se rebeló ante un llamado judicial."
117 "Fue dado de baja un mayor que se rebeló ante un llamado judicial."
118 "Expectativa en las unidades militares," *La Razón*, April 17, 1987.
119 "Las Órdenes de Alfonsín," *La Razón*, April 17, 1987.
120 "Hablan los sublevados," Unspecified Newspaper, April 17, 1987.
121 "Expectativa en las unidades militares."
122 "Ernesto Guillermo Barreiro: La fuga del mayor interrogador," *La Razón*, April 19, 1987.

Analyses of the rebellion have largely focused on the demands of the officers: the rebels rejected the trials for the disappearances as unconstitutional, demanded an amnesty, and insisted on the honor of the armed forces as an institution.[123] Did President Alfonsín give in to the demands of the rebels when he proposed the *Due Obedience Law*? I suggest that a focus on the performative force of the rebellion helps to understand the *Due Obedience Law* as a more complex response to a crisis: the rebellion unfolded as a performance of disobedience in direct response to demands that junior officers be responsible for their past actions. The officers' disobedience in the present led the President to reconsider the value of individual responsibility and conscience-based disobedience in the military. These officers did not disobey the 1976 orders to detain, torture, and kill; but they disobeyed the 1985 orders to answer to civilian courts. In response to this parody of liberal subjecthood, Alfonsín stressed the value of obedience in the present and grew increasingly willing to honor obedience to orders in the past. In a message to the nation on April 16, 1987, President Alfonsín declared that "democracy means liberty, but it also means order. It means the guaranteed and unrestricted exercise of all the rights inherent in the human condition, but it also means the complete submission, without exceptions, to the judicial system."[124] More specifically: "The commanders and officers of the armed forces only have one obligation: to obey the orders of their superiors and of the highest commander. This is why they have received the ... weapons that belong to the nation."[125] In this speech, given two days before the meeting at which Alfonsín is alleged to have made concessions to the rebels, Alfonsín promised "we will reaffirm in concrete actions the criteria for responsibility that will allow for the definitive reconciliation" of the country.[126] Even before the meeting with the rebellious officers, Alfonsín understood the rebellion as an embodiment of disobedience and agency that was dangerous for the country and its democratic institutions. His response was to ask for present obedience in return for offering a legal fiction honoring past obedience.

Due Obedience, Revisited, 1987: "Article 1 of This Law Denies the Human Quality to Certain Citizens, [and] Subtracts Them from the Realm of Criminal Law"

The 1987 military rebellion changed the way that politicians and courts approached the question of obedience. The crisis was widely interpreted as a breakdown of hierarchy and obedience, making "due obedience" seem a natural solution to the problem defined as disobedience. The discourse of obedience, order, and hierarchy, long favored by the military commanders and their conservative civilian allies, started to appeal to wider audiences.

123 "Hablan los sublevados." 124 "La democracia no se negocia," *La Razón*, April 18, 1987.
125 "La democracia no se negocia." 126 "La democracia no se negocia."

Conservatives were alarmed that the crisis showed signs of "anarchy" and "fragmented the chain of command."[127] Rebel leader Aldo Rico claimed that he only "assumed the command and responsibility" during the rebellion because he saw "the fundamental disorder" at the Infantry School.[128] Others saw that the most urgent task was to "re-establish the functioning of the chain of command and the subordination to strict compliance" because "this constitutes the cardinal principle of military organization."[129] The government extended this discourse of order and subordination from the present into the past: in his dictum on the due obedience excuse, Attorney General Juan Gauna argued that democratic ideals of obedience should not be applied to the crimes of the dictatorship: "... the rule of law mandates that we base the decision not on the concept of obedience that is suitable in a democracy that respects individual dignity, but on the concepts that regrettably had validity at the time the acts were committed."[130] Gauna concluded that most officers could not question or modify orders but "were only able to transmit or execute orders" and should therefore not be held responsible for their actions.[131] President Alfonsín declared at the conclusion of the crisis, "we are not against the military as long as they fulfill their duties."[132]

Initially, the President's advisors hoped that the Supreme Court would conveniently define due obedience abstractly and generously in its appeals judgment in the *Camps* case.[133] Yet Supreme Court Justices declared that a general redefinition of due obedience was the task of Congress, not the courts.[134] Meanwhile, the Supreme Court used the procedural means at its disposal to stop the pending trials.[135] In the *Causa ESMA*, the dates for the public portion of the trial had been set for April 23 onward.[136] Less than forty-eight hours before the scheduled opening of the public trial, the Supreme Court demanded the complete case file in order to decide on a jurisdictional question, thereby suspending the proceedings in *Causa ESMA*.[137]

Congress passed the *Due Obedience Law* on June 8, 1987. The law established an irrefutable presumption that officers below a certain rank "cannot be punished" for crimes in connection with the dirty war "because

127 Sergio Crivelli, "Un panorama poco alentador," *La Prensa*, April 23, 1987.
128 " 'Soy el único responsable,' afirmó Rico ante el juez," *Clarín*, April 26, 1987.
129 Italo A. Luder, "Autocrítica e integración nacional," *Clarín*, March 8, 1987.
130 "La eximacion de causas penales a oficiales y jefes," *La Prensa*, May 14, 1987.
131 "La eximacion de causas penales a oficiales y jefes."
132 "Los discursos de Alfonsín ante el pueblo en Plaza de Mayo," *La Razón*, April 20, 1987.
133 Carlos Santiago Nino, "The Duty to Punish Past Abuses of Human Rights Put Into Context: The Case of Argentina," *Yale Law Journal*, Vol. 100 (1991), p. 2629.
134 "Precision sobre obediencia debida," *Clarín*, May 2, 1987.
135 See Nino, "The Duty to Punish Past Abuses," pp. 2628–2629.
136 *Causa 761/ESMA*, April 9, 1987, Vol. 19, p. 4019.
137 Supreme Court, Resolution, April 23, 1987, *Causa 761/ESMA*, Vol. 20, p. 4260; for reactions, see: See Alberto Riobó, "Los motives de la resolución," *La Razón*, April 22, 1987; "A 48 horas del juicio oral, la Corte requirió la *Causa ESMA*," *La Razón*, April 22, 1987.

they have acted under due obedience."[138] Mid-ranking officers who have not commanded military zones or subzones were presumed to not have acted with responsibility unless a court established the opposite within thirty days. Where the obedience stipulations of the law apply, "it is legally established that the respective persons acted under coercion and subordination to higher authority and in fulfillment of orders, without the ability or possibility of scrutinizing the appropriateness or legitimacy of these orders, or of exercising opposition or resistance."[139] The only crimes to which this presumption did not apply were those that were thought to have been committed on private initiative: rape, the abduction and illegal adoption of children of the disappeared, and fraud involving real estate.[140] Thus, the law stipulated for groups of persons united by nothing but their formal military rank that they acted under specified circumstances that would establish their irresponsibility. The law preempted any individual assessment of responsibility in court. After all, the crisis to which the law was meant to provide a response was triggered by the demand that junior officers testify in court, not by the conviction of any of them.

The *Due Obedience Law* resonated with the post-crisis emphasis on hierarchy and obedience as the pillars of military order. Yet the junior officers destined to benefit from the law did not uniformly embrace it. The law offered them impunity on the basis of a blanket excuse, but not a justification.[141] Norberto Cozzani, one of the two convicted junior officers, commented on the due obedience project in process: "If due obedience, conceived as the irresistible compliance with irrational orders from the highest commanders, is the path towards denying the criminal accountability of all the subordinate officers, one does a disservice to the truth and enshrines an unjustified stain that affects the entire armed forces."[142] "My conscience," he added, "does not allow me to accept liberty at the price of this moral abandonment."[143] Never, Cozzani told the reporters, did he receive "any order from my superiors that implied the execution of a criminal plan, nor was I forced by any irresistible force to commit actions that my moral conscience disapproved of."[144] Cozzani's problem was not that the law offered impunity for acts previously considered "atrocious or aberrant," but that benefiting from the law, he would see himself redescribed as a fearful and obedient soldier rather than a conscientious and responsible agent.

The representatives of the victims in *Causa ESMA* challenged the *Due Obedience Law* as unconstitutional. While these complaints were being considered, the Appellate Chamber had to determine who among the remaining

138 Law 23.521, *Ley de Obediencia Debida*, Art. 1, section 1, available at www1.umn.edu/humanrts/research/argentina/ley23-521.html.

139 Law 23.521, Art. 1 section 2. 140 Law 23.521, Art. 2.

141 See Austin, "A Plea for Excuses."

142 "Un cabo rechazó la obediencia debida," *Clarín*, May 16, 1987.

143 "Un cabo rechazó la obediencia debida." 144 "Un cabo rechazó la obediencia debida."

defendants had decision-making capacity according to the requirements of the *Due Obedience Law*. The prosecution argued that all the remaining defendants had held positions in which they participated in the making of decisions and had authority to give orders. They took the defendants' statements made to the Supreme Council of the Armed Forces and converted the proud claims of agency and historical responsibility into imputations of criminal responsibility:

> To think that a commander who gives an order according to a directive received from his superiors acted like a telephone operator who simply relays a message would reveal a fundamental misunderstanding about the functioning of the military organization.
>
> In *Causa 13*,[145] it was proven that personnel of the Navy stationed at the ESMA. illegally detained persons, many of whom were tortured. It was also proven that these actions were ordered and authorized by the Commander in Chief of the Navy.[146]

The prosecutors conceptualized the Navy as a well-organized system devoted to the commission of crimes.[147] Regular reports and supervision ensured that even spontaneous actions on the ground were integrated into an institutional system:

> This form of command constitutes active conduct and not an omission because it implies authorizing subordinates to commit certain acts, providing them with support personnel, notifying other forces so that they would not interfere in the operations, and providing logistical support that was necessary for executing the tasks.
>
> In addition, had the commander given a different order, the subordinate personnel would have changed their form of conduct. There are no records showing that at any point orders were given to prevent torture.[148]

On the basis of these considerations, the prosecution asked the court to uphold all the remaining indictments because the officers had sufficient discretion and power to be held responsible. The defense lawyers contested that none of the accused had such decision-making capacity because responsibility for military matters was located at the top, in the person of the commander in chief. The court mainly followed the prosecution arguments and methodology:

> All the accused stated affirmatively that the chain of command was functioning properly, that they knew what was done in the ESMA, that this [conduct] followed orders that were given, and that the faithful compliance with these orders was closely supervised. At the same time, all those subordinates who are suspect of having executed the acts and are excluded from this trial for legal reasons have corroborated that all they did was in

145 The trial of the juntas.

146 Julio Strassera and Luis Moreno Ocampo, June 30, 1987. *Causa 761/ESMA*, Vol. 22, pp. 4488–4489.

147 Strassera and Moreno Ocampo, June 30, 1987, pp. 4490–4492.

148 Strassera and Moreno Ocampo, June 30, 1987, p. 4493.

compliance with what was ordered through the regular chain of command and that the School [ESMA] was closely supervised by these authorities.[149]

From these observations, the Court concluded:

It is prima facie proven in this case that in the Navy School of the Mechanics, a large number of persons suspected of having some link to subversion were kept in clandestine detention. Many of these persons were tortured in order to obtain information from them. The fate of the vast majority of these detainees is unknown. *These facts in conjunction with the wide and emphatic assumptions of responsibility in the statements of the defendants lead to the conclusion that these acts could be attributed to them.*[150]

The Court only revoked the indictments of the two lowest-ranking officers who were still on trial. These constructions of responsibility were appealed to the Supreme Court: the victims' representatives objected to the *Due Obedience Law*'s stipulations of irresponsibility.[151]

The representatives of the victims objected to the *Due Obedience Law* on philosophical and political, rather than on purely pragmatic, grounds. Their lawyer Alicia Oliveira claimed that the law:

[P]uts the notion of "passive or blind obedience" into operation and converts officers, sub-officers, and soldiers of our armed forces and security forces into automata determined to "comply with every order, however exorbitant it may seem." This acceptance is ontologically and ethically improper in a democratic regime.

It is obvious that behind the supposed state of ignorance or of irresistible physical force, [this law] penetrates irreversibly into the concept of the intelligent free will, a human will that can incur errors concerning its objects or concerning the legality of its action, or can suffer a restriction of its area of self-determination, but it still differs from the mere fact of nature and marks the difference between the subject that perceives and the reality that transcends it. *Article 1 of this law denies the human quality to certain citizens, [and] subtracts them from the realm of criminal law.*[152]

Oliveira argued that this conceptualization of responsibility implies a concept of obedience that a democratic society cannot live with – neither in relationship to the past nor to the present. While Oliveira objected that such subjectivities were not suitable for democratic citizens, Attorney General Jaime Malamud Goti defended the *Due Obedience Law* and its generous application on political grounds.[153] Malamud Goti identified "decision-making capacity" with a position of power in which the defendant had "liberty of action" [*libertad de determinación*].[154] Malamud Goti's standard for reconstructing

[149] Strassera and Moreno Ocampo, June 30, 1987, pp. 4526–4527.

[150] Strassera and Moreno Ocampo, June 30, 1987, p. 4528. Emphases added.

[151] *Causa 761/ ESMA*, Vol. 21, pp. 4265–4270, 4271–4282, 4283–4302, 4303–4311, 4314–4319.

[152] Alicia Oliveira, *Plantea Inconstitucionalidad*, June 12, 1987. *Causa 761/ESMA*, p. 4314. Emphases added.

[153] Jaime Malamud Goti, December 24, 1987. *Causa 761/ESMA*, Vol. 23, pp. 4732–4737.

[154] Malamud Goti, December 24, 1987, p. 4735.

the defendants as responsible persons who can be accused of crimes was not their *unforced participation* in crimes, but their own initiative and *individual contribution* to the system:

> The decision-making capacity is established by proving that the accused effected an individual contribution to the perfection of the criminal plan elaborated by the commanders in chief, thus distinguishing this concept from the mere possibility of executing orders with more or less efficiency.[155]

In Malamud Goti's interpretation, only former Navy Commanders of Operations Antonio Vañek and Julio Antonio Torti were deemed to have possessed the power and decision-making authority required for criminal responsibility under the *Due Obedience Law*. According to the Navy's own regulations, the Commanders of Operations had "the specific authority to issue the norms that were necessary for putting the strategic directives of the commander in chief into practice, and to direct the entire Navy in the execution of operations with the alleged goal of fighting subversion."[156] All other defendants, in contrast, "have not contributed anything to the specification of the perverse methods devised by their superiors."[157]

In his defense of the *Due Obedience Law*, Malamud Goti stressed the political context:

> One should not ignore the fact that the crimes that have occurred are of an exceptional seriousness, and that a wide sector of our society is involved in them through action or omission, directly or indirectly. These facts oblige the law to ensure that only the most responsible persons are judged, leading *to this situation that some citizens today wrongly consider an abdication of justice, but which is in reality the most efficient way of achieving the strengthening of the institutions that guarantee the conciliation and liberty of the Argentine citizens*. This should be acknowledged as the highest pursuit of this ideal of justice that is so frequently invoked in the writings of the appellants.[158]

Malamud Goti reminded the Supreme Court that the continued existence of democracy in the face of military threats was a basic precondition for achieving ideals of justice.[159] There was no suggestion from Malamud Goti that the *Due Obedience Law* captured a moral truth about the dictatorship. Instead, the law was presented as a compromise designed to maintain the conditions that would make broader social change possible.

The Supreme Court followed the position of the Attorney General in argument and result: It upheld only the indictments of Vañek and Torti. How much agency must an officer have had to be held responsible? The Supreme Court, following the Attorney General, raised the bar considerably:

[155] Malamud Goti, December 24, 1987, p. 4735.
[156] Malamud Goti, December 24, 1987, p. 4736.
[157] Malamud Goti, December 24, 1987, p. 4736.
[158] Malamud Goti, December 24, 1987, pp. 4733–4734. Emphases added.
[159] For a similar argument, see Nino, "The Duty to Punish Past Abuses," p. 2620.

The concept of "decision-making capacity" that is also used by the law is connected to the faculties possessed by commanders who, in exercising their command, could autonomously elaborate and decide on the application of directives that were a separate contribution to the order from their superiors and that would contain illegal authorizations unconnected to any necessity of putting a general plan of operations devised by the superiors into practice.[160]

The Supreme Court focused judicial attention away from acts that were already ordered by the junta members. Each defendant was held responsible only insofar as he individually added new elements of injustice to the preexisting practices and orders: the Supreme Court looked for liberal subjects who "autonomously" decided on orders, and it could not find them in the Navy. The commonplace "mere participation" in the disappearances went excused as the standard for responsibility shifted from will and agency to a hypothetical autonomous contribution. Obedience to immoral orders became retroactively acceptable. More than a few junior officers openly objected to the democratic regime, and any suggestion that they do not have to obey orders they deem immoral would thus have endangered the fragile civilian control over the military. These responsibility ascriptions show a marked shift in discourse in response to the 1987 rebellion: whereas the immediate post-dictatorship discourse stressed responsibility and morality, the post-1987 legislation and government position emphasized obedience over agency and subordination over conscience. For the political elites, controlling the trials and the military hinged on reasserting a hierarchal pact of obedience and responsibility.

CONCLUSION

Criminal trials for state violence are political: in evaluating past atrocities, they also affirm ideas about responsibility, morality, and obedience that can become foundational for democratic politics. As public arenas in which norms are debated, witnesses testify to violations, and defendants can be found guilty and subjected to criminal punishment, these trials are mechanisms for social shaming, assertion of norms, and exclusion of those identified as perpetrators. In Argentina in the 1980s, the government repeatedly tried to limit the scope and duration of trials because it was worried that too many trials lasting too long would provoke a military backlash. Yet the ability of the executive to curtail or steer the trials turned out to be limited to redefining the standards for criminal responsibility for specific sets of crimes. Responsibility ascriptions were widely understood to be flexible, political, and mechanisms to regulate the number of possible trials. The deep societal disagreements about the military dictatorship, disappearances, and torture were not directly addressed. Instead, the President, Congress, and the courts kept modifying the conditions under which officers could be held responsible for these actions.

[160] Malamud Goti, December 24, 1987, p. 4741.

In reconstructing the story of *Causa ESMA* and its contexts through the lens of responsibility, I highlighted the ways in which discussions and invocations of responsibility produce meanings in excess of the narrow issue at hand. Responsibility and obedience are categories through which law understands persons, and through which persons understand their roles and their place in institutions. The interaction between categories of responsibility and persons described as (ir)responsible can be complex, messy, and unpredictable:[161] on the one hand, subjectivities and accounts of one's actions are shaped by norms.[162] In their testimonies, junior officers drew upon the prevailing legal constructions of responsibility to make sense of their actions, assess the consequences they would face, and make demands on their superiors or the courts. Yet junior officers also reemployed these constructions to challenge courts and their superiors. They were "at one acted upon and acting."[163] The new legal constructions of junior officers – first as active agents of violence, and then as coerced and obedient – responded to political demands and changed the way that junior officers thought of themselves and acted. Some officers accepted trials and punishment as appropriate.[164] Others reacted differently: seeing that they could no longer benefit from a pact of obedience and superior responsibility, they felt betrayed by their commanding officers and disobeyed them – in the present.

Responsibility means different things to different people. Rather than finding an "essence" or definition of the term, this chapter has traced some of the things that actors in Argentina's dirty war trials did *with* responsibility. Given that responsibility is open to different interpretations and uses, we can expect cracks and tensions in the ways that people *do* and *talk about* responsibility. Some of these cracks are easily decried as hypocritical: Ernesto Barreiro, the junior officer who told the nation that his conscience mandated him to maintain his honor and refuse to testify in court, later fled the scene of the rebellion when he feared that he would be captured. His initial gesture of military honor did not match his inglorious exit from the rebellion. More broadly, many junior officers wanted a broad vindication of their active participation in violence. At the same time, they expected that their superiors would continue to take paternalistic responsibility for them. When the 1987 *Due Obedience Law* was passed, officers were conflicted: although a number of them resented being portrayed as unthinking or coerced soldiers, many welcomed the wide and collective impunity that the law afforded to them.

The President and many citizens, however, were no less torn in their expectations about responsibility: they did not want to sanction obedience to

[161] See Hacking, *The Social Construction of What?*

[162] See Butler, *Giving an Account of Oneself.*

[163] Judith Butler, *Precarious Life: The Power of Mourning and Violence* (London: Verso, 2004), p. 16.

[164] Ibarlucía, "La Confesión de un asesino."

criminal orders in the past. Yet they insisted that the military obey the President as the Commander in Chief in the present. The problem was not only that their responsibility constructions leaked from the past into the present and back. More fundamentally, citizens and governments of many democratic states expect that the military obey them, but they also reserve the right to be appalled when this obedience leads to violence that they later disapprove of. They advocate for laws that penalize obedience to immoral orders in order to "express the symbolic importance of individual accountability" although they know "that soldiers will in fact follow orders, whether legal or illegal."[165] The stress on individual responsibility for atrocities after World War II coincides with the rise of organizations that do not in fact provide the grounds on which such agency and responsibility practices could flourish. Thinking of responsibility ascriptions as social practices that are bound up with accounts of the self, fantasies of agency, institutional norms, and ideas about citizenship is a first step to critically assessing the work that responsibility ascriptions are made to do in trials and in accounts of past violence.

[165] Minow, "Living Up to Rules," p. 54.

13

The *Microsoft* Case as a Political Trial

William H. Page and John E. Lopatka

The government's monopolization case against Microsoft was not a political trial in the same sense as the historic prosecutions of enemies of the state, like activists, revolutionaries, or ousted despots – what Jens Meierhenrich and Devin Pendas elsewhere in this volume call *destructive* trials.[1] The government's prosecution of Eugene Debs under the Sherman Act, among other laws, for disobeying an injunction against the Pullman Strike of 1894 might have been political in this sense.[2] *Microsoft* was different. The government's case – actually two cases, one brought by the federal government and one by a group of states – charged that Microsoft had impeded the distribution of software products that might have undermined the Windows monopoly of personal computer operating systems.[3] Netscape's Navigator web browser and Sun Microsystems's Java technologies were "middleware," applications software with platform capabilities. Navigator and Java had the potential, according to the government, to develop into an applications platform to rival Windows. Software developers could then have written their programs to the middleware platform, which could run on any underlying operating system, not just Windows. Microsoft allegedly thwarted this threat by deploying a host of anticompetitive practices that prevented Navigator and Java from gaining the critical mass of usage that would have made them a credible platform.

As technical as this summary may sound, *Microsoft* was a political case after all, for three reasons: notoriety, ideology, and interest-group pressure, all of

[1] Jens Meierhenrich and Devin O. Pendas, "'The Justice of My Cause Is Clear, But There's Politics to Fear': Political Trials in Theory and History," in this volume.

[2] Cf. Gerard N. Magliocca, "Constitutional False Positives and the Populist Movement," *Notre Dame Law Review*, Vol. 81 (2005), pp. 821, 860–864.

[3] William H. Page and John E. Lopatka, *The Microsoft Case: Antitrust, High Technology, and Consumer Welfare* (Chicago: University of Chicago Press, 2007), pp. 28–32.

which played a role in its prosecution and resolution. First, *Microsoft* was a *cause célèbre*. It vilified and threatened to dismember the most successful corporation in the "new economy"[4] and consequently aroused intense emotions in popular discourse and intense scrutiny in the popular press.[5] In an important sense, the performance of *Microsoft* extended far beyond the courtroom in the District of Columbia where it was tried. A case achieving this degree of notoriety implicates politics because it seeks an authoritative decision of "a contentious legal question of political significance."[6] Second, *Microsoft* exposed in a new context the ideological conflicts at the heart of antitrust policy. After more than a century, antitrust has become a part of the regulatory establishment, but it still rests on an uneasy compromise between laissez-faire and dirigiste ideologies with roots in the nineteenth century – what we will call the evolutionary and intentional visions of antitrust.[7] Partisans of the modern versions of these ideologies sharply disagree about the appropriate functions of antitrust enforcement. This disagreement is submerged in the ordinary run of cases, but it resurfaces in large-scale, controversial cases, such as *Microsoft*.[8] Finally, *Microsoft* was the product of an unusually wide-ranging and sophisticated lobbying campaign funded by Microsoft's rivals. Whether out of self-interest or principle, these rivals urged the federal antitrust agencies, state attorneys general, and Congress to rein in what they claimed was a rogue monopolist. These efforts went far beyond the usual importunities that the enforcement agencies field every day. Most important, the lobbying included the articulation of a highly influential narrative of how Microsoft's conduct had crushed rivals and perpetuated its monopoly. Microsoft was slow to react and less effective than its competitors and the government, but it too marshalled political and public support.

In this chapter, we attempt to identify which of these political dimensions had the most important effect on the shape and eventual outcome of the case. We argue that the federal and state cases and especially their judicial resolution

[4] Richard A. Posner, "Antitrust in the New Economy," *Antitrust Law Journal*, Vol. 68 (2001), p. 925, where he defines the new economy to include computer software, Internet businesses, and "communications services and equipment designed to support the first two markets."

[5] One measure of the public interest in the case was the extent of media coverage. Between the time trial began and about the time the district court issued its first remedial order, breaking the company in two, the *New York Times* alone published 114 articles on the case. Joel Brinkley and Steve Lohr, *U.S.* v. *Microsoft: The Inside Story of the Landmark Case* (New York: McGraw-Hill, 2000), pp. 337–340.

[6] Meierhenrich and Pendas, "'The Justice of My Cause Is Clear, But There's Politics to Fear,'" p. 51.

[7] William H. Page, "Ideological Conflict and the Origins of Antitrust Policy," *Tulane Law Review*, Vol. 66 (1991), pp. 1–68.

[8] Donald I. Baker, "Antitrust and Politics at the Justice Department," *Journal of Law and Politics*, Vol. 9 (1993), pp. 291, 292. Baker observes that in cases involving monopolies in large markets, "it is much more difficult for the prosecutor to stick his head down and say 'I'm just enforcing the law' as if he were bringing his 795th mail fraud indictment of the year."

are best understood in terms of ideology, rather than naked interest-group pressure. The simple interest-group hypothesis has never explained the enactment and evolution of antitrust law very well, and it does not explain *Microsoft*. Both antitrust law and *Microsoft* are products of a subtler process, one characterized by conflicting and shifting conceptions of the capacity and limitations of the market and the government. These conceptions, or visions, are deeply held views of the public interest, and its relationship to conflicting private interests. They are not neatly separable from special interest pressures. Groups invoke these conceptions to press arguments for regulation in service of their own interests, using narratives to "envision and attempt to enact a new normative reality"[9] in which they can thrive. The narrative that Microsoft's rivals articulated was the best example of this sort of advocacy. But arguments in these terms are persuasive only if they resonate with the policymakers' understanding of the public interest. Administrators and courts must routinely distinguish arguments that credibly advance the public interest from those that invoke it only as lip service. When a special interest group succeeds in persuading the government that an action that benefits the special interest also advances the public interest, the result can be fairly attributed to the interaction of the special interest's narrative with the ideological outlook of its audience, the government policymaker.

In the next Part, we describe the role of politics in antitrust generally, distinguishing the roles of interest-group dynamics and political ideologies. In the following Part, we use that background to examine the events that led to the filing of the *Microsoft* case, and the courts' eventual resolution of the issues.

ANTITRUST AND POLITICS

Antitrust has always had an important but misunderstood political dimension.[10] In its early years, antitrust was a popular movement that arose in opposition to the trusts – enormous new concentrations of capital that formed in the late nineteenth century in many national markets.[11] The trusts

[9] Meierhenrich and Pendas, "'The Justice of My Cause Is Clear, But There's Politics to Fear,'" p. 41.

[10] Some scholars have, for example, distinguished political and economic values in antitrust law. According to Robert Pitofsky, antitrust incorporates non-economic concepts, including the fear that concentrated economic power might threaten democracy. See his "The Political Content of Antitrust," *University of Pennsylvania Law Review*, Vol. 127 (1979), pp. 1051, 1053–1055. Cf. Harlan M. Blake and William K. Jones, "In Defense of Antitrust," *Columbia Law Review*, Vol. 65 (1965), pp. 377, 382–384, who argue that antitrust serves the political objectives of minimizing political interference in the economy and the enlargement of individual liberty.

[11] Richard Hofstadter, "What Happened to the Antitrust Movement?," *The Paranoid Style in American Politics, and Other Essays* (New York: Vintage, 2008), p. 188; Hans B. Thorelli, *The Federal Antitrust Policy: Origination of an American Tradition* (Baltimore: Johns Hopkins Press, 1955), pp. 76–83.

seemed to blur the line between public and private power and to cast doubt on the legitimacy of the market as an institution of social ordering.[12] The states had little inclination or, it was believed in those early years, constitutional authority to attack interstate monopolies.[13] Congress's response was the Sherman Act of 1890, which created civil and criminal penalties for "monopoliz[ation]"[14] and for agreements "in restraint of trade."[15] As courts began to interpret these provisions over the next two decades, antitrust continued to play a prominent role in national politics, particularly during the administrations of Theodore Roosevelt and William Howard Taft.[16]

A new round of political controversy over the trusts erupted after the Supreme Court's controversial 1911 decision in *Standard Oil Co. of New Jersey*.[17] The government in that case attacked John D. Rockefeller's oil empire, which was a holding company in legal form but a trust in effect. Standard Oil, controlling 90 percent of U.S. oil production, had been created largely by the acquisition of competing facilities and protected, according to the Court, by certain exclusionary practices, such as predatory pricing and controlling pipelines.[18] Though the Court upheld the complaint and affirmed a remedial order breaking up the company, it did so not by condemning the company's acts as per se illegal, but by application of an opaque "rule of reason"[19] that potentially allowed a broad and perhaps forgiving inquiry into the economic conditions surrounding any anticompetitive conduct. Frustrated by the Court's apparent timidity, Congress at the instigation of President Woodrow Wilson responded, this time by adopting in 1914 the Clayton and Federal Trade Commission Acts,[20] which were intended to supplement the Sherman Act.[21] The Clayton Act defined more explicitly than had the Sherman Act certain practices that experience had shown could be harmful, including discriminatory pricing, exclusive dealing arrangements, and interlocking directorates; most of these practices were outlawed only when they tended to "lessen competition." The Clayton Act also bolstered private enforcement by allowing judgments won by the government to be used as prima facie evidence against the defendants in subsequent antitrust cases. The Federal Trade Commission Act created what was expected to be an expert agency

[12] William Letwin, *Law and Economic Policy in America: The Evolution of the Sherman Antitrust Act* (Chicago: University of Chicago Press, 1965), pp. 69–70.

[13] Thorelli, *The Federal Antitrust Policy*, pp. 100, 155–162. If we believe Thorelli, "states before 1890 made no determined attempts to enforce their [antitrust] laws."

[14] 15 U.S.C. § 2. [15] 15 U.S.C. § 1.

[16] Ellis W. Hawley, *The New Deal and the Problem of Monopoly: A Study in Economic Ambivalence* (Princeton: Princeton University Press, 1966), pp. 4–9.

[17] *Standard Oil Co.* v. *United States*, 221 U.S. 1 (1911). [18] *Standard Oil*, 221 U.S. at 42–43.

[19] *Standard Oil*, 221 U.S. at 62.

[20] Clayton Act, Pub. L. No. 63–212, chapter 323, 38 Stat. 730 (1914); Federal Trade Commission Act, Pub. L. No. 63–717, chapter 311, 38 Stat. 717 (1914).

[21] Letwin, *Law and Economic Policy in America*, pp. 270–278.

charged with identifying and halting "unfair methods of competition," which might be specific practices defined in the Clayton Act when they indeed threatened to "lessen competition" or entirely novel practices.

Public choice scholars have argued that Congress adopted the Sherman Act and later antitrust laws not to advance any coherent concept of the public interest, but to protect special interests.[22] These scholars point to evidence that antitrust enforcement has regularly helped inefficient firms, and infer that Congress must have intended the law to have this effect[23] and could not have been merely misguided.[24] But if the Sherman Act was intended to benefit special interests, one might expect to find some evidence of that intent in the voluminous legislative histories of the Sherman Act and subsequent antitrust laws. With the exception of the Robinson–Patman Act in 1936,[25] however, those histories reveal no desire to protect particular interest groups, other than consumers.[26] More important, the text of the Sherman Act does not identify particular beneficiaries. Senator Sherman himself conceded in debate that the meaning of the statute's general terms "must be left for the courts to determine in each particular case."[27] It seems unlikely that a Congress intent on benefiting special interests would have ceded to a conservative judiciary the task of giving meaning to a major statute. The courts have properly assumed that Congress wanted them to interpret statutes to serve the public interest.[28]

There was politics in the enactment of the statute, but it was not simple interest-group pressure. In confronting the issue of the trusts, Congress was torn

[22] William F. Baxter, "The Political Economy of Antitrust," in Robert D. Tollison, ed., *The Political Economy of Antitrust: Principal Paper by William Baxter* (Lexington: Lexington Books, 1980); George J. Stigler, "The Origin of the Sherman Act," *Journal of Legal Studies*, Vol. 14 (1985), pp. 1–12; Gary D. Libecap, "The Rise of the Chicago Packers and the Origins of Meat Inspection and Antitrust," *Economic Inquiry*, Vol. 30 (1992), pp. 242–262; Donald J. Boudreaux et al., "Antitrust before the Sherman Act," in Fred S. McChesney and William F. Shughart, eds., *The Causes and Consequences of Antitrust: The Public-Choice Perspective* (Chicago: University of Chicago Press, 1995), pp. 255–270. Stigler concludes that the Clayton Act was designed to hinder large efficient firms for the benefit of smaller inefficient ones. Stigler, "The Origin of the Sherman Act," pp. 4–5. Others find that the law was designed to benefit large, established firms at the expense of new entrants or expanding competitors. Robert B. Ekelund, Jr., et al., "Business Restraints and the Clayton Act of 1914: Public or Private-Interest Legislation," in McChesney and Shughart, eds., *The Causes and Consequences of Antitrust*, pp. 271–286.

[23] William F. Shughart, "Public-Choice Theory and Antitrust Policy," in McChesney and Shughart, eds., *The Causes and Consequences of Antitrust*, pp. 7, 10–11; Thomas J. DiLorenzo, "The Origins of Antitrust: An Interest-Group Perspective," *International Review of Law and Economics*, Vol. 5 (1985), pp. 73–90.

[24] Fred S. McChesney and William F. Shughart, "The Unjoined Debate," in McChesney and Shughart, eds., *The Causes and Consequences of Antitrust*, pp. 345–347.

[25] Hugh C. Hansen, "Robinson-Patman Law: A Review and Analysis," *Fordham Law Review*, Vol. 51 (1983), pp. 1113, 1119–1124.

[26] McChesney and Shugart, "The Unjoined Debate," p. 349. [27] 21 Cong. Rec. 2460 (1890).

[28] Jonathan R. Macey, "Promoting Public-Regarding Legislation Through Statutory Interpretation: An Interest Group Model," *Columbia Law Review*, Vol. 86 (1986), pp. 223–268.

between two ideologies of the market and the state: the evolutionary and intentional visions.[29] In the evolutionary vision, the market, framed by common-law rules of property and contract, is a venue for value-enhancing exchange among a myriad of participants.[30] The economic structure and the distribution of wealth that emerge from freely reached bargains reflect a social optimum that the state should not disturb, except in rare cases. In this vision, the trusts were mainly the natural product of technological change in production and transportation. To the extent trusts had unjustified monopoly power, it was because tariffs protected them from foreign competition.[31] Government action against the trusts, in this view, should be limited to removing barriers to entry by foreign firms.[32] In the intentional vision, by contrast, markets are inherently coercive. They allow players with larger endowments of wealth and knowledge to exploit others, with the aid of the state's mechanisms for enforcement of contractual and property rights.[33] The outcomes of market transactions thus reflect the conscious actions of powerful actors, and market structures tend toward monopoly. The trusts, in this vision, proved that markets could not break down monopolies; only government was capable of imposing democratic control and legitimacy.[34]

The Sherman Act was a legislative compromise between these visions and their corresponding prescriptions for the role of the state. The state intervened in the market by providing public and private rights of action against the trusts and other restraints of trade. This innovation was a radical break with the common law, which had merely refused to enforce agreements in restraint of trade.[35] But the statute accepted the market as a means of economic ordering. It did not rely on direct regulation of prices, state ownership, or any other form of continuous governmental intervention; instead, it limited intervention to sporadic public and private lawsuits aimed at penalizing or enjoining illegal conduct and thus restoring the norm of competitive markets.[36]

[29] Page, "Ideological Conflict and the Origins of Antitrust Policy," pp. 1–67. This account draws on Thomas Sowell, *A Conflict of Visions: Ideological Origins of Political Struggles* (New York: William Morrow, 1987).

[30] Page, "Ideological Conflict and the Origins of Antitrust Policy," pp. 11–15.

[31] Page, "Ideological Conflict and the Origins of Antitrust Policy," pp. 31–32.

[32] Page, "Ideological Conflict and the Origins of Antitrust Policy," pp. 31–32.

[33] Page, "Ideological Conflict and the Origins of Antitrust Policy," pp. 12–15.

[34] Page, "Ideological Conflict and the Origins of Antitrust Policy," pp. 32–33.

[35] Letwin, *Law and Economic Policy in America*, p. 81; Thorelli, *The Federal Antitrust Policy*, p. 53.

[36] The antitrust compromise was not unique in nineteenth-century regulation. William Novak observes that in state and local regulation "nineteenth century Americans could find room for a political faith between the Scylla of socialism and the Charybdis of economic liberalism, skeptical of the claims that a good society could only come from a surrender to either the state or the civil society." William J. Novak, *The People's Welfare: Law and Regulation in Nineteenth-century America* (Chapel Hill: University of North Carolina Press, 1996), p. x.

Since passage of the Sherman Act, the political branches have continued to play a role in making antitrust policy. On the federal level, for example, presidents nominate both the judges whose decisions shape the law and the agency heads who decide what cases to bring on behalf of the government. In this process, the ideology of the governing party necessarily influences the outlook of key decision makers in the system. Franklin Roosevelt, for example, made antitrust enforcement a major element of his program in the Second New Deal of the late 1930s.[37] The enforcement program of Thurman Arnold, Roosevelt's choice to head the Justice Department's Antitrust Division, had a lasting effect on antitrust law. Congress conducts regular oversight hearings in which members question enforcement officials about their programs and decisions, sometimes with special reference to the needs of voters in their districts. [38] In some instances, Congress has made procedural and substantive revisions.

More dubiously, the states also influence federal antitrust policy. Congress in the Hart-Scott-Rodino Act of 1976 authorized state attorneys general to bring federal antitrust actions for monetary relief as parens patriae on behalf of their citizens.[39] The same officials can also seek injunctive relief against threatened harm in their states from antitrust offenses.[40] These statutory provisions effectively commission politicians elected or appointed to a statewide office as public enforcers of the federal antitrust laws. As we explain in the next part, the states played a central role in the *Microsoft* litigation.

Despite these executive and legislative actions, antitrust policy has never returned to any degree of prominence in national party politics. Over the past century, antitrust has been domesticated and institutionalized as a national policy (enforced by two federal agencies and many state agencies), a legal specialty, and an academic field.[41] Even a major government monopolization case such as *Microsoft* arises within a framework of judicially developed legal standards and economic theory. In practical terms, this configuration of the antitrust establishment has placed the generalist federal appellate courts at the controls of antitrust policy. The insulation of the federal judiciary from naked political pressure diminishes the role of interest-group dynamics in antitrust law.[42]

[37] William H. Page, "Legal Realism and the Shaping of Modern Antitrust," *Emory Law Journal*, Vol. 44 (1995), pp. 1, 18–20.

[38] William E. Kovacic, "The Federal Trade Commission and Congressional Oversight of Antitrust Enforcement," *Tulsa Law Journal*, Vol. 17 (1982), pp. 587, 631–634.

[39] Codified at 15 U.S.C. § 15c.

[40] See Clayton Act § 16, 15 U.S.C. § 26. States may also sue for injuries to state property interests, see Clayton Act § 4, 15 U.S.C. § 15, and may function as public enforcers of state antitrust laws, which now tend to track the federal antitrust laws at least in their substantive provisions. See generally *California* v. *ARC Am. Corp.*, 490 U.S. 93, 101 (1989), which noted that "Congress has not pre-empted the field of antitrust law."

[41] Hofstadter, "What Happened to the Antitrust Movement?," p. 188.

[42] Ronald A. Cass, "Judging: Norms and Incentives of Retrospective Decision-Making," *Boston University Law Review*, Vol. 75 (1995), pp. 941–997; William M. Landes and Richard

But the federal judiciary is not insulated from ideology, which remains the primary political determinant of antitrust policy. [43] As we noted earlier, the textual openness and ideological ambiguity of the Sherman Act leave the courts with enormous discretion to define the frequency and extent of antitrust interventions according to their evolving conceptions of the public interest.[44] In exercising this discretion courts in different eras have drawn on the evolutionary or intentional visions for guidance, depending upon the prevailing ideology of the times.[45] Thus, the content of antitrust law is partially determined by the influence of the two visions at various stages in its history. In the formative period of Sherman Act jurisprudence, the Supreme Court looked primarily to the evolutionary vision.[46] From the late 1930s through the mid-1970s, however, the Supreme Court adopted numerous per se rules, strict merger standards, and an expansive definition of monopolization.[47] Just as the decisions in the formative period of antitrust reflected the evolutionary vision of the era, the sweeping liability rules of the post-Depression era and the lawsuits they spawned reflected the dominant intentional vision. Courts of this era readily accepted claims of market coercion, the idea that large firms could easily protect their dominant positions by imposing on their dealers a variety of restraints.[48] This era also saw the private treble damage action emerge as a leading form of antitrust enforcement.[49] Many of these private lawsuits protected the plaintiffs from more efficient rivals or systems of distribution.[50] Some of the government actions of the period, like the *IBM* case,[51] filed in 1969, also protected inefficient firms and inhibited hard competition.[52] Within the intentional vision, however, the goal of these actions was not simply to protect inefficient firms, but to open channels of trade and to advance populist social values.

A. Posner, "The Independent Judiciary in an Interest-Group Perspective," *Journal of Law and Economics*, Vol. 18 (1975), pp. 875, 885–887.

[43] Eric A. Posner, "Does Political Bias in the Judiciary Matter?: Implications of Judicial Bias Studies for Legal and Constitutional Reform," *University of Chicago Law Review*, Vol. 75 (2008), pp. 853–884.

[44] Macey, "Promoting Public-Regarding Legislation Through Statutory Interpretation," p. 223.

[45] Page, "Legal Realism and the Shaping of Modern Antitrust," p. 1.

[46] Page, "Legal Realism and the Shaping of Modern Antitrust," pp. 44–66.

[47] Page, "Legal Realism and the Shaping of Modern Antitrust," pp. 29–42.

[48] *FTC* v. *Texaco, Inc.*, 393 U.S. 223, 229 (1968), which deemed "inherently coercive" Texaco's sale of tires, batteries, and accessories to its service station operators; and *Simpson* v. *Union Oil Co.*, 377 U.S. 13, 24 (1964), which held that a system for "consignment" of gasoline to service station operators "coercively laced [the operators] into an arrangement under which their supplier is able to impose noncompetitive prices on thousands of persons whose prices otherwise might be competitive."

[49] Richard A. Posner, "A Statistical Study of Antitrust Enforcement," *Journal of Law and Economics*, Vol. 13 (1970), pp. 365, 371.

[50] William H. Page, "Antitrust Damages and Economic Efficiency: An Approach to Antitrust Injury," *University of Chicago Law Review*, Vol. 47 (1980), pp. 467, 467–468.

[51] *In re* IBM Corp., 687 F.2d 591 (2d Cir. 1982).

[52] John E. Lopatka, "United States *v.* IBM: A Monument to Arrogance," *Antitrust Law Journal*, Vol. 68 (2000), p. 145, 145 n. 4.

In the late 1970s, however, the courts and enforcement agencies began to move away from per se rules and toward standards that allowed even dominant firms to compete vigorously.[53] This change reflected the growing acceptance among courts and antitrust enforcers of the Chicago School of antitrust analysis, which brought a new form of the evolutionary vision to the interpretation of business practices.[54] As in earlier periods, the shift to a new antitrust vision reflected political changes in the federal judiciary and in the larger society.[55] Under the Chicago School view, antitrust was about promoting economic efficiency as a means of protecting the welfare of consumers. Guided by this conception, courts rejected claims that antitrust law should protect firms from more efficient rivals. In the most dramatic expression of the shift in perspective, the Department of Justice dropped its monopolization case against IBM,[56] and soon afterward settled its monopolization suit against AT&T.[57] The Chicago School framework, adapted to accommodate the judiciary's concern with legitimacy in legal processes,[58] remains dominant to this day.

Beginning in the mid-1980s, however, a post-Chicago School began to emerge that questioned the generalizations of Chicago scholars about the efficiency of practices that had been routinely condemned in the pre-Chicago era.[59] Post-Chicago economic models use game theory to show that, in carefully defined circumstances, practices such as tying, exclusive dealing, and predatory pricing as well as others can be anticompetitive. Although accepting much of the Chicago critique of earlier judicial opinions, these models challenge the suggestion of some Chicagoans that most practices traditionally of concern to antitrust courts increase efficiency or, at worst, merely redistribute wealth. By exposing market failures and advocating antitrust remedies, post-Chicago

[53] John E. Lopatka and William H. Page, "Bargaining and Monopolization: In Search of the 'Boundary of Section 2 Liability' Between *Aspen* and *Trinko*," *Antitrust Law Journal*, Vol. 73 (2005), pp. 115, 121–122.

[54] William H. Page, "The Chicago School and the Evolution of Antitrust: Characterization, Antitrust Injury, and Evidentiary Sufficiency," *Virginia Law Review*, Vol. 75 (1989), pp. 1221–1308.

[55] Page, "The Chicago School and the Evolution of Antitrust," p. 1300. See also Ivan T. Berend, *An Economic History of Twentieth Century Europe* (Cambridge: Cambridge University Press, 2006), p. 273, who argues that the globalization of the economy since 1970 has gone "hand in hand with the emergence of neo-liberal economics."

[56] *In re* IBM Corp., 687 F.2d 591 (2d Cir. 1982).

[57] *United States* v. *AT&T Co.*, 552 F. Supp. 131 (D.D.C. 1982).

[58] See Page, "Legal Realism and the Shaping of Modern Antitrust," pp. 50–51. According to Page, the evolution of antitrust law since the mid-1970s reflects the influence of the Legal Process school of jurisprudence, which sought "to restore legitimacy to the lawmaking function of judges [by] refocus[ing] analysis on the mechanisms by which legal decisions, with their attendant policy choices, were to be made."

[59] The starting point was Herbert Hovenkamp, "Antitrust Policy after Chicago," *Michigan Law Review*, Vol. 84 (1985), pp. 213–284. See also Herbert Hovenkamp, "Post-Chicago Antitrust: A Review and Critique," *Columbia Business Law Review*, Vol. 2001 (2001), pp. 257, 266–267. For a recent overview, see Daniel A. Crane, "Chicago, Post-Chicago, and Neo-Chicago," *University of Chicago Law Review*, Vol. 76 (2009), pp. 1911–1934.

analysis lends support to the intentional vision and to modified forms of pre-Chicago doctrine. Significantly, however, unlike manifestations of the intentional vision in earlier eras, post-Chicago analysis acknowledges that the public interest is defined by some concept of economic efficiency.[60] The product of post-Chicago economics most important by far to the *Microsoft* litigation was the economic theory of network effects.

MICROSOFT AND POLITICS

We argued in the last part that politics has played an important role in antitrust law over the past 120 years through the decisions of judges and enforcement officials animated at different times and in different ways by the evolutionary and intentional visions. *Microsoft* is best understood in this historical context. The complicating factor in *Microsoft* is the unusual role of interest-group pressure. There were three antitrust investigations of Microsoft before 1995, and lobbying by Microsoft's rivals accompanied each of them. But the most important investigation, begun by the Antitrust Division in 1996, involved unusually intense lobbying at every stage. This investigation culminated in the filing on May 18, 1998, of the federal and state monopolization cases.[61]

The primary impetus for both cases was a white paper[62] authored by Netscape attorneys Gary Reback and Susan Creighton[63] and submitted to the Department of Justice in August 1996. The paper also found its way into the hands of an antitrust lawyer in the Texas Attorney General's office, Mark Tobey.[64] The white paper provided the factual and theoretical core of both the federal and state complaints against Microsoft. It was the centerpiece of a well-funded lobbying campaign, but also offered a persuasive narrative

[60] Jonathan B. Baker, "Recent Developments in Economics that Challenge Chicago School Views," *Antitrust Law Journal*, Vol. 58 (1989), pp. 645, 646.

[61] The states' original complaint was slightly broader than the Justice Department's complaint, asserting claims that Microsoft monopolized a market of office productivity suite software and illegally bundled its Outlook Express e-mail software and other unnamed applications with Windows 98. But the federal and state cases were consolidated, and the states filed an amended complaint that conformed to the federal government's complaint. See John R. Wilke, "States Narrow Suit Against Microsoft, Drop 'Office' Claims," *Wall Street Journal*, July 20, 1998.

[62] Gary Reback and Susan Creighton, *White Paper Regarding the Recent Anticompetitive Conduct of the Microsoft Corporation* (unpublished manuscript on file with the authors, 1996). The brief acknowledged assistance from economists Brian Arthur and Garth Saloner. For descriptions of Reback and Creighton and a colorful account of the events leading up to the preparation of the white paper, which was originally intended to be published as a book, see John Heilemann, *Pride before the Fall: The Trials of Bill Gates and the End of the Microsoft Era* (New York: Harper Collins, 2002), pp. 11–20.

[63] Joseph Farrell and Garth Saloner, "Installed Base and Compatibility: Innovation, Product Preannouncements, and Predation," *American Economic Review*, Vol. 76 (1986), pp. 940–955.

[64] Brinkley and Lohr, *U.S.* v. *Microsoft*, pp. 6–7.

showing how Microsoft's conduct threatened to reduce competition in network markets. This narrative, which drew upon the post-Chicago economic theory of network effects, was a compelling expression of the intentional vision.

Lobbying: Form and Substance

Microsoft's rivals waged a political campaign against the company at the Department of Justice, on Capitol Hill, in statehouses, and in the press. The campaign consisted of at least five components. First, Microsoft's rivals communicated directly with decision makers at the Antitrust Division of the Department of Justice. The most important of these communications were the white paper, noted above and described more fully below, and a day-long presentation in April of 1998 by a group of experts assembled by Microsoft's competitors. The group included Dennis Carlton, a distinguished University of Chicago economist retained by Sun Microsystems, who laid out a sophisticated argument for a structural remedy.[65] Communications continued during the litigation and the shaping of the remedy. Shortly before the district court issued its anticipated findings of fact, this form of lobbying became a two-way street. Joel Klein, head of the Antitrust Division, began urging industry executives to endorse publicly the government's proposal for significant relief, which would eventually take the form of a structural decree.[66] Wary of an adverse public reaction to a dramatic remedy, Klein believed that the government needed political support to break up Microsoft, just as Microsoft's rivals believed they needed political support to induce the government to sue.

Second, Microsoft's rivals urged the states also to sue. The first depositions in what became the governments' case against Microsoft were taken of Netscape executives in August of 1997.[67] Enlisting the aid of the states was important. The states were an alternative source of a public antitrust action against Microsoft, and their interest in pursuing a case could prod the Department of Justice into bringing an action, lest the federal government appear weak in fighting monopolists. The lobbying of the states became particularly significant in the remedial phase of the litigation.[68] Judge Thomas Penfield Jackson, who had been assigned the *Microsoft* case, had asked Richard Posner, a preeminent antitrust scholar, law professor, and appellate judge, to

[65] Heilemann, *Pride before the Fall*, pp. 91–94.

[66] Heilemann, *Pride before the Fall*, pp. 199–211.

[67] Heilemann, *Pride before the Fall*, pp. 22–24.

[68] For example, shortly after Judge Jackson released his findings of fact, the Iowa Attorney General speaking on behalf of all the states in the case declared that "the states are determined to stay in court 'until we get a serious remedy for the serious competitive harm.' " John R. Wilke, "Microsoft Hopes for GOP Savior, but States Are Problem," *Wall Street Journal*, November 9, 1999.

broker a settlement.[69] Commenting on his experience, Judge Posner later wrote that "it was only after four months of almost full-time mediation that, faced with the intransigency and incompetence of the states, I decided the case would not settle, and threw in the towel."[70] Others believe that the Department of Justice and Microsoft were themselves unable to reach an accord.[71] Undoubtedly, however, the states' involvement complicated the settlement negotiations. When the Justice Department, Microsoft, and a group of states eventually did reach an agreement after the first appellate decision in the case, another group of states balked and pursued more extensive relief.

Third, firms made statements to the press to generate media attention and to increase pressure on the agency. Scholars have noted the campaign's use of "high-ground thematics," identifying the cause with the consumer interest, and "personalization," demonizing Microsoft's leaders, especially Bill Gates.[72] Moreover, early in the campaign, Reback attacked the incoming Assistant Attorney General for Antitrust Joel Klein for "being soft on Microsoft's marketing tactics." He also complained that "[t]he issue of when to intervene in the market, and the benefits that consumers get by market intervention, has been heavily politicized,"[73] implying that Microsoft or allied politicians were influencing the decision. Klein responded that "I can assure you that what we do here is not political,"[74] but the press coverage may have had some effect, at least in the early stages of the case. According to one former head of the Antitrust Division, these public and private complaints in 1996 "cornered" Klein: "Whatever he thinks of the complaints, he has to investigate."[75]

Fourth, the rivals worked with existing organizations and created new ones to advance their cause. In late 1997, for example, Ralph Nader organized a conference on "Appraising Microsoft and Its Global Strategy,"[76] at which

[69] John R. Wilke and David Bank, "Microsoft Judge Turns Up Heat for Pact – At a Meeting Last Week, Jackson Said the Time Is 'Propitious' to Settle," *Wall Street Journal*, November 23, 1999; Heilemann, *Pride before the Fall*, p. 2; Ken Auletta, *World War 3.0: Microsoft and Its Enemies* (New York: Random House, 2001), p. 306.

[70] Richard A. Posner, "Federalism and the Enforcement of Antitrust Laws by State Attorneys General," in Richard A. Epstein and Michael S. Grieve, eds., *Competition Laws in Conflict* (Washinton: AEI Press, 2004), p. 265, n. 7.

[71] Heilemann, *Pride before the Fall*, pp. 4–5, 211–213.

[72] Walter Lance Bennett and Jarol B. Manheim, "The Big Spin: Strategic Communication and the Transformation of Pluralist Democracy," in Walter Lance Bennett and Robert M. Entman, eds., *Mediated Politics: Communication in the Future or Democracy* (Cambridge: Cambridge University Press, 2000), pp. 279, 289–293.

[73] Karen Donovan, "New Antitrust Head Klein Gets High Marks," *National Law Journal*, September 2, 1996.

[74] Donovan, "New Antitrust Head Klein Gets High Marks."

[75] Donovan, "New Antitrust Head Klein Gets High Marks."

[76] Jeri Clausing, "Nader Conference Levels Sights on Microsoft," *New York Times*, November 21, 1997.

Reback and representatives of Sun and Netscape spoke. In April 1998, Microsoft's rivals formed the "Project to Promote Competition and Innovation in the Digital Age," or ProComp, in order "to get Justice to file an antitrust lawsuit [against Microsoft] and win it."[77] The organization's name obviously was chosen to promote the theme that Microsoft's actions threatened consumers, not merely its competitors. Also blurring ProComp's identity as an instrument of competitors was the participation of Judge Robert Bork, a leading Chicago School theorist of an earlier era – albeit as a paid representative of Netscape.[78]

Fifth, and finally, Microsoft's competitors successfully lobbied Senator Orrin Hatch of Utah (home of one of the rivals, Novell) to convene hearings of the Senate Judiciary Committee.[79] Microsoft's competitors used the hearings, conducted in March and July 1998, to lambaste the company, complaining especially about Microsoft's practice of incorporating new functions into Windows.[80] One editorial observed that the "real goal [of the hearings] was to give Senators and Microsoft's competitors a chance to portray Mr. Gates as a modern-day robber baron."[81] Indeed, in announcing the hearing on "market power and structural change in the software industry," Senator Hatch described Microsoft's threat to competition in language of network effects that echoed the work of Saloner.[82] The enlistment of Hatch, a prominent Republican, also provided ideological cover by making support for enforcement action appear to be in the antitrust mainstream.

Microsoft was slow to respond. Bill Gates believed that Microsoft had simply competed hard, as it was entitled – indeed, encouraged – to do, and that federal antitrust authorities had targeted Microsoft unfairly.[83] Gates thought that the latest investigation would blow over. But when the campaign against Microsoft grew more intense, Microsoft mounted its own public relations and lobbying

77 Mary Mosquera, "Anti-Microsoft Group Wants Antitrust Lawsuit," *TechWeb News*, April 20, 1998; Rajiv Chandrasekaran, "Opponents of Microsoft Open Drive for Wider Antitrust Case," *Washington Post*, April 21, 1998.

78 Ellen Frankel Paul, "Hayek on Monopoly and Antitrust in the Crucible of *United States* v. *Microsoft*," *New York University Journal of Law and Liberty*, Vol. 1 (2005), pp. 167, 201.

79 Several months before the hearings took place, lawyers on Hatch's staff met with Silicon Valley executives in the offices of Reback's law firm to gather negative information on Microsoft. Heilemann, *Pride before the Fall*, p. 23.

80 See John R. Wilke and David Bank, "Mr. Gates Goes to Washington: Microsoft's Chief Concedes Hardball Tactics," *Wall Street Journal*, March 4, 1998; Jeri Clausing, "Senate Panel Hears from Microsoft Rivals," *New York Times*, July 23, 1998; James V. Grimaldi, "Gates Bows Out as Senate Panel Revisits Microsoft – Software Giant Calls Hearing a Stacked Deck," *Seattle Times*, July 22, 1998.

81 " 'Bull's Eye' Bill," *Wall Street Journal*, March 4, 1998.

82 See Orrin G. Hatch, "Washington vs. Microsoft: Beware High-Tech Monopolies," *Wall Street Journal*, March 3, 1998.

83 Auletta, *World War 3.0*, pp. xvii–xxv.

campaign, adopting many of the same techniques as its rivals.[84] For example, by March 1998, stung by negative perceptions in the technology community and among consumers, Microsoft hired new Washington lobbyists.[85] Later, it gathered allies, such as Symantech, Compaq, and CompUSA, and retained a distinguished economist, Gregory Mankiw of Harvard, to argue (successfully) that the DOJ should not try to delay the release of Windows 98.[86] It instructed its lobbyists to try to persuade Congress to reduce the Antitrust Division's proposed budget.[87]

This description of the lobbying campaigns says almost nothing about their substantive content. In considering the role of political influence in a complex antitrust case, however, it is important to distinguish communications that contain empty rhetoric from those that contain evidence and economic analysis. Netscape's white paper illustrates the point. It was, as we have just shown, the opening move of a multipronged lobbying campaign aimed at exerting political pressure on the government to file suit. But it also presented a sophisticated legal and economic argument that Microsoft's conduct directed at Netscape's Navigator and Sun's Java would thwart innovation and reduce competition in Internet markets.

The framework for the white paper's argument was the economic theory of network effects, which began to develop during the 1980s to explain high-technology markets like the ones in which Microsoft competes.[88] Certain durable goods (such as video disk players) are used with numerous complementary goods over their useful life. When the durable good embodies a standard that is incompatible with those of its rivals, the producers of the goods will compete intensely for market share. After a "tipping point" is reached, the market may become "locked in" to one product standard: new consumers prefer to buy the dominant product, because a greater variety of complementary products are

[84] Dan Carney, "Microsoft's All-Out Counterattack," *Businessweek Online*, May 15, 2000, www.businessweek.com/2000/00_20/b3681219.htm. The article describes Microsoft's creation of an aggressive, well-funded lobbying operation in response to the government/s lawsuit. See also Maurice E. Stucke, "Does the Rule of Reason Violate the Rule of Law?," *U.C. Davis Law Review*, Vol. 42 (2009), pp. 1375, 1446–1447, who argues that vague legal standards in antitrust law give enforcers greater discretion and thus encourage firms to lobby government agencies for favorable action. Stucke suggests that Microsoft's inattention to lobbying in the mid-1990s "exposed [it] to the government's antitrust prosecution" but that Microsoft responded by funding a formidable lobbying operation.

[85] Don Clark, "Mr. Gates Goes to Washington: Master Programmer Updates His Code," *Wall Street Journal*, March 4, 1998. The biggest challenge for public-relations specialists was to craft a more favorable image of Gates. One writer quipped that Gates's "handlers . . . have perhaps the easiest job on the planet getting him media attention – and the hardest making him seem more affable." Clark, "Mr. Gates Goes to Washington."

[86] Lisa Napoli, "Microsoft Rounds Up Allies to Defend Windows 98," *New York Times*, May 7, 1998.

[87] Auletta, *World War 3.0*, p. 268.

[88] An early important statement is Michael L. Katz and Carl Shapiro, "Systems Competition and Network Effects," *Journal of Economic Perspectives*, Vol. 8 (1994), pp. 93, 94.

available to use with it, and developers prefer to produce complementary products for consumers to use with the dominant product, because the dominant product has a larger installed base of users. The owner of a standard might win in the early standards competition based on a very small advantage or mere luck, and might remain dominant, even if a product incorporating a different standard with better intrinsic qualities emerges. This implication of the theory cast some doubt on the evolutionary vision's tenet that firms win in the marketplace because their products are better.

The white paper argued that Microsoft dominated the market for PC operating systems because of network effects and was trying to keep its position by violating the antitrust laws. Microsoft's Windows operating system, according to the white paper, was "threatened by the introduction of new technology," the Netscape browser along with Sun's Java technologies, "that is a partial substitute – and, in time could become a complete substitute – for the monopoly product."[89] Microsoft had originally acquired its monopoly by "leveraging off of its operating system monopoly ... first to Windows, and then to all major desktop applications."[90] It had integrated its earlier MS-DOS operating system with a graphical interface called Windows, then gradually moved its MS-DOS developers to Windows as the new platform for their applications.[91] In time Windows became a dominant operating system in itself and subsumed MS-DOS. Microsoft feared that Netscape's browser could displace Windows in the same way.

The browser, the white paper argued, is "a 'front end' that allows the user to access resources and information across a network" and might, in Bill Gates's words, "replac[e] Windows as the mainstream set of software standards"[92] and thus weaken the network effects that protect the Windows monopoly. Consequently, Microsoft first offered to divide the browser market with Netscape. When that failed, Microsoft bundled its Internet Explorer browser with Windows at no charge and formed various exclusive contracts with computer manufacturers and Internet businesses that were the main channels of distribution for the Netscape browser. The white paper argued that this conduct amounted to illegal monopolization under a variety of theories, including predatory pricing,

[89] Reback and Creighton, *White Paper Regarding the Recent Anticompetitive Conduct of the Microsoft Corporation*, p. 164.

[90] Reback and Creighton, *White Paper Regarding the Recent Anticompetitive Conduct of the Microsoft Corporation*, p. 26.

[91] Reback and Creighton, *White Paper Regarding the Recent Anticompetitive Conduct of the Microsoft Corporation*, pp. 27–32.

[92] Reback and Creighton, *White Paper Regarding the Recent Anticompetitive Conduct of the Microsoft Corporation*, p. 49.

tying, and exclusive dealing. It also emphasized that "because the predation takes place in a market subject to network effects ... the effects of the predation are magnified."[93]

Distinguishing Influences: Agencies and Courts

The puzzle in evaluating the role of politics in *Microsoft* is to distinguish naked efforts to induce the government to impede a rival from legitimate efforts to alert the government to harmful conduct and to present evidence and theory to argue that government action would advance a coherent account of the public interest. No bright line separates these activities; they probably fall on something approaching a continuum. Nevertheless, a distinction can be made. Some observers have suggested that, because the Antitrust Division began its investigation and filed its case after extensive lobbying, it must have done so simply to benefit the whining rivals who funded the campaign.[94] Others go further and suggest that a campaign of this scale using these tactics threatens traditional pluralist democracy, because it "challenge[s] the basic assumptions about information transparency, stability of interests, and political coherence of interest organizations on which the quality of democratic communication among specific interests, general publics, and policy makers depends."[95] Both criticisms assume that, when an agency is subjected to intense lobbying, it will bend to the will of the lobbyists and consciously make enforcement decisions that harm the public interest.

This analysis rests on an oversimplified view of the determinants of administrative action. More important, it ignores the role of the courts, which ultimately decide the outcome of any case the agency chooses to bring. Because the courts are independent of the political branches, they are not subject to direct pressure from interest groups, and can weed out claims brought for

[93] Reback and Creighton, *White Paper Regarding the Recent Anticompetitive Conduct of the Microsoft Corporation*, p. 141.

[94] Gerald F. Seib, "Libertarians Choose Sides as Antitrust Case Expands," *Wall Street Journal*, June 9, 1998, quotes Milton Friedman as saying that Sun's and Netscape's advocacy shows that antitrust "tend[s] to become prey to special interests." Thomas Sowell maintained that the government was simply "trying to protect competitors." See his "Microsoft's Sin: Not Thinking like a Lawyer," *Chicago Sun-Times*, June 5, 1998. Bill Gates insisted that the government was listening not to consumers but to "a handful of our competitors who want the government to help them compete by preventing Microsoft from enhancing its products." See Bill Gates, "Why the Justice Department Is Wrong," *Wall Street Journal*, November 10, 1997. Fred S. McChesney, finally, described the "Microsoft extravaganza" as an instance of "overt politicization of the antitrust process" in his "Economics Versus Politics in Antitrust," *Harvard Journal of Law and Public Policy*, Vol. 23 (1999), pp. 133, 134. See also McChesney and Shughart, "The Unjoined Debate," pp. 341, 343, who argued that earlier lobbying of antitrust enforcers to take action against Microsoft was an instance of "the now-familiar story of unsuccessful firms appealing to government for antitrust action that would handicap a highly successful rival."

[95] Bennett and Manheim, "The Big Spin," p. 295.

protectionist reasons. The antitrust injury doctrine requires courts to screen private lawsuits brought for perverse reasons; courts should be capable of doing so in the case of government suits. Because the agencies know this, one might argue, they would bring only cases they are likely to win. This constraint should be even more powerful in an era like the present one in which the many members of the federal judiciary have adopted the evolutionary vision.

Admittedly, the independent judiciary will not always inoculate enforcement agencies against interest-group pressure. An agency official might conceivably decide it is advantageous to be seen working zealously for a lost cause. Or an agency might, for protectionist reasons, use regulatory devices that courts cannot review – it might, for example, drop a justified case or use informal means, like jawboning, to deter firms from competing with a favored firm. But we are concerned in this chapter with the role of lobbying in *Microsoft*, where the government did sue and eventually achieved a partial victory in court. Moreover, we have the benefit of the white paper, a comprehensive and lucid statement of the rivals' substantive position. We are thus able to measure the lobbyists' substantive arguments against both the governments' claims (in the complaint and later in the case) and the judicial outcome. The similarities and differences should give us some basis for assessing the role of politics in the case. To the extent the white paper persuaded agency officials to file a case supported by economic theory, the best inference is that the agency's decision to file was not based on simple interest-group pressure, but at least in part on a coherent account of the public good.

The antitrust issues posed by Microsoft's behavior were exceptionally difficult. Every practice challenged could be understood through the use of accepted economic analysis as competitively benign, and the white paper demonstrated that the same practices could be sensibly understood as exclusionary. The *Microsoft* litigation undoubtedly served a decisive function in resolving these issues. But the issues were difficult in large measure because they involved a "new economy," one based on information and high technology, and one that required new economic learning. *Microsoft* represented the new economic order, and the government could set the rules for the emerging economy through resolution of the issues there. In this sense, *Microsoft* served a didactic function for the government. The closely followed, intensely scrutinized, very public trial of Microsoft afforded the government a dramatic opportunity to instruct economic actors in the new economy on the code of conduct it would enforce through the antitrust laws. To the extent the white paper's arguments persuaded the courts, the inference that the government thought it was pursuing the public interest becomes stronger. The power of the white paper is confirmation of the narrative's practical legal force and its capacity to shape normative reality in a decisive political trial.

The Department of Justice and the states embraced the white paper. Both of the complaints tracked the white paper's narrative of events: Microsoft first sought to co-opt a budding rival, and when the rival spurned its overture,

Microsoft set about to crush the rival and another that emerged. The complaints tracked the white paper's legal arguments for liability, both with respect to the antitrust claims available and the conduct that satisfied the elements of those claims. In all, the congruence between the white paper and the governments' arguments throughout the course of the litigation is striking. The congruence was not coincidental. The underlying events were many and ambiguous; the technology that lay at the heart of the industry was not easy to understand; the legal issues were complicated; the economic analysis was sophisticated. It is inconceivable that the government arrived at its positions during the litigation independently, having merely been tipped off by lobbyists to the existence of wrongdoing.

The government's acceptance of the white paper's account proves that the lobbying was effective, but it does not explain why. The most likely hypothesis is that the government officials found that the white paper made a compelling argument as to how best to promote the public interest. It is possible, of course, that the officials wanted to promote the interests of Microsoft's rivals, and adopted the white paper's account as the most plausible way of giving those interests a public-interest veneer. But the Antitrust Division was reluctant to dive head first into a major monopolization case against Microsoft. If its interest was merely in doing the bidding of Microsoft's rivals, that was not evident.[96]

It is also significant that the courts at least partly embraced the white paper's analysis. A federal court's endorsement is stronger evidence that the lobbying was not only effective, but at least arguably consistent with a principled vision of the public interest. The district court found in favor of the government (and implicitly the white paper) on virtually every important issue of contested fact and adopted nearly all of the government's characterizations of those facts.[97] It also agreed, in a later opinion, with most of the governments' arguments on the legal implications of the facts.[98] It found that Microsoft unlawfully maintained a monopoly in personal computer operating systems, that it attempted to monopolize the Internet browser market, and that it engaged in illegal tying. The only legal claim the court rejected was that Microsoft engaged in illegal exclusive dealing under Section 1 of the Sherman Act, a meaningless decision in Microsoft's favor because the court found that the same conduct violated Section 2 of the Sherman Act. Just as important, the district court ordered radical, structural relief: Microsoft would be split in two, one firm limited to producing operating systems and one to applications.[99]

[96] See generally Heilemann, *Pride before the Fall*, pp. 27–33.

[97] *United States* v. *Microsoft Corp.*, 84 F. Supp. 2d 9 (D.D.C. 1999), aff'd in part, rev'd in part, 253 F.3d 34 (D.C. Cir. 2001) (per curiam).

[98] *United States* v. *Microsoft Corp.*, 87 F. Supp. 2d 30 (D.D.C. 2000), aff'd in part, rev'd in part, 253 F.3d 34 (D.C. Cir. 2001) (per curiam).

[99] *United States* v. *Microsoft Corp.*, 97 F. Supp. 2d 59 (D.D.C. 2000), aff'd in part, rev'd in part, 253 F.3d 34 (D.C. Cir. 2001) (per curiam).

Although by the end of the trial Judge Jackson had embraced the governments' analysis, we now know that his credibility and legal objectivity were tainted. Beginning at least two months before he issued findings of fact, Judge Jackson gave a series of secret interviews to reporters covering the case.[100] The interviews were "embargoed," the judge insisting that the reporters agree not to publish his comments until the case had left his courtroom.[101] In the interviews, later published, Jackson displayed a strong distaste for Microsoft in general and Bill Gates in particular. He said that "Gates & Co.'s 'crime' was hubris – a refusal to acknowledge that the nation's antitrust laws applied to them."[102] He said Gates was like "a smart-mouthed young kid who ... needs a little discipline," and that Microsoft executives "don't act like grown-ups."[103] So convinced was Judge Jackson of Microsoft's wrongdoing and stubbornness that he shocked all parties to the litigation by entering a structural remedy without holding a separate evidentiary hearing.[104] Even if Judge Jackson started the litigation with no animus toward Gates and Microsoft and only formed his opinion based on evidence presented during litigation, as Jackson insisted, his vitriol raises a suspicion that his legal decisions were not based entirely on the strength of the arguments made in the white paper and by the government. On appeal, the District of Columbia Circuit Court held that Judge Jackson committed "deliberate, repeated, egregious, and flagrant" violations of three canons of the code of judicial conduct for federal judges and a provision of the United States Judicial Code.[105]

Nevertheless, the appellate court did not throw out Judge Jackson's findings of fact, choosing instead to remove him from proceedings in the case after remand. Most important, the court of appeals itself embraced critical elements of the governments' case. In an opinion that was per curiam ("through the court," rather than attributed to individual judges) the court affirmed the district court's conclusion that Microsoft had unlawfully maintained a monopoly in the operating system market by integrating the Internet Explorer browser with Windows, forming restrictive distribution agreements with Internet service providers, and imposing limits on the ability

[100] See *United States* v. *Microsoft Corp.*, 253 F.3d 34, 108 (D.C. Cir. 2001) (per curiam).

[101] *Microsoft*, 253 F. 3d at 108.

[102] Ken Auletta, "What Kept Microsoft from Settling Its Case," *New Yorker*, January 15, 2001, p. 41.

[103] *Microsoft*, 253 F. 3d at 110. He also compared Microsoft's behavior to that of drug traffickers and gangland killers, *Microsoft*, 253 F.3d at 110, and to Japan at the end of World War II. *Microsoft*, 253 F. 3d at 111 (quoting Peter Spiegel, "Microsoft Judge Defends Post-trial Comments," *Financial Times*, October 7, 2000.

[104] See Heilemann, *Pride before the Fall*, p. 220. He quipped that he had imposed a drastic remedy to get Microsoft's attention, just as a North Carolina mule trainer in an old story "whopped [the mule] upside the head" with a 2-by-4 to get the mule to "do all kinds of wonderful tricks." *United States* v. *Microsoft Corp.*, 253 F.3d 34, 111 (D.C. Cir. 2001) (per curiam) (quoting Brinkley and Lohr, *U.S.* v. *Microsoft*, p. 278).

[105] *Microsoft*, 253 F. 3d at 107.

of computer manufacturers to delete Internet Explorer or to promote independent middleware.[106]

Through these holdings the court assented to the theory first developed comprehensively in the white paper. The assent was qualified, however. The court rejected all of the government's claims that Microsoft had reduced competition by giving its products and services away free or by producing better products. These holdings stripped from the case the arguments in the white paper that most clearly represented simple pleas for protection from better and cheaper products. The court also rejected the conclusion that Microsoft had attempted to monopolize the browser market, finding that the plaintiffs had not proven the existence of a browser market protected by entry barriers. (Confusingly, though, the court also found that Microsoft had maintained its operating system monopoly by foreclosing competition in the browser market.[107]) Finally, the court reversed the finding of illegal tying, holding that a special tying standard should apply to platform software.[108] This decision, among others, ensured that Microsoft would not be required to distribute its Internet Explorer browser only separately from its Windows operating system; it would be required only to allow others to delete the browser and to add or substitute a different browser if they chose to do so. It thus stripped from the case another of the white paper's claims that Microsoft should be required to make its products less capable in order to improve its rivals' ability to compete.

The appellate court also gave Microsoft a major victory in setting aside the district court's divestiture order. The court concluded that the district court erred in failing to conduct an evidentiary hearing on remedies and in failing to provide adequate reasons for its decree. Moreover, the reduced scope of liability the appellate court found required a fresh consideration of remedies.[109] More important, the court signaled unmistakably that a structural remedy would be inappropriate.[110]

Heeding the message of the appellate court, the Department of Justice and a group of states negotiated a settlement when the case returned to the district court, this time to a different judge who found the settlement to be consistent

[106] *Microsoft*, 253 F. 3d at 50–80. [107] *Microsoft*, 253 F. 3d at 80–84.

[108] *Microsoft*, 253 F. 3d at 84. It remanded the case to the district court, allowing the governments to pursue it based on the correct legal standard. *Microsoft*, 253 F. 3d at 95–97. The governments chose not to pursue it, though, undoubtedly because the conduct underlying the tying claim was part of the conduct that supported the monopoly maintenance claim. Given that the governments succeeded on the latter claim, they could obtain all possible relief against tying as relief against monopoly maintenance.

[109] *Microsoft*, 253 F. 3d at 98.

[110] It reasoned that a court might find a causal connection between exclusionary behavior and the suppression of incipient competition sufficient to support liability for monopoly maintenance, but not sufficient to support structural relief. See id. at 106. The appellate court would almost certainly find the necessary connection lacking if on remand the district court imposed a structural remedy. The court instructed that remedial provisions had to focus on conduct found unlawful.

with the public interest and entered a corresponding consent decree.[111] A small group of states refused to settle and pursued the litigation, but the new district judge entered a remedy in their case virtually identical to the consent decree,[112] and the appellate court affirmed both of the final judgments.[113]

The final judgment imposed a set of conduct restrictions on Microsoft. Microsoft was required, for example, to give computer manufacturers more freedom to modify Windows by deleting access to certain functions and adding other software.[114] Collectively, the provisions allowed Microsoft to maintain the integrity of Windows as a software platform by preserving code on which producers of applications relied, while allowing computer manufacturers and end users readily to use competing products.

The most provocative provisions, characterized by the court as "forward-looking,"[115] required Microsoft to disclose various application programming interfaces, technical information, and communications protocols that pertain to interoperation between middleware and the operating system and between personal computer operating systems and servers.[116] These provisions were not tied directly to any conduct found unlawful, and the provision mandating the disclosure of communications protocols between personal computers and servers proved especially frustrating to the court, because industry participants were not interested in using them.[117]

In all, the influence of the white paper can be seen in the way the federal and state governments framed their cases, in the decisions of the district court

[111] *United States* v. *Microsoft Corp.*, 231 F. Supp. 2d 144 (D.D.C. 2002), aff'd sub nom., 373 F.3d 1199 (D.C. Cir. 2004). The *Microsoft* case began during the Clinton administration, and the consent decree was entered during the George W. Bush administration. One might be tempted to infer that the Justice Department's willingness to accept a far less aggressive remedy than the agency had originally sought was a function of the change in political party in the White House. But a more likely explanation is that the government recognized that the district court, guided by the appellate court's opinion striking down the original structural remedy, would not impose structural relief, and the appellate court would not affirm it even if the district court imposed it. That assessment proved accurate.

[112] *New York* v. *Microsoft Corp.*, 224 F. Supp. 2d 76 (D.D.C. 2002).

[113] *Massachusetts* v. *Microsoft Corp.*, 373 F.3d 1199 (D.C. Cir. 2004).

[114] *United States* v. *Microsoft Corp.*, No. Civ.A. 98-1232 (CKK), 2002 WL 31654530, at *2–3 (D.D.C. November 12, 2002). In addition, Microsoft was prohibited from discriminating in licensing Windows against OEMs that promoted non-Microsoft products. Id. at *1–2. End users had to be given a simple means of removing easy access to Microsoft's browser. *Microsoft*, 2002 WL 31654530, at *4–5. The settlement also prevented Microsoft from entering into exclusive or otherwise restrictive distribution and promotion agreements with Internet access providers and others. *Microsoft*, 2002 WL 31654530, at *4.

[115] *Microsoft*, 231 F. Supp. 2d at 190. [116] *Microsoft*, 2002 WL 31654530, at *3–4.

[117] *New York* v. *Microsoft Corp.*, 531 F. Supp. 2d 141, 158–164 (D.D.C. 2008); William H. Page and Seldon J. Childers, "Software Development as an Antitrust Remedy: Lessons from the Enforcement of the Microsoft Communications Protocol Licensing Requirement," *Michigan Telecommunications and Technology Law Review*, Vol. 14 (2007), pp. 77–136; John E. Lopatka, "Assessing Microsoft from a Distance," *Antitrust Law Journal*, Vol. 75 (2009), pp. 811, 839.

finding liability and initially ordering relief, and, to a lesser extent, in the appellate court's liability determination and the ensuing proceedings and remedies. After this winnowing, the eventual influence of politics on *Microsoft* had less to do with interest-group pressure than with the persuasiveness of the white paper's narrative. The white paper convinced the governments and ultimately the courts that the markets in which Microsoft operated would not be restored to competition absent government intervention. The acceptance of the argument by the Antitrust Division of the Clinton administration and by Judge Jackson was likely aided by their adherence to some version of the intentional vision.[118]

There is little reason to believe that most members of the DC Circuit also took that ideological view. The court nevertheless endorsed some of the key elements of the white paper's narrative. We can perhaps see traces of the influence of ideology in the many tensions (if not outright inconsistencies) in the reasoning of the court's formally unanimous, unsigned opinion.[119] These tensions indicate that the opinion did not have a single author with a single view of the government's case. The court's decision to issue such an opinion per curiam, a form usually reserved for obvious or routine decisions, may reflect a broadly political desire to mask the role of ideology in the resolution of such a controversial and celebrated case. Whatever the reason, the outcome is the clearest evidence of the persuasiveness of the white paper's narrative. It represents a rare, if limited, victory for the intentional vision in modern antitrust.

CONCLUSION

A trial is political because of its purpose and the practices that enact and mediate that purpose.[120] Political lobbying prodded the government to bring the case and shaped the litigation. But the purpose of the case was not simply to bring about an outcome favored by powerful economic interests. The more fundamental purpose, revealed only after trial and appellate procedures and even then only after extensive mediation and negotiation, was to ratify the essential claims of a powerful narrative with important political consequences. The outcome is political because it represents a victory for the intentional vision, which claims intervention in markets is necessary, even in the "new economy," to restore competition and ensure markets serve the public interest.

118 For an account of the Division's perspective, authored by its Deputy Assistant Attorney General (and a distinguished economist), see Daniel Rubinfeld, Competition, Innovation, and Antitrust Enforcement in Dynamic Network Industries, Address before the Software Publishers' Association, March 24, 1998, available at www.usdoj.gov/atr/public/speeches/1611.htm.

119 John E. Lopatka and William H. Page, "The Price of Unanimity: The D.C. Circuit's Incoherent Opinion in Microsoft," *The Antitrust Source*, November 2001, available at www.abanet.org /antitrust/at-source/01/11/price.pdf.

120 Meierhenrich and Pendas, "'The Justice of My Cause is Clear, But There's Politics to Fear.'"

14

The Trials of Khodorkovsky in Russia

Richard Sakwa

In a dawn raid on his plane in Novosibirsk on October 25, 2003, Mikhail Khodorkovsky, the head of the Yukos oil company, was arrested.[1] This event has spawned a mountain of literature and provoked a debate that shows little sign of diminishing. By that time Khodorkovsky had become one of the world's richest and most powerful men, while Yukos had been transformed from a ramshackle conglomeration of Soviet production, refining, and distribution units into a vertically integrated oil company that was set to go global. It was Russia's second-largest producer, and if the plans in 2003 to merge with Roman Abramovich's Sibneft oil company had been completed, it would have become the country's biggest oil company, with 40 percent or more of its stock ready to be sold to an American company. On all counts, this looked like a success story, but it was precisely at this moment that the Russian authorities struck. After a long period of detention, in May 2005 Khodorkovsky was sentenced to nine years in jail (reduced to eight on appeal) and Yukos was broken up. In March 2009 a second trial began, and in December 2010 Khodorkovsky and his leading colleague Platon Lebedev were given another long sentence, to be served concurrently with the first, that would see them in jail until 2016. In December 2012 the Moscow City Court reduced their sentences by two years, and on August 6, 2013, the Supreme Court cut a further two months from their sentences, bringing forward their anticipated release to August 23 and May 2, 2014, respectively. However, on November 12, 2013, Khodorkovsky wrote to President Vladimir Putin requesting a pardon, although he insisted that "The issue of admission of guilt was not raised."[2] On December 19 Putin signed the pardon, and early next morning Khodorkovsky was released and flew to Berlin.

[1] The material in this chapter draws on Richard Sakwa, *Putin and the Oligarch: The Khodorkovsky-Yukos Affair* (London: I. B. Tauris, 2014).

[2] "Khodorkovsky's First Message in Freedom," December 20, 2013, available at www.khodorkovsky.com/featured-articles/khodorkovskys-first-message-in-freedom/.

The two cases against Khodorkovsky represent a distinctive type of political trial.[3] They share the fundamental characteristic of other political trials: they were an exercise in power, demonstrating to all who was the ultimate source of authority in the land; they were salutary, in that they acted as a warning to others that they could share this fate if they challenged the authorities; and they were system-forming, in that the trial reshaped the political and social landscape to allow a reconfigured policy constellation to predominate. Khodorkovsky's first trial was accompanied by the break-up and effective expropriation of Yukos, with the bulk of its assets transferred at a steep discount to a favored state-owned oil company, Rosneft. Gazprom, the giant gas production and distribution company, had hoped to benefit but after severe internal factional struggles Rosneft won, but Gazprom was compensated in September 2005 by the acquisition of Sibneft.

There are distinctive elements to the whole affair. It was a one-off, which suggests that the shock factor was so large that no other trial of a business leader was necessary. It also indicates that special factors were involved in the attack on Khodorkovsky that ultimately were not replicable. This point is reinforced by the launching of the second trial when Khodorkovsky was already safely incarcerated in a prison camp near Chita in Russia's Far East. His first sentence would have ended in late 2011, allowing him to return to active life just as Russia entered another electoral cycle, with parliamentary elections in December 2011 and the presidential contest in March 2012. Putin's return to office for a third term in 2012 was accompanied by mass protests against electoral fraud and the stifling tutelary nature of the Putin system as a whole. By late 2013 the protests had largely fizzled out, and accompanied by some mild reforms, Putin was firmly back in the saddle and could afford to be magnanimous. Khodorkovsky was no longer perceived to be a political threat, and with the Sochi Winter Olympics due to be staged in February 2014, Russia rid itself of one of its most intractable human rights embarrassments.

This was a *decisive* trial, in the language of the Introduction to the book. A fundamental political question was resolved: the sovereignty of the administrative regime could no longer be challenged. There was an element of didacticism involved, acting as a warning to others, but this was a consequence, rather than a cause, of the event. Equally, although there was a destructive dynamic at work, the relatively constrained nature of the attack left the bulk of the oligarchs at liberty, and even Khodorkovsky remained an active commentator on Russian political affairs. As we shall see, this exercise of sovereign regime power used the procedures of the constitutional state in a way that subverted the substantive legalism that is at the heart of a constitutional order. In performative terms, the Khodorkovsky trials exposed the regime's

[3] Cf. Jens Meierhenrich and Devin O. Pendas, "'The Justice of My Cause Is Clear, But There's Politics to Fear': Political Trials in Theory and History," in this volume.

machinations, and although they pandered to the populist animus against "oligarch" power, they inflicted substantive damage on the regime's legitimacy. In revealing the exercise of raw power, although disguised as a remedial act of justice, the regime exposed its operative practices to external critique.

The attack on Khodorkovsky marked a watershed in Putin's presidency. If before the international community was willing to believe in Putin's liberal reformist credentials, as the Yukos affair developed and Russia adopted a harder line in international politics, the regime that he led was increasingly considered as authoritarian. The struggle against Khodorkovsky and his associates revealed Putin's political style, the way that specific factions were able to seize the policy agenda over certain issues, and exposed the tensions in the whole Putinist style of governance. Coming at a time when primary commodity sales were enjoying a price boom, and thus the Kremlin was showered with the accompanying bonanza, competition over the appropriation and application of resources intensified. The *silovik* faction (those with a background in or aligned with the security services) took advantage of this to press forward their attack on one of the most egregiously independent business leaders. The liberal model of economic development that had hitherto predominated in the energy sector was now bent to the will of factional interests, although liberals did not lose their positions entirely. These two factors – the struggle against the "over-mighty" oligarch and competition over control of rents – exacerbated fissures that are inherent in Russia's political system and intensified the struggles at the heart of the state. Like the Dreyfus affair in Third Republic France, the case throws a deep and harsh light on the nature of the political system.

CONTEXT

The Yukos oil company was established in the early 1990s, and within a decade it had grown to become one of the world's major players. By the end of its first decade the company improved its corporate governance, rejecting some of the worst predatory and ruthless aspects of the 1990s, so that by 2003 it had become a model for the development of Russian corporate capitalism. However, in that year the government launched a sustained assault against the company's leading executives and associates, and by October of that year Khodorkovsky himself was in jail. The charges against him and his colleagues focused on tax avoidance and fraud, but as we shall see, numerous other factors were involved, including Khodorkovsky's alleged political ambitions. In the second trial from 2009 the Yukos executives were effectively charged with embezzlement of the oil on which they had allegedly failed to pay tax in the first case. At issue was the fundamental question: the appropriate relationship between the state and private capital, and who would determine key issues of economic policy and strategic development. Two logics of modernity collided, each coherent and valid in its own terms, and the clash gave rise to the Yukos affair.

The Khodorkovsky trials helped establish the boundaries between the state and big business. The fall of the communist system in 1991 and the emergence of an independent Russia in December of that year prepared the way for a traumatic shift to market democracy. This entailed a revolutionary transformation of social and political relations as the Soviet planned economy was dismantled and a market system installed in its place. However, as Alexis de Tocqueville stressed, even the most radical of revolutions incorporates much of the ancien régime into its operative practices. This was exacerbated in Russia by the absence of an alternative elite ready to take power, and instead much of the old Soviet *nomenklatura* (office-holding class) was incorporated wholesale into the new order.

With President Boris Yeltsin at its head between 1991 and 1999, Russia became a capitalist democracy, but it did so in a revolutionary way – that is, law, constitutionality, the regular operation of institutions, were subordinated to the imperative of change. This was a hybrid revolution because the transformation was designed precisely to create the conditions where extraordinary politics no longer needed to apply, and where law and institutions would be able to operate autonomously. It is this tension which gave rise to a dual state, in which law and institutionalized procedures (the constitutional state) were balanced by the emergence of an arbitrary and shadowy administrative regime operating with a degree of autonomy from the legal political order above and popular representative institutions from below (above all political parties and parliament).[4] Putin's assumption of the presidency in 2000 represented a new phase of Russia's hybrid revolution, when contradiction itself became a mode of governance. Every act and institution was imbued with a double valance. The phrase "dictatorship of law," with which Putin launched his presidency, neatly encapsulates the contradictory character of his leadership. The law was used instrumentally, to achieve overtly political goals – the cutting down to size of someone who perceived to be an over-mighty subject.

Putin's first two presidential terms (2000–2008) were used to restore the privileges of the state against the declared willfulness of "oligarchs," the conventional name for the small group of super-rich individuals who profited from the revolutionary change in property ownership in the 1990s (we use the term purely in that sense), as well as regional leaders and other political and social actors. Putin's regime, however, was unwilling to subordinate itself to the constraints of the constitutional state or the supervision of popular representative institutions, and thus it stood outside of the process – the restoration of the power of the state – which it declared to be its goal.

[4] Richard Sakwa, "The Dual State in Russia," *Post-Soviet Affairs*, Vol. 26 (2010), pp. 185–206; Richard Sakwa, *The Crisis of Russian Democracy: The Dual State, Factionalism and the Medvedev Succession* (Cambridge: Cambridge University Press, 2011).

The powers of the administrative regime were intensified as "managed democracy" undermined the free play of autonomous political actors. The administrative regime assumed the power to decide who was a friend or enemy, and thus in Schmittian terms became sovereign. Although Putin and his successor from 2008, Dmitry Medvedev, expressed distaste for the term "sovereign democracy," which became current following the Beslan school hostage crisis of September 2004, the concept effectively encapsulates the aspirations of the regime in both domestic and foreign policy. Equally, although both Putin and Medvedev repudiated revolution as a form of political action, and hence with scrupulous attention to detail ensured that the prerogatives of the administrative regime were inscribed in legislative acts and remained in formal conformity with the letter of the constitution, in practice once again a type of revolutionary expediency came into contradiction with the revolution's attempt to transform Russia into a law-based democratic capitalist state. The abusive application of judicial procedures to pursue political goals characterized the Putinite form of tutelary politics.

It is in the forks of this contradiction that the Yukos affair developed, and in which Khodorkovsky was brought low. Khodorkovsky himself was no stranger to the contradictory essence of Russia's post-communist revolution, and thus he was both Putin's antagonist and at the same time he was a protagonist of the contradiction that Putin's regime reflected. In gaining his assets Khodorkovsky had not hesitated to bend the rules and ruthlessly to exploit the courts and legislative lacunae to build his empire.[5] We should be wary, therefore, of unduly romanticizing Khodorkovsky's resistance to the consolidation of Putin's statism and model of political economy, although giving due weight to his dignity and courage in adversity; or indeed, of aligning with the Putinite view that this "over-mighty subject" embodied a threat to the government's ability to forge policies and strategies that represented the interests of the many and not the few. We should also distinguish between the attack on Khodorkovsky personally and the assault against the Yukos oil company, although in practice the two campaigns are almost inseparable. The reason for this fusion is that the logic of the two events had a common source: to remove a challenge to the regime's putative prerogatives in the political sphere; and to assert those same prerogatives in economic life. The attack on Yukos was a consequence of the personal attack on Khodorkovsky, but soon gained a life of its own as economic predators pounced on the vulnerable company and achieved a partial redistribution of the property settlement of the 1990s.

The assault on Yukos was not part of a predetermined plan that was systematically implemented, but reflected a gradual enlarging of appetites as the first stage – the humbling of Khodorkovsky – encountered surprisingly little resistance. In broader terms, the Khodorkovsky trials represented

[5] Khodorkovsky admits as much in a letter to the writer Ludmila Ulitskaya on June 5, 2009, Mikhail Khodorkovskii, *Stat'i, dialogi, intervyu* (Moscow: Eksmo, 2010), p. 124.

a confrontation between the two great forces of modernity, the state and the market and their associated conceptions of freedom. Khodorkovsky represented the rising power of the nascent bourgeoisie in Russia, while Putin defended classic statist positions, asserting the primacy of the political over social forces. Thus the case represents a reprise of some of the issues raised by Carl Schmitt in Weimar Germany, and in particular his concern that the social was swallowing the political.[6] Khodorkovsky may well have become a political victim of the Russian regime, but his challenge was explicit and sustained. His first trial was a political signal that the era of the power of independent tycoons was over, and henceforth big business could make money but only on condition that it made no overt political demands, and thus accepted its subaltern place in the political order. The second trial was more personal, as Putin fought to keep Khodorkovsky from engagement in the 2011–2012 succession operation, but even from jail Khodorkovsky became one of the defining forces in Russian politics. Lacking authoritative leaders, the opposition comprised a confused ragbag of incompatible aspirations. One can only imagine what would have happened if Khodorkovsky had been free to place himself at the head of the protest movement.

THE RISE OF YUKOS

By the time of his arrest in 2003 Khodorkovsky was top of the Forbes Russia list with $3.7 billion.[7] For many he represented the exemplary "oligarch" who made his fortune during the period of anarchic privatization (known in Russian as *prikhvatizatsiya*, "piratization") in the 1990s.[8] The "chaotic 1990s" casts a long shadow over Russia, and the legitimacy of the property settlement of the period is still questioned. Khodorkovsky was born in Moscow to a Jewish-Russian family of modest means on June 26, 1963. Like Putin, he spent his first years in a cramped communal apartment, and his family only moved into a separate flat in 1971 (it would be another six years before Putin's family received an apartment of their own). His parents were typical Moscow technical intelligentsia. His father, Boris Moiseevich, and his mother, Marina Filippovna, were both chemical engineers and spent their working lives at the "Kalibr" factory turning out precision measuring equipment. Like another of the leading oligarchs of the era, Roman Abramovich, Khodorkovsky started earning extra income from an early age, working in a bakers, as a carpenter, and then for four years he headed a building brigade (the *shabashniki*), including work in Moldova and the Baikal-Amur Mainline (BAM) railway.

[6] Carl Schmitt, *The Concept of the Political*, translated by George Schwab (Chicago: Chicago University Press, 1996).
[7] "Kratkii kurs istorii milliarderov," *Izvestiya*, March 1, 2003, p. 2.
[8] David E. Hoffman, *The Oligarchs: Wealth and Power in the New Russia* (New York: PublicAffairs, 2002), pp. 100–126.

In 1981 Khodorkovsky entered the renowned Mendeleev Institute of Chemical Engineering, graduating in 1986. He was a model Soviet citizen, and rose to become deputy head of the Komsomol (Communist Youth League, VLKSM) organization in his institute. He was elected a member of the Sverdlovsk Komsomol district committee and then became deputy head of the Frunze district Komsomol committee, at which time he joined the Communist Party of the Soviet Union (CPSU). It was in this district that all the top members of the VLKSM Central Committee were registered, providing many contacts that came in useful later. Khodorkovsky graduated just at the time when opportunities dramatically expanded as a result of Mikhail Gorbachev's perestroika. The green light was given for the development of a "Komsomol economy" that provided the seedbed for a post-communist entrepreneurial class, acting as privileged auxiliaries to the formal economy.

Youth entrepreneurship quickly turned into a massive money laundering exercise. With partners from the Mendeleev Institute, in December 1986 Khodorkovsky opened a private café, traded new technologies to Soviet enterprises, imported computers, and sold Polish, Armenian, and French cognac. Above all, Khodorkovsky took advantage of legislation adopted in 1987 that allowed the creation of private commercial banks. He established a cooperative intended to introduce scientific innovation into production, although it largely focused on the hugely lucrative business of selling computers. By December 1988 Khodorkovsky had created one of the first banks, which in May 1990 was formally registered as "Menatep." In December of that year it was one of the first companies in Russia to issue what at the time passed for shares. Persistent rumors suggest that some of Menatep's early funds were provided by the Komsomol Central Committee, and even that it used "party money" from the CPSU itself.[9] Khodorkovsky admitted later that he relied on protection from the state committee on science and technology to ward off challenges from the police and security services. Attempts to rein in the Komsomol economy were futile. Nevertheless, up to the August 1991 coup Khodorkovsky considered himself "a loyal Communist Party member";[10] and if the Soviet order had not dissolved he would no doubt have been at the head of Chinese-style capitalism within a socialist framework.

Soon after launching himself in business, Khodorkovsky in 1987 was joined by Leonid Nevzlin, who quickly rose to become his deputy. Another of Khodorkovsky's associates in this early period was Vladislav Surkov, who later as a deputy head of the presidential administration shaped "sovereign democracy."[11] In January 1990 the bank was joined by the financial genius

[9] Marshall I. Goldman, *The Piratization of Russia: Russian Reform Goes Awry* (London: Routledge, 2003), p. 147.

[10] Rose Brady, *Kapitalizm: Russia's Struggle to Free Its Economy* (New Haven: Yale University Press, 1999), p. 55.

[11] Ol'ga Kryshtanovkaya, *Anatomiya rossiiskoi elity* (Moscow: Zakharov, 2005), p. 303.

Platon Lebedev, who would go on to become its head. Menatep soon overtook most of its competitors, in particular because of its masterful ability to convert the Soviet "wooden" ruble into convertible cash. State enterprises diverted virtual ruble resources (*beznalichnye*) through the accounts of the new banks, and in return they received real currency. In effect, this was a license to print money. With the fall of communism and the coming to power of Yeltsin in Russia in 1991, Menatep's fortunes soared, above all by exploiting close links to the government.[12] Khodorkovsky occupied a number of governmental and advisory posts.

In 1992 Menatep shifted its focus from purely financial activities to create Rosprom, a holding company to manage its industrial interests. In the early 1990s Menatep was flooded with more cash than it knew how to handle. In his characteristic manner Khodorkovsky thought in grandiose terms, and used this money to create a major industrial empire. He bought up any available company, including the Apatit mineral fertilizer company in Murmansk region that was later to play such a fateful role in the Yukos affair. By March 1996, through Rosprom, Menatep had controlling shares in 29 industrial enterprises and major holdings in another 50.[13] Most of these companies were bought in investment auctions, in which money had to be found after purchase. In the case of the Apatit plant, the company was bought cheaply, but the condition of the purchase was to invest in the company. Fearing that the old Apatit management would simply steal transfers or misuse them, Menatep took over the management of the company, paid the wages, optimized taxes, and invested in infrastructure, or so Menatep argued. These indirect investments were the basis for the judicial resolution of charges that Menatep had made the requisite investment in Apatit, until the case was reopened on political grounds.[14]

From 1992 the oil industry was broken up into a number of what were intended to become vertically integrated companies on the Western model, as well as being regionally concentrated. The Yukos oil company was created in April 1993 as a result of the merger of two state-owned entities, and was Russia's second-largest oil producer. The 1992 privatization program for the oil industry stipulated that the state would initially retain a controlling interest. However, the pressing financial needs of the government, with the budget deficit by 1995 reaching 10 percent of GDP, led to the disbursement of the state's share. Seizing the opportunity, a number of leading banks offered credit to the government on security of government shares in privatized enterprises,

[12] For an account of this early period, see Paul Klebnikov, "The Oligarch Who Came in from the Cold," *Forbes*, March 18, 2002, available at www.forbes.com/forbes/2002/0318/110_print.html.

[13] Natal'ya Gotova, "Mikhail Khodorkovskii ukhodit v promyshlennost," *Segodnya*, March 29, 1996.

[14] Valerii Panyushkin, *Mikhail Khodorkovskii: uznik tishiny* (Moscow: Sekret Firmy, 2006), pp. 63–65, 213–217.

the notorious "loans-for-shares" scheme.[15] Menatep was put in charge of processing the bids for the Yukos auction, allowing it to gain 45 percent of the company's stock for $159 million, $9 million above the starting price. The associated investment tender in December 1995 saw a further 33 percent of Yukos stock going to Menatep for $150 million, with the bank pledging to invest a further $300 million over the next three years. The bottom line was that Khodorkovsky and his partners paid a total of $350 upfront for control of 78 percent of Yukos stock, suggesting that the total value of the company was $450, although at the same time they were taking on some $3 billion of debt. With later share emissions that further diluted the state's holding, by autumn 1996 Menatep owned 90 percent of Yukos stock. When the shares began trading in 1997, Yukos's market capitalization was $9 billion, and reached some $15 billion by early 2002. In 1996, however, Khodorkovsky was still joking that the winners of the loans-for-loans auction were "a collection of bankrupts," although he personally was not doing so badly.[16]

In that year Khodorkovsky played an active role in the hard-fought presidential contest that saw Yeltsin elected for a second term. Uncertain of the outcome, in the notorious "Appeal of the Thirteen" of April 1996 a group of top oligarchs called on Yeltsin to come to terms with his main challenger, Gennady Zyuganov at the head of the Communist Party of the Russian Federation (CPRF).[17] Khodorkovsky was one of the initiators of the letter together with Boris Berezovsky, another of the leading tycoons, urging that Zyuganov be offered the post of prime minister with enhanced powers, while Yeltsin would remain president. However, instead of the elections being postponed to save the country from catastrophic divisions, the oligarchs generously funded Yeltsin's campaign, and by hook and by crook he was re-elected. It was in this campaign that the oligarchs first made their political mark, among whom a group of "seven bankers" (*semibankirshchina*) predominated. In a notorious interview, Berezovsky claimed that the seven had been responsible for Yeltsin's re-election and controlled 50 percent of the Russian economy: "We hired [Anatoly] Chubais [the liberal minister responsible for privatisation] and invested huge sums of money to ensure Yeltsin's election. Now we have the right to occupy government posts and enjoy the fruits of our victory."[18] Their grip on the media was no less tight, controlling 70 percent of

[15] Daniel Treisman, "'Loans for Shares' Revisited," *Post-Soviet Affairs*, Vol. 26 (2010), pp. 207–227.

[16] Pavel Khlebnikov, *Krestnyi otets Kremlya Boris Berezovskii, ili istoriya razgrableniya Rossii* (Moscow: Detektiv Press, 2001), p. 262; the book had earlier come out in English as Paul Klebnikov, *Godfather of the Kremlin: Boris Berezovsky and the Looting of Russia* (New York: Harcourt, 2000).

[17] "Get Out of the Impasse," *Current Digest of the Post-Soviet Press*, Vol. 48 (1996), pp. 1–3; "Vyiti iz tupika!," *Kommersant*, April 27, 1996, p. 1.

[18] The seven bankers were Boris Berezovsky, Vladimir Potanin, Mikhail Khodorkovsky, Vladimir Gusinsky, Alexander Smolensky, Mikhail Fridman, and Pyotr Aven. Chrystia Freeland,

the Moscow press and radio and 80 percent of national television.[19] In an interview with *Nezavisimaya gazeta*, Khodorkovsky made no bones about the relationship between politics and business: "Politics is the most lucrative field of business in Russia. And it will be that way forever."[20] Oligarchs now firmly entered the lists as the most influential politicians, with Berezovsky between 1997 and 2000 consistently ranking as the top oligarch and in 1998 and 2000 listed as the fourth most influential person in the country, although Khodorkovsky of all the major oligarchs ranked lowest, in those years placed only 25th and 60th, respectively.[21]

Menatep had established a close relationship with Yukos, so it was already an insider at the time of the auctions. Unlike some other oil companies, Menatep then played a major part in the further development of the enterprise.[22] If the first stage in Yukos's development was assembling the company and giving it a rudimentary corporate structure, the second was privatization of its stock, the bulk of which went to Menatep, then the third stage was transforming ownership into control. The methods used to achieve this reflected the harshest period of "robber baron" capitalism in Russia. In the case of Nefteyugansk, the capital of Yukos's main oil-producing subsidiary Yuganskneftegaz (YNG), there were even accusations of the murder of the mayor, Vladimir Petukhov, on June 26, 1998. To achieve control a whole range of "informal corporate governance practices" were applied, including share dilution, asset stripping, transfer pricing, undermining shareholder voting rights, and forced bankruptcies. As Adachi notes, these practices "performed important functions in relation to the conversion of post-Soviet former state enterprises into functional firms, able to perform as business units in a market economy."[23] Yukos became notorious for the vigorous application of these methods, but out of it emerged a competitive vertically integrated company. By 1999 Yukos was Russia's largest oil company in terms of total recoverable reserves, 85 percent of which were in the massive West Siberian YNG concession.[24]

In the early 2000s big business began to transform itself from morally dubious "oligarch capitalism" into respectable national capital. Although Joel

John Thornhill, and Andrew Gowers, "Moscow's Group of Seven," *Financial Times*, November 1, 1997. Petr Aven is listed when in fact the seventh was Vladimir Vinogradov, head of Inkombank.

[19] Goldman, *The Piratization of Russia*, p. 2.

[20] Cited by Andrei Piontovsky, "Modern-Day Rasputin," *Moscow Times*, November 12, 1997.

[21] Kryshtanovkaya, *Anatomiya rossiiskoi elity*, p. 330.

[22] Valery Kryukov and Arild Moe, *The Changing Role of Banks in the Russian Oil Sector* (London: Royal Institute of International Affairs, 1998).

[23] Yuko Adachi, "The Ambiguous Effects of Russian Corporate Governance Abuses of the 1990s," *Post-Soviet Affairs*, Vol. 22 (2006), p. 67. See also her *Building Big Business in Russia: The Impact of Informal Corporate Governance Practices* (London: Routledge, 2010).

[24] David Lane and Iskander Seifulmulukov, "Company Profiles: LUKoil, YuKOS, Surgutnefteftgaz, Sidanko," in David Lane, ed., *The Political Economy of Russian Oil*, Part 1 Appendix (Lanham: Rowman & Littlefield Publishers, 1999), pp. 111–124, 114.

Hellman had argued that the initial winners of economic liberalization would block further reforms,[25] the oligarchs had already begun to change themselves before the state-bureaucratic apparatus moved against them. As world oil prices and exports rose, Khodorkovsky in October 1999 announced an ambitious investment program.[26] In the early 2000s most major Russian oil companies launched a transparency drive, with the notable exception of Surgutneftegas.[27] Khodorkovsky was in the vanguard of this transformation, changing Yukos from one of the most ruthless and predatory companies to a symbol of a more open and transparently managed enterprise. It adopted Western accounting standards and issued clear financial accounts every three months, and in 2002 Menatep published a list of its main shareholders. Pumping 2 percent of global oil output, Yukos took advantage of the rise in energy prices, tripling in just two years to reach $33 per barrel by 2000. The company's transformation was accompanied by Khodorkovsky's reinvention of himself as an enlightened capitalist. Khodorkovsky was one of the most successful oligarchs to shift from finance to industrial capital, a process hastened by the 1998 financial collapse. As one of Russia's best performing companies, Yukos gained significant sympathy in the West in its later struggle with the Kremlin, and it made the assault against the company appear all the more irrational and politically motivated. The problem was that Khodorkovsky had forgotten his own insight. In an interview in the late 1990s he announced that if the prime minister asked him to resign as head of his bank, he would do so without hesitation: "That's how Russia is organized. The state is always the dominant force in the economy."[28]

THE FALL OF YUKOS

With Putin's ascent to power in 2000 a new model of state–business relations was imposed, dubbed the policy of "equidistance." No business tycoon would be allowed to have a privileged relationship with the state; they would all be held equally at arm's length. Within the state, however, a group of economic entrepreneurs emerged with their own agendas, the *siloviki* and their allies in state-controlled enterprises. The new system worked well enough in the first

[25] Joel S. Hellman, "Winners Take All: The Politics of Partial Reform in Postcommunist Transitions," *World Politics*, Vol. 50 (1998), pp. 203–234.

[26] In 1999 Yukos invested R1.7 billion, but planned to increase this to R11 billion in 2000, of which R8.35 billion would go directly into raising output, Tat'yana Lysova, "Kuda devat' den'gi," *Vedomosti*, October 25, 1999.

[27] Surgut covered its ownership structure in a complicated cross-holding scheme, and in 2003 stopped publishing GAAP-compliant financial reports, Catherine Belton and Neil Buckley, "On the Offensive: How Gunvor Rose to the Top of Russian Oil Trading," *Financial Times*, May 14, 2008.

[28] Chrystia Freeland, *Sale of the Century: Russia's Wild Ride from Communism to Capitalism* (New York: Crown, 2000), p. 157.

years of Putin's leadership. Some of the more egregiously political of the so-called "oligarchs" were humbled, notably Vladimir Gusinsky at the head of the Media-Most media empire, and Berezovsky, and both ended up in exile. The business community as a whole was not unhappy to see them go, since their flamboyant model of political capitalism tended to discredit the market system as a whole. Yukos continued to thrive, and moved toward the Western model of corporate governance. By early 2003, as noted, there were plans to merge with Sibneft, which would have created a major world energy company. At the same time, Yukos assumed a higher political profile and Khodorkovsky increasingly made little secret of his political ambitions. There were many reasons for the estrangement between the regime and Yukos, and personally between Putin and Khodorkovsky.

The assault against the oligarchs "as a class" was renewed in the run-up to the December 2003 parliamentary elections and the March 2004 presidential campaign, a time when the Kremlin sought to disarm serious political opposition and to ensure its predominance in political and economic decision-making. One of the key bodies shaping this new narrative was the Council of National Strategy (SNS), founded in 2002 by Stanislav Belkovsky and Iosif Diskin.[29] In May 2003, the SNS issued a report called "The State and the Oligarchs," which signaled the beginning of the political assault on Yukos. The report argued that since 1995 Russia had been pursuing the path of "oligarchical modernisation," and as the economic power of the oligarchs increased, so too did their political influence. The report signaled that the Yukos affair was framed as a way of resisting the encroachments of big business on the prerogatives of the state. Having completed the privatization of the economy, the oligarchs were now privatizing politics. The report warned of the dangers of "a creeping oligarchical coup" whereby the country's system of governance would be changed to ensure "the union of super-big business and executive power." Khodorkovsky was named ten times in the report and Yukos twenty-five times, with Abramovich coming in second with nine and twenty-two mentions for Sibneft. In the end, however, only the former was singled out for attack.[30]

A number of factors determined that the assault would be directed against Khodorkovsky and Yukos. In December 2001 Khodorkovsky established the Open Russia Foundation, modeled on George Soros's Open Society Institute (OSI), to support civil society development, and thereafter Khodorkovsky loudly proclaimed his social mission, and thus trespassed on the paternalistic state's territory. A number of policy issues came between the Kremlin and Khodorkovsky. Pipeline networks today create the sinews of geopolitical

[29] The SNS included twenty-three experts across the political spectrum, a number of whom disagreed with the findings of the report and resigned, Vladimir Pribylovsky, "What's the Scandal About?," *Moscow Times*, June 11, 2003, p. 8.

[30] "Gosudarstvo i oligarkhiya," available at www.strategeia.ru/news_453.html.

order, establishing new diplomatic realities that once built endure for generations, bringing together some countries and regions while marginalizing others.[31] Russia's oil exports are controlled by Transneft, the state-owned monopoly, regulated by a complex system of access quotas. In November 2002 four Russian companies (Yukos, Lukoil, TNK, and Sibneft) formed a consortium to build a $3.5 billion oil pipeline from Western Siberia to Murmansk, with a planned annual capacity of around $100 million tonnes, to open in 2007. The line would have by-passed the Transneft system and opened up world markets (above all America) to exports. A further issue that divided Yukos from the Kremlin was the plan to build a 2,400 km oil pipeline from Angarsk to Daqing in Manchuria, the center of China's oil refining industry.

The merger of Yukos and Sibneft was announced on April 22, 2003, in a deal that would have created Russia's biggest and the world's fourth-largest oil company in terms of production. At first the merger appears to have been condoned by the Kremlin, but fears that the Yukos-Sibneft company, which was due to come into operation on January 1, 2004, would create a giant beyond the Kremlin's influence tilted opinion against the merger. The new company would have challenged the state's claimed prerogatives over energy and broader security questions; and the attack on Yukos was the outcome. The Kremlin's alarm was heightened by Khodorkovsky's plan to sell a 25 percent stake, and possibly 40 percent or more, of the new super-company to ChevronTexaco, ExxonMobil, or some other company (Khodorkovsky was sending out mixed signals, although the former was the most likely purchaser). Elena Tokareva, the head of the *Stringer* journal, argues that "From 2002 the Yukos corporation entered the political phase of its development and its main efforts were no longer directed even to producing oil but focused on buying power in the country as a whole, and whole regions." Yukos launched a whole range of political projects which, in Tokareva's view, provoked the state to respond, and the tax question was no more than a tactic to avoid talking about political issues.[32]

From this perspective, consumed by hubris, the Menatep-Yukos leaders ignored the warning signs. Thane Gustafson endorses this view in his magisterial study of the Russian oil industry. The aggressive use of transfer pricing, the high-handed pipeline negotiations with China, the attempts to shape the oil tax regime in parliament, and, above all, Khodorkovsky's arrogant personal manner and his increasingly accentuated interest in political and social affairs broke with the imposed conventions of the Putin system and provoked the attack. Gustafson eschews systemic explanations, such as the consolidation of a predatory state or fears associated with the sale of Yukos-Sibneft shares to an American company, and instead argues, "Without the factor of personality, in short, the contest and the privatized oil industry

[31] Rafael Kandiyoti, *Pipelines: Flowing Oil and Crude Politics* (London: I. B. Tauris, 2008).
[32] Elena Tokareva, *Kto podstavil khodorskovskogo* (Moscow: Yauza, 2006), p. 129.

would arguably not have descended into such a bitter confrontation among a small group of powerful men, which in turn served as the convenient instrument for one leadership faction to gain the edge in the making of policy."[33] Khodorkovsky thought he was leading a crusade for the soul of Russia, and instead, as so often in Russian history, he came to be seen as alien and threatening: "Khodorkovsky and Yukos were attacked because they were seen by a wide range of Russian elite opinion as a foreign body and a threat."[34]

At a fateful meeting of business leaders with Putin on February 19, 2003, Khodorkovsky addressed the painful topic "Corruption in Russia: A Brake on Economic Growth." Khodorkovsky provided some opinion polling data and other statistics, including the assertion that corruption had reached $30 billion a year, a quarter of the state budget, and that according to the Indem Foundation 72 percent of Russians feared going to court because the bribes were too high.[35] As Khodorkovsky went on Putin's expression became ever harder, and at this comment he exclaimed that it was wrong to presume guilt like this. This was not enough to stop Khodorkovsky, and he urged that corruption should be made a shameful phenomenon. He then cited the example of Rosneft's takeover of Severnaya Neft, and openly challenged Putin over the acquisition. According to Victor Gerashchenko, who would go on to head the Yukos board, Khodorkovsky was not deterred and spoke again, appealing to Putin to endorse the oil pipeline to China. According to Gerashchenko Putin unequivocally said "no"; there was a project to build a line to Nakhodka, "and that was the plan that would be implemented." Khodorkovsky insisted that his pipeline would use private capital and not state funds, but Putin was adamant. Still Khodorkovsky refused to remain silent, and to the astonishment of those present he declared, "Vladimir Vladimirovich, you do not understand the importance of establishing relations with China ...," and sat down.

"After this meeting," according to Gerashchenko, "Khodorkovsky was told unequivocally to leave Russia. He would not budge an inch: "what did I say that was wrong?" he demanded.[36] Those present later reported that the exchange had been marked by a high degree of personal animosity. Nevzlin correctly alleges that as a result of the meeting Igor Sechin and Viktor Ivanov, two key Putin allies in the presidential administration, were instructed by Putin to begin gathering evidence against Yukos.[37] Khodorkovsky himself realized

[33] Thane Gustafson, *Wheel of Fortune: The Battle for Oil and Power in Russia* (Cambridge: Belknap Press of Harvard University Press, 2012), p. 316.

[34] Gustafson, *Wheel of Fortune*, p. 273.

[35] Mikhail Khodorkovskii, "Korruptsiya v. Rossii – tormoz ekonomicheskogo rosta," PowerPoint presentation, available at www.khodorkovsky.ru/faq/2636.html, in section "Voprosy i otvety: Za chto on sidit."

[36] Victor Gerashchenko, "I Encountered Total Disregard for the Law," *Novaya gazeta*, July 10, 2008, translated and available at www.khodorkovsky.info/timeline/136489.html.

[37] Valerii G. Shiryaev, *Sud mesti: pervaya zhertva dela Yukosa* (Moscow: OGI, 2006), p. 17.

that Yukos faced difficult times, and soon after warned a meeting of Yukos department heads that the company would be attacked, and those who were not ready should leave.

This did not deter Khodorkovsky from active engagement in the parliamentary elections, due to be held in December 2003. He supported not only liberal parties, notably the Yabloko grouping with which he had long been associated, but also the CPRF. When asked by Putin about this, Khodorkovsky denied that Yukos was funding the Communists, but agreed that he had funded them in a personal capacity – a distinction that Putin considered moot. Yukos had long been an active lobbyist in the State Duma, and between 2001 and 2003 influenced the legislation on the taxation of energy resources, the indexation of the energy resource tax, export duties on crude oil and petroleum products, and amendments to the production-sharing agreement (PSA) law. The Kremlin was clearly irked at the company's lobbying power and its ability to block the passage of laws in parliament that would have removed these and other tax loopholes. No sooner was Yukos weakened than these laws were pushed through the Duma in late 2003. It is clear that on a whole number of policy issues Yukos was perceived as a threat to the Kremlin's management of the economy.

Khodorkovsky became the most intransigent proponent of the view that the economy should be disembedded from social control, and in particular from state supervision. He was pushing the Polanyian elastic band far to the side of the view that economic life should enjoy an autonomous existence and, indeed, should shape the socio-political sphere. Kimmage puts this well:

> Once upon a time, a Russian oil company called Yukos and a man named Mikhail Khodorkovsky embodied a dream – that the free market, perhaps more than any other force, could and would complete Russia's transformation from a struggling post-communist question mark into an economically prosperous democracy ruled by reasonable laws and anchored in the institution of private property.[38]

The partisans of this view, Kimmage notes, were always more numerous in the West than in Russia. The transformation of Yukos appeared to demonstrate the redemptive power of transparent corporate governance, international accountants, and investment in social projects. Khodorkovsky himself had also undergone a transformation: "With an almost messianic fervor, he had adopted his new cause to the point where he seemed to be waging a quest for martyrdom. No longer the young man who would give up his bank if the government asked, Khodorkovsky had turned into a quixotic crusader almost eager for prison."[39]

[38] Daniel Kimmage, "Putin's Restoration: Consolidation or Clan Rivalries?," in Geir Flikke, ed., *The Uncertainties of Putin's Democracy* (Oslo: NUPI, 2004), pp. 129–143, at p. 129.

[39] Peter Baker and Susan Glasser, *Kremlin Rising: Vladimir Putin's Russia and the End of Revolution*, Revised edition (New York: Scribner, 2007), p. 286.

BASMANNY JUSTICE

The assault against Yukos signaled the Kremlin's determination to restore its authority in the country. On June 19, 2003, one of Yukos's senior security officials, Alexei Pichugin, was arrested and later charged with organizing up to five contract killings, and on June 26 the Prosecutor-General's Office (PGO) conducted a search of Yukos's Moscow headquarters. On July 2 the head of the Menatep international finance group (Yukos's main shareholder), Lebedev, was arrested in connection with $280 million worth of share acquisitions in 1994 in Apatit, as well as with tax evasion by Menatep subsidiaries in the Tomsk region. The fundamental charge against him was of large-scale fraud. Nevzlin and Khodorkovsky were questioned as witnesses in the Lebedev case. Khodorkovsky visited the United States soon after the attack on Yukos began, but he made it clear that he would return to confront whatever fate had in store for him. Months of pressure culminated in Khodorkovsky's arrest on October 25. He then spent the next two years in the Matrosskaya Tishina pre-trial detention center (SIZO – investigative isolator) in Moscow, despite appeals from an international group of defense lawyers to allow him out on bail, since it was clear that he had no intention of fleeing the country. The planned merger between Yukos and Sibneft was suspended and then reversed. Numerous other cases were launched against associates of the Yukos company, notably a young lawyer retained by Yukos, Svetlana Bakhmina, who was given a severe prison sentence despite having under-age children. Vasily Aleksanyan, the terminally ill former general counsel and vice president of Yukos, was denied essential medical treatment in custody after refusing to implicate Khodorkovsky.

The political nature of the case was reflected in the Kremlin's refusal to accept a solution that would allow the Yukos company to pay its alleged tax arrears and remain a viable company. At various points the "Yukos affair" could have come to a negotiated solution. According to some estimates, more than 70 offers to the government to settle the debts went unanswered.[40] Given the enormous revenues generated by the Yukos oil company at a time when Brent crude reached over $50 a barrel, a repayment plan for the tax arrears could easily have been arranged, and was repeatedly offered by Yukos executives, although liability was not admitted. On November 19, 2004, Yukos was landed with another $6 billion tax demand, bringing the total tax bill to $20 billion. By the time Khodorkovsky's trial ended in May 2005 the total tax bill had risen to $27.5 billion. The tax bill in some years (2001, 2002) exceeded the total revenue of the company in that year. The way that the tax bills were handled makes it clear that the case was about far more than legitimate tax recovery. All companies had in the past engaged in extreme tax-minimization schemes, including transfer pricing, but at the time these loopholes were legal. By freezing Yukos's bank accounts and setting deadlines that were impossible

[40] "Gosudarstvo raspravilos s Yukosom," *Izvestiya*, December 30, 2004.

to meet, the courts and tax authorities drove Yukos into bankruptcy and forced the sale of its assets (above all YNG) to companies controlled by the Russian government. The refusal to accept a negotiated settlement demonstrates that the Kremlin was playing for higher stakes: the destruction of Yukos and the reorganization of the Russian energy sector.

The trial of Khodorkovsky and his associates has been described as a "kangaroo court."[41] Lawyers conducting the case were subject to searches and other forms of harassment that drove them to appeal to legal advocacy organizations to defend their rights. The case was accompanied by repeated breaches of advocacy rules.[42] Anton Drel, the lead lawyer representing Khodorkovsky, was summoned for questioning by the PGO on October 17, 2003, in contravention of Article 8 of the law on the rights and duties of lawyers, which states that a defense attorney cannot be summoned for questioning or to give evidence in a current case, and also Article 56 of the Russian Criminal Code. There were numerous searches of the law offices of companies associated with the Yukos case. On October 9, 2003, Drel's offices were searched and documents connected with the Yukos case confiscated, clearly violating attorney–client privilege. At the time of the search the FSB (the successor to the KGB security police) knew that Drel was at a court hearing representing Lebedev. The investigations were accompanied by improper searches, often executed with a show of force, without proper search warrants, incomplete records of the materials confiscated, and without the subjects of the search or their representatives being present, as stipulated by law. The "Koralevo" orphanage supported by Yukos, run by Khodorkovsky's parents, was raided by armed men in the presence of the children.

While Pichugin was accused of murder and attempted murder, the charges against Khodorkovsky and Lebedev focused on economic crimes, covering eleven charges against seven articles of the Russian Criminal Code.[43] There was no reason to believe that either would attempt to leave the country to avoid trial. In addition, Pichugin was held in the Lefortovo detention center, run at the time by the FSB in contravention of Russia's Council of Europe commitments. Pichugin was allegedly interrogated with the help of the injection of psychotropic drugs, in an attempt to get evidence that could have turned him into a witness for the prosecution. There are allegations that Lebedev was treated inhumanely while in detention, above all by not being provided with adequate medical assistance. Lebedev suffers from diabetes mellitus and a heart

[41] Sarah E. Mendelson and Theodore P. Gerber, "Soviet Nostalgia: An Impediment to Russian Democratization," *The Washington Quarterly*, Vol. 21 (2008), p. 92.

[42] These are listed in *Constitutional and Due Process Violations in the Khodorkovsky/Yukos Case*, A White Paper Prepared by Defense Lawyers on Behalf of Mikhail Khodorkovsky, Platon Lebedev, and Alexei Pichugin (Moscow, n.d.), compiled by Robert Amsterdam and Charles Krause.

[43] Details in Mariya Lokotetskaya and Lyudmila Romanova, "Sud idet: Lebedev i Khodorkovskii ponyali, v chem ikh obvinyayut i ne priznali vinu," *Gazeta*, July 16, 2004, p. 3.

condition. Indeed, he was arrested in hospital and taken initially to Lefortovo before being transferred to Matrosskaya Tishina.

The first trial of Khodorkovsky and Lebedev began on July 11, 2004, and lasted nearly a year. This was the most important trial in the country's post-Soviet history. It took place in the Meshchansky court in Moscow, but the decision on whether bail should be given and other key procedural issues were decided by the Basmanny court. This court specializes in "political" cases and is closely associated with the procuracy, with the prosecution team working out of the investigative division of the PGO based in the Basmanny district of Moscow, hence the term "Basmanny justice."[44] The Yukos affair revealed the ability of the regime to apply "telephone law"; that is, to influence judicial outcomes.[45] The Yukos affair was a classic case of a "prosecution to order" (*zakazannoe delo*) accompanied by the malpractices of "Basmanny justice." The two main charges in support of the view that Khodorkovsky and his colleagues did not get a fair trial is that they were kept in pre-trial detention without due cause, and that prosecutors were allowed to confront the defendants without lawyers being present. A constant criticism is that the defendants had great difficulty communicating freely with their defense lawyers.

Giving evidence in February 2005 Khodorkovsky argued that he did not consider himself guilty on any of the charges: "Everything they accuse me of was normal business practice." Khodorkovsky vigorously defended his record: "I categorically object to the criminal-artistic presentation of normal business practices." He argued that the prosecution had "thought up accusations" in matters with which he had no connection. Khodorkovsky's basic argument was that he was being charged for crimes that did not even exist, about events that were torn out of context, and based on materials that were distorted.[46] Khodorkovsky's legal team offered detailed rebuttals of the charges. For example, on April 5, 2005, Genrikh Padva noted that the date at which Khodorkovsky was alleged to have created a "criminal group" was sometimes stated to have been in 1990, in other documents in 1993, and elsewhere in 1995 or 1997.[47] On April 7, 2005, Padva argued that Menatep had actually saved the situation with the Apatit plant, and he stressed that the company's shareholders had suffered no loss and its directors had been fully aware of the sales plan.[48]

The trial came to a close on April 11, 2005. In his final statement on that day Khodorkovsky declared his innocence and stated that he would not ask for

[44] *Basmannoe pravosudie: Uroki samooborony: Posobie dlya advokatov* (Moscow: Publichnaya reputatsiya, 2003), available at www.ip-centre.ru/books/Basmannoe.pdf.

[45] Alena Ledeneva, "Telephone Justice in Russia," *Post-Soviet Affairs*, Vol. 24 (2008), pp. 324–350.

[46] Dmitrii Simakin, "Khodorkovskii: 'Eto kriminal'no-khudozhestvennoe delo," *Nezavisimaya gazeta*, February 28, 2005, p. 7.

[47] Dmitrii Simakin, "'Prestupleniya voobshche ne bylo': Genrikh Padva nachal dolguyu rech' v zashchitu Khodorkovskogo," *Nezavisimaya gazeta*, April 6, 2005, p. 1.

[48] Dmitri Simakin, "V poiskakh zerna istiny," *Nezavisimaya gazeta*, April 8, 2005, p. 7.

clemency. He asserted that he "did not want to be president," and condemned the damage that the "home-grown bureaucracy" had inflicted on the country. He was proud of his work over the past fifteen years, creating by 2004 the largest and most transparent oil corporation in Russia, arguing that he had sought to work for the good of the country. On no point had the prosecution been able to prove his guilt. He would not ask for leniency, but would "strive for justice."[49] He emotionally thanked his family for their support, movingly speaking of his wife Inna as "a real comrade-in-arms and Decembrist."[50] At the end of his 39-minute speech the court burst into a spontaneous prolonged standing ovation, with the exception of the prosecution team and the judges. On May 31 Khodorkovsky was found guilty of nine offences out of the eleven with which he was charged, with the indictment of repeated forgery of documents dropped; and Lebedev on eight charges, also against six articles of the RF Criminal Code. Khodorkovsky received a nine-year sentence (reduced on appeal to eight) to a general-regime penal colony, minus the 18 months he had served in pre-trial detention. Lebedev, the head of Menatep, received the same term.[51] The sentence was only one year short of that demanded by the prosecution, and its severity took many observers aback. There is little doubt that the sentence was agreed with the Kremlin. Their lawyers immediately announced that they would appeal.

Even before the judgment was delivered, on May 13, 2005, the Prosecutor General announced that further charges could be laid against Khodorkovsky and Lebedev. Appearing on NTV on June 6, 2005, the deputy Prosecutor General, Vladimir Kolesnikov, warned that other leading business figures could be in the firing line: "I can say one thing, [Khodorkovsky's] case will not be the last. We have got plenty of cases in the cartridge clip."[52] His words proved prophetic, since we now know that the PGO was preparing a second trial even before the first was over. Some of Khodorkovsky's lawyers also became the target of accusations of "unprofessional conduct" as part of a continuing process of intimidation. The Moscow department of the Federal Registration Service unsuccessfully called for three (Anton Drel, Denis Dyatlov, and Yelena Levina) to be disbarred, and then tried to strip Yury Schmidt, who was preparing the appeal to the European Court of Human Rights (ECtHR), of his license, a request refused by the St. Petersburg Lawyers' Chamber. There

[49] Ekaterina Butorina, "Nepravil'nyi oligarkh: Mikhail Khodorkovskii skazal sudu poslednee slovo," *Vremya novostei*, April 12, 2005, p. 1; Anfisa Voronina, "Poslednee slovo," *Vedomosti*, April 12, 2005.

[50] Marina Gridneva and Lina Panchenko, "Sego dnya: 'Ne vinovat, snisokhozhdeniya ne proshu'," *Moskovskii komsomolets*, April 12, 2005, p. 3. Later Khodorkovsky was jailed where the Decembrists had been exiled (Chita), and Inna could truly reveal her "Decembrist" qualities.

[51] Dmitrii Simakin and Mikhail Tolpegin, "Upraytili: Rasprava nad Khodorkovskim i Lebedevym byla ozhidaema, no vse ravno shokirovala svoei zhestokost'yu," *Nezavisimaya gazeta*, June 1, 2005, p. 1. Lebedev's sentence was later reduced on appeal to eight years.

[52] Peter Lavelle, "The Kremlin's 'Cartridge Clip'," *Untimely Thoughts: Analysis*, June 7, 2005.

were also attempts later to disbar Karinna Moskalenko, in charge of presenting Khodorkovsky's case to the ECtHR. The persistent refusal of the advocate bodies in Moscow and St. Petersburg to approve these disbarments led to the legislative initiative of Putin in spring 2008 to allow courts to disbar advocates on request from the state registration service.

Although Khodorkovsky and Lebedev had been sentenced earlier primarily on charges of tax evasion, the new charges announced on February 5, 2007, focused on embezzlement of over $23 billion through fraud and money-laundering.[53] Once again the transfer pricing schemes came under scrutiny, with crude oil produced by the YNG, Tomskneft and Samaraneftegaz production subsidiaries allegedly delivered on paper at reduced prices to companies registered in the tax-benefit zones in Mordovia, Evenkia, and other regions, and then sold on at market prices, thus severely reducing tax liabilities. Such tax optimization schemes, according to lawyer Pavel Ivlev, who had earlier represented Yukos, continued to be practiced by Rosneft. Yury Schmidt pointed out the absurdity of the new charges, which suggested that Khodorkovsky and Lebedev stole their own oil and then tried to launder the profit of what had been normal cash flows from the sale of a product that was at the core of the company's business.[54]

In December 2006 Khodorkovsky and Lebedev were moved from their respective camps to the investigative prison in the city of Chita. Their second trial began in March 2009 in the Khamovniki Court in Moscow. The logical incompatibility of the two trials became clear. The first trial found the two guilty of fraud and tax evasion, but the legality of the extraction and sale of the oil was not questioned, the proceeds of which were part reinvested in the company and part distributed to shareholders. The new trial accused the defendants of embezzling all of the oil produced by the three main Yukos production subsidiaries for a period of six years; embezzling the shares held by a Yukos subsidiary in one of the production companies and five other companies; and laundering the proceeds of the allegedly embezzled oil and the shares in the indirect subsidiaries. Over the course of 19 months the court sat 280 times and examined 188 volumes of evidence, as well as numerous other documents such as minutes of shareholder meetings. A total of 81 witnesses testified in court, 52 for the prosecution and 29 for the defense. As in the first trial, procedural obstacles were placed in the way of counsel defending the accused. For example, the judge rejected a request for adequate access with their clients.

In the first trial Khodorkovsky and Lebedev were held in an iron cage, whereas in the second trial they were held in a glass box (known colloquially as the "aquarium"), which inhibited discussions with their lawyers or the

[53] The new charges were based on Articles 160 and 174 of the RF Criminal Code.

[54] Yurii Schmidt, "Chto dal'she," October 25, 2007, available at www.khodorkovsky.ru/cassation/comments/7430.html.

passing of documents. The defense motion to summons Bruce Misamore, the former chief financial officer of Yukos, who could give crucial evidence, was refused. A large part of the early stage of the trial was limited to the prosecution simply reading out parts of the charges, in what appears to have been a deliberate attempt to drag out proceedings and to dampen international interest. Given the seriousness of the case, it would have been reasonable to expect the case to have been heard at a higher instance, that is, by the Moscow City Court, where the trial would have been heard by a panel of three judges or a jury.[55] Instead, the case took place before a single judge, Viktor Danilkin, in a district court. The double jeopardy issue was frequently raised, since the previous case had dealt with associated issues.[56] Article 50.1 of the Russian constitution prohibits a repeat conviction of someone already found guilty on charges related to circumstances of another crime. The logical incompatibility of the two trials soon became clear.

Khodorkovsky provided a detailed rebuttal of the charges. The amount of oil which Khodorkovsky and Lebedev were charged with embezzling was greater than Yukos's entire production for the relevant period. They were alleged, moreover, to have done this without alerting the attention of the company's independent auditors, PricewaterhouseCoopers, or the Russian authorities, or indeed the prosecutors in the first trial. The charges were essentially in contradiction to those of which the men were convicted in their first trial; they had been convicted of failing to pay taxes on output which was now alleged to have been stolen, although this issue was not even raised at the first trial. If the charges presented in the second trial were correct, then there would not have been any revenue to be taxed, thus rendering the first trial void.

The verdict was delivered on December 27, 2010, just before the New Year holidays. Danilkin began by pronouncing Khodorkovsky and Platonov guilty, and then raced through his 350-page summary, which repeated almost verbatim the prosecution case – and in certain instances even exceeded prosecution claims. On December 30 the two were sentenced to 13.5 years in a penal colony, including time already served, which meant that the two would not be free for seven more years. The new sentence attracted widespread international criticism. It was also accompanied by a major scandal when the court's press secretary and aide to the presiding judge, Natalya Vasileva, announced on February 14, 2011, that the judge had not written the verdict himself, as prescribed by law, but had been influenced by unnamed figures in the Moscow

[55] The case is made by Otto Luchterhandt, *Report of the Presidential Council of the RF for the Development of Civil Society and Human Rights on the Results of the Public Scholarly Analysis of the Court Materials of the Criminal Case against M. B. Khodorkovsky and P. L. Lebedev* (tried by the Khamovnichesky District Court of the City of Moscow; the verdict issued on December 27, 2010) (Moscow, 2011), p. 210.

[56] Ferdinand Feldbrugge makes this point in his submission, *Report of the Presidential Council*, pp. 63–64.

City Court.[57] The latter is ruled with a heavy hand by Olga Yegorova, and she had been involved in a number of scandals when reformist judges had been dismissed and those who acquitted too many defendants were censured. It appeared that the lid was now coming off to reveal how the Khodorkovsky trial had been manipulated by outside forces.

CONCLUSION

Post-communist Russia has developed as a peculiar amalgam of a modern constitutional state (the "stationary bandit" described by Mancur Olson) and a semi-autonomous administrative regime (the "roving bandits").[58] The Yukos case exposed the fault lines in this construction, as well as the multiple identities of the regime itself. The Yukos affair was not a Stalinist-type operation planned in advance and implemented methodically, but was provoked by a set of actions and reactions without a single common cause. Different factions within the regime had different agendas, but gradually an "affair" (*delo*) took shape embedded within a narrative that also evolved as the case advanced. While the attack on Khodorkovsky was undoubtedly selective, it was far from arbitrary. Putin targeted those who had flaunted their closeness to power in the most provocative manner, or had allegedly abused their dominance of the media. Putin was setting the rules of the political game, and in attacking a few oligarchs he was disciplining the rest. There was an implicit threat: toe the line if you wish to keep the assets "gained" in the 1990s.[59] By 2003 this was no longer enough. Volkov sees the Yukos case "as the strengthened state terminating the implicit and informal contract it had with the oligarchs, and proceeding to create an alternative system or relations with business in which formal rules will have more weight."[60] In this sense, the Yukos affair was decisive, allowing the administrative regime to consolidate its power.

Khodorkovsky also by 2003 sought to move beyond the consultative regime, and his various initiatives effectively meant that Yukos became a distinctive type of party substitute, a mega-party acting as a type of state within the state striving to dominate political parties, parliament and the public sphere, and this Putin

57 Natal'ya Vasil'eva, "'Prigovor byl privezen iz Mosgorsuda, ya tochno znayu': Otkrovennoe intervyu o dele Yukosa pomoshchnika sud'i Khamovnicheskogo suda," www.gazeta.ru, February 14, 2011, available at www.gazeta.ru/politics/2011/02/14_a_3524202.shtml.

58 Mancur Olson, *Power and Prosperity: Outgrowing Communist and Capitalist Dictatorships* (Oxford: Oxford University Press, 2000). The Yukos affair suggests that the shift from roving to stationary bandits, which for Olson signaled the beginning of civilization, good government, and ultimately democracy, is incomplete in Russia.

59 For an analysis of this, see Alekseĭ A. Mukhin, *Novye pravila igry dlya bol'shogo biznesa, prodiktovannye logikoi pravleniya V. V. Putina* (Moscow: Tsentr politicheskoi informatsii, 2002).

60 Vadim Volkov, "The Yukos Affair: Terminating the Implicit Contract," *PONARS Policy Memo*, Vol. 307 (2003), p. 2.

and his associates found intolerable. The Yukos affair represented a conflict between two modernizing agents, the state and big business. As a result of the affair, however, the nascent "bourgeoisie" was seriously weakened as a collective actor and a major independent force in Russian politics was eliminated from the game, allowing the state to become the dominant player in the form of what became known as the "vertical of power."[61] The Khodorkovsky trials represented a political struggle between the state (and sub-sections of the state), and a powerful business concern in which judicial proceedings were used to advance particular interests and to demonstrate to other actors who ultimately was sovereign in Russia.

The whole ensemble of procedural and normative violations described earlier is reminiscent of the grand "affairs" (such as the "Leningrad Affair" in the late 1940s), of an earlier era of Soviet history, when one strand led to another, and the snowball effect came to implicate people who were far from the original case. This is how the "Khodorkovsky Affair" will no doubt be remembered long after the present leadership has passed into history. An open letter in support of Khodorkovsky's and Lebedev's defense team by a number of prominent human rights activists, including Elena Bonner, Ludmila Alexeeva, and Lev Ponamarev, drew comparisons with the great purges of the 1930s, and in particular the way that after a long trial new charges were discovered. They noted:

> When arbitrariness rules in the country, when controlled "justice" is used as a stick to beat people with and law becomes a travesty, every courtroom that hears a political trial turns into a battleground for truth and justice. The battle fought there is very often unequal, so it's all the more important to express solidarity with those who defend victims of political persecution. The new charges in the Yukos case are a gauntlet thrown down to society, a signal that all appearances have been thrown to the four winds. The pressure put on Khodorkovsky and Lebedev's lawyers, aimed at their humiliation, is testament to the fact that the authorities are using all their influence to assist the prosecution.[62]

At the root of the Yukos affair lies a deep paradox: whether the selective application of law can, if only partially, reflect the aspiration to universal justice; or whether the selective application of law is always unjust.[63]

Khodorkovsky's travails in court acted as a warning for the business community not to over-step the line. The disciplinary effect of the trial was exemplary and demonstrated that ultimately there was no defense against the

[61] Aleksei Zudin, "Gosudarstvo i biznes v. Rossii: evolyutsiya modeli vzaimootnoshenii," *Neprikosnovennyi zapas: Debaty o politike i kul'ture*, available at www.nz-online.ru/print.phtml?aid=80018067.

[62] "Every Courtroom That Hears a Political Trial Turns into a Battleground for Truth and Justice," February 27, 2007, available at www.khodorkovsky.info/society/documents/134906.html.

[63] *Khodorkovskikh chtenii*, Konferentsii "Rossiiskie al'ternativy," July 10, 2007, available at www.polit.ru/dossie/2007/10/05/conf.html.

state. The case represented the instrumentalization of law, subordinating it to the power system. The lack of judicial independence was clearly evident. Moskalenko notes that the Yukos case breached fundamental principles not only of due process but also "of the very idea of justice." She argues that "This trial demonstrated that the judiciary could ignore rules, human rights, and clear evidence, in its submission to pressure by the executive." In particular, she insisted that Khodorkovsky's detention was in clear breach of domestic and international norms, and the Procuracy decided the venue in which the case would be heard, infringing the rules on court jurisdiction. Moreover, the case against Khodorkovsky was reopened after receiving a letter from Putin, but the letter was not placed in the case file although the Prosecutors' response is logged: "It is not understood how President Putin is allowed to instruct the head of the main prosecutorial body on legal questions." The case also revealed how a dissenting judge could be dismissed from office.[64] While all law may ultimately be political, there is a fundamental difference when it is placed at the service of an administrative regime. Due process may undoubtedly be used instrumentally within the framework of a constitutional state, but there is a qualitative difference with the abuse of judicial process when used to destroy a regime's political enemy.

The selective, decisive, and politically inspired use of law in the Putin era was confirmed by Medvedev's recognition of "legal nihilism." On May 20, 2008, Medvedev called for an independent court system when he addressed a meeting with senior judges and legal officials in the Kremlin: "[Unjust] decisions, as we all know, do happen and come as a result of different kinds of pressure, like telephone calls and – it cannot be denied – offers of money."[65] The Yukos affair graphically illustrated the instrumental use of the law. Although Khodorkovsky had twice been found guilty by the courts, in the end it was the regime that was on trial. In a number of letters, dialogues, and interviews issued from prison, Khodorkovsky issued withering criticism of the regime and broader analysis of Russian political development.[66] In line with a long Russian tradition, jail gave him the freedom to become a critic of public authorities.

The attack on Khodorkovsky had far-reaching consequences. First, it reinforced the sovereignty of the administrative regime. The power system affirmed that it could decide who was friend or foe, and drive through this decision with an implacable logic that threatened its own declarations in favor of the consolidation of the rule of law, constitutionalism and the autonomous power of the state. The Yukos affair achieved the disciplining of the oligarchs as a class, and by the same token, undermined the social power of classes in general. With Khodorkovsky humbled, the other oligarchs were cowed and

[64] Karinna Moskalenko, "The Judicial System in Practice," in Jennifer Moll, ed., *Blueprint for Russia* (London: Foreign Policy Centre, 2005), pp. 41–42.

[65] Available at www.kremlin.ru/text/appears/2008/05/201007.shtml.

[66] Sakwa, *Putin and the Oligarch*, pp. 162–201.

hurried to make their peace with the state on the regime's terms. The bourgeoisie and the middle class were unable to impose their hegemony, while the voice of the workers throughout the post-communist world remains marginalized. Statism as a principle was reinforced while the regime was left with no serious competitors. The second outcome lies in the realm of political economy, consolidating a distinctive model of *dirigisme*. This was a state-directed economic strategy that fell short of state capitalism, and even more state corporatism, but a rather more interventionist state created state corporations in what it considered strategic sectors of the economy as part of a state-directed modernization strategy. The Yukos case demonstrated that while the post-communist Russian system was in favor of the market, it would intervene to limit the autonomy of market *forces*. The final outcome is rather more paradoxical. The trials exposed the contradictions at the heart of the system of rule known as sovereign democracy. A political system is most powerful when its ruling practices are invisible and internalized in the life of the society as normal. The Khodorkovsky trials exposed the influence of "telephone law" and other limitations on judicial independence, and thus undermined the legitimacy of the regime in its entirety. The regime itself was as much on trial as the defendants. The politicized trials of Mikhail Khodorkovsky ultimately exposed the regime itself to a political trial in the domestic public sphere and international public opinion.

15

Nashiri in Gitmo

The Wages of Legitimacy in Trials before the Guantanamo Military Commissions

Lawrence Douglas

Compared to Nuremberg's magnificent Palace of Justice, a Renaissance-revival showpiece where American prosecutors tried Nazi war criminals after World War II, the Expeditionary Legal Complex (ELC) at Guantánamo Bay provides little to please the eye. Enclosing the facility, which houses Gitmo's military courtroom, is a 10-foot chain-linked fence covered with dark green sniper netting and two coils of dense razor wire. Unseen soldiers keep watch from mobile guard-towers. Around the fence runs a second security perimeter made of bright orange Jersey barriers, seemingly the work of a counter-terror specialist strongly influenced by Christo and Jeanne-Claude. Photographing the complex is strictly forbidden, except from one specific point which has been marked by a 3′x3′ spray-painted square on a walkway; here one is allowed to stand and take a picture, though my attempt to do so is interrupted by two soldiers puttering by in a golf-cart-like vehicle called a "mule," who bark at me until my escort, an unflappable sergeant from the Division of Public Affairs, politely informs them of the picture-taking rule. Sheepish, they drive off. Still, my sergeant dutifully examines my photo to make sure my lens hasn't strayed; asked to account for such precautions, he deadpans, "So al Qaeda doesn't know where to go when they land with their submarines . . ."[1]

The courthouse building, which can only be glimpsed from inside the fenced complex, looks like a Costco warehouse, a simple windowless aluminum structure colored Naples yellow with a pitched roof. This is where the trial of Abd al-Nashiri, the senior al Qaeda lieutenant alleged to have masterminded the bombing of the USS *Cole* in a Yemeni harbor in 2000, will be held sometime in the not too distant future.[2] Still wending its way through pre-trial motions, the Nashiri case is one of two presently before the commission; the 9/11 case against

[1] Author's notes.

[2] The trial, once scheduled to begin on December 4, 2014, has been subject to numerous delays. As of this writing, no trial date has been set.

Khalid Sheik Mohammed (KSM) and four co-defendants is also slowly heading toward trial. These cases involve the only capital charges to emerge out of al Qaeda crimes, and represent not only the most important cases to be submitted to the military commission but also the most significant to come before a military court since leading Nazi functionaries stood trial in occupied Germany. In his opening address before the International Military Tribunal (IMT) in Nuremberg, Robert Jackson, who had taken a leave from his position on the Supreme Court to head the American prosecution, put the task facing the tribunal poetically, "To pass these defendants a poisoned chalice is to put it to our own lips."[3] Jackson understood that along with Nazi functionaries, law itself stood on trial at Nuremberg; the unusual tribunal had to demonstrate that it was something other than, as one prominent critic put it, a "high-grade lynching party."[4]

The daunting problem of legitimacy that vexed Nuremberg remains paradigmatic of political trials that involve crimes of war. At its most basic, criminal law draws a line between violence that is authorized by the state in the form of a punishment, and violence that is prohibited by the state as a delict (or, alternatively, by the international community).[5] In the overwhelming majority of criminal cases, this distinction is never called into question – least of all, is the state's authority to draw it. In most cases, trials operate on settled terrain in which the systemic motives and purposes of the prosecution and the rationale for the imposition of a sanction remain beyond the terms of legitimate dispute. Not so with political trials. A Paul Schervish had observed, "A political trial is an explicit occasion in which adversarial parties contend over the normative legitimacy of the legal order as a whole rather than just over the distribution of outcomes within the existing legal dispensation."[6]

War crimes trials, in particular those involving novel law and institutional arrangements, inevitably become a site of such normative contestation. In such cases, the distinction between the internal police powers of the state and its external war-making powers is volatized. Here the distinction between the criminal, as the subject of regulatory punishment, and the enemy, as a target

[3] International Military Tribunal, *Trial of the Major War Criminals before the International Military Tribunal, Nuremberg 14 November 1945–1 October 1946*, vol. 2, (Nuremberg: International Military Tribunal, 1947), p. 101.

[4] The remark came courtesy of Jackson's Supreme Court colleague, Harlan Fiske Stone; Raymond Brown, "The American Perspective on Nuremberg," in Herbert Reginbogin and Christoph Johannes Maria Safferling, eds., *The Nuremberg Trials: International Criminal Law Since 1945* (Munich: Saur, 2006), p. 24.

[5] See Hans Kelsen, *Pure Theory of Law* (Berkeley: University of California Press, 1967).

[6] Paul G. Schervish, "Political Trials and the Social Construction of Deviance," *Qualitative Sociology*, Vol. 7 (1984), p. 195. See also Jens Meierhenrich and Devin O. Pendas, "'The Justice of My Cause Is Clear, But There's Politics to Fear': Political Trials in Theory and History," in this volume.

of military force, threatens to collapse.[7] The charge of "victors' justice," against which Nuremberg toiled, captures this volatility. In the name of punishing criminals, victors' justice uses the cover of legality in order to serve the "destructive" end of eliminating an enemy.[8] The challenge that faced Jackson at Nuremberg was to show that the law, through its processes and incriminations, was not simply serving as a tool of military reckoning. Rather, it was capable of judging and condemning acts of atrocity through procedures that were fair and incriminations that stated meaningful crimes. Put somewhat differently, if, as I have argued elsewhere, Nuremberg was designed to serve a didactic end, a critical dimension of its didactic work was to demonstrate the power of the rule of law to gain dominion over the worst atrocities without distorting its sober operations. [9]

The military commissions at Guantánamo Bay face a similar, if not more extreme, challenge. At Gitmo, the specter of the "poisoned chalice" finds a less literary expression in the form of a stuffed animal belonging to Richard Kammen, a civilian lawyer who heads Nashiri's defense team. Gray with pink ears, it stands no more than six inches tall. A court security officer first mistook the animal for a bunny, a touch of cute ornamenting the defense's table. But the MP should have looked more closely, for rare indeed is the bunny that carries a joey in a pouch. He also might have noticed a second kangaroo, this a gold pin, glimmering on the lapel of Kammen's suit jacket in the spot where one has grown accustomed in such settings to seeing an all but obligatory American flag. As Kammen, an accomplished lawyer with four decades of trial experience, dryly observes, his choice of lapel pin "is not meant to express my love of Australian wildlife."[10]

History has more than vindicated Nuremberg; how it will treat the Guantánamo military commissions is another matter. The props of a defense lawyer hardly settle the issue, but they do serve as an all-too-tangible reminder of the extraordinary challenge that the military commissions face: to demonstrate that a tribunal originally born of an impatient contempt for due process can now prove itself a viable institution of American law. If the commissions are to answer Kammen's stark normative challenge, they will have to *show* that if originally designed as an executive instrument for the elimination of enemies, they now serve as a legally normalized, autonomous, and fair tribunal capable of submitting crimes of war to the bench of justice.

7 See Otto Kirchheimer, *Political Justice: The Use of Legal Procedure for Political Ends* (Princeton: Princeton University Press, 1961). See also Meierhenrich and Pendas, "'The Justice of My Cause Is Clear, But There's Politics to Fear.'"

8 See Meierhenrich and Pendas, "'The Justice of My Cause is Clear, But There's Politics to Fear.'"

9 Lawrence Douglas, *The Memory of Judgment: Making Law and History in the Trials of the Holocaust* (New Haven: Yale University Press, 2001).

10 Author's interview with Richard Kammen.

BUSH'S EXTRAORDINARY COURT: ELIMINATING THE ENEMY

On the morning of October 12, 2000, the USS *Cole*, a navy destroyer with a crew of nearly 300, arrived in Yemen's Port of Aden on a refueling stop. Shortly before noon on the same day, a fiberglass motor boat operated by two suicide bombers and laden with several hundred pounds of explosives blew a gaping 40-foot-wide hole in the *Cole*'s hull, killing seventeen crewmen and injuring dozens more.[11] "The people of Yemen partied on shore the night we were attacked," Joe Pelly, a now-retired senior chief petty officer who was on the *Cole*, remembered.[12] With President Ali Abdullah Saleh publicly blaming the bombing on Mossad and Yemeni parliamentarians railing for jihad against America, an FBI team sent to Aden confronted what one agent described as "the most hostile environment the FBI has ever operated in."[13] Nonetheless, the team broke the case. The alleged chief architect of the attack was identified as a Saudi Arabian of Yemeni descent named Abd al-Rahim al-Nashiri. Nashiri had fought with the Taliban against the Northern Alliance before joining al Qaeda sometime around 1998. Quickly, he emerged as one of Osama bin Laden's most valued associates, allegedly becoming the head of al Qaeda in the Arabian Peninsula. Evidence indicated that Nashiri had prepared an earlier strike against another navy destroyer, the USS *The Sullivans*, but that a skiff filled with explosives had gotten stuck at low tide and become swamped under its excess weight. Later investigators also linked Nashiri to an attack on a French tanker, *The Limburg*, that killed one crewmember and leaked tens of thousands of gallons of oil into the Gulf of Aden.

American operatives caught up with Nashiri in Dubai in October 2002. But for nearly four years after his capture, Nashiri's whereabouts were unknown. Former U.S. officials[14] later indicated that Nashiri was first held in Afghanistan in a secret CIA location called "the Salt Pit," then flown to a CIA "black site" prison in Thailand; from there, he was ferried to another CIA prison in Poland (in 2014 in a suit brought by Nashiri, the European Court of Human Rights found Poland complicit in CIA torture and ordered the Polish government to pay the plaintiff 100,000 euros in damages);[15] next he was rendered to Morocco, and later still to Romania (the ECHR has yet to decide Nashiri's suit against the Romanian government). It wasn't until September 2006, nearly four

[11] Kirk S. Lippold, *Front Burner: Al Qaeda's Attack on the USS Cole* (New York: Public Affairs, 2012).

[12] Author's notes.

[13] Lawrence Wright, *The Looming Tower: Al-Qaeda and the Road to 9/11* (New York: Vintage, 2007), p. 365.

[14] Larry Siems, *The Torture Report: An Investigation into Rendition Detention and Interrogation under the Bush Administration*, The Torture Report Chapters, December 2, 2009, available at www.thetorturereport.org/report/chapter-3-black-sites-lies-and-videotapes.

[15] See *al Nashiri* v. *Poland*, Judgment, July 24, 2014 available at http://hudoc.echr.coe.int/eng?i=001-146044

years after his capture, that Nashiri was transferred along with thirteen other "high value detainees" to Guantánamo Bay. According to Bush, the decision to belatedly send Nashiri and KSM to Gitmo to stand trial before a military commission represented a determination to bring to justice the perpetrators of al Qaeda's most extreme crimes. But it certainly was born of something else, too: a recognition that without a highly visible success, yet another signature act in Bush's beleaguered presidency was destined to abject failure.

Trial by military commission has played a long, if less than continuous, role in American legal history.[16] As early as 1780, George Washington convened a Board of General Officers to weigh charges of espionage against British Major John André, later executed by order of the commanding general. The tribunals established by General Winfield Scott during the Mexican–American war (1846–1848) firmly established military commissions by name, and over 400 persons were tried by these exceptional courts over the course of the hostilities.[17] Military commissions received extensive use during the American Civil War with as many as 6,000 trials conducted by these exceptional courts. President Andrew Johnson convened such an instrument to try the conspirators in the assassination of Abraham Lincoln, presumably out of fears that a civilian jury in DC might have southern sympathies and fail to convict.[18] During World War II, the United States used military commissions to try a wide variety of suspected war criminals. The United States was the prime mover in the creation of the IMT responsible for trying twenty-two major Nazi war criminals in Nuremberg, and also mounted an extensive trial program against hundreds of former Nazis in its German occupation zone.[19] Military commissions were also used to try German spies and saboteurs on domestic soil and a substantial number of Japanese war criminals in both the Philippines and Tokyo.[20]

Despite these precedents, George Bush's decision, announced in a brief executive order from November 13, 2001,[21] to try "certain non-citizens in the war against terrorism" before military commissions represented a dramatic

[16] See generally Fionnuala Ni Aolain and Oren Gross, eds., *Guantanamo and Beyond: Exceptional Courts and Military Commissions in Comparative Perspective* (Cambridge: Cambridge University Press, 2013).

[17] David Glazier, "The Development of an Exceptional Court: The History of the American Military Commission," in Ni Aolain and Gross, eds., *Guantanamo and Beyond*, p. 44.

[18] See David Glazier, "Precedents Lost: The Neglected History of the Military Commission," *Virginia Journal of International Law*, Vol. 46 (2005), pp. 1–85.

[19] See Lawrence Douglas, "From IMT to NMT: The Emergence of a Jurisprudence of Atrocity," in Kim Christian Priemel and Alexa Stiller, eds., *Reassessing the Nuremberg Military Trials: Transitional Justice, Trial Narratives and Historiography* (New York: Berghahn, 2012).

[20] See Louis Fisher, *Military Tribunals and Presidential Power: American Revolution to the War on Terrorism* (Lawrence: University of Kansas Press, 2005).

[21] Administration of George W. Bush, 2001, *Military Order – Detention, Treatment, and Trial of Certain Non-Citizens in the War Against Terrorism*, November 13, 2001, available at www.law.cornell.edu/background/warpower/fr1665.pdf.

break from practice. Historically, military commissions had been used in a narrow range of cases – when, say, martial law had been declared or the crimes committed were incident to acts of the battlefield, where civilian courts could not practically be convened. Indeed, General Scott's original decision to create commissions was born of practical necessity, as the existing law of court-martial was believed to lack extra-territorial application in the case of the war with Mexico. In the case of Bush's order, the "global war on terror" rendered the very idea of a battlefield something of a misnomer. More to the point, the order came at a time when American civilian courts were fully functioning. Civilian federal courts – also known, by virtue of the Constitution's enabling language, as Article III courts – had established an impressive, though not unblemished,[22] record of trying and convicting terror suspects – from home-grown insurgents, such as the Oklahoma City bomber Timothy McVeigh, to the "blind Sheikh" Omar Abdel-Rahman, sentenced to life imprisonment in connection with the first World Trade Center bombing in 1993. Critics, however, argued that civilian courts, with their indulgent procedures, grandstanding defense attorneys, lax treatment of sensitive intelligence, unreliable juries, and endless appeals, were ill-equipped to deal with terror cases.[23]

These concerns were not entirely without merit. In particular bars against hearsay and "chain of custody" requirements for seized evidence mean, as one expert has put it, that civilian courts are "not always best equipped to deal with every aspect of enemy misconduct."[24] Nonetheless, Bush's conclusion that "the nature of international terrorism" made it "not practicable to apply ... principles of law and the rules of evidence generally recognized"[25] in criminal cases came not from the law enforcement or intelligence communities, which largely continued to store their faith in the federal court system, but from

[22] During pre-trial discovery in the "blind Sheikh" trial, prosecutors supplied the defense with a list of unindicted co-conspirators. This list in turn was passed on to Osama bin Laden, whose name appeared on it. Andrew McCarthy, a prosecutor of Abdel-Rahman's who has since become a vocal critic of civilian trials for terror suspects, has often used this as an example of the unreliability of Article III courts in cases involving sensitive national security matters. Others, however, have observed that the problem was not with the system per se; a pretrial protective order would have protected against the document's dissemination. See Benjamin Weiser, "Top Terror Prosecutor Is a Critic of Civilian Trials," *New York Times*, February 9, 2010, available at www.nytimes.com/2010/02/20/nyregion/20prosecutor.html?pagewanted=2.

[23] For a review of the debate, see American Bar Association Standing Committee on Law and National Security, "Trying Terrorists in Article III Courts: Challenges and Lessons Learned," *National Strategy Forum*, July 2009, available at www.americanbar.org/content/dam/aba/migrated/natsecurity/trying_terrorists_artIII_report_final.authcheckdam.pdf; also John T. Parry and Song Richardson, eds., *The Constitution and the Future of Criminal Justice in America*, Part 7 (Cambridge: Cambridge University Press, 2013).

[24] Gary D. Solis, "Contemporary Law of War and Military Commissions," in Ni Aoláin and Gross, eds., *Guantanamo and Beyond*, p. 80.

[25] Administration of George W. Bush, 2001, *Military Order – Detention, Treatment, and Trial of Certain Non-Citizens in the War Against Terrorism.*

officials within the political branches – in particular, from Vice President Cheney and his chief of staff, David Addington, who believed the threat posed by al Qaeda required a new legal paradigm that permitted, in the words of one Pentagon official, "taking the gloves off."[26]

Rather than work from existing models, Bush, Cheney, and Addington sought to radically reshape the structure, method, and purposes of trials undertaken in the name of this ill-defined global war. Historically, as one authority has noted, U.S. military commissions had "comported to domestic legal standards" – that is, had largely tracked the law of court-martial – and indeed had exceeded the "international norms of the day."[27] Admittedly, there were lapses, particularly in the case of the commission convened by President Roosevelt to try the handful of Nazi saboteurs who landed on domestic shores in June 1942. Roosevelt's decision to bypass the civilian court system was in large measure prompted by a desire to conceal information of the weakness of America's coastal defenses and of the FBI's intelligence failures. Although the closed trial of the Nazi saboteurs was controlled by procedures that "dramatically depart[ed] from court-martial standards,"[28] a hastily convened Supreme Court upheld the President's authority to convene such a commission in *Ex parte Quirin*,[29] a decision that even as stalwart a supporter of executive power as Antonin Scalia described as "not this Court's finest hour."[30]

In the decades following the Court's ruling, *Ex parte Quirin* had largely fallen into desuetude; the case never so much as received passing mention in a course on Law and War that I took as a student at the Yale Law School in the 1980s. In the wake of 9/11, however, Bush officials resurrected the precedent with a vengeance. Roosevelt's dreary commission and the fact that the Court had upheld the executive's authority to convene encouraged the Bush administration in its radical experiment with military commissions. By the terms of this plan, norms meant to protect the dignitary rights of the accused and processes designed to instill confidence in the accuracy of verdicts could all be jettisoned as "not practicable" in cases involving alien terror suspects. Suspects could be denied access to the evidence against them. Confessions extracted through coercion or even torture could be used to incriminate. Trials could be closed to the public. Verdicts would be final, with dramatically curtailed forms of appellate review. In contrast to the lumbering work of trying cases before civilian juries, trial by military commission would hum along at a clip.[31]

26 Jane Mayer, *The Dark Side: The Inside Story of How the War on Terror Turned into a War on American Ideals* (New York: Doubleday, 2008).

27 Glazier, "The Development of an Exceptional Court," p. 37.

28 Glazier, "The Development of an Exceptional Court," p. 49.

29 317 U.S. 1 (1942).

30 542 U.S. 507 (2004), at 569 (Scalia dissenting).

31 See generally Jess Bravin, *The Terror Courts: Rough Justice at Guantanamo Bay* (New Haven: Yale University Press, 2013).

But speed was hardly the only goal. Whatever legitimate concerns critics of Article III courts might have had, the Bush proposal seemed to go far beyond what was needed to create an instrument more sensitive to the evidentiary and security issues raised by complex terror cases. Indeed, the Bush proposal seemed designed simply to facilitate convictions, and in this respect represented a disturbing derogation of due process. More disturbing yet, the procedures appeared to be designed to conceal from the public knowledge of the systematic abuses that made possible the acquisition of at least some of the evidence against the accused. In Bush's formulation, trial by military commission would permit the administration to have its cake and eat it too: it could mistreat and even torture suspects in an effort to acquire actionable intelligence of future attacks, but could also use whatever evidence gathered through abuse in trials of those accused of past wrongdoing. Or, as David Cole has put it, it would create "an avenue for short circuiting legal processes that might hold us accountable for our wrongs."[32]

That was the theory. In practice, Bush's experiment with military commissions assembled a record of unseemly missteps that frustrated the cause of justice and damaged America's standing abroad. Basic questions of procedure led to rancorous debates among commission members. Prosecutors labored aimlessly without adequate leadership, institutional support, or legal tools, frustrated by the CIA's steadfast refusal to share evidence and disillusioned by the realization that virtually all cases were tainted by allegations of detainee abuse if not outright torture.[33] In its landmark 2006 holding in *Hamdan* v. *Rumsfeld*,[34] the Supreme Court brought down the entire ill-conceived and shoddily constructed edifice, declaring Bush's military commission in violation of both the Uniform Code of Military Justice and Common Article Three of the Geneva Conventions (and leading Donald Rumsfeld to quip, "So I'm going to go down in history as the only secretary of defense to have lost a case to a terrorist?").[35]

Barack Obama assumed the presidency committed to reforming Bush's misbegotten tribunal, if not abolishing it altogether. The Military Commissions Act (MCA) of 2009 built on an earlier, less than impressive effort by Congress in 2006 to transform Bush's scheme into a workable instrument of American justice. The 2009 revisions did not solve all the problems; perhaps most troublingly, the MCA (2009) left intact the scheme in which only *alien* unprivileged enemy belligerents could be brought before a military commission. A military commission would have no jurisdiction over an American who fought on the side of al Qaeda; he would be tried by civilian court. As a historical matter, there

[32] David Cole, "Military Commissions and the Paradigm of Prevention," in Ni Aoláin and Gross, eds., *Guantanamo and Beyond*, p. 99.

[33] Bravin, *The Terror Courts*.

[34] 548 US 557. See also Jonathan Mahler, *The Challenge:* Hamdan *v.* Rumsfeld *and the Fight over Presidential Power* (New York: Farrar, Straus, Giroux, 2008).

[35] Quoted in Bravin, *The Terror Courts*, p. 306.

was no reason to exempt Americans from the jurisdiction of military commissions; in fact, General Scott's original commissions were designed specifically to apply to American soldiers. The fact that the matter of venue would continue to be resolved not by the nature of the conduct but by the nationality of the suspect did nothing to help the commissions overcome their legitimacy deficit. The message seemed still to be: good enough for aliens but not for Americans.

As a second matter, the MCA (2009) continued to list as triable offenses certain acts – such as "providing material support for terrorism" and "conspiracy" – that lacked a clear basis in the international law of armed conflict.[36] These problems came to head when a panel of the DC Circuit Court of Appeals reversed the conviction of Salim Hamdan, the mild-mannered cab driver and former bin Laden chauffeur whose previous challenge had brought down Bush's military commissions.[37] Tried by a reconstituted commission under the 2006 law, Hamdan was convicted of "providing material support" to al Qaeda and handed, from the perspective of Bush officials, an embarrassingly lenient sentence. Hamdan served out his term and in 2008 returned to his native Yemen, but continued to press his appeal. In October 2012, a DC Circuit Court panel concluded that material support did not represent a violation of the international law of war, a decision that cast serious doubt on whether any conspiracy charge would likewise survive appellate review.[38]

Also, when it came to deciding what to do with the 9/11 defendants, the Obama administration waffled badly. It first announced, on the eighth anniversary of Bush's executive order, what many jurists had urged from the outset: it would bring KSM and his confederates to federal court to stand trial. Then, in the face of opposition from New York's Mayor Bloomberg, who openly fretted about the security nightmare posed by shuttling KSM to lower Manhattan, and from Congress, which barred the use of public funds to bring Guantanamo detainees to the United States to stand trial, Obama reversed course. The 9/11 case would stay in Gitmo.

The vehement argument over where to try KSM turned into a larger ideological clash on the military commissions themselves, with supporters convinced that any transfer would toll the premature death knell of the system before it could prove its mettle, and opponents hopeful that moving

[36] Title 10, section 950t, United States Code, available at www.gpo.gov/fdsys/pkg/USCODE-2011-title10/pdf/USCODE-2011-title10-subtitleA-partII-chap47A-subchapVIII-sec950t.pdf.

[37] See *Hamdan* v. *United States*, No. 11–1257, decided October 16, 2012, available at www.cadc.uscourts.gov/internet/opinions.nsf/722A4A4B384D5EC985257A99004D77C0/$file/11–1257-1399811.pdf.

[38] In June 2015, a three-judge panel of the DC Circuit set aside Ali al-Bahlul's conspiracy conviction. In September 2015, the court vacated its June ruling and granted the government's petition for a rehearing en banc. As of present writing, the DC Circuit Court's en banc ruling has not been handed down.

the 9/11 case would put the legal mooncalf out of its misery before it could do more damage to America's world standing. Both sides appeared to overlook the fact that administration lawyers had never considered transferring the *Cole* case to civilian court. Nashiri had orchestrated attacks on military targets in a foreign port and so would be charged with violations of the law of armed conflict. Regardless of what happened to KSM, Nashiri would stand trial before the military commission.

THE OBAMA COMMISSION: MAKING VISIBLE THE RULE OF LAW

As chief prosecutor of the military commission, General Mark Martins follows in the tradition of the great Nuremberg jurists, Jackson and Telford Taylor, but also a far less auspicious line: he is the sixth chief prosecutor in the commission's ten-year existence, some of his predecessors having been forced out or resigned in frustration. On a cloudless day in mid-June in an old hangar that houses the Media Operations Center at Gitmo, Martins begins his press conference with a reminder and an expression of thanks. The reminder is to drink plenty of water; the summer sun is powerful at Gitmo, brutal by midday, and Martins warns us of the dangers of dehydration. This gesture – the seasoned soldier acting as guardian of his less-experienced charges – is protective but not condescending. The thanks are directed to the small group of journalists that has traveled down for this week's pretrial hearings. Here again the tone is understated and sincere. Martins is well aware of the crucial role that reportage will play in shaping the public's understanding of the commission. Legitimacy, a court's most precious endowment, is, as the Supreme Court once observed, a "product of substance and perception."[39] The creation of solid substance means little if all anyone sees is the bad old stuff.

Before becoming chief prosecutor in 2011, Martins worked closely with legislators and Obama administration lawyers to redesign the commission, which now, he emphasizes, looks a great deal like an Article III court, or rather, like a mix between a federal court and a conventional court-martial.[40] Statements acquired through torture or inhumane interrogations are barred. Come trial, guilt will be determined by a military jury, called a "panel," and the government must prove its case beyond a reasonable doubt. In certain respects the commission represents an improvement over the court-martial system, as defendants facing capital charges, such as Nashiri, must be provided "learned counsel" (lawyers with extensive experience in death penalty cases, like Rick Kammen), a provision not granted to ordinary soldiers facing a death-qualified

[39] 505 U.S. 833, at 865, *Planned Parenthood* v. *Casey*, available at http://supreme.justia.com/cases/federal/us/505/833/case.html.

[40] See Jennifer K. Elsea, *Comparison of Rights in Military Commission Trials and Trials in Federal Courts*, Congressional Research Service Report, March 21, 2014, available at www.fas.org/sgp/crs/natsec/R40932.pdf.

court-martial. Differences remain between the military commissions and civilian courts – why else create a separate system? For example, the commissions permit hearsay that would likely be barred in an Article III court. And yet the trial of the major Nazi war criminals before the IMT at Nuremberg and the twelve so-called "successor" trials staged by the American military of Nazi functionaries, also in Nuremberg, were all controlled by relaxed evidentiary norms that permitted hearsay.[41] As Martins notes, hearsay is also permitted in the UN'S Yugoslavia and Rwanda tribunals, as well as the International Criminal Court. I recall a conversation I had some years ago with Sir Geoffrey Nice, the British barrister and human rights activist who prosecuted Slobodan Milosevic. "It is well nigh impossible," Nice remarked, "to conduct complex war crimes prosecutions, where evidence often comes from sensitive sources, using standard common law rules of evidence."[42] Far from describing a deficiency, the admissibility of certain hearsay statements arguably describes an attraction of the revamped commissions.

More than just its chief prosecutor, Martins has become, by virtue of his impeccable credentials and reputation for integrity, the public face for the commission, its best last chance of demonstrating a commitment to the rule of law. First in his class at West Point, Rhodes scholar, Army Ranger, J.D. from Harvard, 2011 recipient of Harvard Law School's Medal of Freedom, Martins is also faultlessly polite and courteous – fair-minded with a scholarly manner and seriousness of purpose that immediately command respect. He has worked tirelessly to get the word out about the revamped commission, by lecturing widely, overseeing the creation of a helpful, well-organized, and easily navigable website, and arranging for public viewing by CCTV of the proceedings at certain locations back in the States. Whether these efforts can alter the perception of illegitimacy, the principal legacy of the commission's disastrous first decade of existence, remains to be seen.

Martins is well aware of the difficulties he faces. In a case in which the system itself stands in the dock, winning a conviction achieves little if the process by which the conviction is secured is seen as little more than an exercise of executive power aimed at the elimination of a political enemy.[43] At the same time, he must win convictions or risk undercutting the very rationale for trying terror suspects before military commissions. And yet one is tempted to say that only by losing his cases could Martins demonstrate to a deeply skeptical, if not openly hostile, community of legal observers that the commission's processes

[41] See Lawrence Douglas, "History and Memory in the Courtroom: Reflections on Perpetrator Trials," in Reginbogin, ed., *The Nuremberg Trials: International Criminal Law Since 1945*.

[42] Author's notes of interview with Geoffrey Nice; see also, Geoffrey Nice and Philippe Vallières-Roland, "Procedural Innovations in War Crimes Trials," *Journal of International Criminal Justice*, Vol. 3 (2005), pp. 354–380.

[43] See Kirchheimer, *Political Justice*; Meierhenrich and Pendas, "'The Justice of My Cause is Clear, But There's Politics to Fear.'"

are fair and comport with the requirements of due process. Yet despite the difficulty of his situation, Martins remains cautiously optimistic. "If ... observers withhold their judgment of the reformed military commissions until they observe a trial firsthand," he says, "I believe that they will see a system that is fair and legitimate, and deserving of their confidence."[44] It is, as he well knows, a big if.

DUE PROCESS AND THE LEGACY OF TORTURE

After the ELC's warehouse exterior, the high-tech courtroom – with its dark wood desks, built-in computer monitors, and sleek black ergonomic office chairs – offers something of a surprise. It looks a great deal like the equivalent international criminal courts in The Hague. The viewing gallery can accommodate just under fifty spectators; today about two-thirds of the seats are taken. Those on the right are reserved for survivors and members of victims' families, who, should they desire privacy, can draw a heavy purple curtain to separate their seats from the journalists, NGOs, and other observers seated on the left. Logistics dictate the placement, though it could just as well be ideology. During my previous visit, I had the chance to talk to a group of survivors and family members of victims, all of whom, not surprisingly, strongly support the commission. When asked what penalty they would like to see Nashiri receive, to a person they said death. Sharon Pelly, whose husband Joe survived the attack, volunteered, "If you need someone to execute him, I'll do it myself."[45]

The journalists and NGOs tend to be far less convinced by the happenings in the courtroom. Typically, the ACLU, Human Rights Watch, and several other NGOs will send down a representative to observe the week's proceedings and to report back a fresh description of the commission's fatal deficiencies; the ACLU's periodic updates often end with the same coda: "Since they began, the ACLU has been visiting Guántanamo Bay to report on the systemic flaws in the Military Commissions and call for its closure. As the trials proceed, the cracks in the façade just keep growing."[46] The journalists on the whole do not disagree. This week's group is modest, just seven of us are on hand to report on the Nashiri motions; next week, when the commission shifts its docket to the 9/11 case, that number will triple as journalists from *Der Spiegel* and the *Irish Times* and *Le Temps* will flock to Gitmo to moralize on American incompetence and malfeasance. This week's group is split between three extremely experienced

[44] Benjamin Wittes, "Mark Martins Address at Harvard Law School," *Lawfare Blog Post*, April 3, 2012, available at www.lawfareblog.com/2012/04/mark-martins-address-at-harvard-law-school/.

[45] Author's notes.

[46] Ian Kysel, "Guántanamo Dispatch: New Revelations of Attorney-Client Surveillance," *ACLU Blog of Rights*, June 14, 2013, available at www.aclu.org/blog/national-security/guantanamo-dispatch-new-revelations-attorney-client-surveillance.

journalists who know the material intimately and three younger bloggers, one of whom spends the week arguing that the true war criminals are George W. Bush and Dick Cheney and writes a post entitled "The Imperialist and Racist Origins of the Guantánamo Penal Colony."[47]

For all the attention given to the commissions' alleged flaws – that they allow hearsay (a defect for many observers), violate rights of confrontation, theoretically permit certain involuntary statements to be used as evidence – the most troublesome aspect of the government's case against Nashiri oddly tends to get overlooked. Yet it is this aspect that is quietly dramatized in the day's first order of business, otherwise a mere formality. At issue is the "un-detailing" of a lawyer from Nashiri's defense, who has received a fellowship to pursue postgraduate work at Harvard. The ultimate permission to leave the team rests with the presiding judge, an army colonel named James Pohl, who is also presiding over the 9/11 case.[48] An experienced jurist with a strong independent streak, Pohl will only agree once he establishes that the change is acceptable to the defendant. Nashiri sits at the far end of the defense table in short-sleeve white prison garb. Small of stature, the defendant looks fit – Kammen confirms that his client is not participating in the hunger strike that presently includes more than 100 detainees – and younger than his stated age of 48. Beardless, but sporting perhaps a day or two of stubble, Nashiri is not particularly devout, rarely if ever making use of the prayer breaks scheduled through the day. He told American investigators that he was a millionaire by age 19, but Kammen dismisses this story as "absolute bullshit."[49] An FBI source once described Nashiri as "someone who would commit a terrorist act 'in Mecca, inside the Kaaba itself' if he believed the cause demanded it,"[50] and yet his demeanor in court is polite and attentive. He stands when Pohl enters the courtroom – a small gesture, but one that Slobodan Milosevic notably withheld during his trial in The Hague. During the proceeding, Nashiri swivels slowly back and forth in his chair, following the simultaneous interpretation on headphones.

The exchange lasts only a couple of minutes. Pohl asks Nashiri if it is his "free and voluntary choice"[51] to let the lawyer leave the team, and whether he likewise accepts Air Force Captain Daphne Jackson, an African-American

[47] Marjorie Cohn and Adam Hudson, "Caging Human Rights: Guantánamo and Beyond," *Truthout* Special Feature, available at http://truth-out.org/news/item/16793-caging-human-rights-guantanamo-and-beyond.

[48] Pohl continues to preside over the 9/11 case. In July 2014, he was replaced as judge in the Nashiri case by Airforce Colonel Vance Spath. Pohl "undetailed" himself in the interest of avoiding scheduling conflicts between the two cases.

[49] Author's notes.

[50] Ali H. Soufan, *The Black Banners: The Inside Story of 9/11 and the War Against al-Qaeda* (New York: Norton, 2011), p. 265.

[51] Office of Military Commissions, *Unofficial/Unauthorized Transcript of the Al Nashiri (2) Hearing (6.11.13 9:03–10:30 at 1770–1774)*, Military Commission Notes Sessions, June 11, 2013, available at www.mc.mil/CASES/MilitaryCommissions.aspx.

JAG, now seated at the defense table and visibly pregnant, as a replacement. Nashiri answers, "Yes, I agree to that," first in Arabic and again in English. The brief respectful back and forth underscores the detailed procedures that now govern the revamped commissions; anyone who denies the reality of these procedures, or dismisses them as mere persiflage, either does not understand how a legal system works or does not want to see how the court actually acts.

All the same, the commissions' present attentiveness to the autonomy and dignity of the accused is hard to reconcile with the backstory of the government's treatment of Nashiri. Like many other detainees, Nashiri was subjected to "enhanced interrogation," cruel and inhumane practices that included stress positions, sleep deprivation, forced nudity, and other forms of degradation. But as one of the highest-ranking al Qaeda figures in captivity, Nashiri also came in for special treatment. Between being shuttled from one CIA black site prison to another, Nashiri was waterboarded and made to endure mock executions. He was bound, stripped, and hooded before a power drill was revved near his skull – torture, plain and simple. The CIA actually maintained videotapes of his waterboarding, but later destroyed these tapes amid concerns about the legal exposure of its interrogators.[52]

The government acknowledges that the legacy of this torture has left Nashiri with PTSD. Indeed, the prosecution petitioned the court to have Nashiri subjected to a psychiatric exam, which the defense acknowledges was conducted with sensitivity, competence, and thoroughness. This exam determined that in addition to PTSD, Nashiri suffers from "major depressive disorder," and "problems related to interaction with the legal system"[53] (we can only look forward to the day when the latter is recognized in the pages of the *DSM*). Nevertheless, the exam found Nashiri fit for trial – able to understand the charges against him and capable of participating in his defense – a conclusion that his lawyers largely accept. For its part, the prosecution concedes that evidence acquired through Nashiri's torture – including, obviously and most importantly, any statements of his determined to have been the result of an overborne will – cannot and will not be used at trial. The prosecution also successfully petitioned the guard force to have Nashiri transported to court without belly chains, as the security precaution apparently strongly reminded the defendant of his years of mistreatment.

But as welcome as these developments are, they also miss the deeper point. The government's position is that the vigilant observation of present procedure suffices to rectify the history of substantive abuse. At first blush, this seems of a piece with the Constitution's due process clause, which bars the government from denying a person "life, liberty or property without due

52 Siems, *The Torture Report*.

53 Office of Military Commissions, *United States* v. *Al Nashiri*, AE104j, available at www.mc.mil/CASES/MilitaryCommissions.aspx.

process of law" – the corollary being that the government can deny all these things if due process is provided. And yet as the Supreme Court has noted, the due process clause has also "been understood to contain a substantive component as well, one 'barring certain government actions regardless of the fairness of the procedures used to implement them.' "[54] In constitutional law, this doctrine of "substantive due process" bars the executive from doing things that "shock the conscience." The standard is admittedly subjective and so has invited controversy, but the doctrine has supplied the basis for holding confessions obtained through government coercion inadmissible at trial.[55] In the famous case of *Rochin* v. *California*, the Court further reasoned, "a conviction which rests upon evidence of incriminating objects obtained from the body of the accused by physical abuse is as invalid as a conviction which rests upon a verbal confession extracted from him by such abuse."[56] In these cases, of course, substantive due process established bars on the admissibility of evidence; it did not stop the government from proceeding in the absence of the barred material; nor did it limit the kind of punishment that the government might seek. And yet this case law developed in response to acts of coercion; how might the doctrine of substantive due process deal with the far graver matter of *torture*, an act that represents the most egregious violation of the liberal respect of the dignity and autonomy of the person?[57] The topic has played virtually no role in Supreme Court jurisprudence, but one answer might be gleaned from the actions of Susan Crawford, a former judge on the United States Court of Appeals for the Armed Services who served as the Convening Authority of the Guantánamo military commission from 2007 to 2010. Confronted with evidence that Mohammed al-Qahtani, the alleged "20th hijacker" of 9/11, had been tortured during his detention at Gitmo, Crawford refused to refer his case for trial.[58] It is not entirely clear whether Crawford's refusal reflected a judgment that conviction would be impossible in the absence of the tainted evidence or because she thought that even if there were sufficient "good" evidence to move forward, she could not in good conscience do so. But if the Convening Authority arguably concluded that the fact of torture should bar the government from trying a suspect altogether, it seems fair to insist that substantive due process demands that capital charges be taken off the table in cases clouded by the specter of the worst government abuse. Perhaps we should conclude that Nashiri's torture casts a pall over any

54 505 US 833, at 846, *Planned Parenthood* v. *Casey* (1992).

55 See 316 U.S. 547, *Ward* v. *Texas* (1942).

56 342 U.S. 165 (1952) at 167 (Frankfurter quoting dissent of California Supreme Court decision denying petitioner's motion for a hearing.)

57 See David Luban, "Liberalism, Torture and the Ticking Bomb," *Virginia Law Review*, Vol. 91 (2005), pp. 1425–1461.

58 See Solis, "Contemporary Law of War and Military Commissions"; and Bravin, *Terror Courts*.

punishment; at the very least we should recall the Supreme Court's lapidary and necessary insight: "death is different."[59]

The problem, of course, is not unique to the military commission, which perhaps explains why it is not front and center of the NGOs' list of complaints: Justice Department prosecutors almost certainly would have sought the death penalty had Nashiri been charged in federal court. But the irony of course is that the military commission must now do better. A federal court need not labor to convince a domestic and international audience of its basic fairness; the military commission enjoys no such luxury. Here again the question of legitimacy is front and center. One can, of course, readily imagine the political pressures that led the government to forward capital charges against Nashiri. *Cole* survivor Joe Pelly openly acknowledges that he takes medication for his PTSD, and also mentions the case of Johann Gokool, a petty officer who lost a foot in the blast and later committed suicide. "We were tortured, too," Pelly says. "Every night I have visions of what I had to deal with that day."[60] Yet however much these expressions of anguish may move us, we court moral danger when we use the same word to describe the suffering of Pelly and the treatment of Nashiri. In seeking the death penalty, the government has frustrated its deeper ambition – to legitimate the work of the military commission.

THE WAGES OF LEGITIMACY

Along with many of the soldiers who guard and maintain the military commission, the journalists and NGOs are quartered in Camp Justice, a grid-like collection of "tents" that dot the former landing strip of the old McCalla Field. The tents, which look like Quonset huts and sleep six, call forth thoughts of Scott and Shackleton thanks to overly aggressive air-conditioning, while the military showers spray nothing but scalding water. It's hardly the most agreeable arrangement, but any thoughts of my own personal comfort seem out of place here. Shaving one morning, I hear a soldier next to me mutter, "I'm so sick of this fucking place"[61] – not, I learn, an uncommon sentiment. Another soldier tells me, "It's not just the detainees who are tired of Gitmo. People don't often think about the stress on the guards."[62]

Gitmo's detention camps occupy but a small part of the naval base, but they have proved toxic to the reputation of the commission, the base, and the nation. If the commission is to succeed in legitimating itself, it will have to sever its connection to the camps. This could happen in one of two ways. A commission official who gives me a guided tour of the Expeditionary Legal Complex places emphasis on the word "expeditionary." The court building,

[59] See Daniel Ross Harris, "Capital Sentencing after *Walton* v. *Arizona*: A Retreat from the 'Death Is Different' Doctrine," *American University Law Review*, Vol. 40 (1991), pp. 1389–1429, available at www.wcl.american.edu/journal/lawrev/40/harris.pdf.

[60] Author's notes. [61] Author's notes. [62] Author's notes.

he notes, was designed to be moved; it could be placed on a barge and relocated, say, to a military base on the continental United States. Admittedly that would additionally delay the already sluggish progress of the Nashiri and 9/11 cases, and other legal and political complications stand in the way, but when asked whether he would push a magic button to move the commission stateside, General Martins looks cautiously tantalized. His only comment is to note that the 2009 law reforming the commissions is silent as to venue. "Guantánamo" appears nowhere in its dense thicket of procedure and provisions.

Or the commission could stay and the camps themselves could finally go. The camps have been in the news again recently, because Obama has renewed his pledge, made on the first week of his first term, to close them down, and because of the detainee hunger strike that prompted his announcement. I had a chance to visit the detention camps during an earlier trip to Gitmo, around the time that the present hunger strike began. If the strike had already started, it certainly wasn't mentioned during my tour; the officer in charge of Camp 6, where most of the remaining 166 detainees are interned, described obesity as one of the biggest problems with his inmate population.[63]

Our first stop was Camp X-ray, a 20-minute drive up Sherman Avenue, Gitmo's main thoroughfare, past the McDonald's and the Subway, past the "high rises" where the lawyers stay and the high school for the dependents of those stationed at the naval base. Eventually we reach a remote spot close to the northeast border with Cuba proper. Closed down eleven years ago, the abandoned camp is small – a reminder that systemic abuse often unfolds in intimate spaces – and now heavily grown over with dried grass, its wooden guard towers warped and sagging. Plans to raze the abandoned camp were put on hold by a federal court order preserving it as a putative crime scene. As the first of Gitmo's numerous camps, it was in use for only 100 days but produced the images that remain indelible in public consciousness: detainees, clad in orange jumpsuits and blackened goggles, prone before open air cages.[64] Just outside the rotting camp are dilapidated wooden huts where, a decade ago, men in polo shirts and chinos would stroll over to conduct "interviews."

Later, we drove over Radio Hill, where the present detention complex is located. Camp Delta, a sprawling facility surrounded by white bollards is now all but empty; presently it houses a behavioral-health clinic. The road cut toward the coast and we passed Camp Iguana, home to the last remaining group of Uighurs, a Turkic ethnic minority some of whose members got caught up in America's dragnet in Afghanistan and Pakistan. The camp is named after Guantánamo's most famous and protected local fauna. Iguanas roam freely

[63] Since the original writing of this chapter, dozens of detainees have been transferred; the present detainee population stands at 61.

[64] See Karen Greenberg, *The Least Worst Place: Guantanamo's First 100 Days* (Oxford: Oxford University Press, 2009); and Jonathan M. Hansen, *Guantanamo: An American History* (New York: Hill and Wang, 2011).

and abundantly – shortly after I arrived for the first time, I was introduced to one named "Holy Fuck," who is often seen resting by the entrance to the commissary and whose name remains as famous as its origin obscure. The speed limit on the base is strictly enforced at 25 miles per hour, and the fine for killing an iguana allegedly runs as high as $10,000. Camp Iguana occupies a spectacular spot on a rocky bluff overlooking the Caribbean, the impressive vista either a reward to the apparently benign Uighurs or a cruel reminder of their continued captivity despite being slated for release over two years ago. The Uighurs are not alone in this regard – 86 detainees slated for release have been waiting two years for their freedom, their transfer delayed by congressional intransigence and presidential inaction.[65]

Camps 5 and 6 house almost all the remaining detainees; Camp 6, modeled after a medium-security prison, is reserved for compliant detainees, who, at least until the hunger strike that gripped the camp in 2013, represented a majority of those remaining at Gitmo. Detainees have the choice of taking language and art courses. There is a library stocked with *Harry Potter* in Arabic and Pashto and other books whose titles resonate provocatively: Gabriel Garcia Marquez's *Notes on a Kidnapping*, H.G. Wells's *The War of the Worlds*, and John Grisham's *The Innocent Man*. There are TV channels and video games. (According to a Public Affairs Officer, one detainee "only wanted a DVD of *Brazilian Butts*. He was very insistent, but that was a 'no'.")[66] "It's a whole lot nicer than where we keep our soldiers," a military lawyer on the tour ruefully commented. "Have you ever seen Leavenworth? What a dump."[67] And yet Leavenworth is a prison, where persons convicted of criminal wrongdoing are incarcerated. After a dozen years of captivity, none of the detainees in Camp 6 have ever been charged with anything.[68] The only thing that has changed is that they are no longer designated "unlawful enemy combatants": Congress improved that in 2009 to "unprivileged enemy belligerent."

Now, during my June visit, the camps are in lockdown. More than forty of the hundred hunger-striking detainees are being force-fed. And yet there is a feeling – optimism would be too strong a word, more a sense that the sheer accumulation of frustration and despair has broken through the inertia, and that finally something will change. Those slated for release might actually be released; those who can be charged with crimes might actually be charged; and the administration might even figure out what do with the forty-six detainees whom it deems too dangerous to release but unable to try, presumably for lack of adequate or usable evidence. I ask a lieutenant colonel in the Marines what he would do with this last group, and his answer in unequivocal: "You can't hold

[65] The last of the Uighurs were released after the writing of this chapter. [66] Author's notes.
[67] Author's notes.
[68] See Owen Fiss, "The War against Terrorism and the Rule of Law," *Oxford Journal of Legal Studies*, Vol. 26 (2006), pp. 235–256.

them forever, no matter how much they want to hurt us. You're talking about 46 guys against the United States military. C'mon."[69]

***

Can a spiral notebook be weaponized? The question consumes an afternoon session, and represents a final challenge facing General Martins: how to deal with Kammen's kangaroo strategy, which aims to show at every turn that the case remains trapped in "a truly bizarre world,"[70] a grotesque simulacrum of law? Approaching his late sixties, Rick Kammen still has something of the bad boy about him. He merrily recalls a trial from years back in which a judge addressed him as "Mr. Kunstler" – a reference to the flamboyant lawyer who represented members of the Chicago Seven – to which Kammen responded, "Good morning, Judge Hoffman."[71] The Indianapolis native speaks with a soothing Midwestern twang but is gifted at making life miserable for the government, perhaps in part because the government, by which I now mean the larger entity of which the prosecution is just a tiny part, is quite good at making life miserable for itself. There are numerous stakeholders in the case – the Joint Task Force that oversees the camps, the intelligence communities, the Secretary of Defense – and General Martins's delicate task is complicated by all of them. Until recently Kammen, who likes to use spiral notebooks, had been allowed to bring his notebooks to his meetings with his client. A new rule changed that: forthwith spiral notebooks are considered contraband. The commander of Gitmo's detention facilities responsible for the change, an army colonel named John Bogdan, soberly explains to the court that the wire from the notebook could be removed and fashioned into a garrote. Kammen is incredulous. "Have you run any experiment on how long it would take to remove the wire ... and turn it into a garrote?"[72] Colonel Bogdan admits that he has not. Kammen hands Colonel Bogdan a spiral notebook, challenging him to fashion a garrote. "We'd like to see how long it takes." A prosecutor leaps to her feet. Objection! Sustained. "Would you allow a three ring binder or is that also too dangerous?" Kammen asks. The commander demurs, "I'd have to see."[73]

At some point, Judge Pohl says, "Are we fighting over spiral notebooks?"[74] Laughter ripples through the courtroom, but not from the prosecution's desk. The last thing that the prosecution wants is to be dragged into a fight over

[69] Author's notes.

[70] *Unoffical/Unauthorized Transcript of the Al Nashiri (2) Hearing*, June 12, 2013; 9:08–10:26 at 1998.

[71] Author's notes.

[72] *Unofficial/Unauthorized Transcript of the Al Nashiri (2) Hearing*, June 13, 2013; 14:32–16:24 at 2402.

[73] *Unofficial/Unauthorized Transcript of the Al Nashiri (2) Hearing*, June 13, 2013; 14:32–16:24 at 2420.

[74] *Unofficial/Unauthorized Transcript of the Al Nashiri (2) Hearing*, June 11, 2013 10:50–11:50 at 1839.

notebooks – spiral or plastic; three-ring or two-hole punched? All the same, it can ill-afford to abandon the beleaguered commander, and so counters with an appeal to principle: is the court really prepared to substitute its judgment of what constitutes a security risk for the experts'? Despite his quip, Judge Pohl, who describes himself as "a linear guy"[75] and who runs his courtroom with a matter-of-fact even-handedness, follows the dispute attentively, his only trace of impatience a habit of repeating, "I got it. Okay, got it."

Then there is the matter of surveillance. As at its sister facilities in The Hague, the ELC's spectator gallery is separated from the court proper by layers of bulletproof and soundproof glass that offer a broad view of the courtroom, but spectators actually follow the proceeding on a series of TV monitors mounted at the front of the gallery. These provide both picture and sound – on a forty-second delay. This arrangement takes some getting used to – you watch, for example, Judge Pohl enter the courtroom, take his seat, and open his mouth; then forty seconds later, the whole thing repeats on the monitors, now with sound.

This protocol – familiar to those who followed the trial of Saddam Hussein, not an association that the commission necessarily wants to invite – is meant to protect classified information from inadvertent leaks. Should sensitive material come under discussion, Judge Pohl or the court security officer can push a button, muting the transmission and illuminating a light by the judge's bench that flashes red, much as if a hockey goal had been scored. During a 9/11 hearing in late January, the hockey light flashed and white noise filled the speakers, all without Judge Pohl lifting a finger. Evidently the mute button had been activated by what the parties called the OCA – the "original classification agency," apparently the CIA – a revelation that left Judge Pohl, who was either utterly unaware of the CIA's power or furious at its brazen use, apoplectic, the prosecution dispirited, and the defense both disturbed and filled with irrepressible *Schadenfreude*. The next morning, Pohl demonstrably summarized in open court what the public had missed during the three-minute gap, reminded anyone who was listening that "only the judge has authority to close the courtroom," and threatened to have a "little meeting" with any "external body" trying to control his proceeding.[76]

Still, the damage had been done. The Nashiri hearing in February, which followed directly on the heels of this episode, became bogged down in a lengthy debate as to whether the entire courtroom was nothing more than, as one defense lawyer put it, a "huge listening device."[77] Members of the defense moved to a far corner of the courtroom to confer in whispers,

[75] *Unofficial/Unauthorized Transcript of the Al Nashiri (2) Hearing*, June 11, 2013 9:03–10:30 at 1798.

[76] *Unofficial/Unauthorized Transcript of the Al Nashiri (2) Hearing* at 1469.

[77] *Unofficial/Unauthorized Transcript of the Al Nashiri (2) Hearing*, February 4, 2013; 13:00–14:39 at 1582.

suspicious (or at least performing the suspicion) that microphones on the defense's desk might be wired to the OCA – now referred to as "the man behind the curtain."[78] The move prompted a prosecutor to dryly observe, "we have some theatrics going on,"[79] a charge as true as it was beside the point. Of course the defense was engaging in theatrics – why else put a stuffed kangaroo on your desk? – and effective theatrics at that. For the suggestion that the very agency responsible for torturing Nashiri now controlled the courtroom and could bring down a curtain of white noise when discussion turned to the matter of Nashiri's abuse struck to the core of the commission's credibility.

Kammen, understandably, was not about to let the matter go away. At issue at the June hearings is a smoke detector that detects no smoke. Nashiri, KSM, and the dozen other "high value detainees" are housed in Camp 7, an ultra-secure facility the very location of which is a secret – except perhaps to anyone who cares to look at Google maps, which shows it ostensibly occupying an isolated spot on Radio Hill. Because even Nashiri's lawyers are not permitted into Camp 7, meetings take place at a separate facility called Echo II; smoke detectors in the meeting rooms were recently discovered to conceal audio monitoring devices. The commander of the camp, the same Colonel Bogdan known for his cautious approach to notebooks, acknowledges the audio capability but steadfastly insists that it never has been used to monitor attorney–client conversations, which all know to be privileged. Kammen manages to make Colonel Bogdan's time on the stand most uncomfortable, as an increasingly glum-looking Bogdan is forced to attempt to explain how he managed not to know or be apprised of the monitoring capability until six months into his command.[80] For its part, the prosecution points out that the defense has proffered not a shred of evidence to prove that monitoring has occurred. It has simply moved from capability to actuality, and now is asking the government to prove that something has not happened, an impossible burden to assume, or as one prosecutor puts it, the defense is "asking us to prove that dragons don't exist."[81] Unfortunately for the prosecution, the day's headlines trumpet the name Edward Snowden and the lineaments of an audacious program of electronic eavesdropping by the NSA. If the NSA essentially eavesdrops on everything always, is it so preposterous to believe the government would

[78] *Unofficial/Unauthorized Transcript of the Al Nashiri (2) Hearing*, February 4, 2013; 9:01–9:56 at 1543.

[79] *Unofficial/Unauthorized Transcript of the Al Nashiri (2) Hearing*, February 4, 2013; 13:00–14:39 at 1593.

[80] *Unofficial/Unauthorized Transcript of the Al Nashiri (2) Hearing*, June 13, 2013; 14:32–16:24, at 2365.

[81] *Unofficial/Unauthorized Transcript of the Al Nashiri (2) Hearing*, June 11, 2013; 10:50–11:50, at 1833.

eavesdrop on a conversation between lawyers and a senior al Qaeda lieutenant?[82]

The last day of proceedings also does little to advance General Martins's larger goal. The motion to be discussed deals with classified material; in fact, its very subject is classified and so is known simply as the "unnamed motion."[83] Members of the press are barred from being present, as is the accused, an arrangement that Kammen claims is unheard of in a capital case. The actual session does not last long, some seventy-nine minutes, and the following week, the military commission website will publish a version of the transcript, alas with whole pages blacked out.[84] In the press conference that directly follows on the heels of the closed session, chief prosecutor Martins is at pains to emphasize that federal law authorizes such closed sessions in civilian court, too, and that the trial in chief will be open and public, relying on evidence available to general scrutiny.

The defense treats the government's rejoinder with skepticism that is largely reflected in the reports of the media and NGOs. But here again, to conclude that the government is merely feigning an interest in transparency is fundamentally to misunderstand its position. More than anything, the prosecution needs to open the trial up, wants to make its procedures and evidence clear to all, for every time it is forced into close session, it revives the history of Nashiri's secret torture.

If the week's sessions make plain enough the exceptional problems that the government faces as it seeks to promote its commission, they also reveal something self-defeating about the arguments of the defense. No doubt Kammen is correct that a federal court, unhampered by the struggle over legitimacy that makes this proceeding at times absurd and more often fascinating, could try the case more smoothly and expeditiously. Yet the very ease of the process would simply hurry Mr. Nashiri toward a likely conviction. Here of course the ironies abound, as speed was to be a key virtue of Bush's original commission; now the need to air questions that would be settled in federal court arguably works to the defense's favor. As for Kammen's artful efforts to paint the prosecution and commission as the unreconstructed toady of the "other stakeholders," the very openness of the debate, the vigor of the adversarial proceeding, the clarity and professionalism of the prosecution's rebuttals, and the steady, patient, practical stewardship of Judge Pohl powerfully suggest that something more complex and interesting is happening in the courtroom.

82 Judge Pohl later found "no monitoring has occurred for at least the prior two years from the date of the hearing, well beyond the 15 September 2011 date of the referral charges in this case." *United States* v. *Al Nashiri*, AE 149K (August 5, 2013).

83 Office of Military Commissions, *Commission AE92*, available at www.mc.mil/CASES/MilitaryCommissions.aspx.

84 See generally *Unofficial/Unauthorized Transcript of the Al Nashiri (2) Hearing*, June 14, 2013; 9:08–10:27, pp. 2468–2522.

Still, if the government is successful in justifying its processes, it will have to come to terms with the substance of what it is trying to do. Unlike General Martins, Kammen is not a student of Nuremberg. But when we share a meal at Reagan Airport during our return home from Gitmo, he removes a Kindle from the backpack where he also keeps his stuffed kangaroo and shows me a book he has read closely.[85] Its subject is the controversial *Malmedy* trial of 1946. Overshadowed by the more famous trials conducted at Nuremberg, the American army staged numerous other prosecutions at Dachau, on the site of the former Nazi concentration camp. The *Malmedy* case involved the prosecution of 73 members of the SS accused of massacring scores of American airmen during the Battle of the Bulge. The trial resulted in dozens of convictions, including numerous death sentences. Later, allegations emerged that American interrogators had beaten and abused their SS captives. Though never fully proven, these charges made front-page news in the *New York Times*, and led, amid escalating Cold War tensions and a strengthened commitment to secure Germany as an ally, to the painful decision to commute all the death sentences. In 1956, the last of those convicted of massacring American soldiers walked out of Landsberg prison a free man. The case and the commutation remain controversial among historians, and the meaning of the incident is far from simple or clear. But it is fair to see it as standing for a principle fundamental to our system of law and justice: that America does not execute men whom it has tortured.

[85] James J. Weingartner, *A Peculiar Crusade: Willis M. Everett & the Malmedy Massacre* (New York: New York University Press, 2000).

Index